Reference and Information Services

AN INTRODUCTION

THIRD EDITION

KAY ANN CASSELL AND UMA HIREMATH

Neal-Schuman

An imprint of the American Library Association

Chicago 2013

Web Extras

Visit http://www.neal-schuman.com/reference-information-services-3E/ to access new readings for each chapter, information about changes in the reference tools described in these pages as well as important new ones, and the original, uncut version of Meghan Harper's chapter on services for children and young adults.

Printed in the United States of America
17 16 15 14 13   5 4 3 2 1

Extensive effort has gone into ensuring the reliability of the information in this book; however, the publisher makes no warranty, express or implied, with respect to the material contained herein.

ISBNs: 978-1-55570-859-7 (paper); 978-1-55570-864-1 (PDF).

Library of Congress Cataloging-in-Publication Data

Cassell, Kay Ann.
    Reference and information services : an introduction / Kay Ann Cassell, Uma Hiremath. — Third edition.
        pages cm
    Includes bibliographical references and indexes.
    ISBN 978-1-55570-859-7
    1. Reference services (Libraries) 2. Electronic reference services (Libraries) 3. Reference books—Bibliography. 4. Electronic reference sources—Directories. I. Hiremath, Uma. II. Title.

Z711.C355 2013
025.5'2—dc23
                                                                                                    2012031068

Cover design by Kimberly Thornton. Images © Shutterstock, Inc.
Text design in Palatino and Univers Condensed by UB Communications.

♾ This paper meets the requirements of ANSI/NISO Z39.48-1992 (Permanence of Paper).

Dedicated to you:
The entrepreneurial librarian of the twenty-first century
providing "anytime, anywhere" reference

Contents

Part II Introduction to Major Reference Sources

Part IV Developing and Managing Reference Collections and Services

Preface

Skill Sets

Reference and Information Services, Third Edition, is about skills, resources, and best practices. Reference service has become much more complex and is in a constant state of flux.

The process of maturing into a worthy reference librarian, skill set by skill set, is challenging, unending, hugely rewarding, and, yes, fun. In this book, we identify these skill sets, analyze them, break them into their component parts, and present them to you, the eternally maturing reference librarian, in ways that are reproducible. The first and second editions of this book were dedicated to the intrepid librarian because the reference librarian at the start of the twenty-first century had to, above all else, be fearless in the face of a technology revolution. This third edition is dedicated to the entrepreneurial librarian who must continually think outside of the box and look for trends and technology that can be adapted to the library setting.

Ambiguity, never a stranger to the field of librarianship in general and information studies in particular, seems particularly acute in the face of dramatic new technologies fostering equally dramatic new ways of doing reference. Google has completed the prodigious digitization of over 20 million manuscripts available for open reference, even as Twitter continues peeping out reedy 140-character reference posts. The solid old desk, across which the static transaction of reference questions and answers was conducted, is being elbowed out or entirely replaced by virtual reference, reference consultation services, "Learning Commons," roving librarians, and mobile technology. Real-life librarians have spawned virtual reference librarians within the dense proliferation of social networks like Facebook. Online searching skills, techniques, and interpretation have overtaken resource-based reference and are imperative to effective reference services in all libraries.

The ferocious pace of change has compelled us to write yet another new edition to update and replace the sources listed in the second edition. Search skills required to locate newly digitized government documents, for example, bear little resemblance to searches through the voluminous GPO publications of a few years ago. An augural job listing by the New York Public Library included this as one of its performance expectations: a knowledge of the library as a "location where new and emerging information technologies and resources are combined with traditional sources of knowledge in a user-focused, service-rich environment that supports today's social and educational patterns of learning, teaching, and research." No pressure intended.

The professional reference librarian must commit to an ongoing understanding of the fundamental concepts, essential resources, search techniques, and managerial tasks inherent to reference, which are underwritten in large part by the wider social and educational patterns of information and research. The chapters contained in this edition support that commitment, even as they ease the pressure of trying to know too much without organized skill sets. The larger universe, where the primacy of information has never been felt more acutely, is kept in strict perspective throughout the text. The updated chapter on Reference 2.0 tools introduced in the second edition now captures more of the restless mutability of emerging technologies and alerts the reference professional to experimental trends and practices that are utilizing new technology in innovative ways. More important, it acknowledges the maturing of virtual reference and the continually rising expectations of the user to access information freely, instantaneously, and often using mobile devices. The chapter on reference work with children and young adults, completely rewritten for this edition, reflects the importance of developmentally appropriate reference resources, a timely mirror to the global emphasis being placed on the relevance of information-seeking behavior at all stages of human development. An entirely new chapter on ethics adds a critical framework for reference librarians having to function within the somewhat unseen but treacherous shoals of information copyright issues and professional codes of conduct. The role of reference librarians as "information trust agents" cannot be underestimated in a universe of unending and complex information transactions. This chapter aims to anchor the expected rules of conduct and alert reference librarians to areas of vulnerability.

While earlier editions provided a mix of print and e-resources, this third edition spotlights electronic resources, in deference to the primacy of online searching over resource-based reference. The book continues to provide free web resources of depth and value useful for budget-conscious institutions faced with continuing global recession, along with a listing of mobile apps available for smartphones, iPads, and other mobile technology. This text also incorporates the valued suggestions of practitioners, including the adoption of the suggestion by an LIS faculty member to provide the uninitiated student with a comprehensive idea of the immense diversity in reference resources through an accessible list of RUSA Outstanding Reference Resources, so that a list of selected titles appears as an appendix. What worked effectively for the first two editions remains but is enhanced with necessary updates. We have taken care to both cull and expand the hundreds of resources listed in the text, with amendments and supplements offered as a Web Extra (http://www.neal-schuman.com/reference-information-services-3E/).

Each of the chapters on resources provides an important section on selection and keeping current in the field. We have continued to treat reference transactions as an organic process that involves understanding both the text and subtext of a question, identifying the best resources, and providing an optimal answer. *Reference and Information Services: An Introduction* differed from traditional reference texts in consciously linking questions to sources, rather than classifying resources and providing a general description of their use. Our approach, firmly grounded in real-world practices, was a direct result of the oft-heard remark from library school graduates who believed their experiences in real transactions felt remote from what they had studied at school. The progression of question → reference interview → search process → resource options → answer was deemed to be a truer representation of what students would face in the real world, and this third edition continues to uphold that structure.

Organization

While this third edition of *Reference and Information Services: An Introduction* is aimed at all reference librarians striving to acquire or affirm the necessary skill sets, it is organized to complement the syllabus of a typical library and information studies course. The four sections that make up the text provide a well-rounded grounding in the fundamental concepts of reference, the arsenal of major resources with which every reference librarian must become familiar to answer basic questions, special topics such as readers' advisory and user instruction (that fall within the purview of reference work), and tools to field the ongoing responsibility of developing and skillfully managing reference departments in the face of constant change and innovation.

Part I: Fundamental Concepts

Chapter 1, "Introduction to Reference and Information Services," provides readers with an overview of the breadth of services housed under the reference rubric and discusses some of the changes in reference service.

Chapter 2, "Determining the Question: In-Person, Telephone, and Virtual Reference Interviews," outlines the first and perhaps most critical step in the reference process. In order to assist the reader the librarian must skillfully determine the user's question or need. Given that reference is, and always will be, predicated on contact and communication, even in times of change, this chapter takes into account in-person, telephone, and virtual reference interviews.

Chapter 3, "Finding the Answer: Basic Search Techniques," is in many ways a conclusion to Part I and a prelude to Part II. Having identified the question, the next step is to construct an answer. This hands-on chapter trains you to organize your thoughts, develop a strategy for the particular request, and find the optimal solution.

Part II: Introduction to Major Reference Sources

The nine chapters in this section focus on how, what, where, who, and when questions as they correlate to authoritative resources, rather than describe types of resources. Included in this section are:

Chapter 4, "Answering Questions about Books, Magazines, Newspapers, Libraries and Publishing, and Bibliographic Networks—Bibliographic Resources"

Chapter 5, "Answering Questions about Anything and Everything—Encyclopedias"

Chapter 6, "Answering Questions That Require Handy Facts—Ready Reference Sources"

Chapter 7, "Answering Questions about Words—Dictionaries, Concordances, and Manuals"

Chapter 8, "Answering Questions about Events and Issues, Past and Present—Databases (and Indexes)"

Chapter 9, "Answering Questions about Health, Law, and Business—Special Guidelines and Sources"

Chapter 10, "Answering Questions about Geography, Countries, and Travel—Atlases, Gazetteers, Maps, Geographic Information Systems, and Travel Guides"

Chapter 11, "Answering Questions about the Lives of People—Biographical Information Sources"

Chapter 12, "Answering Questions about Government and Related Issues—Government Information Sources"

Each of these chapters begins with an overview of materials and how they are used to answer the particular type of question. We provide sample questions (and answers) for which those sources are best used and describe the major print, electronic, and web-based materials available. There is also guidance for collection development and maintenance practices; further considerations and special information particular to the topic; a final list of the "Top Ten" reference sources in the subject area; and a list of recommended free websites. The "Recommended Resources Discussed in This Chapter" are standardized as title entries for easy discovery. As each chapter is uniformly structured, you will find it conducive both to advanced reading in preparation for service and as an effective reference source at the desk.

Part III: Special Topics in Reference and Information Work

Chapter 13, "When and How to Use the Internet as a Reference Tool," addresses one of the most challenging and ubiquitous reference resources to have emerged in our times. Outlining the strengths and weaknesses of the Internet as a reference source, this chapter also contains a five-step approach to using the Internet in reference transactions.

Chapter 14, "Readers' Advisory Work," discusses both the history of readers' advisory (RA) and its current practice. While RA is sometimes housed in departments other than reference (Adult, Children's, or Young Adult Services), the librarian sitting at the reference desk should and often must be prepared to field all questions, including an RA question. This chapter, authored by Cindy Orr, describes the most common types of RA queries, best practices and common mistakes in RA, and a list of recommended resources.

Chapter 15, "Reference Sources and Services for Children and Young Adults," authored by Meghan Harper, discusses a developmentally appropriate approach to reference work with children and young adults. Librarians must be conscious of both reading and development levels of children and young adults. The chapter also discusses reference service for children with special needs and includes recommended titles for reference collections for children and young adults. Harper's excellent chapter in its entirety is available as a Web Extra (http://www.neal-schuman.com/reference-information-services-3E/).

Chapter 16, "Information Literacy in the Reference Department," discusses the importance of information literacy in all types of libraries and offers suggestions for one-to-one classroom instruction and distance learning. In the right transaction, instruction can be a very appropriate and valued response to a query.

Part IV: Developing and Managing Reference Collections and Services

The selection of fast-disappearing or format-changing reference material has never required as much dexterity and flexibility as in the current climate. Management skills are essential for the library professional, as is the development of assessment tools that continually measure the library's success in cresting and controlling the ebb and flow of changing reference collections and services.

Chapter 17, "Selecting and Evaluating Reference Materials," provides sources for review and evaluation criteria. You will also find guidance for managing the materials budget, assessing collections, weeding titles, writing policy, and marketing the collection.

Chapter 18, "Ethics in Reference," authored by Angela Ecklund, tackles the sometimes difficult but very important issues of professional codes of ethics, plagiarism, copyright and intellectual property, as well as access to information and censorship. This is a new chapter for this edition that we hope will provide guidance to the reader.

Chapter 19, "Managing Reference Departments," looks at staff, service, and department organization. This chapter provides options for managers and considerations for decision making. While aimed at the manager, it is also a helpful glimpse for any professional into the form and function of today's reference departments.

Chapter 20, "Assessing and Improving Reference Services," moves from the day-to-day practice of reference work to the vision and development of future services. In times of budget stringency especially, there is heightened emphasis on assessment and accountability. From why we should assess to what and how to assess to what we should do with our findings, this chapter encourages a hands-on and proactive approach to improvement.

Chapter 21, "Reference 2.0," provides a comprehensive snapshot of the many tools and sites mined from Web 2.0 technology and used to enhance reference services by innovative libraries across the United States, Great Britain, and Canada.

Finally, Chapter 22, "The Future of Information Service," looks ahead to the models, materials, and services that will continue to evolve and define reference services in the foreseeable future.

Round 3

In asking the user to absorb the skill sets provided in this book as a means to navigate fearlessly through the shifting sands of reference, we have been rather fearless ourselves. We have invited stringent critiques from theoreticians and practitioners, students and faculty, as well as colleagues and friends on the ideas, organization, choices, and usability of the text. Our personal egos have been temporarily suspended in the search for an objectively good product. The four members of the Advisory Board (listed on the verso of the title page) have been invaluable in helping us toward this goal. We have been in safe hands and we hope to pass that security on to you.

David Lankes, a Mover and Shaker at Syracuse University, talks of libraries as facilitators of knowledge-creation and reference as conversation and participatory networking. Round 1 of this book was birthed through intense conversation. We could see our fetal ideas gain bone, muscle, and tissue as we held focus groups at ALA conferences, deconstructed scores of reference syllabi, poured through publishers' catalogs and websites, and immersed ourselves in "participatory networking" with both aspiring students and grizzled practitioners. It was a heady experience. Round 2 was a process of fine-tuning, of quieter contemplation, of more in-depth questioning and expanded experience. Comprehensiveness, currency, and readability were the ternion values undergirding all additions, subtractions, and edits to the text. Round 3 has focused on tethering multiformat reference tools and services to the larger movements in society to provide context to the choices we have made. Crowdsourcing, cloud computing, and the remarkable *immediacy* of mobile technology are all feeding and being fed by a whole new style of information seeking and reference research. The product you hold amalgamates the energetic fire of its birth; the controlling waters of intensive calibration and expansion that marked Round 2; and the recognition of reference as part of a dynamically changed information universe in this Round 3 of the book.

We hope this combination will find its resonance in your individual development as intrepid and entrepreneurial reference librarians of the twenty-first century.

Acknowledgments

This book could not have accrued without the collective strengths provided by a number of people. We thank:

Charles Harmon, who has been a continuing source of positive energy and ideas through the entire project. Thanks also to Amy Knauer, who has kept us on track.

The members of our Advisory Board, Marie Radford, Anita Ondrusek, Eileen Abels, and Steve Task.

Reference librarians everywhere who shared their ideas.

Our many friends for their understanding and support.

Kay thanks:

Marina I. Mercado for her support, patience, and love.

The library school students I have taught for helping me to shape my ideas about reference service.

Uma thanks:

Bala, always Bala.

Part I
Fundamental Concepts

1
Introduction to Reference and Information Services

Virtual reference and electronic resources dominate the current conversation on reference and information services. Although the mission and goals of reference and information services remain much the same, the way they are being provided is constantly changing. The development of subscription and free electronic resources has changed the sources of information available, while virtual reference has made it possible to reach users no matter where they are. Librarians and library users are constantly bombarded with a wide range of information choices that must be evaluated for authenticity and accuracy. Whether at home on their computers or wandering through the stacks, many people feel as though they are drowning in a sea of information. New media and technologies link us to this new and growing body of knowledge and enable librarians to assist users virtually as well as face-to-face. Reference services are at once a life raft, map, and compass to those who feel adrift. In providing users with a combination of personalized services in a timely manner, libraries reaffirm their centrality as twenty-first-century public institutions par excellence.

For all its contemporary relevance, the concept of reference service is over a century old. In 1876, according to Genz (1998), Samuel Green, librarian of the Worcester Free Public Library in Massachusetts, developed the idea of having librarians assist the user in the selection of books to suit their needs. This served a dual function, increasing the use of his library's collection and thereby demonstrating the need for the library. Green saw the role of the public library as one of welcoming users by having a pleasant and cultivated female staff. Some forty years later, in 1915 at the thirty-seventh meeting of the American Library Association, a paper on reference work was delivered by W.W. Bishop, the superintendent of the Reading Room of the Library of Congress. Bishop defined reference work as "the service rendered by a librarian in aid of some sort of study" holding that it was "an organized effort on the part of libraries in aid of the most expeditious and fruitful use of their books" (Genz, 1998: 511).

Charles Williamson further developed the idea of reference service in his 1923 report "Training for Library Service: A Report Prepared for the Carnegie Corporation of New York," which included a course description for reference work:

> A study of the standard works of reference, general and special encyclopedias, dictionaries, annuals, indexes to periodicals, ready reference manuals

of every kind, special bibliographies, and the more important newspapers and periodicals. Works of similar scope are compared, and the limitations of each pointed out. Lists of questions made up from practical experience are given, and the method of finding the answers discussed in the class. (Genz, 1998: 513)

More recently, several authors, including William A. Katz (2001) and Richard E. Bopp and Linda C. Smith (2011), wrote reference texts in which they continued to refine the role of the reference librarian over the subsequent decades.

Perhaps the most important point to remember is that reference service seeks to fulfill the greater mission of the library by assisting individual users. Despite the many transformations that have been wrought on reference work by developments of our information society and paradigm shifts in the self-understandings of the library, much has remained the same. First and foremost, it is still a service in which the librarian interacts with a patron on a one-to-one basis, whether it is in person or virtually. This level of personal service has become even more important in the twenty-first century in light of the alienating and depersonalizing effects of many information technologies. On the other hand, the way in which librarians provide such service has changed considerably—it now extends beyond face-to-face assistance thanks to the availability of the telephone, e-mail, and the technology for chat and instant messaging (IM) reference, and even social media such as Facebook and Twitter.

Ethics

Ethical awareness and engagement is a crucial aspect of all library services, and the ideals that have been established for the profession generally apply fully to those working in reference services. Just as a therapist would do his patients little good if he did not keep their information confidential, reference librarians must follow certain standards of behavior if the service they provide is to be effective. The American Library Association's current Code of Ethics, last revised in 2008, provides a useful guide. This code upholds a variety of the principles essential to the modern library.

The code encourages librarians to provide the same high level of service to all library users and to provide information that is "accurate, unbiased and courteous." This statement is at the heart of good reference service, which strives to provide good quality information and information to all. Reference staff must understand what constitutes a good reference interaction and must strive to meet that standard with each user query (Bunge, 1999).

The code calls for upholding the principles of intellectual freedom and resisting attempts to censor library materials. Resource selection is reflected in this statement, as librarians are encouraged to provide information on a subject from many points of view. The code goes on to insist on the user's right to privacy and confidentiality in requesting and using library resources. Reference librarians must be particularly cognizant of this professional obligation. They must respect the privacy of a user by keeping their reference interview and the resources used confidential.

Intellectual property rights, addressed in the code, are of increasing importance in libraries. Librarians must keep current with changes in intellectual property laws, especially copyright, and keep their users aware of these laws. Librarians must know when copying is covered under the "fair use" provision of the law and when copying violates the copyright law. This is more than a good in itself; it also helps protect the institution, its employees, and its users from claims of copyright infringement and intellectual dishonesty.

The relationship between personal interests and professional responsibilities is discussed in the code. The respectful treatment of coworkers and colleagues and the safeguarding of the rights of all employees are encouraged. Library employees are cautioned not to put private interests ahead of library interests. This means that employees should be circumspect in their dealings with library vendors and others outside the library so their decisions are made on professional merit and are not influenced by personal interest.

The code also cautions library employees not to put personal convictions or beliefs ahead of library interests. This is of special significance to reference librarians. Sometimes a librarian must help a user research an area that is personally against the librarian's beliefs or philosophy. By putting professional duties first, the librarian can successfully assist the user and provide the information needed.

Other professional library organizations have their own codes of ethics. These include, among others, the American Society for Information Science (ASIS), the Society of American Archivists, the Medical Library Association, and the American Association of Law Libraries. A more in-depth discussion of ethics is presented in Chapter 18.

Kinds of Information Service

Information service is the process of resolving information needs of users in response to a particular question, interest, assignment, or problem and building positive relationships with users (Radford, 1999). The Reference and User Services Association (RUSA) of the American Library Association defines reference transactions, sometimes referred to as reference service, as "information consultations in which library staff recommend, interpret, evaluate, and/or use information resources to help others to meet particular information needs" (RUSA, 2008). These reference transactions can take place in person, on the telephone, or virtually via e-mail, chat reference, instant messaging, texting, Twitter, or video conferencing. Librarians are also creating websites, answer archives, and links to "frequently asked questions"—all of which are designed to anticipate user questions and help people find information independently. Traditional reference desk service continues to be highly valued by library users in many settings, but newer forms of virtual communication such as e-mail, chat reference, and IM have grown tremendously in popularity. Consequently, it is all the more important for librarians to understand the range of inquiries that can be expected, allowing them to provide a full and ready answer, regardless of the form through which the query arises or through which the answer is delivered.

Answering Reference Questions

In light of the immense diversity and range of possible questions, being approached by a patron with an information need can seem like a daunting prospect. Indeed, much of the difficulty of information services arises from uncertainty about the kind of service or breadth of information called for by a given question. Categorizing reference questions by type is a useful way to make sense of such concerns. Three common types of reference questions are ready reference questions, research questions, and bibliographic verification.

Ready reference questions such as "Where is Harry Truman's Presidential Library?," "Who won the 2011 World Series?," "What is the capital of Nepal?," or "Where can I find a copy of the Declaration of Independence?" can be readily answered using a general reference source. The librarian may be tempted to tell the user the answer to simple ready reference questions. Yet here the saying that "giving a man a fish feeds him for a day while teaching him to fish feeds him for a lifetime" helps to explain the importance of providing instruction when possible. No matter how simple they initially seem, ready reference questions provide the opportunity for teachable moments. Taking into consideration users' needs and willingness to engage in instruction, librarians should lead users through the process of looking up the information rather than simply provide the solution.

Librarians who assist users with ready reference inquiries on a regular basis sometimes choose to create a "ready reference" section of the most commonly used resources, either in print or on the library's website, to answer quick questions. Typically, such sections include a general all-purpose encyclopedia, dictionaries, almanacs, and handbooks. Librarians should keep the sources up-to-date and also should avoid depending so heavily on this subset of the collection that other sources are overlooked by library users and librarians. Ready reference questions have diminished due to the ease of answering basic questions through search engines such as Google, though a study found that for chat reference about 30 percent of the questions were ready reference (Connaway and Radford, 2011). Thus, ready reference remains a cornerstone of information services, and librarians should be ready to provide it at any time.

Research questions are more complex, may take much longer to answer, and typically require multiple sources of information. These are often the questions that require the user to consider a variety of sources and viewpoints and to subsequently draw conclusions. Sometimes questions that initially seem like ready reference questions are found to be far more complex, as previously hidden facets of the user's inquiry are revealed. Here, the variety of possible sources increases with the complexity of users' questions. Librarians should, for example, guide users in the use of bibliographic sources, databases, and other reference resources. Likewise, users with complex questions may need guidance as to how to find or request the full text of articles for which only citations are given in a search of electronic databases, allowing them to move beyond cursory surveys of the literature.

Research questions, especially if the user is unable to fully articulate the nature of his or her query, require librarians to ask additional questions through the reference interview as a means of understanding the nature of the request before setting out to help the patron answer it. The librarian will need to determine how much information is needed, what level of information is needed, and what other sources have already been consulted. As is discussed in Chapter 3, information services call for mutual engagement, especially with more complex questions. Reference librarians should never be passive participants, pointing the way to an answer. Instead, they should play the part of dynamic guides, collaborating with users on their search for information and knowledge.

Naturally, the extent of such engagement may vary from one circumstance to another. Different types of libraries tend to have their own standards for how long librarians should spend with users on research questions. Many public libraries recommend that users be given five or ten minutes of personal assistance and then asked to return if more help is needed. A university library may have a similar standard, or depending on the institution, the librarian may invite the user to make an appointment for more in-depth research assistance. Some libraries may suggest that users call or e-mail ahead of their visit so the librarian can be prepared to offer the best possible assistance. Many libraries now offer consultation services for which the user makes an appointment in advance, which allow the librarian to spend more time with the user. Librarians may also refer users to other libraries with more specialized materials in the area of the users' research or offer to call back or e-mail if additional information is found.

Finally, a library user may seek *bibliographic verification* when he or she has already obtained the information needed but must verify the sources. Sometimes this service is a matter of fact checking, while on other occasions users may have completed their research but lack full citation information. As users increasingly depend on electronic databases for information, compiling and formatting bibliographic citations becomes easier. Verifying and citing material found on webpages is more difficult since the information needed for the citation is not always easy to find.

Readers' Advisory Service

Readers' advisory service, sometimes considered a type of information service, is the quest to put the right resources in the hands of the right reader. Public and school librarians especially are increasingly expected to provide an answer to the question, "Can you help me find a good book?" Fortunately, as demand has increased, so too has the ease of providing this service. While there is no substitute for a librarian's own knowledge or experience, many new technologies serve to make readers' advisory far easier than it was in the past. Many online databases, for example, have functions that automatically recommend other books for those who like a given title. Others have searchable lists of works by genre, helping readers match their favorite books to others like them. As always, however, remember that readers' advisory, like other reference work, is predicated on the interaction between a librarian and a library user. Asking directed questions, listening carefully to the user's responses, and tailoring assistance accordingly is the basis of excellent, truly helpful service.

Readers' advisory service is generally associated with public libraries and school libraries and may be employed by those looking for fiction or sometimes literary nonfiction. In academic libraries, it is far less common as users rarely come in searching for a good book to read. Even so, readers' advisory may be needed to help lay researchers looking to deepen their knowledge of a particular field. A patron who has read and enjoyed Stephen Ambrose's *Undaunted Courage*, but is troubled by allegations about Ambrose's questionable accuracy and academic honesty, may want to know the titles of books about the Lewis and Clark expedition that are both reputable and engaging. Successful readers' advisory librarians are skilled at asking users questions that enable them to assist in finding books of interest. They must know a great deal about various genres of fiction and nonfiction and be intimately familiar with their library's collection. Significantly, it is important that they be able to convey their expertise in a friendly and conversational manner. Truly mastering readers' advisory service requires a great deal of skill and practice. The basics are explored in more detail in Chapter 14.

Information Literacy

Information literacy, formerly often referred to as *user instruction*, may range from showing an individual how to use the library's online catalog and basic print and electronic reference sources to formal classroom sessions about conducting research in the library. The basic component of information literacy includes demonstrating how, when, and why to use various reference sources in an integrated way that will capture the user's attention at the teachable moment.

In today's educational settings, the ease of using electronic resources often results in a failure to teach more traditional research strategies. While finding superficial information has grown easier, in-depth information has become increasingly difficult to find for many students. In the library, too, approaches to instruction may vary. Librarians often question whether to simply answer questions posed by users or to teach users how to employ the available resources. This may be contingent on the mission or purpose of the library. Academic institutions may call on their librarians to help students understand how to engage effectively and independently in the research and information evaluation process. Public librarians, by contrast, may try to teach users about reference sources in a more informal manner as they lead users to the answers they seek. Thus, while instruction is always an important part of reference work, the degree to which librarians go about providing it is highly contingent on the type of library and the way it has defined its role in library instruction.

In any case, all reference librarians must be skilled at helping users find information and answers quickly and be ready to teach users how to use the reference sources that are available. The best reference librarians develop an intuition for when to be information providers and when to be information literacy instructors. In some libraries, only specific, designated librarians are charged with conducting library instruction courses. Nevertheless, an increasing number of librarians are required to participate in their libraries' information literacy program, and library school graduates are expected to be capable of teaching basic classes on the use of library resources. As should be clear, even those librarians not charged with providing formal instruction have the opportunity to teach informally those they assist. The various aspects of information literacy are covered in greater depth in Chapter 16.

Selecting and Evaluating Print and Electronic Resources

Selecting and evaluating print and electronic information for the library's collection can be as professionally rewarding as providing expert information service. Reference librarians' involvement in selecting and evaluating titles for the collection helps them develop rich knowledge of the sources at their disposal, increasing their effectiveness.

The responsibility for selecting reference materials depends largely on the size and scope of the library. In large academic libraries, selecting reference materials may be assigned to subject bibliographers whose work may be limited to collection development responsibilities. On the other side of the continuum, the evaluation and purchase of resources in very small libraries may be the work of a single reference librarian or coordinator of reference. A range of shared selection and evaluation possibilities between these points include reference materials selection committees or group assignments.

The question "What makes a resource a reference source?" has long been debated in our profession. For the purpose of this discussion, reference sources are those resources set aside to be consulted for specific information rather than to be read as a whole. In other words, reference sources contain content meant to be "looked up." Typically, one turns to a reference source in search of something in particular rather than to the text as a whole. Reference collections are always on hand either in the library or electronically, making for a consistently available body of knowledge. Note that labeling narrative or nonreference resources as "reference" to ensure that a popular volume is always available may lead to bloated reference collections, and, thus, this is not generally recommended. Finally, with the addition of electronic reference sources that have become increasingly available to remote library users from their homes, dorm rooms, offices, and elsewhere, reference collections encompass much more than print books and are available twenty-four hours a day.

As the present trend toward shrinking budgets for reference collections, lean reference collections, and the elimination of duplication among print and electronic collections continues, the careful evaluation and selection of reference materials is essential. Libraries should determine the criteria that will be used in selecting sources for their reference collections. The following criteria may help determine whether a print or electronic resource is a worthy addition to a library's collection: scope, quality of content, appropriateness for audience, format, arrangement, authority, currency, accuracy, ease of use, unique coverage, and cost.

Some libraries select reference materials by reading reviews in the library professional literature, such as *Library Journal*, *Choice*, and *Booklist*'s "Reference Books Bulletin." Other institutions insist on physically reviewing reference sources at exhibits at library association conferences or through special arrangements with publishers of reference materials. Most libraries employ a combination of these two. A more extensive discussion of selection and evaluation takes place in Chapter 17.

Creating Finding Tools and Websites

Another strategy employed by many reference departments is the creation of finding tools, subject or research guides, and pathfinders for library users. Here, librarians act as guides, mapping out the best routes through familiar territory and pointing out interesting sites along the way. Subject or research guides are often prepared by academic libraries using LibGuides (http://www.springshare .com/libguides/) as a template for frequently requested subjects, such as African studies, criminal justice, and intellectual property. Similarly, public libraries may prepare guides that address frequently asked questions of a quotidian nature, such as finding job information, checking the credentials of a health care provider, or researching a family tree. Depending on the topic, audience, and needs, these guides may assist the user to identify a selection of appropriate reference books, relevant databases and search terms, a selection of current and authoritative websites, and tips for searching the library's catalog for additional materials.

Librarians also create websites of carefully evaluated links and other resources organized by topic. Who better than a librarian to organize information, pointing users to "the best" sources and helping them steer clear of the dubious? Web-based finding tools are available to users 24/7, they can be updated as often as needed, and they can include direct links to websites and electronic reference tools. Depending on the circumstance and the nature of a library's web presence, such resource guides can be either general, providing direction to broadly targeted reference resources, or subject specific. General all-purpose lists of librarian-selected web resources include the *Internet Public Library* (http://www.ipl2.org/) and *INFOMINE* (http://infomine.ucr.edu/). Examples of library subject-specific guides include the New York Public Library's *Best of the Web* (http://www.nypl .org/collections/nypl-recommendations/best-of-web) and the University of Washington's *Information Gateway* (http://www.lib.washington.edu/subject/). Larger libraries, whether academic or public, often produce these guides. Smaller libraries may be better served by developing bibliographies for specific areas in which they have subject specialists and linking to a general reference website like the *Internet Public Library*.

Promotion and Marketing

Promotion and marketing of libraries and reference service is becoming more important than ever. With expanding e-resource collections and e-services, library collections may be less visible to the public, so it is even more important for libraries to call attention to them in order to encourage use by their community. Promoting reference service among individual library users can go a long way toward achieving this goal, especially insofar as it demonstrates how the library can serve them. In large communities—urban public libraries, for example—promoting the library through individual users is not enough to attract new users, and major marketing or publicity campaigns become important. In academic, school, and special libraries, promotion and marketing are equally essential. Use of print and online newsletters, websites, information literacy instruction, and meetings with faculty and staff can provide opportunities to promote the library's resources.

Evaluating Staff and Services

Libraries may seek to routinely evaluate their reference collections or reference service. In her book *Evaluating Reference Services: A Practical Guide,* Jo Bell Whit-latch (2000: 1) wisely emphasizes the importance of defining the purpose of the evaluation before setting a strategy: "The most important questions you must ask" according to Whitlatch, are "Why am I evaluating reference services" and "What do I plan to do with the study results?"

Assessing the quality of the reference interaction, from either the user's or the librarian's perspective, will help determine how effective the reference service is. Evaluating reference staff is one way to do this and will also help to ensure quality reference service. The American Library Association's Reference and User Services Association (2004) has developed "Guidelines for Behavioral Performance of Reference and Information Service Professionals" that are intended to be used in the training, development, or evaluation of library professionals and staff. The performance of reference librarians is typically evaluated on both the information conveyed to the user and the satisfaction of the interaction for the library user.

The following factors are covered by the ALA guidelines:

- *Approachability:* Are users able to identify that a reference librarian is available to help?
- *Interest:* Does the librarian demonstrate a high degree of interest in the reference transaction?
- *Listening/inquiring:* Does the librarian identify the user's information need in a manner that puts the user at ease? Are good communication skills used throughout the transaction?
- *Searching:* Is the librarian skilled at creating search strategies that yield accurate and relevant results?
- *Follow-up:* Does the librarian determine if the user is satisfied with the results of the search/interaction? (RUSA, 2004)

These performance guidelines may form the backbone of a library's staff evaluation instrument, whether the instrument is a simple self-evaluation checklist, a peer-evaluation tool, or a formal evaluation system influencing earning potential.

In addition to evaluating staff, the library may measure its productivity or efficiency with quantitative measures that include the number of questions answered and the frequency with which print and/or electronic sources are consulted. Smaller libraries may count the number and type of all in-person questions answered by the reference staff. Larger libraries frequently rely on quarterly one-week periods to estimate the number of questions answered over the course of a year. Depending on the available resources, data may be recorded using hand-held computers, by making hash marks on a form, or by any means in between.

A variety of other evaluation strategies are also available to libraries. For example, another useful measurement is assessing the quality of the resources available. Departmental evaluations can include issues of resource allocation such as how the library's budget allocates for library staff, print and electronic resources, computers and networks, and buildings. Evaluation methods frequently used to gauge users' satisfaction with reference services and sources include questionnaires, surveys, focus groups, observation, and interviews.

It is crucial that library administrators determine what is to be measured and against what standards before choosing the preferred method of evaluation. There are many sources available for detailed information on designing evaluation instruments for libraries. Librarians should carefully consider these aspects: selecting the best method; developing and field-testing the instrument; administering the survey, questionnaire, or interview; planning the observation; avoiding interviewer bias; and scores of ethical issues. Analyzing data and developing conclusions and recommendations may require advanced training, and in some cases libraries may need to hire evaluation experts. These and other questions are considered in greater depth in Chapter 20.

The Changing Nature of Reference

As the form of the library has evolved in the years since Samuel Green's seminal pronouncements in 1876, so, too, has the nature of reference services. Today, it stretches far beyond the walls of the library and has far loftier ends than welcoming users to the library with a "cultivated female staff." Academic libraries and some special libraries in particular have already seen a slowing of traffic to the physical library and increasing use of the library's online resources. Users can ask questions 24/7 through virtual reference and expect an immediate response. Likewise, they can access electronic resources that the library provides through its website. Virtual reference is growing quickly; the appeal of chat, instant messaging, and Twitter and other technology-based services, such as mobile technology, point to a generational paradigm shift ahead. These online reference services have the advantage of being convenient and necessary in our fast-paced world.

In numerous forms and fashions, technology continues to change reference services. Librarians must be ready to learn new technology and adapt to the needs of users unable to imagine a world without technology. Like few other professionals, librarians must be willing to ride the waves of such change, adapting to meet the needs of their users. Whether it is a smartphone, an iPad, or a laptop, users will want to receive and read their information via the technology of their choice.

New models of reference are also developing to meet different user needs. Libraries are adding more points of service, such as an information desk near the front of the library, a reference service point combined with other library services, or an in-depth reference center where a user can sit down with a librarian and work out a plan for researching a paper. In other situations, librarians rove the library to help users who do not approach the reference desk and librarians meet individually with users to discuss their reference or research needs.

These and other new strategies are changing the way information services are offered. As we look ahead, we must be aware that reference work will no doubt be based increasingly on electronic means of communication. At the same time, it will continue to be a personal service, although not necessarily face-to-face. There will be more emphasis on electronic materials, while some older materials will still need to be consulted in print format. Even so, the way we find information and convey it is as fundamental today as it ever was. In the chapters ahead, we explore the cutting edge of contemporary reference, demonstrating how to keep this crucial service central to the modern library.

Recommendations for Further Reading

Agosto, D. E., L. Rozakis, C. MacDonald, and E. Abels. 2011. "A Model of the Reference and Information Service Process: An Educators' Perspective." *Reference and User Services Quarterly* 50, no. 3: 235–244. Provides an overview of current trends in the delivery of information services, models of practice, and the role of the librarian in education. Reference today is found to be a more collaborative, evaluative process than in the past.

Alexander, L., J. Blumenthal, K. Downing, B. MacAdam, K. R.Gurpreet, K. Reiman-Sendi, N. Scholtz, and L.A. Sutch. 2011. "Mlibrary: Concepts for Redefining Reference." *Journal of Library Administration* 51, no. 4 (April 22): 326–342. Examines the evolution of library reference services over the course of ten years at the University of Michigan's Library. This study of one library provides general insights into how reference has changed in this period, including the reconfiguration of space in the reference room, reference inquiry trends, shifts in the role of academic librarians, the emergence of new information needs, and new technology.

Austin, B. 2004. "Should There Be 'Privilege' in the Relationship between Reference Librarian and Patron?" *The Reference Librarian* no. 87/88: 301–311. Explores whether privilege should be extended to the librarian-patron relationship.

Connaway, L. S., T. J. Dickey, and M. L. Radford. 2011. "'If It Is Too Inconvenient I'm Not Going After It.' Convenience as a Critical Factor in Information-Seeking Behaviors." *Library and Information Science Research* 33, no. 3: 179–190. Presents the findings of two multiyear empirical studies on how perceived convenience affects information-seeking behavior. The findings are put in the context of gratification theory. Convenience is shown to affect users' choice of resources, satisfaction with the resources, and the time horizon of the search process.

Ismail, L. 2010. "What Net Generation Students Really Want: Determining Library Help-seeking Preferences of Undergraduates." *Reference Services Review* 38, no. 1: 10–27. Discusses the results of a survey of undergraduates at Marywood University, which, to the surprise of the university's librarians, indicated that students preferred in-person reference encounters to virtual reference. Underscores the benefit of assessing the needs and preference of users before investing too exclusively in new models of service.

Jacoby, J. A., and N. P. O'Brien. 2005. "Assessing the Impact of Reference Service Provided to Undergraduate Students." *College and Research Libraries* 66, no. 4 (July): 324–340. Reports on how reference service can help students to learn to do research and to use the library.

Kilzer, R. 2011. "Reference as Service, Reference as Place: A View of Reference in the Academic Library." *The Reference Librarian* 52, no. 4: 291–299. Examines how reference and research models are trending toward a distributed variety of services at point of need. Explores the traditional concept of "reference as place" and reinterprets this concept in light of reference services as they exist today. Shows that proactive methods and collaboration between universities and campus entities are increasing in importance.

Landesman, M. 2005. "Getting It Right—The Evolution of Reference Collections." *The Reference Librarian* no. 91/92: 5–22. Presents the history of the development of reference collections.

Nunn, B., and E. Ruane. 2011. "Marketing Gets Personal: Promoting Reference Staff to Reach Users." *Journal of Library Administration* 51, no. 3 (March 24): 291–300. Suggests that an outreach campaign address the lack of awareness of reference services by promoting the personal aspect of reference through person-to-person interactions, word-of-mouth recommendations, and establishing relationships with faculty and students.

O'Connor, L., and K. Lundstrom. 2011. "The Impact of Social Marketing Strategies on the Information Seeking Behaviors of College." *Reference and User Services Quarterly* 50, no. 4: 351–365. Applies social marketing, "the application of commercial marketing techniques to the resolution of social and health problems," to academic library outreach. Shows how social marketing strategy results in some positive changes in information-seeking behavior among college students, specifically a reduction in procrastination and an increase in help seeking. However, does not show an effect on the selection of materials.

Rix, W. 2009. "Reference Collections and Staff: Retaining Relevance." *The Reference Librarian* 50, no. 3: 302–305. Addresses how reference collections have changed and how staff have adapted over the last twenty years. Also discusses how to weed print resources and options for making new use of the space.

Smith, D. A., and V. T. Oliva. 2010. "Becoming a Renaissance Reference Librarian in Academe: Attitudes toward Generalist and Subject Specific Reference and Related Profession Development." *Reference Services Review* 38, no. 1: 125–151. Discusses librarians' attitudes about general and specialized reference questions and the level of subject-area preparation needed by academic librarians at the reference desk. Also addresses professional development and confidence level.

Bibliography and Works Cited

American Library Association. 2008. "Code of Ethics of the American Library Association." American Library Association. http://www.ala.org/advocacy/proethics/code ofethics/codeethics.

Bopp, R. E., and L. C. Smith. 2011. *Reference and Information Services: An Introduction*. Englewood, CO: Libraries Unlimited.

Bunge, C. 1999. "Ethics and the Reference Librarian." *The Reference Librarian*, no. 66: 25–33.

Connaway, L. S. and M. L. Radford. 2011. *Seeking Synchronicity: Revelations and Recommendations for Virtual Reference*. Dublin, OH: OCLC Research. Available: http://www.oclc.org/reports/synchronicity/default.htm.

Genz, M. D. 1998. "Working the Reference Desk." *Library Trends*, 46, no. 3 (Winter): 505–525.

Katz, W. A. 2001. *Introduction to Reference Work*. 2 vols. New York: McGraw-Hill.

Radford, M.L. 1999. *The Reference Encounter: Interpersonal Communication in the Academic Library*. Chicago: Association of College and Research Libraries.

RUSA (Reference and User Services Association). 2004. "Guidelines for Behavioral Performance of Reference and Information Service Providers." June. American Library Association. http://www.ala.org/rusa/resources/guidelines/guidelinesbehavioral.

———. 2008. "Definitions of Reference." American Library Association. http://www.ala.org/ala/mgrps/divs/rusa/resources/guidelines/definitionsreference.cfm.

Whitlatch, J. B. 2000. *Evaluating Reference Services: A Practical Guide*. Chicago: American Library Association.

2

Determining the Question: In-Person, Telephone, and Virtual Reference Interviews

The reference interview is a challenging experience because the librarian and the user must communicate effectively so that the librarian understands the user's need. The reference interview requires a balance of skills. It is both an art and a science, requiring both responsiveness to the individual user and a structure within which to work. While librarians should learn the elements of a good reference interview, they must also recognize that these steps need to be adapted to each situation. Each reference interview will be slightly different since each user and each question are different. The overall structure has three phases: "establishing contact with the user, finding out the user's need, and confirming that the answer provided is actually what was needed" (Ross, Nilsen, and Radford, 2009: 5). Within this framework, librarians must learn to improvise like expert jazz musicians.

For librarians, giving the right answer to the right question is the most important part of the reference interaction. Yet, studies and experience show that users react to the manner in which the reference interview is conducted, paying special attention to both verbal and nonverbal cues. They are more likely to return to a librarian who has handled their request respectfully whether or not their information need has been completely fulfilled. As librarians learn the elements of a good reference interview, they will also understand that they will need to adapt the elements of the interview to the specific situation. Conduct is as important as content, as is found in good customer service.

Why Do the Reference Interview?

Sometimes it seems like the questions asked by users are very straightforward, prompting librarians to wonder why the reference interview is necessary at all. Upon looking into the matter, however, the librarian often discovers that the real question was not the first one asked. Users tend to believe they can ask a short question and get enough information to proceed on their own. In such circumstances, the ambiguity of their initial inquiry often leads to confusion. A user might, for example, ask for books about stars when, in fact, the user wants to know the constellations one can see south of the equator or is seeking information about the home addresses of movie stars. As another example, a user might ask for books on baking when the user actually wants to find out about the chemistry involved in the rising of yeast rather than recipes for bread. In philosophy, errors prompted by the multiple meanings of words are known as "category mistakes," the grouping of dissimilar concepts under a single shared label. Errors of this kind may not have profound consequences in the library world, but they do delay delivery of the correct response to the user. By asking additional clarifying questions, the librarian can avoid such problems, focusing on the meaningful content of the user's request (Dewdney and Michell, 1996).

What We Know about the Reference Interview

Many authors have written about the nature of reference interactions. Robert S. Taylor (1968), in his article "Question Negotiation and Information Seeking in Libraries," explored the reference interaction from the point of view of question negotiation. Taylor discussed "the five filters through which a question passes and from which the librarian selects significant data to aid him in his research" (p. 183). Elaine Z. Jennerich and Edward J. Jennerich (1997) approached the reference interview as a "creative art" and a "performing art." Mary Jo Lynch (1978) studied the reference interview in public libraries and asked how reference librarians know when to interview a user, through what channels a librarian gathers information without asking questions, and what are the characteristics of an effective question sequence.

Brenda Dervin and Patricia Dewdney's (1986) article "Neutral Questioning: A New Approach to the Reference Interview" proposed the neutral questioning model—a user-oriented approach to answering reference questions. Patricia Dewdney and Catherine Sheldrick Ross (1994) continued the research in this area by looking at the reference interview from the user's point of view. They asked Master of Library and Information Science students to visit libraries and ask questions of interest to them and to report on the results. Only 59.7 percent said that they would return to the same librarian (Dewdney and Ross, 1994).

Marie Radford, in her 1998 article in *Library Trends*, turned her attention to nonverbal communications. She identified five factors indicated by users that were critical in their decision as to whom to approach. They were initiation, availability, proximity, familiarity, and gender. Mary Jane Swope and Jeffrey Katzer (1972) studied the question of why people don't ask for assistance and found that dissatisfaction with their previous assistance, the belief that their query was too simple, and the disinclination to bother the librarian affected their decision not to ask for assistance.

Intercultural communication has been explored by Wang and Frank (2002) and Walker and Clark (2011). Wang and Frank pointed out that both language and cross-cultural communication barriers affect academic librarians' work with international students and suggested many ways for librarians to close that gap. Walker and Clark also emphasized the language barriers for international students that may affect their ability to understand slang, colloquialisms, and even library terminology. Most recently, research has turned to the area of virtual reference and what are the best practices for chat reference, instant messaging (IM), and text messaging. The work of Mon and Janes (2007), Radford, Connaway, and colleagues (2011), Kwon and Gregory (2007), and Luo (2011) helps us to better understand virtual reference.

Conducting the Reference Interview

The reference interview is composed of several parts, each of which is discussed in turn in the following pages:

- Establishing rapport with the user
- Negotiating the question
- Developing a successful search strategy and communicating it to the user
- Locating the information and evaluating it
- Ensuring that the question is fully answered—the follow-up
- Closing the interview

Establishing Rapport with the User

When users arrive at the library or contact a librarian virtually (whether by phone, e-mail, chat reference, or IM), they expect to find someone willing to assist them. To make the initial approach easier, librarians must find ways to signal, verbally and/or nonverbally, that they are approachable. In "An Exploratory Study: A Kinesic Analysis of Academic Library Public Service Points," Edward Kazlauskas (1976) found that raising the eyebrow and lowering it when someone approaches, maintaining eye contact, nodding, and smiling all help make the initial encounter more positive and comfortable. Kazlauskas also identified behaviors that make the librarian less approachable: lack of immediate acknowledgment of user, failing to change body stance as the user comes closer, covering the eyes with the hand, reading, tapping one's finger, and twitching of the mouth.

Marie L. Radford (1998: 699) "observed reference interactions for thirty-seven hours, interviewing 155 users who approached thirty-four librarian volunteers." Her purpose was to discover behaviors that influenced which librarian the user approached. She identified five factors indicated by users that positively shaped user decisions:

- *Initiation.* The librarian begins the interaction by using one of the following nonverbal signals: eye contact, body orientation, movement toward the user, or verbal enforcement.
- *Availability.* The librarian indicates availability by turning around, moving toward the patron, using eye contact, or otherwise signaling attention to the user nonverbally.
- *Proximity.* Users decide whom to approach based on their physical distance from the librarian.
- *Familiarity.* The user had previously met or been helped by a particular librarian.
- *Gender.* Users found it more comfortable to approach a female librarian.

The librarian can also look approachable by roving through the library reference area and helping users who may need assistance. Many users may not be comfortable initiating a conversation with a librarian when they need help, so roving gives users a less formal opportunity to seek assistance. As they roam, librarians can simply ask users if they are finding what they need. They can approach users whom they have already assisted or perhaps users who have not approached the reference desk but appear to need some assistance.

When serving users who telephone or send their requests by e-mail or chat reference, the librarian can make the process easier by greeting the user in a friendly, upbeat manner (e.g., "Hello. How can I help you?") and by responding to the information provided by the user. For example, the user may say he or she is using virtual reference rather than visiting the library because of an illness. The librarian might respond by saying, "I hope you will be better soon" (Ross, Nilsen, and Radford, 2009: 204).

Whatever the circumstances, the user must feel that the librarian is interested in his or her question. In person, the librarian can accomplish this by facing the patron when speaking and listening and by maintaining eye contact with the patron. The librarian signals his or her understanding of the user's question by responding verbally or by nodding. When the user contacts the library virtually, the librarian must stay in contact with the user by conveying in words his or her interest in the question. For example, the librarian could say, "What an interesting question," and then follow up by writing that he or she is still trying to find resources for the user.

Negotiating the Question

Once the possibility of dialogue has been established, the next step is to determine the patron's query. Many approaches to negotiating the question have been suggested by researchers and practitioners. Brenda Dervin and Patricia Dewdney (1986) have suggested "sense-making" as a way of finding out exactly what the user wants. Sense-making is user oriented and approaches the reference interview in an organized way designed to ensure that the librarian understands what the user really needs. This method calls for an understanding of the user's situation, the gap that led to the question, and how the user plans to use the information. Dervin and Dewdney argue that it is important to understand that the "gaps individuals face (i.e., the questions they have) depend upon the way in which they see the situation and how they are stopped. The kind of answers they want is dependent on how they expect to use or be helped by the answers" (p. 507). Two questions, alike in form, may not, in the end, be at all similar if the users who ask them differ in their views of the situation. Dervin and Dewdney went on to develop a further approach to questioning called "neutral questioning" which grows out of "sense-making." Neutral questioning involves asking open questions that will help the librarian discover the true nature of the question. Dervin and Dewdney state that, through questions, the librarian must assess the situation, assess the gaps, and assess the uses of the information. They suggest that the most useful neutral questions are the following:

> What kind of help would you like?
> What have you done about this so far?
> What would you like this book (information) to do for you? (Dervin and Dewdney, 1986: 512)

An example of this questioning in action is the following:

> Do you want annual reports? What sort of details do you want? If you could tell me the kind of problem you're working on, I'll have a better idea of what would help you. (Dervin and Dewdney, 1986: 510)

This form of questioning can be tailored to the needs of each individual by focusing on how the information will be used. Once learned, neutral questioning is not a long process because it is adapted to the needs of the individual. Neutral questioning can help librarians avoid the kind of category mistakes described earlier in this chapter. It also helps facilitate other forms of disambiguation, by ensuring that all possible information about the user's request is made known. Users may ask where books on a certain subject are, thinking that they can browse when they get to the section and find what they are looking for on their own. Other patrons may need some specific information and think the library does not have it just because a particular book is not on the shelf—unaware that a librarian may be able to answer the question with another source.

For a positive reference interview to take place, the librarian must listen carefully to the user and ask clarifying questions as necessary. The librarian must begin with open-ended questions, giving the user a chance to express reference needs. Often, the first question asked by the user does not really describe what the user is seeking. The librarian must ask probing, open-ended questions such as these: "Please tell me more about your topic." "What do you want to know about [the topic]?" "What additional information can you give me?" The librarian should continue with clarifying questions that may be a combination of open-ended or closed-ended questions until it is clear what the user wants. These clarifying questions might include the following:

Open-ended questions	Closed-ended questions
How much information do you need?	Do you need current or historical information?
What have you already found?	Do you need factual or analytical information?
What format for the information do you need?	Can you read languages other than English?

The librarian should rephrase the question to be sure that he or she really understands what is needed by the user. Of course, it goes without saying that the librarian should remain objective and not make judgments about the subject of the question. The same is true of a virtual reference question. The librarian must ask the same open-ended questions to give the user a chance to type out their information.

Although the librarian should begin with open-ended questions that allow users to express their question more fully, there is also a place for closed-ended questions. Once the librarian understands the question, he or she may want to narrow the search with some clarifying, closed-ended questions. The important thing to remember about closed-ended questions is that the response from the user will be brief. For example, if the librarian asks the user, "Do you want books or just articles?," the user may respond with a one-word answer, such as "books" or "articles." Sometimes a mix of open- and closed-ended questions works best. As the librarian listens to the user's question, he or she must not make assumptions about the user or the question. Assumptions may lead the librarian in the wrong direction, bringing the search up short. By working to avoid the always mistaken belief that the horizon of the user is the same as the librarian's own, the librarian can extend the limits of his or her vision.

For this interchange to be truly effective, the librarian should include the user in the search. For example, the librarian may turn the monitor toward the user to show the user the information being located in the database. This will enable the librarian to continue to test whether he or she is proceeding in the right direction, and it will be less isolating for the user. As the exchange proceeds, including the user will give the librarian the opportunity to offer other information about how to use the library that may be helpful to the user in the future.

In the course of assisting the user, the librarian may need to help the user to reframe the question. The question may be too general or too specific, and the librarian must then work with the user to better formulate the question. For example, the user may ask for information on the Civil War but actually want information on the Battle of Gettysburg. The librarian should try to find out in carefully crafted phrases how the information will be used and what level of material is needed.

Finally, the librarian should paraphrase the question back to the user to be sure that the understanding is mutual. For example, "If I understand you correctly, you want information on the coral reefs in Key West, especially their geology, location, and water temperature." It is easy to misunderstand the user's question, so every effort should be made to make sure the user's needs are being clearly communicated.

Developing a Successful Search Strategy and Communicating It to the User

Once the subject is clear, the librarian should construct a search, selecting search terms and identifying the most appropriate sources for the particular user. If the librarian has little knowledge of the subject, he or she should partner with the user in selecting the subject terms. No one, even a subject specialist, can ever expect to be an expert on that which might be of interest to library patrons, and the reference encounter is often as much a chance to learn as it is to teach. So long as one knows where to begin looking, the reference process can be exciting for both librarian and user. As the search is developed, the librarian should explain as much about the search as he or she thinks is of interest to the user. The librarian should also respect the user's time frame and work to assist the user to the fullest extent possible within that time frame, taking into consideration how busy the service desk or virtual queue is.

Of the many kinds of information available on most subjects, the librarian must determine what information will fit the user's needs. Does the user want more general information or more technical information? The librarian can judge this only by continuing to communicate with the user. The user may also have a preference as to the format of the information, the amount of information, and the level of the information. Ideally, the librarian will discover much of this information in the earlier phase of determining the question. It is important for the librarian to keep constantly in mind all that he or she knows about the user's needs and work to plan the search accordingly.

Locating the Information and Evaluating It

Whatever the extent of a reference query, the librarian should continually check in with the user to determine whether the material discovered meets the user's needs. This process should continue until the user has the information required or the user has resources to examine.

The librarian should provide instruction on the use of the resources to the user if the user is unfamiliar with them. Online resources especially may need some explanation in order for the user to make the most effective use of these materials. Evaluating the information is important to be certain that the sources selected are of high quality. The librarian should do this using the guidelines for selection and evaluation of reference materials. See Chapter 17 for more information on evaluation and selection.

Ensuring That the Question Is Fully Answered—The Follow-Up

The follow-up question is of great importance to the reference interview. It is necessary to check with users to see whether they have had their questions answered. The librarian may want to ask if the users found the information they sought or say, "Please come back if you don't find what you are looking for, and we can look somewhere else," or the librarian may simply check in with users while roving. Gers and Seward (1985) stated that the follow-up question "may be the single most important behavior because it has the potential for allowing one to remedy lapses in other desirable behaviors" (p. 34). Dewdney and Ross (1994) found that librarians often fail to ask follow-up questions. This can result in a situation where the user lacks needed information but is unable to express the discrepancy.

Closing the Interview

Like the closing moves of a chess game, the conclusion of a reference interview is a highly specialized art. Once it has been confirmed that the user has all of the information he or she desires, the consulting librarian should find a way to bring the conversation to a close without making the patron feel summarily dismissed.

Christopher Nolan (1992) suggests that a reference department should develop goals for the interview, making it easier to know when the conversation should be brought to a close. He further states that "three factors are involved in the end of most interviews: knowledge or content of the interview, dynamics of the interpersonal interaction, and institutional or policy components" (p. 515). Keep in mind that, as is suggested elsewhere in this book, reference and information services are one of the primary means to spotlight the value of the library itself, so the interview should close on an open note. For example, the librarian can make a follow-up comment that will encourage the user to return to the library, such as "Feel free to return if you need further assistance on this question or have other questions." Also, as Radford, Radford, and colleagues (2011) have discussed, when getting the complete answer is not possible, it does not mean that the interview is unsuccessful; a careful referral if the user agrees can also be a good conclusion.

Problematic Strategies in the Reference Interview

The Imposed Query

Most librarians and researchers have based their evaluation of the reference interview on the assumption that the questions were self-generated. This is not always true. Melissa Gross (1998) defines and discusses the imposed query as "a process in which the imposer or end user passes the question to another who will act as the agent in the transaction of the query and then return to the imposer with the answer or resolution" (p. 291). Although we do not know all of the implications of the imposed query, it is logical to assume that the assumptions and stereotypes of both the person who asked the question and the person who transmits the query will affect the outcome. Gross points to the need for more research in this area. One example of the imposed query is when a parent arrives in the library asking for information for his or her child's homework assignment. Another example might be that an executive asks an assistant to research a subject but provides little direction. In either case, the person who needs the information is not present and the person talking to the librarian may or may not be clear as to the actual information need. It is helpful to the librarian to identify this situation as the imposed query, so the librarian will realize that the person asking the question may not be able to clarify the question for the librarian, making it more complicated to provide help.

The Communications Trap

Sometimes the problem between the user and the librarian is one of communication. The article "Oranges and Peaches: Understanding Communication Accidents in the Reference Interview" points out this problem (Dewdney and Michell, 1996: 520–521). This article begins by describing a scenario in which a student arrives at the library, claiming that he has been assigned a book to read titled *Oranges and Peaches*. The librarian is unable to find a book by this title and asks the student for the author. The librarian does not ask the student any open-ended questions or sense-making questions in order to get information on the context of the request. Finally, the student does provide additional information, and the librarian realizes that the student is looking for Darwin's *On the Origin of Species*.

Sometimes the librarian misunderstands the question because the pronunciation of the key words is slightly different or the librarian hears the word and relates it to something familiar to him or her. In another example, Dewdney and Michell (1996: 527–528) describe a user who arrives at the library asking for material on Socrates, but the librarian has just been weeding in the sports section and hears it as "soccer tees." There are, of course, many words that sound the same but have completely different meanings, for example, China/china, Turkey/turkey and Wales/whales. Other communication accidents happen when the user asks a question that he or she has heard from someone else. The solution to these miscommunications is, first, to restate the question, allowing the user the opportunity to rephrase it, and, second, to ask follow-up questions, helping to introduce context into the discussion.

Behaviors to Avoid

Librarians should take care not to fall into the many traps that can easily occur during the reference transaction.

Keep in contact with the user. It is tempting just to start typing on the computer once the user has asked a question. This is extremely confusing to the user, who neither knows what the librarian is doing nor if the librarian really understood the question. Before beginning a search, be sure that the question is clear by restating it and explaining to the user what is being searched. If possible, let the user see the screen so he or she can follow the search. If the librarian goes elsewhere to get the information for the user, the librarian should try not to be out of sight of the user for any length of time so that the user knows the librarian is still working on the question.

Avoid negative closure, that is, a dismissive behavior that falls short of providing full service. In a negative closure, the librarian is more interested in getting rid of the user than in answering the question and sends the user away without the information needed. Here are some examples of this:

- The librarian provides an unmonitored referral. This is when the librarian sends the user somewhere else without any clear direction. For example, the librarian gives the user a call number and suggests looking in that area or points to a particular area and suggests browsing there. Similarly problematic would be a situation in which the librarian refers the user elsewhere in the library or to an agency without confirming that the user will actually find information there.
- The librarian suggests that the user should have done some work before asking for help.
- The librarian tries to get the user to accept information more easily available than what the user needs.

- The librarian suggests that the information will not be found for one of a number of reasons, such as too hard, obscure, or elusive or simply not available in the library and perhaps not in any library.
- The librarian tries to convince the user not to pursue the question.
- The librarian leaves the desk and does not return.
- The librarian, through a nonverbal action such as turning away from the user, indicates that the interview is over. (Ross and Dewdney, 1998: 151–163)

Ross and Dewdney (1998) offer recommendations for more positive behavior rather than the negative closure. They recommend that when the librarian refers the user to another part of the library or to another library or information source, the librarian should verify that useful information will be found by the user. The librarian should also encourage the user to return if the user does not find the information needed. Roving reference can help identify users who need more help or who need help but have not talked to a librarian. If the reference interaction is virtual, the librarian might suggest a visit to the library for further information or encourage the user to contact the library again for more assistance.

Another behavior to avoid is simply not listening to the user. It is difficult to listen intently to each user's question, but the librarian must do this in order to understand as completely as possible the user's question. To not listen closely and ask pertinent questions can lead to assumptions that will send the librarian in the wrong direction. For example, the librarian might be asked about abortions and immediately go to the health section, only to find out the person wanted to know about aborting space flights.

Librarians should also avoid playing twenty questions with the user, whereby the librarian just keeps asking closed-ended questions hoping to discover what the user wants. These closed-ended questions often result in the user not being able to fully explain the question as well as with open-ended questions.

Finally, the librarian should avoid making the user feel stupid. Most users do not know library jargon. They may use "bibliography" instead of "biography" or they may use "reference book" when they mean a circulating nonfiction book. The librarian must learn to use less library jargon and to understand the patrons (Cramer, 1998).

The Telephone Interview

The telephone interview is one step removed from the face-to-face interview. It does have the advantage of getting immediate feedback from the user. Although the librarian cannot see the user, the librarian can hear the tone and inflections in the user's voice and can ascertain how he or she is communicating.

The librarian should develop a pleasant speaking voice to aid in phone communication, aiming to sound approachable and attentive. As always, it is important to rephrase the user's questions to clarify the meaning and to ask open-ended questions. In this virtual context, it is doubly important that the user be kept informed as to how the search process is proceeding and that silent time be kept to a minimum. Once the answer has been found, follow-up questions should be asked to confirm that the question has been properly answered. The librarian should also cite the source where the answer can be found and should encourage the user to call again or visit the library (Ross, Nilsen, and Radford, 2009).

Answering Questions Virtually

Using virtual reference software to provide reference assistance has become part of the lives of most reference librarians. Answering questions by e-mail, chat reference, IM, and text messaging is not so different from answering questions face-to-face (FtF). The problem is that virtual reference lacks the advantage of the FtF reference interview where the user's tone of voice, facial expressions, and body language help the librarian to judge whether he or she is communicating well with the user. What is a handicap for some is, however, an advantage for others who cannot leave home or do not communicate well verbally, making it a powerful means to support the mission of many libraries to make their resources available to all (Ross, Nilsen, and Radford, 2009).

Librarians should approach the virtual reference question in the same way as a face-to-face one. In e-mail reference, the structure of the reference interview is still a well-designed form that captures essential information. This is the best way for the librarian to get information from the user. Collecting enough information is essential because it is hard to go back, ask follow-up questions, and get a response from the user. Librarians should try to provide the best answer possible but leave open the possibility of users asking additional questions if their questions have not been fully answered.

Chat reference, IM, and text messaging have considerable potential for the reference interview because they are done in real time. When providing chat reference, the librarian should not assume that the user does not have time for the reference interview. The fact that the user has chosen not to come to the library does not indicate that the user is impatient or in a hurry (Kern, 2003). The librarian should greet the user by name and acknowledge the receipt of the question. He or she should then proceed to do a reference interview, asking the user open-ended questions. The librarian should explain that the questions are aimed at ensuring that he or she understands the user's question and should restate the question back to the user. It is also important to tell the user what steps are being taken because the user cannot see what the librarian is doing. The librarian should read carefully the user's reply for clues as to whether he or she is communicating well. Nora Wikoff (2008) suggests that better staffing of chat reference services would mean that librarians would have more time to conduct a reference interview and to be sure that the users received the information needed. Wikoff also forecasts that "the chat virtual reference medium may lead to a restructuring of the reference interview to take advantage of what the chat virtual reference format offers" (p. 240).

IM is faster than chat reference because of the nature of the software, but these messages often lack context. Librarians may not have contact information to follow up, and it is difficult to know when the question is finished. Librarians must be succinct when responding to IM or text messaging queries. They should also try to get an e-mail address if they want to do some follow-up. If the information needed is not available electronically, librarians should arrange to get the print information to users by fax or other convenient means (Ronan, 2003).

In a study at the University of Guelph, Rourke and Lupien (2010) compared chat reference and IM interactions. They found that patrons used the two services differently. More research-oriented questions were asked via chat reference, and more directional and policy and procedure questions were asked via IM. Thus, the two services complemented each other.

The virtual reference librarian should aim to be approachable in wording responses to the user. Just as in the FtF interview, the librarian will want to strive to make the user comfortable with the process so that the user will return to the library. Follow-up should encourage the user to use the library virtually or in person. Recent research shows that the same mistakes happen in virtual reference as in FtF interviews, that is, the lack of the reference interview, unmonitored referrals, and failure to ask follow-up questions (Nilsen, 2005). Straw (2000) comments that "a well-written response not only answers a question eloquently, but it also tells the user about the importance that the library places on the question" (p. 379). Mon and Janes's (2007) study confirms this. They found that librarians providing e-mail reference who used more words in their answers tended to be thanked more often, whereas librarians who resorted to the "canned" responses or the FAQs received fewer thank-yous.

RUSA Guidelines—An Integrated Approach

The Reference and User Services Association Board of Directors approved the most recent guidelines for the reference interview, "Guidelines for Behavioral Performance of Reference and Information Service Providers," in June 2004. These guidelines cover approachability, interest, listening/inquiring, searching, and follow-up. Each of these five areas includes general guidelines, in-person guidelines, and guidelines for telephone, e-mail, and chat reference. For the first time, the guidelines have been tied to virtual reference as well as in-person reference. This provides the librarian with a way to begin to blend the various ways of answering a reference question, rather than treating virtual reference separately as had been the case when the technology was first emerging. These guidelines stress the need for good communication skills, whether the question is asked in person or virtually, stating, "In all forms of reference services, the success of the transaction is measured not only by the information conveyed, but also by the positive or negative impact of the patron/staff interaction. The positive or negative behavior of the reference staff (as observed by the patron) becomes a significant factor in perceived success or failure."

- *Approachability.* "Approachability behaviors, such as the initial verbal and non-verbal responses of the librarian, will set the tone for the entire communication process and will influence the depth and level of interaction between the staff and the patrons."

- *Interest.* "A successful librarian must demonstrate a high degree of interest in the reference transaction. While not every query will contain stimulating intellectual challenges, the librarian should be interested in each patron's information need and should be committed to providing the most effective assistance."
- *Listening/inquiring.* "The reference interview is the heart of the reference transaction and is crucial to the success of the process. The librarian must be effective in identifying the patron's information needs and must do so in a manner that keeps patrons at ease."
- *Searching.* "The search process is the portion of the transaction in which behavior and accuracy intersect. Without an effective search, not only is the desired information unlikely to be found but patrons may become discouraged as well."
- *Follow-up.* "The reference transaction does not end when the librarian leaves the patrons. The librarian is responsible for determining if the patrons are satisfied with the results of the search and is also responsible for referring the patrons to other sources, even when those sources are not available in the local library." (RUSA, 2004)

Kwon and Gregory (2007) documented that the revised RUSA guidelines are effective in chat reference and made recommendations for future revisions of the guidelines as well as pointed out the need to study e-mail and IM reference.

Cultural Differences

Librarians should try to understand and respect the cultural differences of users. Some users may have trouble asking their questions. If users are difficult to understand, librarians could ask them to write out their questions. Librarians should avoid jargon and speak slowly and distinctly. Users struggling with spoken English might appreciate handouts that they can read. Other issues to be aware of involve differences in body language and personal space issues. In some cultures, it is acceptable for people to stand very close to the person to whom they are speaking; in the United States, strangers generally stand about an arm's length away for comfort. Etiquette also differs among cultures. In some countries, it is important to greet someone formally before beginning the conversation, while in others it is important to shake hands first. For others, gender may be an issue. No matter what the cultural differences, it is important to treat all people with respect.

Improving Our Skills

Doing a good reference interview takes skills that come only with practice. The new librarian should continually evaluate his or her abilities and try to improve them.

- Practice looking approachable. This means being relaxed and open and not looking so busy that the person will hesitate to ask a question.
- Practice active listening skills. Listening to the nuances as well as the words of the user will help the librarian to be sure that they understand the question.

- Develop knowledge of reference sources. Continuing to build knowledge of reference resources is essential in assisting the user.
- Practice posing questions. Think about how to craft and ask questions that will elicit more information from the user and help the librarian to better understand the question.
- Practice follow-up questions and closing the interview. Both are essential in making sure the question is answered and making it comfortable for the user to return again.
- Shadow more experienced colleagues or mentors to gain better skills in negotiating reference questions. This can be done both for FtF and virtual encounters.

A Look Ahead

As we look to a future that is a mix of FtF, telephone, and virtual reference, the importance of the reference interview remains. It has been proven to be an important key to successfully answering user questions. It is also important in having the user feel that the librarian has tried his or her best to answer the question. It is interesting that the user values the behavior of the librarian often more than the answer. Consequently, the development of good people skills is of great importance no matter the form of the reference interview. Kathleen Kern (2003) summed up the reference interview as follows: "we need to remember that the type and quality of the service we offer must depend on our philosophy of reference service and not on the mode of communication with the user" (p. 49). As the ways we work to help library users continue to change, we would do well to keep these words in mind, remembering that it is an orientation toward excellent service that leads to satisfied users.

Recommendations for Further Reading

Bobrowsky, Tammy, Lynne Beck, and Malaika Grant. 2005. "The Chat Reference Interview: Practicalities and Advice." *The Reference Librarian* no. 89/90: 179–191. Offers practical information on how to conduct a virtual reference interview via chat.

Breitbach, William, and J. Michael DeMars. 2009. "Enhancing Virtual Reference: Techniques and Technologies to Engage Users and Enrich Interaction." *Internet Reference Services Quarterly* 14, no. 3/4: 82–91. Presents strategies and technologies for making virtual reference interviews more effective, including freely available technology, such as web-based screencasting tools, that can be used quickly to overcome typical communication difficulties encountered in chat reference.

Carr, Allison, and Pearl Ly. 2009. "'More Than Words': Screencasting as a Reference Tool." *Reference Services Review* 37, no. 4: 408–420. Explains how images and videos of complex search strategies created on-the-fly can improve the quality of communication in chat reference, e-mail and FtF reference interviews. Suggests that screencasting could replace the detailed written instructions of the past.

Connaway, Lynn Siligini, and Marie L. Radford. 2011. *Seeking Synchronicity.* Dublin, OH: OCLC. Presents a research report on virtual reference service that will inform the development of VRS and the role of interpersonal communication in the reference interview.

Fagan, Judy Condit, and Christina M. Desai. 2002/2003. "Communication Strategies for Instant Messaging and Chat Reference Services." *The Reference Librarian* no. 79/80: 121–155. Discusses effective ways to communicate using IM and chat reference.

Hicks, Alison, and Caroline Sinkinson. 2011. "Situated Questions and Answers: Responding to Library Users with QR Codes." *Reference and User Services Quarterly* 51, no. 1: 60–69. Presents a case study of a QR code pilot program at the University of Colorado at Boulder designed to connect users in the physical stacks and other spaces with virtual reference libraries. Suggests that QR codes, by consolidation of research services, allow reference librarians to provide instant, customized assistance to previously disconnected campus spaces.

Kern, M. Kathleen. 2009. *Virtual Reference Best Practices, Tailoring Services to Your Library.* Chicago: American Library Association. Provides a wealth of up-to-date information on how to set up a virtual reference service.

Miller, Faye, and Jake Wallis. 2011. "Social Interaction and the Role of Empathy in Information and Knowledge Management: A Literature Review." *Library and Information Science* 52, no. 2: 122–132. Presents an overview of research on the social role of empathy in the changing nature of information science and explores the idea that empathy can be taught to information professionals using virtual environment.

Naylor, Sharon, Bruce Stoffel, and Sharon Van Der Laan. 2008. "Why Isn't Our Chat Reference Used More? Finding of Focus Group Discussions with Undergraduate Students" *Reference and User Services Quarterly* 47, no. 4 (Summer): 342–354. Documents the reasons the Milner Library at Illinois State University's chat reference service was not better used.

Owen, Tim Buckley. 2006. *Success at the Enquiry Desk: Successful Enquiry Answering— Every Time.* 5th ed. London: Facet. Provides a helpful and up-to-date manual on the particulars of providing reference service.

Park, Jung-ran, Guisu Li, and Amy Burger. 2010. "Opening and Closing Rituals of the Virtual Reference Service of the Internet Public Library." *Journal of Documentation* 66, no. 6: 807–823. Examines opening and closing rituals in IPL's e-mail-based online reference interactions in order to assess how IPL librarians and users verbally construct social space in an asynchronous medium. Measures the indicators of verbal politeness and structural politeness, and suggests that IPL and IFLA standards are being met.

Portree, Martha, R. Sean Evans, Tina M. Adams, and John J. Doherty.. 2008. "Overcoming Transactional Distance; Instructional Intent in an E-mail Reference Service." *Reference and User Services Quarterly* 48, no. 2 (Winter): 142–151. Discusses how customization of the e-mail response is an important part of the transaction. Documents how librarians provide instruction and as a result interact more directly with the user.

Radford, Marie L., Gary P. Radford, Lynn Silipigni Connaway, and Jocelyn A. DeAngelis. 2011. "On Virtual Face-Work: An Ethnography of Communication Approach to a Live Chat Reference Interaction." *The Library Quarterly* 81, no. 4: 431–453. Applies the ethnographic theories of Erving Goffman to transcripts of virtual reference interactions in order to examine how "maintaining face" is an integral part of a successful reference interaction. Discusses how user satisfaction is affected by perceived social relationships, fear, respect, deference, and the flow of communication. Suggests that even misspellings and typos have communicative value in virtual interactions.

Ronan, Jana. 2003. "The Reference Interview Online." *Reference and User Services Quarterly* 43, no. 1 (Fall): 43–47. Discusses how chat reference communication norms for virtual communities can be applied to real-time chat reference service following the RUSA "Guidelines for Behavioral Performance of Reference and Information Service Professionals."

Rozaklis, Lily, and Craig M. MacDonald. 2011. "A Typology of Collaborative Communication in a Digital Reference Environment." *The Reference Librarian* 52, no. 4: 308–319. Describes the virtual environment of *ipl2*'s *Ask an ipl2 Librarian* service, in which librarians collaboratively determine the nature of users' questions.

RUSA (Reference and User Services Association). 2004. "Guidelines for Behavioral Performance of Reference and Information Service Providers." *Reference and User Services Quarterly* 44, no. 1 (Fall): 9–13. Discusses the RUSA guidelines for providing digital reference service.

Shenton, Andrew I. K. 2010. "How Comparable Are the Actions of a School-Based Intermediary Responding to Inquiries and the Information-Seeking Behavior of Young People?" *The Reference Librarian* 51, no. 4: 276–289. Examines the theory that the gap in knowledge between school library users and school-based information professionals is shrinking. Disputes this theory with the conclusion that the type of knowledge used in the information profession, literacy of resources, and wayfinding is not comparable to the "bricks" of knowledge with which students build their projects.

Stover, Mark. 2004. "The Reference Librarian as Non-Expert: A Postmodern Approach to Expertise." *The Reference Librarian* no. 87/88: 273–300. Explores the reference interview using the "postmodern psychotherapeutic view of the therapist as a non-expert."

Ward, David. 2004. "Measuring the Completeness of Reference Transactions in Online Chat Virtual Reference." *Reference and User Services Quarterly* 44, no. 1 (Fall): 46–57. Examines the effectiveness of online chat reference and to see if the questions were answered completely.

Ward, David. 2005. "How Much Is Enough? Managing Chat Length." *Internet Reference Services Quarterly* 10, no. 2: 89–93. Discusses how to handle long chat reference sessions, including both policies and suggested practices.

Ward, David. 2005. "Why Users Choose Chat: A Survey of Behavior and Motivations." *Internet Reference Services Quarterly* 10, no. 1: 29–46. Examines why people choose chat reference and their overall satisfaction with the service.

Ward, Joyce, and Patricia Barbier. 2010. "Best Practices in Chat Reference Used by Florida's Ask a Librarian Virtual Reference Librarians." *The Reference Librarian* 51, no. l (Winter): 53–68. Presents typical issues, such as incomplete questions, misunderstandings, and technical issues, that interfere with positive outcomes in chat reference interactions. Recommends solutions and provides chat reference transcripts as examples.

Westbrook, Lyn. 2009. "Unanswerable Questions at the IPL: User Expectations of E-mail Reference." *Journal of Documentation* 65, no. 3: 367–395. Examines difficult and hard-to-categorize reference questions received at the IPL for what they reveal about both users' expectations and librarians' expectations.

White, Marilyn Domas. 1981. "The Dimensions of the Reference Interview." *RQ* 20, no. 4 (Summer): 373–381. Discusses the importance of explaining to the user what is happening during the reference interview.

White, Marilyn Domas. 1998. "Questions in Reference Interviews." *Journal of Documentation* 54, no. 4 (September): 443–465. Discusses the types of questions asked in a presearch interview.

Bibliography and Works Cited

Cramer, Dina C. 1998. "How to Speak Patron." *Public Libraries* 37, no. 6 (November/December): 349.

Dervin, Brenda, and Patricia Dewdney. 1986. "Neutral Questioning: A New Approach to the Reference Interview." *RQ* 25 (Summer): 506–513.

Dewdney, Patricia, and Gillian Michell. 1996. "Oranges and Peaches: Understanding Communication Accidents in the Reference Interview." *RQ* 35, no. 4 (Summer): 520–536.

Dewdney, Patricia, and Catherine Sheldrick Ross. 1994. "Flying a Light Aircraft: Reference Service Evaluation from a User's Viewpoint." *RQ* 34, no. 2 (Winter): 217–230.

Gers, Ralph, and Lillie J. Seward. 1985. "Improving Reference Performance: Results of a Statewide Study." *Library Journal* 110 (November 1): 32–36.

Gross, Melissa. 1998. "The Imposed Query: Implications for Library Service Evaluations." *Reference and User Services Quarterly* 37, no. 3 (Spring): 290–299.

Jennerich, Elaine Z., and Edward J. Jennerich. 1997. *The Reference Interview as a Creative Art.* 2nd ed. Englewood, CO: Libraries Unlimited.

Kazlauskas, Edward. 1976. "An Exploratory Study: A Kinesic Analysis of Academic Library Public Service Points." *Journal of Academic Librarianship* 2, no. 3: 130–134.

Kern, Kathleen. 2003. "Communication, Patron Satisfaction, and the Reference Interview." *Reference and User Services Quarterly* 43, no. 1 (Fall): 47–49.

Kwon, Nahyun, and Vicki L. Gregory. 2007. "The Effects of Librarians' Behavioral Performance on User Satisfaction in Chat Reference Services." *Reference and User Services Quarterly* 47, no. 2 (Winter): 137–148.

Luo, Lili. 2011. "Text Reference Service: Delivery, Characteristics, and Best Practices." *Reference Services Review* 39, no. 3: 482–495.

Lynch, Mary Jo. 1978. "Reference Interviews in Public Libraries." *Library Quarterly* 48, no. 2 (April): 119–142.

Mon, Lorri, and Joseph W. Janes. 2007. "The Thank You Study" *Reference and User Services Quarterly* 46, no. 4 (Summer): 53–59.

Nilsen, Kirsti. 2005. "Virtual Versus FtF Reference: Comparing Users' Perceptions on Visits to Physical and Virtual Reference Desks in Public and Academic Libraries." Paper presented at Reference and Information Services Section, World Library and Information Congress, Oslo.

Nolan, Christopher W. 1992. "Closing the Reference Interview: Implications for Policy and Practice." *RQ* 31, no. 4 (Summer): 513–523.

Radford, Marie L. 1998. "Approach or Avoidance? The Role of Nonverbal Communication in the Academic Library User's Decision to Initiate a Reference Encounter." *Library Trends* 46, no. 4 (Spring): 699–717.

Radford, Marie L., Lynn S. Connaway, Patrick A. Confer, Susanna Sabolcsi-Boros, and Hannah Kwon. 2011. "'Are We Getting Warmer?' Query Clarification in Live Chat Virtual Reference." *Reference and User Services Quarterly* 50, no. 3 (Spring): 259–278.

Radford, Marie L., Gary P. Radford, Lynn Silipigni Connaway, and Jocelyn A. DeAngelis. 2011. "On Virtual Face-Work: An Ethnography of Communication Approach to a Live Chat Reference Interaction. *The Library Quarterly* 81, no. 4: 431–453.

Ronan, Jana Smith. 2003. *Chat Reference, A Guide to Live Virtual Reference Service.* Westport, CT: Libraries Unlimited.

Ross, Catherine Sheldrick, and Patricia Dewdney. 1998. "Negative Closure: Strategies and Counter-Strategies in the Reference Transaction." *Reference and User Services Quarterly* 38, no. 2 (Winter): 151–163.

Ross, Catherine Sheldrick, Kirsti Nilsen, and Marie L. Radford. 2009. *Conducting the Reference Interview.* 2nd ed. New York: Neal-Schuman.

Rourke, Lorna, and Pascal Lupien. 2010. "Learning from Chatting: How Our Virtual Reference Questions Are Giving Us Answers." *Evidence Based Library and Information Practice* 5, no. 2: 63–74.

RUSA (Reference and User Services Association). 2004. "Guidelines for Behavioral Performance of Reference and Information Service Providers." American Library Association. http://www.ala.org/rusa/resources/guidelines/guidelinesbehavioral.

Straw, Joseph E. 2000. "A Virtual Understanding: The Reference Interview and Question Negotiation in the Digital Age." *Reference and User Services Quarterly* 39, no. 1 (Summer): 376–379.

Swope, Mary Jane, and Jeffrey Katzer. 1972. "Why Don't They Ask Questions?" *RQ* 12, no. 2 (Winter): 161–166.

Taylor, Robert S. 1968. "Question Negotiation and Information Seeking in Libraries." *College and Research Libraries* 29, no. 3 (May): 178–194.

Walker, Claire and Amanda Clark. 2011. "Meeting the Reference Expectations of ESL Students: The Challenges of Culture." *College and Research Libraries News* 72, no. 1 (January): 20–23.

Wang, Jian, and Donald G. Frank. 2002. "Cross-Cultural Communication: Implications for Effective Information Services in Academic Libraries." *Portal: Libraries and the Academy* 2, no. 2: 207–216.

Wikoff, Nora. 2008. "Reference Transaction Handoffs; Factors Affecting the Transition from Chat Virtual Reference to E-mail." *Reference and User Services Quarterly* 47, no. 3 (Spring): 230–241.

3

Finding the Answer:
Basic Search Techniques

All the right questions have been asked in the reference interview. What next? In a perfect reference world, as epitomized in the following children's poem, the questions are asked, understood, and answered to the complete satisfaction of the user.

> *The Firefly*
> "How DO you make your bottom glow?
> How DO you make your sitter light?"
> The firefly cleared his throat and said,
> "Bioluminescence is the oxidation of an enzyme
> or protoplast called lucifern or luciferase."
> I thanked him and went home to bed.
> —*Jack Kent*

During a reference interaction, however, the absence of that vocal, erudite firefly makes for a more challenging exchange. As described in the previous chapter, the reference interview is not merely conversation. It is skilled conversation with a definite purpose. It requires the use of preestablished procedures and practiced skills to be effective. The conscious use of such tools as keeping eye contact to signal being approachable, repeating the user's question to verify meaning, and asking open-ended questions to elicit further details are not a function of individual personality but requirements for which every reference librarian should be trained.

A less-studied aspect of the reference interview is the reference answer. The assumption is that once the user's question is fully understood, reference librarians will, like the firefly, clear their throats and spill out a completely formed answer. As even the most experienced librarian can vouch, the clearing of one's throat is the closest one approaches to this perfect scenario. The reference answer, much like the interview, benefits greatly from preconditioning, practice, and a conscious adoption of answering tools. With these tools, the reference answer is less vulnerable to the randomness of the librarian's knowledge coinciding with the user's idiosyncratic questions. A professional interaction is ensured regardless of the personalities involved.

Tools of the Answering Trade

Questions, queries, quests, and quizzes—the range of user needs is vast. It is both the most exhilarating and the most terrifying aspect of the reference librarian's job. The following is a list of requests received during one day at an academic library:

- I need examples of funerary sculpture from the eighteenth century.
- Do you have articles about deforestation in the Dominican Republic in Spanish?
- I have to write about how the Internet has negatively affected American society.
- Do you have an outline map of Georgia?
- What is the date for the first Seder in 2013?
- I need to do a paper on the relation between monasteries and printing.
- Are there cookbooks in this library?
- Which New Jersey governor signed the Declaration of Independence?
- For my senior thesis, I have to research the life of Emily Brontë.
- How can I tell if a journal has been peer reviewed?

The act of leaping reflexively from one type of answering level to another can be done by everyone, much as hitting back at an approaching tennis ball is done. To *effectively* leap, however, requires much the same dedicated training as a professional tennis player who learns to hit balls with a combination of skill and instinct. Answering skills can be developed, just as questioning skills can be developed, in a successful reference interview. As the reference interview proceeds, the librarian should simultaneously consider the following three steps to avoid a scattershot search:

1. Categorize the answer.
2. Visualize how the final answer will appear.
3. Test the waters to check if the answer is proceeding in the right direction.

Step 1: Categorize the Answer

Time-Consuming or Quick?

Sorting an answer along a continuum ranging from ready reference to time-consuming is of immense help:

- It helps in avoiding panic and frustration on the part of both the librarian and the user by setting up a level of expectation. Reference professional standards listed in the "Guidelines for Behavioral Performance of Reference and Information Service Providers" recommend conducting a "search within the patrons' allotted time frame" or clearly stating the "expected turnaround time" in the case of remote reference (RUSA, 2004).
- It also helps in organizing the flow of a reference interaction. Alerting the user that finding the answer could take 5 minutes or 15 minutes or 1 hour or more allows the user to plan his or her time more effectively.
- It assigns a more professional stamp on the interaction. For telephone reference, if the answer does not fall in the realm of ready reference, the librarian can say, "I will call you back with an answer within fifteen minutes." This way, the user is not left dangling in a seemingly endless abyss of waiting for the phone to ring.

- It alerts the librarian to possible complications. Approximations of a time value for each answer can sometimes be miscalculated, but most questions in school, public, and academic libraries are answerable within 15 minutes of research. If not, the question may be based on incorrect assumptions, or it might need to be upgraded to an in-depth research question rather than a quick reference question, or a referral may be in order. The question on the New Jersey governor who signed the Declaration of Independence, for example, was printed on a school assignment sheet and occupied two reference librarians. Almost one hour was squandered before it was finally deduced that such a governor simply did not exist. It was suggested that perhaps the assignment was alluding to the New Jersey governor who signed the Constitution rather than the Declaration.

Simple or Complex?

The READ scale (http://readscale.org/) was developed to gather reference statistics; however, it is also a useful tool to help calibrate between simple and complex answers. Simplicity allows the librarian to think "within the box" and allot relatively little time to finding the answer:

- A question can be simple because it is pedestrian. An outline map of Georgia State, for example, has no hidden complexities. It is a graphic. Moreover, it is an ordinary graphic that can be found in well-established sources, such as the Outline Maps folder published by Facts on File, or printed via a simple Google images search.
- A question can be simple because it falls within the purview of the librarian's own interests and therefore the resources are highly familiar. Locating, explaining, and presenting the best resources does not require fresh initiative or the rapid acquisition of "knowledge on the fly."
- A question can be deceptively simple, such as the earlier example of a request for cookbooks, which proceeded to develop into a search for obscure recipes for cocktails that could use cardamom as an ingredient. In such cases, when original searches balloon into quite another direction, time and simplicity estimates must be recalculated.

Current or Retrospective?

It can be useful to delineate questions that require current information from those which do not. Literary critiques, biographies, histories, word etymologies, and etiquette books are subject areas that require currency but do not put a premium on it. Stock reports, directories, almanacs, and statistical yearbooks do. Deciding on whether the question is retrospective helps to veer the search process to appropriate formats. The earlier example question on the life of Emily Brontë would most definitely benefit from an exhaustive print biography. Searches on a database for current articles on Brontë would be more likely to provide a single, scholarly perspective on some aspect of her work. The example question on the first Seder of 2013, on the other hand, would be most efficiently answered by an Internet search.

Specific or Cross-Disciplinary?

Being alert to differences in questions aimed at facts versus analyses helps in structuring the search process. Factual information can usually be found in one classification area, though not necessarily one source. Analyses requiring cross-disciplinary perspectives will have to be broken down into their component parts in order to select multiple classification areas. See, for example, the difference between the following two inquiries:

- What are the different kinds of illegal drugs?
- I need to do a five-page report on the impact and incidence of illegal drug abuse in the teenage population of the United States.

In the first question, the Dewey area of the 360s or the Library of Congress call numbers in the RC566–RC568 area would amply cover a listing of all of the different kinds of illegal drugs. In the second assignment, however, additional research would have to cover drug culture (306 or HV5825), impact of drugs on teen health (613 or RA564.5), criminal statistics (310 or KDZ32), overviews such as those found in *CQ Researcher* (909 or H35), and databases for articles.

Single Source or Multisource?

Questions requiring no more than a single source are usually closed-ended questions. "I was born on January 10, 1976; what day of the week was that?" The question requires one perpetual calendar. There is no need for further confirmation or evaluation. *The World Almanac* or the *Time Almanac* at http://www.infoplease .com/ would suffice. A question on the "impact of ancient Roman architecture on the perceived power of Rome," on the other hand, would draw from multiple sources, dealing at minimum with the history of Rome and the dynamics of architecture and architectural forms.

User Appropriate?

Academic librarians are faced with students attempting to pick up resources for absentee friends, just as public librarians are invariably approached by parents wanting resources for "the Civil War," "the Holocaust," or "a famous African American." A printed sheet in their hands, a slight disconnect in their enthusiasm for the subject, and a successful reference interview should establish their role as middlemen, rather than as end users of the information. For such "imposed queries" (Gross, 2001), ascertaining the age, grade level, reading level, or purpose of the end user's needs is critical in choosing the appropriate answer source. A question on the workings of democracy in America could be answered with Tocqueville's dense treatise or with *Cliffs Notes'* simple explanations in American Government. Assignments may also have restrictions on type of source (e.g., no *Wikipedia*, peer-reviewed journal articles, etc.) that need to be identified.

Step 2: Visualize How the Final Answer Will Appear

This book describes hundreds of important resources. While envisioning the exact resource to consult for each question is an unlikely scenario, it is both possible and advisable to triangulate onto the category of sources. Indexes, guides, directories, catalogs, dictionaries, journals, statistical yearbooks, government publications, almanacs, websites, and databases—the strengths of each are established so that a move toward any one appropriate category or format is a logical first step. Most reference librarians follow the visualizing search strategy technique without consciously practicing it. The librarian who spends time looking for the "oversize commercial atlas that was right here in the business section" has admittedly used a visualization tool but has been stumped by the change in shape, as the publication has morphed into two smaller-sized publications, as was the case with the 135th edition of the *Rand McNally Commercial Atlas and Marketing Guide*. Conscious practice improves the visualizing process. As Tim Owen (2012: 27) suggests, "You can't see the fine detail, and you don't know yet whether there is a source ... [but] ... conjure up a picture in your mind's eyes of what the final answer will look like."

The focal points for successful visualization of answer resources are not color and size, but a rapid mental slide show of whether the answer would be in:

- print/Internet/database,
- textual/graphical/statistical formats, and
- Reference/Circulating/Children.

While the first step of categorizing the answer is essential in visualizing the answer source, shuffling through rapid images of format, category, source type, and reading-level appropriateness not only helps triangulating onto the right resources but aids the process of continuing to ask the right follow-up questions. Here are three questions on Africa:

1. What were some of the causes and effects of imperialism in Africa?
2. What are current crime statistics for countries in the African continent?
3. Is the African setting necessary for character and plot development in the novels of J. M. Coetzee?

Given the breadth of information and the analytical requirements inherent to Question 1, a circulating book or online encyclopedia may be the first choice in resource visualization. For Question 2, current crime statistics for all countries might be most accessible through the Internet with globally vested sites such as that offered by the United Nations at http://www.uncjin.org/Statistics/ WCTS/wcts.html. Unless a specific critical study of all aspects of Coetzee's works exists, a database of literary criticism such as Gale's Literature Resource Center might be the best bet for answering Question 3.

Step 3: Test the Waters to Check If the Answer Is Proceeding in the Right Direction

In basketball, players are urged to use soft-focus techniques and peripheral vision to be aware of the entire playing area. While providing answers, it is useful to use a similar technique to gauge continually whether the answer is proceeding in the right direction.

Creative Browsing

Float a trial balloon with introductory information and check user response. Calibrate accordingly. As studies have shown, individual research can be highly nonlinear. Users are far more likely to recognize the information they need when they see it than to know all of the details of what they need before they start. For example, a somewhat taciturn user asked this question: "Where is your section on airplanes?" A reference interview of some length established that the user needed "pictures of planes flying together." Faced with an illustrated encyclopedia of aircraft, the user showed interest but continued to want more material. At this point, the ongoing verbal interview was not producing new insight, so the librarian floated a trial balloon by asking the user which type of illustration was closest to what he wanted. He pointed to a V-formation of military aircraft but remembered that the V was disrupted at one point during the flight. This was the clue that it was the classic "missing man formation" aerial maneuver enacted at parades and funerals to honor MIAs. This further piece of information led the user to remember that he had seen it in a broadcast of President Reagan's funeral. This was the exact image he wanted and the librarian was able to get it for him.

In short, the more inchoate the question and the more limited the ability to draw clues from a reference interview, the greater is the value of trial balloons in locating the right answer.

Subcategorizing

Draw the user into various subcategories of the question to see if any strike the right chord. As the user shows interest in one category over another, focus on the chosen material and add to it.

For example, a user was interested in sexually transmitted diseases (STDs). The topic, being of a somewhat sensitive nature, was treated to a less than exhaustive interview. Presented with monographs, statistical data material, a dictionary of diseases, an illustrated encyclopedia of diseases, and a quick sample of online sites, the user was most interested in graphic images of people afflicted with STDs. In this case, the online option worked best, as the user was a concerned mom who wanted gory pictures to scare her adolescent son into following the straight and narrow.

Overviews

Provide a range of synopses of material and ask, "Do any of these appear to answer your question?" While ready reference questions require a single source, broader queries can be answered through different perspectives, thus requiring different resources. However, as Joseph Janes (2003: 38) has correctly pointed out, "users often want a response that is good enough—not perfect but optimal." The user rather than the librarian, though, must necessarily decide the optimal response. One way to navigate between the lines separating the overzealous librarian flooding the user with material and the Spartan librarian assuming the optimal choice is to provide "bites." A quick look at the "About" icon in an e-resource or a scan of the preface, table of contents, or back-page blurb in a print resource is enough to provide a sweeping overview of the kinds of perspectives available to answer the question.

Whether the user is gently pushed into creatively browsing through the material to clarify the research and enable the librarian to select the right answer source, or the librarian organizes the range into subcategories from which the user can choose, or the user is provided with a quick and sweeping overview of the resources available, the end result is still the same. The librarian tests the waters to see if the initial response to a question is heading into the right answer field.

Types of Answers

Like all of human language and communication, the phrase "reference answer" conceals as much as it conveys. An "answer," far from being a uniform entity, can be of many different types and, more pertinently, provide various levels of utility for the user. Even in the Web 2.0 universe of crowdsourcing and frequently asked questions (FAQs), which had heretofore been immersed in the exploration of more and more advanced data-mining and natural-language processing techniques, a number of newer algorithms, such as "maximum entropy models" (Zheng et al., 2011), are being designed to gauge the actual quality of answers. Indices of reliability, accuracy, and content analysis are being fine-tuned to act as "answer quality measures" (Fichman, 2011), so that a basic retrieval of information is no longer enough. Both during and after a reference interaction, it helps to be clear about what kind of answer was given to a user and whether another level of utility could have been possible.

Levels of Utility
Value-added answer ← Skilled answer ← Elementary answer

While all of these three broad answer gradations are helpful to the user, the highest level of utility can be assumed to derive from the value-added answer.

Value-Added Answers

The value-added answer goes a step beyond merely providing the right resources. It organizes the material, prioritizes the resources, keeps an eye open for potential research needs being generated by the material, and presents the answer with élan.

- On paper, providing a cover letter annotating the various sources so that their relevance is made clear goes a long way to adding value to an answer. Corporate and law librarians are perhaps the best practitioners of value-added answers. Not only are the right resources to the question selected, but the relevance of each resource is made clear so that answers are presented as professional time-saving reports. Such reports, of course, are far from the 15-minute answers averaged by desk reference, or the 12 to 13 minutes averaged for live chat reference, and can take up to weeks or months to prepare (Williams, 2002).

- In-person answers can benefit greatly from professional tips and the librarian's perception as to why one source is more relevant or reliable than another. If six print resources have been presented to the user, for example, the librarian can point out that the top two resources are the ones to begin with, as they contain the most relevant information and are from highly reputable publishers. Alternatively, if different resource formats have been presented, the librarian can explain why a certain website would provide the most current updates, or how a database has a better chance of leading the user to a richer range of sources through hyperlinks.

- Answers provided via e-mail can employ simple cut-and-paste methods to consolidate the relevant facts from a variety of websites or database articles. With citations provided for each extract, the user has the option to do further research, if necessary. If not, the user is provided with a high-utility answer that has saved both time and energy.

- In live or chat reference, thinking ahead and out of the box makes for a value-added answer. For example, a user had a question on the control of pests without the use of pesticides. The librarian was able to locate a perfect environmental website and a transcript of a radio interview on the subject. Most librarians would stop at this point, having provided a complete answer. This librarian picked up on the minor clue that the information was for a college paper and did a follow-up question on whether the user had access to a style guide to cite websites and transcripts. The user was most appreciative.

- The librarian can also include concerns, suggestions, and possible referrals in all formats, so that the user has the best possible overview of a topic before starting the research process.

Skilled Answers

Value-added answers, however desirable, can be quixotic in the working life of many librarians. Often, there is just not enough time or staff to provide the "icing on the answer cake." At this point, the skilled answer adequately serves the purpose. To provide such an answer, the right resources are located, sifted, and judged so that only the best sources are selected for research consumption. As an interesting research project reported, "information seekers will readily sacrifice content for convenience. Convenience is thus one of the primary criteria used for making choices during the information-seeking process" (Connaway, Dickey, and Radford, 2011: 27). Value-added answers must be able to address the need for user convenience.

Sifting through all of the material available on a subject, especially in a large library with vast resources, is almost as daunting as having no information at all. While there is some truth and much humor in Roy Tennant's (2001) aphorism that librarians like to search and users like to find, a complete and calibrated answer includes both the challenge of a search and the satisfaction of a find. Fast and effective ways to vet multiple sources and create a hierarchy of utility for the user include the following:

- Check the table of contents to get a quick overview of subjects and pertinent keywords included. If online versions do not have a table of contents page, speed-check for selected subject keyword counts to get a sense of the relevance of the text to the search.
- Locate keywords in the index to see if there is a long list of entries or pages on the subject.
- Skim through the preface to gauge the focus of the author.
- When available, review excerpts on book jackets; these may also provide a clue to the strengths of the resource.
- Past experience with certain websites, publishers, or series can be used to expound on resource choices. For example, a Gale encyclopedia can be expected to have glossaries, boxes highlighting interesting important facts, enlivening illustrations, and extensive cross-references; a DK publication is guaranteed to have spectacular graphics; *CQ Researcher* can be relied upon to provide an unequivocal overview, chronology, statistics, and evaluative account of hard-to-find sociocultural issues; and the U.S. Census website will provide reliable demographic statistics.

In chat reference, too, the skilled answer requires professional weighing of resources. For example, a user asked a question about Turner syndrome. The librarian located two authoritative websites. One was the acclaimed *Merck Manual* and the other was a special-interest national organization, the Turner Syndrome Society. The user wrote back to say that he or she was confused because the occurrence rates listed in the two sites differed. Here was the librarian's assured answer: "That's a tough call; they are both reputable sites. While the *Merck* is a reference book, the site for the Turner Syndrome Society may be more in touch with the actual statistics because they deal exclusively with the condition" (Mary-Jean Gurzenda, Q&A NJ live reference, April 26, 2005).

Elementary Answers

There are occasions when you simply do not have the right resources or you do not have the time to provide a value-added or skilled answer. In such cases, it is best either to strategize, so that you are able to gain more time, or to make use of the right referrals, if you believe the resources are simply not available at your own institution.

Collaboration

If the resources are not available, a strong system and ethic of referrals is both valid and highly useful for the user. As mentioned in Chapter 9, keeping a list of the nearest medical, legal, and business libraries is essential to all library reference services. The areas are specialized and invariably may require more in-depth research. Creating a webpage with a list of databases available in other open-access libraries is also helpful. At the Harvard University Library website, links to catalogs far beyond the university are offered so that it is possible to check the British Library Catalog and Germany's Karlsruhe Virtual Catalog.

Encouraging the increasingly sophisticated system of electronic bookmarking can help when sufficient resources do not appear to be available. Traditionally, librarians have a list of "Favorites" bookmarked on reference desk computers. This tradition has carried over to roving librarians with laptop computers. However, with each computer needing to be bookmarked individually, there is a pattern of irregularity in what gets bookmarked in one and forgotten in another. With continuing innovations in social bookmarking that allow for vetted links to be accessed from any computer, as well as refinements in categorizing these links through "tags," the sharing of organized e-resources is easily harnessed. Sites such as Connotea (http://www.connotea.org/), CiteULike (http://www.citeulike .org/), Diigo (http://www.diigo.com/), LibGuides (http://springshare.com/ libguides/), and Pinboard (http://pinboard.in/), to name only a few, provide convenient tools to organize and share e-resources. Screen-sharing tools such as Join Me (https://join.me/) allow for a seamless exchange of page views and document sharing. Acquiring the skill to use these new collaborative tools is good practice; reference librarians "must become comfortable transferring their expertise to a web environment, seeking out the bountiful sites that exist online and using tools such as bookmarking sites strategically to better organize and share those resources for the benefit of their institutions" (Redden, 2010: 226).

Strategizing

When time is scarce, some methods can stave off the inclination to simply not answer users' questions or to keep them waiting indefinitely.

- Ascertain whether the question can be "tabled" and answered at your convenience or whether it requires an immediate response.
- Send over an appropriate link or provide an introductory resource such as an encyclopedia to get the research started.
- In face-to-face settings, escort users to the right area to browse and inform them you will be rejoining them in a certain number of minutes.

Common Pitfalls in Reference Answering

Wrong Information

The pressure to "just answer" can sometimes be overwhelming. Take, for example, the following scenarios: An irate user on the telephone who wants the location and number for a gas station "right now" because she's running out of gas on some highway; the trusting teenager who asks a trivial question for which your mind draws a blank; the new coworker who is at the desk with you and looking to you for reference know-how—the world of human reference can be fraught with the pressure to "just answer." The point to remember is "do not do it."

Anticipating the pressure and recognizing that it is part of every reference librarian's experience helps in developing a resistance to "just answering." Wrong information can range from being irksome to dangerous. Rather than just answering, compromises can always be negotiated. The highway driver can be asked to pull over to the shoulder so you can conduct a more reliable search. The teenager can be drawn into a minute of conversation as you Google the trivia. The new coworker can learn along with you as you consult with a colleague.

Inappropriate Information

A poor cousin to wrong information is inappropriate information. Heaping a researcher with resources on African American culture because of an inability to find a specific resource on Kwanzaa is counterproductive. It not only may not answer the question but also wastes the time of the researcher. In addition to librarian lassitude, a poor reference interview is usually at the root of inappropriate information. The school librarian who pulled out multiple biographies of Karl Marx even though the student had continued to expand on his need for a Marx biography as part of a book report for Black History Month could easily have established the confusion between Marx and Malcolm X. The futile medical information piled on the user who needed to research "Wounded Knee" is a painful product of poor reference interviews leading to inappropriate information.

Avoidance

Avoidance of difficult questions is highly unprofessional and unethical. It is usually an outcome of momentary panic in the face of a seemingly impenetrable question. Remembering a few helpful tips when faced with a panic attack will guard against falling prey to avoidance techniques.

- Develop handy referral systems both within and outside the reference area. Knowing other staff members' special interests or aptitudes can assist in referring users to the right person in the event of a difficult reference question in that area.
- Keep pathfinders, how-tos, "knowledge bases," and referral lists on intractable subjects to prevent avoidance tactics. An interesting online incarnation of this can be found in the virtual reference service cooperative QuestionPoint (http://www.questionpoint.org/), and its creation of a "global knowledge base." The base is a collation of Q&A pairs, fed by nearly 500 libraries worldwide, with the aim of storing communal knowledge for repeated future use.
- Establish a context for the question. Technical jargon, for example, can be intimidating on its own, but it is considerably tamed when located within a subject context for which material is accessible. The user looking for "Mott insulator transitions in Bose condensates" is really looking for a basic textbook on condensed matter physics.
- Attack questions from different angles. If all of the books on the Reformation in sixteenth-century Europe are out, you can still help a user by providing biographies of Martin Luther.
- If a resource simply cannot be located for a query, play Sherlock Holmes for a moment and reasonably deduce what institution might have a vested interest in creating, organizing, or advertising such information. An overview

of soybean production in Argentina, for example, would most likely be located in online sites for organizations such as the Ministry of Economy and Production for the government of Argentina or the Economic Research Service of the U.S. Department of Agriculture.

- Finally, do not succumb to feeling that you must know everything. If the topic is unfamiliar, get familiar with it. Ask the user for clarifying information, or else consult a ready reference resource. Even wildly unfamiliar concepts and words can be decoded with a dictionary, an encyclopedic entry, or a quick browse on the Internet. Having understood the word, the question no longer appears as unapproachable.

"Disappearing into the stacks," as one study found (Ross and Dewdney, 1998), is quite simply unthinkable.

Poor Knowledge of Resources

No librarian can escape from the inevitable errors committed by not knowing the reference collection. Most librarians have, at some point in their career, forgotten a perfect resource available in their collection; however, the experience must be avoided at all costs. The best way to minimize the margin of error is to consciously refresh familiarity with resources on an ongoing and unremitting basis. Studying a new acquisition as it is received provides bedrock knowledge that is both incremental and absorbed at an unhurried pace. Shelf reading, weeding, swapping stories of successful answering resources with colleagues, and testing alternate sources with hypothetical questions are all ways of getting intimate with the collection. Challenging oneself to choose subject areas outside of one's comfort zone or area of expertise and working to become more familiar in these fields also proves helpful in the long run.

Lack of Follow-Up

A less obvious but equally egregious error in answering reference questions is not following up after providing the resources. Even live reference usually has a preset message requiring the user to write back if "further information is required." However, a telling analysis of 859 transcripts from the virtual reference service QuestionPoint found that only 50 percent of librarians thought of asking a follow-up question, despite it being prescribed as a highly recommended query clarification technique (Radford et al., 2011). As mentioned in Chapter 2 on the reference interview, user questions tend to grow roots as more research is done. It is good practice to return to the user to see if anything else is required.

Inadequate Search Skills

The most powerful deterrent to answering complex questions, however, is an underlying sense of inadequacy in searching skills. This is easily remedied. All reference librarians can become proficient search strategists if they consciously practice the art of "searching," rather than fall into the habit of "browsing." Search skills can be practiced with three major tools of reference:

1. The local library catalog
2. Electronic databases (e-indexes and full-text journals)
3. The Internet

Given that Internet searching has sounded a dominant note in the past few decades, Chapter 13 is devoted to the study of finding answers on the Internet. The other two search strategy tools are outlined in the following sections.

The Library Catalog

As one reference veteran correctly remarked, the catalog is the "first-resort tool for identifying and locating reference works in the library and, if the catalog record includes links, on the Web" (personal communication, December 29, 2005).

Catalogs in the majority of libraries use the Library of Congress Subject Headings (LCSH). A conscious recognition of the structure of authority headings goes a long way in honing the art of catalog searches. The LCSH, for example, can offer "magic searches" (Kornegay, Buchanan, and Morgan, 2005) based on the efficacy of its form subdivisions. Form subdivisions, of little value in pre-online cataloging times when author and title searches predominated, allow "librarians to combine the precision of the cataloger with the freewheeling style of a Googler" (Kornegay, Buchanan, and Morgan, 2005: 46). They do this by establishing what the material "is," rather than what it is "about." So, for example, if a user is searching for primary documents on the Revolutionary War, a search strategy that recognizes form subdivisions would look like this:

<Revolutionary War—Diaries>
OR
<Revolutionary War—Correspondence>
OR
<Revolutionary War—Sources>

By directing the search to what the material "is," namely primary documents such as diaries, correspondence, and sources, the search avoids the necessary irrelevancies associated with random topical keyword searches. It also obviates the necessity for having any prior knowledge of a controlled vocabulary, as would be required for a strict subject search where the search string would have to look like this to get the same results:

<United States—History—Revolutionary War, 1775-1783—Diaries>

While the list of form subheadings runs into the thousands, a study of actual usage found a highly skewed pattern with barely 100 subdivisions being used 90 percent of the time (O'Neill et al., 2001). It is therefore both a productive and feasible exercise for reference librarians to keep a list of some of the most-used form subdivisions. The following is a selected list of 20 common LCSH form subdivisions:

Common LCSH Form Subdivisions	
Periodicals	Case studies
Biography	Dictionaries
Bibliography	Pictorial works
Directories	Guidebooks
Statistics	Indexes
Maps	Databases
Handbooks	Study guides
Poetry	Interviews
Fiction	Popular works
Scores	Tables

Similarly, in an effort to train new reference librarians, a list of "25 high-performance subdivisions" was created by the reference staff of the Hunter Library of Western Carolina University and reported in a study (Kornegay, Buchanan, and Morgan, 2005). Princeton University's reference cataloging offers a lengthier list of selected subdivisions at http://library.princeton.edu/departments/tsd/katmandu/reference/formsubdiv.html. Having a kit of subdivisions that anchor topical keywords to subject areas allows a speedy and effective search of the online library catalog.

The popularity of social tagging in the Web 2.0 universe is bringing into question the continued use of form divisions that derive from controlled vocabulary sets. Studies suggesting an eventual combination of social annotations and formal classifications have been proliferating, with some finding that successful searches are enhanced with the incorporation of folksonomies into the creation of metadata (Lu, Park, and Hu, 2010).

Electronic Databases

A bewildering array of interfaces prompts one to believe that databases are very different creatures. Although the differences in databases must be acknowledged, some basic search patterns and strategies prove effective, regardless of whether one is looking for images in *AccuNet/AP Multimedia Archive* or global equity pricing in *Mergent Online*.

STEP 1 INVOLVES IDENTIFYING THE RESEARCH TOPIC.
Writing out the topic, either as a full sentence or as a list of concepts central to the topic, is critical in establishing the framework for starting the search. Database searches can quickly derail with misleading or unnecessary keywords. Search strategy worksheets and search tips, such as those created by the Humboldt State

University (http://library.humboldt.edu/infoservices/sstrawrksht.htm), help researchers to organize their search strings in a methodical and productive way. Worksheets such as the one designed by the J. Paul Leonard Library at San Francisco State University (reproduced as Figure 3-1) can be used to clarify the initial topic for both the researcher and the reference librarian.

STEP 2 REQUIRES IDENTIFYING THE APPROPRIATE DATABASE.

Database collections typically resemble a suburban mall. There are a few "big name" databases highlighted by the library, accompanied by a host of smaller or more subject-specific acquisitions. Each of these has an "About" or "Help" icon that lists the scope and focus of the collation. Combining a comprehensive "big name" database with a more specialized subject database can result in a well-balanced search. Randomly wandering through a mall of databases in search of specific information can conversely be an enervating, even fruitless, experience. While federated searching aims to address this problem, familiarity with specialized databases can help greatly in reducing the sheer multiplicity of results typically associated with general searches. The Top Ten source lists provided at the end of each chapter in Part II of this book are a good starting point.

STEP 3 ENCOURAGES BECOMING FAMILIAR WITH THE SEARCH SCREEN AND SEARCH FUNCTIONS.

A number of major databases are subscribing to a somewhat similar form interface where the entry box for search terms is typically followed by a set of limiters. The limiters are of tremendous value and should be exploited to the fullest extent possible. Searches can be variously limited by date ranges, full-text availability, peer-reviewed entries, within-text searches, subject descriptors, and formats. Boolean operators such as AND, OR, and NOT are also available to narrow, broaden, or eliminate unnecessary terms in a search string. Other standard search tools such as proximity operators, truncations, wildcards, and plurals are also part of the database search-polishing arsenal. A key describing which polishing tools can be found in any given database is always included. Sometimes the tools are nested within an "Advanced Search" button and will perform more effectively than the "Basic Search." Figure 3-2 is an example of an archetypal form interface where the search terms are fine-tuned with a set of Boolean operators and followed up by a set of date, title, language, image, and other limiters.

STEP 4 URGES A SEARCH THAT USES SUBJECT HEADINGS OR/AND REFINES KEYWORDS.

If keyword searches using the advanced limiters do not produce the desired results, be prepared to step up to a higher level of search strategizing. Refer to the controlled vocabulary inherent to each database. This can be done by consulting the thesaurus attached to most databases, or by retrieving the subject descriptors listed in every individual record. Most thesauri list terms with broader, narrower, and related terms as well. These can be methodically used to dredge up more accurate material. Multiple studies have shown, for example, that using MeSH (Medical Subject Headings) reduces the retrieval of extraneous citations and markedly improves the efficacy of searches (Richter and Austin, 2012). Alternately, retrieving subject headings listed in an initial search entry can achieve the

Figure 3-1. Database Search Strategy Worksheet

Database Search Strategy Worksheet

Name_____ Date_____

Reference Librarian_____

Please fill out this form to help the Reference Librarians assist you in determining the best databases and search strategy for your topic.

I. State your research topic (in complete sentence).

Example: How has the relationship between blacks and Jews historically been portrayed in the popular media?

II. List any limitations such as language, period of time, periodical title, etc.

III. Concept terms you think might be useful in searching your topic.

Use another sheet of paper if your search has more than three concepts. Note: Terms within the same columns are connected by the Boolean operator "OR" and are called a "set." Sets are connected by the operator "AND."

Sources for relevant terms:

- natural language; that is, familiar words you know
- database thesaurus (see if one is available for the specific database you are using)
- subject headings and descriptors in relevant citations records you find
- terms from encyclopedias, textbooks, coursework, etc.

Concept 1	Concept 2	Concept 3	
Example: Blacks African Americans Afro-Americans Negroes	Jews Jewish	Mass Media Radio Film Newspapers	Broadcasting Television Movies

AND   AND

Search statement example: (black* or African American*) and Jew* and (mass media or broadcast* or televis* or film*)

The asterisk (*) symbol in this statement is used to truncate. Truncation symbols vary among databases. Look in the database help sections to find which symbol is used.

Source: San Francisco State University, J. Paul Leonard Library, http://www.library.sfsu.edu/.

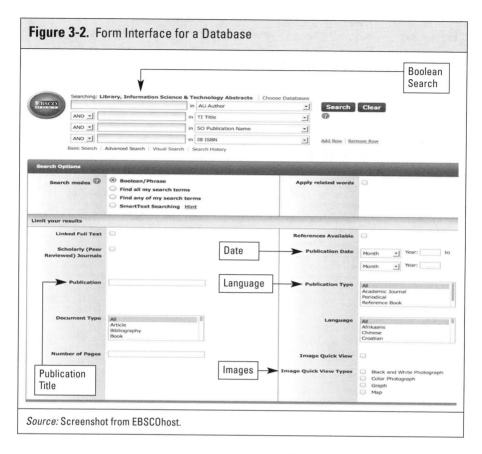

Figure 3-2. Form Interface for a Database

Source: Screenshot from EBSCOhost.

same results. A great many databases are set up with subject headings. Many of these headings are linked and allow for a one-click entry to new descriptors. Institutions such as the Alvin Sherman Library of Nova Southeastern University in Florida provide detailed individualized instructions to aid users in creating the most effective database search. Figure 3-3 provides a small sample of the instructional pages.

STEP 5 EVALUATES THE RESULTS.

The librarian can speedily evaluate the results by both the number of documents returned and the occurrence of search keywords in the title, subject keywords, or abstract prefacing the document. Much like Goldilocks entering the bears' house and trying out things until she found them to be "just right," the number of documents returned in a search indicates whether the terms used were "just right." For the most part, searches that result in fewer than ten documents may suggest an overly cautious search string that might be broadened by truncating the term or using the <OR> operator. More than 200 documents can be frequently defeating and may benefit from <AND> or <NOT> operators or any of the given limiters offered by the database. Any number in between is a good indication that the search string was "just right."

Figure 3-3. Refining a Database Search

◫ **Additional Features**

The Thesaurus is a controlled vocabulary list of subjects and related terms used to standardize the indexing in the database. You can select and search for synonyms, related, and preferred terms.

To use the Thesaurus

- click the **Thesaurus button**–left side of screen
- select **one or more databases**
- enter a **term** or **phrase**
- click **Start**

The results screen displays your term, or a related term, in a hierarchy. The report includes the database(s), and how many related records are available.

To clear the terms entered

- click **Clear** in the bottom taskbar

Search Thesaurus For:

| computers | | Start |

Select one or more databases.
Enter a subject.
Click **Start**.

The Thesaurus is a list of suggested subject headings and related terms in the database's controlled vocabulary. You can look up and get information about subjects covered.

Thesaurus in Education Full Text.

http://www.nova.edu/library/dils/lessons/wilsonwebeducation/
Alvin Sherman Library, Research, and Information Technology Center, Nova Southeastern University

Source: Created by the Distance and Instructional Library Services department of the Alvin Sherman Library, Research, and Information Technology Center at Nova Southeastern University in Ft. Lauderdale, Florida.

Search words are frequently highlighted by databases so that a quick eye-balling of the title, descriptors, and abstract is sufficient to suggest whether the result is worthwhile. Most results are also arranged in reverse chronological order, so that the timeliness of the articles can be gauged immediately. Some databases tab the results into scholarly and general categories; others list the citation and the number of words so that they need to be checked to evaluate levels of appropriateness.

STEP 6 PULLS TOGETHER THE SEARCH RESULTS INTO AN ORGANIZED WHOLE.
Having conducted a successful search, it is important to remember that database results, unlike print material, disappear unless immediately organized. The results can be printed so that a hard copy is available. They can be saved on flash drives or exported directly into software such as EndNote or RefWorks. Students and staff at Yale University, for example, have open access to import citations into RefWorks. The globally renowned scientific database SpringerLink adopted CiteULike, a bookmarking website, so citations can be instantly stored, shared, tagged with personal ratings, and exported. Alternately, the results can be e-mailed, a welcome

management addition for users who do not have the immediate means to print hard copies and for research collaborators who want to alert members to pertinent research. The results can also be tagged as the search is being conducted. This is particularly useful when an introductory or overview of a research field is conducted and a large number of entries are being scanned for possible relevance.

However careful the original search strategy, it is vital to keep in mind that the strategy has to be constantly revisited and redefined as the research process continues. New subject descriptors suggest different tacks to the same topic. Indexed terms are certainly not graven in stone, and "related" terms can vary quite noticeably among databases. Searches may also have to be repeated over time to account for any significant time lags. As the UWS Library (2010) at the University of the West of Scotland has noted, "MEDLINE is notoriously slow to index non-U.S. specialty journals."

With the ongoing development of federated searching and open URL link resolvers, which allow a single query interface to trawl across multiple databases (Linoski and Walczyk, 2008), the future trend of database searching appears to be striving for increased search friendliness. Summon, WebFeat, EDS, Serials Solutions' Article Linker, MuseGlobal's Muse Search, and Innovative Interfaces' Web Bridge are just some of the "next generation services" that "radically enhance resource integration and move us on from the isolated data silos of the present" (Rapp, 2012: 37).

Raison d'être: Finding the Answers

Finding answers is what we do as reference librarians. All of our skills in collection development, format management, and reference interviewing find their full flowering in the effective answering of user questions. It is quite simply our raison d'être.

Clarity in establishing the processes that go into the making of an answering strategy is a good thing. Deconstructing the process can appear as a slow-motion exercise that confirms and validates what the experienced reference librarian does almost instinctively, or it can provide an instructive framework to condition and hone the librarian's techniques in answering queries of wildly different provenance. Either way, it aims to emphasize the pedagogical aspects of search strategies and the answering process.

Recommendations for Further Reading

Dawson, Heather. 2011. *Know It All, Find It Fast for Academic Libraries*. London: Facet. An effective version of the earlier best-selling *Know It All, Find It Fast: An A–Z Source Guide for the Enquiry Desk* by Bob Duckett, Peter Walker, and Christinea Donnelley. Cross-referenced and comprehensive, this book is a helpful guide for reference librarians confronted with unfamiliar inquiries.

Eurodesk. Available: http://www.eurodesk.org/edesk/. This website is an example of an answering process set up on "How to answer European questions." Designed for Eurodesk, an online support site for professionals working with young people in the European region, the site establishes an "enquiry answering checklist" and gives examples of successfully answered questions that followed the process.

"The Exchange." A one-time regular column in *RQ/Reference and User Services Quarterly*, "The Exchange" is an interesting way to study the asking and answering of tricky reference questions, some of which were never answered. The compilation of questions and answers is available to RUSA (Reference and User Services Association) members at http://www.ala.org/.

National Health Service (NHS). Sponsored by the NHS, a national British pharmacy service available online at http://www.ukmi.nhs.uk/, aims to provide collaborative and evidence-based information on medicines and supplies an interactive template for "standard search patterns" such as one for drug interactions. Templates such as these can be useful for searches that are repeated often. In academic libraries, subject-specific templates can be developed based on curricula. In public libraries, genealogy searches, relative car prices, personal finance resources, doctor information, and researching a house, are some general areas that one can find ready answers with prepared pathfinders.

Project Wombat. Since 1992, Stumpers-L was a popular reference electronic discussion list where librarians could post challenging questions that had "stumped" them. As of January 2006, Project Gutenberg hosted the new version of this site, known as Project Wombat, named after the mascot of the earlier discussion list. Available at http://project-wombat.org/, the list has various levels of subscription so that the user can choose between unmoderated and filtered lists.

Walsh, John. 2011. "The Use of Library of Congress Subject Headings in Digital Collections." *Library Review* 60, no. 4 (June): 328–343. A report both commissioned and publicized by the Library of Congress suggested that the Library of Congress Subject Headings (LCSH) were becoming less necessary in an emerging research world where "we think of Google as the catalog." The debate between the use of free-text searching as epitomized by information searches online, and the use of controlled vocabulary as traditionally espoused in both print and online research, sharpened following the LC report, as discussed by Norman Oder in "The End of LC Subject Headings?" 2006. *Library Journal* (May 15): 14. This study finds that LCSH is still "the most popular choice for subject access in digital libraries."

Bibliography and Works Cited

Barnes, Laura. 2011. "Social Bookmarking Sites: A Review." *Collaborative Librarianship* 3, no. 3 (July): 180–182.

Bell, Suzanne S. 2012. *Librarian's Guide to Online Searching*. 3rd ed. Englewood, CO: Libraries Unlimited.

Case, Donald O. 2012. *Looking for Information: A Survey of Research on Information Seeking, Needs, and Behavior*. 3rd ed. London: Academic Press.

Connaway, Lynn Sillipigni, Timothy J. Dickey, and Marie L. Radford. 2011. "'If It Is Too Inconvenient I'm Not Going After It': Convenience as a Critical Factor in Information-Seeking Behaviors." *Library and Information Science Research* 33, no. 3 (July): 179–190.

Fichman, Pnina. 2011. "A Comparative Assessment of Answer Quality on Four Question Answering Sites." *Journal of Information Science* 37, no. 5: 476–486.

Gross, Melissa. 2001. "Imposed Information Seeking in Public Libraries and School Library Media Centers: A Common Behaviour?" *Information Research* 6, no. 2 (January).

Hacker, Diana. 2010. *Research and Documentation in the Electronic Age*. 7th ed. Boston: Bedford/St. Martins.

Janes, Joseph. 2003. *Introduction to Reference Work in the Digital Age*. New York: Neal-Schuman.

Kent, Jack. 2005. "The Firefly." *Cricket* 32, no. 11 (July): 4. ©2005 by Jack Kent.

Kornegay, Becky, Heidi Buchanan, and Hiddy Morgan. 2005. "Amazing, Magic Searches." *Library Journal* 130, no. 18 (November): 44–46.

Linoski, Alexis, and Tine Walczyk. 2008. "Federated Search 101." *Library Journal Net Connect* 133 (Summer): 2–5.

Lu, Caimei, Jung-ran Park, and Xiaohua Hu. 2010. "User Tags versus Expert-Assigned Subject Terms: A Comparison of Library Thing Tags and Library of Congress Subject Headings." *Journal of Information Science* 36, no. 6 (November): 763–779.

Nagy, Andrew. 2011. "Defining the Next-Generation Catalog." *Library Technology Reports* 47, no. 7 (October): 11–15.

O'Neill, Edward T. O., Lois Mai Chan, Eric Childress, Rebecca Dean, Lynn M. El-Hoshy, and Diane Vizine-Goetz. 2001. "Form Subdivisions: Their Identification and Use in LCSH." *Library Resources and Technical Services* 45, no. 4: 187–197.

Owen, Tim Buckley. 2012. *Success at the Enquiry Desk: Successful Enquiry Answering—Every Time.* 6th ed. London: Facet Publishing.

Radford, Marie, Lynn Silipigni Connaway, Patrick A. Confer, Susanna Sabolcsi-Boros, and Hannah Kwon. 2011. "'Are We Getting Warmer?' Query Clarification in Live Chat Virtual Reference." *Reference and User Services Quarterly* 50, no. 3 (Spring): 259–279.

Rapp, David. 2012. "Discovery at Dartmouth." *Library Journal* 137, no. 3 (February 15): 36–39.

Redden, Carla S. 2010. "Social Bookmarking in Academic Libraries: Trends and Applications." *The Journal of Academic Librarianship* 36, no. 3 (May): 219–227.

Richter, Randy R., and Tricia M. Austin. 2012. "Using MeSH to Enhance PubMed Search Strategies for Evidence-Based Practice in Physical Therapy." *Physical Therapy* 92, no. 1 (January): 124–132.

Ross, Catherine Sheldrick, and Patricia Dewdney. 1998. "Negative Closure: Strategies and Counter-Strategies in the Reference Transaction." *Reference and User Services Quarterly* 38, no. 2 (Winter): 151–163.

RUSA (Reference and User Services Association). 2004. "Guidelines for Behavioral Performance of Reference and Information Service Providers." June. American Library Association. http://www.ala.org/rusa/resources/guidelines/guidelinesbehavioral.

Sauers, Michael P. 2009. *Searching 2.0.* New York: Neal-Schuman.

Saxton, Matthew L., and John Richardson. 2002. *Understanding Reference Transactions.* Boston: Academic Press.

"SpringerLink." 2008. *Online* 32, no. 6 (November–December): 14.

Tennant, Roy. 2001. "Avoiding Unintended Consequences." *Library Journal* 126, no. 1 (January 1): 38.

UWS Library. 2010. "Advanced Online Searching and Research Features." University of the West of Scotland. http://www.uws.ac.uk/workarea/downloadasset.aspx?id=2147490368.

Williams, Sinead. 2002. "Teaming for Research Excellence." *Online* (November/December): 31–35.

Zheng, Xiaolin, Zhongkai Hu, Aiwu Xu, DeRen Chen, Kuang Liu, and Bo Li. 2011. "Algorithm for Recommending Answer Providers in Community-Based Question Answering." *Journal of Information Science* 38, no. 1: 3–14. http://jis.sagepub.com/content/38/1/3.

Part II
Introduction to Major Reference Sources

4

Answering Questions about Books, Magazines, Newspapers, Libraries and Publishing, and Bibliographic Networks—Bibliographic Resources

Overview

Bibliographic resources remain vital in the age of electronic resources. They represent an organized and consistent way to present information about books, periodicals, newspapers, and media, whether they are in print or in an electronic format. Though this same information can be found piece by piece on the Internet, a bibliographic resource provides a way to compare and contrast information collected from many sources. With these resources in hand, the librarian can answer questions about everything from recently published novels and electronic journals to films and media distributors. Many requests of this kind arise from users' need to verify citation information for texts that they have previously consulted or to verify the existence of new sources. Bibliographic resources can also assist in such tasks as finding a copy of a book published at the end of the eighteenth century, copies of a nineteenth-century magazine, or the address of a new publisher. Further, they can help users find libraries with special collections and publishers who publish books in a specific subject area. This chapter introduces the reader to the questions that call for these resources and the means of answering them.

Bibliographies are essentially lists of books or other materials that can be organized by author, title, or subject. They record pertinent information about each item listed, including its author, title, edition, place of publication, publisher, and date of publication. The particulars of a bibliography's organizational structure inform and delimit the ways it can be used. For example, the bibliographic information may differ depending on whether the information is meant to facilitate verification of the title, location of a specific copy, or purchase of an in-print book. Bibliographies may be comprehensive—attempting to include everything within the scope of the bibliography—or selective. Some bibliographies are current and are regularly updated. Others are no longer published and record the existence of materials at a particular time and place. These are retrospective bibliographies. In the future, most bibliographies will be compiled in an electronic format, making them easier to produce, more flexible to search, and easier to keep current.

Bibliographies have a long and distinguished history. Even before the rise of print, records were kept of written materials. As early as the seventh century BC, the Library at Sennacherib at Nineveh kept a list of clay tablets (Harmon, 1989: 16). In the fourteenth century, we find a catalog compiled by Franciscan monks, *Registrum Librorum Angliciae*, which listed manuscripts in more than 180 English monasteries (Harmon, 1989: 17). One of the first bibliographies to be printed was a bibliography of ecclesiastical writers in chronological order, compiled by Johann Triheim, abbot of Spanheim, and published in 1494 (Stokes, 2003). Trade bibliographies began to be published with the invention of the printing press in the fifteenth century, as the need to make the public aware of new publications arose. In 1545, Conrad Gesner published *Bibliotheca Universalis*, a universal bibliography that listed 12,000 books arranged by the author's name, followed by an *Appendix* in 1555 with 3,000 additional works (Macles, 1961). Libraries began to print catalogs of their collections in the eighteenth century, including Leyden (1710), Oxford (1738), and Bibliothèque Royale (1743) (Harmon, 1989: 21). Scholars have compiled bibliographies either to record all books published in a single location or a single country, or a complete or selective list of books published on a certain topic, or a list of the works written by one author. These bibliographies have enabled librarians and scholars to know what books have been published and often where they can be found.

How Bibliographies Are Used

Bibliographies are used to do the following:

* Identify or verify information
* Locate materials
* Select materials for the collection

A bibliography can be used to identify or verify information about a book or other type of material. For example, there may be two books with the same title. The bibliographic record, which includes the author, title, publisher, date of publication, and other useful information, may help to distinguish one from the other; the date of publication or the place of publication may be a guide as to which book it is. A list of books by date or by country can be used to verify the existence of a book. The *National Union Catalog* is an example of a bibliography used to both verify and locate books and other materials. In this case, it listed materials held by the Library of Congress and by the many participating libraries. Bibliographies can also provide information for collection development by identifying new or retrospective titles on a certain subject. A library trying to build a new collection in a certain subject area may find bibliographies useful.

Questions Answered by Bibliographies

Q: Where can I find the name of the author of the book, *The Greater Journey*?

A: If this book is in print or available as an e-book, the answer can be found in *Books in Print*, which lists books available for purchase. Otherwise, it could be found in a library catalog or in *WorldCat*, which lists books and other types of materials owned by libraries.

Q: Where is the periodical *Library Journal* indexed?

A: This information can be found in a directory of periodicals such as *Ulrich's Periodicals Directory*.

Q: What publishers might be interested in publishing my book on how to do organic gardening in the city?

A: The directory *LMP, Literary Market Place*, is one source of information on this topic since it provides information on publishers and what subject areas they publish.

Q: Are there any academic libraries in Fort Worth, Texas?

A: The *American Library Directory* is a good source for this information.

Q: What books have recently won the Pulitzer Prize?

A: *BooksInPrint.com* can be searched for this information.

Major Bibliographic Resources Used in Reference Work

National Catalogs and Bibliographies

National bibliographies provide listings of materials that are published in a particular country and often include materials received through the legal deposit. Each book or other material listed has been examined and cataloged, thus providing a high degree of accuracy. A national bibliography can answer the following questions: What books has a specific author written? What books have been published on a subject in a particular country?

The United States

Although there is no single, central national library covering all publications in the United States, the Library of Congress serves many of the functions of a national library. There is no legal deposit requirement that all published materials must be deposited in a national institution (often the national library), and it is not needed for copyright protection. However, since 1978 copies of all copyrightable works published in the United States must be deposited at the Copyright Office at the Library of Congress, but "not all works deposited are selected for inclusion in the collections of the Library of Congress" (Balay, 1996: 48). Because of this, all items published in the United States are not available in one location.

THE NATIONAL UNION CATALOG

The *National Union Catalog* (*NUC*) began as the card catalog of the Library of Congress in 1901. The first printed author catalog was produced in 1942 and included catalog cards from 1898 to 1942 from the Library of Congress and from other research libraries. In 1956, the *NUC* added the collections of other libraries to the *NUC* book catalog. From 1968 to 1981, the pre-1956 card catalog was published as the *National Union Catalog: Pre-1956 Imprints*, which was an author or main entry only catalog. This was published in both print and microfilm, called REMARC records. Today, the *NUC* is available free through the Library of Congress at http://catalog.loc.gov/ (only books cataloged by the Library of Congress are included) and for a fee on the bibliographic network, OCLC. It includes books, maps, music, serials, visual materials, and many other materials. The Library of Congress itself has a collection of 151 million items that includes 34.5 million books, 66.6 million manuscripts, 13.3 million photographs, 5.4 million maps, 6.4 million pieces of sheet music, and 1.3 million moving images.

The *NUC* is a good source of retrospective bibliographic information and can be used to verify information on earlier editions of the writings of an author and to verify the existence of a particular work. Although most information from the *NUC* can be found in *WorldCat*, some bibliographic information is only available in the NUC.

LIBRARY CATALOGS

Access to library catalogs online has made it easier to both identify and locate books, magazines, newspapers, manuscripts, maps, audiovisual materials, and other materials. In addition to its own catalog, the Library of Congress has an extensive list of online library catalogs on its website (http://catalog.loc.gov/). The New York Public Library's online catalog (http://catalog.nypl.org/) is an extensive database of U.S. and international titles owned by the New York Public Library. The NYPL site also provides mobile access.

When a catalog lists the records of several libraries, it becomes a union catalog. Many library consortia have union catalogs to make it easier for their members to identify and locate library materials. For example, the Five Colleges consortium in Massachusetts (Amherst College, Hampshire College, Mount Holyoke College, Smith College, and the University of Massachusetts Amherst) has an online union catalog (http://fcaw.library.umass.edu:8991/F). Another example is "Tri-Cat," a union catalog for three medical center libraries in New York City: Memorial Sloan-Kettering Cancer Center, The Rockefeller University, and Weill Medical College at Cornell University (http://lib3.rockefeller.edu/). On an international level, *WorldCat* lists the holdings of libraries from all over the world and provides users with access to materials needed often close to their own location. A public version of *WorldCat* (http://www.worldcat.org/) is now available through Google. Users can find a copy of the book in a library near them or find out how popular a title is by how many libraries own it. *WorldCat* is also available through a mobile app. All of these online catalogs, whether from a large library such as the New York Public Library, a union catalog or *WorldCat*, are tremendous resources for other libraries because they verify the existence of a particular resource which a user may be able to borrow, read online, or read or examine on site.

The United Kingdom

In the United Kingdom, the *British National Bibliography* (*BNB*) provides selective coverage of printed and electronic publications published since 1950. "The *BNB* is the single most comprehensive listing of U.K. titles. U.K. and Irish publishers are obliged by law to send a copy of all new publications, including serial titles, to the Legal Deposit Office of the British Library. The *BNB* also contains details of forthcoming books." Most items listed in the *BNB* are available at the British Library. The *General Catalogue of Printed Books to 1975* and supplements to 1998 are available in print and are based on the country's legal deposit. *Catalogue* is now part of *Explore the British Library* (http://explore.bl.uk/), a newly designed online catalog which provides access to this world-renowned library collection.

Canada

In Canada, the Library and Archives Canada (LAC) maintains *AMICUS*, an online catalog listing records from 1,300 Canadian libraries, and has provided free online access to *Canadiana*, Canada's National Bibliography, since 1998. It "lists and describes a wide variety of publications produced in Canada, or published elsewhere but of special interest or significance to Canada" (http://www.collections canada.gc.ca/canadiana/index-e.html). Among the publications included are books, periodicals, sound recordings, video recordings, government documents, and electronic documents. "*Canadiana* provides standard cataloguing information for each item listed." *New Books Service* is a free, monthly service providing pre-publication information on books in English and French (http://www.collections canada.gc.ca/newbooks/index-e.html).

Trade Bibliographies

Trade bibliographies are bibliographies usually produced commercially by the publishers and booksellers in a country to provide information on what is in print, what is out of print, and what will be published. The primary purpose of a trade bibliography is to provide information about what materials are available for purchase. The materials listed are supplied by the publishers. Because one primary reason for having a trade bibliography is to help people obtain the needed information in order to locate and purchase the book, price, publisher, and ISBN (International Standard Book Number) are listed. The ISBN system allows each book published to have a distinctive number. The number includes a country code, a publisher identifier, a title identifier, and a checkdigit. The materials listed have not been examined by the publisher compiling the information.

A trade bibliography can also answer questions such as these: Is this book still in print? What books by a certain author are still in print? What recent books on a particular subject have been published? Is this advertised book available or forthcoming?

Books in Print is a comprehensive annual trade bibliography for books, audio books, and video titles published or distributed in North America. *Books in Print* is available online through Bowker and in print. The online version combines in-print, out-of-print, and forthcoming titles. Librarians can use *Books in Print* to verify information about specific titles and to identify titles on a particular subject. *Fiction Connection* and *Non-Fiction Connection*, which are online readers' advisory sites, are provided at no cost. A *Global Books in Print* is also available that includes the United States, Canada, Europe, and Australia. This is a useful tool for a library that needs to buy and locate materials outside the United States.

U.S. Retrospective Bibliography

A series of bibliographies make up the U.S. retrospective bibliography. These bibliographies are useful for establishing the existence and sometimes the location of books published before the twentieth century. For many scholars doing research on the history of the United States and the work of early authors and scholars, these bibliographies are a necessary part of their work. Charles Evans, a librarian, compiled *American Bibliography: A Chronological Dictionary of All Books, Pamphlets, and Periodical Publications Printed in the United States from the Genesis of Printing in 1639 Down to and Including the Year 1800*. It is considered "the most important general list of early American publications . . . [it] includes books, pamphlets and periodicals, arranged chronologically by dates of publication. [It] gives for each book author 's full name with dates of birth and death, full title, place, date, publisher or printer, paging, size and, whenever possible, location of copies in American libraries" (Balay, 1996: 45). In each volume, there are indexes by author, subject, and printers and publishers. An author-title index to the whole set was published in 1959. It is now available in a digitized format with full text of the materials listed as *Early American Imprints, Series I. Evans* (1639–1800).

Ralph R. Shaw and Richard H. Shoemaker continued the Evans bibliography with *American Bibliography: A Preliminary Checklist for 1801–1819*. This bibliography was intended to fill the gap between the end of Evans and the beginning of Roorbach in 1820. Shaw and Shoemaker also include library locations. It was followed by Richard H. Shoemaker 's *A Checklist of American Imprints for 1820–1829* and *A Checklist of American Imprints for 1830–1846*. This is also available on microform and online.

Orville Roorbach, a bookseller, published *Bibliotheca Americana: 1820–1861*. This "trade catalog of American publications, including reprints," was intended for use by booksellers (Balay, 1996: 46). The four volumes are arranged alphabetically by author and title and provide the publisher and sometimes the date of publication. Though incomplete and sometimes inaccurate, it is all we have for this period. James Kelly compiled *The American Catalogue of Books . . . January 1861 to January 1871*, picking up where Roorbach ended. It is also a trade bibliography providing similar information to Roorbach (Balay, 1996: 6). It is arranged alphabetically by author and title.

Joseph Sabin's *A Dictionary of Books Relating to America from Its Discovery to the Present Time* lists books, pamphlets, and periodicals published in the Western Hemisphere and elsewhere with locations. It was published in 1936, having been finished by others. Arranged by author, each entry includes title, place, publisher, date, format, paging, and often information about the contents (Balay, 1996: 45). John Edgar Molnar published an author-title index to Joseph Sabin's *Dictionary of Books Relating to America in 1974. Sabin Americana 1500–1926* is now available in a digitized format with full text of many of the documents listed in the *Dictionary*.

American Catalogue of Books 1876–1910 was both a national and trade bibliography. The first volume lists the books under author and title, and the second volume by subject. It "aims to include, with certain exceptions, all books published in the U.S. which were for sale to the general public" (Balay, 1996: 46).

The *United States Catalog* is an in-print list published by H.W. Wilson from 1899–1927. This was followed by *Cumulative Book Index*, subtitled "A world list of books in the English language," which was published by H.W. Wilson from 1928–1999. Each volume is a listing of works published in English anywhere in the world during that time period. Authors, titles, and subjects are arranged in one alphabet.

American Book Publishing Record Cumulative 1876–1949 and *1950–1977* are early Bowker publications arranged by Dewey number with author and title indexes, with separate volumes for fiction and juvenile fiction. They document books published during this period. This publication continues to the present and is published monthly with an annual volume.

Periodicals and Newspapers

Libraries receive many questions about periodicals and newspapers. For example, where is a magazine published? Where is this journal indexed? What is the subscription price of this magazine? When did the journal begin? How much does it cost to advertise in this magazine or newspaper? One of the top sources for information about current domestic and international magazines, journals, and newspapers is *Ulrich's Periodicals Directory*, which lists over 220,000 domestic and foreign serial publications including magazines, journals, newspapers, irregular serials, and online serials. *Ulrich's* provides bibliographic information about each title including address, subscriber information, a brief description of the serial, where the serial is indexed, whether the serial is available online, and the history of the serial as well as the ISSN (International Standard Serials Number). The ISSN, like the ISBN, provides a way to distinguish similar titles from one another. A listing of online databases is also included. The print version is a four-volume work arranged by subject. The online version, *Ulrichsweb*, lists titles from over 242 countries including active, suspended, ceased, and forthcoming titles.

Magazines for Libraries is a source of recommendations for periodicals. Arranged by subject, it describes each magazine, evaluates it, and recommends what kind of libraries might want to purchase this magazine. It is particularly useful for public libraries, school libraries, and community college libraries. More than 5,400 magazines and databases are reviewed. Title and subject indexes are included. *Magazines for Libraries* reviews are also included in *Ulrichsweb*.

Although *Ulrich's* is often the first choice of librarians for information on periodicals and newspapers, other directories provide similar information or supplement it. *The Standard Periodical Directory* is a smaller directory of periodicals listing over 62,000 U.S. and Canadian magazines and newspapers. It is published annually and is known for listing many house organs and trade publications not listed elsewhere. The online version is titled *MediaFinder*. The *International Directory of Little Magazines and Small Presses* is a source of information about little magazines and presses that may or may not get listed in the standard directories. Each magazine or press is described in nonevaluative terms. Subscription information is also provided.

As the number of electronic journals and databases increases, users and librarians need to know what journals and databases are available electronically, their subscription price, and their availability. The *Gale Directory of Databases*, a listing of databases, database products, online services, and database vendors and distributors, is available in print and online in the *Gale Directory Library*. This reference work is a comprehensive listing of current information covering over 20,000 on databases and database products in English and other languages. For example, the librarian can find out what databases are available from ProQuest or from EBSCO. The librarian can also find out how to contact the publisher of the database.

A number of other publications help librarians and users sort out the information on journals that are available electronically. *NewJour* (http://library .georgetown.edu/newjour/) is a free listing of all journals and newspapers available electronically. Users of the list are encouraged to send in new titles to add to the list. *Fulltext Sources Online (FSO)*, edited by Mary B. Glose, is "a directory of publications accessible online in full text, from 30 major aggregator producers." *FSO* is also available in print, published two times a year. As open access journals have begun to flourish, the *Directory of Open Access Journals (DOAJ)* lists over 3,700 free, full-text scholarly journals on all subjects and in all languages with many searchable at the article level (http://www.doaj.org/). *Gale Directory of Publications and Broadcast Media* is both an online and print publication, listing periodicals and newspapers as well as radio and television stations and cable companies in the United States and Canada. This directory provides subscription rates, circulation, key staff, and advertising rates for both publications and media. It is organized geographically with city subdivisions for magazines, newspapers, radio, and TV, and also includes a subject index. This directory is part of the *Gale Directory Library*.

Earlier compilations of serials titles and their locations were recorded in two volumes, which serve as a way to verify and locate serials titles that have been in existence for a long period of time or were being published before 1999. They are *Union List of Serials in the U.S. and Canada before 1950*, which ends in 1949, and *New Serials Titles* that continued the *Union List of Serials* and ceased publication in 1999.

Nonprint Materials

The nonprint equivalent to *Books in Print* simply does not exist. Librarians trying to identify, verify, and order DVDs, CDs, videos, and audiotapes must search a series of sources in order to locate the information they need. *Video Source Book* provides information on a wide range of videos from children's features to documentaries to straight-to-video movies. The videos are arranged alphabetically by title, and the list includes a detailed description. Six indexes are also available including subject, awards, and distributors. The *Internet Movie Database* (http://IMDB.com/), now owned by Amazon.com, is a large online movie (feature film) database begun about 1990. For each movie the database provides the name of the director, the writing credits, the characters in the movie, the running time, and viewer comments. It also indicates the formats available (VHS, DVD) in the United States, the United Kingdom, Canada, and Germany. For educational, documentary, instructional, and independent productions, there is the *NICEM Film and Video Finder Online* that is available by subscription. A print version is also available. This database covers over 640,000 items in all formats of media, for all age levels, and provides both ordering information and MARC records. *Bowker's Complete Video Directory* lists feature films, documentary, and special-interest videos in four volumes with basic information needed in order to locate the titles. In addition to VHS listings, it lists Beta, 3⁄4", U-matic, 8 mm, and laser disc formats. *Books Out Loud: Bowker's Guide to Audiobooks* (formerly *Words on Cassette*) provides detailed bibliographic information on audiobooks, both cassettes and CDs, including a content summary and an author/reader/performer index.

Bibliographies of Bibliographies

Theodore Besterman's *A World Bibliography of Bibliographies* is a retrospective bibliography of bibliographies separately published and arranged by subject. It includes information through 1963. Over 115,000 bibliographies in 40 languages are listed. It is an important contribution to the history of bibliography. Alice F. Toomy produced a supplementary volume that spanned 1964–1974.

Publishing and Library Resources

Questions about publishing and libraries come from the public and from librarians themselves. Librarians and users often want basic information about a publisher, its location, and what types of material it publishes. They are often looking for a publisher to publish a book they plan to write. *Publishers, Distributors and Wholesalers of the United States* is available in print. The list of publishers is extensive, including small press and audiovisual publishers. Updated annually, it provides full contact information on publishing companies, distributors, and wholesalers in one alphabet. With over 186,000 entries, it can help the user find information on the fields of activity, trade imprints, and subsidiaries. The *American Book Trade Directory* lists over 20,000 retail and antiquarian book dealers, wholesalers, and distributors in the United States in a geographical arrangement. Librarians can use this directory to locate subject specialists, distributors of hard-to-find books and other materials, retail stores for specialized materials including books in languages other than English, and library collection appraisers.

Publishers Directory lists over 30,000 U.S. and Canadian publishers (both major publishers and small and specialized publishers), distributors and wholesalers listing contact information, key personnel, and the number of titles published. It is available online as part of the *Gale Directory Library*.

The *Library and Book Trade Almanac* is available in print. It provides reports on national and international library and book trade trends, new legislation, and news of the book trade and library world. The latest statistics, ranging from the number of books published by subject to the average prices, are included. It is a good place to find the latest information on book, periodical, and audiovisual prices.

Literary Market Place is a guide to the American book publishing industry. An annual publication, it provides information on every aspect of the publishing business including publishers, what kinds of material they publish, and key personnel and related areas such as literary agents, translators, book fairs, printers, and manufacturers. This is a very useful reference work for authors and others working in the publishing industry.

American Library Directory, an annual publication available online and in print, is arranged by state and then by city and provides information and statistics about academic, public, special and government libraries in that city, including special collections and key personnel.

World Guide to Libraries lists more than 42,500 libraries in 200 countries. This work is arranged by continent and country and then by type of library. All essential information about each library is listed including address, telephone, fax, e-mail, collections, and statistics.

Directory of Special Libraries and Information Centers, both a print and online publication, covers over 35,000 special libraries and information centers. Volume 1 provides information on subject-specific resource collections maintained by businesses, educational institutions, nonprofit organizations, government entities, and so on. There are international listings as well as North America. Volume 2 provides geographical and personnel indexes. It is also part of the *Gale Directory Library*.

Bibliographic Control

> Bibliographic control includes the standardization of bibliographic description and subject access by means of uniform catalog code, classification systems, name authorities, and preferred headings; the creation and maintenance of catalogs, union lists, and finding aids; and the provision of physical access to the items in the collection. (*ODLIS*, 2012)

Bibliographies perform this function of bibliographic control by organizing material by author, title, and subject so that the item can be identified and then locating a library owning the material so that it can be accessed. The best example of bibliographic control is the online library catalog. Cataloging each item in a library collection provides the means to retrieve each item in a variety of ways. Cataloging also provides consistency so that the same form of an author's name or a title is used each time, and a standard set of subject headings is used.

The three elements that have made possible bibliographic control on an international level are Machine Readable Cataloging (MARC) records, the International Standard Bibliographic Description (ISBD), and Anglo-American Cataloguing Rules (AACR2) (Gorman, 2001). MARC records were developed by the Library of Congress and have been used since 1968. "MARC is the way we encode the results of the cataloging process" (Gorman, 2001: 308). The structure of the MARC record has standardized the format of the data for each item cataloged. The ISBD "was seen . . . as a means of standardizing the presentation of descriptive data so that it could be machine-translated into MARC" (Gorman, 2001: 308). Finally, the AACR2 was an effort to "bring uniformity to cataloguing practice in the English-speaking world" (Gorman, 2001: 308). The standardization has resulted in all permutations of a name being linked and a standard list of subject headings controlled by a thesaurus for consistency. Verification and access are the results of bibliographic control. The more comprehensively an item is indexed, the more accessible it will be since it can be searched from more access points.

In addition to individual library catalogs, there are also union catalogs that combine the catalogs of several libraries and make it possible to search for information and locations across several catalogs at one time. Bibliographic utilities also help the librarian to identify and locate books and other materials. The most noteworthy of these bibliographic utilities is OCLC (Online Computer Library Center). OCLC is a nonprofit membership organization with over 71,000 member libraries from 112 countries. Libraries use OCLC to locate, acquire, catalog, and borrow library materials. *WorldCat*, its union catalog, provides access to "nearly 900 million pieces of information about who holds what and where" (http://www.oclc.org/membership/). The presence of bibliographic utilities has increased the standardization of cataloging and has greatly improved access to books and other materials.

Collection Development and Maintenance

Selection and Keeping Current

Librarians can turn to several sources to identify bibliographies. The primary source is the *Guide to Reference*, an online-only resource that replaces Balay's *Guide to Reference Books*. Listing a wide range of reference resources, it is organized by subject area and has good search capability. It provides an informative annotation on each resource listed. The *Guide to Reference* has expanded its coverage to include many online resources as well as books and databases. On a yearly basis, *American Reference Books Annual* provides a comprehensive annotated list of reference books published in a specific year in the United States and Canada. It is available in print and online. The British equivalent to the *Guide to Reference* is the *New Walford Guide to Reference Resources*, a three-volume work that is constantly revised. It is a good companion to *Guide to Reference* in that it includes more European resources in addition to British resources.

Evaluating Bibliographic Resources

The basic criteria for evaluating any type of materials also apply to bibliographies. They include: accuracy, authority, scope, arrangement, methodology, bibliographical content, and currency.

- *Accuracy* is the most important criterion for bibliographies. Since bibliographies are used to verify information about a book or other type of material and often to locate it, the accuracy of the information is of the utmost importance. Each unit of the bibliographic record must be correct.

- The *authority* of the compiler and publisher helps the librarian or user to evaluate the credibility of the work.
- The *scope* can make a big difference particularly in subject bibliographies. The librarian will want to know if a subject bibliography covers the same ground as another bibliography or covers different dates or different types of material. The preface or introduction to the bibliography often describes the scope of the bibliography.
- The *arrangement* can make the bibliography easier or more difficult to use. How is the main body of the bibliography arranged—by author, title, subject, date, geography, and so forth? And what indexes are provided to have alternative ways to access the material?
- The introduction of a bibliography usually describes both the scope and the *methodology* of the work. For example, it is important to know if the compiler examined each work listed in the bibliography. If not, the bibliography may not be very useful since listing items not examined usually produces some errors.
- *Bibliographical content* should be examined to see if the bibliographical entries include enough information to help the user to verify the titles and to proceed to locate them.
- A bibliography should be *current* within the boundaries of the work. The dates and material it covers should be inclusive unless otherwise stated.

Further Considerations

In a search for bibliographic information for books, periodicals, or nonprint materials, there are certain basic considerations. First, it is important to know if the title is current or older. Sometimes the user does not know, so the librarian must try all sources—those listing current material and those listing older material. However, if the item is current, the librarian should start the search with bibliographic sources that list current material, such as trade bibliographies or library catalogs. If a price and publisher are needed to order the item, a current trade bibliography such as *Books in Print* is a good beginning source. Many libraries also use the databases developed by library vendors such as Baker and Taylor and YBP, which provide bibliographic information and reviews from standard review sources. If a user wants to find a book in the library, then either the library's own catalog or a union catalog such as OCLC's *WorldCat* can be a good starting place unless the item is too recent to be listed.

For periodicals, librarians can use *Ulrich's Periodicals Directory* to find subscription information and to verify the title. Library catalogs usually list the periodicals the library owns and the holdings. For information about electronic serials, librarians can turn to *Fulltext Sources Online*.

If the librarian understands the user's needs, it will be easier to determine the appropriate bibliographic source. Often more than one appropriate source is available. Even in this electronic world, a need exists to verify, identify, and locate materials. Bibliographies provide needed access to all formats of materials.

THE TOP TEN BIBLIOGRAPHIC RESOURCES

Title	Print	Online
American Library Directory. 1923–. Medford, NJ: Information Today.	Annual	Subscription http://www.americanlibrarydirectory .com/
Books in Print. 1905–. New Providence, NJ: R.R. Bowker.	Annual	Subscription http://www.bowker.com/
Gale Directory of Databases. 1993–. Farmington Hills, MI: Gale Cengage Learning.	Annual	Subscription http://www.gale.cengage.com/ DirectoryLibrary/
Gale Directory of Publications and Broadcast Media. 1969–. Farmington Hills, MI: Gale Cengage Learning.	Annual	Subscription http://www.gale.cengage.com/ DirectoryLibrary/
Guide to Reference. 2008. Chicago: American Library Association.		Subscription http://www.guidetoreference.org/
Literary Market Place (*LMP*). 1940–. Medford, NJ: Information Today.	Annual	Subscription http://www.literarymarketplace .com/
New Walford Guide to Reference Resources. 2005–. London: Facet Publishing.	3 vols.	
Publishers, Distributors and Wholesalers of the U.S. 1978–. New Providence, NJ: R.R. Bowker.	Annual	Subscription http://www.bowker.com/
Ulrich's Periodicals Directory. 1932–. New Providence, NJ: R.R. Bowker.	Annual	Subscription http://www.ulrichsweb.com/
WorldCat. 1971–. Dublin, OH: OCLC.		Subscription http://www.worldcat.org/

RECOMMENDED FREE BIBLIOGRAPHIC WEBSITES

British National Bibliography. http://bnb.bl.uk. All materials published in the United Kingdom are listed here.

Canadiana. http://www.collectionscanada.gc.ca/canadiana/index-e.html. This is the primary source to identify and verify Canadian materials.

Internet Movie Database (*IMDB*). http://www.imdb.com/. The best source for information on all aspects of film—actors, directors, and so forth.

Library of Congress Catalog. http://catalog.loc.gov/. The Library of Congress's large collection makes it an excellent source for identifying and verifying titles.

New York Public Library Catalog. http://catalog.nypl.org/. The New York Public Library has another large and sometimes unique collection that is useful in identifying and verifying titles.

NewJour. http://library.georgetown.edu/newjour/. This source provides a listing of all new e-journals.

Recommended Resources Discussed in This Chapter

American Bibliography: A Chronological Dictionary of All Books, Pamphlets, and Periodical Publications Printed in the United States from the Genesis of Printing in 1639 Down to and Including the Year 1800. 14 vols. Charles Evans. Chicago: Self-published, 1903–1959. Also available online as *Early American Imprints, Series I: Evans, 1629–1800,* from Readex.

American Bibliography: A Preliminary Checklist for 1801–1819. Ralph R. Shaw and Richard H. Shoemaker. 22 vols. New York: Scarecrow, 1958–1966. Available digitized from Readex.

American Book Publishing Record. Amenia, NY: Grey House Publishing, 1876–. Monthly with an annual volume.

American Book Publishing Record Cumulative 1876–1949. 15 vols. New York: Bowker, 1980.

American Book Publishing Record Cumulative 1950–1977. 15 vols. New York: Bowker, 1979.

American Book Trade Directory. Medford, NJ: Information Today, 1915–. Annual.

American Catalogue of Books . . . January 1861 to January 1871. 2 vols. James Kelly. New York: Wiley, 1866–1871.

American Catalogue of Books 1876–1910. 8 vols. in 13. New York: Publishers Weekly, 1880–1911.

American Library Directory. Medford, NJ: Information Today, 1923–. Annual. Also available online: http://www.americanlibrarydirectory.com/.

American Reference Books Annual. Littleton, CO: Libraries Unlimited, 1970–. Annual. Also available online: http://www.arbaonline.com/.

Bibliotheca Americana: 1820–1861. 4 vols. Orville Roorbach. New York: Roorbach, 1852–1861.

Books in Print. New Providence, NJ: Bowker, 1948–. Annual. http://www.bowker.com/. Also in print from Grey House Publishing.

Books Out Loud: Bowker's Guide to Audiobooks. 2 vols. Amenia, NY: Grey House Publishing, 2012.

Bowker's Complete Video Directory. Amenia, NY: Grey House Publishing, 2011.

British National Bibliography. http://bnb.bl.uk/.

Canadiana. http://www.collectionscanada.gc.ca/canadiana/index-e.html.

A Checklist of American Imprints for 1820–1829. Richard H. Shoemaker. 10 vols. New York: Scarecrow. Available digitized from Readex.

A Checklist of American Imprints for 1830–1846. Richard H. Shoemaker. Metuchen, NJ: Scarecrow, 1964–1971. Available digitized from Readex.

Cumulative Book Index. 1928–1999. New York: H.W. Wilson.

A Dictionary of Books Relating to America from Its Discovery to the Present Time. 28 vols. Joseph Sabin. New York: Sabin, 1868–1936. Also available as Sabin Americana 1500–1926, from Gale Digital Collections: http://www.gale.com/digitalcollection/.

Directory of Open Access Journals. Lund, Sweden: Lund University Libraries. http://www.doaj.org/.

Directory of Special Libraries and Information Centers. Farmington Hills, MI: Gale. Annual. Also available online in *Gale Directory Library:* http://www.gale.cengage.com/DirectoryLibrary/.

Explore the British Library. http://catalogue.bl.uk/.

Fulltext Sources Online. Mary B. Glose, ed. Medford, NJ: Information Today, 1989–. Semiannual. Also available online: http://www.fso-online.com/.

Gale Directory of Databases. Farmington Hills, MI: Gale, 1993–. Annual. Also available online in *Gale Directory Library:* http://www.gale.cengage.com/DirectoryLibrary/.

Gale Directory of Publications and Broadcast Media. Farmington Hills, MI: Gale, 1990–. Annual. Also available online in *Gale Directory Library:* http://www.gale.cengage.com/DirectoryLibrary/.

Guide to Reference. Chicago: American Library Association, 2008–. http://www.guideto reference.org/.

International Directory of Little Magazines and Small Presses. Paradise, CA: Dustbooks, 1965–. Annual.

Internet Movie Database (IMDB). http://www.IMDB.com/.

Library and Book Trade Almanac. Medford, NJ: Information Today, 1957–. Annual.

Library of Congress Catalog. http://catalog.loc.gov/.

Literary Market Place: The Directory of the American Book Publishing Industry. Medford, NJ: Information Today, 1940–. Annual. Also available online: http://www.literarymarket place.com/.

Magazines for Libraries. New Providence, NJ: Bowker, 1969–. Also available online: http:// www.ulrichsweb.com/.

National Union Catalog, Pre-1956 Imprints. A Cumulative Author List Representing Library of Congress Printed Cards and Titles Reported by Other American Libraries. 1968–1981. 754 vols. London: Mansell.

New Books Service. Ottawa: Library and Archives Canada. http://www.collectionscanada.gc .ca/newbooks/index-e.html.

New Serials Titles. Washington, DC: Library of Congress, 1953–1999.

New Walford Guide to Reference Resources. 3 vols. Ray Lester, ed. London: Facet Publishing, 2005–.

New York Public Library Catalog. http://catalog.nypl.org/.

NewJour. http:/library.georgetown.edu/newjour.

NICEM Film and Video Finder Online. Albuquerque, NM: Access Innovations. http://www .nicem.com/.

Publishers Directory. Farmington Hills, MI: Gale. Annual. Also available online in *Gale Directory Library*: http://www.gale.cengage.com/DirectoryLibrary/.

Publishers, Distributors and Wholesalers of the United States. Amenia, NY: Grey House Publishing, 1978–. Annual.

The Standard Periodical Directory. New York: Oxbridge, 1989–. Annual. Also available online as *MediaFinder*: http://www.mediafinder.com/.

Ulrich's Periodicals Directory. New Providence, NJ: Bowker, 1932–. Annual. Also available online: http://www.ulrichsweb.com/.

Union List of Serials in the U.S. and Canada before 1950. New York: Wilson, 1965.

A World Bibliography of Bibliographies. 4th ed. 5 vols. Theodore Besterman. Laussane: Societaas Bibliographica, 1965–1966.

World Guide to Libraries. Munich: K. F. Sauer; distributed by Gale, 1966–.

WorldCat. Dublin, OH: OCLC, 1971–. http://www.worldcat.org/.

Recommendations for Further Reading

Duckett, Bob. 2010. "T. J. Wise and the City Librarian: Bibliographical Research—1917 Style." *Library and Information History* 26, no. 1: 43–55. An account of the labor-intensive process for compiling bibliographies in the days before electronic databases, for those interested in the history of bibliographic research. The paper describes the efforts of a well-known bibliographer attempting to publish a complete bibliography of the works of the Brontë family.

Goedeken, Edward A. 2010. "So Poor We Can't Even Pay Attention: Identifying Important Serials for Political Science during the Great Recession." *The Serials Librarian* 59, no. 3–4: 334–345. Presents approaches for determining the most important academic journals for local needs, based on both reputation and citation information. The example used is political sciences, but the method can be readily adapted to other disciplines.

McTavish, Jill R., Diane Rasmussen Neal, and C. Nadine Wathen. 2011. "Is What You See What You Get? Medical Subject Headings and Their Organizing Work in the Violence against Women Research Literature." *Knowledge Organization* 38, no. 5: 381–397. An examination of the factors that complicate the use of authoritative subject headings on the topic of violence against women in the National Library of Medicine's standardized thesaurus, known as MeSH. The project demonstrates how the terminology used to describe the topic differs by field, such as health, sociology, and psychology. The project also demonstrates how subject headings change over time due to trends in scholarship, politics, and social construction.

Park, Ji-Hong, and Jiyoung Shim. 2011. "Exploring How Library Publishing Services Facilitate Scholarly Communication." *Journal of Scholarly Publishing* 43, no. 1: 76–89. Examines how new models in scholarly communication, including that of the open access institutional repository, are changing the way that articles are vetted and discovered. The article concludes that the development of a platform within the academic community for knowledge sharing and creating awareness of new research is a high priority.

Paynter, Robin A., Rose M. Jackson, and Laura Bowering Mullen. 2010. "Core Journal Lists: Classic Tool, New Relevance." *Behavioral and Social Sciences Librarian* 29, no. 1: 15–31. Reports on the use of core journal lists and elaborates on the variety of new and emerging metrics for judging the importance of journals.

Rolla, Peter J. 2009. "User Tags versus Subject Headings: Can User-Supplied Data Improve Subject Access to Library Collections?" *Library Resources and Technical Services* 53, no. 3: 174–185. Discusses the subject of bibliographic control. Some members of the library community advocate for the use of user-supplied tags in addition to librarian-supplied subject headings in the catalog. This article compares tags and controlled descriptors created for the same records to highlight differences and to demonstrate the usefulness of each.

Stout, Nancy. 2009. "What Would Thoreau Think? A Representative List of Green Periodicals for the 21st Century." *The Serials Librarian* 57, no. 3: 233–243. Offers notes on the social importance of specialized catalogs and an annotated bibliography of periodicals on ecology and advocacy.

Walker, Christopher H. 2011. "Cost and Value of Bibliographic Control. A Report of the Heads of Technical Services in Large Research Libraries Interest Group ('Big Heads'), American Library Association Annual Conference, Washington, DC, June 2010." *Technical Services Quarterly* 28, no. 2: 184–186. Highlights the cost and importance of bibliographic control in large research libraries.

Bibliography and Works Cited

Balay, Robert. 1996. *Guide to Reference Books*. Chicago: American Library Association.

Gorman, Michael. 2001. "Bibliographic Control or Chaos: An Agenda for National Bibliographic Services in the 21st Century." *IFLA Journal* 27: 307–313.

Harmon, Robert B. 1989. *Elements of Bibliography: A Simplified Approach*. Rev. ed. Metuchen, NJ: Scarecrow Press.

Macles, Louise Noelle. 1961. *Bibliography*. Translated by T. C. Hines. New York: Scarecrow Press.

ODLIS (Online Dictionary for Library and Information Science). 2012. "Bibliographic Control." Accessed July 12. http://www.abc-clio.com/ODLIS/odlis_b.aspx.

Stokes, Roy B. 2003. "Bibliography." In *Encyclopedia of Library and Information Science*, edited by Miriam A. Drake. New York: Marcel Dekker.

5
Answering Questions about Anything and Everything—Encyclopedias

Overview

The basic informational core of any library was the encyclopedia. The thinking mind's dream, the needy mind's crutch, and every librarian's staple, the encyclopedia was quite simply the closest approximation to a bookish God, omniscient and omnipresent. A librarian at the desk, in fact, was often confused for an encyclopedia. "Excuse me, just one quick question: In what years was the French and Indian War fought?" Professional dignity could be maintained only with a quick dive into the nearest encyclopedia.

The easy availability of an encyclopedia for the past 200 years has effectively obscured the original encyclopedia's breathtaking vision and magnitude of purpose. To provide succinct, user-friendly information on *all* areas of cumulative human activity would be considered impossible in a pre-Internet age, if it did not already exist in the form of the encyclopedia.

Given the ubiquity of today's World Wide Web and the proliferation of Web 2.0 technology, the era of the printed multivolume general encyclopedic tome is over. In its place, there is a proliferation of electronic and open source encyclopedias that strive to retain the authority of the past even as they capture the immediacy of ongoing current events.

Structure and Use of Encyclopedias

The etymology of the word "encyclopedia" is supposedly from *enkyklios paideia,* Greek for a "well-rounded education." While the inspiration of an encyclopedia to foment a well-rounded education has not changed since the days of Aristotle, changes in the audience and choices in the format have resulted in a bewildering variety of encyclopedias.

The earliest scholars who compiled information primarily for their own use did not have user-friendliness in mind. The information collated was idiosyncratic in both content and arrangement. Yet the act of collating diverse information into a cohesive unit must have fed into a basic human need since variations of encyclopedic undertakings can be found in all parts of the world over many centuries.

By the eighteenth century, the first prototype of the modern encyclopedia was presented in the form of John Harris's *Lexicon Technicum,* a compilation of alphabetically arranged articles written by multiple experts with a copious bibliography.

The three major structural elements of the modern encyclopedia were slotted into place and have continued. Since then, the basic structure has been relatively unvarying, but encyclopedia choices have matured in response to different needs and innovations. Broadly, they are as follows.

Age Appropriateness

There is a welcome recognition that knowledge is not the preserve of the adult scholar alone. Age-focused encyclopedias have overtaken the field so that today, it is impossible to equate the encyclopedia with exclusive and sophisticated research needs, as was the case in past centuries. Encyclopedias for elementary school readers, middle-school students, and young adults in high school are primary audience foci as are all levels of adult readers.

Focus

Given the vast demographics that are now the target audience, encyclopedias are either general or specialized. Their breadth of coverage and ease of reading distinguish them from general titles. Specialized encyclopedias are known for intensity of focus on a single subject and in-depth accounting of all aspects related to that subject, and they are, in fact, becoming the only type of encyclopedia that continues to be published in print format.

Scope

Print encyclopedias come in all sizes to suit all needs and all pocketbooks. There are the single-volume encyclopedias with brief entries or highly specialized topics. The impressive multivolume series can be breathtaking in their scope to cover anything and everything. The scope of online encyclopedias is potentially infinite as suggested by the continual increase in articles populating *Wikipedia*, which registered 100,000 articles in English in 2003 and 3,964,297 in May 2012, with the total number at over 22 million articles in almost 300 languages (http://stats.wikimedia.org/).

Format

In the past decade, the formats available to encyclopedias have grown from simple print to a dizzying array of choices. Cheap little diskettes, courtesy of CD-ROM technology, and DVDs have been surpassed by online availability that is easily accessible, frequently updated, and either free or available through subscriptions. The future of encyclopedias is most definitely anchored to its online avatar. More interestingly, with the increasing popularity of open source, user-generated models, the avatar itself is morphing and maturing in ways that would have been unthinkable to creators of the traditional encyclopedic format.

Since the purpose of an encyclopedia is to be all encompassing, the potential to fall short is acute. It is imperative then that every reference librarian is completely clear about both acquiring and using the right encyclopedia for the right reasons. Questions on whether one should purchase a general encyclopedia rather than use freely available resources must be honestly considered by every reference librarian. At a minimum cost of hundreds of dollars for a general, multivolume set, the financial premium for carefully evaluating and making the most productive choice is also relatively steep.

Questions Answered by Encyclopedias

Adult or child, layperson or professional, the act of reaching out to an encyclopedic source, be it multivolume or a single volume, print or electronic, is conditioned by certain basic expectations.

Ready Reference

Q: Is Agricola a drink?

A: According to *Grolier Online*, "Agricola" was a Roman general who lived AD 40–93.

While Google searches have replaced the role of print encyclopedias for quick ready reference, online and embedded encyclopedias continue to provide reliable and direct information on any topic. From straightforward biographies and country studies to more abstract conceptual ideas such as "values," the general encyclopedia is presumed to have it all.

Accessibility

Q: What are the workings of an electric motor?

A: The *World Book* has a clear three-page description with color graphics that is not technically abstruse and shows exactly how a motor works.

Entries in any encyclopedia are also geared toward high accessibility. From the simplicity of alphabetized entries, to the text of the writing that eschews specialized jargon, encyclopedias are primed to be easily digested. Anyone who has turned to the *World Book* to define "ethics" will feel the immense sense of gratitude that a good encyclopedic account can engender. Complex intellectual constructs such as deontology and teleology are worded in simple explanations and couched within a clear context that makes the dense study of ethics seem approachable.

Scope

Q: I need to compare the economic, social, and political features of Japan with Germany.

A: *Lands and Peoples* has specific sections on the land, people, economy, history, and government of both nations. The *Grolier Online* version can create a customized side-by-side comparison chart as well.

Accessibility is traditionally married to scope as well, so that users expect to get a fully outlined sketch of any topic. If it is a country that is researched, an encyclopedia is expected to briefly cover a description of the people, topography, government, economy, and history. If it is a biography, the important dates and achievements that merited an entry on the person are expected. The dimensions and definition of any topic are covered, however briefly, in an encyclopedia.

One-Stop Source

Q: My sixth-grader needs to do a report on arch construction and give descriptive examples of such architecture; where can she start?

A: *The New Book of Knowledge* defines and describes arch structures. You can also check for examples in the related articles mentioned about the Arc de Triomphe, Romanesque architecture, and bridges.

The "mall mentality" so pervasive in the modern era also applies to searches in an encyclopedia. It is frequently used as a one-stop source for multifaceted subjects so that if research on Picasso as a founder of the Cubist movement is required, entries for both the artist and Cubism are handily available. In *Questia*, the bold new initiative owned by Gale Cengage Learning, searches made in the embedded *Columbia Encyclopedia*, Sixth Edition, provide both the encyclopedic entry and links that lead to full-text books and articles on the subject, as well as tools to cite sources and format papers. This all-inclusive resource at http://www.questia .com/ is also available as an app for iPad and smartphone usage.

Cross-References

Q: Help! I know nothing about it and need to do a twenty-page report on the history and heritage of Korean Americans in my community.

A: The *Gale Encyclopedia of Multicultural America* will help and the *World Book*'s entry on Asian Americans provides additional resources that you can check out for more in-depth research.

While breadth of topics covered is the prime expectation of any encyclopedia, depth of coverage is not. Instead, users have come to rely on bibliographies and cross-references to extend their research in any subject. The system of cross-references in an encyclopedia was introduced as early as 1410 so that it is, by now, firmly embedded in user expectations. Encyclopedias are frequently used as shortcuts to find out where specialized information is available by consulting the bibliographic "further resources" and "recommended reading" lists included in all encyclopedias.

Synopses

Q: I am writing a novel set in the late nineteenth century and need a brief overview of how much training and what kind of training was required to be a physician.

A: It took barely two years of "deplorable" education to complete medical college in the United States. An interesting synopsis of "Medical Education" provided in Great Britain, Germany, and America can be read in the 1911 *Encyclopaedia Britannica*.

The encyclopedia is also useful in defining the years in which it was produced. As a definitive account of human experience, the encyclopedia reports and testifies to the various differing stages of human thinking. The standard encyclopedic description of marriage in 2005 was "the legal agreement between a man and a woman." With same-sex marriages continuing to acquire social currency and legal legitimacy, more recent descriptions have been attempting to capture the increased shades of meaning, so that the current *Encyclopaedia Britannica* describes it as "a legally and socially sanctioned union, usually between a man and a woman." Much as changing definitions in dictionaries offer tantalizing glimpses into human sociology, encyclopedic entries expand on those glimpses to provide a fuller, synoptic picture of the era in which they are written.

A more political interpretation is in the subtle power of the encyclopedia as not just a sociocultural synopsis of the times but as an active tool for the structuring of knowledge. For example, the creators of the *Australian Encyclopaedia* of the early 1900s were reportedly guided by the imperative to create a cohesive national identity and selected their encyclopedia entries accordingly (Kavanagh, 2010).

Value Add-Ons

Q: Where can I research Middle Eastern national anthems and get to hear them as well?

A: *LookLex Encyclopaedia* (formerly the *Encyclopaedia of the Orient*) at http://www .i-cias.com/e.o/ has a description of anthems as well as music clips you can hear.

Depending on the encyclopedia, users have also come to expect "extras." Maps, photographs, illustrations, diagrams, statistical tables, primary text or excerpts from historic documents, and multimedia attachments on electronic encyclopedias that run the gamut of audio and video configurations are all increasingly feeding into user expectations. In all probability, the writers and compilers of thirteenth-century encyclopedias were the first to comprehend the human need for visual accompaniments as they delicately etched miniature illustrations and curlicue letterings into their laborious copying of encyclopedias. Those tiny, idiosyncratic additions to the script have certainly extended a long way to the multimedia encyclopedias that are continuing to develop since their inception in the 1990s.

The kinds of questions print encyclopedias are less suited to answer are as follows.

Analytical Phrases

Analytically connected nouns such as *the impact of Turkish immigrants in Germany* are better suited to monographs than to an encyclopedia. Structured to explain "Turkey" and "immigration" and "Germany" as separate entities, print encyclopedias would not be the source to consult for a merged analysis of divergent topics. Electronic encyclopedias with the capacity for Boolean searching and hyperlinks may prove more productive, but the search could be random and require multiple links.

Current Issues

Print encyclopedias are also intrinsically unsuited to dynamic, quick-developing areas of information such as statistics. Demographic figures, economic transactions, or sports tallies are best accessed from other sources. Online encyclopedias, however, are constantly updated and can be accessed for this kind of information.

New Technology

Rapidly growing fields such as computer technology are prone to entry lags in both print and online encyclopedias. The 2004 print editions of the major encyclopedias do not mention *MP3* technology or *blogs* or *zines*. The 2008 print editions do not include *RSS feeds* or *Ning*. Perhaps the traditional encyclopedia's age-old need to provide a well-rounded perspective on any topic provides a built-in brake against rushing into describing ongoing technological advancements.

The first editor of the venerable *Britannica* declined to edit the revised edition because the publishers wanted to include biographies of living persons. "How can we know if their lives merit an entry?" (Kogan, 1958: 274) was his impassioned argument, elements of which account for a more restrained entry of dynamic developments. A.J. Jacobs, the editor of *Esquire*, who purportedly read all 33,000 pages of the *Britannica*, wryly wrote that Madonna was one of the few popular icons entered, though "you could tell the editors wrote the entry while wearing one of those sterile full-body suits people use when containing an Ebola outbreak" (Jacobs, 2004: 191). This restraint is less evident in the online versions of the major encyclopedias that must compete with the ever-bountiful and easily accessible *Wikipedia*, where the only restraint to including topics is a "notability" guideline that states subjects must have "received significant coverage in reliable sources that are independent of the subject" (http://en.wikipedia.org/wiki/Wikipedia:Notability).

Major Encyclopedic Resources Used in Reference Work

While there is an inchoate expectation that encyclopedias are expected to answer anything and everything, there are in reality two major types of encyclopedias:

- *General:* Those that do answer everything
- *Specialized:* Those that answer anything to do with a specific subject

Type	Description	Examples
General	Covers all areas of information	• *Encyclopaedia Britannica* • *Encyclopedia Americana* • *World Book Encyclopedia*
Specialized	In-depth coverage of one area	• *Encyclopedia of Consumption and Waste* • *The Grove Encyclopedia of American Art* • *Dirr's Encyclopedia of Trees and Shrubs*

Both general and specialized encyclopedias can typically be acquired in multiple formats so that reference libraries either have a choice among print, DVD, CD-ROM, apps, and online versions; or combination purchases that include two or more options. They can be single or multivolume print editions. Electronic versions provide multimedia options with audio and video in addition to text.

General Encyclopedias

William Smellie, the colorful, individualistic editor of the premier edition of the *Encyclopaedia Britannica* of 1768, was determined to expand the traditional audience for an encyclopedia from a limited, learned group, to an unlimited democratic one. "Utility," he wrote, "ought to be the principal intention." He then went on to expand on his utilitarian strategy "to diffuse the knowledge of Science" so that "any man of ordinary parts, may, if he chuses, learn the principles of Agriculture, of Astronomy, of Botany, of Chemistry, etc." (Kogan, 1958: 10–11).

"Utility" and "the greater good of the greatest number" continue to underwrite the relative popularity of encyclopedias. The descriptions of current works have been crafted to establish both their structural framework and present analytical reviews on their "utility" to the public. The structural components will focus on the LURES of each encyclopedia.

We have created LURES as a handy mnemonic to remind the busy reference librarian to check the following:

- Level of user
- Updating policies
- Research aids
- Electronic availability
- Special features

The analysis, deriving from the structure, will point out each encyclopedia's distinctive strengths, weaknesses, and overall utility.

The *World Book Encyclopedia*

Edition: 2012. Volumes: 22. Articles: 17,360. Illustrations: 27,500. Index entries: 170,000. Online at http://www.worldbook.com/.

L   The *World Book Encyclopedia* is a general encyclopedia that is aimed primarily at the reference needs of school-age students and secondarily as a general reference tool for families, educators, and the public.

U   It is the only major encyclopedia that still has a print version published annually, with additions of new articles and selected revisions of existing articles and graphics. The additions derive from an ongoing "Classroom Research Project" that continually tests the actual use of the encyclopedia in selected North American classrooms.

R   The *World Book* has an extensive system of cross-referencing that is additionally backed by a highly comprehensive index. "Related articles" point the user to other aspects of a topic. "Additional resources" provide a bibliography for further reading on more than 1,500 articles.

E   It is available as a DVD that contains more articles than the print version, far fewer illustrations, and various electronic "perks" such as over two hours of videos, animation, and sounds and a handy embedded search engine. *World Book Online* is a veritable cornucopia of multilevel, multipronged encyclopedias available at http://www.worldbookonline.com/ through a paid subscription that is offered to individuals on an annual, one-month, and even a three-day basis. *World Book Kids, Student, Discover, Advanced, Spanish*, and *French* are all part of the online offering. In addition, the online versions have more articles than the print version as well as hyperlinks, videos, primary source documents, citation builders, state-of-the-art multimedia, and daily updates.

S   The encyclopedia has certain unique features. It provides an instructional section in the final volume that aims to introduce the user to the basics of research and communication skills. It also adds on an annual *Year Book* supplement to cover major world events. A special graphics feature utilizes transparency in color overlays to display dual aspects of a single subject, so that the picture comes alive.

Analysis

The *World Book*, while ostensibly designed for the school-age student, is unarguably one of the most popular general encyclopedic sources used by all ages today. It marks high on readability, with articles that are clear and frequently illustrated. Technical words are italicized and defined. Larger articles employ a graduated, simple-to-complex method that mirrors the process of human learning. Difficult entries are appended with an outline, so that the user can opt to get a bird's-eye view of the subject as well as develop a sense of the interrelationships within the subject. Questions at the end of major articles help focus the user on the most important aspects of a difficult field. An average of 100 new articles are added each year in the print version, along with rewrites, updates, and new maps and illustrations. In terms of Smellie's mission of "utility," the encyclopedia scores very high.

Overall Utility

Think salt. This is a source of basic information that is a staple for very different genres of libraries. It is both attractive and accessible. Currently, it is the only major general encyclopedia, aimed at all ages, that has continued to steadily print an annual revised and updated edition in addition to its online edition and software choices. The only constituency for which it is inadequate is the one requiring in-depth information.

Encyclopedia Americana

Edition: 2006. Volumes: 30. Articles: Over 45,000. Illustrations: Over 23,000. Index entries: Approximately 353,000. Online subscription as part of a bundle available at http://go-passport.grolier.com/.

L   Like the *World Book*, it is advertised as a resource for "Grades 8–up." The inclusion of articles on subjects like "ceratopsia," "seaborgium," and "margino-cephalia," however, attest to its aim to be something more than a resource for school students.

U   The print version, traditionally published on an annual basis, broke with tradition by not issuing a new edition since 2006 when over 9,500 pages had been either revised or added.

R It has a very detailed and singular index so that the ratio of articles to index entries averages four entries for each article. Information that has not been covered by a full-length article, but is contained within a larger subject, is also indexed. Major subjects have complete outlines included in the index. Cross-references are provided both within and at the end of each article. Bibliographies aimed at representing "divergent points of view" are provided.

E The *Americana* is available as part of a packaged bundle of eight databases, collectively called *Grolier Online*, and offered via subscription at http:// go-passport.grolier.com/.

S The editors pride themselves on several features such as the unusual coverage of era surveys. Articles on each of the centuries are provided as separate entries. "Almost book length" articles have been written on issues such as the World Wars. A glossary of unwieldy or technical terms is provided with the index, listing all the words in the glossaries.

Analysis

Touted as being "prominent among Abraham Lincoln's scanty store of books" (preface), the *Encyclopedia Americana* has been part of the reference landscape since 1829. Does the fact that it is the first encyclopedia to be published in the United States give it added cache? Perhaps. The *Encyclopedia Americana* has been a familiar sight to generations of users and is therefore a trusted resource. Ostensibly a source for Americana, it is in reality not so limited and can be consulted for extensive general research. In fact, it has more than double the number of entries of the *World Book*, though far fewer illustrations. However, its greatest strength does lie in its fierce coverage of both the big and the small events of American history. Primary documents such as the Bill of Rights, the Declaration of Independence, and the Gettysburg Address can be found in the *Encyclopedia Americana*. A great many of the articles are signed, including short 100-word articles such as the one on "twill" and the 200-word article on "algorithm." Even before it ceased publication, the encyclopedia had been periodically criticized for being slow to include important current events in its print format. Given that the online version is just one part of the larger Grolier bundle, and that the last print edition has not been updated since 2006, suggests the *Americana* landscape has irrevocably dimmed.

Overall Utility

In terms of retention, the greatest selling point of the *Americana* is contained in its title. Medium-sized libraries acquiring the *World Book* have no pressing need for the *Americana*, but might feel vulnerable when faced with questions regarding such topics as *Lochner v. New York*, the U.S. Coast Guard, Alan Greenspan, the Carnegie Institution of Washington, or the House Un-American Activities Committee. While being a solid general-purpose encyclopedia, the *Americana* has, in the past, been most trustworthy in its provision of domestic information. However, its flagging commitment to updates and revisions greatly compromises the overall utility of the resource.

Encyclopaedia Britannica

Edition: 2007. Volumes: 32. Articles: 64,900. Illustrations: 24,000. Index entries: 215,000. Print discontinued. Online at http://www.britannica.com/.

L   The *Encyclopaedia Britannica* is globally renowned as a general informational resource, yet the style, presentation, structure, and content of the entries are unabashedly directed to a higher level of readership.

U   The final print version has been revised multiple times with a revision of articles on topics such as Pluto, stem cells, and nutrition. *Book of the Year* is an annual supplement that covers major events throughout the world and is included at no additional charge to all subscribers.

R   "The Great EB," as it is popularly known, has an elaborate system of research aids that can be overwhelming. Two full volumes are devoted to the indexing of entries. Over 500,000 cross-references are also allied to the index entries. The one-volume *Propaedia*, aimed at aiding the user to clarify topics through intellectual structure rather than alphabetical convenience, tends instead toward mind-numbing erudition.

E   Given that the print version is no longer published, the *Britannica* is available in an increasing variety of nonprint formats: DVD, apps, and online. The software, which is available for less than $50.00, can be tailored to suit three age levels. The *Britannica Ultimate Reference Suite* has over 100,000 articles and 19,000 graphics, as well as entries from the encyclopedia's famous past authors such as Sigmund Freud, Marie Curie, and Orville Wright. A "research organizer" offers software glitz that allows for note taking, saving bookmarks, and formatting reports. The online reference site is also available for younger (School Edition), experienced (Academic Edition), and all-purpose (Library Edition) readers. Over 3,000 audio-video animations plus links to 166,000 websites and full-text articles from EBSCO, combine to provide a formidable online presence. The most intriguing development of the online site, however, has been the adoption of modified open source entries at http://www.britannica.com/. The modification consists of three categories of content: that created by the existing community of experts, by users, and by the encyclopedia itself, which integrates any part of the first two to create an "EBchecked" topic. In addition to the wiki facet, *Britannica* has added a cluster of Web 2.0 connectivity content such as widgets, blogs, and Twitter feeds.

S   To present what is "special" about the Great EB is to imply that there is something quotidian about it. There really isn't. Defined by a complex tripartite structure; an index that is analytical; nonstandardized vocabulary; an authorship that reads like a Who's Who of global and historical personalities; and a hoary history, the encyclopedia is unique at all levels.

Analysis

The *Britannica* claims well over 200 years of experience in delivering the "world standard in reference." Marketing hyperbole aside, the *Britannica* can rightly claim preeminence in name recognition. With past contributors like Einstein and Trotsky, and current ones like former presidents Bill Clinton of the United States and Mary Robinson of Ireland, its credentials are stellar. The twelve-volume *Micropaedia* is the core resource for general reference, providing breadth of coverage in short, authoritative articles. The *Macropaedia* offers depth of coverage on selected topics. International coverage has always been of a high order so that even non-biographical or non-geographical subjects such as AIDS receive a global perspective. The *Britannica* is harder to navigate than most current print encyclopedias.

The *Micropaedia* is designed with small font and three columns, separated by narrow margins that leave very little white space. Ease of readability is not a prime consideration as evident in the variant style of articles and the non-standardized vocabulary. There is no controlled vocabulary, and a great many of the *Macropaedia* articles read more like academic treatises than as general reference resources.

Overall Utility

It is hard to imagine libraries without the venerable and indomitable *Britannica*. It was the source that was consulted when something could not be found in a more accessible, general reference encyclopedia. Ultimately, despite the discontinuation of a print edition, it remains the encyclopedia with the most gravitas. That reputation has been transferred effectively to the award-winning *Britannica Online* version as well. The integration of traditional content with breaking Web 2.0 technology appears seamless. Speedy edits and updates are handled through the adopted "push-to-publish" technology, while thousands of content sharing widgets and integrative tools allow for the high utility value provided by metasearches, interactive whiteboards, and mobile access.

Multimedia Encyclopedias

All the major print editions have been eclipsed by digital or software versions. The formidable *Collier's Encyclopedia*, in publication since 1950, could only be found in parts of the *Encarta* digital encyclopedia, until that too was discontinued by 2010. The continuation of annual updates of the print version of *Encyclopedia Americana* remains a matter of serious conjecture. Globally, the honorable *Brockhaus* of Germany, printed since 1808, ceased publication after the printing of its twenty-first edition in 2005–2007. While general encyclopedias were one of the earliest entrants into providing online editions, subject encyclopedias can now be found in multiple formats. *SAGE eReference*, for example, was launched in January 2007 to provide electronic versions of its products at http://sage-ereference.com/.

Wikipedia

While all of the general encyclopedias in the preceding section are available in non-print formats, the dream of early encyclopedists to cater to the masses and generate a utilitarian source of encyclopedic information has led, in the twenty-first century, to a point where the masses are feeding information to the masses. *Wikipedia*, born on January 15, 2001, is an online encyclopedia that offers "free-content," so that anybody is free to take the information, free to provide the information, and free to edit existing information. In the brave new world of burgeoning open source software that feeds off voluntary authorship, *Wikipedia* hopes to be the ultimate people's encyclopedia. As of 2012, there were 22 million multilingual articles percolating in *Wikipedia*, of which almost 4 million were in the English language (http://stats.wikimedia.org/). Reportedly, 53 percent of adult American Internet users accessed *Wikipedia* (Pew Internet and American Life Project, 2011), making it the sixth most visited website on the Internet (http://www.alexa.com/), though quite possibly the resource of first resort accessed by students.

"*Wikipedia* is always present in the classroom—whether it's invited to attend or not" (Erikson, 2012). While educators continue to warn against using *Wikipedia* as a cited source for research, in the face of its phenomenal usage statistics, the encyclopedia has seen a definite rise in legitimacy since its birth over a decade ago. The distrust of accuracy in material associated with the source is yielding to ways of capitalizing on its values and the acquisition of "new media literacies" (Jenkins, 2007) that allow users to recognize the nature of open source information. In tandem, the many advantages of looking to *Wikipedia* for current information, useful hyperlinks, non-Western resources, popular culture, and more global coverage of topics are gaining increased recognition.

As a nonprofit venture, *Wikipedia* itself is also continually striving toward increased credibility as seen in its establishing of "trust ratings" for its contributors. An Education Program set up in 2011 is intended to "mobilize and empower the next generation of human-knowledge generators" with review editors and writers from academia, thereby moving toward the ideal of creating neutral, referenced, notable, and verifiable articles (http://outreach.wikimedia.org/wiki/Wikipedia_Education_Program).

Other Open Source Encyclopedias

Citizendium, born in March 2007, was also fathered by Larry Sanger of *Wikipedia*. The sole aim of this encyclopedia was to shore up the single greatest criticism leveled at collaborative, open source ventures, namely, their lack of accountability. Touting itself as the "world's most trusted encyclopedia and knowledge base," *Citizendium* has more than 16,000 carefully vetted articles.

Google's relatively short-lived entry to open source online encyclopedias was launched as a beta project in 2008. *Knol*, as it was named, differed from *Wikipedia* in that the contributors had to sign their names and could even include a photograph and biography of themselves. Authors could also control the level of collaboration that they wanted from the community at large, choose between three different creative commons licenses, and exercise their option to include advertisements. In the "spring cleaning" of 2011, Google requested *Knol* authors to transfer their articles to an alternate publishing site at http://www.annotum.org/ by April 2012, thereby fueling the school of thought that believes such ventures to be inherently fragile.

Yet, a host of other beta sites, such as *Scholarpedia* for "scholarly" peer-reviewed articles on a limited number of subjects, testifies to the continuing attraction of wiki encyclopedias despite their alleged temporality. Most dramatically, "the

Great EB," which has long touted itself as "the world's most famous and authoritative source of information" based on the authority of its contributors, guardedly opened the field to user-community input at its online site.

Subject-specific, open source, collaborative encyclopedias are also making an appearance. *Proteopedia*, for example, which is aimed at biochemists and biologists, introduced the linking of text with spectacular three-dimensional information on biomacromolecular structures. Since its inception in 2007 through February 2012, some 81,575 articles have been created by "page contributors, content donators and editors"; updates occur weekly.

Bundled Encyclopedias

The "bundling" of encyclopedic resources is an additional characteristic of nonprint resources. "Our greatest challenge is treading the fine line between too big and too niche," states Kevin Ohe of the Greenwood Publishing Group when speaking of electronic resource bundling (Roncevic, 2006: 10). The "fine line" is apparent in the newer bundles of online encyclopedias being offered by various publishers. While online editions were typically provided as a clutch of general and specific encyclopedias, the specific needs of specific user groups are also being introduced. So, for example, Britannica targets its online general encyclopedias for different types of libraries such as the academic, public, and school libraries. Grolier and EBSCO cater to different age groups such as the elementary, middle, and adult student. Oxford University Press is collating its subject encyclopedias into portal sites such as the breathtaking *Oxford Music Online* that provides "the most extensive and easily searchable online music resource available" (http://www.oxfordmusiconline.com/public/). Greenwood Publishing has fed more than 600 of its print editions on terrorism and security issues to create the online *PSIO: Praeger Security International Online*.

Although bundled encyclopedic offerings can appear to be prohibitively expensive, they serve multiple purposes and may be viewed in the budget as an accretion of many different line items. Conversely, the lengthy shopping list of resources bundled together may be dazzling in terms of what is included but for the most part may not be relevant to institutional needs.

Use of Multimedia Encyclopedias

Multimedia encyclopedias have plenty to offer. The early CD-ROM versions that were simple transpositions of print to electronic format have gained both confidence and the necessary technology to burgeon into spectacular multimedia extravaganzas. A quick search for "Antarctica," for example, can explode into a mesmerizing display of interactive pictures, sounds, streaming video, multiple hyperlinks, animation, atlases, and timelines. Of course, the option to consult merely the text always exists, but invariably, the lure of a click into multimedia proves irresistible and fascinating. The factor of visual seduction segues neatly into some of the major considerations to keep in mind when reviewing the acquisition and use of an electronic encyclopedia. Reviews and ratings for the top ten encyclopedia software packages can be accessed at http://encyclopedia-review.toptenreviews.com/.

Options in Learning Styles

Electronic encyclopedias provide information in a variety of mediums—textual, auditory, and visual. If the education pundits are correct in believing that each person has the propensity to absorb information effectively through individualistic applications of all five senses, then the variety of choices inherent in an electronic format is certainly very appealing. The small print account of the Roman Empire as presented in the *Britannica* can blur before the eyes of a teenager who may respond more enthusiastically to the same subject when presented with voice-over narration and changing images as presented in *Grolier Online*.

Information Searching

Electronic encyclopedias can simplify and accelerate the process of information searching. Hyperlinks that leap from one aspect of an entry to a related one assist the careful user in covering vast ground in a short time. Keyword search capabilities can take researchers directly into multiple sources useful to their search.

Updates

Updating facts, figures, and statistical, biographical, and technological data is far easier to accomplish in an online resource. The researcher can thereby be relatively sure of the accuracy of current information. Quick editing also allows a majority of electronic encyclopedias to include popular culture, an area that most print encyclopedias are wary of covering.

Scope

Electronic articles are typically longer than print versions, since ultimate shelf space and production cost per page is not the issue as with print encyclopedias. In addition to longer articles, a greater number of articles are the norm. There is, of course, a flip side to the obvious charms of nonprint encyclopedias.

- The usage mechanisms need a more complex infrastructure in order to provide multiple services at the same time. Print encyclopedias need shelving space. Many users can consult different volumes at the same time. Electronic encyclopedias need hardware, software, computer know-how on the part of the user, computer accessibility, and possible investments in multimedia apparatus such as headphones—in short, a far greater investment in infrastructure.
- The traditional allure of browsing through encyclopedias so that information on the Hebrides islands could just as well lead to a nonpertinent, yet exhilarating romp through the alphabetically proximate city of Hebron and the goddess Hecate is tamed in the electronic format. Browsing through hyperlinks is more suited to relevant related topics. The element of serendipitous knowledge, for which print encyclopedias are universally beloved, is dramatically muted in the more linearly conceived search technology of electronic encyclopedias.
- Librarians are a breed of professionals well suited to constant technological change. Yet the vulnerability never lessens. Electronic encyclopedias, in the past decade alone, have sprouted hydra-headed formats. CD-ROM technology led to a flurry of death announcements on the print encyclopedia in the 1980s. Paid subscriptions to online encyclopedias, with online access to patrons, led

to another flurry of epitaphs on CD-ROM technology. The advent of free online encyclopedias has left the publishing world, the librarians, and the users poised for future changes. Open source encyclopedias further complicate the current scenario. While the ongoing sense of vulnerability to change is certainly a function of time, it is vulnerability that has never been engendered by the solid rows of print encyclopedias present in every library.

- Current user acceptance or use of online encyclopedias can also create a unique set of problems for the reference librarian. An alphabetical print resource requires little instruction, and so the user has instant control. Electronic encyclopedias invariably require a set of instructions and, especially in public libraries, a process to sign up for the use of a computer. Troubleshooting can come in many forms. *Wikipedia*, for example, can be a "frame buster" that is hard to send directly; in order to send articles electronically the user must instead employ a "copy and paste" method. Each unaware user needs to be informed individually. A sense of immediate control over the information resource is relatively lacking in the electronic format.

Specialized Subject Encyclopedias

Language has a peculiar impact on the way an object is perceived. Subject encyclopedias, unconsciously allied with the more popularly known general encyclopedias, are, in practice, acquisitions that cater to a very different constituency. The subject encyclopedia is "encyclopedic" only in that it is a comprehensive source of information arranged for easy access. The use of a specialized encyclopedia, however, is wholly different. Users are, for the most part, seeking relatively in-depth information on a highly specific topic—a topic that would merit perhaps a few pages in a general encyclopedia. Acquiring a subject encyclopedia, then, is really the equivalent of acquiring multiple books on a single topic, directed at a particular group of users. Acquiring a subject encyclopedia does not fulfill the traditional encyclopedia's "utilitarian" dictum of providing the "greatest good for the greatest number."

Being alert to this critical distinction can help the reference librarian choose among the thousands of subject encyclopedias that continue to flood the market at an ever-increasing pace. For the general encyclopedia, for which there is always a perceived need, the primary consideration is one of reliability. For the subject encyclopedia, the primary consideration would have to be demand or need. If there is an established constituency for the subject, only then can other considerations such as relative accuracy, reliability, and scope come into focus.

The word *subject* is also host to two important variations. Some subjects are really single topics such as the prize-winning three-volume *Encyclopedia of the World's Zoos*. Others are multiple topics within a field of knowledge, such as the well-established fifteen-volume *Encyclopedia of Religion* or the nine-volume *International Encyclopedia of the Social Sciences*, Second Edition. Single-topic encyclopedias require a crystal-clear demand for the topic, whereas some subjects encompassing a field of topics can be essential purchases for even the smallest libraries. For example, the valuable *Routledge Encyclopedia of Philosophy*, winner of an American Library Association (ALA) Honorable Mention in 1999, or the more recent *The Encyclopedia of Philosophy* are handy compilations of philosophers, most of whom cannot be located in single-volume works. Similarly, the 2003 Dartmouth winner, the *Garland Encyclopedia of World Music*, is a comprehensive single purchase that covers vast areas of minor entries, not locatable in either the general encyclopedia or a topical manuscript. The absolute relief felt by a librarian in locating an account of "Tumbuka healing," in which African music is the equivalent of a prescription drug, is a feeling regularly engendered in reference librarians using subject encyclopedias. Multitopic research fields such as Canada or broadcasting or Judaism are well served by indispensable subject encyclopedias such as *The Canadian Encyclopedia*, the *Encyclopedia of Television*, and *Encyclopaedia Judaica*. Equally noteworthy subject encyclopedias like the *Encyclopedia Sherlockiana*, the *Encyclopedia of Country Music*, or the *Encyclopedia of Body Adornment* are undeniably worthy acquisitions in and of themselves but can be perceived as idiosyncratic luxury items unless the reference librarian has perceived a strong need in the constituency. A handful of multidisciplinary titles are of use to any and every library. *The McGraw-Hill Encyclopedia of Science and Technology* covers a wide range of scientific topics written in an authoritative yet understandable style, with *McGraw-Hill AccessScience 2.0 (MGHAS2)* as the online version. The thirty-four-volume *Dictionary of Art*, despite its deceptive title, is an encyclopedic compendium of Western and non-Western art, art themes and cultural influences, artists and their biographies, art critics and art collectors, all supplemented with both color and black-and-white images. *Grzimek's Animal Life Encyclopedia* is the definitive compilation of information on insects, fishes, amphibians, reptiles, birds, mammals, and other orders. Each order is discussed and brought alive with representative examples of species within the order. Photographs, illustrations, and maps provide graphic enhancements. Anything that runs, flies, leaps, crawls, slithers, and swims can be located in this seventeen-volume work. The *International Encyclopedia of Political Science* is an impressive global collaboration that aims to provide a comprehensive and comprehensible overview of political life across regions and through time. Finally, the *Gale Encyclopedia of Multicultural America*, although not as generically relevant as science, politics, art, and animals, is a useful addition to all libraries within the United States, land of immigrants. Historical background information, patterns of settlement, and cultural mores associated with 152 groups are described along with useful contact information on organizations and research centers that are relevant for further research.

Some of the most copious publishers of subject encyclopedias are the following:

- *ABC-CLIO:* Publisher of the "Companion" series that focuses on popular American issues. Also owner of the *Greenwood Publishing Group* that includes Greenwood Press, Praeger Publishers, Heinemann USA, GEM, and Libraries Unlimited, thereby constituting one of the more copious publishers of reference encyclopedias.
- *Berkshire Publishing Group:* Entered the world of independent publishing as recently as 2005, and yet has forged a strong profile with "Outstanding Reference" recognition from *Library Journal* and ALA, among others.

- *Facts on File:* Publishes encyclopedias specifically for school and library consumption, with curriculum-based subject areas as the guiding framework.
- *Gale Cengage Learning:* Publisher of some of the most user-friendly subject encyclopedias and distinguished by its composite style, Gale products are also expanded by imprint publications from the likes of U•X•L and Macmillan Reference USA.
- *Garland Science* and *Routledge Reference* of the Taylor and Francis Group: Specialize in scholarly niche publications.
- *Oxford University Press:* The behemoth of American university presses and a global publisher of reference encyclopedias.
- *Scribner's:* Despite its relatively smaller output, Scribner's looms large in the world of subject encyclopedias, as it has been awarded ALA's prestigious Dartmouth medals and Honorable Mentions multiple times. In 1999, Charles Scribner's Sons joined Thomson Gale.

Librarians should contact publishers directly if interested in updates of existing editions, or put out feelers about forthcoming plans or suggestions for future publications. A handy "Publisher Index" listing all the major producers of reference resources can be found in the annual reference supplement issued by *Library Journal* every November.

Reference librarians looking to fill a subject demand can check on a somewhat dated, yet wonderful resource: the two-volume *Subject Encyclopedias* by Allan N. Mirwis (1999). The best picks from recent publishers can be culled from RUSA's annual Outstanding Reference Sources as well as the annual Dartmouth medal winners. Both lists are available at http://www.ala.org/.

Encyclopedias for Children and Young Adults

Children's encyclopedias also cover vast swathes of information but are usually short, heavily illustrated, and graphically simple with larger fonts and user aids.

- Aimed at grades 3–8, *The New Book of Knowledge* is available only as a database.
- The print version of Grolier's six-volume *Lands and Peoples* has not seen an update since 2005 but is available as one of the *Grolier Online* databases. It is aimed at grades 6–12 but can be used by upper-elementary students as well.
- *Compton's by Britannica* (2010), the incarnation of the earlier *Compton's Encyclopedia*, has been an effective teaching tool since 1922 when it was first published specifically for middle and high school students.
- For upper-elementary students, *My First Britannica* (2008) is a pleasing thirteen-volume resource, hosted by the venerable Britannica publishing house.
- An alphabetic general encyclopedia aimed at the elementary student can be found in the thirteen-volume *The World Book Discovery Encyclopedia*.

A full account of these resources and more can be found in Chapter 15.

Collection Development and Maintenance

Selection and Keeping Current

A number of established professional publications are available to assist in finding the right encyclopedia. Among the most well-known sources are these:

- *Booklist* provides an annual update of existing encyclopedias in the September issue.
- *Word-of-mouth* opinions expressed by veteran reference librarians should always be welcomed. Preferred usage recommendations are one of the best indications of a good encyclopedia.
- *ARBAonline* (derived from *American Reference Books Annual*)
- *Kirkus Reviews*—special editions
- *Encyclopedia Software Review* (http://encyclopedia-review.toptenreviews.com/) offers collated reviews of nonprint encyclopedias.
- *Reference Reviews* (http://www.gale.cengage.com/reference/) has guest columnists who provide handy, comprehensive, and current reviews of encyclopedias, both online and in print. While hosted by Gale, which is a part of Cengage Learning, the reviews are not restricted to Gale products.

Evaluating Encyclopedic Resources

Around the year 1230, Bartholomew de Granville published one of the most popular early encyclopedias, the *De proprietatibus rerum*, or *The Properties of Things*. A typical entry described:

> Of A Maid:...a woman is more meeker than a man, she weepeth sooner. And is more envious, and more laughing, and loving; and the soul is more in a woman than in a man... (Steele, 2006: 22)

Despite intense competition among encyclopedias in the thirteenth century, de Granville's descriptions of the properties of things such as the meek, weeping, envious, laughing, loving woman with more soul, evidently struck the right chords. It was translated into multiple languages from its original Latin, and was a bestseller for over three centuries. Fifty to sixty fatted calves had to be slaughtered to provide enough vellum for a single copy, and multiple scribes and illuminators had to be employed, so that the process of acquiring the right encyclopedia was a far bloodier and exorbitant acquisition than it is today. The owning of an encyclopedia was certainly a luxury reserved for the aristocracy. With the technological breakthrough of the printing press and the sociopolitical establishment of democratic ideals, the notion of an encyclopedia as everyman's resource became more entrenched. Today, we are inundated with scores of encyclopedias: general, age-specific, subject-specific, illustrated, and multiformatted. Our energies are best spent in whittling down the choices to emerge with what best suits individual and institutional needs. In theory, this could prove to be a daunting task. In practice, the worth of an encyclopedia is relatively easy to gauge. Given the thousands of articles that continue to describe de Granville's ageless "properties of things," it is instructive to pick a few topics with which the reviewer is knowledgeable. A checklist composed of the following questions, *in order of preference*, can gird the reviewer with a sure sense of what is a work of quality and what deserves to be purchased.

Question 1: Is this encyclopedia reliable?

Above all else, reliability is essential. Given the thousands of articles penned by thousands of contributors, it is possible to gauge the reliability factor only through well-established indicators of authority. The list of contributors should be professionally qualified or known authorities on a subject. The publisher should be reputable. Both factors must be mirrored in articles that are accurate and current to the best of your knowledge. It is best to do the following:

- Choose a topic with which you are highly familiar or have a specific question that needs to be answered.
- Establish a list of expectations, preferably in writing, prior to gauging the article. If, for example, your field of expertise is the U.S. Civil War, set up an "a priori" checklist:
  - When was the Civil War waged?
  - Where were the major battles fought?
  - Who were the primary personalities involved in the war?
  - What were some of the probable causes of the war?
  - How did the war come to an end?
  - Why is the war so important in the context of American history?
  - Are there other reliable sources listed for continued research?
- Large subject topics such as the Civil War would merit the entire gamut of the reference librarian's reviewing arsenal of who, what, where, why, when, and how probes. Others, like a biography, might merit a more specific list such as this:
  - Who the person was
  - Why the person was famous
  - When the person was born and other significant dates
  - Availability of additional resources

Authoritative answers to an "a priori" set of questions that you are able to confirm is a simple and satisfying way of developing an educated preference for a much-used resource. In addition, you gain "added vision" while reading through professional critiques of encyclopedias, so that the ongoing evaluations offered by reference pundits have added resonance rather than the niggling uncertainty of a received truth.

Question 2: The source is reliable, but is it suitable for our constituency and the mission of our institution?

A clear perspective on the target audience can be mapped in terms of the following:

- Age/reading level: child, young adult, adult, or all age groups
- Purpose: general knowledge, in-depth research

- Institutional size: small, medium, large
- Institutional type: public, academic, special

A child looking for general information on a subject in a small public library will both want and expect a very different encyclopedic source from an adult historian expecting to conduct research in a large special library.

Question 3: The source is both suitable and reliable, but can we afford to purchase it?

In increasingly financially strapped libraries, the relevance of cost cannot be underestimated. Given the variety of formats in which encyclopedias can now be found, the variation in cost adds to the flexibility of choice.

- If the *Britannica* is available online for free, and the online version is a fraction of the price of print, what are the factors that would urge buying one format over another, or in addition to another?
- Are yearly updates necessary, or can the constituency live with a general encyclopedia set for five years, so that the average cost per year is less?

Question 4: Once the reference librarian has established that the encyclopedia is reliable, suitable, and affordable, it is time to ask this question: will it hold the user's interest?

Perfectly comprehensive sources of information are undervalued or underused because of poor readability factors. The layout, graphics, font size, paper, and binding quality all contribute toward a print source that is accessible. For online versions, quick loading, clean graphics, and updated web links are of the essence in holding user interest.

Additional Criteria

If the major questions have been answered, additional criteria can help fine-tune the acquisition process.

- What is the scope of the encyclopedia? The length, breadth, and intensity of coverage for all entries can be assessed.
- How are subjects treated? Are the entries intended for scholarly research or as popular information sources? Distinguishing between the two types is critical to both evaluation and user recommendation. Signed works and lengthy bibliographies supporting each entry are typically aimed at the serious researcher.
- Is there any bias, either unconsciously evident or explicitly professed, in any of the entries? Controversial topics such as abortion and stem-cell research are potentially fertile areas to check for bias.
- Is the encyclopedia necessary because it is unique and would constitute a niche publication? Niche publications appear infrequently and may need to be acquired when available rather than when actively needed.
- Is the encyclopedia a rich resource for preresearch queries? Does it have a high potential for providing a guide to further research through suggested readings and the availability of cross-references?

A unique, unbiased publication with great sources for further research is, however, of little value if the first four criteria have not been met. The bottom line in evaluation then is as follows:

1. The encyclopedia must be reliable.
2. The encyclopedia must be suited to the needs of the institution and its stakeholders.
3. The encyclopedia must be affordable.
4. The encyclopedia must be designed to hold user interest.

Further Considerations

The *World Book Encyclopedia* and the *Britannica Student Encyclopedia* were the only major general encyclopedias to be updated in print in the recent past. The sturdy, old, all-purpose general encyclopedia appears to be reemerging in navigable online formats. Not surprisingly, they seem to resemble the search engines to which print encyclopedias appeared to have lost out at the start of the new millennium. A striking example can be found in the Great EB, which announced it would be ending its 244 reign in the realm of print as of 2012. However, in its latest *Britannica Online* garb, the encyclopedia is supported by a galaxy of corollary reference materials such as a dictionary, atlas, and access to thousands of vetted Internet links and e-books. It is "whiteboard ready" and allows for integration with interactive learning management systems such as Moodle. Widgets allow for customizing, and the entire offering may even be found as an iPad app for $1.99 a month. Given its powerful name recognition and reputation for reliability, and its concerted new bid to function with the accessibility and agility of a search engine, it is possible we are seeing the evolution of the general encyclopedia as both scholarly synopses and interactive portal.

The choice facing the current reference librarian, then, is increasingly one of retention rather than active acquisition of the general encyclopedia in print format. Instead, questions of acquisition have dramatically gravitated toward online resources. With online encyclopedias, the reference librarian must also bear the onus of being alert to bundled products. The updated *Grolier Online*, for example, covers subscription to eight individual encyclopedias. The *Encyclopedia of Sustainability Science and Technology* (2012) is bundled along with over 140 handbooks, encyclopedias, and dictionaries, all huddled together under the *SpringerReference.com* umbrella. The *Gale Virtual Reference Library* has over 700 encyclopedias in its collation of over 4,000 e-books. *Credo Reference* offers at least 11 general encyclopedias and hundreds of subject ones in its 550+ collection.

Curiously, the printing of subject encyclopedias continues along with online counterparts. According to a study (East, 2010), in the ten years between 1999 and 2009, the number of subject encyclopedias reviewed in the journal *Reference and User Services Quarterly* saw negligible change. In fact, it rose from 63 to 66 reviews, thereby demonstrating the continued publication of these reference resources. While librarians might question the value-for-money invested in these resources, even a cursory survey of *Reference 2012* published by *Library Journal* attests to the continuing production of subject encyclopedias.

Encyclopedias represent a continuing purchase or subscription cost, either in print or as part of online databases. Even after careful evaluation, an assessment of constituency needs and the reference department's mission plan are critical to making a choice. Visualizing some real-life scenarios can help prime the reference librarian in choosing the best possible options.

- You are head of reference in a medium-sized public library, serving a mixed-age constituency of 40,000 people. Your annual budget for reference acquisitions is $24,000.00, and you have ten public computers. Would you…
  - Budget for the thirty-two-volume final print edition of *Encyclopaedia Britannica* 2010 at $1,095.00?
  - Consider the 56,000,000-word *Encyclopaedia Britannica Online* with its added access to the encyclopedia as well as the *Student, Elementary*, and *Concise* versions for $69.95 the first year?
  - Purchase the $30.00 DVD version of the *Encyclopaedia Britannica*?
  On what factors would you base your decision?
  - Computer-literate constituency and the demand for online information?
  - Option of remote access for online and a community that owns PCs?
  - Computer availability—can library afford a dedicated computer?
  - Shelf space for print?
  - Combination purchase possibilities?
- You are the chair of a small academic library with a total student population of 7,295. Your annual budget for reference acquisitions is $38,000.00. Would you…
  - Purchase the well-received twenty-volume *Digital Encyclopedia of Applied Physics* for $6,644?
  On what factors would you base your decision?
  - Large physics department?
  - Competing needs of other departments?
  - At $295.00 per volume, option to buy some print volumes rather than the entire set?
  - At $1,662.00, option to buy an annual subscription?
  - Existing collection of older *Encyclopedia of Modern Physics* adequate?

Recommended Resources Discussed in This Chapter

Alexa. http://www.alexa.com/.
Annotum. http://www.annotum.org/.
ARBAonline. http://www.arbaonline.com/.
Booklist. http://www.booklistonline.com/.
Britannica Student Encyclopedia. Chicago: Encyclopaedia Britannica, 2012.
Brockhaus. http://www.brockhaus.de/.
The Canadian Encyclopedia. Historica Foundation. http://www.thecanadianencyclopedia.com/.
Citizendium. http://en.citizendium.org/.
Compton's by Britannica. Chicago: Encyclopaedia Britannica, 2010.

TOP TEN ENCYCLOPEDIAS

Title	Print	Online
Compton's by Britannica. 2010. Chicago: Encyclopaedia Britannica.	26 vols.	Subscription http://corporate.britannica.com/
Dictionary of Art. 2003. New York: Oxford University Press.	34 vols.	Subscription http://www.groveart.com/ http://www.oxfordartonline.com/
Encyclopaedia Britannica. 2010. Chicago: Encyclopaedia Britannica.	32 vols.	Free and subscription http://www.britannica.com/
Encyclopedia Americana. 2006. Danbury, CT: Grolier.	30 vols.	Subscription http://grolier.com/
Encyclopedia of Religion. 2004. Farmington Hills, MI: Thomson Gale.	15 vols.	eBook subscription http://www.gale.com/
Grzimek's Animal Life Encyclopedia. 2003–2004. Farmington Hills, MI: Thomson Gale.	17 vols.	eBook subscription http://www.galegroup.com/
International Encyclopedia of Political Science. 2011. Thousand Oaks, CA: SAGE Publications.	8 vols.	Subscription to SAGE Reference Online http://www.sagepub.com/
The McGraw-Hill Encyclopedia of Science and Technology. 2012. New York: McGraw-Hill Professional.	20 vols.	Subscription http://www.mhest.com/index.php
The New Book of Knowledge. 2008. Danbury, CT: Grolier.	21 vols.	Subscription http://go.grolier.com/
The World Book Encyclopedia. 2012. Chicago: World Book.	22 vols.	Subscription http://www.worldbookonline.com/

Credo Reference. http://www.credoreference.com/.

Dictionary of Art. Jane Turner, ed. New York: Oxford University Press, 1996.

Digital Encyclopedia of Applied Physics. George L.Trigg, ed. Hoboken, NJ: John Wiley and Sons, 2004–2011. http://mrw.interscience.wiley.com/emrw/9783527600434/home/.

Dirr's Encyclopedia of Trees and Shrubs. Michael A. Dirr. Portland, OR: Timber Press, 2011.

Encyclopaedia Britannica. Chicago: Encyclopaedia Britannica, 2010. http://www.britannica.com/.

Encyclopaedia Judaica. 2nd ed. Michael Berenbaum, ex. ed. Farmington Hills, MI: Macmillan Reference, 2006.

Encyclopedia Americana. Danbury, CT: Grolier, 2006. http://go-passport.grolier.com/.

Encyclopedia of Body Adornment. Margo DeMello. Westport, CT: Greenwood Press, 2007.

Encyclopedia of Consumption and Waste. Carl A. Zimring and William L. Rathje, eds. Thousand Oaks, CA: SAGE Publications, 2012.

Encyclopedia of Country Music. 2nd ed. New York: Oxford University Press, 2012.

Encyclopedia of Homelessness. David Levinson, ed. London: SAGE Publications, 2004.

RECOMMENDED FREE ENCYCLOPEDIA WEBSITES

Britannica. http://www.britannica.com/. More than 25,000 short entries with a tab for additional content that provides basic bibliographic information is offered by the free version of the Great EB. Attempts to read more than the short entry lead to a frustrating blackout of the item page.

Encyclopedia.com. http://www.encyclopedia.com/. Nearly 200,000 reference entries from sources that include *Oxford's World Encyclopedia*, the sixth edition of the *Columbia Encyclopedia*, and subject-specific medical, computer, and science encyclopedias, power this resource.

Fact Monster. http://www.factmonster.com/encyclopedia.html. A children's resource, which is part of *Infoplease*, but includes *The TIME for Kids Almanac* in addition to the *Columbia Encyclopedia*.

Infoplease. http://www.infoplease.com/encyclopedia/. The *Columbia Electronic Encyclopedia* of 2007 with its 80,000 cross-references and 57,000 articles make up this free encyclopedia.

Wikipedia. http://www.wikipedia.org/. As the sixth most visited site, the charms of this open source, collaborative encyclopedia are hard to ignore, even as each entry needs to be approached with due caution.

Encyclopedia of Modern Physics. Robert A. Meyers, ed. San Diego, CA: Academic Press, 1990.

The Encyclopedia of Philosophy. 2nd ed. Donald Borchert, ed. Farmington Hills, MI: Macmillan Reference, 2005.

Encyclopedia of Protestantism. Hans Hillerbrand, ed. New York: Routledge, 2003.

Encyclopedia of Religion. 2nd ed. Farmington Hills, MI: Thomson Gale, 2004.

Encyclopedia of Sustainability Science and Technology. Robert A. Meyers, ed. Berlin, Germany: Springer SBM, 2012.

Encyclopedia of Television. Horace Newcomb, ed. New York: Taylor and Francis, 2004.

Encyclopedia of the World's Zoos. Catherine E. Bell. Chicago: Fitzroy Dearborn, 2001.

Encyclopedia of World Dress and Fashion. Joanne B. Eicher, ed. 10 vols. New York: Oxford University Press, 2010–2011.

Encyclopedia Sherlockiana. Matthew E. Bunson. New York: Hungry Minds (now Wiley), 1997.

Encyclopedia Software Review. http://encyclopedia-review.toptenreviews.com/.

Gale Encyclopedia of Multicultural America. Farmington Hills, MI: Thomson Gale, 1999. 2nd ed., 2003, available only online: http://www.gale.cengage.com/.

Garland Encyclopedia of World Music. Ruth M. Stone, James Porter, and Timothy Rice. New York: Garland Publishing, 1999.

Grolier Online. http://go.grolier.com/.

The Grove Encyclopedia of American Art. Joan Marter, ed. New York: Oxford University Press, 2011.

Grzimek's Animal Life Encyclopedia. 2nd ed. Farmington Hills, MI: Thomson Gale, 2003–2004.

International Encyclopedia of Political Science. Bertrand Badie, Dirk Berg-Schlosser, and Leonardo Morlino, eds. Thousand Oaks, CA: SAGE Publications, 2011.

International Encyclopedia of the Social Sciences. 2nd ed. William A. Darity Jr., ed. Farmington Hills, MI: Macmillan Reference, 2007.

Kirkus Reviews. https://www.kirkusreviews.com/.

Knol. http://knol.google.com/k. Defunct as of April 2012.

Lands and Peoples. Danbury, CT: Grolier, 2005.

LookLex Encyclopaedia (formerly the *Encyclopaedia of the Orient*). http://www.i-cias.com/e.o/.

The McGraw-Hill Encyclopedia of Science and Technology. 11th ed. New York: McGraw-Hill Professional, 2012. Also available online: http://www.mhest.com/index.php.
My First Britannica. Chicago: Encyclopaedia Britannica, 2008.
The New Book of Knowledge. http://teacher.scholastic.com/products/grolier/program_TNBON.htm.
On the Properties of Things: De proprietatibus rerum. John De Trevisa. Gloucestershire: Clarendon Press, 1988.
Oxford Music Online. http://www.oxfordmusiconline.com/public/.
Proteopedia. http://www.proteopedia.org/.
PSIO: Praeger Security International Online. http://www.abc-clio.com/.
Questia. http://www.questia.com/.
Routledge Encyclopedia of Philosophy. Edward Craig, ed. New York: Taylor and Francis, 1998.
Scholarpedia. http://www.scholarpedia.org/.
Subject Encyclopedias. Allan N. Mirwis. Phoenix, AZ: Oryx Press, 1999.
Wikipedia. http://www.wikipedia.org/.
The World Book Discovery Encyclopedia. Chicago: World Book, 2009.
World Book Encyclopedia. Chicago: World Book, 2012. http://www.worldbookonline.com/.

Recommendations for Further Reading

American Reference Books Annual. 2012. Westport, CT: Libraries Unlimited. Also available online: http://www.arbaonline.com/. *ARBAonline* provides access to more than 20,000 reviews submitted within the decade. In addition, up to 200 new or updated reviews are entered at the start of each month. The print edition, organized by subject, has a section on "Dictionaries and Encyclopedias."
ARBA Guide to Subject Encyclopedias and Dictionaries. 1997. 2nd ed. Englewood, CO: Libraries Unlimited. Though dated, this selection of subject dictionaries and encyclopedias culled from ten years of ARBA reviews provides a broad overview of the breadth of material available. New reviews can be found in *ARBAonline* (http://www.arbaonline.com/).
Callahan, Ewa S., and Suasan C. Herring. 2011. "Cultural Bias in Wikipedia Content on Famous Persons." *Journal of the American Society for Information Science and Technology* 62, no. 10 (October): 1899–1915. Given *Wikipedia*'s openness to authorship and editing, the relevance of neutral point of view (NPOV) has come under sustained scrutiny. In this representative article, the authors limit their study to American and Polish coverage of famous people and conduct a series of quantitative surveys. Their results are somewhat inconclusive but serve as an instructive example of what constitutes both the lure and the vulnerability associated with *Wikipedia*—its bypassing of traditional, formal authorship.
De Laat, Paul B. 2012. "Open Source Production of Encyclopedias: Editorial Policies at the Intersection of Organizational and Epistemological Trust." *Social Epistemology* 26, no. 1 (January): 71–103. The article provides an interesting philosophical underpinning to how six prominent and successful encyclopedias (*Wikipedia, h2g2, Scholarpedia, Citizendium, Knol,* and the *Encyclopedia of Earth*) deal with the elephant in the room—trust.
East, John. W. 2010. "'The Rolls Royce of the Library Reference Collection': The Subject Encyclopedia in the Age of Wikipedia." *Reference and User Services Quarterly* 50, no. 2 (Winter): 162–169. An interesting article that questions the importance of subject encyclopedias, even as it records the steady publication and purchase of these

resources by academic libraries. The role of federated search engines and platforms that aim to replicate the easy accessibility of *Wikipedia* are also discussed as tools to facilitate the use of expensive ("Rolls Royce") subject encyclopedias.

"Encyclopedia Update, 2011." 2011. *Booklist* 105, no. 2 (September 15): 50–52. Authored by Mary Ellen Quinn, the ever-reliable annual update covers three major online encyclopedias in some detail. The accounts are descriptive rather than analytical. The January 1 and 15, 2008, issues of *Booklist* also describe encyclopedias in global languages.

Jacobs, A. J. 2004. *The Know-It-All: One Man's Humble Quest to Become the Smartest Person in the World*. New York: Simon and Schuster. A compelling and entertaining memoir that testifies to the age-old allure of encyclopedias, this book tells of Jacobs' attempt to read through all 32 volumes of the *Encyclopaedia Britannica*.

Kavanagh, Nadine. 2010. "'What Better Advertisement Could Australia Have?' Encyclopaedias and Nation-Building." *National Identities* 12, no. 3 (September): 237–252. It is the author's contention that "encyclopaedic objectivity is an illusion. Encyclopaedias construct knowledge." The case study to prove this thesis is the 1925 *Australian Encyclopaedia*, which was published with the explicit and exclusionary idea of establishing a unified national culture in the new nation. So, for example, animals that made it as entries in the encyclopedia were kangaroos and emus, but not elephants and tigers. Lord Tennyson's son, a political official in Australia, was included, but not the great poet himself.

Kister, Kenneth F. 1994. *Kister's Best Encyclopedias: A Comparative Guide to General and Specialized Encyclopedias*. 2nd. ed. Phoenix, AZ: Oryx Press. Though it has been almost two decades since its publication, this is a thoughtful resource for understanding the immensity and internal organization of encyclopedic resources.

Kogan, Herman. 1958. *The Great EB: The Story of the Encyclopaedia Britannica*. Chicago: University of Chicago Press. This is an engrossing account of the making of the *Encyclopaedia Britannica* and the towering ambitions that were passed from one visionary to the next so that the *Britannica* became a reality. It reads like a novel.

Pink, Daniel. H. 2005. "The Book Stops Here." *Wired Magazine* 13, no. 3 (March). Pink provides a quick tour of encyclopedia production principles from the One Smart Guy model (Aristotle), to the One Best Way model (*Britannica*), to the One For All model (*Wikipedia*).

Bibliography and Works Cited

Ash, Katie. 2012. "As Print Fades, Encyclopedias Endure in Schools." *Education Week* 31, no. 26: 10.

Carriveau, K. L., Jr. 2012. "SpringerReference.com." *CHOICE: Current Reviews for Academic Libraries* 49, no. 5 (January): 844.

Carroll, Jann. 2011. "From Encyclopaedias to Search Engines: Technological Change and its Impact on Literacy Learning." *Literacy Learning: The Middle Years* 19, no. 2 (June): 27.

Cohen, Noam. 2008. "Start Writing the Eulogies for Print Encyclopedias." *The New York Times* (March 16): 3.

East, John, W. 2010. "'The Rolls Royce of the Library Reference Collection': The Subject Encyclopedia in the Age of Wikipedia." *Reference and User Services Quarterly* 50, no. 2 (Winter): 162.

Erikson, Edward. 2012. "Wikipedia in My Classroom." (April 2). http://blog.wikimedia.org/2012/04/02/wikipedia-in-my-classroom/.

Foster, Andrea. 2008. "What Google's New Encyclopedia Means for Students and Professors." *Chronicle of Higher Education* 55, no. 2 (September 5): A17.

Jacobs, A.J. 2004. *The Know-It-All: One Man's Humble Quest to Become the Smartest Person in the World.* New York: Simon and Schuster.

Jenkins, Henry. 2007. "What Wikipedia Can Teach Us about New Media Literacy." Available: http://www.henryjenkins.org.

Jonker, Travis. 2012. "Grolier Gets a Revise: A Close Look at Reference Mainstay Grolier Online, Newly Updated." *School Library Journal* 58, no. 1 (January): 51.

Kavanagh, Nadine. 2010. "'What Better Advertisement Could Australia Have?' Encyclopaedias and Nation-Building." *National Identities* 12, no. 3 (September): 237–252.

Kogan, Herman. 1958. *The Great EB: The Story of the Encyclopaedia Britannica.* Chicago: University of Chicago Press.

"Life Isn't 2-D, So Why Should Our Encyclopedias Be?" 2008. *Pharma Business Week* (September 8): 106.

McArthur, Tom. 1986. *Words of Reference: Lexicography, Learning, and Language from the Clay Tablet to the Computer.* Cambridge, NY: Cambridge University Press.

Pew Internet and American Life Project. 2011. "Wikipedia, Past and Present" (January 13). http://pewinternet.org/Reports/2011/Wikipedia.aspx.

Quinn, Mary Ellen. 2011. "Encyclopedia Update 2011." *Booklist* 105, no. 2 (September 15): 50–52.

Rand, Angela Doucet. 2010. "Meeting at the Student-Wikipedia Intersection." *Journal of Library Administration* 50, no. 7/8 (October–December): 923–932.

Roncevic, Mirela. 2006. "E-reference on a Mission." *Library Journal* (September 15): 10.

Steele, Robert. 2006. *Mediaeval Lore from Bartholomew Anglicus.* Middlesex, UK: Echo Library.

6

Answering Questions That Require Handy Facts—Ready Reference Sources

Overview

Moments of flamboyance in reference transactions are rare. When exhibited, they are invariably through the dramatic simplicity of a ready reference resource. Über-Google librarians seemingly pull out of a hat a string of reliable and relevant dates, events, statistics, rankings, names, chronologies, and facts to ease the itch of patron queries that are short, factual, and nonanalytical. Most important, these answers are not embedded in a million "results" and therein lies the continuing relevance of ready reference in the new era.

Ready reference work includes all the joys and tribulations of instant gratification. It is quick. It is immediate. It is fun. It contributes to the stereotype of the all-knowing reference librarian. It also requires the reference librarian to assemble a stable of ready reference sources that are handy and entirely familiar. Information seekers of the post-Google era now look for information on their own before approaching a library professional, thus changing the nature of ready reference questions both in quantity and in level of difficulty. It is important for the reference librarian to develop a more powerful stable that reflects this change.

With the relatively easy availability of full-text sources online, resources that were not created to be used as ready reference are accessible enough to be used in that way. A quote from *Romeo and Juliet*, for example, no longer requires a quotation book or concordance, but may be handily located in freely available online versions of the entire play. Yet, a significant number of library websites continue to have an icon directing the user to ready reference sources. A survey of ARL library websites found that almost 95 percent had created pages for such sources (Singer, 2010). The pages are variously termed as "quick reference" as at the Purdue University Library (http://www.lib.purdue.edu/eresources/readyref/); "virtual reference desk" as at the University of Delaware Library (http://www2 .lib.udel.edu/ref/virtual/index.htm); or just plain "reference desk" as at the Library of Michigan (http://web.mel.org/). These sources testify to the need for vetted sites that aim to provide a more productive and streamlined search for information.

While online resources and the ability to "bookmark" and create "knowledge bases" have expanded the scope and range of ready reference resources, there continues to be a traditional substratum of established reference works to provide a footing for answering this genre of questions. This chapter delineates some of those handy reference resources specifically collated to cover the major who, what, which, where, when, and how questions faced by a reference librarian.

How Ready Reference Is Used

The need for ready reference sources is felt in these situations:

- Quick, rather than multistep, answers are required.
- Factual, rather than analytical, information is required.
- Relative facts need to be located in a single source.
- The information required is wide ranging but not deep.
- Citations for primary research are required.
- The data found in a random Internet search are of dubious accuracy.

Ready reference is not necessarily "simple" reference. As Marydee Ojala writes, "it's the easy-sounding, fact-based questions that may be more difficult to answer" (Ojala, 2001: 59). There is usually only one right answer. Selecting the right resource to find these right answers is the first step in ready reference work.

Questions Answered by Ready Reference

Q: What is the Earth's distance from the sun?
A: 91.4–94.5 million miles according to the *World Almanac*.

Q: Where are the Amtrak and Greyhound stations located in Mobile, Alabama?
A: The address, telephone, and toll-free numbers are listed in *City Profiles USA*.

Q: How much would it cost to register copyright on a new computer software application?
A: $35—the *Copyright* website at http://www.copyright.gov/ can provide more detailed information.

Q: Who publishes historical romances in Virginia?
A: The *Literary Market Place* has a comprehensive list.

Q: Which character in the play version of *The Diary of Anne Frank* steals food?
A: Mr. Van Daan, according to the *MagillOnLiterature Plus* database.

Q: How do I address a letter to the Pope?
A: *Emily Post's Etiquette* suggests "Your Holiness" or "Most Holy Father."

Q: In the United States, how many single women below the age of 29 years with less than a high school diploma had a child in 2010?
A: The *Statistical Abstract of the United States*, 2012 (Table 90) reports a total of 480 women of which 52.5 percent were not living with a partner.

Major Ready Reference Resources Used in Reference Work

It is traditional to discuss differences between almanacs and yearbooks; annuals and compendiums; directories and indexes; and the many ready reference sources available to a librarian. While ready reference resources emphasized in this chapter include almanacs, fact sheets, directories, consumer reports, synopses, handbooks, chronologies, and yearbooks, selecting from this range of resources becomes easier if standard questions are visualized as falling into these question categories: who, what, where, which, when, and how. The subjects falling under the question categories can be interchangeable, and certainly not obedient to the examples given in this chapter. The generalized query is best served with an encyclopedia, an almanac, or web portals such as *ipl2* (http://www.ipl.org/), *Bartleby* (http://www.bartleby.com/), *LibrarySpot* (http://www.libraryspot.com/), and *Credo Reference* (http://www.credoreference.com/).

Type	General Sources	Specific Source	Example
Who	Telephone books, government directories, almanacs	http://www.anywho.com/	I need a telephone number for 5 Main Street, Anytown, USA.
What	Consumer and citizen guides, college guides, grant books; occupation handbooks	http://www.cem.va.gov/	What are the eligibility requirements to be buried in a U.S. national cemetery?
Which	Literary synopses, yearbooks	*Masterplots*	Which Russian character murdered a greedy, old pawnbroker?
Where	Relocation directories, almanacs	*City Profiles USA*	Can I get the crime statistics, weather averages, and school rankings for Boise, Idaho?
When	Timelines and events, chronologies, almanacs	*Chase's Calendar of Events*	What celebrities were born in the month of July?
How	Etiquette, statistics, manuals, almanacs	*Robert's Rules of Order*	What is the minimum number of people required to form a quorum?

General Facts

Almanacs are the epitome of a ready reference resource. They are crammed with general information that is concise, factual, and structured to broadly answer who, what, where, which, when and how questions. The earliest almanacs, dating back to the 1300s, were usually focused on the calendar and on weather. They gradually expanded to include a little bit of everything. Benjamin Franklin's beloved 1733 publication *Poor Richard's Almanac* even included lists of road names and a bit of poetry.

Poetry and road names have fallen by the wayside, yet the tradition of providing the widest common denominator of popularly requested facts continues to mark the successful almanac. In fact, the success of the almanac to provide wide-ranging and comprehensive data has, in tense times, been charged with assisting terrorists with "target selection and pre-operational planning" information, as was the case following 9/11 when heavily marked almanacs detailing American railways, dams, and reservoirs were found in the apartment of an al-Qaida sleeper agent. Librarians, among others, were quick to respond to the FBI bulletin warning against almanac-toting individuals with the retort that "Almanacs don't kill. People do" ("FBI Almanac Alert," 2004).

United States

The most respected and used almanac in America is the annual *World Almanac and Book of Facts*. Published since 1868, and an annual since 1886, the *World Almanac* is crammed with facts, features, rankings, directories, and information. The index is comprehensive and a critical key to opening up the riches of the *Almanac*. The print edition is 1,008 pages and available in both paperback and hardcover editions. It is available in e-book format and is part of the Infobase Publishing eBook Master Collection for schools and libraries. A Kindle edition is available through Amazon.com. The *World Almanac for Kids* is available as an online database.

Marketed as a dual-format resource, the annual *Time Almanac* is prominently linked to the free website *Infoplease* (http://www.infoplease.com/). Rather than the traditional table of contents and index bracketing the almanac, a detailed index prefaces the book. Graphical tabs listing the major sections replaces the table of contents, with "health and nutrition" given special focus and highlighted in red. Like the *World Almanac*, the *Time Almanac* has incorporated index marks on the edge of the book to facilitate quick delineation of different sections in the book. Free access to the website provides a distinct advantage to the almanac. There is a children's version of the almanac as well, the *TIME for Kids Almanac*, with a free website at *Fact Monster* (http://www.factmonster.com/).

Canada and the United Kingdom

While a great many reference works are globally useful, regardless of the place of publication, the almanac gains in value when directed to a specific audience. Users looking up the *World Almanac* or the *Time Almanac* will find universal facts on statistics, measures, calendars, science, biographies, and news, but they will also find a great deal of information on the U.S. government, political structure, and personalities. So, a copy of the *Canadian Almanac and Directory* and the hoary *Whitaker's Almanack* also would be worthwhile investments to ensure ready access to Canadian and British facts.

Whitaker's Almanack continues a tradition that began in 1868, with the pledge to register "the people, institutions and processes [that] keep the modern world's cogs turning." In addition to global cogs involving statistics and general information, *Whitaker's* is an invaluable fount of facts on the United Kingdom. Summaries of the year's newsworthy events are supplemented with distinctly local information such as the winner of the Irish Derby, the year's productions at the Royal Opera

House in Covent Garden, and local government listings that allow the user to verify, for example, whether Exeter is a parliamentary constituency. The table of contents divides the information into major categories and the all-important index is comprehensive. The almanac is not available online, though sample entries and web links to useful sites can be found at http://www.whitakersalmanack.com/.

The Canadian Almanac and Directory, published since 1847, prides itself on being Canada's preeminent sourcebook. It combines the essence of an almanac with that of multiple directories. In addition to providing scores of statistics, maps, weights and measures, national awards, Canadian symbols, and local forms of address, it also lists information on businesses, agencies, associations, health care facilities, publishers, provincial utility companies, and more. A bilingual article on the history of the country marks this "snapshot of Canada" as uniquely Canadian. It is available online at http://www.greyhouse.ca/almanac.htm and includes monthly updates.

Local Facts

An essential component of ready reference is accessible local information. The resources for this can be diverse and less than formal. The onus of collating a useful collection is squarely on the reference librarian, based on the demands of the users. Some resources that can answer the who, what, when, where, which, and how questions of a municipality are the following:

- Town directory
- Town map
- List of elected officials and representatives
- Local government, institutions, agencies, and associations
- Visitor information
- List of services such as nearest fax, notary public, passport services, post office
- Transportation and directions to the library
- Local datasheet

The Parsippany–Troy Hills Public Library System in New Jersey had taken the initiative in producing a pathfinder titled "New to Parsippany" that listed all services needed by a new resident. Given the high number of immigrants in the region, the pathfinder included information about ESL (English as a Second Language), adult education, and the certification of foreign transcripts, along with the more traditional facts of local day care, employment, newspapers, and service agencies. The pathfinder has since been supplanted by online links to "Selected Websites" in the region. Such online links can be found on most library sites, such as the Monona Public Library in Wisconsin (http://www.mononalibrary .org/local.html), the Jacobs Library of the Illinois Valley Community College (http://www.ivcc.edu/library.aspx?id=4038), and the Tisch Library at Tufts University, Boston (http://www.library.tufts.edu/tisch/subject/general.htm). The Richland County Public Library in South Carolina was even more ambitious and looked into creating not only local links, but a formal database of local resources that could supply a ready index for articles printed in community media as well as a community obituary index (Griffis, Cooper, and Headley, 2010).

The "Who" Facts

The "who" questions are typically answered by telephone directories or by biographical directories. Letting your fingers do the walking with the ubiquitous telephone directory is good practice for the reference librarian. Given its commonality and public familiarity with usage, the "Super Pages" tend to be forgotten. They do, however, provide a slew of value add-ons in addition to business and name listings that can prove very handy to the busy librarian. Contact information for community agencies such as those for domestic violence, senior citizens, blood banks, and substance abuse are located in the telephone directory. Frequently needed numbers for local, county, state, and federal government offices are also listed in the Blue Pages of the phone directory. Verizon adds a Community Magazine to its directory, with area maps, graphics of airport and stadium layouts, local attractions, a recreation guide, and a calendar of events. Online telephone directories are highly effective resources as well; *AnyWho* (http://www.anywho.com/), *Superpages* (http://www.superpages.com/), and *Switchboard* (http://www.switchboard.com/) are all worthy sites to locate persons or businesses. Reverse lookups are also possible in all three. *Switchboard* also offers search capabilities for web addresses, area codes, and zip codes. An online source available at http://inter800.com/ locates 800/888 numbers by listing the product, service, or company name.

Specialty directories can be a positive addition to the basic telephone directory. Publishers like Gale Group and Omnigraphics produce a series of specialty directories, some of more value to ready reference than others. Omnigraphics specializes in rearranging or expanding upon telephone directories that facilitate a more exact search. The *Toll-Free Phone Book USA* and *Headquarters USA* are annual directories with alphabetical listings of organizations. Entries through yellow-page-style subject classifications provide additional access. In addition to their titular focus, the directories list complete mailing addresses and telephone numbers for the organizations.

Some directories act like yellow pages with a particular focus. The *National Directory of Corporate Giving* and the *National Directory of Nonprofit Organizations* are two examples. The former profiles over 1,000 funding sources in the United States. In addition to contact information, giving priorities and preferences are also analyzed. The latter lists names, addresses, telephone numbers, and annual revenues for over 180,000 nonprofit organizations. Popularly known as a "criss-cross directory," the *Cole Cross Reference Directories* and the *Hill-Donnelly Cross Reference Directory* provide succinct answers to questions posed by users who have an address but are in search of a name or telephone number. Small business owners planning a marketing strategy as well as new homeowners scouting a particular area also use it extensively. Listings are most easily located either by the telephone number or by the address. Special sections include color-coded pages that provide locations via census tracts, zip codes, and street names. A "relative affluence rating" or income level estimate based on census data as well as medians of home value and income level accompanies each listing.

With 36,400 post offices serving more than 141 million homes, farms, and businesses through "snow, rain, heat and the gloom of night," the U.S. Postal Service publishes the detailed two-volume *National Five-Digit Zip Code and Post Office Directory*. The resource lists all the post offices in the country as well as the zip code for each named street. Arranged by state, each section is preceded by a map of the state, with three-digit zip code divisions outlined. A useful feature in Volume 2 is the listing of both new and discontinued zip codes as well as details of classes of mail and special services. The online version is freely available at http://www.usps.com/. The "com" designation is based on the status of the Postal Service as an independent establishment of the Executive Branch, but users are redirected even if they type in "gov." An online site for Canadian postal information is available at http://www.canadapost.ca/segment-e.asp. It provides information on postal (zip) codes and reverse searches, as well as a list of Canadian municipalities with defunct "old names" listed alongside.

Who's Who in America has been a familiar resource in America for over a century. First published in 1898, the current edition of *Who's Who* is a two-volume set that lists over 100,000 "high achievers." The value of this resource is that it covers living Americans about whom not much may be found otherwise. The mini-biographies are built around at least 20 set characteristics. Facts may be located not only for the glitterati, the literati, and the accomplished but relatively anonymous leaders of business, science, education, and the arts. There are two indexes to help the user find a name. One is by geographical location and the second is through an occupational category. *Who's Who in the World* is a valuable companion volume with the same format and coverage of over 50,000 global personalities. The publications are available online via subscription at http://www.marquiswhoswho.net/. The online version is updated daily, and it is possible to search by name, gender, religion, and other access points. The online version also incorporates a total of 20 other *Who's Who* publications that focus on subject specialists. The subject coverage is useful for academic and special libraries but not necessary for the average public or school library.

A subject-special version of who is who can be found in the annual *Literary Market Place*, popularly known as the *LMP*. Given that the percentage of books published in the United States has risen at an exponential rate, the value of the *LMP* has risen in tandem. With many years of publishing history, the two-volume *LMP* has established itself as a reliable and exhaustive resource for the North American book-publishing world. The resource includes contact information for publishers, literary agents, and editorial services in America and Canada. The entries are alphabetical, as well as by subject, geographic location, and type of publication. The confusing world of imprints, subsidiaries, and distributors is also listed. A calendar of book trade and promotional events is provided along with relevant awards and prizes. The information is updated throughout the year and revised annually in print. The online version, available at http://www.literary marketplace.com/, has both the *LMP* and the *International Literary Market Place* and is updated continuously. Users have the option of free access to limited information such as a list of small presses or of becoming paid annual or even weekly sub-scribers, with access to all the information contained in both publications.

The "What" Facts

The "what" questions typically cluster around specific concerns of consumers. In an age of dizzying choice, what to choose based on what criterion is a recurring responsibility. From the more trivial questions of what is the best restaurant, vacuum cleaner, MP3 player, or car to the more weighty ones of what occupation, college, or government aid is available, consumer guides have increasingly become a staple of reference libraries. Monthly issues of *Consumer Reports* and the annual *Consumer Reports Buying Guide* are marketed as the consumer's most authoritative guides for "doing homework" on potential purchases. With ratings on home products that range from canned soups to minivans, the format is designed to aid the consumer in scoping the market, gauging trends, evaluating specific features, and scanning relative prices and advantages. The synoptic *Buying Guide* is linked to the monthly *Reports*, which studies products in great detail. The *Buying Guide* is handy in providing short overviews of popular items but is more valuable as a comprehensive and cumulative index to the *Reports*. As a nonprofit organization, *Consumer Reports* has staked much of its authority on the fact that it is independent of manufacturers' bias. It buys all the products it tests and accepts neither advertising nor free samples from commercial companies. The online version has a four-year searchable archive and can locate items by keyword or through an alphabetical index, or by category. It is available for a fee at http://www.consumerreports.org/. It also includes a special section on "Canada Extra" for Canadian ratings on local goods.

A comprehensive source for pricing information on both new and used cars is the *Edmunds Guides*. No longer in print version, the *Edmunds Guides* are available online at http://www.edmunds.com/ and are popular, as the first free auto web-site for car ratings. They continue to provide free access to ratings as well as value add-ons such as a monthly payment calculator and used vehicle listings by geo-graphic location. The small, yellow *N.A.D.A. Appraisal Guides*, also available online at http://www.nadaguides.com/, are another staple of ready reference and provide quick, continually updated prices on used and new vehicles of all types. *Kelley Blue Book*, available in print since 1926 and online at http://www.kbb.com/, is yet another respected source for pricing on new and used cars.

A clear, well-organized synopsis of major occupational groups in the United States, the handy biennial *Occupational Outlook Handbook* (*OOH*) is the resource to consult when the user needs to know what qualifications are required to be a recreational therapist; or what is the exact nature of an account collector's job; or if there is any future in a job as a machine setter. A great many of the 822 occupations detailed by the federal government are presented in organized sections describing the nature of the job, working conditions, current employ-ment statistics, future job outlook through the year 2020, required training, median earnings, related jobs, and sources for further information that include the union or association covering the job type. The structure of the descriptions for each occupation is unvarying, providing ideal material for quick reference. The information is also freely available online at http://www.bls.gov/ooh/. Given that the *OOH* is updated only once in two years, it is supported by the *Occupational Outlook Quarterly* that is released both in print and online.

Information sources on financial assistance also abound. There are homes that are sold for a single dollar to local governing bodies. There are special education grants for infants with handicaps. There are guaranteed loans for veterans in need of housing. The *Government Assistance Almanac* from Omnigraphics is a user-friendly and commercial version of the government behemoth the *Catalog of Federal Domestic Assistance*, freely available at http://www.cfda.gov/. With a comprehensive listing of domestic financial aid available through government agencies, the almanac lists the purpose of the grant, eligibility, range, and scope of aid and assistance provided, as well as a referral to the grant agency's head-quarters, telephone number, and Internet address. The Omnigraphics edition, with its detailed index, is far easier though less comprehensive to use than the *Catalog*, which contains far more detailed information such as grant deadlines, renewal policy, and application procedures. Another advantage provided by the website is the easy access to all formal grant applications, including the generic Form 424 used for most assistance grants.

Billions of dollars in grants are awarded annually by independent, company-sponsored, community, and grant-making foundations. The *Foundation Directory* provides in-depth information about some 10,000 of the largest of such foundations. First published in 1960, the *Directory* is updated and revised annually based primarily on the tax returns of relevant foundations. It aims at both describing and providing contact information to all major grant-giving institutions. Entries are arranged by geographic state, though seven supplementary indexes, including a subject index, provided additional searching capabilities. The *Directory* does not cover grants to individuals. At http://foundationcenter.org/, the *Foundation Directory Online* is available at five levels of coverage, the *Basic*, *Plus*, *Premium*, *Platinum*, and *Professional*. It is updated weekly and covers more than 100,000 U.S. foundations and corporate donors, over 2.4 million grants, and over half a million key decision makers.

There was a time in the not-too-distant past when ready reference would include a messy collection of print catalogs and curricula from colleges and universities across the nation. While this collection is supplanted by the comprehensive online presence of individual educational institutions, wide-ranging information that can aid the college consumer still depends on collated guides. Peterson's multiple guides to graduate schools are available both in print and online at http://www.petersons.com/. They provide a definitive source for graduate and professional programs in accredited institutions, both in the nation and abroad. Profiles that cover the field of study, enrollment statistics, typical costs, computer and library facilities, housing, and contact information are provided for more than 1,800 institutions. Peterson's annual compilation of undergraduate institutions also delivers rounded profiles of junior and community colleges. In addition to the information provided for graduate colleges, these volumes state whether the institution is state supported; has an urban, suburban, or small-town campus; and the levels of difficulty in getting admission—from noncompetitive to most difficult. Barron's *Profiles of American Colleges*, College Board's *College Handbook*, and the *U.S. News Best Colleges* are all worthy publications to aid the college consumer.

In addition to mainstream colleges, selections of specialized directories based on community interest are also of value to a collection. *The Handbook of Private Schools* lists selected, nonpublic educational institutions. *American Trade Schools Directory* is a loose-leaf publication that has an amendment service to continually update the listings of schools for classified occupations that run the gamut from acupuncturist and accountant to welder and X-ray technician. The Law School Admission Council, in cooperation with the American Bar Association, publishes the annual *Official Guide to ABA-Approved Law Schools*. Peterson's also has a whole series of subject-specific school directories such as the ones for *Visual and Performing Arts*, *Nursing Programs*, and *MBA Programs*.

The "Which" Facts

"Which" questions are interchangeable with "what" questions, but tend to hone in on fewer or single options. Which chemical substance? Which song? Which film? Which drug? Which association? Which nonprofit company? Which poem, short story, drama? Ready reference in the "which" question field is scopic in range and more intimate in detail. Following are a few representative examples that should help you extrapolate rules for the "which" typology.

Masterplots is an ever-growing multivolume series that parses major bodies of literature such as fiction, drama, poetry, and short stories. Aimed at facilitating an understanding of all major literary works, this classical reference source has been around since 1949. In addition to a synopsis, some works are appended with critical evaluations, story segments, and review essays that have annotated bibliographies. The twelve-volume *Masterplots*, Fourth Edition, is a collection of all literary genres, whereas other series such as the two-volume *Critical Survey of Graphic Novels* focus on one genre. The six-volume *Magill's Survey of American Literature* and six-volume companion *Magill's Survey of World Literature* offer biographies, bibliographies, abstracts, and analyses of 339 U.S. and Canadian authors and 380 globally renowned authors, respectively. A handy category list groups authors by genre, country, gender, and ethnic identity so that those questions on "which female Chinese-American poet..." or "which 18th century African dramatist..." are handily located. Currency is anchored by *Magill's Literary Annual*, which critically evaluates around 200 significant examples of noteworthy writing published in the previous year.

The *CRC Handbook of Chemistry and Physics*, currently in its ninety-second edition, has long been the definitive text to find reliable and exhaustive data on globally agreed properties of organic/inorganic compounds and chemical/physical data. A CD-ROM version allows quick searches by keyword, physical properties, chemical name, or molecular formula. Ready reference is also facilitated with a cross-table searching tool that allows single searches to collate all material on a topic described in different sections of the printed text.

The "When" Facts

Published as a thirty-two-page booklet in 1957 by the Chase brothers, the annual *Chase's Calendar of Events* is currently considered the most accessible and authoritative compilation of both famous and trivial events and holidays. The publication is arranged by each day of the calendar, so that all special events, celebrations, and birthdays of famous people on a particular day are clumped together. Presidential proclamations, religious observances, anniversaries of famous events, astronomical phenomena, and sponsored events provide the bulk of entries listed. A detailed index at the end of the book lists all events alphabetically so that a search is possible both by the name of the event or by the date on which it is celebrated. Obscure events also flood the pages of *Chase's*, as it is open to everyone to submit entries that will be added at the discretion of the editor. So, for example, Independence Day on July 4 is listed along with the World's Greatest Lizard Race in Lovington, New Mexico. National and state days of other countries around the world are also included.

For quick facts on what happened on a certain day in history, the "Anyday" page at http://www.scopesys.com/anyday/ provides an ambitious, global list of births, deaths, holidays, religious observances, and trivial and nontrivial happenings around the world from ancient times. A perpetual calendar for the years from 1901 to 2100 is located at http://www.vpcalendar.net/. The site also provides handy information on the exact years that define centuries and millennia as well as the dates of seasons in both hemispheres and Australia.

The *American Decades* and *American Eras* series are comprehensive sources for chronologies, headlines, and facts required for a specific time period in U.S. history. The series presents the eras of pre-twentieth-century America and the decades of twentieth-century America in composite capsules that cover the major events, laws, entertainment, business, government, and personalities of the age. The source is a unique addition to "when" references because it covers dates of more abstract entities than the more easily located births, deaths, anniversaries, and calendar events. Cultural, social, and economic trends are covered; so, for example, the date for Levittowns, the first prototypes of mass-produced suburban complexes, can be located through an exhaustive index. The *UXL American Decades* series is a children's version of this resource and is available in both print and as an e-book.

The "Where" Facts

Ranked by *Library Journal* as one of the top twenty best reference resources of the millennium, the *Statesman's Yearbook* is an annual one-stop source for the social, political, geographic, and economic profiles of all the countries of the world. More general information such as time zones and ISO (International Organization for Standardization) country codes can also be found in the first part of the book. Published since 1864, the information is concise, authoritative, annually updated, and supplemented with a foldout color world map with flags from all 193 countries. An interactive online version available free with the purchase of the print edition can be accessed at http://www.statesmansyearbook.com/public/. It is updated on a regular basis, has links to over 2,000 other related sites, and access to PDFs of all past *Yearbook* issues since 1864. Similar information, updated frequently, can be found in *The World Factbook* at the Central Intelligence Agency website (https://www.cia .gov/library/publications/the-world-factbook/index.html). This site also contains one of the most current resources for checking on chiefs of state and cabinet ministers of nations and territories, as the information is updated on a biweekly basis.

Omnigraphics publishes a host of descriptive directories aimed at users looking for pertinent information on U.S. cities. The *Moving and Relocation Directory* and *City Profiles USA* are two examples. The *Directory* provides a list of over 100 major cities that are deemed to be "popular relocation locations." Much of the information provided is from primary sources, collected by contacting individual offices and firms. Statistics such as the "quality of life indicator" come from government sources. Whereas some of the features that have been included—such as time zone maps and area code tables—can be found in general almanacs, the directory is unique in its compiling of a comprehensive factual profile of the selected cities. Chambers of commerce, local moving companies, banks, television and radio stations, mass transit and telecommunications, employment agencies, and property appreciation rates are some of the included features listed for each of the 121 cities.

The "How" Facts

"How" questions are of two types: the "how many" variety that require statistical resources and the "how to" sort that require manuals.

How Many

Published since 1878, the preeminent print resource for statistical queries was the annual *Statistical Abstract of the United States*. While this resource was the prime example of a reference workhorse that was easier and faster to use in print (Singer, 2010), on October 1, 2011, the U.S. Census Bureau announced the termination of data collection for its Compendia program which underwrote the *Abstract* and referred users to individual sites listed in the source notes for each given table. The online version at http://www.census.gov/compendia/statab/ continues to be an exhaustive portal into the social, economic, and political profile of the United States, parsed into thirty sections and 1,406 tables. However, the process of providing ready reference is no longer as "ready." Each table is documented with a source that includes website information when applicable and must be approached as an individual resource. Links to both macro and micro data on counties, cities, states, and metropolitan areas are available at the site, but its genius as a one-stop print resource for collated statistical information so ideal for ready reference might be compromised for the future, unless ProQuest and Bernan Press continue publication as promised.

Use of the U.S. Census website (http://www.census.gov/) can quickly transform a ready reference question into a lengthy reference session. The site is rich. Despite clear icons, detailed instructions, and fast-loading screens, it is well worth the time of any reference librarian to get familiar with the vast information and search strategies available for the site. Keep in mind that the three factors of subject, time period, and location determine the data category, and developing a search string for popularly asked questions goes a long way in making the best use of this seemingly infinite statistical resource. A search string for demographic information on the U.S. Census website would look like this:

- Click on: American FactFinder
- Click on: Geographies
- Select geographic area: e.g., Kalamazoo County
- Select and Add
- Click on: Race and Ethnic groups/Ancestry Group
- Select specific groups: e.g., Irish and German
- Add and Close
- Select DP-1 table and Go

Using this search string in *American FactFinder* (http://factfinder2.census.gov/), it would take the librarian or end user a few scant minutes to answer relatively complex questions such as this: *"In Kalamazoo County, Michigan, are there a larger number of inhabitants claiming Irish or German ancestry?"* While the search strings evolve along with a changing web and must be updated periodically, the habit of setting up a few search strings for dense but rewarding websites makes for effective ready reference.

A similarly well-endowed statistical site is *FedStats* at http://www.fedstats .gov/. It acts as a portal to over 100 major federal agencies that expend more than $500,000 on any statistical activity. The information can be accessed either through the agency, by subject, alphabetically, or by keyword searches. The information is monitored and revised by each individual agency, so that the sites are not standardized, and the librarian must be prepared to conduct different search strings for each search.

How To

A classic resource that has been around since 1922, *Emily Post's Etiquette* was revised and rewritten in 2011 by a great-granddaughter-in-law, Peggy Post. The new edition includes netiquette, online dating, and cell-phone etiquette in addition to the traditional issues of manners, table settings, ceremonies, and how to address correspondence. This book also covers changing social realities so that, for example, a divorcee announcing her daughter's engagement is provided with clear guidelines as to how to phrase the invitation. A section on addressing Canadian government officials is also included. The index is comprehensive, and the structure of the book is readily evident in the nine area sections laid out in the contents page. More recently, the *Etipedia* was created as an online etiquette reference resource.

The reigning authority on parliamentary procedures, *Robert's Rules of Order Newly Revised* was first published in 1876. It is an invaluable resource for checking on the correct procedure for conducting an institutional meeting. The composition of a meeting, the call to order, the bringing and passing of a motion, the types of motions, rules of quorum and debates, voting procedures, disciplinary action, and the taking of minutes are laid out in formal detail. The index is both clear and comprehensive so that the locating of abstruse issues is convenient. A website at http://www.robertsrules.com/ offers twenty frequently asked questions and provides an open forum to ask and answer questions. However, the fourth edition published in 1915 is public domain and can be freely accessed at a number of sites such as http://www.rulesonline.com/ and http://www.bartleby.com/176/.

A host of e-government and legal questions also fall into this category and must be fielded by most reference librarians of public and academic libraries. How to research a deed, register to vote, file income tax, and file for a divorce are timeless questions that have gained in volume since the upsurge of online-only restrictions. Web resources listed in Chapters 9 and 12 provide lists of sites useful to address this category of "how to" questions.

Collection Development and Maintenance

Selection and Keeping Current

Having an accessible selection of multiple resources for each question category is a reasonable strategy as billions of facts are accommodated at different levels of coverage and currency by each resource. An efficient way to keep current with new websites is to subscribe to a monthly newsletter provided by the hardworking team at the *ipl2*. The free newsletter at http://theipl.wordpress.com/ keeps abreast of reliable information sites.

"Current awareness services" such as search alerts, table of contents, and citation alerts are possible through RSS (really simple syndication). Web-based RSS readers like Google Reader or Bloglines are free and regularly supply fresh content and real-time updates to relevant sites without having to actively look for it beyond the initial act of subscribing to the feed.

To keep a stable of ready reference online resources fresh and up-to-date, it is advisable to check in with some of the more reliable sources of recommendation. The Reference and User Services Association (RUSA), for example, has a committee that produces the "Best Free Reference Web Sites" each year. The list is published in the fall issue of the *Reference and User Services Quarterly* with an online version on the RUSA website.

Evaluating Ready Reference Resources

Ready reference covers a wide range of materials. While authority, scope, cost, format availability, usability, reliability, and comprehensiveness are important in evaluating these materials, the prime directives are accuracy and currency. Ready reference must provide up-to-date facts that are definitive. Whereas keeping up on professional literature and reviews is the bedrock of validating resources, it is the reference librarian who is responsible for the following:

- Establishing which source serves which category of question
- Gauging whether the source is consistently accurate and current

Whether online or in print, the information provided needs to be constantly vetted for reliability. Most print sources have years of publishing experience and authority to back their use. Yet ready reference, with its compulsion for quick factual answers, draws heavily from online sources. Ninety-five percent of academic library websites have a ready reference section of selected sources that have presumably been selected by professionals. Public, school, and special libraries either provide an open access ready reference section or collate their own "favorites" bookmarked for quick personal access. Social bookmarking services like Delicious (http://delicious.com/) have refined online ready reference by allowing all the staff computers in a library to share a single set of "favorites." These sites can be monitored by doing the following:

- Checking for dead links
- Checking the citation sources for verifiability
- Being alert to sites with commercial endorsements that have a vested interest
- Cross-checking answers to establish whether answers are consistently accurate
- Checking the updating timetables for each site

Further Considerations

In 1957, a futuristic article predicted that a ready reference image database would be searchable by the simple act of "pushing a series of buttons on a huge robot that then popped up like a toaster" with the requested result (Singer, 2010). Well, the pop-up toaster is here and it is called the Internet. With so much of ready reference currently answerable through online or electronic resources, keeping lists of reliable sites, setting up RSS feeds for pertinent updates, and becoming wholly familiar with the content and structure of resources in each of the question categories allows this genre of reference to be handled deftly. Verifying the answer in more than one resource, print or online, is also key to accuracy.

The world of ready reference is as infinite as the minds of humans. Attempting to prefigure the range of queries is a paralyzing exercise. Almanacs, encyclopedias, dictionaries, and a selection of even five trusted resources for each category of the who, what, which, when, where, and how questions will arm the reference librarian with the tools to successfully answer 99 percent of ready reference questions. In the past, the stouthearted librarians of the New York Public Library would prove this time and again as they boldly ventured into schools to play the game "Stump the Librarian." Students questioned the librarians, who then found an answer within three minutes from a small traveling collection of ten to fifteen ready reference tools in print. The good news? The librarians always won.

The following list is a sampling of some of the questions they fielded:

- This is my name in hieroglyphics: ⌐ ⚲ ⚲. What is it?
- What years constitute 10 BC?
- What does it mean to die a "natural death"?
- How long can a person lie on a bed of nails?
- What percent of the globe's land is arable?

Today, the same questions would not necessarily require a bag of printed sources when a single tablet with online access could suffice. The Norwich

University in Vermont, with its "monstrous" reference desk, "built for keeping ready reference materials," was recently replaced with a more appropriate design with "minimal storage space"(Ahlers and Steiner, 2012). The well-known ready reference wheel used for almost half a century by the Milwaukee Public Library that was automated to bring ready reference resources to librarians seated around it at the touch of a button, was retired in 2011. However, digital approximations of the "wheel" can be found in any number of iterations such as the wiki-based "Virtual Notebook" being tried out at the Purdue University Libraries; the "Assistance Guide" wiki at the University of Texas at Austin (Bejune and Morris, 2010); the burgeoning universe of online reference knowledge bases (Bosančić, 2010); or the widespread 24/7 Ask-A-Librarian services offered around the globe. The world of ready reference has most certainly evolved. Its continued existence testifies to its continued need. The effectiveness and reliability of resources to fill that need, be it online or in print, continue to remain the responsibility of the reference librarian.

TOP TEN READY REFERENCE SOURCES

Title	Print	Online
Chase's Calendar of Events. 2012. New York: McGraw-Hill.	Annual	
Consumer Reports. New York: Consumers Union of United States.	Monthly	Subscription http://www.consumerreports.org/
Credo Reference (Formerly Xrefer). Boston: Credo Reference.	Ongoing	Subscription http://www.credoreference.com/
ipl2. Philadelphia: Drexel University, College of Information Science and Technology.	Weekly updates	http://www.ipl.org/
Local telephone directory	Annual	http://www.superpages.com/ http://www.switchboard.com/ http://www.anywho.com/
Occupational Outlook Handbook. 2012–2013. Washington, DC: U.S. Department of Labor.	Biennial	http://www.bls.gov/ooh/
The Statesman's Yearbook. 2012. New York: Palgrave Macmillan.	Annual	Subscription http://www.statesmansyearbook.com/
Statistical Abstract of the United States. 2012. Ann Arbor, MI: ProQuest/Bernan Press.	Annual	http://www.census.gov/compendia/statab/
Time Almanac. 2013. Upper Saddle River, NJ: Pearson Education.	Annual	http://www.infoplease.com/
World Almanac and Book of Facts. 2012. New York: World Almanac Books.	Annual	

RECOMMENDED FREE READY REFERENCE WEBSITES

Bartleby. http://www.bartleby.com/. Encyclopedias, dictionaries, thesauri, style books, quotation books, gazetteers, fact books, anthologies in the public domain, this site is akin to the attic of a historic home, packed with unique treasures and a rich, if idiosyncratic, source of ready reference answers.

Census.gov. http://www/census.gov/. A labyrinthine resource worth studying as it provides a rich vein of statistical information on the demographics of the United States.

Geohive. http://www.geohive.com/. The site is a handy almanac of global statistics, with reliable links to international statistical organizations.

Infoplease. http://www.infoplease.com/. "All the knowledge you need" reads the byline of *Infoplease*. It is one of the few free online versions of a popular general almanac and contains the necessary vastness of resources required for effective ready reference.

ipl2. http://www.ipl.org/. The site selects, evaluates, and organizes online web resources in a variety of subjects that make it a thoughtful resource for ready reference answers. This site also offers a 24/7 "Ask An ipl2 Librarian" service.

Recommended Resources Discussed in This Chapter

American Decades. Farmington Hills, MI: Gale Cengage Learning, 1996–2011.

American Eras. Farmington Hills, MI: Gale Cengage Learning, 1997–1988.

American FactFinder. http://factfinder2.census.gov/.

American Trade Schools Directory. San Diego, CA: Croner Publications, 1953–series.

Anywho. http://www.anywho.com/.

Bartleby. http://www.bartleby.com/.

Canadian Almanac and Directory, 2012. Toronto, Ontario: Grey House Publishing Canada, 2011. Also available online: http://www.greyhouse.ca/almanac.htm.

Catalog of Federal Domestic Assistance. http://www.cfda.gov/.

Chase's Calendar of Events, 2013. New York: McGraw-Hill, 1957–. Annual.

City Profiles USA. 10th ed. Detroit: Omnigraphics, 2010.

Cole Cross Reference Directories. 2012. Available in multiple formats online: http://www.coledirectory.com/.

College Handbook, 2013. New York: College Board, 1962–. Annual.

Congressional Directory. Washington, DC: Government Printing Office, 1995–. Updates available online: http://www.gpoaccess.gov/cdirectory/index.html.

Consumer Reports. New York: Consumer's Union of United States, 1936–. Monthly. Also available online: http://consumerresports.org/.

Consumer Reports Buying Guide 2012. New York: Consumers Union of United States, 1935–. Annual.

Copyright. http://www.copyright.gov/.

CRC Handbook of Chemistry and Physics. 92nd ed. W.M. Haynes, editor-in-chief. Boca Raton, FL: CRC Press, 1914–. Annual.

Credo Reference. http://www.credoreference.com/.

Critical Survey of Graphic Novels. Bart H. Beaty and Stephen Weiner, eds. Pasadena, CA: Salem Press, 2012.

Edmunds Guides. http://www.edmunds.com/.

Emily Post's Etiquette. 18th ed. Peggy Post. New York: HarperCollins, 2011. Also available online: http://www.emilypost.com/.

Etipedia. http://www.emilypost.com/etipedia/.

FedStats. http://www.fedstats.gov/.

Foundation Directory. New York: Foundation Center, 1978–. Annual. Also available online: http://foundationcenter.org/.

Geohive. http://www.geohive.com/.

Government Assistance Almanac 2012. Detroit: Omnigraphics, 1985–. Annual.

The Handbook of Private Schools. Boston: Porter Sargent Publishers, 1915–. Annual.

Headquarters USA 2012. Detroit: Omnigraphics, 1977–. Annual.

Hill-Donnelly Cross Reference Directory. Tampa, FL: Hill-Donnelly Corporation, 1917–. Annual. Also available online: http://lp.hilldonn.com/hd/.

ipl2. http://www.ipl.org/.

Kelley Blue Book. http://www.kbb.com/.

LibrarySpot. http://libraryspot.com/.

Literary Market Place 2012. Medford, NJ: Information Today, 1965–. Annual. Also available online: http://www.literarymarketplace.com/.

MagillOnLiterature Plus. http://www.ebscohost.com/public/magillonliterature-plus.

Magill's Literary Annual. John D. Wilson and Steven G. Kallman, eds. Pasadena, CA: Salem Press, 1977–. Annual.

Magill's Survey of American Literature. Steven G. Kellman, ed. Pasadena, CA: Salem Press, 2006.

Magill's Survey of World Literature. Steven G. Kellman, ed. Pasadena, CA: Salem Press, 2009.

Masterplots. 4th ed. 12 vols. Lawrence W. Mazzeno, ed. Pasadena, CA: Salem Press, 2010.

Moving and Relocation Directory. 8th ed. Detroit: Omnigraphics, 2012.

N.A.D.A. Appraisal Guides. Costa Mesa, CA: National Appraisal Guides, 2012. Also available online: http://www.nadaguides.com/.

National Cemetery Administration. http://www.cem.va.gov/.

National Directory of Corporate Giving. 17th ed. New York: Foundation Center, 2011.

National Directory of Nonprofit Organizations. Farmington Hills, MI: Gale Cengage, 2012.

National Five-Digit Zip Code and Post Office Directory. Baton Rouge, LA: Claitor's Publishing Division, 2012. Also available online: http://www.usps.com/.

Occupational Outlook Handbook. 2012–2013. Washington, DC: U.S. Government Printing Office, 1945–. Biennial. Also available online: http://www.bls.gov/ooh/.

Occupational Outlook Quarterly. Washington, DC: U.S. Government Printing Office, 2012. Also available online: http://www.bls.gov/ooq/home.htm.

Official Guide to ABA-Approved Law Schools 2013. Newtown, PA: Law School Admission Council and the American Bar Association, 2012. Also available online at: http://www.lsac.org/.

Peterson's Guides. Lawrenceville, NJ: Peterson's. Also available online: http://www.petersons.com/.

Profiles of American Colleges. 30th ed. New York: Barron's Educational Series, 2012.

Recommended Reference Books for Small and Medium-Sized Libraries and Media Centers. Shannon Graff Hysell, ed. Santa Barbara, CA: Libraries Unlimited, 2011.

Robert's Rules of Order Newly Revised. 10th ed. Henry M. Robert. New York: Perseus Book Group, 2000.

The Statesman's Yearbook 2012. New York: Palgrave Macmillan, 1864–. Annual. Also available online: http://www.statesmansyearbook.com/public/.

Statistical Abstract of the United States. U. S. Census Bureau. Washington, DC, 1878–. Annual. Freely available online: http://www.census.gov/compendia/statab/.

Superpages. http://www.superpages.com/.

Switchboard. http://www.switchboard.com/.

Time Almanac 2013. Upper Saddle River, NJ: Pearson Education, 1947–. Annual.

TIME for Kids Almanac, 2013. New York: Time for Kids, 2000–. Annual.
Toll-Free Phone Book USA 2012. Detroit: Omnigraphics, 2011.
U.S. News Best Colleges, 2013. New York: U.S. News and World Report L.P., 1985–. Annual.
UXL American Decades. Farmington Hills, MI: UXL (Gale), 2003–2012.
Whitaker's Almanack 2012. London: Bloomsbury Publishing, 1868–. Annual. Also available online: http://www.whitakersalmanack.com/.
White Pages. http://www.anywho.com/.
Who's Who in America 2013. New Providence, NJ: Marquis Who's Who, LLC, 2012.
Who's Who in the World 2013. New Providence, NJ: Marquis Who's Who, LLC, 2012.
The World Almanac and Book of Facts 2013. New York: Infobase Publishing, 1868–. Annual.
The World Almanac for Kids 2013. New York: Infobase Learning, 1995–. Annual.
The World Factbook. https://www.cia.gov/library/publications/the-world-factbook.

Recommendations for Further Reading

Agosto, Denise A., and Holly Anderton. 2007. "Whatever Happened to 'Always Cite the Source'?" *Reference and User Services Quarterly* 47, no. 1: 44–54. Citations are an established "best practice" for all reference transactions. An unobtrusive test conducted on twenty-five libraries in the United States and Canada found that ready reference questions like the population of Montana and the location of the Southern Poverty Law Center were answered without citing the source. The study brings out one of the pitfalls of ready reference, namely, the disregard for citing sources in the process of providing "quick" reference.

Bejune, Matthew M., and Sara E. Morris. 2010. "The Development of the Virtual Notebook, A Wiki-Based Ready Reference Technology." *Reference and User Services Quarterly* 50, no. 1 (Fall): 27–34. An instructive case study in the evolution of ready reference technologies at Purdue University and the current use of a wiki-based "Virtual Notebook." In the words of the authors, "While the use of the Virtual Notebook has yet to reach the level expected by the researchers, there is no doubt that a wiki can be helpful in supporting reference and user services within a distributed library environment."

Bell, Suzanne S. 2012. *Librarian's Guide to Online Searching.* 3rd ed. Santa Barbara, CA: Libraries Unlimited. Given that ready reference requires both speed and accuracy, this book is invaluable in training reference librarians to navigate database searches with ease and confidence. Bell uncovers the inherent structure of databases, describes the tools of efficient searching, and provides helpful exercises and visual screenshots to enhance the text. The material effectively teaches ways for reference librarians to get adept at online retrieval.

Bishop, Bradley Wade, Diana Sachs-Silveira, and Traci Avet. 2011. "Populating a Knowledge Base with Local Knowledge for Florida's Ask a Librarian Reference Consortium." *Reference Librarian* 52, no. 3 (July-September):197–207. While the article is aimed at shoring up potential weaknesses in virtual reference, the study also serves to highlight the importance of both creating a ready reference knowledge base and populating it with information that is needed for a local constituency.

Ford, Charlotte. 2008. "Finding Facts Fast: Ready Reference." In *Crash Course in Reference.* Santa Barbara, CA: Libraries Unlimited. A review and listing of ready reference resources that can be added to a basic reference collection is provided in this chapter of a book that provides a broad overview of reference services.

Hogan, W. P. 2011. "Gale's Ready Reference Shelf." *CHOICE: Current Reviews for Academic Libraries* 48, no. 6 (February 28): 1046. The article discusses the pros and cons of using Gale's integrated ready reference resource that accesses fifteen of the most popular databases in one search. The more than 320,000 entries make for large results that need to be tamed to be of use. Those interested in this article might also want to check samples of actual searches that can be seen at the Gale site: http://www.gale.cengage .com/customer_service/sample_searches/grrs.htm.

Mudrock, Theresa. 2002. "Revising Ready Reference Sites: Listening to Users Through Server Statistics and Query Logs." *Reference and User Services Quarterly* 42, no. 2 (Winter): 155–163. This article is a strong reminder to reference librarians that ready reference sites must constantly evolve according to the needs of users. Usability heuristics, feedback, and usage statistics can be employed to structure the evolution. Mudrock provides a practical example as applied to the University of Washington Libraries at Seattle.

Singer, Carol, A. 2010. "Ready Reference Collections: A History." *Reference and User Services Quarterly* 49, no. 3 (Spring): 253–264. The author provides a comprehensive tour from the origins of ready reference in the nineteenth century to its current embrace of online sources. She holds that "[r]eady reference collections were originally formed, and still exist, because they perform a valuable function in providing convenient access to information that is frequently used at the reference desk."

Sowards, Steven, W. 2005. "Visibility as a Factor in Library Selection of Ready Reference Web Resources." *Reference Services Review* 33, no. 2: 161–172. By studying the ready reference websites of 100 libraries, Sowards deduces that reference librarians typically select sites that receive recognition soon after the site is launched. It is also educative to check the sites that are included in different kinds of libraries.

Bibliography and Works Cited

Ahlers, Deborah, and Heide Steiner. 2012. "The Approachable Reference Desk." *College and Research Libraries News* 73, no. 2 (February): 70–73.

Bejune, Matthew M., and Sara E. Morris. 2010. "The Development of the Virtual Notebook, A Wiki-Based Ready Reference Technology." *Reference and User Services Quarterly* 50, no. 1 (Fall): 27–34.

"Best Free Reference Web Sites: 13th Annual List." 2011. American Library Association. http://www.ala.org/.

Bosančić, Boris. 2010. "A Blueprint for Building Online Reference Knowledge Bases." *Reference and User Services Quarterly*, 50, no. 2 (Winter): 152–161.

Brunning, Dennis. 2012. "Credo Reference Interview with John Dove (President) and Carol Helton." *Charleston Advisor* 13, no. 3 (January): 58–60.

Brynko, Barbara. 2011. "Sweet: The Rise of Credo Reference." *Information Today* 28, no. 5 (May): 1. Available: http://www.infotoday.com/.

"FBI Almanac Alert Prompts Unintended Reactions." 2004. *American Libraries* (January 4). http://www.ala.org/ala/alonline/currentnews/newsarchive/alnews2004/alnews-jan2004/fbialmanacalert.cfm.

Fernandes, Maria Isabel. 2008. "Ready Reference: Thoughts on Trends." *Community and Junior College Libraries* 14, no. 3: 201–210.

Griffis, Debby, Wilhemina Cooper, and Stephen Headley. 2010. "Creating a Local Resources Index/Database." *Serials Librarian* 58, no. 1–4 (January–June): 215–218.

Guz, Savannah Schroll. 2011. "Best Databases: Best Overall: Credo Reference." *Reference 2012: Supplement to Library Journal* 136, no. 19 (November 15): 6.

Ojala, Marydee. 2001. "Don't Sweat the Small Stuff: Business Ready Reference Decoded." *Online* 25, no. 1 (January–February): 59–61.

Singer, Carol, A. 2010. "Ready Reference Collections: A History." *Reference and User Services Quarterly* 49, no. 3 (Spring): 253–264.

7

Answering Questions about Words— Dictionaries, Concordances, and Manuals

Overview

Humans may have started with a primordial grunt, but they sure have extended it. Fungible and pusillanimous; zephyr and logodaedalian; mook and zax; every nuance and twitch in human existence morphs into a word that aspires toward universal and timeless communication.

Dictionaries make a valiant attempt to list all the words in a language along with meanings, usage, pronunciation, grammatical provenance, and syllabication. Although there are many different types of dictionaries, they share one major characteristic: they provide definitions. Alexander Theroux, in fact, chose to refer to a dictionary as a "definitionary" (Saussy, 1989: xv).

In the past few years, the convenience and authority of definitions available through online dictionaries, apps, and those embedded in word processing software has led to a rapid increase in the proliferation of online sources and a noticeable sluggishness in the updating and publishing of traditional print dictionaries. New formats suggested by the emerging tools of Reference 2.0 are also coming into play so that collaborative, free-content dictionaries such as *Wiktionary* and *Wordia* are available options.

How Dictionaries Are Used

- A question requiring a definition should automatically prompt a reference librarian to consult a dictionary. The need for definitions ranges across many types of words—simple, archaic, slang, idiomatic, foreign, literary, and technical.
- In addition to simple meanings, the etymology and usage of a word can also be clarified by a quick dictionary search. Confusion over the spelling of words, even everyday ones that might "embarrass/embarass," is referred to a dictionary.
- Dictionaries act as invaluable pronunciation and syllabication guides as well. These are accomplished through phonetic symbols, supplemented with keys to the symbols used. Online and electronic versions provide audio pronunciations.
- The root history of words can be found in dictionaries so that users get to know etymologies such as "algebra" being the sum of the Arabic fractions "al" (the) and "jabara" (to reunite).

- Dictionaries list classes of words, so simpler grammatical quandaries can be directed to a dictionary. The principal forms of the word are also included.
- Even a general dictionary provides synonyms for many words. More in-depth needs can be met with a dictionary of synonyms.
- A visual or illustrated dictionary provides text as well as graphical representations to provide further clarity to a word.
- A dictionary of regionalisms provides specialized definitions of less universal usage. It can, for example, help the reference librarian direct a Maine user to the genealogy rather than the gardening section when asked about "seed folk."

Questions Answered by Dictionaries

Definitions

Q: I have been directed to "shelve my alb" in the second half of the play; is that integral to the Stanislavski school of method acting?

A: Er, no. An alb is merely a full-length white linen ecclesiastical vestment with long sleeves, according to the eleventh edition of *Merriam-Webster's Collegiate Dictionary*.

Orthography

Q: Is the wit of Wilde "mordint" or "mordent"?

A: Neither. To paraphrase Wilde, "to foul one spelling may be regarded as a misfortune; to foul two smacks of carelessness." Wilde's "mordant" wit can be checked in *The American Heritage Dictionary*.

Pronunciation

Q: When people say "nuclear" with a "nu-cu" sound, do I get a "me-graine" or a "my-graine"?

A: You may want to indulge in a "my-graine," according to *The New Oxford American Dictionary*.

Etymology

Q: Is "juggernaut" a bona fide English word?

A: According to the *Oxford English Dictionary*, "juggernaut" is the English incarnation of Jagannath, a bona fide Hindu god.

Grammar

Q: What is the transitive verb of "sequence"?

A: If you sequence transitive verbs after the root noun, as directed by *NTC's American English Learner's Dictionary*, you would transit to "sequenced."

Synonyms

Q: Is there a better word for "nice"?

A: There are 80 nicer synonyms for "nice" in *Roget's New Millennium Thesaurus*, available at http://thesaurus.reference.com/.

Visual Images

Q: What are the differences between a thumb knot, a reef knot, and a butterfly knot?

A: Textual explanations are bound to tie one up in knots. Refer instead to the *Ultimate Visual Dictionary*'s "Ropes and Knots" page for photographic representations.

Regionalisms

Q: I just moved to northern Illinois and my neighbors asked me to "scramble." Should I be insulted?

A: Accept your potluck invitation graciously, after checking the *Dictionary of American Regional English*.

Major Dictionaries Used in Reference Work

The use of dictionaries then, is ubiquitous, interesting, and widespread. Given such usage, the types of dictionaries that exist are many: general purpose, specialized, abridged, unabridged, rhyming, slang, polyglot, historical, illustrated, and etymological to name a few. Given such richness, the librarian has an important mandate to be aware of the choices, both online and in print, so that the reference collection has the right mix of dictionary selections to suit constituency needs.

General Dictionaries

"A definition is a snapshot of a word at rest" (McQuade, 2003: 1688). General dictionaries strive to provide that perfect snapshot. Depending on the number of "words at rest" that are captured in a publication, a general dictionary can be unabridged with over 265,000 entries; abridged with over 139,000 entries; or pocket-sized with anywhere from 30,000 to 55,000 entries (Reitz, 2004).

Unabridged Dictionaries

In unabridged dictionaries, depth and breadth of information is the prime directive rather than currency of words.

The twenty-volume *Oxford English Dictionary* (*OED*) took forty-four years to complete. With more than 590,000 entries that have multiple corollary word forms, extensive etymology, date of first recorded use of a word, and a "sense perspective" that includes the usage and status of the word, the *OED* with its "21,370 large pages of very small print" (Hoyle, 2008: 4) is the accepted authority of international English. While a second printing was published in 1989, a completely revised and updated version is continually in the works. The revisions and additions are being added to an accessible database rather than kept in storage for a printed third edition. Available both online and on CD-ROM, the *OED Online* is updated quarterly. The online version, available at http://www.oed.com/, is the most comprehensive version currently as it contains the second edition of the dictionary, a three-volume Additions Series, quarterly updates, a Historical Thesaurus, and all the drafts for the third edition. The site is intuitive and highly useful as a resource for questions on detailed usage and etymology of words. While all dictionaries provide definition, pronunciation, and basic etymology, the *OED Online* adds a timeline charting alphabetical or chronological word usage, variant spellings, and historical quotations as well. Publishers of the *OED* have stated that a third edition in the printed format appears to be "unlikely" but may not be ruled out entirely (Jamieson, 2010). The "Preface to the Third Edition" can be found online at the site.

Webster's Third New International Dictionary, Unabridged is the direct descendant of Noah Webster's 1828 opus, *An American Dictionary of the English Language*. The cumulative weight of historical expectation is evident in the 470,000 descriptive entries that fill out the book. While the current edition, produced after "700 editor-years of effort," dates to 1961, an addenda section has kept the dictionary somewhat updated to 2002. A CD-ROM version is available as well with 476,000 entries, color illustrations, and 13 search options. An online version is also available at https://member.m-w.com/subscribe.php for a monthly or annual fee.

The *Random House Webster's Unabridged Dictionary*, Second Edition, is available on CD-ROM as well as a 2,300-page hardcover book. Both versions have 315,000 entries of which 1,000 are new words updated to 2001. In the print version, the updates are not integrated into the main text, but provide relative currency to the dictionary. A 2006 release of the same edition combines the book and CD-ROM. It is the smallest of the three unabridged behemoths and the most affordable. The entries are short, focus clearly on American English, and provide a reliable source for American pronunciation. There is no online version of this dictionary.

Abridged Dictionaries

THE UNITED STATES

With over 90,000 words, more than 4,000 color graphics, and a longstanding commitment to providing detailed usage information, *The American Heritage Dictionary*, Fifth Edition, is a respected standard in abridged dictionaries. The print version of the fifth edition comes with a free app to access the dictionary on mobile devices, with basic definitions and pronunciation freely available at http://ahdictionary.com/. It is also a popular choice for embedded lookups in e-books so that a double-click (e.g., on any word in a Stephen King title available through Glassbook's open software) provides a definition from *The American Heritage Dictionary*. The CD-ROM version has certain value-added features such as the ability to enlarge all thumbnail illustrations; supply audio pronunciation to words; and provide optional search limiters including the ability to block "vulgar" words. Contemporary words such as "tweet" and "crowdsourcing" and "crunk" are included in the latest version.

Clarity, simplicity, and speed of access seem to be the motivation behind the relatively recent *New Oxford American Dictionary* (*NOAD*), Third Edition. With 350,000 words, over 100,000 example sentences, and the publishing weight of the Oxford University Press to back it, the *NOAD* is establishing itself as a dictionary that goes to the heart of a definition. Rather than listing all the senses of a word in sequence, the "core" or most literal definition of a word is provided, along with related or less literal submeanings, all of which are derived from the 2-billion-word *Oxford English Corpus*. The pronunciation guide is harder to navigate, since a guide is provided at the start of the book, rather than applied to each word.

Merriam-Webster's Collegiate Dictionary, Eleventh Edition, has more than 100 years of authority undergirding the current edition. With 225,000 entries in the eleventh edition, supported by 42,000 usage examples, it continues to be "runner-up to the Bible" as the "second best-selling English hardcover book in history" (McQuade, 2003: 1688). The new edition openly touts a belief in the "convergence" of formats to provide multiaccessibility, so that print, online, and CD-ROM versions are all provided as a single package. The online version is independently available at http://www.m-w.com/ and on AOL, with a huge clutch of value-added features such as a thesaurus, word stories, word of the day, kids' dictionary, and a message board to exchange word trivia. Some sections, such as "Signs and Symbols" available in print, are not included online. In its latest avatar, an enhanced version of the dictionary is now available for iPhones.

THE UNITED KINGDOM

Winston Churchill's droll observation that "England and America are two countries divided by a common language" is most evident in the distinctive collection of abridged dictionaries published in the United Kingdom. Unlike the venerable *OED*, which maintains a commanding global profile despite its British roots, the abridged dictionaries published in the United Kingdom are uniquely and unabashedly British.

"It's nice, rich, handy, modern. Obtain it!" is a charming anagram of the inimitable *Chambers Dictionary*, Ninth Edition (http://www.anagramgenius.com/archive/chambe.html), which continues to be floated even though the dictionary published its twelfth edition. Over 100 years old, the *Chambers* continues to pepper the collection with fey definitions such as "channel surf—switching rapidly between different television channels in a forlorn attempt to find anything of interest." These, of course, are not the norm, and the 620,000 definitions making up the 2011 edition have clear definitions and include terms from dialects and historical forms. It is available as an app at http://www.chambers.co.uk/.

The *Bloomsbury Concise English Dictionary*, by contrast, is the British edition of *Encarta Webster's Dictionary of the English Language*. It eschews the British tradition of using the IPA (International Phonetic Alphabet) and has its own phonetic system. It is also distinguished by user-friendly additions such as cross-references to almost 1,000 of the most common misspelled words and labeling of words considered obscene.

The *Oxford Dictionary of English* 2010 has a total of 355,000 terms that have been updated based on the massive *Oxford English Corpus* database. Since its first edition in 1998, popular usage words such as "muggle," "data smog," and "vuvuzella [the sound of the 2010 World Cup]" have been included. In the Oxford tradition, words have also been supplemented with brief etymologies.

The *Collins English Dictionary* is the most populist British dictionary in that its latest edition has, for better or worse, included highly "young" words—slang, dialect, and chat-group abbreviations that complement the collation of words derived from the 4.5-billion-word *Collins Corpus*. Uniquely British terms like "stealth tax" (indirect tax) and "alarm clock Briton" (moderate income worker with school-going children); new words like "Arab Spring" and "mumpreneur";

abbreviations like SOHF (sense of human failure); and dialect such as "thraiping" (thrashing) distinguish the *Collins*, just as much as the pointed beheading of monarchical terms distinguishes it within British circles. As an outraged citizen pointed out, "Tudor" has simply been defined as a style of architecture in the *Collins*. It also provides usage hints, so that the definition of a common word such as "actual" is followed by the hint that excessive use of the word in a sentence should and can be avoided, as it is "actually" unnecessary. Logodaedalians (wordsmiths) in the United Kingdom are up in arms as the current editors propose to shave away archaic words to make place for 2,000 new entries (Adams, 2008). The dictionary is available online at http://www.collinslanguage.com/ and as an app through iTunes.

CANADA

Recognizing the subtle and not-so-subtle differences in English pronunciation, usage, and spelling fostered by different cultures in different countries, the Oxford University Press has created a uniquely *Canadian Oxford Dictionary*. Compiled by Canadians, examining Canadian sources and perspectives, the 2004 edition has 130,000 terms and various appendices. Words such as "scraper," for example, include the Canadian usage of removing not only ice, but mud and paint as well. Canadian acronyms like "BQ" for Bloc Québécois, expressions like "jam buster," and spellings like "traveller" and "humour" make this a strong Canadian dictionary resource. Given "changing market conditions," the Canadian dictionary division of the publishers, Oxford University Press, was disbanded in 2008 so that the work of updating the dictionary has been outsourced to freelance lexicographers ("Oxford Closes Canadian Dictionary Division," 2008). An online version can be found embedded in the Premier Edition at http://www.oxfordreference.com/. The *Nelson Canadian Dictionary of the English Language* (until recently known as the *ITP Nelson*) has over 150,000 terms. It includes extensive Canadian biographies, history, government, and folklore and uses Canadian spelling. However, the source has not been updated since 1997. In a country where a governmental ruling stated a preference for the "-our" spelling to the "-or," Gage Publications, while slow in adopting the usage, has currently updated the familiar *Gage Canadian Dictionary*. Distinctive Canadian words like "snowbird—a Canadian who goes south for the winter" also make the *Gage* a useful Canadian resource. It is marketed as a dictionary "written by Canadians for Canadians." An updated usage guide with "First Names and First People language" can be found in the reissued *Guide to Canadian English Usage* (Fee and McAlpine, 2011). An informative online presence focusing on Canadian spelling is *Dave VE7CNV's Truly Canadian Dictionary of Canadian Spelling* (http://www.luther.ca/~dave7cnv/cdnspelling/cdnspelling.html).

Specialized Word Sources

Learners' Dictionaries

English, as spoken in McDonald's rather than by the Queen, is becoming the dominant lingua franca of the world; as a result there appears to be a rising market for dictionaries for learners. How is this different from a regular or even an abridged dictionary? For one thing, "less is more" (Dahlin, 1999), and the prime directives are not comprehensiveness and depth of meaning, but simplicity, ease of use, and frequency of words in daily American communication. This is largely calculated from computational analyses of electronic word corpora that cover popular media reports. So, for example, a learner's dictionary is far more likely to include an MTV word like "dude" than an obscure one like "ophiophagus" (serpent eating). All the major publishers of dictionaries such as NTC, Cambridge, Merriam-Webster, Random House, and Macmillan have published recent editions of learner's dictionaries.

The *Macmillan English Dictionary*, for example, bases its dictionary on the enlightening fact that 90 percent of all text consists of only 7,500 words. These are the words that are highlighted along with 80,000 examples of usage. For easy online access, the dictionary can also be freely added as a searchable site in browser toolbars (http://www.macmillandictionary.com/). *NTC's American English Learner's Dictionary* selects 22,000 basic words that are defined and used in context, but eschew other traditional dictionary additions like etymology and synonyms of a word. *The American Heritage Dictionary for Learners of English* has over 40,000 words, with attention paid to the more confusing aspects of English such as homonyms, idioms, and synonyms. A reference section with basic grammar and American factoids is included. An electronic version is also available (http://www.houghtonmifflinbooks.com/epub/learners.shtml). With nearly 100,000 words and phrases and more than 160,000 usage examples, the 2008 publication of *Merriam-Webster's Advanced Learner's English Dictionary* is aimed at an international market in which proficiency in the use of English, and American English in particular, is being attempted by an estimated 1 billion nonnative speakers around the world. It includes a free e-book version as well as a website available at http://www.learnersdictionary.com/.

Visual Dictionaries

In a visual dictionary, the words presented are not alphabetical, but grouped under subjects. The focus is on providing a pictorial of the word. Since terms are illustrated, selection is limited to the noun family. *The Firefly Visual Dictionary* (Corbeil and Archambault, 2002) has 35,000 terms organized into 17 chapters. Insects, geology, sports, and architecture all find pictographic representation in full color. DK, known for its splendid graphics, publishes the *Ultimate Visual Dictionary* (2011) with fancier artwork, incorporating cutaways and exploded views that display internal structures. It is also available as an e-book. *The Firefly Five Language Visual Dictionary* (Corbeil and Archambault, 2009) covers 35,000 words in English, Spanish, French, German, and Italian, illustrated with over 6,000 color images. The role of the visual dictionary comes into sharp focus when, for example, a muskrat and a mole are both described as blunt-nosed and short-eared, but the homeowner needs to identify which one is destroying his summer garden. Visual dictionaries are also handy for those perennial school assignments that require labeling parts of the anatomy or the layers of the earth or the structure of an insect. A free visual dictionary can be found online at http://visual.merriam-webster.com/. Over 6,000 images organized with fewer than fifteen broad subject headings are included. The site may be easily searched with a keyword that conveniently generates read-alike results.

"Gated" Word Dictionaries

The user in search of words "gated" to a particular community, class, age group, region, or profession is best directed to dictionaries of slang, jargon, argot, regionalisms, or idioms. Dictionaries of slang usually collate colloquialisms recurring within groups. Slang, by definition, is particularly vulnerable to passing fads so that what was "groovy" earlier and "sweet" today will, in all probability, be entirely different a few years from now. Publications such as the award-winning, multivolume *Green's Dictionary of Slang* (Green, 2011) defines 10.3 million slang words collated from all the different English-speaking countries. *Stone the Crows: Oxford Dictionary of Modern Slang* (Ayto and Simpson, 2008) includes over 6,000 words and phrases in the second edition of this compilation of slang derived from the *OED* database. The multivolume *Historical Dictionary of American Slang* has more than 300,000 slang words that date back to Colonial America, more of which will be added once the final volumes are published. *A History of Cant and Slang Dictionaries* (Coleman, 2004–2010) is a four-volume opus that studies the recording of slang from 1567 through modern times. For current slang, online options are a wise choice. Everything from hip-hop, to London, to street drugs and sex slang is available. For slang being used in the United Kingdom, a handy directory can be accessed through http://www.peevish.co.uk/slang. Particularly useful for virtual reference that caters to a high percentage of young adult users is *Urban Dictionary* at http://www.urbandictionary.com/, which is also available as a widget for keeping up with the most recent updates at http://www.apple.com/. With both "exact" and "inexact" search options, the site provides meanings for urban slang as well as chat argot like g2g (got to go) and emoticons like :) which is a happy face, but not as happy as :O.

The preeminent dictionary for American regionalisms is the multivolume, exhaustive, and ambitious *Dictionary of American Regional English* (*DARE*). Launched in 1960, the final volume was completed only in 2012. It alphabetically documents regional words unlikely to be found in standard dictionaries. The meaning of a word, spelling, pronunciation, area of usage, and actual recorded use is provided along with some maps that display the geographical distribution of the word. *DARE* is both a dictionary of unfamiliar terms like "Irish confetti" (bricks and stones used while fighting), as well as an engrossing historical record of American culture, with an explanatory website available at http://dare.wisc.edu/.

AAD

AAD? The need for Acronyms and Abbreviations Dictionaries in every reference library has never been felt more keenly. A string of letters that abbreviate a word (Mr.), initial a term (www), or synopsize a proper noun (UN) is a growing trend in human communication. Electronic communication, with its natural affinity for short forms, has added to the global legitimacy and relevance of truncations.

The most distinguished source for decoding these truncations is the Gale Group's multivolume *Acronyms, Initialisms, and Abbreviations Dictionary*. Arranged alphabetically in the contracted form as well as a reverse expanded version, users can consult the dictionary both to decode an acronym and to discover the accepted truncation for a given term. In the newest edition, terms were added primarily from areas dealing with the Internet, education, medicine, and associations. Contractions for bus and railroad stations, navigation systems, and stock exchange symbols were also included.

Available since the 1950s, a single-volume source can be found in the 267,000 entries of the *Abbreviations Dictionary* (Stahl and Kerchelich, 2001). The entries not only include abbreviations, initialisms, and acronyms, but symbols such as emoticons, signs such as $ (listed under "D"), and eponyms or "designations derived from names" such as "Legionnaire's disease." The entries are in alphabetical order, with signs listed under the first letter of the term it signifies. A person who does not know what "μ" stands for will therefore find it hard to locate it under "m," but is aided by the different subject areas that are also listed. The volume includes abbreviations for U.S. states, Canadian provinces, territories, and capitals, and both British and Irish counties.

Acronym Finder (http://www.acronymfinder.com/) is an extensive online dictionary with over five million entries. Search strategies allow for both exact searches and inexact ones that can use wildcard truncations, "begins with," and reverse lookups. Parented by the well-regarded STANDS4 LLC, a free online reference provider, *Abbreviations* (http://www.abbreviations.com/) is a large and comprehensive directory and search engine for acronyms, abbreviations, and initialisms on the Internet. For the reference librarian who refers a user to any of these word sources, it is critical to establish the context usage of a contracted term. Acronyms invariably stand for multiple terms, so that "AA," for example, could stand for Alcoholics Anonymous as well as American Airlines or Aerolineas Argentinas. It may even represent a bond rating, a bra size, or the width of a shoe.

Rhyming Dictionaries

Rhyming dictionaries were created to help poets, song makers, and verse creators. They list phonetic endings in alphabetical form so that if users need words to rhyme with "blue," they would look up the phonetic suffix of "oo." *Words to Rhyme With* (Espy, 2006) has a separate section on "eccentric" words that are difficult to partner with a rhyme, such as "aardvark." *Random House Webster's Rhyming Dictionary* (2008) is an expanded version of the earlier pocket edition and includes 60,000 words with cross-references and a glossary of poetic terms. The *Oxford Rhyming Dictionary* (Upton and Upton, 2004) has over 85,000 words in 40 sound groups, but uses British pronunciation. Derived from Carnegie Mellon University's "Pronouncing Dictionary," a machine-readable collection of over 125,000 words, *RhymeZone*, an online rhyming source available at http://www.rhymezone.com/, has been freely available for over ten years and organizes rhymes by syllable or letter sound.

Metadictionaries

The online medium seamlessly lends itself to consolidating diverse resources while scavenging for individual requests. Why restrict oneself to a single dictionary resource when a simple click can trawl through so many more? This is the motivation behind the metadictionary.

For example, *OneLook* (http://www.onelook.com/) is host to 19,398,235 words (as of July 7, 2012) culled from 1,062 dictionaries that includes everything from the well-known *Compact OED* and *Merriam-Webster's Online Dictionary*, Eleventh Edition, to lesser-known sources such as *Luciferous Logolepsy* and *The Phrontistery*. The dictionary also provides for a reverse feature that allows users to describe a concept in order to find a word.

Another popular metadictionary, *Dictionary.com* (http://dictionary.reference.com/), is free and user friendly. A simple search box at the top of the page in which the word or an approximation of the word can be typed is all that is presented. Over 900 online sources such as *The American Heritage Dictionary* and *The World Factbook* provide an answer with the source for each entry listed below the answer. It is also available as a free app at http://itunes.apple.com/. Metadictionaries, then, act as hosts rather than producers of dictionaries. The spottiness of sources that contribute to an answer makes them a less than fully reliable reference resource, but certainly constitutes a handy site to add to the "Favorites" of a busy reference desk.

Special Constituency Dictionaries

Children's Dictionaries

The reference world of word sources for children focuses on all-purpose dictionaries. The market for children's dictionaries is geared toward three types of institutions: the school library, the public library, and the family library. For the family, hundreds of desk-sized print dictionaries are available with 12,000 to 15,000 words and a grab bag of bonus information aimed at the student. *A Student's Dictionary*, for example, adds on political factoids about the United States, weights and measures, and global trivia such as the seven continents and the eight planets. These publications are handy but not geared for purchase by reference collections. The definitions are spare, the binding fragile, and the entry is usually without synonyms or etymology or context usage. Reliable publishers of children's dictionaries for reference collections are Macmillan, American Heritage, World Book, and Merriam-Webster's.

It is a pleasure to use the *Macmillan Dictionary for Children*. The physical construction includes sturdy binding, large fonts, colorful guidewords, and over 3,000 captioned color illustrations and photographs. The 35,000 entries have clear definitions, parts of speech, abbreviations, synonyms, etymology, pronunciation, and context usage.

The educational psychologist Edward Lee Thorndike and the lexicographer Charles Lewis Barnhart aimed at producing dictionaries that were not "dumbed-down" versions of an adult dictionary. Thorndike-Barnhart has expanded its publications to a cluster of children's dictionaries, the *Thorndike Barnhart Children's Dictionary, Junior Dictionary, Intermediate Dictionary*, and *Student Dictionary*.

The *World Book Dictionary*, also derived from Thorndike-Barnhart files, has been published in print since 1963 and the online version (http://www.worldbook

.com/all/item/1382-dictionary-package-2012) is continually updated. The most recent print edition (2005) has more than 225,000 entries and 3,000 illustrations, while the online version has 248,000 entries, making it one of the largest dictionaries accessible to children.

The *DK Merriam-Webster Children's Dictionary*, with 35,000 entries and 3,000 visually arresting photographs and illustrations, is a reliable and delightful resource for ages eight to the lower teens.

Details about dictionaries for children may be found in Chapter 15.

Bilingual Dictionaries

With porous national boundaries and an increasingly intimate world, the relevance of bilingual dictionaries appears heightened. The large "foreign language" tomes that traditionally graced academic libraries have multiplied into a dizzying variety of unabridged, dual, pocket-sized, and desk dictionaries suitable for academic, public, corporate, and personal libraries. The *LEO dictionary*, a mobile app, covers definitions for seven languages and includes conjugation tables and audio files as well (http://www.apple.com/webapps/searchtools/leodictionary_leogmbh.html).

Cassell, NTC, Oxford, HarperCollins, and Random House are familiar names of brands and publishers that offer a range of bilingual dictionaries. While classic and European languages dominated the industry a century ago, today's landscape offers an extravagant choice of languages. Bilingual dictionaries are conveniently arranged so that the word can be looked up both by its English translation and in the original language.

The Cassell series has had more than 120 years of experience in publishing. *Cassell's Latin Dictionary*, first published in 1854, continues to be a classic addition for the serious researcher. *Cassell's Italian Dictionary* is typical of the later publications that are geared for both the beginner and the advanced speaker. Given that the many dialects of Italian would require multiple synonyms, the dictionary has "translate[d] rather than define[d]" words. In the Italian-English section, pronunciation is eschewed given the phonetic nature of Italian spelling, but included in the English-Italian section.

The Oxford University Press publishes a variety of world language dictionary series. The *Oxford Starter* series, the *Oxford-Duden Pictorial* dictionaries, the *Oxford-Hachette* and *Oxford-Paravia* dictionaries, and the *Compact, Pocket, Concise, Basic* series are all geared at varying levels of readership. Over forty different languages are published with most current projects in the area of pocket and desk editions. A complete list of editions more suited for library reference collections can be accessed at http://www.askoxford.com/.

McGraw-Hill's *Vox/NTC* series has also established itself as an aggressive publisher of world language sources, especially known for its Spanish language series. *Larousse* is the traditional choice for French dictionaries. In the area of world language dictionaries, sometimes even the smallest of publishers become urgent sources of reference acquisition. For example, after the conflict in Kosovo and the sudden influx of Albanians into the United States in the late 1990s, the frantic scramble for stocking libraries and other places with Albanian dictionaries heightened the role of Hippocrene, a small New York press that was able to offer the only *Albanian-English/English-Albanian Practical Dictionary* in print.

Given the nexus between politics and the demand for world language dictionaries, the reference librarian is well advised to acquire the major language dictionaries, as well as keep alert to changing local demographics or global events that can create a sudden demand for lesser-known language groups.

Subject Dictionaries

A burgeoning use of the word "dictionary" is in the area of subject dictionaries. These dictionaries also define words, but triangulate over an isolated subject area and focus with laser-sharp intensity on any and every word connected with that area. Be it medical, legal, business, scientific, technical, computer, mathematical, electronic, religion, or gardening, every subject appears to be inspiring its own dictionary.

Although it is entirely probable that a word presented in a subject dictionary could also be found in an unabridged dictionary, subject dictionaries tend to do the following:

- Provide more depth in definition. Some definitions are quasi-encyclopedic in coverage. For example, in *The Harvard Dictionary of Music*, the definition of "electroacoustic music" runs over a page.
- Be informed by subject specialists and rate high on reliability. *Black's Law Dictionary*, *Stedman's Medical Dictionary*, or *Dorland's Illustrated Medical Dictionary* are authoritative additions to most reference collections. An online version of *Dorland's* is also available for a fee at http://www.dorlands.com/.
- Complete gaps in coverage for relatively smaller fields such as librarianship. *ODLIS*, or the *Online Dictionary for Library and Information Science*, is an exhaustive glossary of well-designed and thoughtfully crafted library terminology. *FOLDOC*, or the *Free On-Line Dictionary of Computing*, supported by the United Kingdom's Imperial College in London, effectively provides over 14,000 definitions in the computing field. *Webopedia* also serves that purpose with daily updates in the world of computer and Internet technology.
- Provide quicker access to updated words. The most dramatic example can be found in the aftermath of the digital revolution, when even pocket-sized computer dictionaries were acquired by reference libraries in an effort to keep up with the torrent of new vocabulary flooding everyday global communication. In 1998, no general dictionary listed terms like "hypertext markup language," and a "mouse" was still just a rodent. The need for a subject dictionary on computer terms was dramatically demonstrated.

In most cases, however, the need is undramatic, and subject dictionaries like *The Dictionary of Aquarium Terms* are acquired only when appropriate to the aims of the institution and the needs of its constituency.

Dictionaries for the Visually and Hearing Impaired

Two major special constituencies for whom authoritative dictionaries are available are the visually impaired and the hearing impaired. While usage of special constituency dictionaries is sporadic, an absence of these dictionaries when needed can be felt very acutely. The need can appear in academic, public, corporate, specialized, and school libraries. Large-print dictionaries typically tend to have shorter definitions, but wider margins and large, clear font sizes. The *Oxford Large Print Dictionary* was first published in 1989 and is derived from the same database as *The New Oxford American Dictionary*. Definitions are clear and supplemented with usage contexts, notes on confusing or variant spellings, and updated biographical and geographical entries. Abbreviations are used sparingly. The Royal National Institute for the Blind provided input on the physical design of the book, so that page quality allows for clarity in type, a maximum of white space is brought about by generous margins and line spacing, and accessible font size.

Webster's New Explorer Large Print Dictionary defines more than 40,000 words with pronunciation. A special section on abbreviations is also included. Approved by the National Association for Visually Handicapped, the guide-words are in eighteen-point font with the entries in fourteen-point font. *Random House Webster's Large Print Dictionary*, published in both the United Kingdom and the United States, is another resource that has received a Seal of Approval from the National Association. The latest edition includes a "New Words" section as well.

Sign language dictionaries are often confused with sign language manuals. Although much overlap occurs between the two, the dictionaries typically provide pronunciation guides, cross-references, and usage context in addition to sign entries with illustrations. *The American Sign Language Dictionary Unabridged* (Sternberg, 1998) has more than 7,000 sign entries accompanied by 12,000 illustrations that are arranged alphabetically. It has been updated to include new signs since it was first published in 1981.

The American Sign Language Handshape Dictionary published by the Gallaudet University Press does not, on the other hand, follow alphabetical order but is organized by a unique system of forty basic "handshapes." The more than 1,600 signs defined in the dictionary derive from these basic handshapes. Illustrations complement the entries and context usage is also provided. An alphabetical Index of English Glossaries at the end of the dictionary provides an alternative way of looking up the right word and sign. More recently, *The Gallaudet Dictionary of American Sign Language* was released with more than 3,000 illustrations and an attached DVD that demonstrates each of the 3,077 signs.

Speaking dictionaries available for handheld devices with handy expansion cards that can be added are also available for this constituency. The *Merriam-Webster Speaking Dictionary and Thesaurus* is an electronic device available at http://www.franklin.com/ that offers *Merriam-Webster's Collegiate Dictionary*, Eleventh Edition, while a Merriam-Webster web application for iPhones and iPods also provides the dictionary and thesaurus in audio format. Free online dictionaries such as the meta-dictionary site available at http://www.dictionary .reference .com/ have partial audio formatting since only some of the dictionaries included, such as *The American Heritage Dictionary*, provide audio pronunciation icons for listening to a word.

Thesauri

Thesauri play a different role from dictionaries. Whereas dictionaries are primarily responsible for defining a word, a thesaurus helps the wordsmith to find the right word. Each word is partnered with strings of synonyms and antonyms. This provides users with both variety and the tools to choose the right shading in meaning. As observed by Mark Twain, "The difference between the almost right word and the right word is really a large matter—it's the difference between the lightning bug and lightning." Thesauri, arranged either alphabetically or by categories, help strike the right word.

Introduced over 150 years ago by Dr. Peter Roget, the term thesaurus is usually synonymous with Roget and hence used by a number of publishers. *Roget's International Thesaurus* is a strong resource. The most recent edition has 330,000 words and phrases organized into more than 1,000 categories arranged according to meanings. The *Oxford American Writer's Thesaurus* is innovative in that it has introduced short articles attached to certain word usages, provides writing tips with a language guide, and features words along with their opposites. It has 25,000 words, supported by 300,000 synonyms and 10,000 antonyms. An online resource is http://www.thesaurus.com/ based on *Roget's New Millennium Thesaurus* and produced by the creators of http://www.dictionary.com/. *Visuwords* is an innovative online graphical dictionary cum thesaurus that projects visual associations of words in the form of a neural network. The free site uses Princeton University's open source database, *Word Net*, to generate both the definition of a word and the many ways in which it connects to other words, associative concepts, and synonyms.

Quotations

Dictionaries often provide quotations to establish the usage of a word. Quotation books exploit that need and provide thousands of memorable quotes that highlight words and concepts. The arrangement of quotation books varies.

The seventeenth edition of the venerable *Bartlett's Familiar Quotations*, for example, is laid chronologically, though supported by an in-depth index of keywords and authors. It contains 25,000 quotations, most of which continue from John Bartlett's original picks of 1855, updated with new quotes from modern personalities like Bill Clinton, Mother Theresa, and Jerry Seinfeld. Bartlett's quotes as listed in the tenth edition can be freely accessed at http://www.bartleby.com/100. It is searchable by keyword as well as through a chronological or alphabetic index of authors and a concordance index and is available as an e-book.

The *Random House Webster's Quotationary* (Frank, 2001), on the other hand, has 20,000 quotations arranged by subject. Chronology plays no part in the arrangement, though cross-references by author are provided. The third editions of the *Oxford Dictionary of Modern Quotations* and the *Oxford Dictionary of Phrase Sayings and Quotations* are both published by the Oxford University Press, with the former arranged chronologically and the latter by subject. *The Yale Book of Quotations*, while considerably smaller with its 12,000 notable quotes, is meticulously researched for original source, emphasizes American material, and is consciously modern and eclectic in its choice of quotes that range from political slogans and television catchwords to children's authors such as Dr. Seuss.

The role of quotation books in providing dramatic or elegant expression to a certain word or concept is straightforward. A few comprehensive quotation books should suffice for that role. Most reference collections, however, tend to stock a variety of books because of the possibility that a user needs to know a specific quote, in which case the chances of finding it increase by varying the range to cover general, humorous, biblical, political, gender focus, and other specialized quote sources.

Concordances

A variation of the quotation book, concordances are an alphabetical enumeration of major words in a book or a collection of books by an author, along with the immediate context of the word. Essential additions to any reference collection are concordances on Shakespeare and the *Bible*.

Much as Roget's, Bartlett's, and Webster's are public domain and used by multiple publishers to sell thesauri, quotation books, and dictionaries, *Strong's Exhaustive Concordance of the Bible*, derivative of nineteenth-century theologian James Strong, is connected with biblical concordances. *Strong's* is a reliable concordance of the *King James Bible*. Concise dictionaries of words in the Hebrew Old Testament and the Greek New Testament are given in addition to the Authorized and Revised English Versions. The prefaced goals of "completeness, simplicity, and accuracy" are evident while using this concordance. *The Unbound Bible*, offered by the Biola University in California, is a free online concordance available at http://unbound.biola.edu/.

The nine-volume compilation *A Complete and Systematic Concordance to the Works of Shakespeare* and its single-volume version, the *Harvard Concordance to Shakespeare*, are both respected choices. The *Harvard* edition focuses on Volumes 4–6 of the nine-volume edition, covering the plays and poems of Shakespeare. The specific play, act, scene, line number, and line row in which the word appears is provided using the modern spelling laid out in *The Riverside Shakespeare*. The *Complete* version has elaborate concordances for characters and individual plays, as well as statistics, stage directions, and so on. James Farrow at the University of Sydney Information Technologies website at http://www.it.usyd.edu.au/~matty/Shakespeare/test.html has developed a well-reviewed online Shakespearean concordance.

Style and Usage of Words

Much as the perfect frame enhances a picture, words can come alive with the right grammar and punctuation. The bullet-spraying panda that eats, shoots, and leaves because of an extra comma struck a punctuation chord in both the United Kingdom and the United States (Truss, 2004). Usage styles have become more elaborate with the explosion of formats, both print and electronic, that need to be cited. The printed book, pamphlet, thesis, or article is compounded by the nonprint CD-ROM, video, CD, or cassette; the oral interview, quote, broadcast, discussion, personal communication; and flourishing websites, databases, electronic discussion lists, chat groups, and so forth. All require citations. Reference librarians must be prepared for two types of questions in the field:

- Grammar and punctuation
- Style and citation guidance

The Chicago Manual of Style is the top choice for the user interested in publication. Originating in the 1890s as a single proofreader's sheet, the sixteenth edition continues to be a crucial tool for countless writers and editors. Preparing a manuscript by dotting the right i's and crossing the right t's, conforming with editorial styles, checking on grammar pitfalls, outlining copyright restrictions, guiding one through the maze of citation differences, providing mathematical copy templates, and designing, producing, and marketing a printed or electronic publication, are all covered in *The Chicago Manual*. It is the source to consult when publication is the goal of the user. There is a CD-ROM version, and an online version available at http://www.chicagomanualofstyle.org/home.html includes sample forms and letter styles.

For the undergraduate and high school student, the Modern Language Association's *MLA Handbook for Writers of Research Papers* is the primary source. Traditionally listed as the bibliographic guide for students, the *MLA* is strong on citation guidance. The *MLA Style Manual and Guide to Scholarly Publishing* (2008) is the standard guide for professional writing. Every reference collection needs to stock the *MLA* simply because users will specifically ask for it by title. The latest edition includes simplified citation formats for electronic sources and helpful guidelines for creating electronic files.

For the professional, specifically the social scientist, the APA's *Publication Manual of the American Psychological Association* (2009) is the most suitable resource. The print manual is aimed at the writing of reports, presentations, and papers. Guides on presenting statistical data, graphics, and metrication are provided in addition to grammar and citation styles. Notes on avoiding plagiarism are also included. Its "frequently asked questions," such as how to cite Facebook or Twitter, are freely available online at http://www.apastyle.org/learn/faqs/index.aspx.

Technological breakthroughs in style management software are resulting in a new generation of management software that can manipulate citations into more than 600 styles including the previously mentioned *APA*, *MLA*, and *Chicago* styles. Products such as Reference Manager, EndNote, RefWorks, 2collab, BibSonomy, and ProCite have the capability to "search Internet databases, organize references, and format bibliographies" (Poehlmann, 2005). Academic libraries have been the first to offer bibliographic management software to students and faculty, such as the free subscription to RefWorks provided to all affiliates of the Johns Hopkins University, EndNote, which is provided to students of Cornell University, and RefWorks and EndNote, which are provided to the community affiliated with the University of Kansas at Lawrence.

Given the different departments in academic institutions, a collection of subject-specific style manuals must also be part of the reference collection. The field of political science, for example, requires the *Style Manual for Political Science*; chemistry would refer to *The ACS Style Guide*; government documents follow *The Complete Guide to Citing Government Information Resources* (Cheney, 2002); journalism favors the *Associated Press Stylebook*; the *AMA Manual of Style* from the American Medical Association guides the medical field; and mathematics is supported by the *Handbook of Writing for the Mathematical Sciences* (Higham, 1998). An all-purpose reference resource that covers basic style guides for multiple professions ranging from chemistry to anthropology and modern language is the second edition of *Cite Right* (Lipson, 2011). Manuals like *The Yahoo! Style Guide* (Barr, 2010) are entirely devoted to the creation and editing of digital content. The list is long and style manual acquisition, as always, would have to draw from a clear consideration of local demand.

For those who are stuck wondering whether to use "that" or "which," split an infinitive, or dangle a participle, the inimitable *Fowler's Modern English Usage* (Burchfield, 2004) has been consulted for more than seven decades. The most recent edition published has departed in controversial ways from the original. It has updated the pronunciation guidelines to cohere with the IPA; provided samples of English usage that are global rather than purely British; and updated "vogue words" and modern usage contexts. For those who are not amused by Burchfield's revised edition, the 1908 version, *The King's English*, has been reprinted in hard copy as *A Dictionary of Modern English Usage: The Classic First Edition* with new contextualizing notes; it may be found online at http://www.bartleby.com/116/.

An admittedly descriptive, rather than prescriptive, usage book has been published in the United Kingdom by Cambridge University Press. *The Cambridge Guide to English Usage* is aimed at the "global and local communicators" of the twenty-first century. Two electronic databases, the *British National Corpus* and the *Cambridge International Corpus*, as well as hundreds of questionnaires, were used to establish patterns that are presented in more than 4,000 alphabetical points of English usage and style.

Collection Development and Maintenance

Selection and Keeping Current

Keeping abreast of developments and updates of dictionaries is accomplished in a number of ways.

- Reading professional reviews
  - *Reference Books Bulletin*, though sectioned into *Booklist*, has its own editorial board and reviews all dictionaries, not just those recommended for purchase.
  - An annual *Supplement to the Library Journal* published in November each year lists recent and forthcoming reference titles with a separate subject listing for dictionaries.

- ○ Updates of prominent dictionaries are reviewed in multiple professional publications such as *Publishers Weekly, Booklist, Library Journal, Choice,* and *School Library Journal.*
- ○ *College and Research Libraries* publishes a semiannual selection of recent reference books that includes reviews of general reference works such as dictionaries.
- ○ Reviews of online and CD-ROM dictionaries are frequently found in *Database.*
- Referring to regularly updated reference works is another way to keep informed. The ALA's *Guide to Reference Books* and *ARBA* are authoritative sources of information.
- A subject-specific monograph such as the 1998 *Guide to World Language Dictionaries* by British librarian Andrew Dalby covers dictionaries for 275 languages in alphabetical order. *Kister's Best Dictionaries for Adults and Young People* reviews 300 English-language dictionaries along with comparative assessments and charts. While dated, it is still a valid resource for insights into the structure of gauging dictionaries and getting a sense of the breadth of material available.
- For an in-depth look at dictionary sources, subscribing to the Dictionary Society of North America is a fertile possibility. Available at http://polyglot.lss .wisc.edu/dsna/, the society is probably the most well-known professional organization of lexicographers. The newsletters and annual journal provide steady insight into the inner dialogues preceding the updating or launching of a dictionary. For a European perspective, membership in EURALEX is possible at http://www.euralex.org/.
- Individual dictionary updates are also possible. The *Oxford English Dictionary,* for example, provides a quarterly newsletter, the *OED News,* which reports research projects and new development initiatives planned for the dictionary. Regular reports on *OED* revisions and new features are guaranteed by signing up for an e-mail listing at http://www.oed.com/news/email.html.

Evaluating Word Sources

Authority and understandability are the prime criteria for evaluating a word source. If the definition of a word is presented in abstract or misleading ways, all other criteria become moot. Since constant and widespread usage of words decides on whether a word enters or is dropped from a dictionary, authority is as important as accuracy. In fact, there are times when the accuracy of a definition is decided by the authority of the lexicographer or lexical institution. For example, is "nigger" a noun or a racial slur, or both? The authority of Merriam-Webster and the Oxford University Press as responsible lexical giants has upheld the secondary definition of a noun despite charges of inaccuracy from the NAACP (National Association for the Advancement of Colored People). Similarly, the second sense of the term "anti-Semitism" as "opposition to Zionism" as defined in *Merriam-Webster's Third New International Dictionary* was criticized by the American Arab Anti-Discrimination Committee but has yet to be revised.

Other criteria for evaluating word sources are currency, cost, format, scope, comprehensiveness, and, of rapidly increasing importance, value-added features. Given the ubiquity of spell-checking software, availability and added access to embedded and machine-readable dictionaries is forging ahead as a criterion for evaluation. Online dictionaries have the unique ability to provide clusters of value-added features such as audio availability so the pronunciation can be heard; variant spellings available through wildcard searches; and hyperlinks to related material such as thesauri, similes, usage examples, and word games. Most large dictionary publishers are adding online availability to the print editions so that it has become an increasingly important component of purchase evaluation.

That said, reference evaluators must keep in mind that dictionaries attempt to be definitive about words, and words by definition are both ephemeral and mutative. As Dr. Johnson laments in his preface to *Cassell's Italian Dictionary* (1977: v), "Every other author may aspire to praise, the lexicographer can only hope to escape reproach."

Further Considerations

Having sampled just a few of the hundreds of dictionaries available, the reference librarian will need to apply the knowledge to these twin tasks:

- Acquisition of word sources
- Information referral

Acquisition

To paraphrase Ranganathan (1963): to every library its own collection of word sources. While general dictionaries, both abridged and unabridged, are staples of every collection, specialized word sources can play out in various permutations depending on the type, size, and in-built expectations of a particular library. Following are a few caveats to keep in mind while acquiring word sources.

- Not all books titled "dictionaries" are really dictionaries. They are merely alluding to the alphabetical arrangement of a book. For example, *A New Dictionary of Irish History from 1800* lends little to the world of words, but a great deal to the world of history instead. Conversely, titles without the word "dictionary" may be just that. Clues can sometimes be found in publications that have "ABC" in the title, such as the classic subject dictionary *ABC for Book Collectors*, wherein a specialized term like "japon vellum" finds definition.
- Word sources can be highly derivative, even incestuous, in their capture of existing words and defining mores. For example, no dictionary listed obscene or "gutter" words until the *American Heritage* decided it was a necessary component of existing communication. Today, it is primarily the children's dictionaries that do not include such words. It is therefore not necessary to compulsively acquire every new title that comes up for purchase.

Referral

To paraphrase Ranganathan (1963) yet again: to every question its own word source. While reference librarians develop a "muscle" to efficiently field a wide variety of questions based on their knowledge of existing word resources, it is helpful to broadly deconstruct just what that "muscle" is.

- *Visualizing:* As the question is asked, fast-forwarding to the final answer helps establish the area for possible resources. If the question is *"What is a chassis?"* the final answer would read *"A chassis is _____."* A simple dictionary would suffice. If the question is *"What's another word for assessment?"* the final answer would read *"Another word is _____."* A simple thesaurus would suffice.
- *Complexity:* Is the question multitiered? Does it require analysis or oblique thinking? *"Was Thomas Edison aware that the use of mercury at his labs could adversely affect the health of his employees?"* With no recorded evidence of whether he did or did not, tracing the definition of "mercury" as it appeared in dictionaries at the turn of the century allowed one researcher to hazard a guess. For the librarian, the area of complexity lies in making the link between the question and the resource to be used.
- *Depth:* How much information does the question suggest? Instead of *"What is angst?"* if the question posed was *"Is angst an English word and can I use it to describe my teen years?"* more depth is required of the answer than a simple definition. A check into the etymology of the word as well as usage would provide a complete answer.
- *Context:* Given the mutability and infiniteness of words, placing words within a larger framework can sometimes ease the reference process. If a word is wholly unfamiliar, the context must be probed. For example, a graduate student wanted to know the meaning of "bovate," a word that could not be found in a general dictionary. The probe helped: *"Do you have the sentence in which this word appears?" "Did you hear this in a particular class at college?"* In this instance, the user had heard the word in the context of Elizabethan history. The possibility that it was an archaic word led the reference librarian to the *OED* where it was defined as a unit of land measure.
- *Format:* In the goal for conducting the most efficient search for the most efficacious answer, print or online resources are very often the personal choice of the librarian, but not always. In the world of word sources, for example, some words are more ephemeral than others and better served by online searches. A virtual reference question that was phrased as *"Are there any statistics available on zeroheros?"* had the librarian frantically looking through *Merriam-Webster's Collegiate Dictionary*, before tracking the definition online to slang for "designated drivers." Current slang and outrageously marginalized words, such as those found in one letter or all-vowel dictionaries, usually suffer premature deaths and are best served by the Internet.

Following is a list of real questions asked at a library that can help exercise the reference "muscle" for answers deriving from word sources:

- *I did a phone interview with the mayor for my term paper. How do I cite his comments in my bibliography?*
- *Is the word "parsimony" ever mentioned in the Bible?*
- *I was reading the novel* The Kite Runner, *and the word "Baba" was used. Is that generic for "father" in Afghanistan?*
- *How do you spell the word that was the title of the poem by British poet William Henley and Timothy McVeigh's last words before he was executed?*
- *What is the most relevant definition of the word "browser"?*

Final Thoughts

"Will This Be the Last Print Dictionary Ever Made?" was the marketing buzz accompanying Houghton Mifflin's release of their five-pound baby, the fifth edition of *The American Heritage Dictionary* (Zimmer, 2011). It has, in fact, been the only major dictionary to publish a print edition in the recent past. The onslaught of modern technology has modified a significant core of what defined a traditional dictionary: its function as the slow-moving arbiter in acknowledging that a word was indeed legitimate and a worthy member of the lexical family. Furious debates followed the presumed laxity of dictionaries that showed permissiveness, as evident in the outcry that surrounded the 1961 update of *Webster's Third*, which presumed to include upstarts like the verb "finalize." This was despite the fact that the edition had taken over 700 editor-years, $3.5 million, and almost 30 years to be updated.

The torrent and speed of online communication necessarily endows language with a plasticity that allows for new usage to become common currency in a very short while. Far more than was evident in a slower past, while the dictionary continues to stand as a responsible mirror of existing usage, its role as a ferocious gatekeeper of formal language is muddied by the needs of speed and timely reflection. Online editions feed into the need for timeliness. They capture the torrent of usage almost instantaneously and are accessible at the flick of a finger. However, the decades spent in winnowing the worth of a word are simply not available. So, for example, we have two definitions for the new word "anchor baby" in the 2011 edition of *The American Heritage Dictionary*. The nonjudgmental definition of the word in the print edition raised the hackles of the Immigration Policy Center in Washington, DC, to the extent that the 200-strong members of the Usage Panel associated with the dictionary were persuaded to redefine the term as an "offensive slur" in the online version (Preston, 2011). The venerable *Oxford English Dictionary* updates its online version every three months, in comparison to the two printed editions it had published since 1928, and includes texting abbreviations like "OMG." *Merriam-Webster* posts the most-used words in "the past 24 hours" and has created an ingenious holding pen for new words that "really should be in the dictionary" but are not, thereby providing both an online snapshot of current usage and holding on to its authority as gatekeeper.

Awareness of the new dynamics in dictionary updates and publication are not only interesting, but help alert the reference librarian to subtleties in definitions such as the increase in qualifiers—"slur," "slang," "idiom," "popular usage" that are an increasing hallmark of dictionary definitions.

TOP TEN DICTIONARY AND WORD SOURCES		
Title	Print	Online
The American Heritage Dictionary. 2011. Boston: Houghton Mifflin.	5th ed.	http://www.ahdictionary.com/
Bartlett's Familiar Quotations. 2002. London: Little, Brown Book Group.	17th ed.	http://www.bartleby.com/100/ 1919 edition http://www.Archive.org/ 1968 edition
Dictionary of American Regional English. 1985–. 2012. Cambridge, MA: Harvard University Press.	5 vols. + 1	100 entries available at http://dare.wisc.edu/
Macmillan Dictionary for Children. 2007. New York: Simon and Schuster Children's Publishing.		
Merriam-Webster's Collegiate Dictionary. 2008. Springfield, MA: Merriam-Webster.	11th ed.	http://www.m-w.com/
MLA Style Manual and Guide to Scholarly Publishing. 2008. New York: Modern Language Association of America.	3rd ed.	
The New Oxford American Dictionary. 2010. New York: Oxford University Press.	3rd ed.	Subscription to "Premium" http://www.oxfordreference.com/
Oxford English Dictionary. 1989. New York: Oxford University Press.	20 vols.	Subscription http://www.oed.com/
Roget's International Thesaurus. 2010. New York: HarperCollins.	7th ed.	http://www.bartleby.com/110/ 1922 edition
Webster's Third New International Dictionary of the English Language, Unabridged. 2002. Springfield, MA: Merriam-Webster.		Subscription http://corporate.britannica.com/ library/online/mwu.html

Recommended Resources Discussed in This Chapter

Abbreviations. http://www.abbreviations.com/.

Abbreviations Dictionary. 10th ed. Dean Stahl and Karen Kerchelich. Boca Raton, FL: CRC Press, 2001. Also available as an e-book: http://www.crcpress.com/.

ABC for Book Collectors. 8th ed. John Carter and Nicolas Barker. New Castle, DE: Oak Knoll Press, 2006.

Acronym Finder. http://www.acronymfinder.com/.

Acronyms, Initialisms, and Abbreviations Dictionary. Farmington Hills, MI: Gale/Cengage Learning, 2012.

The ACS Style Guide: A Manual for Authors and Editors. 3rd ed. Annie M. Coghill and Lorrin R. Garson, eds. New York: Oxford University Press, 2006.

Albanian-English English-Albanian Practical Dictionary. New York: Hippocrene Books, 2006.

RECOMMENDED FREE DICTIONARY WEBSITES

Acronym Finder. http://www.acronymfinder.com/. More than four million acronyms, abbreviations, and initialisms are searchable in this popular site. They can be located by either keyword or through listed categories such as "Information Technology."

The American Heritage Dictionary of the English Language. http://www.bartleby.com/61/. The fourth edition of this reputable dictionary is freely available through this site. Ninety thousand entries with 70,000 audio pronunciations, 900 visual illustrations, language notes and word-roots build up to make this a powerful free online dictionary resource.

Dictionary.com. http://dictionary.reference.com/. This site is quick, reliable, and effective. It is a multisource dictionary service, with the pleasing simplicity of a clean interface featuring a simple blue search box. It also features a thesaurus and translation dictionary that can toggle between 20 different languages.

Merriam-Webster's Collegiate Dictionary. http://www.merriam-webster.com/. The eleventh edition is freely available at this site along with a thesaurus, and medical and Spanish-English word search capability.

Netlingo. http://netlingo.com/. Updated daily, the site is invaluable in navigating the ever-changing shores of "cyberterms," the terminology, acronyms, and emoticons that populate the online universe.

Research and Documentation Online. http://bcs.bedfordstmartins.com/resdoc5e/index.htm. The information on this site, also available in a print book, *Research and Documentation in the Electronic Age*, Fifth Edition, 2010, by Diana Hacker and Barbara Fister, is a comprehensive style guide for scholarly citations. It also gives examples with real sample papers.

AMA Manual of Style: A Guide for Authors and Editors. 10th ed. New York: Oxford University Press, 2007. Also available online: http://www.amamanualofstyle.com/.

The American Heritage Dictionary for Learners of English. Boston: Houghton Mifflin, 2002. Also available online: http://www.houghtonmifflinbooks.com/epub/learners.shtml.

The American Heritage Dictionary of the English Language. 5th ed. Boston: Houghton Mifflin, 2011. Also available online: http://www.ahdictionary.com/.

The American Sign Language Dictionary Unabridged. Martin L. A. Sternberg. New York: HarperCollins Publishers, 1998.

The American Sign Language Handshape Dictionary 2nd ed. Washington, DC: Gallaudet University Press, 1999. Available on DVD: http://gupress.gallaudet.edu/.

The Associated Press Stylebook. New York: The Associated Press, 2012. Also available online: https://www.apstylebook.com/.2010.

Bartlett's Familiar Quotations. 18th ed. John Bartlett. Boston: Little, Brown, and Company, 2012. Also available as an e-book: http://www.hachettebookgroup.com/.

Black's Law Dictionary. 9th ed. Bryan A. Garner, ed. Eagan, MN: West Publishing Company, 2009. Also available as an app: http://itunes.apple.com/.

Bloomsbury Concise English Dictionary. London: A&C Black, 2006.

The Cambridge Guide to English Usage. Cambridge, UK: Cambridge University Press, 2004.

Canadian Oxford Dictionary. 2nd ed. Katherine Barber, ed. New York: Oxford University Press, 2004. Also available online: http://www.oxfordreference.com/.

Cassell's Italian Dictionary. New York: Macmillan, 1977.

Cassell's Latin Dictionary. London: Cassell, 1977.

Chambers Dictionary. 12th ed. Edinburgh: Chambers Harrap, 2011. Also available online: http://www.chambers.co.uk/.

The Chicago Manual of Style. 16th ed. Chicago: University of Chicago Press, 2010. Also available online: http://www.chicagomanualofstyle.org/home.html.

Cite Right. Charles Lipson. 2nd ed. Chicago: The University of Chicago Press, 2011.

Collins English Dictionary. 30th anniversary ed. New York: HarperCollins, 2010. Also available online: http://www.collinslanguage.com/.

A Complete and Systematic Concordance to the Works of Shakespeare. Marvin Spevack, comp. New York: G. Olms, 1968.

The Complete Guide to Citing Government Information Resources. 3rd ed. Debora Cheney. Bethesda, MD: Congressional Information Service, 2002.

Dave VE7CNV's Truly Canadian Dictionary of Canadian Spelling. http://www.luther.ca/~dave7cnv/cdnspelling/cdnspelling.html.

Dictionary. http://www.dictionary.com/.

Dictionary of American Regional English. Joan Houston Hall, chief ed. Cambridge, MA: Harvard University Press, 1985–2012. Also available online: http://dare.wisc.edu/.

The Dictionary of Aquarium Terms. John H. Tullock. New York: Barron's, 2000.

A Dictionary of Modern English Usage: The Classic First Edition. H. W. Fowler. David Crystal, ed. Oxford: Oxford University Press, 2009. Also available online: http://www.bartleby.com/116/.

DK Merriam-Webster Children's Dictionary. New York: DK Publishing, 2008.

Dorland's Illustrated Medical Dictionary. 32nd ed. New York: Elsevier/Saunders, 2011. Also available online: http://www.dorlands.com/.

Encarta Webster's Dictionary of the English Language. 2nd ed. New York: Bloomsbury, 2004.

Etymology. http://www.etymonline.com/.

The Firefly Five Language Visual Dictionary: English, Spanish, French, German, Italian. Jean-Claude Corbeil and Arianne Archambault. New York: Firefly, 2009.

The Firefly Visual Dictionary. Jean-Claude Corbeil and Arianne Archambault. New York: Firefly, 2002.

FOLDOC. Denis Howe, ed. http://foldoc.org.

Fowler's Modern English Usage. Rev. 3rd ed. R. W. Burchfield. Oxford: Oxford University Press, 2004.

Gage Canadian Dictionary. Scarborough, Ontario: Thomson Nelson, 2000.

The Gallaudet Dictionary of American Sign Language. Clayton Valli, editor-in-chief. Washington, DC: Gallaudet University Press, 2006.

Green's Dictionary of Slang. Vol. 1–3. Jonathon Green. London: Oxford University Press, 2011. Also available online: http://www.greensdictionary.com/.

Harvard Concordance to Shakespeare. Marvin Spevack, comp. Cambridge, MA: Belknap Press, 1973.

The Harvard Dictionary of Music. 4th ed. Don Michael Randel, ed. Cambridge, MA: Belknap Press, 2003.

Handbook of Writing for the Mathematical Sciences. 2nd ed. Nicholas J. Higham. Philadelphia: SIAM, 1998. Also available as an e-book: http://epubs.siam.org/.

Historical Dictionary of American Slang. Jonathan E. Lighter, ed. New York: Oxford University Press, 1994–.

A History of Cant and Slang Dictionaries. Julie Coleman. New York: Oxford University Press, 2004–2010.

LEO dictionary. http://www.apple.com/webapps/searchtools/leodictionary_leogmbh.html.

Macmillan Dictionary for Children. New York: Simon and Schuster, 2007.

Macmillan English Dictionary. 2nd ed. New York: Macmillan, 2007. http://www.macmillandictionary.com/.

Merriam-Webster's Advanced Learner's English Dictionary. Springfield, MA: Merriam-Webster, 2008. Also available online: http://www.learnersdictionary.com/.

Merriam-Webster's Collegiate Dictionary. 11th ed. Springfield, MA: Merriam-Webster, 2008. Also available online: http://www.m-w.com/.

Metadictionary. http://www.onelook.com/.

MLA Handbook for Writers of Research Papers. 7th ed. New York: Modern Language Association of America, 2009. Also has a companion website: http://www.mlahandbook .org/.

MLA Style Manual and Guide to Scholarly Publishing. 3rd ed. New York: Modern Language Association of America, 2008.

Nelson Canadian Dictionary of the English Language. Scarborough, Ontario: ITP Nelson, 1997.

A New Dictionary of Irish History from 1800. D. J. Hickey and J. E. Doherty. Dublin, Ireland: Gill and Macmillan, 2003.

The New Oxford American Dictionary. 3rd ed. New York: Oxford University Press, 2010. Also available online: http://oxforddictionaries.com/.

NTC's American English Learner's Dictionary. Richard A. Spears, ed. New York: McGraw-Hill, 1998.

ODLIS (Online Dictionary for Library and Information Science). Joan M. Reitz. 2007. http://www.abc-clio.com/ODLIS/odlis_A.aspx.

OED Online. http://www.oed.com/.

OneLook. http://www.onelook.com/.

Oxford American Writer's Thesaurus. Christine A. Lindbergh, ed. New York: Oxford University Press, 2008.

Oxford Dictionary of English. Oxford: Oxford University Press, 2010.

Oxford Dictionary of Modern Quotations. 3rd ed. Elizabeth Knowles, ed. New York: Oxford University Press, 2008.

Oxford Dictionary of Phrase Sayings and Quotations. 3rd ed. New York: Oxford University Press, 2006.

Oxford English Dictionary. 2nd ed. John Simpson and Edward Weiner, eds. New York: Oxford University Press, 1989.

Oxford Large Print Dictionary. New York: Oxford University Press, 2002. Reissued in 2006 as the *Oxford Large Print Dictionary, Thesaurus, and Wordpower Guide.*

Oxford Rhyming Dictionary. Clive and Eben Upton, eds. New York: Oxford University Press, 2004.

Oxford Starter Bilingual Dictionary series. New York: Oxford University Press. Copyright varies.

Publication Manual of the American Psychological Association. 6th ed. Washington, DC: American Psychological Association, 2009. Also available online: http://www.apastyle .org/manual/.

Random House Webster's Large Print Dictionary. New York: Random House, 2007.

The Random House Webster's Quotationary. Leonard Roy Frank. New York: Random House Reference, 2001.

Random House Webster's Rhyming Dictionary. New York: Random House Reference, 2008.

Random House Webster's Unabridged American Sign Language Dictionary. New York: Random House Reference, 2008.

Random House Webster's Unabridged Dictionary. New York: Random House Reference, 1997.

RhymeZone. http://www.rhymezone.com/.

Roget's International Thesaurus. Barbara Ann Kipferer, ed. New York: HarperCollins Publishers, 2010.

Shakespeare concordance. http://www.it.usyd.edu.au/~matty/Shakespeare/test.html.

Stedman's Medical Dictionary. 28th ed. Philadelphia: Lippincott Williams and Wilkins, 2005. Also available online: http://www.stedmans.com/.

Stone the Crows: Oxford Dictionary of Modern Slang. 2nd ed. John Ayto and John Simpson, eds. New York: Oxford University Press, 2008.

Strong's Exhaustive Concordance of the Bible. Peabody, MA: Hendrickson Publishers, 2007.

A Student's Dictionary. Charleston, SC: The Dictionary Project, 2004.

Style Manual for Political Science. Washington, DC: American Political Science Association, 2001.

Thesaurus.com. http://www.thesaurus.com/ and http://thesaurus.reference.com/.

Thorndike-Barnhart Children's Dictionary. Upper Saddle River, NJ: Pearson Education, 1998.

Thorndike-Barnhart Intermediate Dictionary. Upper Saddle River, NJ: Pearson Education, 1996.

Thorndike-Barnhart Junior Dictionary. New York: HarperCollins, 1997.

Thorndike-Barnhart Student Dictionary. Upper Saddle River, NJ: Pearson Education, 1998.

Ultimate Visual Dictionary. Revised and updated. New York: DK Publishing, 2011.

The Unbound Bible. http://unbound.biola.edu/.

Urban Dictionary. http://www.urbandictionary.com/. Also available is a widget for updates: http://www.apple.com/downloads/dashboard/justforfun/urbandictionary wordofthedaywidget.html.

Visuwords Online Graphical Dictionary. http://www.visuwords.com/.

Webopedia. http://www.webopedia.com/.

Webster's New Explorer Large Print Dictionary. Darien, CT: Federal Street Press, 2006.

Webster's Third New International Dictionary, Unabridged. Springfield, MA: Merriam-Webster, 2002. Also available online: https://member.m-w.com/subscribe.php.

Wiktionary. http://www.wiktionary.com/.

Wordia. http://www.wordia.com/.

Words to Rhyme With. 3rd ed. Willard Espy. New York: Facts on File, 2006.

World Book Dictionary. Chicago: World Book, 2005.

The World Factbook. https://www.cia.gov/library/publications/the-world-factbook/index .html.

The Yahoo! Style Guide: The Ultimate Sourcebook for Writing, Editing, and Creating Content for the Digital World. Chris Barr. New York: St. Martin's Press, 2010.

The Yale Book of Quotations. Fred R. Shapiro, ed. New Haven, CT: Yale University Press, 2006.

Recommendations for Further Reading

Coleman, Julie. 2004–2010. *A History of Cant and Slang Dictionaries*, Volumes I–IV. New York: Oxford University Press. Coleman provides us with an exhaustive and fascinating multivolume account of the colorful history of slang in the English-speaking world. The history is supported with the etymology of slang words, and the context within which they were embedded. Also featured are the spiritualists, criminals, soldiers, journalists, aristocrats, schoolboys, and others who made up a motley crew of slang lexicographers through the ages.

Dalby, Andrew. 1998. *A Guide to World Language Dictionaries*. London: Library Association. This evaluative single-volume collation of dictionaries covering 275 languages from around the world provides the most updated information in the area of language dictionaries. The listings are both annotated and listed alphabetically, so it is not necessary to have additional knowledge of language groups.

Harris, Roy. 2008. "Defining the Undefinable." *Times Higher Education* 1827 (January 10): 20. Harris, an emeritus professor of general linguistics at the University of Oxford, prolific author, and co-editor of the journal *Language and Communication*, presents us with a brief but stimulating essay on the importance of dictionaries to the self-understanding of society and the need to address a society where definitional anarchy in dictionaries is the norm.

Kabdebo, Thomas, and Neil Armstrong. 1997. *Dictionary of Dictionaries and Eminent Encyclopedias*. New Providence, NJ: Bowker-Saur. This edition provides a comprehensive and evaluative bibliography of 24,000 subject, online, historical, and language dictionaries and encyclopedias. While an updated edition would be welcome, the resource continues to be useful in providing an overview of the breadth of dictionaries available.

Kister, Kenneth. 1992. *Kister's Best Dictionaries for Adults and Young People: A Comparative Guide*. Phoenix, AZ: Oryx Press. Kister has written the definitive study of dictionaries. While the facts describing each dictionary are obsolete, the essays on the history, typology, and comparative evaluation of dictionaries continue to be powerful.

Reitz, Joan M. 2004. "ODLIS: Online Dictionary for Library and Information Science." Available: http://www.abc-clio.com/ODLIS/odlis_A.aspx. Also available in print as the *Dictionary for Library and Information Science*, Westport, CT: Libraries Unlimited. First popularized as an online resource, the author has now published this wonderful resource in a print version as well. Definitions for all kinds of dictionaries are provided in a clear style with helpful "compare with" suggestions for relevant entries.

Romero, Joseph M. 2004. "Life Among the Lexicographers." *Humanities* 25, no. 2 (March/April): 20. This is both a well-researched and elegant article on the creation of a unique dictionary, the *Dictionary of American Regional English*.

Wallraff, Barbara. 2004. "Dictionaries." *The New York Times Magazine*, October 5: 18. Written by the author of *Your Own Words*, this article alerts users to the fallibility of dictionaries in terms of differing and idiosyncratic entries and styles.

World Wide Words. http://www.worldwidewords.org/reviews/re-fou1.htm. Michael Quinion, an established British lexicographer, author, and contributor to the *Oxford English Dictionary*, is the creator of this delightful online newsletter on the English language and reviews of new books dealing with language.

Yates, Sarah. 2011. "*Black's Law Dictionary*: The Making of an American Standard." *Law Library Journal* 103, no. 2 (Spring): 175–198. The article presents an analytical account of the history and evolution of Black's dictionary and identifies the factors leading to its current position as the preeminent legal resource over other deserving candidates. While focused on legal dictionaries, the analysis also suggests the many elements that lead to the rise and fall in the authority and popularity of dictionary resources as a whole.

Bibliography and Works Cited

Adams, William Lee. 2008. "War of the Words." *Time International* (Europe Edition) 172, no. 16 (October 20): 42.

Alford, Henry. 2005. "Not a Word." *The New Yorker*, August 29: 62.

Andriani, Lynn. 2008. "Merriam-Webster Joins Learner's English Market." *Publishers Weekly* 255, no. 28 (July 14): 6.

Dahlin, Robert. 1999. "You're as Good as Your Word." *Publishers Weekly* 246, no. 46 (November 15): 33.

Fee, Margery, and Janice McAlpine. 2011. *Guide to Canadian English Usage*. 2nd ed. New York: Oxford University Press.

Hacker, Diana, and Barbara Fister. 2010. *Research and Documentation in the Electronic Age*. 5th ed. New York: St. Martin's Press.

Hoyle, Ben. 2008. "Mafflard Left with Onomatomania after Reading Oxford Dictionary from A to Z." *The Times* (London, England), October 4: 4.

Jamieson, Alastair. 2010. "Oxford English Dictionary 'will not be printed again.'" *The Telegraph,* August 29. http://www.telegraph.co.uk/culture/books/booknews.

McQuade, Molly. 2003. "Defining a Dictionary." *Booklist* (May 15): 1688.

"Merriam-Webster's Collegiate Dictionary now available for iPhone and iPod Touch." 2008. *Science Letter* (September 30): 3714.

Nunberg, Geoffrey. 2011. "Not Another Word." *The New York Times,* Sunday Book Review Essay, September 25: 35.

"Oxford Closes Canadian Dictionary Division." 2008. *Canwest News Service* (October 1). http://www.canada.com/components/print.aspx?id=c74519ed-c8d5-4312-869b-af7508dd65cc.

Poehlmann, Christian. 2005. "Software Reviews." *Technology and Libraries* 21, no. 1 (November 16). http://www.ala.org/lita/ital/21/1/software.

Preston, Julia. 2011. "Anchor Baby: A Term Redefined as a Slur." *The New York Times,* December 9: A17.

Quinn, Mary Ellen, and Christine Bulson. 2008. "Atlas and Dictionary Update, 2008." *Booklist* 104, no. 18 (May 15): 80, 82.

Ranganathan, S. R. 1963. *The Five Laws of Library Science.* Bombay, India: Asia Publishing House.

Reitz, Joan M. 2004. "ODLIS: Online Dictionary for Library and Information Science." http://www.abc-clio.com/ODLIS/odlis_A.aspx.

Saussy III, George Stone. 1989. *The Logodaedalian's Dictionary of Interesting and Unusual Words.* Columbia, SC: University of South Carolina Press.

Truss, Lynne. 2004. *Eats, Shoots and Leaves: The Zero Tolerance Approach to Punctuation.* New York: Gotham Books.

Zimmer, Ben. 2011. "Is This the Last Print Dictionary?" *The Boston Globe,* November 6. http://www.bostonglobe.com/ideas/2011/11/05/this-last-print-dictionary/r7yVwU8xINyKRaKNNEIi8M/story.html.

8

Answering Questions about Events and Issues, Past and Present— Databases (and Indexes)

Overview

Databases and indexes are today the most used library reference sources. They provide access to both current and historic periodical articles as well as newspapers, book information, dissertations, conference proceedings, interviews, and much more. Many users need short articles rather than a whole book or need to be able to combine a number of short articles in order to understand an issue or subject. Most indexes provide only the citation for each article, whereas databases provide full-text articles. Some indexes and databases are available free, such as *Google Scholar* and open access databases, while many others are available as subscriptions that are usually paid for on an annual basis. Understanding the differences between the various databases and indexes is a necessity for librarians and users in order to choose appropriate databases to research a particular subject.

History

Indexes first came into being in the nineteenth century. The first index ever published was *Poole's Index to Periodical Literature* 1802–1906. It indexed articles from 479 American and English periodicals by subject only. For many decades, printed indexes provided access to periodicals and newspapers. Today we have few paper indexes, but even before the more recent shift to digital media, new ways of presenting indexes began to take shape in the 1960s. Dialog, beginning in 1966, and BRS (Bibliographic Retrieval Service), beginning in 1976, provided an interface that allowed librarians to search a large number of indexes by computer. Mead Data Central released the online databases *Lexis* in 1973 and *Nexis* in 1980, respectively. By 1982, Dialog and BRS introduced flat rate simplified versions for home use. In 1985, Infotrac, a videodisc product that enabled the user to search databases in one alphabet, was produced by IAC (Information Access Company). CD-ROMs provided an even better and more economical way to store large amounts of data in a small space, and libraries were able to network CD-ROMs to serve their public. Libraries began to lease databases, often loading the information on their own in-house servers so users could access the information through the OPACs (Online Public Access Catalogs) (Machovec, 1995). The advent of the World Wide

Web made it possible for libraries to subscribe to databases that the user could view over the web and to provide full text for many or all articles. This has revolutionized indexes and made it possible to give access to massive amounts of regularly updated information while guaranteeing flexible, easy access.

How Databases Are Used

Databases and indexes help users to identify journal articles, newspaper articles, book chapters, conference proceedings, and other resources. Indexes dissect what is inside a periodical or newspaper so that the user has access to the individual articles. This enables the user to more easily find a specific article or material on a specific subject. Databases often provide the full text as well as the citation.

Databases are used to find articles in periodicals and newspapers and other resources such as dissertations, book reviews, and conference proceedings. They are most often employed to research topics of current interest or to update information on a subject. In some cases, they can also be used to help understand a contemporary debate, as a variety of material can be found on any controversial topic from many different points of view. It is also helpful to use periodical and newspaper databases to research a subject not yet written about in books. For example, new medical treatments are usually discussed in journals, newspapers, and magazines long before receiving treatment in longer print media, thanks to the quick turnaround of periodical publishing. Most indexes are now full-text databases that allow users to access the complete article along with the bibliographic citation. Also advantageous with today's databases is their easy searchability by subject, keyword, and author, a feature that sometimes makes them preferable to printed reference resources. Along these lines, in addition to material published in periodicals and newspapers, indexes sometimes allow quick access to the contents of reference books, further streamlining the searching process.

Indexes are also useful for doing retrospective research. Many indexes have been in business for many years and have digitized their complete run, for example, the *MLA International Bibliography*. This enables researchers to quickly search for older material. The digitization of newspapers from the beginning of their publishing has also provided an excellent tool for researchers.

As always, it is important to understand the kind and quality of information desired by the user before starting a database search. If the user just wants general, non-scholarly articles on a subject, then multidisciplinary periodical and newspaper databases are probably the proper place to begin. Should the user's interests be more specialized, however, it is important that a more appropriate subject-specific database be chosen.

Libraries have spent a great deal of time designing their electronic resources pages to lead the user to specialized databases. Simply pointing out resources is, of course, not enough, so user instruction is also important in this regard. Librarians can design tutorials or courses that introduce the user to specialized databases in their field of study and demonstrate how to use them. Federated searching using products such as Serial Solutions' Central Search can also help users search appropriate databases by allowing the user to search across several databases at the same time without having to know the names of specific databases and learning individual searching protocols for each database. The area of full-text databases is a rich one and useful to both the librarian and the user.

Questions Answered by Databases

Q: Where can I find information on Hispanic immigrants to the United States?

A: The answer can be found in a general full-text periodical database such as *Academic Search Premier* or in a more specialized index such as *PAIS International.*

Q: Where can I find articles on companies that provide day care for working mothers?

A: A general full-text periodical database such as *ProQuest Research Library* will have articles on this subject. Newspaper databases would be good sources as well.

Q: How can I locate information about the effect of the Internet on American society?

A: A general full-text periodical database such as *Academic OneFile* will have articles on this, or consult a more specialized database such as *Social Sciences Full Text.*

Q: Where can I find five articles of criticism for the Faulkner short story, "A Rose for Emily"?

A: Use a subject database like *Humanities Full Text* that will have full text for many articles. If you need to find more in-depth material, use the *MLA International Bibliography.*

Q: Where can I find articles on deforestation in Mexico?

A: *PAIS International*, from the political and economic perspective, or *BIOSIS Previews*, with scientific articles on the environment, would be good places to go.

Q: What is the best place to look for research about the psychological effects of adoption on children?

A: *PsycINFO* is the best resource to consult for psychological topics. Be sure to use the online thesaurus of subject headings to select the best terms for your search.

Q: Where can I find information about which digital cameras are the best?

A: General full-text periodical databases, such as the *Reader's Guide Full Text* which include consumer magazines such as *Consumer Reports* and computer magazines, are a good source of information.

Major Databases Used in Reference Work

Databases can be multidisciplinary or specialized covering a particular subject area. Multidisciplinary periodical databases provide a way to do research on a wide range of topics. They index periodicals that are widely used, usually providing the full text. General newspaper databases do the same for newspapers. Some index a single newspaper such as the *New York Times* while others index several newspapers. The subject databases can be as specific as *Oceanic Abstracts* or as broad-based as *ERIC* (*Educational Resources Information Center*) or the *PAIS International*.

Multidisciplinary Periodical Databases

Several companies, including EBSCO, ProQuest, and Gale Cengage Learning, dominate the database field. All of these companies to a greater or lesser extent act as conglomerates, continually buying other companies or leasing content in order to offer more databases to libraries. Some databases produced by outside organizations are available by subscription from more than one company. Each of these companies has its strengths and weaknesses, but overall the librarian will find any of them quite satisfactory. The choice a library makes should be predicated on the criteria important to their specific situation such as cost, coverage, and user-friendly interface.

Academic Search Complete, EBSCO's largest multidisciplinary database, indexes and abstracts 13,000 journals of which 9,000 are full text. Covering a wide range of subjects from the sciences, social sciences, and humanities to law, music, and many interdisciplinary subjects such as women's studies and area studies, this database indexes many peer-reviewed (i.e., reviewed by others in the field before being published) and scholarly journals. EBSCO also offers several other multidisciplinary databases to fit the needs of different types and sizes of libraries. *Academic Search Elite* is designed for smaller academic libraries but would also be useful in community college libraries and public libraries. The database indexes and abstracts over 3,700 titles including over 2,100 full-text periodicals. Coverage dates from 1985. For libraries wanting a richer collection of resources there is *Academic Search Premier*, which indexes and abstracts over 8,500 titles with 4,700 full-text titles and back files beginning in 1975. EBSCO also has three databases especially designed for public libraries. *MasterFILE Complete* is the largest of the databases with more than 2,000 full-text periodicals back to 1922, 1,000 reference books, and a large image file. *MasterFILE Premier* and *MasterFILE Elite* index fewer titles. These databases available through EBSCO have good search facility. They are searchable by keyword in the article title, subject descriptors, author, and abstract fields.

ProQuest Central is not only ProQuest's largest multidisciplinary database but also the largest of the multidisciplinary databases with 19,370 titles and over 13,000 titles in full text. It indexes journals, magazines, and newspapers as well as dissertations and company reports and is useful to all types of libraries, providing information on a wide range of subjects including business, humanities, education, social sciences, and sciences. The titles indexed begin in 1995. Its search methods are the usual—Boolean operators, advanced search, and natural language—with complete subject indexing and a controlled vocabulary. *ProQuest Research Library* is a full-text database that covers the top 150 core academic subject areas with over 3,850 titles and over 2,600 with full text beginning in 1971. *CBCA* (*Canadian Business and Current Affairs*) *Complete* is a database of Canadian periodicals that includes bibliographic citations and a great deal of full text. It indexes more than 1,700 titles and 600 full-text titles with coverage back to the 1970s.

Gale Cengage Learning's largest multidisciplinary full-text database, *Academic OneFile*, is geared to undergraduate students, graduate students, and faculty. It indexes over 14,000 periodical titles as well as newspapers (including the *New York Times* and the *London Times*) and wire services. The majority of the titles are full text and peer reviewed, and back file full-text coverage begins in 1980. Another of Gale Cengage Learning's full-text databases is *Expanded Academic ASAP*, which includes material for the undergraduate but is also useful for high schools and public libraries. *Expanded Academic ASAP* indexes over 5,300 titles, of which 3,000 are full text. *General OneFile* indexes 8,000 full-text titles, 3,600 of which are peer reviewed. This database indexes five newspapers with full text of the *New York Times* from 1985 to date as well as 500 travel guides, NPR (National Public Radio) audio programs, and TV video files. The Gale Cengage Learning indexes have good searching capability and the ability to limit searches by full text, by refereed publications, by date, and by journal title.

Recently the H.W. Wilson Company, which had the longest record in the index business beginning at the end of the nineteenth century, was purchased by EBSCO. It was known for the quality of its indexing and its name and subject authority files. Its databases are now being folded into EBSCO's database collection.

The *Readers' Guide to Periodical Literature*, a Wilson database which began publication in 1890, is a general database that is useful in high schools, public libraries, and four-year colleges. Indexing more than 400 periodicals, the *Readers' Guide* now publishes *Readers' Guide Full Text Mega Edition* with the full text of over 200 publications back to 1994 and with indexing and abstracts of 400 periodicals dating back to 1983. *Readers' Guide Abstracts* indexes and abstracts over 300 periodicals. In addition, there is *Readers' Guide Retrospective 1890–1982*, which provides the earlier years of the index in electronic format. *OmniFile Full Text Mega Edition* combines full text, abstracts, and indexing from six Wilson databases, *Education Full Text*, *General Science Full Text*, *Humanities Full Text*, *Readers' Guide Full Text*, *Social Sciences Full Text*, and *Business Abstracts with Full Text*, back to 1982. It also includes full text of titles indexed in five of Wilson's other subject databases. This database includes the full text of articles from more than 3,000 publications back to 1994 and abstracts and indexing from over 3,600 publications. The broad coverage makes this database useful as a general multidisciplinary database.

LexisNexis has several multidisciplinary reference databases aimed at academic institutions, public libraries, and high schools, all providing a variety of full-text information on current events, legal issues, and issues in the news that can be searched by keyword as well as by subject headings. LexisNexis is not a good place to find articles for research papers but rather a great source for finding pieces of information about people, companies, and so forth. The extensive searching capability of the LexisNexis products makes this group of databases extremely useful. The range of publications indexed in the LexisNexis group of databases goes far beyond the usual magazines and newspapers and includes reports, official documents, television and radio broadcast scripts, wire services, conference proceedings, and organizational newsletters. *LexisNexis Academic* provides national and international current events information as well as legal information, business and financial news, information on companies, and medical and science information from more than 10,000 publications, documents, and access to 2,500 full-text newspapers. *LexisNexis Library Express* is a database designed for public libraries. Somewhat similar to *LexisNexis Academic*, it provides access to full-text newspapers, magazines and journals, broadcast transcripts, wire services, and business and legal information.

FirstSearch from OCLC (Online Computer Library Center) provides access to *WorldCat* and a collection of databases including *WorldCat Dissertations and Theses, CAMIO (Catalog of Art Museum Images Online), eBooks and eAudiobooks,* and *ArchiveGrid.*

Dialog, one of the earliest companies in the field, is still a player providing databases from many different publishers covering such subjects as science and technology, business, energy and environment, food and agriculture, medicine, social sciences, and reference. It is now called *ProQuest Dialog* and has just moved to a new platform.

JSTOR is a not-for-profit developed to provide long-term preservation of an archive of important scholarly journals. Complete journals on subjects in all fields from volume 1 are available. The most current years are now being made available. Libraries must become a participant in JSTOR to subscribe to this service. Participant fees are based on the type of library (http://www.jstor.org/).

Google Scholar (http://scholar.google.com/) is a free service that provides limited access to scholarly literature. Most of the access is to citations and abstracts; each entry indicates the number of times the article has been cited. All subjects are covered; articles, books, theses, papers, and so forth, are indexed. Libraries can link to their full-text holdings.

Access: The Supplementary Index to Periodicals indexes about eighty-five popular periodicals including city and regional magazines not indexed elsewhere. It often provides the first indexing for a new periodical and is available in print from 1975 to the present and electronically from 1987 to the present.

Alternative Press Index, founded in 1969, is a biannual subject index to more than 300 alternative, radical, and left-wing periodicals, newspapers, and magazines often not found in other indexes. The online coverage dates from 1991. It is international and interdisciplinary in scope covering such topics as labor, indigenous peoples, feminism, ecology, gays and lesbians, and socialism.

Newspaper Databases and Indexes

Newspaper databases are exceedingly useful to libraries and library users. These databases provide access to current and retrospective articles in many newspapers—often many more than the library might subscribe to. Many provide the full text of newspapers from smaller towns and cities. *Newspaper Source Plus* (EBSCO) provides full text for over 1,000 U.S. newspapers including *The Christian Science Monitor, USA Today,* and *The Washington Post,* selective full text from regional U.S. newspapers, and TV and radio news transcripts.

InfoTrac Custom Newspapers (Gale Cengage Learning) offers libraries access to 1,000 U.S. national, regional, and local newspapers as well as international newspapers. Libraries can select the titles they want.

ProQuest Newsstand allows libraries to develop a customized database of full-text newspapers from the over 525 daily national and international newspapers offered with a core of *The New York Times, USA Today, The Wall Street Journal, The Washington Post, The Guardian, El Norte, The Jerusalem Post,* and the *South China Morning Post.* Coverage begins for many titles in the 1980s and 1990s. In addition to current newspapers, ProQuest also offers its *Historical Newspapers,* which provide a unique primary source for libraries. This collection is continuing to grow. Libraries can subscribe to the full text of major newspapers such as the *New York Times* from 1851–2006, *Wall Street Journal* from 1889–1992, *Washington Post* from 1877–1993, *Christian Science Monitor* from 1908-1996, and *Los Angeles Times* from 1881–1986. The full text of many more newspapers is available.

Newsbank offers access to the full text of many newspapers. *America's News* provides complete full-text electronic editions to more than 1,900 U.S. news sources. A second database, *Access World News,* includes not only full-text newspapers from the United States but also newspapers from many other countries, translated into English when written in other languages.

Subject-Based Indexes

Although many users prefer to use the general databases, they should be introduced to the subject-based databases since many journals are not indexed in the general databases. Subject-based databases index more specialized journals, newspapers, reports, conferences, and documents than general databases. When researching a subject in depth, it is necessary to use subject-based databases to find more detailed and usually more scholarly material. Databases in major subject areas are described in the following paragraphs.

Science and Technology Databases

Two databases that have for many years been the only science databases for the layperson are the *General Science Index* and the *Applied Science and Technology Index. General Science Full Text* (EBSCO, formerly Wilson) is designed for the student and nonspecialist. It includes the full text of more than 100 periodicals from 1995 to date, as well as abstracts and indexing for 300 periodicals from 1984 to date. The subjects covered include astronomy, chemistry, biology, food and nutrition, physics, mathematics, and the earth sciences. *Applied Science and Technology Full Text* (EBSCO, formerly Wilson) provides full text of articles from more than 220 journals from 1997 to date, as well as abstracts and indexing of 800 periodicals from 1983 to the present. The subjects covered include automotive engineering, transportation, petroleum and gas, plastics, robotics, textiles, the food industry, construction, and more. There is also *Applied Science and Technology Retrospective 1913–1983.* A new database, *Applied Science and Technology Source* (EBSCO), covers 1,200 full-text journals in the same subject areas as *Applied Science and Technology Full Text. Science Full Text Select* (EBSCO, formerly Wilson) is a database that includes the full text from three databases— *General Science Full Text, Applied Science and Technology Full Text,* and *Biological and Agricultural Index Plus*—packaged together and aimed at public libraries, high school libraries, and community college libraries. This product covers 400 journals.

Science in Context (Gale Cengage Learning) includes articles from newspapers, journals, and the text of science reference titles, as well as links to websites and audio and video clips. Aimed at a wide user base from students to the general public, it focuses on earth science, life science, the history of science, physical science, space science, and science and society. *Biology Digest* (Plexus Publishing) covers all aspects of the life sciences from 1987 to the present. Intended for high school and undergraduate students, it provides abstracts of journal articles ranging from botany and ecology to biochemistry, physiology, and zoology and is updated nine times a year.

For academic audiences, many in-depth subject databases meet specific needs. Among these, *SciFinder Scholar* is the online version of *Chemical Abstracts* and includes *CAplus* database and the *CAS* (Chemical Abstracts Service) *Registry* database as well as information on chemical substances and reactions. This database covers biomedical sciences, chemistry, engineering, and materials science and includes citations and abstracts from journals, conference proceedings, patents, and dissertations from 1907 to the present. *BIOSIS Previews* is a comprehensive index to life science and biomedical research covering biology, biochemistry, genetics, zoology, environmental sciences, and many more subjects. It provides citations and abstracts to more than 5,000 international journals from 1926 to the present. *SciVerse Scopus* (Elsevier) is an indexing and abstracting service of peer-reviewed literature covering more than 19,500 science, technology, and medical (STM) sources (journals, conference proceedings, scientific websites, and more) as well as the social science and historical material from 5,000 publishers back to 1996. This large, powerful database provides good searching capability. Many more scientific databases exist for those specializing in specific fields. For the geosciences, the *GeoRef* database produced by the American Geological Institute covers all aspects of geology of North America from 1693 to the present and geology for the rest of the world from 1933 to the present. Topics range from environmental geology to marine geology. This database includes bibliographic information and index terms for geoscience journal articles, books, maps, conference papers, reports, and dissertations as well as the publications of the U.S. Geological Survey. *Oceanic Abstracts* (ProQuest/CSA) includes citations and abstracts for literature on marine biology and physical oceanography, fisheries, aquaculture, and much more from 1981 to the present. *Zoological Record Plus*, now produced by Thomson Scientific and formerly by BIOSIS and the Zoological Society of London, covers the literature of zoology and animal science. This database provides bibliographic references to serial publications, books, and other kinds of publications that are indexed by a well-developed online thesaurus. It is regarded as the unofficial register of taxonomic names and systematics. *MathSciNet* is an international bibliographical resource for the literature of mathematics and statistics. Begun in 1940 and produced by the American Mathematical Society, *MathSciNet* provides libraries full-text access to the material for which they have journal or online subscriptions. *INSPEC*, produced by the Institution of Electrical Engineers, provides bibliographic access to science and technology literature in physics, electrical engineering, electronics, computers, computing, and information technology. More than 5,000 journals are indexed as well as conference proceedings, books, dissertations, and reports. Produced cooperatively by the Institute of Electrical and Electronics Engineers in the United States and by the Institution of Engineering and Technology in the United Kingdom, *IEEE Xplore*, which is also called *IEEE/IEE Digital Library*, covers the fields of electrical engineering, electronics, computer science, information science, materials science, physical science, and biomedical engineering. Full text is provided for 151 journals as well as conference proceedings and standards beginning in 1980. The *ACM Digital Library* is an important database for computer science produced by the Association for Computing Machinery. Sources including journals, maps, newsletters, and conferences are indexed with a great deal of full text.

Education Databases

Education is represented by three resources. *Education Full Text* (EBSCO, formerly Wilson) is the *Education Index* with the full text of articles from 350 journals from 1996 to the present and abstracts and indexing for 770 back to 1983. *Education Full Text* indexes journals not indexed by *ERIC* (Education Resources Information Center). Its subject coverage ranges from Distance Education and Educational Technology to Parent-Teacher Relations and Teacher Methods. *Education Index Retrospective: 1929–1983* provides electronic access to the back files of this index. A new resource from EBSCO is *Education Source*, which includes over 1,700 full-text journals and the full text of more than 550 books and monographs.

ERIC (Education Resources Information Center) (http://www.eric.ed.gov/) is a free database funded by the U.S. Department of Education since 1966. It has been online since 1996. *ERIC* provides broad subject coverage in the field of education and extends into some related fields such as library science. It includes citations and abstracts from over 1,000 educational and education-related journals, books, reports, and other relevant materials, many with full text. One of its strengths is that it provides full-text access to a great deal of grey literature in the subject areas covered. The *Current Index to Journals in Education* and the *Resources in Education Index* are now part of *ERIC* online.

Social Science Databases

The social sciences are a rich area for databases due to the changing nature of information in this field. *Social Sciences Full Text* (EBSCO, formerly Wilson) includes the full text of more than 360 publications from 1972 to the present. Its content covers social science journals published in the United States and elsewhere and includes such diverse subjects as international relations, ethics, anthropology, mass media, and urban studies. It indexes over 750 publications. *Social Sciences Index Retrospective 1907–1983*, which provides electronic access to the retrospective indexing of social science journals, is also available. *Sociological Abstracts* (ProQuest/CSA) is a resource for literature in the social and behavioral sciences that includes a wide variety of sociological research. With back files to 1952, it provides indexing and abstracting of articles in more than 1,800 journals as well as books, conference papers, and dissertations. The subjects covered include culture and social structure, family and social welfare, rural and urban sociology, and social development. *SocINDEX with Full Text* (EBSCO) complements *Sociological Abstracts* and covers many aspects of sociology including criminology, ethnic and racial studies, and gender studies. Full text is available for 890 journals as far back as 1908 as well as books and conference papers. Author profiles for the most prolific and cited authors are a useful addition. Produced by the National Association of Social Workers, *Social Work Abstracts* (EBSCO) indexes over 900 journals and dissertations providing citations and abstracts back to 1965. This index covers a wide range of subjects in the social work field including human services, child and family welfare, aging, and substance abuse. *PAIS International*, published since 1914, covers such subjects as government, legislation, public policy, economics, sociology, and political science. The online version begins in 1972. Owned by ProQuest/CSA, it indexes journals as well as books, government documents, grey literature (printed materials not commercially produced), research reports, and conference reports. As its title suggests, it is international in scope and indexes material in English, French, German, Italian, Portuguese, and Spanish. Although this is an index only, not a full-text source, it is a very good one indexing material not found elsewhere. *PAIS Archive 1915–1976* is also available, providing a historical perspective on many social and public policy issues. *Project MUSE* is a collection of more than 400 not-for-profit scholarly journals that can be searched across the full text of all the journals or one journal at a time. It provides both citations and abstracts, and full text. This database covers the digital humanities and social sciences. A recently added book collection represents the publications of a consortium of university presses. Johns Hopkins University Press manages this venture that includes journals from the United States and abroad from publishers such as Duke University Press, Indiana University Press, Edinburgh University Press, and the Liverpool University Press.

SIRS Issues Researcher (ProQuest) is a reprint service providing full-text material from more than 1,700 magazines, newspapers, journals, and government publications as well as multimedia with a focus on social sciences, economics, political science, and current events worldwide. This database index is designed for high schools and community colleges. It does not index complete journals or newspapers, but instead selectively indexes articles.

Historical Abstracts (EBSCO) is a bibliography of world history from 1450 to the present (excluding the United States and Canada). It includes English-language abstracts from journals of history and the social sciences and articles from 3,100 academic historical journals since 1955 in more than 40 languages. It provides the full text of more than 380 journals and 140 books. It is multidisciplinary in approach and can be used for researching sociology, psychology, women's studies/gender studies, religion, anthropology, political science, multicultural studies, and so forth. Citations for books and dissertations are also included.

America: History and Life (EBSCO) provides citations, abstracts, and the full text of articles on U.S. and Canadian history and related fields from prehistory to the present in more than 1,700 journals. As with *Historical Abstracts, America: History and Life* is interdisciplinary and can be used to research many different disciplines including cultural studies, gender studies, and literary studies. There are links to more than 215,000 articles.

The *History Reference Center* (EBSCO) provides 57,000 historical documents as well as the full text of reference books, encyclopedias, and nonfiction books. This database also includes historical photographs and maps and the full text of 150 historical periodicals.

U.S. History in Context (Gale Cengage Learning) is a collection of primary source documents, reference documents, more than 2,000 photographs, maps, and illustrations, and full-text coverage of history-related scholarly journals. Person, time period, and subject can be searched. *World History in Context* (Gale Cengage Learning) provides full-text primary and secondary sources for the study of world history for all countries and all parts of the world. If the library subscribes to both the U.S. and World databases, they can be cross-searched.

Humanities Databases

Humanities has been the last area to develop electronic resources, probably due to the nature of the scholarship that has relied more heavily on book material. *Humanities Full Text* (EBSCO, formerly Wilson) includes the full text of 330 journals from 1910 to date and indexes over 700 periodicals. The subjects covered include classical studies, history, literature, and religion as well as original works of fiction, drama and poetry, book reviews, and reviews of ballets, theater, film, and so forth. The *Humanities and Social Science Index Retrospective: 1907–1983* is also available indexing the *International Index*, the *Humanities Index*, and the *Social Science Index*. *Humanities Source* (EBSCO) is a new full-text database with citations and abstracts and the full text of 1,400 journals.

FRANCIS is a multidisciplinary and multilingual database produced by the Institut de l'Information Scientifique et Technique with citations and abstracts in English and French to more than 4,000 journals, books, and other documents as far back to 1972. The coverage includes the humanities and social sciences with an emphasis on European publications. The *ATLA Religion Database*, produced by the American Theological Library Association, indexes journals representing all major religions and denominations. Its wide coverage extends to archeology and social issues as well as art. More than 1,600 journals with back files to 1908 are indexed in over 60 languages.

Language and Literature Databases

The Modern Language Association (MLA) produces the *MLA International Bibliography*. It is a subject index for literature and linguistics with more than 4,400 periodicals indexed as well as books and dissertations that dates back to the 1920s. It is international in scope and includes bibliographic records in French, Spanish, German, Russian, Portuguese, Norwegian, and Swedish. The *MLA International Bibliography* has its own thesaurus. It is an excellent index for researching literary criticism or any other aspect of literature even though it does not have full text. It is available through several database vendors.

Two literature resources, *Literature Resources from Gale* and *Literary Reference Center Plus*, are the result of integrating several literature databases into one easy-to-search database. *Literature Resources from Gale* combines three major Gale databases, *Contemporary Authors*, *Dictionary of Literary Biography*, and *Contemporary Literary Criticism* as well as *Litfinder*, *MLA International Bibliography*, and other resources into one large searchable full-text database. Users can search for both literary criticism from periodicals and books and biographical information about authors. *Literary Reference Center Plus* (EBSCO) provides information on authors and literature. It includes plot summaries, literary criticism, author biographies, book reviews, poetry, short stories, and author interviews. It is aimed at the general public, high school students, and undergraduates. Another of these literature databases, aimed at a more scholarly audience, is *Literature Online* (ProQuest/Chadwyck Healey), a collection of full-text literary criticism and reference materials as well as the full text of poetry, prose, and drama in English. It includes *ABELL* (*Annual Bibliography of English Language and Literature*) that provides full-text access to 312 current literary journals and the *MLA International Bibliography*. *Linguistics and Language Behavior Abstracts* (ProQuest/CSA) covers all aspects of the international literature on linguistics and the language sciences providing citations and abstracts to journals, books, and dissertations.

Music Indexes

The world of music scholarship is represented by two databases. The *Music Index* abstracts articles in 480 music periodicals from many countries with subject and author indexing. This index provides access to information on all aspects of music and musicians. The original print index began in 1949; the digitized content began in 1970. *Répertoire International de Littérature Musicale* (*RILM*) provides citations and abstracts for more than 950 scholarly journals as well as books, bibliographies, conference proceedings, dissertations, films, videos, and much more beginning in 1967. International in scope, it indexes music articles in nonmusic journals as well as in music journals.

Art Databases

Art has three strong databases that complement one another. Used together they provide wide coverage in art. *Art Full Text* (EBSCO, formerly Wilson) includes the full text of articles from more than 270 journals from 1997 to the present, as well as article abstracts and indexing of 600 publications from 1984 to the present. It is international in scope including material in languages other than English and a wide variety of subjects such as antiques, architecture, art history, costume, and crafts. *Art Index Retrospective: 1929–1984* provides indexing of more than 600 publications. *Art Source* (EBSCO) is a new database that includes 600 full-text journals and more than 220 full-text books as well as 63,000 images and abstracts of art dissertations

ARTbibliographies Modern (ProQuest/CSA) provides indexing and abstracts for journal articles, books, exhibition catalogs, PhD dissertations, and exhibition reviews on all aspects of modern and contemporary art including crafts, photography, theater arts, and fashion, as well as painting and sculpture from the nineteenth century forward. The coverage dates from 1960. Material in both English and in sixteen other languages is included. This index has a well-developed thesaurus.

The *International Bibliography of Art* (ProQuest/CSA) is a bibliography of scholarly writing about the history of Western art. It is the successor to the *Bibliography of the History of Art*. All aspects of art are covered from paintings and sculpture to crafts and folk art. Indexing more than 500 journals, the citations include detailed abstracts. This bibliography is the successor to *Répertoire d'Art et d'Archéologie* from 1973–1980 and the *International Repertory of the Literature of Art* from 1973–1989.

The *Avery Index to Architectural Periodicals* is the only index devoted to architecture and design as well as related subject areas. Produced by the Avery Architecture and Fine Arts Library at Columbia University, it provides indexing and abstracts for over 700 journals.

Library and Information Science Databases

Library science databases include *Library Literature and Information Science Full Text*, *Library and Information Science Abstracts (LISA)*, and *Library, Information Science and Technology Abstracts (LISTA)*, and *Library, Information Science and Technology Abstracts with Full Text*. *Library Literature and Information Science Full Text* (EBSCO, formerly Wilson) includes periodical articles, conference proceedings, pamphlets, books, and theses on library science. *Library Literature* indexes 390 periodicals dating back to 1980 with full text of articles from 155 periodicals back to 1997. It is international in scope and can be searched by keywords, subject headings, personal names, title words, publication, year, and type of article. *Library Literature and Information Science Retrospective: 1905–1983* provides access to the early years of this index. *Library and Information Science Source* (EBSCO) is a new database with full text of over 460 journals and some monographs. International in scope, it encompasses all aspects of library science and information science.

Library and Information Science Abstracts (ProQuest/CSA) is an international index with abstracts of over 440 periodicals from more than sixty-eight countries in more than twenty languages beginning in 1969. It covers all aspects of library science and information science. *LISA* has its own online thesaurus. *LISTA* (*Library, Information Science and Technology Abstracts*) (EBSCO) is an index with abstracts of journal articles, books, research reports, and conference proceedings. *LISTA* covers librarianship, classification, bibliometrics, information retrieval, and information management. *Library, Information Science and Technology Abstracts with Full Text* provides full text for more than 560 journals and some monographs back to the mid-1960s.

Psychology Databases

PsycINFO, published by the American Psychological Association since 1967, has long been the major database in the field of psychology. It is arranged into twenty-two major categories including psychological, social, and behavioral sciences, and related fields such as psychiatry, neuroscience, medicine, and social work. The scholarly, peer-reviewed, online bibliographic index provides comprehensive coverage of more than 1,000 journal titles relevant to psychology and covers more than 1,800 titles including books, dissertations, and reports. The publications included come from more than fifty countries in twenty-eight languages.

Each listing includes the bibliographic citation and abstract. A separate thesaurus has been developed to guide users through the subject headings. This thesaurus is necessary because of the complex and specific vocabulary within the field of psychology. A separate database, *PsycArticles*, provides full-text access to the articles from more than eighty journals. Most go back to volume 1. *PsycINFO* is available from several of the major database vendors.

Psychology journals can also be searched through *Psychology and Behavioral Sciences Collection* (EBSCO), a comprehensive database with about 400 full-text titles covering topics such as emotional and behavioral characteristics, psychiatry and psychology, mental processes, anthropology, and observational and experimental methods. EBSCO's *Academic Search Complete*, *ProQuest Central*, and Gale's *Health Reference Center Academic* are also sources of information on psychology.

Ethnic Databases

The *Black Studies Center*, which covers the black experience, includes the *International Index to Black Periodicals Full Text* (ProQuest/Chadwyck Healey), an index to scholarly and popular material in Black Studies, which began in 1902. There are citations for retrospective records from 1902–1997. From 1998 forward there are citations and abstracts for 150 journals, newspapers, and newsletters published in the United States, Africa, and the Caribbean as well as full-text coverage of forty-two core Black Studies titles. This database provides bibliographic and full-text resources for a wide range of related issues including economics, history, religion, sociology, and political science. It is both international and interdisciplinary in scope. Other resources in the *Black Studies Center* include *The Chicago Defender* from 1910–1925, the *Black Literature Index*, and the *Schomberg Studies on the Black Experience*.

Ethnic Newswatch (ProQuest) is a full-text online database that covers 1990 to the present. It includes a wide variety of newspapers, magazines, and journals from the ethnic, minority, and native presses not available in other indexes. A total of 340 titles are now indexed in subject areas ranging from Jewish studies to African American, Native American, and Hispanic studies. It is searchable in both English and Spanish with titles in both languages. This unique database provides the researcher with alternate points of view on subjects of current interest.

HAPI Online (*Hispanic American Periodicals Index*) indexes and abstracts books, articles, reviews, bibliographies, literary works, and material appearing in 600 scholarly journals published in Latin America, the Caribbean, and the United States from 1970 to the present. It is also available online and links to full-text articles. *HAPI* is produced by the UCLA Latin American Center.

Business and Medical Databases

Among the excellent business databases are *Business Source Premier* (EBSCO), *ABI/INFORM Complete* (ProQuest), *Business and Company ASAP* (Gale Cengage Learning), *Factiva*, and *Business Source Complete* (EBSCO). These business databases offer the librarian and user a good deal of choice and are discussed in more depth in Chapter 9 as are the following medical and consumer health indexes: *PubMed, MedlinePlus, Health Source* (EBSCO), *Health Reference Center*

Academic and *Health and Wellness Resource Center* (Gale Cengage Learning), and *CINAHL*.

Open Access Journals

The amount of full text available in online databases has grown due to open access journals. These journals, produced with alternative business plans so that the user does not have to pay for access, are particularly important in the sciences. Many are to be found through *HighWire Press* (http://highwire.stanford.edu/) and through the *Directory of Open Access Journals* (http://www.doaj.org/), both of which can be searched by subject. Many government databases provide access to open access journals and articles. They include *arXiv.org* (http://arxiv.org/), which offers access to e-prints in the sciences; the Department of Energy *Information Bridge* (http://www.osti.gov/bridge/), which provides full-text articles and bibliographic citations in all areas related to energy; *E-Print Network* (http://www.osti.gov/eprints/) offering e-prints primarily in physics but also in related scientific areas; *NIST Virtual Library* (http://www.nist.gov/nvl/), which includes databases and other information to support the work of NIST (National Institute of Standards and Technology); and *PubMed Central* (http://www.ncbi.nlm.nih.gov/pmc/), which provides access to free journal literature in the biomedical and life sciences from the National Library of Medicine.

Citation Indexes

Citation indexes help researchers follow an idea from the original scholar to others who have cited the original scholar in their work. A researcher can also determine which scholars have influenced others or how a basic concept is now being used. Originally, there were three citation indexes: the *Science Citation Index*, the *Social Sciences Citation Index*, and the *Arts and Humanities Citation Index*. These three citation indexes are now part of *Web of Science* (Thomson Reuters), an international citation index with coverage of 12,000 high-impact journals with links to the full text of articles cited. Coverage begins in 1900 and continues to the present. Librarians should introduce their users to the *Web of Science* if they are writing substantial research papers. *Google Scholar* also lists for each article the number of times the article has been cited.

Databases for Special Types of Material

ProQuest Dissertations and Theses lists United States, Canadian, British, and European dissertations and master's theses from 1861 to the present. Abstracts exist for dissertations since 1980 and theses abstracts began in 1988. More full text is being added. This is a valuable resource for researchers providing in-depth research on many subjects.

Essay and General Literature Index (EBSCO, formerly Wilson) indexes books, about 300 single- and multiauthor collections, and twenty selected annuals and serials annually. It is a unique source of essays found in book collections that include literary criticism and essays on a wide variety of subjects from leadership to courage. The online coverage begins in 1985. Users can search by keyword, subject, title, author, and date of publication as well as by names of fictional characters and titles of literary works. This database has no full text but can be linked to the library's catalog. *Short Story Index* (EBSCO, formerly Wilson) indexes short stories by author, title, subject, genre, and technique. The online version goes back to 1984. This work indexes both collections of short stories and stories from periodicals. Most of this database simply provides bibliographic information, but there is full text for 5,000 stories. This database helps the user to locate short stories that are in multiauthor collections or in periodicals. *Short Story Index Retrospective: 1915–1983* is also available.

The *Play Index* (EBSCO, formerly Wilson) is now available electronically from 1949 to date. This valuable resource indexes more than 31,000 plays published individually or in collections. Full-length plays, radio and television plays, one-act plays and monologues are indexed. Users can search by author, title, subject, style, genre, and cast type. This resource provides the librarian with a way to find individual plays in collections.

LitFinder (Gale Cengage Learning) is a source for finding the full text of poems, short stories, essays, speeches, and plays. This easy-to-use database allows searching by title, subject, author nationality, gender, and date. International in scope, it covers all time periods. Users can locate the text of more than 135,000 works of literature as well as additional information sources.

Book Review Digest Plus (EBSCO, formerly Wilson) has been published since 1905. In addition to the bibliographic citation, each entry includes a summary of the book and excerpts from reviews. In order to be listed, a book must have two reviews of nonfiction and three reviews of fiction. The electronic version covers 1983 to date and includes book reviews from over 5,000 periodicals. Over 225,000 full-text reviews are now included. This index is useful for readers' advisory work and collection development as well as finding reviews of books. *Book Review Digest Retrospective 1905–1982* provides the earlier years of *Book Review Digest. Book Review Index Online Plus* (Gale Cengage Learning) includes the entire back file of the print index from 1965 to the present. More than 5.6 million review citations on more than 2.5 million titles are listed. There are links to full text from other Gale databases, and it does cover many more titles than *Book Review Digest.*

The *Columbia Granger's Poetry Database* provides online access to poetry found in anthologies and collected works. It includes more than 220,000 poems in full text as well as biographical information and critical essays. The poems are indexed by subject, first line, author, and title.

Databases for Children and Young Adults

Librarians can choose from several databases for young people. *Primary Search*, designed for elementary schools and children's rooms, is aimed at grades four through six. It provides full text of more than eighty of the most popular elementary school magazines. It indexes such titles as *Highlights for Children, National Geographic Kids, National Geographic World, Ranger Rick, Cricket,* and *Science World* as well as a number of children's reference resources. *Middle Search Plus*, designed for middle and junior high school students, is aimed at grades seven through nine. It provides full text of more than 150 popular middle school magazines. It indexes both kids' magazines and easy-to-read adult magazines such as *Time*, *National Geographic*, *Sports Illustrated*, *Popular Science*, and *Popular Mechanics* as well as some reference book information. *eLibrary Elementary* (ProQuest) offers 130 full-text magazines, newspapers, reference books, and transcripts as well as maps, images, and multi-media resources concentrating on general interest areas including social science, general science, humanities, and business. This database is designed for K–6 students. *InfoTrac Junior Edition* (Gale Cengage Learning) is aimed at junior high and middle school students. This full-text online database indexes more than 300 general interest magazines of which 230 are full text. Several reference sources have been added including the *Columbia Encyclopedia*, *Merriam-Webster's Biographical Dictionary*, and *Merriam-Webster's Collegiate Dictionary* (Tenth Edition). *InfoTrac Student Edition* (Gale Cengage Learning), designed for secondary school students, indexes 1,200 magazines of which 1,100 are full text. It also includes newspaper articles, reference books, and maps on a wide spectrum of topics, along with some of the same reference works as *InfoTrac Junior Edition*. *Readers' Guide to Periodical Literature* (EBSCO, formerly Wilson), discussed elsewhere in this chapter, is suitable for high school students.

Collection Development and Maintenance

Selection and Keeping Current

Databases are expensive, so librarians must take care in selecting them. Although there are a few databases which are free, such as *Google Scholar*, government databases, and open access sources, most have an annual subscription fee. In many cases, there is now more than one database in a particular subject area so that librarians have a choice and can make decisions based on the selection of materials indexed, the price, and other criteria that are important to a particular library.

Databases continue to change rapidly as publishers try to expand their coverage and better fit their products to the market. Most database publishers have several products, usually for different types of libraries and often different size packages so libraries can choose which package they need and can afford. The very large packages of databases called "The Big Deal" have become unaffordable for some libraries that must now search for other alternatives. The publishers continue to develop new products as well as acquire smaller companies or form partnerships with other companies. Major publishers are also developing linking agreements in order to offer more full-text services to their users. This evolving field makes it difficult to keep current. Many periodicals such as *Library Journal*, *Choice*, *Computers in Libraries*, *Online*, and *Searcher* report on new database products. These same periodicals also include full-length articles from time to time summarizing the state of the field or a particular part of the field. The publishers themselves are active in contacting libraries as they develop new products or upgrade existing ones.

Evaluating Databases

Due to the large number of databases now available, the evaluation of databases requires a careful examination of a number of factors:

- Authority of publisher
- Scope/subjects covered
- Number and quality of periodicals/newspapers/resources indexed
- Number of titles with full-text coverage
- Currency and frequency of updating
- Accuracy of citations
- Subject headings/controlled vocabulary and access points
- Statistics and training for staff
- Cost

The publisher of the database is of prime importance since the track record of a publisher will usually tell a great deal about what the librarian can expect in terms of quality. Librarians also want to be assured that the publisher will stay in business. This is particularly important with databases since they are a major subscription, and the library needs assurance that the database will continue.

The librarian should consider the scope of the database, that is, the subjects covered and the beginning date of coverage. Often more than one choice in a subject area is available, so the librarians should strive to get the best fit of the subject coverage and the dates included for their particular library and its users. The number of periodicals or newspapers indexed and their quality should be examined. This is not just a numbers game. Any publisher can state that it has more periodicals and newspapers indexed than another. But this can be a hollow statistic if the periodicals and newspapers indexed are not of good quality. In fact, indexing articles of lesser quality only serves to make it more difficult to find the better quality material. To determine where particular periodicals are indexed, the librarian can check *Ulrich's* or *Magazines for Libraries*. Since many databases offer a great deal of full text, it is important to find out if full text is offered for the periodicals most needed. The librarian can check a resource such as *Fulltext Sources Online*. Sometimes none of the databases offer the full text of a particular periodical because the publisher of the periodical has not agreed to it. But sometimes only one database has the rights to a certain periodical that is in high demand. Another issue surrounding full text is whether the whole periodical has been included in the full text. Sometimes only the main articles in a periodical are provided while smaller articles, columns, letters to the editor, and even book reviews are omitted. The currency of the database is of utmost importance, as is the frequency of the updating. Unfortunately one cannot assume that just because a database is available electronically that it is up-to-date. Pick a current subject in the news and check it out in several databases to determine how fast they are updating their databases. The librarian should also note the accuracy of the indexing, especially the bibliographic citations. Frequent errors indicate that the quality control of the database is below acceptable standards.

Examine the consistency and the depth of the subject headings used. Many databases use the Library of Congress Subject Headings or the Sears List of Subject Headings. Other subject-based databases such as the *MLA International Bibliography* and *PsycINFO* develop a thesaurus to provide more specificity in the range of subject headings offered. The use of controlled vocabulary in order to have consistency and to expand the subject headings to include the terminology in that field is important to a database, so using an authoritative list of subject headings is absolutely necessary.

Compare the searching power of various databases. Are some of them more user friendly than others? Do they allow Boolean searching? What fields can you search? Note whether it is easy to find what you want.

Some services are not seen by the public but are important to the librarian. First, the library needs to have statistics on the use of each database. The company producing the database must be able to supply these statistics on a regular basis to enable the library to determine how much each database is being used. Second is the issue of training staff. Since each database is slightly different from the other, staff needs training on each new database. Many companies are prepared to send a trainer to introduce the database to the staff. This is an important benefit. Finally there is the cost. Costs vary tremendously, and most publishers negotiate individually with a library or group of libraries. Publishers usually have more than one way of determining the cost, so it is wise to be familiar with the various possibilities. Many now offer flat fees for their databases. Often publishers' fees are based on the size of a user group. For example, in a university, it might be based on the number of students and faculty. Sometimes companies offer "pay per view" plans to attract infrequent users. Publishers may also be willing to charge based on simultaneous uses. In this case, the library pays for a certain number of simultaneous uses depending on how much they judge the database will be used. In any case, costs can be steep for databases, and for this reason libraries often join consortia so that the price for the database can be spread over several libraries and thus lower the cost.

Further Considerations

What to Do When There Is No Full Text

Users have become accustomed to having full text in databases. But not all databases have full text. For example, the *MLA International Bibliography*, an essential index for those researching literature, has no full text. So what is a librarian or a user to do? First, the software programs Serials Solutions or EBSCO A-to-Z can be used to find out if the full text of an article is available in another database owned by the library. Link resolver software can be used to direct the user to full text of an article in another database owned by the library. If the library does not own the full text online, the librarian should turn to the library's print collection to see if the periodical is owned by the library and is available in bound volumes or in microform. If this is also unsuccessful, the library could either order the article through interlibrary loan or turn to a document delivery service such as

Ingentaconnect (http://www.ingentaconnect.com/)), or the British Library Direct (http://www.bl.uk/reshelp/atyourdesk/docsupply/productsservices/bld/index .html/) and purchase the needed article.

Searching

One of the most difficult parts of the rich array of general and subject databases is that the searching protocols differ from company to company and from database to database. Librarians must become familiar with the databases owned by their library. Librarians in an institution often work together to become knowledgeable about databases. Each studies different databases and then shares the information with the others. It is important to look at both the similarities and differences between databases. Librarians need to know the basics of doing a search in each database and understand some of the useful additional features. Many vendors will provide training on their databases, and libraries should take advantage of this.

Mobile Access

Users now want to search databases no matter where they are. With the new smartphones, more searching is possible. In response, database companies are developing a mobile app for their databases to meet the needs of users. Among the database vendors with mobile access are the following: EBSCO, IEEE, JSTOR, LexisNexis, MLA, and the American Chemical Society. Many more vendors will soon offer mobile access to their databases.

Final Thoughts

Databases are one of the most useful and most popular reference tools available in a library. The advent of so much full text has made it much easier for the user to find the full-text articles and other resources. Each new software innovation such as federated searching and article linker makes it even more seamless to the user, who is always in a hurry. As more databases develop, librarians will have more choices. Just as with reference books, duplication in databases is not always necessary. Libraries need to develop plans and annually reevaluate their holdings, including looking at use statistics for each database.

Recommended Resources Discussed in This Chapter

Academic OneFile. Farmington Hills, MI: Gale Cengage Learning. http://www.gale.cengage.com/.
Academic Search Complete. Ipswich, MA: EBSCO. http://www.ebscohost.com/.
Academic Search Elite. Ipswich, MA: EBSCO. http://www.ebscohost.com/.
Academic Search Premier. Ipswich, MA: EBSCO. http://www.ebscohost.com/.
Access: The Supplementary Index to Periodicals (1975–). Evanston, IL: John Gordon Burke Publisher. http://www.magazineresearchcenter.com/.
Access World News. Naples, FL: Newsbank. Subscription. http://www.newsbank.com/.

THE TOP TEN DATABASES AND INDEXES

Title	Print	Online
Academic OneFile. Farmington, MI: Gale Cengage Learning.		Subscription http://www.gale.cengage.com/
Academic Search Complete. Ipswich, MA: EBSCO.		Subscription http://www.ebscohost.com/
Alternative Press Index. Baltimore, MD: Alternative Press Center.	Quarterly	Subscription http://www.altpress.org/
JSTOR. New York: ITHAKA.		Subscription http://www.jstor.org/
LexisNexis Academic. New York: Reed Elsevier.		http://www.lexisnexis.com/
Omnifile Full Text Mega Edition. Ipswich, MA: EBSCO.		Subscription http://www.ebscohost.com/
PAIS International. Ann Arbor, MI: ProQuest.		Subscription http://www.proquest.com/
ProQuest Central. Ann Arbor, MI: ProQuest.		Subscription http://www.proquest.com/
ProQuest Dialog. Ann Arbor, MI: ProQuest.		Subscription http://www.proquest.com/
ProQuest Newsstand. Ann Arbor, MI: ProQuest.		Subscription http://www.proquest.com/

ACM Digital Library (1985–). New York: Association for Computing Machinery. http://portal.acm.org/dl.cfm.

Alternative Press Index (1969–). Baltimore, MD: Alternative Press Center. Also available online: http://www.altpress.org/.

America: History and Life (1964–). Ipswich, MA: EBSCO. http://www.ebscohost.com/.

America's News. Naples, FL: Newsbank. http://www.newsbank.com/.

RECOMMENDED FREE DATABASE WEBSITES

Directory of Open Access Journals. http://www.doaj.org/. Through this database open access articles can be searched.

ERIC. http://www.eric.ed.gov/. This excellent education database is produced by the U.S. Department of Education.

Google Scholar. http://scholar.google.com/. This site indexes a wide variety of journal articles. Some full text is available free of charge.

Highwire Press. http://highwire.stanford.edu/. This site provides free access to many journal articles.

LISTA (*Library, Information Science and Technology Abstracts*). http://www.libraryresearch.com/. This is the LISTA database available at no charge.

Applied Science and Technology Full Text (1997–). Ipswich, MA: EBSCO. http://www.ebscohost
.com/.

Applied Science and Technology Retrospective 1913–1983. Ipswich, MA: EBSCO. http://www
.ebscohost.com/.

Applied Science and Technology Source. Ipswich, MA: EBSCO. http://www.ebscohost.com/.

Art Full Text (1984–). Ipswich, MA: EBSCO. http://www.ebscohost.com/.

Art Index Retrospective: 1929–1984. Ipswich, MA: EBSCO. http://www.ebscohost.com/.

Art Source. Ipswich, MA: EBSCO. http://www.ebscohost.com/.

ARTbibliographies Modern (1960–). Ann Arbor, MI: ProQuest/CSA. http://www.proquest
.com/.

Article First. Dublin, OH: OCLC. http://www.oclc.org/.

ATLA Religion Database (1949–). Chicago: American Theological Library Association. Available from more than one vendor.

Avery Index to Architectural Periodicals (1934–). New York: Columbia University. http://
www.ebscohost.com/.

Biological and Agricultural Index Plus. Ipswich, MA: EBSCO. http://www.ebscohost.com/.

Biology Digest (1989–). Medford, NJ: Plexus Publishing. Also available online through Newsbank: http://www.newsbank.com/.

BIOSIS Previews (1990–). Philadelphia: Thomson Reuters. http://www.thomsonscientific
.com/.

Black Studies Center. Ann Arbor, MI: ProQuest. http://www.proquest.com/.

Book Review Digest (1905–). Ipswich, MA: EBSCO. http://www.ebscohost.com/.

Book Review Digest Plus (1983–). Ipswich, MA: EBSCO. http://www.ebscohost.com/.

Book Review Digest Retrospective 1905–1982. Ipswich, MA: EBSCO. http://www.ebscohost
.com/.

Book Review Index Online Plus (1965–). Farmington Hills, MI: Gale Cengage Learning. http://www.gale.cengage.com/.

Business Abstracts with Full Text (1982–). Ipswich, MA: EBSCO. http://www.ebsco
host.com/.

CBCA Complete. Ann Arbor, MI: ProQuest. http://www.proquest.com/.

Columbia Granger's Poetry Database. New York: Columbia University Press. http://www
.columbiagrangers.org/.

DialogClassic. Ann Arbor, MI: ProQuest. http://www.dialog.com/.

Education Full Text (1983–). Ipswich, MA: EBSCO. http://www.ebscohost.com/.

Education Index Retrospective: 1929–1983. Ipswich, MA: EBSCO. http://www.ebsco
host.com/.

Education Source. Ipswich, MA: EBSCO. http://www.ebscohost.com/.

eLibrary Elementary. Ann Arbor, MI: ProQuest. http://www.proquest.com/.

E-Print Network. Washington, DC: U.S. Department of Energy, Office of Scientific and Technical Information. Available online for free: http://www.osti.gov/eprints/.

ERIC (1966–). Washington, DC: U.S. Department of Education. Available online for free: http://www.eric.ed.gov/. Also available from other vendors.

Essay and General Literature Index (1985–). Ipswich, MA: EBSCO. http://www.ebsco
host.com/.

Ethnic Newswatch (1990–). Ann Arbor, MI: ProQuest. http://www.proquest.com/.

Expanded Academic ASAP. Farmington Hills, MI: Gale Cengage Learning. http://www
.gale.com/.

FirstSearch. Dublin, OH: OCLC. http://www.oclc.org/.

FRANCIS (1984–). Paris: Institut de l'Information Scientifique et Technique. Available from more than one vendor.

General OneFile. Farmington Hills, MI: Gale Cengage Learning. http://www.gale.cengage.com/.

General Science Full Text (1984–). Ipswich, MA: EBSCO. http://www.ebscohost.com/.

GeoRef (1966–). Ann Arbor, MI: ProQuest/CSA. http://www.proquest.com/.

Google Scholar. Available online for free: http://scholar.google.com/.

HAPI Online (*Hispanic American Periodicals Index Online*) (1970–). Los Angeles: UCLA Latin American Center Publications. http://hapi.ucla.edu/.

Health Reference Center Academic (1980–). Farmington Hills, MI: Gale Cengage Learning. http://www.gale.cengage.com/.

HighWire Press. Palo Alto, CA: Stanford University. Available online for free: http://highwire.stanford.edu/.

Historical Abstracts (1955–). Ipswich, MA: EBSCO. http://www.ebscohost.com/.

History Reference Center. Ipswich, MA: EBSCO. http://www.ebscohost.com/.

Humanities and Social Science Index Retrospective: 1907–1983. Ipswich, MA: EBSCO. http://www.ebscohost.com/.

Humanities Full Text (1984–). Ipswich, MA: EBSCO. http://www.ebscohost.com/.

Humanities Source. Ipswich, MA: EBSCO. http://www.ebscohost.com/.

IEEE Xplore (1988–). IEEE/IEE (Institute of Electrical and Electronics Engineers and the Institution of Engineering and Technology). http://ieeexplore.ieee.org/.

Information Bridge. Washington, DC: U.S. Department of Energy. Available online for free: http://www.osti.gov/bridge/.

InfoTrac Custom Newspapers. Farmington Hills, MI: Gale Cengage Learning. http://www.gale.cengage.com/.

InfoTrac Junior Edition. Farmington Hills, MI: Gale Cengage Learning. http://www.gale.cengage.com/.

InfoTrac Student Edition. Farmington Hills, MI: Gale Cengage Learning. http://www.gale.cengage.com/.

INSPEC (1969–). Institution of Electrical Engineers. http://www.theiet.org/publishing/inspec/.

International Bibliography of Art (2008–). Ann Arbor, MI: ProQuest/CSA. http://www.proquest.com/.

International Index to Black Periodicals Full Text. Ann Arbor, MI: ProQuest. http://www.proquest.com/.

JSTOR. New York: ITHAKA. http://www.jstor.org/.

LexisNexis Academic. Bethesda, MD: LexisNexis Academic and Library Solutions. http://www.lexisnexis.com/.

LexisNexis Library Express. Bethesda, MD: LexisNexis Academic and Library Solutions. http://www.lexisnexis.com/.

Library and Information Science Abstracts (1969–). Ann Arbor, MI: ProQuest. http://www.proquest.com/.

Library and Information Science Source. Ipswich, MA: EBSCO. http://www.ebscohost.com/.

Library, Information Science and Technology Abstracts (*LISTA*). Ipswich, MA: EBSCO. http://www.ebscohost.com/.

Library, Information Science and Technology Abstracts with Full Text. Ipswich, MA: EBSCO. http://www.ebscohost.com/.

Library Literature and Information Science Full Text (1980–). Ipswich, MA: EBSCO. http://www.ebscohost.com/.

Library Literature and Information Science Retrospective: 1905–1983. Ipswich, MA: EBSCO. http://www.ebscohost.com/.

Linguistics and Language Behavior Abstracts. Ann Arbor, MI: ProQuest/CSA. http://www.proquest.com/.

Literary Reference Center Plus. Ipswich, MA: EBSCO. http://www.ebscohost.com/.

Literature Online (LION). Ann Arbor, MI: ProQuest/Chadwyck Healey. http://www.proquest.com/.

Literature Resources from Gale. Farmington Hill, MI: Gale Cengage Learning. http://www.gale.cengage.com/.

LitFinder. Farmington Hill, MI: Gale Cengage Learning. http://www.gale.cengage.com/.

MasterFILE Complete. Ipswich, MA: EBSCO. http://www.ebscohost.com/.

MasterFILE Elite. Ipswich, MA: EBSCO. http://www.ebscohost.com/.

MasterFILE Premier. Ipswich, MA: EBSCO. http://www.ebscohost.com/.

MathSciNet (1940–). American Mathematical Society. http://www.ams.org/.

Middle Search Plus. Ipswich, MA: EBSCO. http://www.ebscohost.com/.

MLA International Bibliography (1922–). New York: Modern Language Association. Available from multiple vendors: http://www.mla.org/bibliography/.

Music Index (1970–). Harmonie Park Press. http://www.ebscohost.com/.

Newspaper Source Plus. Ipswich, MA: EBSCO. http://www.ebscohost.com/.

NIST Virtual Library. Washington, DC: National Institute of Standards and Technology. http://www.nist.gov.nvl.

Oceanic Abstracts (1981–). Ann Arbor, MI: ProQuest/CSA. http://www.proquest.com/.

Omnifile Full Text Mega Edition (1982–). Ipswich, MA: EBSCO. http://www.ebscohost.com/.

PAIS Archive 1915–1976. Ann Arbor, MI: ProQuest/CSA. http://www.proquest.com/.

PAIS International (1972–). Ann Arbor, MI: ProQuest/CSA. http://www.proquest.com/.

Play Index (1949–). Ipswich, MA: EBSCO. http://www.ebscohost.com/.

Poole's Index to Periodical Literature (1802–1906). Boston: Houghton Mifflin.

Primary Search. Ipswich, MA: EBSCO. http://www.ebscohost.com/.

Project MUSE (1995–). Baltimore, MD: Johns Hopkins University Press. http://muse.jhu.edu/.

ProQuest Central. Ann Arbor, MI: ProQuest. http://www.proquest.com/.

ProQuest Dialog. Ann Arbor, MI: ProQuest. http://www.dialog.com/.

ProQuest Dissertations and Theses. Ann Arbor, MI: ProQuest. http://www.proquest.com/.

ProQuest Historical Newspapers. Ann Arbor, MI: ProQuest. http://www.proquest.com/.

ProQuest Newsstand. Ann Arbor, MI: ProQuest. http://www.proquest.com/.

ProQuest Research Library. Ann Arbor, MI: ProQuest. http://www.proquest.com/.

PsycArticles (1988–). Washington, DC: American Psychological Association. http://www.apa.org/.

Psychology and Behavioral Sciences Collection. Ipswich, MA: EBSCO. http://www.ebscohost.com/.

PsycINFO (1967–). Washington, DC: American Psychological Association. http://www.apa.org. Available from multiple vendors.

PubMed Central. Washington, DC: National Library of Medicine. Available online for free: http://www.ncbi.nlm.nih.gov/pmc/.

Readers' Guide Abstracts. Ipswich, MA: EBSCO. http://www.ebscohost.com/.

Readers' Guide Full Text Mega Edition (1983–). Ipswich, MA: EBSCO. http://www.ebscohost.com/.

Readers' Guide Retrospective 1890–1982. Ipswich, MA: EBSCO. http://www.ebscohost.com/.

Readers' Guide to Periodical Literature (1890–). Ipswich, MA: EBSCO. http://www.ebscohost.com/.

Répertoire International de Littérature Musicale (RILM) (1967–). Ipswich, MA: EBSCO. http://www.ebscohost.com/.

Science Full Text Select. Ipswich, MA: EBSCO. http://www.ebscohost.com/.

Science in Context. Farmington Hills, MI: Gale Cengage Learning. http://www.gale.cengage.com/.

SciFinder Scholar (1907–). Columbus, OH: American Chemical Society. http://www.acs.org/.

SciVerse Scopus. New York: Reed Elsevier. http://www.scopus.com/.

Short Story Index (1984–). Ipswich, MA: EBSCO. http://www.ebscohost.com/.

Short Story Index Retrospective: 1915–1983. Ipswich, MA: EBSCO. http://www.ebscohost .com/.

SIRS Issues Researcher (1988–). Ann Arbor, MI: ProQuest. http://www.proquest.com/.

Social Sciences Full Text (1995–). Ipswich, MA: EBSCO. http://www.ebscohost.com/.

Social Sciences Index Retrospective 1907–1983. Ipswich, MA: EBSCO. http://www.ebscohost .com/.

Social Work Abstracts. Washington, DC: National Association of Social Workers Press. http://www.naswpress.org/.

SocINDEX. Ipswich, MA: EBSCO. http://www.ebscohost.com/.

Sociological Abstracts (1952–). Ann Arbor, MI: ProQuest/CSA. http://www.proquest.com/.

U.S. History in Context. Farmington, MI: Gale Cengage Learning. http://www.gale.cengage .com/.

Web of Science. Philadelphia: Thomson Reuters. http://www.thomasscientific.com/. Combines *Science Citation Index*, *Social Science Citation Index*, and *Arts and Humanities Citation Index*.

World History in Context. Farmington, MI: Gale Cengage Learning. http://www.gale.cengage .com/.

Zoological Record Plus. Ann Arbor, MI: ProQuest/CSA. http://www.proquest.com/.

Recommendations for Further Reading

Blicher, Heather, and Stephanie Bedell. 2011. "Picture It: Where in the World Is Your Librarian? A Bibliographic Experiment." *Young Adult Library Services* 9, no. 4: 33–35. Describes a playful public library program designed to introduce young adults to their library's indexes and databases, as well as some trusted web resources.

Chua, Alton Y. K., Khasfariyati Razikin, and Dion H. Goh. 2011. "Social Tags as News Event Detectors." *Journal of Information Science* 37, no. 1: 3–18. Discusses the relatively new possibility of examining text-based patterns in social tags to detect news events, both retrospectively and with immediacy.

Dermody, Kelly, and Norda Majekodunmi. 2011. "Online Databases and the Research Experience for University Students with Print Disabilities." *Library Hi Tech* 29, no. 1: 149–160. Presents the findings of a study revealing the frustrating experience of students using screen reading software to conduct research in proprietary databases. Barriers to the students' progress are discussed, and it is suggested that both database design and current information literacy practices for sight-impaired students are partly to blame.

Dixon, Lydia, Cheri Duncan, Jody Condit Fagan, Stefanie E. Warlick, and Meris Mandernach. 2010. "Finding Articles and Journals via Google Scholar, Journal Portals, and Link Resolvers: Usability Study Results." *Reference and User Services Quarterly* 50, no. 2: 170–181. Examines user satisfaction and success rates in performing searches in *Google Scholar*, journal portals and the link resolver form. The results revealed that users were more satisfied with the usability of *Google Scholar*, and changes were made to the library website's information architecture to make pathways more intuitive.

Farmer, Lesley S. J. 2009. "The Life Cycle of Digital Reference Sources." *The Reference Librarian* 50, no. 2: 117–136. Describes a strategy for coping with the dynamic nature of subscription electronic reference sources, from assessment and collection to archiving, preservation, and deselection.

Little, Geoffrey. 2011. "We Are All Digital Humanists Now." *The Journal of Academic Librarianship* 37, no. 4: 352–354. Provides an overview of the ways by which digitized and born-digital material are changing research in history and other fields in the humanities.

Luyt, Brendan, and Daniel Tan. 2010. "Improving Wikipedia's Credibility: References and Citations in a Sample of History Articles." *Journal of the American Society for Information Science* 61, no. 4: 715–722. Examines a series of *Wikipedia* articles on historical events to determine the quality of the sources used and the accuracy of citations. The results suggest that editors of *Wikipedia* rely heavily on Internet and journalistic sources. There is a call for historians and librarians to improve *Wikipedia* so that it meets it highest potential.

Malkmus, Doris. 2010. "'Old Stuff' for New Teaching Methods: Outreach to History Faculty Teaching with Primary Sources." *portal: Libraries and the Academy* 10, no. 4: 413–435. Primary sources are increasingly being used as course material in undergraduate history classes, creating a need for reference librarians knowledgeable about local archives and available digital primary sources. The article also outlines outreach strategies aimed at history faculty and other faculty.

Martin, Rebecca A. 2010. "Finding Free and Open Access Resources: A Value-Added Service for Patrons." *Journal of Interlibrary Loan, Document Delivery and Electronic Reserve* 20, no. 3: 189–200. Provides guidance to searching and accessing open access and public domain resources. The argument is made that training librarians to evaluate the resources and to increase visibility and ease of use for these free resources may lower subscription costs for libraries.

Tomaiuolo, Nicholas. 2010. "Kicking Tires: Information Literacy Students Compare Google Scholar with EBSCO's Academic Search Premier." *Searcher* 18, no. 10: 20–32. A thoughtful look at what drives students to use *Google Scholar* instead of library databases and how to educate students on the essential differences, advantages and disadvantages, of the two. The article also presents student assessments and the methods used to garner them.

Bibliography and Works Cited

Diakoff, Harry. 2004. "Database Indexing: Yesterday and Today." *The Indexer* 24, no. 1 (October): 85–88.

Golderman, Gail, and Bruce Connolly. 2003. "One-Stop Shopping." *NetConnect* (Summer): 30–35.

Machovec, George. 1995. "Identifying Emerging Technologies." In *The Impact of Emerging Technologies on Reference Services and Bibliographic Instruction*, edited by Gary M. Pitkin, 1–24. Westport, CT: Greenwood Press.

9

Answering Questions about Health, Law, and Business— Special Guidelines and Sources

Overview

Medical, legal, and business questions constitute some of the most specialized, sensitive, and expensive areas of reference. The eternal realities of birth, death, and taxes that color all human existence feed inexorably into an urgent and steady stream of questions on health, legalities, personal finance, and business.

> *"I have taken only one abortion pill, but wish to stop. Will that affect my pregnancy?"*

Hmm...

> *"If I donate my house to charity, will I fall below the poverty line so I could apply for Medicaid?"*

Well...

> *"What was the value of $300 in 1829 America relative to the current dollar in terms of the Consumer Price Index and the GDP per capita?"*

Er...

Like most medical, legal, and business questions, these three demonstrate the hallmarks that mark this as a "handle with care" area of reference work.

- The questions are invariably weighty.
- The answers are typically multilevel so that some degree of specialized knowledge becomes necessary.
- A strong code of ethics must govern the answers.
- The resources swallow a significant percentage of reference budgets and require constant updates.
- Finally, and most important, reference librarians, who are trained in the art and science of answering questions, must be constantly aware that they are nonspecialists and should calibrate their responses accordingly.

A careful balance that requires preestablished parameters of appropriate service combined with in-depth knowledge of available reference resources and referrals is the responsibility of every reference librarian. The American Library Association (ALA) recognized this responsibility early in 1992 and set up specific guidelines for medical, legal, and business responses. While subsequently updated, the guidelines have since been sunsetted in 2011 for lack of review. However, it stands as a useful reminder that the stated role of the reference staff is a vital first step in organizing reference services in these areas. "Libraries should develop written disclaimers. . . . The level of assistance and interpretation provided to users should reflect differing degrees of subject expertise between specialists and non-specialists" (RUSA, 2001). Why is the line between the specialist and the nonspecialist so important in these areas? After all, librarians have unflinchingly responded to questions about SQml, Kantian metaphysics, electrical codes, and pointillism without any specialized knowledge of computer science, philosophy, construction, or art. The answer lies in the nature of the beast.

How Medical, Legal, and Business Resources Are Used

The Nature of the Beast

Medical, legal, and business questions are of a different order based on seven characteristics distinctive of these three areas of research.

CRITICALITY

The psychologist Abraham Maslow (1943) had argued that there was a hierarchy of needs so humans would fulfill their wish to be a ballerina, for example, only if they had first fulfilled their need for basic security. So also, there is a hierarchy of criticality in providing the right reference resource. In all probability, the obsolete cancer resource has far more of a negative impact than an obsolete book of linguistics. The right resource for the pro se litigant battling for child custody is potentially more critical than the right resource for dining etiquette. Medical, legal, and business issues, while not always of dramatically inflated consequence, have a powerful built-in predilection for criticality. The issues they cover can conceivably fall into Maslow's first level of need (health, financial, and civic security) and must be recognized as such.

KNOWLEDGE

A medical doctor takes approximately six years to complete a professional education, and a lawyer is ready to face the bar after three years of specialized study. The level of professionalism is marked by a distinctive and highly specialized vocabulary. Given the density, even consumerist keys to the information can require further decoding. The traditional crutches used by reference librarians while searching in unfamiliar territory, namely the index, table of contents, or "About" icons on a website, are sometimes not enough, so that "staff must have the knowledge and preparation appropriate to meet the routine legal, medical, and business information needs of their clientele" (RUSA, 2001). It helps, for example, to know how a bill passes into public law, so that when a user wants to know more about a citation preceded by "P.L." rather than "H.R.," the librarian is clear about looking into laws rather than resolutions. A crash course in basic legal structure is possible through publications like *Legal Research in a Nutshell* (Cohen and Olsen, 2010) or *Legal Research: How to Find and Understand the Law* (Elias, 2009) or *Finding the Answers to Legal Questions* (Tucker and Lampson, 2010). Business resources such as investment reports can be deciphered after a quick study of guides such as *Business Information: How to Find It, How to Use It* (Lavin, 1992).

RESTRAINT

However knowledgeable the librarians, they can only play "doctor on television." Even lawyers who have become librarians, of whom there appear to be an appreciable number, must show restraint in the dispensing of legal advice. Instead, the role of providing guidance to resources and instruction in the use of resources must be adopted both formally as a written directive and behaviorally. The latter can be very hard to do given the neediness and urgency of many users. A strong referral system and relevant pathfinders are both a necessary antidote and a mandatory addition to medical, legal, and business reference services.

ETHICS

The "guess what" quotient of medical, legal, and business questions can be high. "Guess what, that woman is going through a messy divorce...that teen wants a book on the treatment of syphilis...that man wants to invest in Saudi oil." Discussing patron issues with coworkers must be scrupulously avoided. Questions can be of a highly personal nature, and confidentiality must be consciously maintained. In addition, the best possible resource recommendation is dependent on a successful interview, so that tact in conducting the interview is a necessity. The user must feel comfortable about providing the fullest possible information relevant to the question.

VOLUME

It is no accident that there are specialized libraries devoted to medical, legal, and business collections. The demand for this information is high. As the hapless pages in even non-specialized public libraries will attest, it is the 300 and the 600 section of the collection that is in never-ending need of shelving and shelf alignment. The 300s and 600s are the meat of public libraries primarily because the volume of questions is significant. Publishers, too, have realized this, as attested by the staggering number of medical consumer books published every year. A survey conducted by Pew also corroborated consumer interest in health with the statistic that 80 percent of Internet users have looked online for medical information (Fox, 2012).

UPDATING

Given the premium on currency of resources in these areas, an inordinate number of print publications are loose-leaf, or require inserts and pocket parts, or are supplemented by regular updates. Reference librarians will need to set clear guidelines on discarding procedures and updating schedules, as well as monitor the correct placement of inserts and loose-leaf substitutions, pocket parts, or additions. The individual nature of these weekly, monthly, bimonthly, or quarterly additions, so unlike the simple edition updates of other reference material, further sets apart these three fields as a more specialized area of reference. Users who do not have to fumble through bloated *Value Line* binders that show no signs of the weekly inserts having been discarded; or miss out on an updated law because the annotated insert is not placed in the back pocket; or face rows of dusty *Mergent's*

Bond Records because staff is not sure whether they are of "some use" are users who will appreciate the librarian's recognition that these resources require informed attention.

EXPENSE

Once again, given the depth of information and overriding need for currency, a significant portion of reference budgets must be kept aside for medical, legal, and business resources. A single volume of *Weiss Ratings' Guides*, for example, may be between $250 and $300. However, the volume is redundant in four months, when a new quarterly appears.

Questions Answered by Medical, Legal, and Business Resources

The need to understand the nature of the beast is not so that the reference librarian shirks responsibility in tackling such questions, but rather approaches such questions with a full awareness of its necessary limiters.

Q: Can you find any recommendations for a Dr. Mount E. Bank, with whom I have a colonoscopy scheduled?

A: I could certainly find you a biographical sketch instead that lists his certifications and specialty background, in the *Official ABMS Directory of Board Certified Medical Specialists*.

Q: I am suing my contractor for bad faith. He claims it is a case of negligence. What is the difference and does it mean he can get away with shoddy construction?

A: *West's Encyclopedia of American Law* explains the difference between bad faith and negligence, but you do need professional legal representation to ensure your rights in the matter.

Q: Who are the top companies in terms of sale figures?

A: The top three are Exxon Mobil Corporation, Wal-Mart Stores, and Chevron Corporation as of May 2012 according to *Hoover's Handbook of Private Companies*. You could analyze their financial viability by checking the revenue history, net incomes, background information, and structure as given in the *Handbook*.

Q: Are there any contraindications to the drug Coumadin?

A: Consult the latest copy of the *Physicians' Desk Reference* for information, and then I would suggest double-checking with your doctor or pharmacist.

Q: My lawyer left a message to say that inheriting my grandfather's mansion could be "damnosa hereditas." Is that good or bad?

A: Bad! "An injurious inheritance" is the definition given by *Black's Law Dictionary*, so you may want to check into the costs of inheriting it.

Clarity in defining the limits of what can and cannot be answered is critical to these areas of reference. A thorough knowledge of existing medical, legal, and business resources, such as the ones described in this chapter, goes a long way in encouraging clarity when faced with a user's real-life question.

Major Health Resources Used in Reference Work

The days of the family doctor who made house calls sounds like a long-forgotten myth in today's frenetic world of specialists and insurance-sensitive health systems. For better or for worse, consumer empowerment in health decisions is the order of the day and replaces the old unthinking reliance on the family doctor. Given this climate of empowerment, both the demand for and the supply of health information have reached epic proportions. The reference librarian therefore plays a vital role in slimming down the large amounts of information published and offering an improved selection of comprehensive and comprehensible medical information.

Medical Dictionaries

Inopexia and pallidotomy, cirrhonosus and amusia—the involved language created to describe the vast functions and malfunctions of the human body is almost mystical in its incomprehensibility. For a prosaic understanding of it, however, a stellar dictionary that can bridge the gap between professional terminology and amateur understanding is vital. Even comprehensible words must be checked in a medical dictionary if the context is one of health. For example, an innocuous word like "bay" that may mean an estuary or a barking sound or a leaf in the nonmedical world is, in anatomy, a recess containing fluid.

- A resource that has provided a bridge for many years is *Stedman's Medical Dictionary*, Twenty-Eighth Edition. With over 107,000 terms accompanied by graphics and photographs, the dictionary is used by both health professionals and laypersons. User-friendly features include, but are not limited to, a separate listing of "high profile terms"; synonyms distinguished by blue print; all subentries positioned on a new line to provide more visual simplicity; densely labeled illustrations; and a detailed index. A free online version is available at http://www.stedmans.com/ and can be searched by keyword with wildcard capabilities. A CD-ROM supplement has a medical spellchecker, as well as videos, animations, four-color images, and the ability to keep a record of search histories. The dictionary is also available for PDAs with searches through headwords and multiple hyperlinks.

- First published as a pocket medical dictionary in 1898, *Dorland's Illustrated Medical Dictionary*, Thirty-Second Edition, currently defines more than 120,000 terms supplemented with over 1,100 color plates. The dictionary is invaluable for its clean line drawings, photographs, and radiographic images. The dramatic inclusion of color graphics after more than 100 years of black-and-white images has further enhanced the usability of the reference, as has the addition of more than 800 complementary and alternative medical terms. Color boxes, tables for complex information, and medical terms printed in bright red to enhance readability all contribute to a resource that is both user friendly and comprehensive. The authority of the resource can be testified by the National Library of Medicine, which uses it to establish Medical Subject Headings (MeSH), its own controlled vocabulary of subject headings. The dictionary is available on CD-ROM and can also be accessed freely at http://www.dorlands.com/.

- Though dated, *Melloni's Illustrated Medical Dictionary*, with its 30,000 terms and 3,000 illustrations, continues to be a popular choice for students of the health sciences. Close to one-third of each page is devoted to careful two-color line drawings that bring life to terms that are boldfaced. Whereas the previous two dictionaries are suitable for practicing physicians and others, this dictionary is primarily for beginning students, nurses, allied health workers, and the amateur user.

Medical Encyclopedias

Thompson Gale, Omnigraphics, and Facts on File publish health series that are comprehensive, authoritative, and user friendly.

General

- The *Gale Encyclopedia of Medicine* and the *Gale Encyclopedia of Alternative Medicine* are reliable general encyclopedias available in print and as e-books. The six-volume "one-stop" work on human diseases, disorders, syndromes, procedures, therapies, and drugs, the *Gale Encyclopedia of Medicine* was first published to rave reviews in 1999. The fourth edition, published in 2011, continues the format of alphabetical entries covering a range of diseases with information on causes, symptoms, diagnosis, prognosis, treatment, and prevention included. The structure of information is standardized, so that looking up information on unfamiliar topics becomes relatively easy. Graphics supplement many of the entries, and a detailed index with a cross-referencing system aids usage.
- With a national statistic that claims more than one-third of adults in the United States use complementary and alternative medicine, the four-volume *Gale Encyclopedia of Alternative Medicine* is a useful addition to reference collections. It presents forty types of alternative medicine, from ancient Indian Ayurveda to the modern Feldenkrais Method of healing. The information is careful to avoid any bias. Resource lists of printed information and relevant institutions are also given. Color photographs of medicinal plants provide an invaluable key to identifying obscure herbs. Side effects and general acceptance levels for each entry are also included.
- The thirty-two-volume *Encyclopedia of Life Sciences*, with more than 4,300 specially commissioned and peer-reviewed articles, is the definitive text for life scientists. "Introductory," "Advanced," and "Keynote" gradients of coverage, specificity, and complexity help in making this a user-friendly resource for students and specialists. Color illustrations, tables, taxonomies, acronyms and synonym listings all contribute toward the user-friendly aspects of these scholarly volumes. A subscription-based online version, *eLS*, with limited free content, is available at http://www.els.net/.

Specialized

- The *Gale Encyclopedia of Children's Health* is a four-volume compilation of pediatric diseases and disorders aimed primarily for children under the age of four years. In addition to a catalog of diseases, the encyclopedia also covers developmental issues, immunizations, and drugs. The volumes are also available as an e-book through the *Gale Virtual Reference Library*. The *Gale Encyclopedia of Surgery and Medical Tests* covers 450 surgical procedures. The information is enhanced with much-needed descriptions of the diagnostic procedure for each type of surgery as well as the aftercare that will be required. Morbidity and mortality rates and alternate techniques are included. The encyclopedia is aimed directly at patients and caregivers, as evident in the defining of medical jargon, the use of second opinions, lists of questions to ask doctors, procedures for hospital admission and presurgery, and an extensive bibliography of support organizations, associations, and literature on the subject. It is also available as an e-book.

- A comprehensive and widely respected source of information for over 3,000 drugs, the *Physicians' Desk Reference* (*PDR*) is a staple of all health collections. Drugs can be located by manufacturer, as well as by product or generic name and category. Usage information includes warnings, dosages, overdosages, contraindications, and use-in-pregnancy ratings. The print edition is published annually and updated monthly via eDrug Updates. Photographs of over 1,800 drugs are included, even though they are inserted as a group rather than as accompaniments to the written descriptions. The free online version, available at http://www.pdrhealth.com/, on the other hand, includes photos with the description, which is written in lay terms. The website also provides information on herbal medicine such as echinacea; over-the-counter drugs such as Alka-Seltzer; and nutritional supplements such as vitamins. A collation of *PDR* and related sources is available on CD-ROM as well as mobile devices.

- *RxList: The Internet Drug Index* is a complete and reliable online drug index which is freely accessible at http://www.rxlist.com/. Founded by pharmacists in 1995, the index covers both brand and generic drug names. Handy tools, such as a "pill identifier," which can put a name to a drug through color, shape, or the identifier code indented on every pill, make this a valuable free drug resource.

- The accessible two-volume *Gale Encyclopedia of Mental Health* covers all disorders listed in the *Diagnostic and Statistical Manual of Mental Disorders*, a dense manual described in the next section. It also covers various therapies and medications. All entries are standardized to include, among other things, coverage of definitions, causes, diagnoses, prevention, and additional resources. The language is relatively clear of jargon and illustrations, photographs, and graphics complement entries. Key terms in any description are highlighted in a definition box to simplify understanding of complex issues.

- The Anatomy Act of 1832 in the United Kingdom allowed for the legal dissection of donated bodies. This was the culmination of many centuries of heated debate and fear over the process of dissection as a way to get to know the workings of the human body. Leonardo Da Vinci, creator of the *Vitruvian Man*, for example, had to face the censure of the Vatican in 1514 for alleged witchcraft associated with his anatomy studies. The act allowed for a detailed new textbook on anatomy to be written in 1858 by Henry Gray. That early book has continued to be extensively revised and expanded to provide current students of anatomy with the definitive *Gray's Anatomy*, Fortieth Edition. Given that previous editions exceeded 2,000 pages, the resource is conveniently available online and as an iPad app.

Handbooks and Manuals

- With the cautionary principle that "memory is treacherous" guiding its publication, *The Merck Manual of Diagnosis and Therapy* has been an aid to physicians since 1899, when a slim version was first published. Albert Schweitzer is said to have carried a copy to Africa in 1913 and Admiral Byrd to the South Pole in 1929. The layman's version of the *Merck*, published as recently as 1997 and since updated, is titled *The Merck Manual Home Health Handbook*. Based on the original *Merck*, the home edition uses everyday language to give in-depth information on a complete range of disorders. The information is supplemented with original graphics. The table of contents lists all entries under various disorders, but the detailed index guides the user so that it is not necessary to know which disorder contains the word abetalipoproteinemia. Marketed as a "not-for-profit" service to the global community, the home manual is freely available at http://www.merck.com/. The site can be searched by keyword, an alphabetical index, or through a subject section such as "blood disorders" or "infections." Once linked, the page displays a navigation area clearly stating the section, chapter, or topic that has been selected. Relevant hyperlinks and diagrams are also included.
- Published primarily as a diagnostic tool, the *DSM-IV-TR* (*Diagnostic and Statistical Manual of Mental Disorders*, Fourth Edition, Text Revision) is published by the American Psychiatric Association. It has become a fixture in libraries because of its unique coverage of psychiatric illnesses and its authority as a source for standard nomenclature of all mental disorders. Prevalence, genetic predisposition, age, gender, culture, and other features are included for each disorder. The presentation is dense and aimed at the professional rather than the lay user. The fourth edition is available for use on PDAs and smartphones. The much-anticipated fifth edition is not due until May 2013. The recent edition can be searched as a subscription database at http://psychiatry online.org/index.aspx.

Medical Directories

Locating a particular doctor or hospital; scanning listings for relevant doctors and medical centers in a certain area of specialization; and vetting doctors and hospitals are frequent requests. Medical directories provide answers for this category of questions.

- The annual three-volume *Official ABMS Directory of Board Certified Medical Specialists* has comprehensive biographies of over 695,000 medical specialists in the United States and Canada, who have been certified by the twenty-four medical specialty boards of the American Board of Medical Specialties.

Certification is voluntary, so it is not necessary that each qualified physician be in the directory. The directory can be used to locate a physician by specialty and by geographical area. It can also be used to verify a specialist's educational background, professional associations, and general credentials. The print edition includes access to a companion website. The CD-ROM version of the directory is updated twice a year and titled *ABMS Medical Specialists PLUS* (Elsevier). The database version, available at http://www.board certifieddocs.com/, is updated daily and has special features such as "alerts" tailored to specific notifications and downloadable records as well as information about more than 800,000 physicians. A free certification search is accessible at http://www .abms.org/, but the user must log in and complete a registration form. Physicians can also be verified by calling the toll-free number, 1-866-ASK-ABMS.

- A popular consumer guide to physicians is Castle Connolly's *America's Top Doctors*. Over 230,000 physicians are surveyed and nominated by their peers to produce this book's list of over 6,000 "top doctors." Selection is highly subjective but provides a first cut to users looking for a starting point in their search for the right physician. Listings are by area of specialization so that twenty-three specialties and ninety subspecialties can be studied for both institutional and physician listings. The information is also available online for an annual fee at http://www.castleconnolly.com/, though a portion of the database can be accessed free after completing a registration form.

- More than 814,000 fully licensed physicians can be found on the freely available *DoctorFinder* provided by the American Medical Association at http://webapps.ama-assn.org/doctorfinder/home.jsp. Physicians who are not fully licensed are best located in the printed *Directory of Physicians in the United States* published by the American Medical Association that covers residents, researchers, teachers, administrators, and retired physicians.

- A unique resource that has not been updated since 2000 is the consumer watch publication from Public Citizen, *20,125 Questionable Doctors: Disciplined by State and Federal Governments*, National Edition. The doctors pilloried in the four volumes are from across the nation and collectively account for more than 34,000 disciplinary actions ranging from fines to license suspensions. Detailed information on whether the physician has been disciplined for substance abuse, sex offenses, or incompetence is included. With a majority of the physicians listed continuing to practice, the volumes provide an authoritative resource for users looking for further information on specific doctors. The Public Citizen group (http://www.citizen.org/hrg) offers a continuing focus on transparency and accountability in the health profession.

- *DIRLINE*, a comprehensive directory of health and biomedical organizations, is a free government website at http://dirline.nlm.nih.gov/. With over 8,500 records of agencies, referral centers, professional organizations, self-help and community groups, and research institutions, the directory can be searched by keyword or a subject search of the disease or condition. The results include an abstract of the organization's aims, history, and budget, as well as complete contact information.

Medical Databases and Indexes

- *PubMed* is both freely accessible and the most extensive bibliographic database for health issues. It covers the information contained in the National Library of Medicine's *MEDLINE*, which has 18 million citations dating back to 1948; *OLDMEDLINE*, with 2 million citations ranging between 1950 and 1965; and special out-of-scope citations primarily from the life sciences. The coverage is not limited to North American journals. While full text is not available on *PubMed*, a "Link Out" feature allows the user to access full-text articles from a specific citation. Many of these links, however, require subscriptions or fees to access the full text, which can be procured through vendors such as EBSCO or Ovid. Available at http://www.pubmed.gov/, the database has the authority of the National Institutes of Health and is invaluable as an index tool for researchers.

- *EMBASE* is a comprehensive biomedical and pharmacological bibliographic database that can be accessed at http://www.embase.com/. It contains more than 19 million indexed records collated since 1947, with more than 600,000 additions made on an annual basis. With 1,800 additional biomedical journals in its repertoire, it is more extensive than *PubMed*, especially in its coverage of European drug trials and pharmaceuticals that are undergoing research and development.

- Gale Cengage Learning at http://www.gale.com/ is responsible for a set of well-known and respected medical databases and indexes to medical journals, newspaper articles, and pamphlets. The two major ones are *Health Reference Center Academic* and the *Health and Wellness Resource Center* available through the Gale PowerSearch platform. Similar in content, though different in interface, access, and search strategies, the Gale databases are user friendly, authoritative, and provide both full-text articles and indexing to additional titles. Indexing covers articles in books, overviews, pamphlets, and journals. The *Academic* database has a built-in translating tool for on-demand document translation as well as the ability to create alerts with RSS Export.

- EBSCO Information Services at http://www.ebsco.com/ parents a host of bibliographic and full-text medical databases of which *Health Source* and *CINAHL* are notable for their coverage and ease in searching. *Health Source*, available as both a *Consumer* and an *Academic* edition, is an extensive database with access to health periodicals, reference books, pamphlets, drug monograph entries, and patient education fact sheets. Full-text documents as well as abstracts and indexes are available, with convenient links that can guide the researcher to more in-depth study. *CINAHL* is less general, but provides the most exhaustive index for issues related to nursing and allied health. *CINAHL Full Text* is the expanded version that allows for full-text searches. Almost 3,000 journals in the nursing field are indexed by this database, as well as nursing dissertations, conference proceedings, and standards of practice. Together, there are more than 2 million records, some of which date back to the early 1980s. Aimed at a more specialized user, full-text articles from more than 600 journals, legal cases, and clinical trials are also available.

- For special reference collections, the subscription-based *Dialog* service is a rich source of medical and pharmaceutical databases; it has 121 million records directly focused on biomedical and pharmaceutical literature. It also includes the 10,000 foundations listed in the *Foundation Directory* that is invaluable for the constant grant seeking required in the medical field.

Health Information Sites

Changes in medical wisdom have far-reaching effects. The miracle cure of today can become the pariah of tomorrow. Fast-changing knowledge of medical research can oftentimes only be available on the Internet, a medium that is capable of handling and disseminating news speedily and globally. Bookmarking at least five to ten valuable websites for medical news and updates is a necessity of good health reference service.

- The National Library of Medicine is the largest medical library in the world. *MedlinePlus*, a component of the aforementioned *PubMed*, was started in 1998 as the library's consumer health website at http://medline plus.gov/. It now covers over 900 topics with over 700 available in Spanish and 18,000 links to authoritative health sites. It is also a strong resource for checking on drugs, clinical trials, hospitals, and physicians. The information is updated daily and fed by both government agencies and health organizations. A medical dictionary and encyclopedia are included. Some of the sources that cover drug information, such as the *USP-DI*, give Canadian brand names as well, so that, for example, Sinutab in Canada can replace an antihistamine like Sinarest in the United States after a quick check of the website.
- While *MedlinePlus* is a valuable all-purpose site, specialized sites such as the National Cancer Institute at the National Institutes of Health (http://www .cancer.gov/) and the American Cancer Society (http://www.cancer.org/) provide authoritative and timely information on specific diseases. Both sites are written in lay terms and cover the various stages faced by cancer patients.
- A valuable site for drug information, *DrugDigest* (http://www.drugdigest .org/) provides the unique *Drug Interactions* database that allows the user to check for interactions between two drugs. Niggling questions on whether one can take an aspirin for headache while taking a particular prescription drug for diabetes are solved by use of this site. More than 6,000 images of pills also help users who need to confirm that what they are about to swallow is indeed what they meant to swallow, especially when pill makers change the shape or color of the pills. Freely accessible to all, the website also includes data from the subscription database *Clinical Pharmacology*.
- An interesting source for up-to-date medical news articles, with a bias toward news from the United Kingdom, is offered by BBC News (http:// www.bbc.co.uk/news/health/). The "Health" section can be checked for current medical stories, as well as searched for archival material by keyword

or through an A–Z index. More extensive yet is the site from the National Library for Health at http://www.evidence.nhs.uk/ that provides medical updates, news, and links to special libraries and acts as a "digital hub" for services across the country.

- Medical updates in the United Kingdom can also be accessed from the *BMJ* (*British Medical Journal*), a popular and highly reputable online site at http://www.bmj.com/ that attracts over 1.5 million unique users each month and was awarded the Medical Publication of the Year in 2008. More dramatic medical updates can be found in the well-known and well-loved journal *The Lancet*, available at http://www.thelancet.com/. *The Lancet* is unabashedly activist in that it publishes both medical science such as its groundbreaking identification of the viral cause of SARS in 2003, and champions public health causes such as child survival and climate change.

Health Statistics

The National Center for Health Statistics (http://www.cdc.gov/nchs/) is the primary source for health statistics. Data collected from birth, death, and medical records as well as through widespread surveys, testing, interviews, and examinations are collated to provide "surveillance information" that can be used to limn the nation's health problems. The site has a simple overview of datasheets so that it is possible to access a rich vein of statistical information with minimal burrowing. Each datasheet has links to a range of additional sources so that more in-depth research is also possible. Hard-to-find statistics on teens with live births (444,899 in 2007) or tuberculosis in the United States (11,545 in 2009) or persons without health coverage (43.0 million in 2007) can be accessed easily.

Major Legal Resources Used in Reference Work

On January 2, 2003, the Judicial Council of the California County Law Librarians decided to include an icon for 24/7 legal reference help in every page of its site. The effect was immediate. From an average of 100 questions per month, the number of legal queries shot up to an astonishing 2,045 questions. There has never been any doubt that we live in an increasingly litigious society. However, the exponential rise in amateur lawyers and pro se litigants has come as a surprise. The person on the street is now potentially able to draw up a living will; expand a home in accordance with local zoning laws; or fight a custody battle. Prohibitive lawyer fees, coupled with extensive access to legal precedent and rules via the Internet, have put the onus of legal responsibility on the common person, and by extension, the neighborhood librarian.

Given this trend, a collection that includes basic printed legal material and access to online resources is a necessary component of reference service in all libraries. While all libraries must have a dictionary to decode legalese and an encyclopedia to cover a breadth of legal topics, more specialized resources such as directories, indexes, and primary and secondary legal material can be acquired based on the needs of the community.

Legal Dictionaries

- Currently in its ninth edition, the invaluable *Black's Law Dictionary* was first published in 1891 under the stewardship of English legalist Henry Campbell Black. It is reportedly the most cited law dictionary in the country and covers more than 45,000 definitions. A large number of the entries are cross-referenced to cases in the *Corpus Juris Secundum* to aid further research. The last edition also provides a useful appendix of more than 4,000 legal abbreviations and another on legal maxims. Pronunciations of arcane legalese such as the feudal "feoffee" are provided, as well as equivalent terms and alternate spellings for more than 5,300 terms and senses. A pocket, an abridged, and a deluxe edition of the dictionary are also available. The dictionary is available as a digital dictionary that can be integrated with individual word processors and web browsers and is searchable on *Westlaw*. It is also available as an app for iPhones, iPads, and iPods, and Androids.
- With more than 10,000 definitions of over 5,000 legal terms defined with phonetic pronunciations, *Ballentine's Law Dictionary* has been a popular alternative to *Black's*. An all-important case citation, from which a particular definition derives authority, is also supplied, thereby providing a starting point of research for many users. It is particularly useful in its coverage of old Saxon, French, and Latin phrases. The *Ballentine's Legal Dictionary and Thesaurus* combines the dictionary with a thesaurus for legal research and writing so that synonyms, antonyms, and parts of speech are also attached to each definition, making for a more exact understanding of each legal term. The appendix includes *The Chicago Manual of Legal Citation* and a guide to doing research.
- Free online legal dictionaries can also be used for quick searches. *Merriam-Webster's Dictionary of Law* can be accessed through *Findlaw* at http://dictionary.lp.findlaw.com/. A basic legal dictionary that can be searched by legal term, by letter of the alphabet, and by all definitions that include the word is located at http://dictionary.law.com/. A historical dictionary of legal terms can be accessed at http://www.constitution.org/bouv/bouvier.htm, where a copy of the indomitable 1856 *Bouvier's Law Dictionary* provides definitions for such legal entities as "female" (the sex which bears young).

Legal Encyclopedias and Yearbooks

- The word "weal" is defined as the common good or the welfare of the community at large. It was also the motivation and acronym of the preeminent legal encyclopedia, *West's Encyclopedia of American Law* (WEAL), recently reissued as the *Gale Encyclopedia of American Law*. The new 1,413-volume set covers over 5,000 legal issues. Terms, cases, statutes, documents, issues, forms, timelines, and over 600 biographies are presented without specialized jargon so that it is accessible to the layperson. With a determined focus to provide "legal ease" rather than "legalese," even complex and far-ranging issues such as *Roe vs. Wade* are condensed into understandable packets of knowledge with the inclusion of lawyer arguments, majority and dissenting opinions, and the reasoning of the judges. Graphics, cross-references, timelines, photographs, and focus boxes enhance the text. The encyclopedia is also available in an e-book format.

- The *American Law Yearbook* annually updates the above encyclopedia and provides expanded versions of entries. Cross-references, timelines, and photographs that accompany the biographies make this a highly user-friendly resource. Each edition carries the U.S. Supreme Court docket as well as other cases not argued at the level of the Supreme Court. The recent inclusion of legal issues pertaining to YouTube, eminent domain law, and steroid scandals amongst athletes attests to the currency of each edition. It is available in e-book format through *Gale Virtual Reference Library*.

Legal Directories

- Published for 140 years, the *Martindale-Hubbell Law Directory* is an established authority for locating and checking on the credentials of law firms and lawyers. The twenty-six-volume print edition lists more than 1 million lawyers and firms in 160 countries. The entries are arranged by geographical location so that smaller libraries have the option of purchasing single volumes that cover their own home state. An extensive indexing system allows searches by name as well. The volumes are also available on a two-disc CD-ROM that allows for twenty-seven different search criteria. Search results can be exported to a spreadsheet or database program, with more than one application running at the same time. Free online access is available via the *Lawyer Locator* at http://www .martindale.com/ and through new mobile apps. Solicitors and law firms in the United Kingdom can also be freely accessed at http://www.lawyerlocator .co.uk/. The biographical information provided is also supplemented with peer ratings and reviews, a unique practice begun since the 1896 edition of the directory. The directory is not only a global standard for information on the legal profession; it also acts as a marketing or fact-checking tool for lawyers as well. All lawyers and law firms can complete the Practice Profile listings, so that an unlisted firm or lawyer is invariably considered to be suspect.
- The *Law and Legal Information Directory* is an annual, single-volume directory with almost 2,000 pages packed with information. Over 21,000 legal agencies, programs, institutions, facilities, and services are listed under different categories as diverse as "National and International Organizations" and "Awards and Prizes." Each listing provides a brief description and contact information.

Legal Databases and Indexes

Subscription databases such as *Lexis*, *Westlaw*, and *LAWCHEK* aim to provide a wide range of legal information relevant to the most heavily used areas of legal research.

- Started as early as 1973, *Lexis* was a pioneer in providing full-text legal information. As the *LexisNexis* database, it continues to be the most authoritative index of legal and government documents, as well as a resource for full-text legal material. Various permutations of the master database are available so that custom packages can be created for different levels of libraries, the primary three being corporate, government, and law libraries. Case law, codes, legal analysis, public records of property, news transcripts, and regulations are all part of the powerful array of legal resources provided by *LexisNexis*. Indexes such as H.W. Wilson's *Index to Legal Periodicals* are also part of the array. The database has continued to expand and in 2005 became the exclusive provider of legal content for a major repository of business intelligence, *Factiva* (http://www.factiva.com/). Given the richness of the database, the endless customization available, and the high costs of purchase, an involved study of each community's legal reference demands must be made before choosing the right package at http://www.lexisnexis.com/.

- *Quicklaw* is the Canadian branch of *LexisNexis* and can be accessed at http://ql.quicklaw.com/. Tailored to Canadian legal information needs, the same mix of case law, court and tribunal decisions, procedures, legal news, and commentary are provided for a fee. Legal information can also be found in French and the website itself is bilingual.

- *LexisNexis UK* is accessible for a subscription fee at http://www.lexisnexis.co.uk/. With lawyer-locator services, studies and citations of English, Irish, Scottish, Commonwealth, and European cases, all 50 volumes of *Halsbury's Laws*, tax and pension information, and fully amended texts of statutes, and so on, *LexisNexis UK* is a comprehensive legal resource for the United Kingdom. An initiative to provide online legal service was inaugurated in June 2005.

- *Westlaw* is another powerful provider of legal documents such as case law, statutes with annotations and court corrections, directories, law reviews, and public records such as real property deeds. While aimed at the legal professional, *Westlaw* has introduced user-friendly search aids such as "Smart Tools" that attempt to flag any word or acronym that appears to be spelled incorrectly or appears out of context. So for example, even a "correct" spelling like "statue" is flagged if it mistakenly appears in the context of the term "statute of limitations." Related terms are also suggested to aid the nonprofessional. Directories can be scanned by single word search terms and words are automatically searched along with their plurals, irregular plurals, and possessives. The density of information offered is tempered with these search enhancements, details of which can be found at the website (http://www.Westlaw.com/). *WestlawNext*, the newest iteration, promises to transform the traditional search process with its new "Google-like" search engine (Wheeler, 2011) and its immediate introduction as an iPad app.

- *LAWCHEK* was created as a direct result of the 1991 American Library Association study that found the most problematic area of reference research in any library was in the field of law. It is aimed at the layperson and the reference librarian. Fashioned as a tutorial for twelve selected legal disciplines found to be the most heavily trafficked areas of public research, *LAWCHEK* provides fee-based access to legal forms, glossaries, guides, letter templates, and legal directories associated with these areas. It is also linked to both state and federal codes and cases. The website can be accessed at http://www.lawchek.com/.

Legal Online Resources

- Winner of the 2005 Webby Awards for best legal website, *FindLaw* (http://www.findlaw.com/) is a popular free site for legal professionals, students, and the layperson. Packed with legal links, information, lawyer directories, forms, and news, the site is a rich source for both primary and secondary legal material.
- *Hieros Gamos* is a respected website for extensive directory listings of lawyers, law firms, expert witnesses, court reporters, investigators, and process servers both in North America and globally. Legal and bar associations, law libraries around the world, legal events, and news are all part of the website available at http://www.hg.org/.
- In January 1995, *THOMAS* became the first and foremost source for free online information on federal legislation. The *Congressional Record Index* supplies an invaluable index. Also available are historical documents; summaries of congressional activity; the legislative process; committee reports and information; and bill text, summaries, and status. Accessible at http://thomas.loc.gov/, the site is easy to use and provides a valuable resource for any information related to legislation in the United States. Summaries of laws and acts could also be accessed by a Google search with the name of the law in quotation marks followed by the word "summary."
- Access to global laws is also becoming freely available. For British law, a good portal to law sources can be found at http://legal-directory.net/. It provides free access to specialized legal information such as family, property, medical negligence, and personal injury law in the United Kingdom. A comprehensive portal to information about Canadian legal resources, set up by the nonprofit Canadian Legal Information Institute, can be found at http://www.canlii.org/.
- In 2012, EBSCO Publishing and H.W. Wilson pooled their legal databases to form a powerful new online resource, *Legal Source*. The database has full-text coverage of over 1,200 law journals; law reviews; and international journals as well as indexing for about 1,400 monographs by members of the bar. Newer fields such as Internet and Information Science Law are covered along with traditional areas such as Estate Planning and Family Law. A free trial was available at http://www.ebscohost.com/academic/legal-source.

Major Business Resources Used in Reference Work

It is a jungle out there. Business resources run the gamut from tissue-thin pamphlets on personal finance to multivolume works on global marketing. The whys and wherefores and how-to's of making, consolidating, and propagating wealth root into a dense thicket of publications on accounting, taxation, banking, human resources, industrial relations, labor, personal finance, international finance, insurance, advertising, company profiles, product development, biographical directories, commodity statistics, rating guides, statistical overviews, and more. Whereas a set of inclusive online or print business dictionaries, encyclopedias, handbooks, indexes, and directories is required of all reference collections, more in-depth acquisition is required primarily in two of the most heavily trafficked areas of business queries: that of personal finance and business entrepreneurship.

Business Dictionaries

- When users are stumped as to whether they should be putting an "accelerator clause" in their lending document or whether a "variable markup policy" is advisable for their small business, it is time to consult the Oxford University Press's *A Dictionary of Business and Management*. First published in 1990 as *A Concise Dictionary of Business*, the 2009 edition has over 7,000 entries, with a focus on e-commerce terms. The definitions provide pithy background information and are strengthened by a systematic web of cross-references, illustrations, synonyms and abbreviations.
- The distinct Economist Series publications the *Dictionary of Business* and the *International Dictionary of Finance* provide simple definitions on a wide range of business activity. Brief analyses of business concepts are also provided, along with cross-references, acronyms, and business jargon. More than 2,000 terms are listed in each dictionary. Given the global nature of business, many of the terms included are common to countries other than the United States. However, the dictionaries are relatively vulnerable in the area of e-commerce, as they have not been updated since 2003.
- Strong in current terminology is *BusinessDictionary*, which is freely available at http://www.businessdictionary.com/. With over 20,000 definitions that can be approached as keywords or through forty-two subject categories, and 115,000 links between related terms, the site also offers a free daily e-newsletter.
- Libraries that require a more specialized breakdown of dictionary meanings in all the various aspects of business can look into the Barron's Educational Series. Separated into the *Dictionary of Business and Economics Terms* with 8,000 entries; the *Dictionary of Marketing Terms* with 4,000 entries; the *Dictionary of Insurance Terms* with 4,500 entries; the *Dictionary of Accounting Terms* with 2,500 entries; the *Dictionary of Finance and Investment Terms* with 5,000 entries, and more, the series is physically small and hard to shelve but useful and inexpensive.

Directories and Handbooks

- The multivolume annual *Thomas Register of American Manufacturers*, published since 1906, ceased publishing print editions in 2007 and is now freely available online at http://www.thomasnet.com/. It is the standard authority for finding information such as contact numbers, addresses, subsidiaries, sales offices, and affiliations for 607,000 companies. There are 67,000 product and service categories listed alphabetically under city and state. Contact information, as well as product details, is accompanied by millions of detailed CAD drawings of component pieces and company catalogs. Searches can be made via keyword and product category or limited by geographic location. Manufacturing information for the United Kingdom, Canada, and twenty-six other countries can be accessed freely at http://www.solusource.com/.

- First published in 1928, the three-volume *Standard and Poor's Register of Corporations, Directors and Executives* is a panoptic directory of 75,000 corporations and 290,000 executives across the United States, Canada, and parts of the world. Volume 1 covers corporations with contact information that includes website addresses when applicable, as well as a brief listing of key personnel, number of employees, products, total sales, and North American Industry Classification System (NAICS) codes. Volume 2 alphabetically lists officers, directors, trustees, and patrons of business organizations, with both contact information and biographical details such as year and place of birth, college and year of graduation, and noncollege fraternal memberships. Volume 3 contains indexes. The entries are democratic in that Bill Gates is given the same space as an officer of a florist company in Kentucky. An extensive system of cross-references is also provided so that a user can locate companies under NAICS codes, geographical location, and subsidiary and parent company information. Tracking the ultimate parent company in a corporate family hierarchy, so that the relation between, say, ABC as a subsidiary of the Walt Disney Company becomes clear, elevates this resource to more than just a simple directory. The annual is further updated through cumulative supplements. An online paid subscription to *NetAdvantage* (http://www.net advantage.standardandpoors.com/) provides access to the *Register* as well as a bundle of other S&P resources.
- "Who Owns Whom" is the succinct description supporting the title of the extensive eight-volume *LexisNexis Corporate Affiliations*. The directory lists over 228,000 international and American companies with revenue in excess of $50 million and $10 million, respectively. A master index can be used to locate the ownership status, corporate hierarchy, nationality, geographic coverage, personnel, Standard Industrial Classification, and brand name correlations for each company. Users wanting to know if the Bridgestone Corporation is American, or if there are links between the Tokyo office of Bridgestone and the Cobra Tire Company in Phoenix, are well served by the clear nexus provided by this resource. The directory is available as a fee-based online subscription at http://www.corporateaffiliations.com/, where the family tree is traced all the way down to the "seventh level of reporting relationships" and covers nearly 700,000 companies.
- Published in 1991 as a single handbook profiling 500 corporations, Hoover's now publishes multiple handbooks that are updated annually. *Hoover's Handbook of American Business* focuses on 750 influential American companies with in-depth coverage of personalities and analyses of successful company strategies. *Hoover's Handbook of Private Companies* profiles 900 such companies including hospitals, charities, universities, and cooperatives. *Hoover's Handbook of World Business* covers 300 public, private, and state-owned businesses located outside the United States, but intimately webbed in today's global market so that the iconic American 7-Eleven stores are shown to be controlled by Ito-Yokado, a Japanese retail monolith. *Hoover's Handbook of Emerging Companies* aims to highlight 600 of the most vibrantly growing small businesses, with in-depth profiles on 200 of them. *Hoover's Handbook of Industry*

Profiles is the latest addition and covers analysis and trends for 300 industries. All five handbooks emerge from a company database of 65 million companies that allows Hoover's Business Press to offer a dizzying variety of online business resources that can be accessed via subscription at http://www .hoovers.com/.

- *Brands and Their Companies* is a useful directory of more than 426,000 brand names. For users wanting to know which company manufacturers the Frisbee toy (Wham-O Manufacturing Company); or what the brand Diazinon is (a household pesticide); or whether Big Time candy is still in production (no), this is the directory to consult. The entries are listed alphabetically by brand name and briefly list the product description and the manufacturer or distributor. Brands no longer in production are marked as such, whereas brands that have morphed into generic words such as "Xerox" are also included. Brands not registered with the patent office are also entered, making this a unique resource for hard-to-find information. The directory is also available as part of the *Gale Directory Library*, a subscription database available at http://www.gale.com/.

Investment Guides

- In the volatile world of financial investing, a steady guide has been provided by *Value Line Investment Survey*. Published since the 1930s, the survey is a weekly investment advisory that comes in three loose-leaf parts. The main part is the *Ratings and Reports* section that covers 1,700 stocks. Each stock is analyzed and graded for timeliness, safety, and volatility. Background information on the company is provided along with a graph charting a decade of price ranges. Given the careful mix of recommendation and information, *Value Line* has become a staple of reference collections. Subscription to an online version can be found at http://www.valueline.com/.
- A *Financial Ratings Series* powered by Weiss Ratings and The Street Ratings publishes a series of quarterly investment guides for both the novice and seasoned investor. The beginning user can be directed to the *Ultimate Guided Tour of Stock Investing*, in which a pith-helmeted cartoon safari leader leads the investor through the wilds of stock figures, analyses, and analysts. However, the bulk of publications are aimed at the practicing and amateur investor. There are *Ratings Guides on Bond and Money Market Mutual Funds, Exchange Traded Funds, Common Stocks, Stock Mutual Funds, Banks and Thrifts, Health Insurers, Life and Annuity Insurers, Property and Casualty Insurers*. A careful system of ratings is established so that each bond, mutual fund, bank, insurance company, and brokerage firm is analyzed and judged according to a stated set of criteria. Weiss, which has been publishing guides for over thirty years, stresses objectivity so that no compensation is accepted from any of the institutions rated. Libraries have the option of buying one annual issue, or subscribing to the quarterly editions that are published for each guide. Individual rating reports are commercially available at http://www .financialratingsseries.com/.

Business Entrepreneurship Aids

- The *Market Share Reporter* is now a combination of both the North American market and the international market that was previously published as the *World Market Share Reporter*. With more than 3,600 entries arranged under SIC/NAICS codes, the *Reporter* acts as a unique resource for users interested in comparing and ranking the market share of companies and their products. Products ranging from top disposable diaper brands (Huggies Ultratrim) to the leading aircraft maker for the defense department (Boeing Company) are listed along with the percentage share of the market and, in some cases, the dollar amounts as well. An alphabetical table of topics is provided along with a table of contents listed in numerical SIC ascending order. Pie and bar charts supplement some of the entries, and each entry cites the source.

- Previously published as the *Source Book of Franchise Opportunities*, *Bond's Franchise Guide* profiles nearly 900 franchises, divided into business categories such as "recreation and entertainment" and "automotive products and services." Each entry provides contact information. The entries are derived from a 40-point questionnaire and are therefore highly detailed, requiring an a priori reading on how to use the data. In addition to contact information, background history, and a description of the business franchiser, criteria for granting a franchise are also given along with legal and financial requirements. Franchise seekers are well served by this resource. It is also available online at http://www.worldfranchising.com/.

Business Databases and Indexes

- A sweeping database with a powerful indexing component, Gale's *Business and Company ASAP* covers over 200,000 directory listings, full-text public relations newswires for up-to-the-minute information, and thousands of entries from business journals, trade periodicals, and management serials from 1980 to the present. The corollary *Business Index ASAP* is integrated so that indexes for the financial section of *The New York Times*, the *Asian Wall Street Journal*, and *The Wall Street Journal* are available. User aids include a controlled vocabulary, a subject guide, cross-references, and customizable search strategies. Subscription information is available at http://www.gale.cengage.com/.

- *Mergent Online* is an incisive business database that provides global business and financial information that includes filings from *Electronic Data Gathering Analysis and Retrieval* as well as *D&B's Million Dollar Directory Plus*; the annual reports of both U.S. public and international companies; financial reports for more than 10,000 Canadian and U.S. companies; and insider trading data that records all transactions within a six-month period. The database provides the tools to compare and analyze up to 200 companies against a set of variables that can be mixed and matched. The ability to create a customized company report is also offered. The database at http://www.mergentonline.com/ is available with several varieties of configurations and can be adapted to suit the needs of basic business information such as looking up a company to more involved cross-border searches.

- Begun as a graduate project in 1971, *ABI/INFORM Complete* (ProQuest) is a pioneer in the online indexing and abstracting of business information. It currently contains about 2 million documents, of which approximately half are in full text. The meticulous 150-word abstracts for which it was renowned have also been pared down to a mix of long and short, indicative entries as a wider variety of business sources are being added to the database. More than 60,000 company profiles; full-text journals from academic publishers such as Kluwer, John Wiley, and Palgrave Macmillan; and entries from thousands of local, national, and international management and business publications are offered by ABI/INFORM at http://www.proquest.com/products/pt-product-ABI.shtml.

- EBSCO's *Business Source* databases come in different packages: *Elite*, *Premier*, *Corporate*, *Complete*, and *Alumni*. The *Premier* and *Complete* include monograph and reference books in addition to articles from serials. A special "business-specific interface" allows for relatively sophisticated fine-tuning of search results so that lists can be limited by preferred sources and search options can be conducted through more than just company name or subject entry. A breakdown of titles available through each database is available at http://www.ebsco.com/. EBSCO's user-friendly and standardized search bars, title list management tools, and comprehensive coverage of business resources make it an attractive choice for all levels of libraries.

- Formerly known as *Dow Jones Interactive*, *Factiva* is an innovative provider of global business content. Indexes, abstracts, and full-text content from over 9,000 resources including *The Wall Street Journal*, *Financial Times*, television and radio transcripts, individual company reports, *Dow Jones* and *Reuters* newswires, and publications from 118 countries succeed in providing a content-rich and wide-ranging business database. The content is universally indexed and enables searches in multiple languages. Subscription information is available at http://factiva.com/.

Collection Development and Maintenance

Selection and Keeping Current

One of the distinctive aspects of medical, legal, and business resources is that once selected, a large number of the publications tend to fall into the category of a "standing order." Whether it is *Mergent's* reports, reviews, and handbooks or individual states' annotated statutes, the overriding need for currency fuels a system of constant updating that can only be feasible as a standing order. The onus of decision making, then, is on the initial selection for which there are a few effective ways for identifying new resources.

Published Reviews

In addition to reviews found in mainstream publications such as *ARBA* (*American Reference Books Annual*, 2012), *Library Journal*, *Reference and User Services Quarterly*, *Booklist*, and *Choice*, reviews can also be located in professional journals.

- For health and medicine, the *Medical Reference Services Quarterly* (book reviews and from the literature), *JAMA: Journal of the American Medical Association* (books, journals, new media), and *New England Journal of Medicine* (book reviews) are relevant resources. Doody Enterprises (http://www.doody.com/) offers subscriptions to review sets, *Doody's Core Titles, Basic* or *Premium*; *Doody's Review Service*, a larger service that integrates the titles in the *Core List*; and *Catalog Connect*, which provides access links to the Doody database from any library catalog. Baker and Taylor's Majors Education Solutions (https://www.majors .com/wws/home.htm) offers complementary collection development resources such as *BestSellers, Forthcoming*, and *Just Released* for new and noteworthy medical titles. *iMedicalApps* (http://www.imedicalapps.com/) offers regular reviews on new and noteworthy mobile-friendly resources such as *Medscape*.
- For legal resources, reviews are available in the *Law Library Journal* (Keeping Up with New Legal Titles). A free monthly online resource can be found in *The Law and Politics Book Review*, sponsored by the Law and Courts Section of the American Political Science Association at http://www.bsos.umd.edu/ gvpt/lpbr.
- A uniquely consolidated update of business resources can be found at the Business Reference and Services Section of the American Library Association. Titled the *Public Libraries Briefcase*, the quarterly column put out by the section provides an organized bibliographical account of both old and updated resources in all the disparate areas of business. The 2011 issue, for example, covers *An Introduction to Researching Private Companies*.

Publisher Sites

As mentioned earlier, the proclivity to publish series is strong among the publishers of medical, legal, and business resources. Librarians looking for new resources on health, for example, can browse through these websites:

- Omnigraphics Health Reference Series at http://www.omnigraphics.com/
- Facts on File Library of Health and Living at http://www.factsonfile.com/
- Thomson Gale encyclopedias at http://www.gale.cengage.com/
- *The R2Library* launched by Rittenhouse Book Distributors at http://www.ritten house.com/ (offers collection building in digital content as well as a *Quarterly Report* of updates that is freely accessible)

Some legal publications aimed at the layperson are published by the following:

- West Nutshell series at http://www.thomson.com/
- Journals and resource series from the American Association of Law Libraries at http://www.aallnet.org/
- Legal products at http://www.reed-elsevier.com/
- Nolo legal series at http://www.nolo.com/

Some business and finance publications can be checked on the following sites:

- Mergent's products at http://www.mergent.com/productsServices.html
- Financial Services pages at http://www.mcgraw-hill.com
- Hoover's books at http://www.hoovers.com/free

Online Catalogs

Given the number of specialized libraries devoted to medicine, law, and business, nonspecialist reference librarians need not reinvent the wheel.

- A periodic check of new titles acquired by specialized libraries such as the National Library of Medicine, which lists a column titled *Bookshelf*, is freely accessible at http://www.ncbi.nlm.nih.gov/ and can provide timely clues.
- The Harvard Business School brings out a list of new business acquisitions by the fifteenth of each month that is arranged under subject headings. *The New Books at Baker* list can be perused at http://www.library.hbs.edu/bakerbooks/recent/index.html.
- *The New Acquisitions* listed monthly by the Lillian Goldman Law Library at Yale Law School provides an alphabetical list that can be accessed at http://www.law.yale.edu/library/acquisitions.asp.

Electronic Discussion Lists and Alerts

In a research world that is increasingly comfortable with the ethos of social networking, joining a subject-specific electronic discussion list can be very rewarding. The larger group of medical, legal, or business librarians are able to contribute toward any and every question that you may have, including that of collection development. The generosity of electronic discussion list participants cannot be underestimated.

- Medical librarians can be tapped via the MEDLIB-L discussion list. E-mail listserv @list.uvm.edu with the message "subscribe medlib-l <firstname lastname>".
- Legal librarians have a vibrant community in LAW-LIB. E-mail listproc @ucdavis.edu with the message "subscribe lawlib <name>".
- Business librarians are available at BUSLIB-L. E-mail listserv@lists.nau.edu with the message "set buslib-l mail".

Questions on the best new resources in a particular area, relative rankings of subject sources, and feedback on specific titles bring on a range of responses in electronic discussion groups that can be original, sincere, and illuminating.

Signing up for announce lists, e-alerts, and RSS feeds from institutions and professional associations can also instantly flag the reference librarian about new or upcoming publications of possible interest to the collection. All of the online catalogs listed in the previous section, for example, offer signups on their sites.

Evaluating Medical, Legal, and Business Resources

While scope, accuracy, authority, and cost are basic criteria for evaluating medical, legal, and business resources, of heightened importance are the factors of currency, usability, and utility.

Currency

The urgent need for current information has resulted in a number of publications that have a constant schedule of updates. The type and frequency of these updates must be registered so that older copies are discarded immediately and updates are processed at a priority level. For resources that do not have an updating service, weeding must be punctilious. No information in these three subject areas is preferable to outdated information. The currency of a publication can be gauged by looking up issues about which new information has been released. What does a 2012 drug reference say about Halaven or Egrifta? Does a legal yearbook document the controversy over "waterboarding"? Is the IPO (initial public offering) entry of Facebook recorded in a profile of companies?

Usability

All three fields are thick with specialized terminology and jargon. Reference resources aimed at the layperson need to be vetted for linguistic and graphic simplicity. Resources that cannot avoid terminology must have boxed definitions, legends, keys, glossaries, highlights, or other aiding devices. The indexes must be infallible as the material is relatively unfamiliar, and pattern recognition on the part of the user will play an important part in navigating through the material.

Utility

Given the thousands of titles available in each of these areas, the resources must be evaluated in direct correlation to their use for the given community. Publishers are prone to produce series or sets of health, legal, and finance publications. The series follow a standard format, share a distinctive look, and attempt to cover the most heavily trafficked areas of public demand. For example, the temptation to buy all of Omnigraphics's distinctive red-and-white hardcover publications on 140 health topics is understandable, but not entirely necessary. A community may need the most updated version of the *Alzheimer Disease Sourcebook* but not the *Depression Sourcebook* or vice versa. The attractive binders of *Entrepreneur's Business Start-Up Guides* provide a uniform layout to almost fifty different businesses and are a valuable addition to libraries, but again, the *Freight Brokerage Service* may be more useful to some communities and the *Gift Basket Service* to others. Keeping the subject demands of the community in focus is one way of not succumbing to the siren call of professional and well-made series.

Further Considerations

Sources Are Not Enough

In the world of medical, legal, and business resources, despite excellent acquisition skills, a worthy collection, and an acute knowledge of the resources available in multiple formats, there may always be the need to do more. Resources must be supplemented with referrals, research guides, disclaimers, alternate sources, and policies for all kinds of usage.

Alternate Sources

What is considered the ideal source for a general reference question must be approached as just one of the sources for a medical, legal, or business question.

There is value in providing alternatives so that the user can make comparisons. This effectively supplants the role of advice and reinforces the role of the non-specialist librarian as the provider, rather than the interpreter, of information. *The Directory of Special Libraries and Information Centers* (2011) is a handy resource to provide a definitive list of alternate sources in special libraries, resource centers, medical collections, and documentation centers that may be consulted.

The importance of a referral sheet cannot be underestimated. A list of the nearest law, medical, and business libraries must always be handy, so that the user can be referred to a greater variety and depth of resources if necessary. A directory of lawyers, doctors, and business professionals must also be available so that the user can access professionals for additional information if required. Care must be taken, however, to resist personal recommendations of any one specific professional.

Disclaimers

Constant reminders on the currency of the resource must be provided. For example, if the *Physicians' Desk Reference* was provided as the resource to consult for a certain drug, the user must be reminded to check for currency on a website such as *DrugDigest* (http://www.drugdigest.org/), as well as to consult with his or her doctor or pharmacist. An instructive case in point is that despite its widely reported recall in 2004, the drug Vioxx had no mention of any controversy in the 2005 edition of the *PDR*.

Research Aids

For popular subject areas, the librarian should consult written or online aids to identify, demystify, and evaluate medical, legal, and business reference sources. It is not only of enormous help as a visual crutch to the user who is faced with specialized information, but provides a guard against the librarian forgetting to include vital pieces of information while explaining a complex document. Sources such as *Business Information: How to Find It, How to Use It* (Lavin, 1992), despite being an older publication, provide a clear X-ray of the skeletal structure of data-rich financial reports, surveys, and analyses. The data packed into a single page of the *Value Line Investment Survey*, for example, are clearly labeled and explained in the book, so that a condensed key can be prepared by librarians for first-time users. An online example of an effective aid to understanding Mergent publications can be found in the New York Public Library's *A Guide to the Mergent Manuals* at http://tinyurl.com/98vxc4.

Remote Access Usage

Finally, provisions must be made for remote access usage, especially telephone reference. To inform a user on the telephone that a certain disease reads as being fatal or to attempt reading aloud the annotations and updates of a certain law is not only awkward but also ripe for misunderstanding and liability. Text-based responses must also be handled with care. Emphasis on in-house resources that the user can consult, compare, and interpret is far preferable in most medical, legal, and business queries.

Reference versus the Radiendocrinator

In the early part of the twentieth century, the entrepreneur William Bailey sold the all-purpose "Radiendocrinator." It professed to cure everything from acne to memory loss by "ionizing the endocrine glands" (Ware, 2002: 3). The cost to the user was what would today amount to over $10,000. With scopic medical, legal, and business resources available to users through their libraries, and effective informational roles played by reference librarians, it is hoped there will be a decrease in the sale of modern-day radiendocrinators.

TOP TEN MEDICAL SOURCES		
Title	Print	Online
Directory of Physicians in the United States. 2011. Chicago: American Medical Association.	42nd ed. 4 vols.	Subscription https://catalog.ama-assn.org/Catalog/
Dorland's Illustrated Medical Dictionary. 2011. Philadelphia: W.B. Saunders.	32nd ed. 1 vol.	http://www.dorlands.com/wsearch.jsp
DSM-IV-TR. 2000. Arlington, VA: American Psychiatric Association.	1 vol.	Subscription http://psych.org/practice/dsm
Gray's Anatomy: The Anatomical Basis of Clinical Practice, Expert Consult, 2009. Philadelphia: Elsevier.	40th ed	http://www.us.elsevierhealth.com/
Medical and Health Information Directory. Farmington Hills, MI: Gale Cengage Learning.	27th ed 3 vols. 10 parts	Part of *Gale Directory Library* http://www.gale.cengage.com/ Directory/Library
MedlinePlus, *ClinicalTrials*, and more. Bethesda, MD: National Library of Medicine.		http://www.nlm.nih.gov/
The Merck Manual of Diagnosis and Therapy, 2011. Whitehouse Station, NJ: Merck Sharp and Dohme.	19th ed. 1 vol.	http://www.merckmanuals.com/
Official ABMS Directory of Board Certified Medical Specialists, 1993–. Philadelphia: W.B. Saunders.	Annual 26 vols.	Subscription http://www.boardcertifieddocs.com/
Physicians' Desk Reference, 1945–. Montvale, NJ: Thompson PDR.	Annual 1 vol.	http://www.pdrhealth.com/
Stedman's Medical Dictionary. 2005. Philadelphia: Lippincott Williams and Wilkins.	28th ed. 1 vol.	http://www.lww.com/

TOP TEN LEGAL SOURCES		
Title	Print	Online
American Jurisprudence. 1998–2013. Eagan, MN: Thomson West.	2nd ed. 83 vols.	Databases, part of *Westlaw* and *LexisNexis* http://www.westlaw.com/ http://www.lexisnexis.com/
Ballentine's Law Dictionary. New York: Cengage Delmar Learning.	1 vol.	Subscription http://www.lexisnexis.com/
Black's Law Dictionary. 2009. Eagan, MN: Thomson West.	9th ed.	Subscription http://www.westlaw.com/
Gale Encyclopedia of American Law. 2011. Farmington Hills, MI: Gale Cengage Learning.	3rd ed. 14 vols.	E-book subscription http://www.gale.cengage.com/
Legal Source. Ipswich, MA: EBSCO.		Subscription http://www.ebscohost.com/
Lexis/LexisNexis. New Providence, NJ: LexisNexis.		Subscription http://www.lexisnexis.com/
Martindale-Hubbell Law Directory. 1931–. New York: Martindale-Hubbell Law Directory.	Annual 26 vols.	http://www.martindale.com/ http://www.lawyers.com/
The New Oxford Companion to Law. 2008. New York: Oxford University Press.	1 vol.	Database Part of *Oxford Reference Online* at http://www.oxfordreference.com/
THOMAS. Washington, DC: Library of Congress.		http://thomas.loc.gov/
Westlaw/WestlawNext. New York: Thomson Reuters.		Subscription http://www.westlaw.com/

Recommended Resources Discussed in This Chapter

Medical

Alzheimer Disease Sourcebook. 5th ed. Detroit: Omnigraphics, 2011. Also available as an e-book: http://www.omnigraphics.com/ebooks.php.

American Cancer Society. http://www.cancer.org/.

America's Top Doctors. 11th ed. New York: Castle Connolly Medical Ltd., 2011.

BMJ (British Medical Journal). http://www.bmj.com/.

CINAHL. http://www.ebscohost.com/academic/cinahl-plus-with-full-text/.

Depression Sourcebook. 3rd ed. Detroit: Omnigraphics, 2012. Also available as an e-book: http://www.omnigraphics.com/ebooks.php.

Dialog. http://www.dialog.com/.

Directory of Physicians in the United States. 42nd ed. Chicago: American Medical Association, 2011.

TOP TEN BUSINESS SOURCES		
Title	Print	Online
Business Source Complete. Ipswich, MA: EBSCO.		Subscription http://www.ebscohost.com/
The Directory of Business Information Resources. 2012. Amenia, NY: Grey House Publishing.	1 vol.	Subscription http://gold.greyhouse.com/
Dun and Bradstreet's Million Dollar Directory. New York: Dun and Bradstreet.		Subscription: http://www.dnbmdd.com/mddi/
Hoover's Handbooks. Austin, TX: Hoover's	Annual Multiple eds.	Subscription http://www.hoovers.com/
LexisNexis Corporate Affiliations. 2011. New Providence, NJ: LexisNexis.	8 vols.	Subscription http://www.corporateaffiliations.com/
Market Share Reporter 2012. 2011. Farmington Hills, MI: Gale Cengage Learning.	Annual 1 vol.	Subscription Part of *Gale Directory Library* http://www.gale.cengage.com/ DirectoryLibrary/
ReferenceUSA. Papillion, NE: ReferenceUSA.		Subscription. http://www.referenceusa.com/
Standard and Poor's NetAdvantage. New York: Standard and Poor's.		Subscription http://www.netadvantage .standardandpoors.com/
Thomas Register of American Manufacturers. 1905–. New York: ThomasNet.		http://www.thomasnet.com/
Value Line Investment Survey. New York: Value Line.	Weekly	Subscription http://www.valueline.com/

DIRLINE. http://dirline.nlm.nih.gov/.

DoctorFinder. http://webapps.ama-assn.org/doctorfinder/home.jsp.

Doody's Review Service. http://www.doody.com/drs/.

Dorland's Illustrated Medical Dictionary. 32nd ed. Philadelphia: W. B. Saunders (Elsevier), 2011. Available as an e-book: http://www.us.elsevierhealth.com/. Also available online for free: http://www.dorlands.com/wsearch.jsp.

DrugDigest. http://www.drugdigest.org/wps/portal/ddigest.

DSM-IV-TR (Diagnostic and Statistical Manual of Mental Disorders). Arlington, VA: American Psychiatric Association, 2000. Also available online: http://psych.org/practice/dsm/.

EMBASE. http://www.embase.com/.

Encyclopedia of Life Sciences. 2007. Malden, MA: John Wiley and Sons. Also available online: http://www.els.net/.

Gale Encyclopedia of Alternative Medicine. 3rd ed. Jacqueline L. Longe, ed. Farmington Hills, MI: Gale Cengage Learning, 2008. Also available online: http://www.gale.cengage.com/.

RECOMMENDED FREE HEALTH, LAW, AND BUSINESS WEBSITES

Health

British Medical Journal. http://www.bmj.com/. This is both a print publication and a free online resource of depth and variety. It is peer-reviewed and the online site is updated daily.

Healthfinder. http://www.healthfinder.gov/. Sponsored by the U.S. National Health Information Center, this site draws from over 1,600 government and nonprofit organizations to provide a wide range of popular health topics.

Mondofacto. http://www.mondofacto.com/. A subject-specific dictionary of terms related to medicine and the sciences, this resource also includes acronyms, eponyms, conventions, and the history of terms.

National Library of Medicine (NLM). http://www.nlm.nih.gov/. As the world's largest medical library, the U.S. National Library of Medicine provides this free website with access to the health database *MedlinePlus, ClinicalTrials, AIDSinfo, Genetics Home Reference, Tox Town, Household Products* and *Haz-Map.*

WebMD. http://www.webmd.com/. Appropriately titled, this site provides timely and reliable health information for the general management of health.

Law

American Law Sources Online (ALSO). http://lawsource.com/also/. This resource provides an extensive compilation of links to freely available sites on U.S., Canadian, and Mexican law sources (cases, statutes), commentary (law reviews), and practice aids (court information, official forms).

FindLaw. http://www.findlaw.com/. A popular, easily navigable site that offers a mix of cases, statutes, news, and legal directories.

Glin. http://www.glin.gov/. This site is an extensive searchable database that freely provides global documents in the legal categories of laws, judicial decisions, legislative records, and legal literature.

Hieros Gamos. http://hg.org/. This is a dense, content-rich site of legal directories from around the world, as well as news, guides, and legal reference material.

THOMAS. http://thomas.loc.gov/. This is the definitive site for U.S. federal legislative information, bills, resolutions, committee information, congressional records, treaties, and presidential nominations.

Business

Big Charts. http://bigcharts.marketwatch.com/. A personal investment research website that offers interactive charts, market commentary, and industry analysis. The "Historical Quotes" tab allows a user to research stock quotes dating back to 1985.

Department of Commerce. http://www.commerce.gov/. The site of the U.S. Department of Commerce has descriptions of all the various departments important for business owners, as well as portals to other pertinent sites that may be of interest to the business owner.

IRS. http://www.irs.ustreas.gov/. Particularly popular in the month of April, this is the main site for the U.S. Internal Revenue Service. Downloadable forms, publications, and tax-related information are packed into this site.

THOMASNET. http://www.thomasnet.com/. More than 607,000 industrial companies (as of 5/5/2012) in North America are listed in this free online resource that no longer publishes its traditional multivolume print edition, *The Thomas Register.*

Gale Encyclopedia of Children's Health. 2nd ed. Kristine Knapp and Jeffrey Wilson, eds. Farmington Hills, MI: Gale Cengage Learning, 2011. Also available online: http://www.gale.cengage.com/.

Gale Encyclopedia of Medicine. 4th ed. Jacqueline L. Longe, ed. Farmington Hills, MI: Gale Cengage Learning, 2011. Also available online: http://www.gale.cengage.com/.

Gale Encyclopedia of Mental Health. 3rd. ed. Laurie J. Fundulian, ed. Farmington Hills, MI: Gale Cengage Learning, 2012. Also available online: http://www.gale.cengage.com/.

Gale Encyclopedia of Surgery and Medical Tests. 2nd ed. Anthony J. Senagore, ed. Farmington Hills, MI: Gale Cengage Learning, 2008. Also available online: http://www.gale.cengage.com/.

Health and Wellness Resource Center. Farmington Hills, MI: Gale Cengage Learning. http://www.gale.cengage.com/HealthRC.

Health Reference Center Academic. Available on CD-ROM and online: http://www.gale.com/.

Health Source—Consumer and Nursing/Academic editions. Ipswich, MA: EBSCO. http://www.ebscohost.com/.

iMedicalApps. http://www.imedicalapps.com/.

JAMA: The Journal of the American Medical Association. Chicago: American Medical Association, 1960–. Also available online: http://jama.ama-assn.org/.

The Lancet. http://www.thelancet.com/.

Medical Reference Services Quarterly. 1982–. Philadelphia: Taylor and Francis. Also available online: http://www.taylorandfrancis.com/.

MedlinePlus. http://medlineplus.gov/.

Medscape. http://www.medscape.com/.

Melloni's Illustrated Medical Dictionary. 4th ed. Ida G. Dox, Biagio John Melloni, Gilbert M. Eisner, and June L. Melloni. Baltimore, MD: Williams and Wilkins, 2001.

The Merck Manual Home Health Handbook. Robert S. Porter, Justin L. Kaplan, Barbara P. Homeier, eds. Whitehouse Station, NJ: Merck and Co., 2009. Also available online: http://www.merckmanuals.com/.

The Merck Manual of Diagnosis and Therapy. 19th ed. Robert S. Porter and Justin L. Kaplan, eds. Hoboken, NJ: John Wiley and Sons, 2011. Also available online: http://www.merckmanuals.com/.

National Cancer Institute. http://www.cancer.gov/.

National Center for Health Statistics. http://www.cdc.gov/nchs.

National Library for Health. http://www.evidence.nhs.uk/.

New England Journal of Medicine. Waltham, MA: Massachusetts Medical Society, 1928–. Also available online: http://content.nejm.org/.

Official ABMS (American Board of Medical Specialties) Directory of Board Certified Medical Specialists 2012. 44th ed. Philadelphia: W.B. Saunders Company, 2011. Also available online: http://www.boardcertifieddocs.com/.

Physicians' Desk Reference—PDR. New York: Thomson Reuters, 1974–. Annual. Also available online: http://www.pdr.net/.

PubMed. Bethesda, MD: National Library of Medicine, National Institutes of Health. http://www.pubmed.gov/.

RxList: The Internet Drug Index. http://www.rxlist.com/.

Stedman's Medical Dictionary. 28th ed. Philadelphia: Lippincott Williams and Wilkins, 2005. Also available online: http://stedmansonline.com/.

20,125 Questionable Doctors: Disciplined by State and Federal Governments, National Edition. Washington, DC: Public Citizen Group, 2000.

Legal

American Law Yearbook. Farmington Hills, MI: Gale Cengage Learning, 2011. Also available online: http://www.gale.cengage.com/.

Ballentine's Law Dictionary. New York: Cengage Delmar Learning, 1994. Also available online: http://www.lexisnexis.com/.

Ballentine's Legal Dictionary and Thesaurus. New York: Cengage Delmar Learning, 1995.

Black's Law Dictionary. 9th ed. Bryan A. Garner, ed. Eagan, MN: Thomson West, 2009. Also available online: http://www.westlaw.com/.

Bouvier's Law Dictionary. John Bouvier. Jamaica Plain, MA: Boston Book Company, 1856. Also available online: http://www.constitution.org/bouv/bouvier.htm.

Canadian Legal Information Institute. http://www.canlii.org/.

Corpus Juris Secundum. Eagan, MN: Thomson West. Copyright varies. Also available online: http://www.westlaw.com/.

FindLaw. http://www.findlaw.com/.

Gale Encyclopedia of American Law. Farmington Hills, MI: Gale Cengage Learning, 2011. Also available online: http://www.gale.cengage.com/.

Garner's Dictionary of Legal Usage. Bryan Garner. New York: Oxford University Press, 2011.

Hieros Gamos. http://www.hg.org/.

Law and Legal Information Directory. Farmington Hills, MI: Gale Cengage Learning, 2012. Also available online: http://www.gale.cengage.com/.

Law Library Journal. Washington, DC: American Association of Law Libraries, 1908–.

LAWCHEK. http://www.lawchek.com/.

Legal Source. http://www.ebscohost.com/academic/legal-source.

LexisNexis. http://www.lexisnexis.com/.

LexisNexis UK. http://www.lexisnexis.co.uk/.

Martindale-Hubbell Law Directory. New York: Martindale-Hubbell Law Directory, 1931–. Also available online: http://www.martindale.com/ and http://www.lawyers.com/.

Merriam-Webster's Dictionary of Law. Linda Picard Wood, ed. Springfield, MA: Merriam-Webster, 1996. Also available online for free: http://dictionary.findlaw.com/.

The New Oxford Companion to Law. Peter Cane and Joanne Conaghan, eds. New York: Oxford University Press, 2008. Also available online: http://www.oxfordreference.com/.

Quicklaw. http://ql.quicklaw.com/.

THOMAS. http://thomas.loc.gov/.

Westlaw. http://www.westlaw.com/.

Business

ABI/INFORM Complete. http://www.proquest.com/products/pt-product-ABI.shtml.

Bond's Franchise Guide. Oakland, CA: Source Book Publications, 2012. Also available online: http://www.worldfranchising.com/.

Brands and Their Companies. Farmington Hills, MI: Gale Cengage Learning, 2010. Also available online: http://www.gale.cengage.com/.

Business and Company ASAP. http://www.gale.cengage.com/.

BusinessDictionary. http://www.businessdictionary.com/.

Dictionary of Accounting Terms. 5th ed. Jae K. Shim and Joel G. Siegel. New York: Barron's Educational Series, 2010.

Dictionary of Business. Graham Bannock, Evan Davis, Paul Trott, and Mark Uncles. New York: Bloomberg Press, 2003.

Dictionary of Business and Economics Terms. 5th ed. Jack P. Friedman. New York: Barron's Educational Series, 2012.

A Dictionary of Business and Management. 5th ed. London: Oxford University Press, 2009. Also available online: http://www.oup.com/.

Dictionary of Finance and Investment Terms. John Downes and Jordan Elliott Goodman. New York: Barron's Educational Series, 2010.

Dictionary of Marketing Terms. Jane Imber and Betsy-Ann Toffler. New York: Barron's Educational Series, 2008.

EBSCO Business Source. http://www.ebscohost.com/.

Factiva. http://factiva.com/.

Financial Ratings Series. Amenia, NY: Grey House Publishing. 2011. Also available online: http://www.financialratingsseries.com/.

Hoover's Handbook of American Business. Austin, TX: Hoover's Business Press, 2011. Also available online: http://www.hoovers.com/.

Hoover's Handbook of Emerging Companies. Austin, TX: Hoover's Business Press, 2011. Also available online: http://www.hoovers.com/.

Hoover's Handbook of Industry Profiles. Austin, TX: Hoover's Business Press, 2010. Also available online: http://www.hoovers.com/.

Hoover's Handbook of Private Companies. Austin, TX: Hoover's Business Press, 2012. Also available online: http://www.hoovers.com/.

Hoover's Handbook of World Business. Austin, TX: Hoover's Business Press, 2012. Also available online: http://www.hoovers.com/.

International Dictionary of Finance. Graham Bannock and William Manser. London: Profile Books, 2003.

LexisNexis Corporate Affiliations. New Providence, NJ: LexisNexis Group, 2012. Also available online: http://www.corporateaffiliations.com/.

Market Share Reporter 2012. Farmington Hills, MI: Gale Cengage Learning, 2011. Also available online: http://www.gale.cengage.com/.

Mergent Online. http://www.mergentonline.com/.

Mergent's Bond Record. New York: Mergent FIS, 1999– (monthly). Also available online: http://www.mergent.com/.

Standard and Poor's Register of Corporations, Directors and Executives. New York: McGraw-Hill, 2011. Also available online: http://www.netadvantage.standardandpoors.com/.

The Street Ratings Guides. Amenia, NY: Grey House Publishing, 2012. Also available online: http://www.financialratingsseries.com/.

Thomas Register of American Manufacturers. http://www.thomasnet.com/.

Value Line. http://www.valueline.com/.

Value Line Investment Survey. New York: Value Line Publications, 1995– (weekly). Also available online: http://www.valueline.com/.

Recommendations for Further Reading

Abels, Eileen, and Deborah P. Klein. 2008. *Business Information: Needs and Strategies*. Bingley, UK: Academic Press. Aimed at achieving a "successful information seeking process" in the area of business information, this resource covers basics such as the nature of users and their needs; as well as complexities in access and industry, company, product and demographic information.

American Library Association, Reference and User Services Association, Business Reference and Services Section. 2001. *Guidelines for Medical, Legal, and Business Responses*. http://www.ala.org/rusa/resources/guidelines/guidelinesmedical. Despite its lack of an update, this clear set of guidelines prepared for both specialist and nonspecialist reference librarians, helps in dealing with issues on the role of staff, the currency and accuracy of sources, and the special care required for off-site users in need of medical, legal, or business questions.

The Directory of Business Information Resources, 2012. 2012. New York: Grey House Publishing. A useful overview of the most relevant business newsletters, trade shows, special associations, trade journals and magazines, industry-specific databases, directories, and websites for almost 100 broadly grouped industries.

Encyclopedia of Business Information Sources. 2008. Farmington Hills, MI: Gale Cengage Learning. The twenty-fourth edition of this book is a dense compilation of an unusually broad spectrum of print, electronic, and online business resources arranged by subject. Within each subject, types of resources such as indexes, directories, almanacs, and databases are listed with a brief description and complete contact information.

Ennis, Lisa A. and Nicole Mitchell. 2010. *The Accidental Health Sciences Librarian.* Meford, NJ: Information Today. "Help! My Degree Is in English" is the first chapter in this quick guide to being a useful health sciences librarian. The National Library of Medicine and its classifications and resources is covered along with common consumer health queries, health-related databases and websites, and technology issues that include Web 2.0 tools such as blogs and RSS feeds.

Fishman, Joel, and Dittakavi Rao. 2010. *Navigating Legal Research and Technology: Quick Reference Guide to the 1,500 Most Common Questions About Traditional and Online Legal Research.* Getzville, NY: Bridge Publishing Group. This resource provides a detailed listing of all the many areas of legal questions faced by the reference librarian. Answers to these questions are to be found in a hybrid of electronic and manual legal resources. Definitions of legal terms are also included. Highly comprehensive and eminently readable.

Huber, Jeffrey T., Jo Anne Bookman, and Jean Blackwell, eds. 2008. *Introduction to Reference Sources in the Health Sciences.* 5th ed. New York: Neal-Schuman. A comprehensive collection of health resources, the fifth edition of this book continues to pinpoint the major bibliographic and informational sources relevant to health reference collections. Print, electronic, and online formats are all included.

Jankowski, Terry Ann. 2008. *The MLA Essential Guide to Becoming an Expert Searcher: Proven Techniques, Strategies, and Tips for Finding Health Information.* New York: Neal-Schuman. The difference between "Googling" a health topic and diving deep into a database is highlighted in this thorough treatise on search strategies and database construction. Specific health databases are discussed and a list of thirty exercises for becoming a skilled health information specialist is provided.

Maatta, Stephanie L. 2012. *Business Information Sources and Services: An Introduction.* New York: Neal-Schuman. This resource provides extensive descriptions of titles valuable to reference questions dealing with marketing, franchising, and even business career issues. The continued development of skills in business librarianship is also included in the last part of the book.

Medical and Health Care Books and Serials in Print. 2012. New York: Grey House Publishing. An extensive listing of over 115,000 books and nearly 24,000 serials related to the health and biomedical field. The two-volume set can be searched by subject and title as well as by author and publisher. It is a useful resource to consult for updates in a field where currency is of paramount value.

The Medical Library Association's Master Guide to Authoritative Information Resources in Health Sciences. 2011. Laurie L. Thompson, Esther Carrigan, Mori Lou Higa and Rajia Tobia, eds. New York: Neal-Schuman. The Brandon-Hill List of selected medical titles relevant to a small library was discontinued in 2004. This guide aims at filling the gap with a concise collection development tool, listing the top ten to twenty titles for thirty-five subject areas as listed in the MeSH schedule.

Tucker, Virginia, and Marc Lampson. 2010. *Finding the Answers to Legal Questions: A How-To-Do-It Manual.* New York: Neal-Schuman. A highly handy resource that covers everything from conducting a legal reference interview, to collection development and the creation of a legal website. The resource is simple and comprehensive.

Wood, M. Sandra, ed. 2008. *Introduction to Health Sciences Librarianship.* New York: Routledge. A wide, informative net is cast over the length and breadth of health resources, services, libraries, and information in original ways that include screen captures and "A Day in the Life of..." accounts of the health reference librarian.

Worley, Loyita. 2006 (update in production for 2013). *BIALL Handbook of Legal Information Management*. Burlington, VT: Ashgate Publishing Company. Though applied to the laws of the United Kingdom, this is an authoritative handbook on critical aspects of law librarianship applicable to all information providers. Search techniques and organization of legal resources along with chapters on the practical management and training of staff in ongoing legal research and ethics combine to provide a compelling focus on legal information services as a whole.

Bibliography and Works Cited

American Library Association. 2011. *ALA Guide to Economics and Business Reference*. Chicago: ALA Editions.

American Library Association. 2011. *ALA Guide to Medical and Health Sciences Reference*. Chicago: ALA Editions.

American Reference Books Annual. 2012. Westport, CT: Libraries Unlimited. http://www.arbaonline.com/.

Cohen, Morris L., and Kent Olsen. 2010. *Legal Research in a Nutshell*. 10th ed. Eagan, MN: Thomson Reuters Westlaw.

Directory of Special Libraries and Information Centers. 2011. 39th ed. Farmington Hills, MI: Gale Cengage Learning.

Elias, Stephen. 2009. *Legal Research: How to Find and Understand the Law*. Berkeley, CA: Nolo.

Fox, Susannah. 2012. "Pew Internet: Health." Pew Internet and American Life Project. March 1. http://www.pewinternet.org/.

Lavin, Michael, R. 1992. *Business Information: How to Find It, How to Use It*. Phoenix, AZ: Oryx Press.

Maslow, Abraham H. 1943. "A Theory of Human Motivation." *Psychological Review* 50, no. 4: 370–396.

Moulton, Sara E. 2008. "Response to a Consumer Health Query." *Journal of Consumer Health on the Internet* 12, no. 3 (July 1): 237–249.

"Outstanding Business Reference Sources: The 2011 Selection of Recent Titles." 2011. *Reference and User Services Quarterly* 52, no. 2 (Winter): 122–126.

Pettinato, Tammy R. 2008. "Dealing with Pro Se Patrons." *Public Services Quarterly* 4, no. 3 (October 1): 283–289.

Ross, Celia. 2008. "Keeping Up with Business Reference." *Journal of Business and Finance Librarianship* 13, no. 3 (January 1): 363–370.

RUSA (Reference and User Services Association). 2001. *Guidelines for Medical, Legal and Business Responses*. American Library Association. http://www.ala.org/ala/mgrps/divs/rusa/resources/guidelines.

Scarr, Carrie. 2008. "Business/Economics." *Library Journal* (Reference Supplement) 133 (November 15): 32–34.

Tucker, Virginia, and Marc Lampson. 2010. *Finding the Answer to Legal Questions: A How-To-Do-It Manual*. New York: Neal-Schuman.

Ware, Leslie, and editors of *Consumer Reports*. 2002. *Selling It*. New York: W.W. Norton.

Wheeler, Ronald E. 2011. "Does WestlawNext Really Change Everything? The Implications of WestlawNext on Legal Research." *Law Library Journal* 103, no. 3 (Summer): 359–377.

Yates, Sarah. 2011. "*Black's Law Dictionary*: The Making of an American Standard." *Law Library Journal* 103, no. 2 (Spring): 175–198.

10

Answering Questions about Geography, Countries, and Travel— Atlases, Gazetteers, Maps, Geographic Information Systems, and Travel Guides

Overview

Geography is an interdisciplinary area of study spanning both earth science (physical geography), which studies the physical features of the earth, and social science (human geography), which studies the relationship between humans and the environment. Today, geography "explores the relationship between the earth and its peoples through the study of place, space and environment. Geographers ask the questions where and what; also how and why" (Unwin, 1992: 13). "Individuals with diverse interests are tied together through their interest in understanding how places or locations affect activities (human or otherwise), how places are connected, and how those connections facilitate movement between places or cause an event at one location to impact another location" (Johnson, 2003: 1).

As our perspectives shift to a more global outlook, the importance of geographic information increases, allowing more learning about the world in which we live. The information provided by geographic sources is remarkable and extensive and includes information in print and electronic formats. Geographic sources provide information in narrative form through gazetteers and other text resources and visually through maps. Although geographic information is available in other information sources, resources specific to the field provide the most precise and accurate information. For example, in an atlas the user can find not only the location of a country or city but also its latitude and longitude and its relationship to other geographic entities.

How Geographic Information Is Used

Geographic information sources are used in a variety of ways. First, they can be employed to find the location of towns, rivers, mountains, countries, continents, and other geographic entities. Geographic sources make it possible for users to more easily visualize the relationship between countries and continents. They do more than just provide directions; they may show the makeup of a particular land area—its mountains, valleys, rivers, and plains. Other geographic tools show the environmental and climatic or ecological factors in an area so we can better understand how this affects the ability of the area, for example, to develop agriculturally. Geographic sources may deal with the past as well as the present. For example, historical maps and atlases trace changing country boundaries to provide the reader with a way to visualize what has happened in a particular country and how history has been affected by these changes.

Questions Answered by Geographic Information

Q: What countries surround Turkey?

A: This answer can be found by looking at a current map of Turkey in an atlas such as the *Times Comprehensive Atlas of the World*.

Q: What is the present name of the country called Burma?

A: A gazetteer such as the *Columbia Gazetteer of the World Online*, which will cross-reference Burma to its present name, Myanmar, can provide this information.

Q: Where is Montevideo located?

A: Either an atlas with a good index such as the *Oxford Comprehensive Atlas of the World* or a gazetteer such as the *Merriam-Webster's Geographical Dictionary* can be used to find this answer. It is a city in the country of Uruguay.

Q: What were the boundaries of the countries in Europe in 1848?

A: This can be found in *Shepherd's Historical Atlas*.

Major Geographic Information Resources Used in Reference Work

Geographic information sources come in many formats. First of all, there are gazetteers. Gazetteers are text-based sources of information about geographic places and features. They are arranged alphabetically and describe as concisely and precisely as possible where, for example, a particular town or mountain range is located and other pertinent facts about it.

In contrast to gazetteers, maps are a way to visualize the world. They take an enormous amount of information and put it into a format that can be more easily understood (Liben, 2008). The most common types of maps are route and street maps that show the streets and highways so that someone can determine the best route to get from one place to another. Topographic maps show the natural land features through the use of color so that the user can see clearly the mountainous areas, the rivers, and the plains. Political maps show the boundaries of major cities, towns, and villages, and the boundaries of countries. Thematic maps usually deal with a narrow theme such as religion, ethnic diversity, or history, using the visual format of maps to convey information.

The digital revolution has brought new possibilities to mapmaking, but the end of the paper map is not in sight. Although digital mapmaking has made it possible to produce interactive maps, to provide for route finding, to search for place name, and to convert maps into electronic form, paper maps still have some distinct advantages. They allow subtleties of color and text that are not possible with digital maps. Maps that appear on a computer screen are limited by the screen resolution. Paper maps also allow the user to look at a wider expanse at one time than is possible on a screen (Ashworth, 2003: 56). Route and street maps are particularly useful in electronic format. Such sites as *MapQuest* (http://www.mapquest.com/) and *BingMaps* (http://www.bing.com/maps/) make it possible for the user to type in their starting location and their destination. These programs then provide a map and written directions to the location. Alternately, these programs allow a user to type in a specific address and get a map of that location. In some major metropolitan areas, websites such as *HopStop* are being developed to help plan routes on foot and via public transportation in cities.

An atlas is a collection of maps with some unifying theme. Atlases may include a series of maps for a particular country or continent, showing both the overview and more specific areas such as a state, province, city, or a world atlas that covers the entire globe. Atlases offer more than maps since they often include other geographic information such as population, the environment, and statistics on countries, with a detailed index. But there are also collections of historical maps that show the changes in political boundaries through time. Thematic or subject atlases have become popular to show visually a particular subject, for example, an atlas on some aspect of history. A third type of map is a globe. Globes provide a way to see the relationship between continents and land masses and provide a more accurate visualization of the earth. There is less geographic detail on a globe. Another source of geographic information is travel guides. Travel guides come in many forms. Some simply list places to see, restaurants, and hotels, while others provide more detailed information about a particular city or country with maps, detailed information on the history and culture of the city or country, and interesting descriptions of historical sites.

Overview Resources

Newly developed resources provide a wealth of geographic information. *World Geography and Culture Online* is an electronic resource that provides ready reference information as well as geographic information and maps all in one resource. There are entries for over 200 countries; each includes a map as well as information on the geography, history, climate, the people, and much more. This electronic resource provides up-to-date news and ways to compare countries and states. Librarians can use this resource to answer a multitude of questions.

The Utrecht University Library hosts *Geosource* (http://www.library .uu.nl/geosource/), which describes its content as "web resources for human geography, physical geography, planning, geoscience and environmental science." The information available ranges from international and professional organizations, to university departments, library collections, and reference sources.

Gazetteers and Geographical Dictionaries

"A gazetteer is an alphabetical list of place names with information that can be used to locate the areas that the names are associated with" (Johnson, 2003: 49). Often users do not need a map but simply want information about the location of a particular city, town, river, or mountain. For this information, the librarian can turn to a gazetteer or a geographical dictionary.

The *Columbia Gazetteer of the World Online* is a well-regarded source of information on geographical places and features. It has over 170,000 detailed entries listing geographical sites such as countries, cities, lakes and mountains, and cultural and historical points of interest worldwide. Country profiles provide brief information on the population, economy, history, and government. The online version of the *Gazetteer* (http://www.columbiagazetteer.org/) is available by subscription, and there is a CD-ROM version as well.

Merriam-Webster's Geographical Dictionary, Third Edition, is a one-volume gazetteer and a good choice for libraries not needing the more extensive *Columbia Gazetteer of the World*. It contains more than 54,000 brief entries with economic, political, and physical data and 250 black-and-white maps. Countries, cities, natural features, and historical sites are listed.

The *Getty Thesaurus of Geographic Names Online* (http://www.getty.edu/research/tools/vocabulary/tgn), a free online gazetteer developed by the Getty Research Institute, lists nearly 1 million place names. It provides information about the preferred name for a place (a place could be a city, a village, or a land feature such as a mountain) and all variants by language and through history. The latitude and longitude is given for each place as well as its hierarchical position. For example, Paris' hierarchical position is World (facet), Europe (continent), France (nation), Ile-de-France (region), Ville de Paris (department), Paris (inhabited place). It also places Paris in its historical hierarchy and adds a note about its history. Sources of information for this thesaurus are listed and include the *Times Atlas of the World*, *Merriam-Webster's Geographical Dictionary*, and the *Encyclopaedia Britannica*.

Geographic Names Information System (GNIS) (http://geonames.usgs.gov/) provides a way to maintain uniform geographical usage throughout the federal government. It lists over 2 million physical and cultural geographic names in the United States, the U.S. territories, and Antarctica and was developed by the U.S. Geological Survey in cooperation with the U.S. Board of Geographic Names. Users can search for names of towns, rivers, streams, valleys, airports, schools, and much more. For example, the search for a town will give the user the elevation, the population, history notes, and the latitude and longitude.

NGA GEOnet Names Server (http://earth-info.nga.mil/gns/html/index.html), a database of 5.5 million foreign place names, is hosted by the National Geospatial-Intelligence Agency. This database provides the standard spellings of all foreign geographic place names.

Geographical Names of Canada (http://www.nrcan.gc.ca/earth-sciences/home) is the site to use to verify place names for Canada in the same way that *GNIS* does for the United States. It can be found in the Geography and Boundaries section of the website.

Worldmark Encyclopedia of the Nations, also available as an e-book, is a five-volume source of information on over 193 countries and dependencies around the world arranged by region. In addition to the detailed information on each country, there are biographical essays on national leaders.

Maps and Atlases

Mapmaking has a long history. Even in ancient times the Babylonians drew maps on clay tablets. The Greeks were among the early mapmakers. The maps of Ptolemy were still being used in the fifteenth century when his book *Geography* was published in 1482 in Latin. The European discovery of America and the explorations of Africa and Asia diminished the importance of Ptolemy's works. Geographers from all over Europe contributed new information and corrected the maps of Ptolemy during the sixteenth century. Among those mapmakers were two Dutchmen, Abraham Ortelius and Gerard Mercator. The invention of printing coincided with these explorations so that new maps could be more easily produced and distributed. "Governments began to use maps as tools not only for foreign conquest and economic exploitation but to establish control at home and for purposes of national defense" (Edson, 2002).

Major World Atlases

Called by *Booklist* the "pinnacle of atlases," the *Times Comprehensive Atlas of the World* is the highest quality general world atlas available. The maps are the work of Collins Bartholomew of Glasgow, Scotland, a highly regarded producer of maps. Its digitally produced maps have light but easy to distinguish colors and a readable typeface. This atlas tries to provide a balanced coverage of all parts of the world and includes extensive mapping of all continents with at least ten maps per continent. Thematic world maps covering such topics as climate, population, energy, and minerals are included. The *Times Atlas* pays careful attention to detail and uses easy-to-read symbols. Its excellent index lists over 200,000 place names at latitude/longitude coordinates and can serve as a gazetteer. The *Times Atlas* does, however, lack city maps.

The *National Geographic Atlas of the World*, though smaller than the *Times Atlas* with fewer pages, maps, and index entries, is nevertheless a very good atlas that particularly excels in U.S. maps. It includes city maps for each continent with the largest number from the United States. Completely revised, it contains the latest information on political and natural changes. A country section provides basic information on all independent countries including the country flag, demographics, and economic information. A group of thematic world maps provide information on environmental issues, natural resources, and human culture.

Oxford Comprehensive Atlas of the World reflects recent changes in country boundaries. This atlas includes 290 pages of maps; a fifty-six-page section on different aspects of world geography including climate change, biodiversity, and global warming; a set of six ocean floor maps; and photos of the planets. It is recommended for its excellent maps.

The *DK Great World Atlas* includes 370 maps, 320 satellite images, and 750 full-color photographs as well as industry maps, communication maps, agricultural maps, and natural resource maps. It has a list of countries of the world with some basic statistical information on each of them. This atlas is very user friendly with good layout of each page.

Many of the publishers of atlases publish a series of atlases in various sizes and at different prices.

Medium-Sized Atlases

Although there is no comparison to the *Times Comprehensive Atlas of the World*, many atlases in the medium-sized category provide good coverage at a moderate price and are very useful in a library.

The *Times Concise Atlas of the World* is a smaller version of the *Times Atlas*. It includes the usual Collins Bartholomew maps, the detailed index of 130,000 place names, and a list of countries with concise information on each country and a picture of the flag. City maps are inset on the page of the country.

The *Hammond World Atlas* is one of a series of Hammond atlases. The new edition of this medium-sized atlas has over 200 digital maps, a sixty-four-page "Thematic Section," with information ranging from the solar system to global warming, and a forty-eight-page "Satellite Image Section." The physical maps are from digital elevation data. The index features 110,000 entries. Major metropolitan areas are dealt with as inserts on regional maps. Commentary relating to each continent precedes each section. The *Hammond World Atlas* uses a smaller scale for countries other than the United States, which makes comparisons difficult. Nevertheless, it is an excellent atlas for its size and price.

The *Oxford Atlas of the World*, which is revised annually, includes 179 pages of full-color, computer-generated maps with an index of 83,000 entries. The major part of this atlas is devoted to maps of the continents including physical maps, political maps, and maps of specific regions. There is a separate section with thirty-one pages of maps for sixty-nine urban areas. A thirty-two-page gazetteer that provides ready reference information is arranged alphabetically with country summaries and official flags. The index uses the latitude and longitude as well as a letter/figure grid reference.

The *HarperCollins New World Atlas* also features Collins Bartholomew maps. It provides a new approach to an atlas with a variety of maps for each continent on such subjects as countries, issues, and environments, and a number of excellent physical/political maps covering all parts of the continent. The index of 80,000 place names is particularly useful.

The Dorling Kindersley *DK Traveler's Atlas* provides physical maps for every section of the world as well as a box with a list of cities and places to see in that country or group of countries and another box with possible activities. Introductions to each continent provide maps on climate, transportation, languages, and standard of living.

Desk and Student Atlases

Smaller atlases are also published by the same publishers. Though not as detailed as larger atlases, they are often useful to students. *Goode's World Atlas* is an excellent compact atlas with world thematic maps, physical/political regional maps, and an index and geographic tables. It is highly recommended. In addition, it is worth considering the following dictionaries in this category: *Oxford Essential World Atlas* and the *National Geographic Concise Atlas of the World*.

Historical Atlases

Maps provide information about the past as well as the present. They can be arranged by theme or by date. *Shepherd's Historical Atlas* is a rich source of historical maps, especially European maps. *Shepherd's* shows the changes in boundaries throughout the ages, providing the user with an understanding of the impact of wars and treaties on the face of Europe.

David Rumsey and Edith M. Punt have produced *Cartographica Extraordinaire: The Historical Map Transformed*. This work reflects the way even historical maps are being transformed by geographic information system (GIS) technology. The maps in this work are also available on Rumsey's website (http://www .davidrumsey.com/). The David Rumsey Map Collection also provides 17,400 free copyright maps specializing in eighteenth- and nineteenth-century maps, focusing on the Western Hemisphere but including historic maps of other continents as well. These maps are searchable by country, state, publication author, or keyword, and can be printed.

Other sources of historical maps online are the *History of Cartography Gateway* (http://www.maphistory.info/), which links to map collections, and the Library of Congress *American Memory Collection* (http://memory.loc.gov/ammem/index .html), which features mostly U.S. maps from 1544 to 2004 in the public domain. Users can search the *American Memory Collection* by cities and towns or by subject, for example, conservation and environment, discovery and exploration, cultural landscapes, military battles and campaigns, and transportation and communication. Yale University provides on its website a selection of maps from its historical map collection. This is a good source of antiquarian maps and historical city maps (http://www.library.yale.edu/MapColl/index.html).

Thematic Atlases

The atlas format is used for thematic maps, which may or may not depend on geography. These atlases usually deal with a narrow theme. Some examples of thematic atlases are the following.

Times History of the World, edited by Richard Overy, begins with a twelve-page "Chronology of World History." It presents a balanced view of world history, including information on social history and on the cultural achievements of the various civilizations.

The *Atlas of World History* provides a series of maps combined with a narrative and photographs for each time period, beginning with the Ancient World and continuing to the year 2000. An alphabetical list of events, people, and places is quite valuable. This atlas provides an added dimension to our understanding of world history through its visual approach.

The *Historical Atlas of the U.S.* provides a visual approach to U.S. history. It alternates the thematic sections, for example, land, people, boundaries, economy, networks, and communities, with the five chronological sections of 1400–1606, 1607–1788, 1789–1860, 1861–1916, and 1917–1988. The atlas includes timelines of U.S. history along with text and photographs. A bibliography includes the sources of the maps and illustrations as well as additional sources of information and an index.

The *Historical Atlas of Canada* is a three-volume interdisciplinary effort to capture the history of Canada—both of the indigenous people and the Europeans. The three volumes are "From the Beginning to 1800," "The Land Transformed, 1800–1891," and "Addressing the Twentieth Century, 1891–1961." The maps range over a wide variety of subjects from population, workforce, and transportation to trade, agriculture, and fishing. This atlas presents its material in clear, easy-to-read maps with accompanying text. The volumes lack an index, but the table of contents is detailed.

Historical Atlas of the North American Railroad by Derek Hayes traces the development of railroads in the United States and Canada from the early nineteenth century to the twentieth century through a series of 400 color maps. The maps are accompanied by a very interesting narrative on the history of the railroads, making good use of primary source material.

Oxford New Historical Atlas of Religion in America, edited by Edwin Gausted, is an excellent atlas that uses both text and maps to show by century and region the growth of each religion. In addition to the more traditional religions, the atlas includes coverage of Muslim, Hindu, Sikh, Buddhism and other religious groups. There are bibliographical references at the end of each section.

The *Barrington Atlas of the Greek and Roman World* by Richard J. A. Talbert is a comprehensive atlas of the classical world that includes all the regions that the Greeks and Romans penetrated between 1000 BC and 640 AD. It is an attempt to re-create the landscape of that time.

Road Atlases and Maps

The best-known road atlas is the *Rand McNally Road Atlas*. This atlas, updated annually, provides maps of every state in the United States, every Canadian province, and a map of Mexico. There are also maps of 300 cities and twenty U.S. national parks. A list of town names by state is available at the end of the atlas as well as a nationwide mileage chart and a map showing interstate mileage and drive time. This atlas is used by people needing to determine the best route to a destination. It is integrated with http://www.randmcnally.com/ via codes on the map pages.

Individual maps are often needed by users. The following are some of the sources of individual maps, both current and historic.

The Perry-Casteñada Library, University of Texas website (http://www.lib.utexas.edu/maps/) has a collection of 250,000 maps of which about 20 percent are digitized and available online. Organized by region and then by country, the collection is strong in historical maps and is a good source for printing out a small-scale map. Online maps of current interest are posted on the homepage. E-mail and chat service is available for those needing further assistance.

The National Geographic Society provides some free maps, and many for purchase from its website. The society's *Map Machine* (http://www.national geographic.com/maps/map-machine) can be used to obtain a free street map. *National Geographic Education* (http://education.nationalgeographic.com/education/) provides free printable country maps at its teacher education page.

The *United Nations Map Library* also has a growing collection of country maps that can be accessed at http://www.un.org/depts/dhl/maplib/maplib.htm.

The *National Atlas of the United States* (http://www.nationalatlas.gov/) is an interactive geological and topographical map produced by the U.S. Geological Survey that provides a wealth of information about the United States on a variety of topics from agriculture to government. Users can access over 400 data layers and can assemble and print maps to meet their needs. Some files require GIS software, but it is, on the whole, a user-friendly site with many printable maps.

The *Atlas of Canada* (http://atlas.nrcan.gc.ca/site/english/index.html) is a bilingual online product. There are many interesting thematic maps showing both current and historic information in visual form on such subjects as the environment, the economy, history, climate, and health.

A more recent addition to online maps is *Google Maps*. At http://maps .google.com/, the user can find a map for a particular location, find a map to locate a business, or get directions from one location to another. In addition to these maps, *Google Earth* (http://www.google.com/earth/index.html) provides satellite maps. Google now has a MyMaps where users can create personalized, annotated maps. Libraries are using this feature to create local maps showing library branches, local historical sites, and other sites of local interest.

The *American FactFinder*, located on the U.S. Census site (http://factfinder2 .census.gov/), provides maps based on historical information. There are both reference and thematic maps that have been developed using census data.

INFOMINE (http://infomine.ucr.edu/), a site developed by librarians, has a selective list of map links primarily of the United States.

For British maps, a good place to start is the British Library Map Collection (http://www.bl.uk/onlinegallery/index.html), which includes old and new maps. Other important map collections in the United Kingdom include the Bodleian Library at Oxford University, the National Library of Scotland, the National Library of Wales, and the Royal Geographic Society.

Librarians will want to buy road and street maps for their community, county, and state. Many good local and regional map companies exist and can be located through the Yellow Pages of local telephone directories. Maps are also produced by city, county, and state governments.

U.S. Government Publications and Maps

Maps are available from many departments of the U.S. government. The largest number of maps is produced by the U.S. Geological Survey (http://www.usgs .gov/). They include geological maps, topographical maps, and GIS maps on a wide range of topics including agriculture and farming, atmosphere and climate, and health and disease. They make aerial photographs available for purchase through *EROS* (*Earth Resources Observation Systems*) *Data Center* (http://eros.usgs .gov/).

The U.S. Census Bureau's Maps and Mapping Resources (http://www .census.gov/geo/www/maps) provides maps that enable the user to visualize the information in the census. The Census Bureau also provides online mapping resources of U.S. locations through the TIGER mapping service. The U.S. Environmental Protection Agency (EPA) has developed *EnviroMapper* (http://www .epa.gov/emefdata/em4ef.home), which provides maps by location showing eligibility for the Superfund monies and information about such issues as hazardous wastes and toxic emissions. The Federal Emergency Management Agency website (http://www.fema.gov/hazard/map/index.shtm) provides multiple hazard maps showing locations vulnerable to floods, landslides, tornadoes, and hurricanes.

A new site under development by the U.S. government combines Data.gov with Geospatial One-Stop to produce a variety of interesting data. It is called *Geo.Data.gov* (http://geo.data.gov/).

The Geography and Map Division of the Library of Congress (http:// www.loc.gov/topics/maps.php) provides both historic and more recent maps showing changes in the U.S. landscape, for example, maps showing the growth and development of the U.S. National Parks.

Canadian maps including topographic, geological, forest, and mining maps as well as aerial photographs and satellite images are produced by the Earth Sciences Section of *Natural Resources Canada* (http://www.nrcan.gc.ca/earth-sciences/home).

GIS Sources

A geographic information system (GIS) uses "computer hardware, software, data and people combined to answer spatially based questions and to provide new ways of looking at geographic information to find solutions or make decisions" (Johnson, 2003: 177). GIS has added a whole new dimension to the study of geography enabling its users to view, analyze, and display geographic information in new ways going far beyond the study and use of maps. Using GIS software requires advanced study or training. Some of the sites providing GIS products are the U.S. Geological Survey's GIS website (http://egsc.usgs.gov/isb/pubs/ gis_poster/), the Census Bureau's *American Factfinder*, and EPA's *EnviroMapper*.

A number of companies provide GIS software packages. These include ArcGIS (ESRI), Maptitude (Caliper), MapInfo Professional (Pitney Bowes), and IntelliGIS (ISS). Open source software, such as GRASS developed by the U.S. Army Corps of Engineers, and MapServer, developed by University of Minnesota, are also available.

Travel Guides

An often overlooked geographic source is travel guides. Travel guides are available from a diverse array of authors and publishers. Although some may seem too subjective to be used as a reference source, others provide a great deal of factual, up-to-date information on cities and countries. Some of the most factual of the guidebooks are the *Michelin Green Guides*, the *Baedeker Guides*, the *Rough Guides*, *Lonely Planet*, and *Moon Handbooks*. All of these guidebooks provide detailed information about the history of a city or country and information about museums and other cultural sites. They often provide maps of the interiors of museums and noted buildings and detailed descriptions of important rooms within these buildings.

There are also useful specialized travel guides providing information on such subjects as accessibility, guides to special kinds of sites such as the national parks, Native American landmarks, and ecotourism sites. In addition, there are guides to campgrounds, for example, *Woodall's Campground Directory*.

Collection Development and Maintenance

Selection and Keeping Current

Information about geographical sources as well as reviews of new monographs and online information sources help the librarian to identify new and updated materials. Geographical sources are regularly reviewed in *Booklist*, *Choice*, *Library Journal*, and *American Reference Books Annual*.

The U.S. government remains a key source of information producing a wide variety of maps. The TIGER mapping service from the U.S. Census Bureau produces detailed maps of locations throughout the United States using census data. Other maps are produced by the National Oceanic and Atmospheric Administration (NOAA), the U.S. Geological Survey (USGS), the U.S. Department of Housing and Urban Development (HUD), the U.S. Department of Defense's National Imagery and Mapping Agency (NIMA), the Environmental Protection Agency (EPA), and others.

Information about new geographic sources is available through the American Library Association's Map and Geography Round Table (MAGERT) newsletter, *base line*, and its electronic discussion list, *maps-l*; the *Information Bulletin* of the Western Association of Map Librarians; and *The Bulletin* published by the Association of Canadian Map Libraries and Archives.

Numerous monographs, such as Mary Lynette Larsgaard's (1998) *Map Librarianship: An Introduction*, Jenny Marie Johnson's (2003) *Geographic Information: How to Find It, How to Use It*, and Barbara Farrell and Aileen Desbarats's (1981) *Guide for a Small Map Collection*, provide information on map librarianship.

In addition to some of the geographic sources listed in this chapter, ALA's Map and Geospatial Information Round Table has suggested in its publication "Helpful Hints for Small Map Collections" that libraries acquire topographic maps of their county and state, city maps of nearby cities, and aerial photographs of their area (Larsgaard and Rankin, 1997). These can be acquired through commercial map dealers or through the U.S. Geological Survey. Libraries needing to acquire maps should look at the catalogs or websites of the major publishers of maps including Times Books, Rand McNally, C. S. Hammond, National Geographic

Society, DK, Michelin (France), and Oxford University Press, as well as publishers of electronic maps including DeLorme and GIS firms such as ESRI.

Evaluating Geographic Resources

The criteria for good-quality accessible maps includes currency and accuracy, authority, legibility, scale and projection, color, symbols, format, index, and price.

The currency of the maps must be a primary consideration. Boundaries continue to change and even place names change. Maps must be current in order to be useful. Before purchasing geographic sources, the currency of the source should be verified by checking to see if current boundaries of countries are shown and to see that it reflects changes in names of cities and countries.

Accuracy is essential for a good-quality map. Accuracy and currency are closely linked, since a large part of accuracy has to do with being up-to-date. Authority is particularly important to mapmaking. The major publishers of maps and atlases are Times Books, Rand McNally, C. S. Hammond, the National Geographic Society, DK and Oxford University Press. Other publishers are known for the quality of their maps. Among them are Collins Bartholomew (Glasgow) and Philips in the United Kingdom and Michelin in France.

Legibility and readability of the map is crucial. This may be influenced by the scale of the map, the color contrast of the map, and the way symbols are used to indicate certain features of the map. "Scale is the ratio of distance on the map to linear distance on the earth" (Monmonier and Schnell, 1988: 15). Scale can be represented as a ratio l:10,000 or 1/10,000 or it can be represented as a bar scale or a verbal scale "one inch equals 64 miles."

Color is often a subtle but important part of mapmaking. A well-done map will be pleasant to look at and yet offer enough contrast to understand the different kinds of land areas. Symbols are used to distinguish between geographic features and make them easier to locate. Symbols must have a good legend and be adequately explained. The use of a good type style is needed to enable the user to easily find the desired information.

Atlases should display a balanced coverage of the world or a balanced approach to the continents or countries that they cover. Mary Lynette Larsgaard (1998) suggests determining the number of pages in an atlas and then counting the number of pages devoted to the United States and the number of pages devoted to Africa as a way to ascertain whether the atlas is providing balanced coverage. Larsgaard also suggests comparing the same area in two or more atlases to determine which atlases are providing the best treatment.

As much as possible, the same scale should be used throughout an atlas. In this way it is possible to compare the size of countries or continents. "Map projection is the method employed to transfer a curved area—a section of earth—to the flat, two dimensional plane of the page" (Sader and Lewis, 1995: 164). All flat maps distort to some extent the shapes and areas. The larger the area covered by the map, the greater is the distortion; the smaller the area, the less distortion there will be. Various methods of projection are used to lessen the distortion. The kind of projection used depends on the use of the map. Different map projections are often used within an atlas to best capture a particular area.

Atlases need to be accessible. This involves the arrangement of the atlas as it moves from area to area, the need for a clear and easy-to-understand legend, and a comprehensive index with both cross-references to other names or spellings and a good grid system. Many indexes use latitude and longitude to describe the location of a particular place while others use a grid system. If it is hard to find specific places after locating them in the index, then the indexing has failed.

Because maps are now produced both on paper and electronically, it is necessary to evaluate whether the format serves the source well. Is this, for example, an appropriate map for an electronic format or would it be better in paper? Sometimes the purpose of the source will dictate which format is more appropriate. If the format is paper, it is important to note the ease of handling the atlas, the convenience of use and the binding, and whether some of the maps fall into the book's gutter, making them hard to read.

Price is the final consideration for any atlas. It may pay to have fewer atlases and purchase those of high quality.

Further Considerations

For many reasons, users need geographic information. They may want to see a map of a particular area of the world to better understand what is happening there. They may want to know where Saudi Arabia is in relation to Iraq, or they may want to know where Bali is in relation to Penang. Maps often provide an understanding of how events affect other countries in a region.

People planning a trip want maps and guidebooks to chart their trip. For example, they might be planning a trip to Thailand and want to know what other countries they could easily visit. Maybe friends have given them names of towns to visit, and they need to see where they are.

A businessperson has just been told that he is being sent to Kiev in the Ukraine. He is researching Kiev to find out about the area, the temperature for the time of year he is going, what he can expect in terms of access to e-mail, and whether he can expect to be able to use a wireless laptop. Maps and guidebooks will provide him with a great deal of information, as will websites.

Recommended Resources Discussed in This Chapter

American FactFinder. U.S. Census Bureau. http://factfinder2.census.gov/. Free.
American Memory Collection. Library of Congress. http://memory.loc.gov/ammem/index .html. Free.
Atlas of Canada. http://atlas.ncran.gc.ca/site/english/index.html. Free.
Atlas of World History. New York: Oxford University Press, 2010.
Barrington Atlas of the Greek and Roman World. Richard J. A. Talbert. Princeton, NJ: Princeton University Press, 2000.
base line: a newsletter of the Map and Geography Round Table. American Library Association. 1981–.
British Library Map Collection. http://www.bl.uk/onlinegallery/index.html. Free.

TOP TEN GEOGRAPHIC INFORMATION SOURCES

Title	Print	Online
Columbia Gazetteer of the World. New York: Columbia University Press.	2nd ed.	Subscription http://www.columbiagazetteer.org/
Google Maps		http://maps.google.com/
MapQuest		http://www.mapquest.com/
National Geographic Atlas of the World. Washington, DC: National Geographic Society	9th ed.	
Oxford Atlas of the World. New York: Oxford University Press.	Annual	
Perry-Casteñada Library Map Collection. Austin, TX: University of Texas Libraries.		http://www.lib.utexas.edu/maps/
Rand McNally Road Atlas. Chicago: Rand McNally.	Annual	
Shepherd's Historical Atlas. Totowa, NJ: Barnes and Noble.	9th ed.	
Times Comprehensive Atlas of the World. New York: Harper Collins.	2011	
World Geography and Culture Online. New York: Facts On File/Infobase Publishing.		Subscription http://www.infobasepublishing.com/ OnlineProductDetail.aspx?ISBN= 0816043795

RECOMMENDED FREE GEOGRAPHIC WEBSITES

American Memory Collection. Library of Congress. http://memory.loc.gov/ammem/index.html. Offers free access to historical maps from the Library of Congress.

Atlas of Canada. http://atlas.ncran.gc.ca/site/english/index.html. Provides access to a wide variety of information and maps on all subjects from people and society to health.

British Library Map Collection. http://www.bl.uk/onlinegallery/index.html. Includes both historical and modern maps of the United Kingdom from the British Library.

Google Maps. http://maps.google.com/. Provides access to current U.S. and international street maps.

MapQuest. http://www.mapquest.com/. Offers access to maps and directions for the United States and beyond.

Perry-Castañeda Library Map Collection. http://www.lib.utexas.edu/ maps/. Includes an astonishing collection of maps, both current and historical, from all over the world.

U.S. Census Bureau. http://www.census.gov/geo/www/maps/. Offers a wide variety of U.S. maps based on the U.S. census.

U.S. Geological Survey. http://www.usgs.gov/. Provides current and historical topographical maps from the U.S. Geological Survey.

The Bulletin. Ottawa, ON: Association of Canadian Map Libraries and Archives. 1968–. Tri-annual.

Cartographica Extraordinaire: The Historical Map Transformed. David Rumsey and Edith M. Punt. 2004. http://www.davidrumsey.com/. Free.

Columbia Gazetteer of the World Online. http://www.columbiagazetteer.org/.

DK Great World Atlas. London: Dorling Kindersley, 2008.

DK Traveler's Atlas. New York: Dorling Kindersley, 2006.

EnviroMapper. Environment Protection Agency. http://www.epa.gov/emefdata/em4ef .home/. Free.

EROS (Earth Resources Observation Systems) Data Center. U.S. Geological Survey. http://eros .usgs.gov/. Free.

FEMA maps. http://www.fema.gov/hazard/map/index.shtm. Free.

Geo.Data.gov. http://geo.data.gov/. Free.

Geographic Information: How to Find It, How to Use It. Jenny Marie Johnson. Westport, CT: Greenwood Press, 2003.

Geographic Information Systems. Reston, VA: U.S. Geological Survey. http://egsc.usgs.gov/ isb/pubs/gis_poster/.

Geographic Names Information System (GNIS). http://geonames.usgs.gov/. Free.

Geographical Names of Canada. http://www.nrcan.gc.ca/earth-sciences/home. Free.

GeoSource. http://www.library.uu.nl/geosource/. Free.

Getty Thesaurus of Geographic Names Online. http://www.getty.edu/research/tools/ vocabulary/tgn. Free.

Goode's World Atlas. Chicago: Rand McNally, 2002.

Google Earth. http://www.google.com/earth/index.html. Free.

Google Maps. http://maps.google.com/. Free.

Guide for a Small Map Collection. Barbara Farrell and Aileen Desbarats. Ottawa: Association of Canadian Map Libraries, 1981.

Hammond World Atlas. 5th ed. Spring House, PA: Hammond, 2010.

HarperCollins New World Atlas. New York: HarperCollins, 2003.

"Helpful Hints for Small Map Collections." Mary Larsgaard and Katherine Rankin. http://www.ala.org/magirt/publicationsab/electronicpubs/larsg.

Historical Atlas of Canada. 3 vols. Toronto: University of Toronto Press, 1987–1988.

Historical Atlas of the North American Railroad. Derek Hayes. Berkeley, CA: University of Cali-fornia, 2010.

Historical Atlas of the U.S. Rev. ed. Washington, DC: National Geographic Society, 1988.

History of Cartography Gateway. http://www.maphistory.info/. Free.

HopStop. http://www.hopstop.com/. Free.

INFOMINE. http://infomine.ucr.edu/. Free.

Information Bulletin. Western Association of Map Librarians. 1970–. Triannual.

Library of Congress. Geography and Map Division. http://www.loc.gov/topics/maps .php. Free.

Map Librarianship: An Introduction. Mary Lynette Larsgaard. Englewood, CO: Libraries Unlimited, 1998.

Map Machine. National Geographic Society. http://www.nationalgeographic.com/maps/ map-machine. Free.

MapQuest. http://www.mapquest.com/. Free.

Merriam-Webster's Geographical Dictionary. 3rd ed. Springfield, MA: Merriam-Webster, 2001.

National Atlas of the United States. http://www.nationalatlas.gov/. Free.

National Geographic Atlas of the World. 9th ed. Washington, DC: National Geographic Society, 2010.

National Geographic Concise Atlas of the World. 2nd ed. Washington, DC: National Geographic Society, 2007.

National Geographic Education. http://www.nationalgeographic.com/education/. Free.

Natural Resources Canada. Earth Sciences Section. http://www.nrcan.gc.ca/earth-sciences/home. Free.

NGA GEOnet Names Server. http://earth-info.nga.mil/gns/html/index.html. Free..

Oxford Atlas of the World. 18th ed. New York: Oxford University Press, 2011.

Oxford Comprehensive Atlas of the World. New York: Oxford University Press, 2008.

Oxford Essential World Atlas. 6th ed. New York: Oxford University Press, 2011.

Oxford New Historical Atlas of Religion in America. Edwin Gausted, ed. New York: Oxford University Press, 2001.

Perry-Castañeda Library Map Collection. http://www.lib.utexas.edu/ maps/. Free.

Rand McNally Road Atlas. Chicago: Rand McNally. Annual. http://www.randmcnally.com/.

Shepherd's Historical Atlas. 9th ed. Revised and updated. Totowa, NJ: Barnes and Noble, 1980.

Times Comprehensive Atlas of the World. New York: Harper Collins, 2011.

Times Concise Atlas of the World. 11th ed. London: Times Books, 2009.

Times History of the World. 5th ed. Richard Overy, ed. New York: Times Books, 1999.

United Nations Map Library. http://www.un.org/depts/dhl/maplib/maplib.htm. Free.

U.S. Census Bureau. http://www.census.gov/geo/www/maps. Free.

U.S. Geological Survey. http://www.usgs.gov/. Free.

Woodall's North American Campground Directory. Guilford, CT: Globe Pequot. Annual.

World Geography and Culture Online. Facts on File. Available by subscription.

Worldmark Encyclopedia of the Nations. 12th ed. Farmington Hills, MI: Gale Cengage, 2007. Also available as an e-book.

Yale University Map Collection. http://www.library.yale.edu/mapColl/index.html. Free.

Recommendations for Further Reading

Berenstein, Paula. 2006. "Location, Location, Location: Online Maps for the Masses." *Searcher* 14, no. 1 (January): 16–25. A discussion of new online maps including *Google Maps*, *Google Earth*, and *Yahoo! Maps*.

Bishop, Bradley Wade. 2011. "Location-Based Questions and Local Knowledge." *Journal of the American Society for Information Science and Technology* 62, no. 8: 1594–1603. Explores the barriers faced by staff fielding location-based questions through a virtual chat reference consortium. Location-based questions account for a large percent of the total reference questions received by this statewide service.

Boyer, Deborah. 2010. "From Internet to iPhone: Providing Mobile Geographic Access to Philadelphia's Historic Photographs and Other Special Collections." *The Reference Librarian* 52, no. 1-2 (December 30): 47–56. Describes a project by the City of Philadelphia's Department of Records to make images and other location-based documents available on PhillyHistory.org through smartphones, while creating the potential for revenue through print sales. The project is treated like a case study, and guidelines for use in similar projects are provided.

DeSanto, Dan. 2011. "The Mobile Future of Place-Based Digital Collections." *Bulletin of the American Society for Information Science and Technology* 38, no. 8: 10–13. Describes a project for a mobile application underway at the University of Vermont's Center for Digital Initiatives to make images from the Long Trail Collection accessible to hikers.

By linking geospatial metadata for the images to *Google Maps*, hikers will be able to use smartphones to discover historical information and images relating to locations on the trail.

Dietz, Cynthia. 2010. "Implementing Geospatial Web Services: A Resource Webliography." *Issues in Science and Technology Librarianship* 61. A valuable bibliography of resources for implementing and understanding geospatial services. Tools, courses, presentations, and tutorials helpful to those seeking to build their own geospatial web service are described, and interoperability challenges are noted.

Dodsworth, Eva. 2010. "Indirect Outreach in a GIS Environment: Reflections on a Map Library's Approach to Promoting GIS Services to Non-GIS Users." *Journal of Library Innovation* 1, no. 1: 24–35. Describes a new geospatial information literacy outreach and instructional program in use at the University of Waterloo Map Library. The program uses workshops, classroom visits, events, networking, and other approaches to introduce a broad range of students to the technology.

Erwin, Tracey, and Julie Sweetkind-Singer. 2010. "The National Geospatial Digital Archive: A Collaborative Project to Archive Geospatial Data." *Journal of Map and Geography Libraries* 6, no. 1: 6–25. Describes a geospatial data preservation and access project funded by the Library of Congress that was a collaborative effort between the University of California at Santa Barbara and Stanford University. Two repositories for the data were created, with federated searching enabled.

Johnson, Mary J. 2011. "Historical Maps Updated." *School Library Monthly* 27, no. 6: 32–34. Lists and reviews interactive online resources that allow students to explore historical maps in new ways. Search strategies and sources for map-related lesson plans are also included.

Lamb, Annette, and Larry Johnson. 2010. "Virtual Expeditions: Google Earth, GIS, and Geovisualization Technologies in Teaching and Learning." *Teacher Librarian* 37, no. 3: 81–85. Presents resources and strategies for teaching with geospatial technology.

Mitchell, Susan. 2003. "Where in the World? An Online Guide to Gazetteers, Atlases and Other Map Resources." *Internet Reference Services Quarterly* 8, no. 1/2: 183–194. An annotated guide to map resources on the web.

Shular, Michele D. 2009. "Turning Genealogists onto GIS." *Journal of Map and Geography Libraries* 5, no. 1: 55–71. Promotes the use of GIS for genealogists, for whom historical map collections and mapping projects provide valuable information. The article also provides examples of how this information can be used to create family histories.

Bibliography and Works Cited

Ashworth, Mick. 2003. "Paper or Pixels: Where to Next for Maps?" *Geographical* (December): 56–60.

Cline, Michael E. 2005. "Mapping Solutions Under $500." *Online* (May/June): 230.

Edson, Evelyn. 2002. "Bibliographic Essay: History of Cartography." Map History/History of Cartography. http://www.maphistory.info/edson.html.

Farrell, Barbara, and Aileen Desbarats. 1981. *Guide for a Small Map Collection*. Ottawa: Association of Canadian Map Libraries.

Johnson, Jenny Marie. 2003. *Geographic Information: How to Find It, How to Use It*. Westport, CT: Greenwood Press.

Kenny, Ann Jason. 2002. "More Than Just Maps." *School Library Journal*. Net Connect (Fall): 45–47.

Larsgaard, Mary Lynette. 1998. *Map Librarianship: An Introduction*. Englewood, CO: Libraries Unlimited.

Larsgaard, Mary, and Katherine Rankin. 1997. "Helpful Hints for Small Map Collections." American Library Association. http://www.ala.org/magirt/publicationsab/electronic pubs/larsg.

Liben, Lynn S. 2008 "Understanding Maps: Is the Purple Country on the Map Really Purple?" *Knowledge Quest* 36, 4: 20–30.

Monmonier, Mark, and George A. Schnell. 1988. *Map Appreciation*. Englewood Cliffs, NJ: Prentice Hall.

Sader, Marion, and Amy Lewis, eds. 1995. *Encyclopedias, Atlases and Dictionaries*. New Providence, NJ: R. R. Bowker.

Unwin, Tim. 1992. *The Place of Geography*. Burnt Mill, England: Longman Scientific and Technical Press.

Wood, Denis, with John Fels. 1992. *The Power of Maps*. New York: Guilford Press.

11

Answering Questions about the Lives of People— Biographical Information Sources

Overview

Many users ask for biographical information about well-known and not-so-well-known people. Where were they born? How old are they? How many times were they married? How many children do they have? Biographical sources answer these and many more questions. Although biographical information is widely available in many other reference sources, biographical resources provide more extensive and often more accurate information about people who are important historically and people who are currently in the news. To these ends, a wealth of biographical sources exists. Some are published by major publishers and others by small, sometimes vanity, presses.

How Biographical Resources Are Used

Biographical sources provide information about the lives of both living and deceased people; these print and electronic resources may concentrate on one country, such as *Who's Who in America*; on people in a certain field, such as *American Men and Women of Science*; or may be more general in nature, such as *Biography.com*. The information may be brief—providing the correct name, dates of birth and death, the field of work of the person and the person's nationality—or may be more extensive, discussing in great detail the person's life and accomplishments and including a bibliography for further research. Since biographical sources are a source of information about people, they can prove helpful to the user who is simply seeking minimal information about a person, including what their field of work is or was, dates of birth and maybe death, and nationality. Sometimes biographical sources are used to determine that the user has the correct person if there is more than one person with the same or a similar name. On the other hand, the user may be looking for more extensive information on a person and should be directed to a source that provides a lengthy biography and perhaps a list of sources for more information. Sometimes biographical sources are used to find well-known people in a certain field such as engineers, jazz musicians, or philosophers. For this reason, some biographical sources have an index by profession.

Questions Answered by Biographical Resources

Q: When did Susan B. Anthony die?

A: The answer can be found in the *American National Biography*.

Q: What are the birth and death dates for Charlotte Brontë?

A: This can be found in *Oxford Dictionary of National Biography*.

Q: How can I find articles about Martha Graham?

A: *Biography in Context* is a good source to check for articles on well-known people.

Q: Where can I find biographical information about Joyce Carol Oates?

A: *Literature Resource Center* can be searched to find this information.

Major Biographical Resources Used in Reference Work

Indexes

Indexes are a good place to begin when uncertain where the biography of a certain person will be found. The *Biography and Genealogy Master Index* indexes over 2,000 biographical reference sources such as biographical dictionaries, *Who's Who*, subject encyclopedias, and literary criticism with biographical information. About 5 million biographical sketches of persons, both living and deceased, from every field and from all areas of the world are included in this index. Listings include the birth and death dates of each person, the source of the biographical information, and if there is a portrait. This index is particularly useful when it is not obvious which biographical source would have information. It is available online and updated semiannually.

Biographies of Contemporary People

For concise information about contemporary people, the user can turn to the *Marquis Who's Who* series of publications. *Who's Who in America* is perhaps the best known of the series. This annual publication provides current biographical information on about 93,000 noteworthy Americans. Some of the entries are new listings; many are updated entries. Questionnaires are sent to those listed to update their information annually. A typical entry includes the person's name, occupation, date of birth, family information, education, career summary, publications, civic and political activities, memberships, and address. This valuable biographical source includes a geographic index, a professional index, a retiree list, and a necrology for those deceased since the last edition.

Marquis also publishes a regional *Who's Who* for each part of the United States such as *Who's Who in the East*, *Who's Who in the Midwest*, *Who's Who in the South/Southwest*, and *Who's Who in the West* as well as others such as *Who's Who of American Women* and professional sources such as *Who's Who in American Art* and *Who's Who in American Politics*. Marquis also publishes a *Who's Who in the World*. The format for all the print *Who's Who* is similar. *Marquis Biographies Online* provides access to more than 1.4 million biographies of people from twenty-four of the "Who's Who" print publications. It covers both people from the past and present and from all walks of life. This online database allows the user to search by such criteria as name, gender, occupation, college/university, date of birth, or a combination of them. According to the publisher, the online subscription database is updated daily. Librarians can also subscribe to parts of this database such as the *Who's Who in America* slice or the *Who's Who in the World* slice.

Who's Who is the British resource that lists contemporary people of note— mostly British but a few Americans as well. With more than 33,000 biographies, this resource follows the usual pattern of listing the name, present position, date of birth, family details, education, and career in order of date, publications, recreations, and address. *Who's Who* is updated through a questionnaire to the people listed. An obituary section with the death date is also included. This database is now available online.

Although *Canadian Who's Who* began in 1910, it did not become an annual reference work until 1980. Questionnaires are sent out annually to update the 14,000 biographical sketches in this work. This work lists date and place of birth, address, family details, education, career information, memberships, and awards or other achievements for each person.

World Who's Who includes information on more than 60,000 noteworthy men and women from all professions and from all parts of the world. A typical entry includes the person's name, nationality, profession, date and place of birth, family information, education, career summary, awards, publications, leisure interests, and contact information. Obituaries are included in addition to a section that lists all the reigning royal families in the world. This online resource allows the user to search by name, nationality, place and date of birth, and profession. Routledge also publishes a series of international "Who's Who" by profession such as *International Who's Who in International Affairs* and *International Who's Who in Classical Music*.

Current Biography provides biographical information on people in the news. Each of its eleven issues per year provides profiles of eighteen to twenty people from the arts, politics, literature, sports, film and television as well as obituaries of people previously profiled. This well-written biographical source is useful for students as well as adults. The articles are 2,000 to 3,500 words in length and include a photograph of the person and a bibliography of additional sources of information. An annual volume compiles the individual issues for the year. *Current Biography Illustrated* is the online version of *Current Biography*. In this format users can search the entire database from 1940 to the present by name, profession, place of origin, birth or death date, ethnicity, and gender.

Newsmakers: The People Behind Today's Headlines is similar to *Current Biography*. Each biography of 1,500 to 3,000 words includes the person's address, date of birth, family details, education, career summary, awards, writings, and a biographical essay. A photo of each person and a bibliography of additional sources of information are included. People listed in each issue come from all walks of life including business, television and film, entertainment, literature, politics and government, and science. This publication provides indexes by nationality, occupation, and subject as well as an obituary section. In addition to the four issues published annually, there is an annual cumulative volume. An e-book of the annual volume is also available.

Biography in Context (formerly *Biography Resource Center*) is an extensive online database providing biographical information about persons currently in the news and those deceased. Each profile includes personal information, career information, the person's writings, "sidelights," and a bibliography for further readings about the person. This Gale Cengage Learning resource includes full text from more than 265 periodicals and more than 600,000 biographies from more than 170 Gale Cengage Learning resources, including *Encyclopedia of World Biography*, *Dictionary of American Biography*, and *Scribner Encyclopedia of American Lives*. The database can be searched by name, occupation, year of birth, nationality, ethnicity, or place of birth.

Biography Reference Bank combines several H.W. Wilson databases into one biography subscription database. This database includes H.W. Wilson *Biographies Plus Illustrated*, *Junior Authors and Illustrators*, and links to other full text from H.W. Wilson publications including *Current Biography*. More than 660,000 people are listed in this database, which can be searched by name, profession, place of origin, gender, ethnicity, birth and death dates, titles of works, and keyword. More than 36,000 images are also included. *Biography Reference Bank* is part of the recent acquisition of H.W. Wilson by EBSCO.

The newest of these online biographical compilations is *Biography Source*. It is the result of the merger of EBSCO and H.W. Wilson and includes over 600,000 in-depth biographies and obituaries. Among the resources indexed in *Biography Source* are *Biography Today*, *Biography*, *Current Biography*, *Cambridge Dictionary of American Biography*, and *Notable American Women*.

Biography.com is a free database that includes 25,000 biographies of well-known people from ancient times to the present. Each entry includes birth and death dates, career information and often a photograph, list of works and related web links. Information for this website comes from *Cambridge Dictionary of American Biography* and *Cambridge Encyclopedia Database* as well as information from the cable station, A&E (Arts and Entertainment).

Biographical Dictionary (http://www.s9.com/) is another online source of biographical information covering more than 33,000 people both past and present. Brief information is given for each person including birth and death dates, profession, position held, and literary and artistic works produced. Anyone can add content to this site.

Who2? (http://www.who2.com/) provides basic information of more than 38,000 people with links to other related websites.

Retrospective Biography

American National Biography is a recent work published in print and available online that is a successor to the *Dictionary of American Biography* (*DAB*). It is a completely new work "that resulted in the more expansive understanding of who is a notable American" (Bryant, 1999: 82). There are 18,000 lengthy biographies that include more women, minorities, and people from other countries who have lived in the United States and made contributions to it than the original *DAB*. Not all people in the *Dictionary of American Biography* are included in the new *American National Biography*. As in the *Dictionary of American Biography*, all persons listed are deceased. This new work is updated quarterly online and can be searched by name, occupation, gender, birth and death dates, birthplace, and ethnic heritage. Entries include a photograph of the person and a bibliography. A useful feature is the hyperlinks to related biographies.

The *Dictionary of American Biography* was commissioned by the American Council of Learned Societies. It has been for many decades the premier source of American biography. The last supplement was published in 1985 and includes people who died before 1980. A total of 19,000 biographies are included in the volumes of this work.

Oxford Dictionary of National Biography, published in 2004, is a major revision of the *Dictionary of National Biography (DNB)*, which was completed in 1900. Available both in print and online, this new version includes both 58,000 new biographies and rewritten or revised biographies of the lives of people included in the thirty-three volumes of the original *DNB* and its supplements. Over 10,000 portraits also appear in this work. The coverage includes Britons from all walks of life who have made their mark in Great Britain or elsewhere, as well as people from other countries who have played a role in British history and life. As in the original *DNB*, people listed in this work are all deceased. Searching online is by person, place, dates, and fields of interest. Three updates online are made each year.

The original *Dictionary of National Biography* covered 29,333 people. It was reissued in 1908–1909 in twenty-two volumes. Additional supplements were published between 1912 and 1996. As is the case with the *DAB*, the *DNB* has been the primary source of biographical information about people of British origin. The *Dictionary of Canadian Biography* states in the introduction that those omitted are those "who have not set forth in what is now Canada, or at least approached its shores" (*DCB*, 1966: xvi). The volumes are arranged in chronological order as determined by the person's death date. Volume 1 covers 1000 to 1700. Each biographical sketch is 400 to 1,200 words. A general bibliography and an index are included at the end of each volume. Fourteen volumes have been published to date. The *Dictionary* is also available in French. The *Dictionary of Canadian Biography Online* is the online version of the *Dictionary of Canadian Biography*, which also includes some of the biographical sketches for the upcoming volume.

World Biographical Information System (*WBIS Online*) compiles biographical articles from digital archives from the eighth century BCE to the twenty-first century and provides facsimiles of the original documents online. This online tool includes 8.5 million digitized biographical articles and is available in German, Spanish, English, French, and Italian. Searches can be done by name, gender, year of birth and death, occupation, and country.

Who Was Who and *Who Was Who in America* are the retrospective versions of *Who's Who* and *Who's Who in America*. Once a person is deceased, he or she becomes part of the retrospective version. *Who Was Who* is grouped in four-year segments. Volume 12, for example, contains the entries of people who died between 2006 and 2010. The entries are as they appeared in *Who's Who* with the death date added as well as posthumous publications. *Who Was Who: A Cumulated Index 1897–2000* provides easy access to *Who Was Who* listing the person's name, birth and death years, and the volume number. *Who Was Who in America* now has twenty-two volumes beginning in 1897 and continuing through 2010–2011. In addition, a historical volume covers the years 1607–1896. This is a specially compiled volume since *Who's Who in America* did not begin until 1899. Parts of *Who Was Who in America* are available online as part of the *Marquis Biographies Online*. The complete *Who Was Who* is available online with links to the *Oxford Dictionary of National Biography*.

The *National Cyclopedia of American Biography* is subtitled "Being the History of the United States as illustrated in the lives of the founders, builders and defenders of the Republic and of the men and women who are doing the work and moulding the thought of the present time." The volumes are groupings of individuals and not in alphabetical order. Each person has a fairly lengthy biography and a photo or line drawing as well. Many of these people were alive when the volume was published. Because the listings are not in alphabetical order, each volume has an index. The uniqueness of this biographical source is that it lists many people (e.g., prominent businesspeople, clergy, etc.) who are not in other biographical sources.

The *Scribner Encyclopedia of American Lives* presents very readable signed biographies of deceased people with a photo of each person and a bibliography. Each volume is arranged in alphabetical order with an occupations index. A new volume is issued every two years. These volumes are supplements to the *Dictionary of American Biography*.

Encyclopedia of World Biography, Second Edition, is a multivolume work that includes in-depth portraits of more than 7,000 persons, both living and deceased, from all time periods and all walks of life both living and deceased. The biographies are very readable and include a bibliography and often a photograph or drawing of the person. Because of the emphasis on the international, it is a good place to find information on persons from other countries such as government officials. A supplement is published annually. This is also available as an e-book that includes the supplements to the *Encyclopedia*.

One-Volume Biographical Dictionaries

Chambers Biographical Dictionary is a large one-volume biographical dictionary that includes 18,000 biographies of "people who have shaped, and continue to shape, the world in which we live" (preface). In a user-friendly format, the dictionary provides short biographical sketches of people both living and deceased. The entries are written in prose describing the achievements of the person. For a few select people the biographical sketch is highlighted in a box with an appropriate quote by or about the person. *Chambers* is available online. It is also published under the title *The Cambridge Biographical Dictionary*.

Merriam-Webster's Biographical Dictionary is a compact one-volume biographical dictionary listing concise biographical information about 30,000 persons from ancient times to the present day who are deceased. It is useful as a ready reference source.

Obituaries

Obituaries are often requested by library users searching for details of someone's life. Because of such easy access to the retrospective issues of the *New York Times*, it is not as necessary to have separate volumes with obituaries; however, these two print volumes can be quite useful and easy to check. The *New York Times Obituaries Index, 1885–1968* and *New York Times Obituaries Index, 1969–1978* are an accumulation of obituaries for these periods of time. It is rather interesting to note the different policies throughout the decades about murders and suicides, but Volume 2 does cover these deaths. *ProQuest Obituaries* is an online source of over 10.5 million full-text obituaries from U.S. newspapers using the newspapers digitized by ProQuest. Users can search by name, date, and keyword. Newsbank has also developed an online obituaries database, *America's Obituaries and Death Notices*, which includes information from a large number of newspapers throughout the United States. Another source to try is *Obituaries.com*, which provides access to obituaries from 700 newspapers in the United States and Canada.

Subject-Based Biographical Tools

Contemporary Authors is an excellent source of information on current authors, especially nonfiction writers whose biographical information can be hard to find. Available in print and electronic formats, it includes a wide range of authors publishing fiction, nonfiction, poetry, and so on. The information provided includes personal information, career information, awards, "sidelights," which is an essay about the author's work, writings by the author, and writings about the author. Periodically, these biographies are updated. Over 120,000 authors are included. *Contemporary Authors* is also part of Gale Cengage Learning's *Literature Resource Center*, which also includes *Contemporary Literary Criticism Select* and the *Dictionary of Literary Biography Online*. The *Dictionary of Literary Biography Online* contains more than 10,000 biocritical essays on authors and their works. This information has been compiled from other Gale Cengage Learning publications and from 260 literary journals. The user can search by name, ethnicity, nationality, genre, literary theme, and literary movement. Websites on the author's life and work are included. The print version of the *Dictionary of Literary Biography* has more content than the online version, so librarians might want to compare the two to decide which version is the best for their users.

Voices from the Gaps: Women Artists and Writers of Color (http://voices.cla.umn .edu/) is maintained and updated by the English Department of the University of Minnesota. This site provides biographical information on North American women artists and writers of color. Users can search by name, racial/ethnic background, or keywords.

The American Historical Association's *Guide to Historical Literature* includes references to biographies throughout each of its three editions (1931, 1961, and 1995). This is an excellent source of biographies from a particular time period.

Directory of American Scholars provides short biographical sketches similar to those found in *Who's Who in America*. Each of the five volumes covers specific disciplines: History; English, Speech, and Drama; Foreign Languages, Linguistics and Philology; Philosophy, Religion, and Law; and Social Sciences. A separate index volume includes an alphabetical index, discipline index, institutional index, and geographical index. This resource provides information about many in the academic world not easily found in other biographical sources.

American Men and Women of Science; A Biographical Directory of Today's Leaders in Physical, Biological and Related Sciences is an invaluable source of information about contemporary scientists in both the United States and Canada who have made significant contributions in their field. The information on 130,000 scientists is provided in a concise format and includes birth date, birthplace, citizenship, family details, specialty field, education, honorary degrees, professional experience, honors and awards, memberships, research information, address, and e-mail. There are seven volumes of biographical information with an eighth volume devoted to a discipline index organized by field of activity, and within each subject the names are arranged by state. Volume 1 also lists the winners of various scientific prizes. This reference work is available online through *Gale Virtual Reference Library* and as an e-book.

The New Dictionary of Scientific Biography, a biographical dictionary for mathematicians and natural scientists, which is often called a *DAB* for scientists, has been updated; it is now a twenty-six-volume set. The additional volumes can be ordered separately, or the whole set can be purchased as an e-book that is part of the *Gale Virtual Reference Library*. The School of Mathematics and Statistics of the University of St. Andrews, Scotland, produces and keeps up-to-date a free website on mathematicians, *Indexes of Biographies* (http://www-history.mcs.st-and.ac .uk/BiogIndex.html). The biographies are quite extensive and are signed.

Notable American Women, 1607–1950: A Biographical Dictionary, Notable American Women, the Modern Period: A Biographical Dictionary, and *Notable American Women: A Biographical Dictionary Completing the Twentieth Century* provide signed scholarly articles on over 2,200 women and document the role of American women in history. The *Palgrave Macmillan Dictionary of Women's Biography* provides biographical information on over 2,100 women both current and from the past. It provides information on many contemporary women from all parts of the world who have received little recognition. The *National Women's History Museum* (http://www.nwhm.org/education-resources/biography/biographies-home/) lists women by area of contribution such as environmentalists, activists, entertainers, and journalists. There is a short biographical sketch for each woman with a photograph and a short bibliography.

Eric Weisstein's World of Biography (http://scienceworld.wolfram.com/ biography/) provides brief biographical sketches of over 1,000 people in the sciences with a short bibliography for each person.

Biographies of philosophers can be found in the *Stanford Encyclopedia of Philosophy*, an open access website (http://plato.stanford.edu/). It provides extensive signed biographies of philosophers updated by experts in the field.

The *Biographical Directory of the United States Congress, 1774 to Present* is now available online (http://bioguide.congress.gov/biosearch/biosearch.asp). Users can search by name, position in Congress (senator, representative, Speaker of the

House, etc.), state, party, and so on. Photos of recent members of Congress are included.

Modern and Contemporary Artists and Art (http://www.the-artists.org/) can be searched by the name of the artist or by art movement, style, or medium in this free website. The listings provide information about the artists and their work. The *Union List of Artist Names* (*ULAN*) is produced at the Getty Museum in California (http://www.getty.edu/research/tools/vocabularies/ulan/index.html). It lists over 293,000 names of artists. Its scope is global, covering antiquity to the present. Each record includes variations of the artist's name, dates of birth and death, geographic locations, relationships such as student-teacher relationships, biographical notes, and the source of the information.

Biographical information on people in the movies can be found on the *Internet Movie Database* site (http://www.imdb.com/). The official database for the Broadway theater is *Internet Broadway Database* (http://www.ibdb.com/). Users can search by show, people, theater, characters, awards, and songs.

Biographical information on over 100 jazz musicians is located at http://www.pbs.org/jazz/biography/ along with audio clips and photographs. It is based on a film by Ken Burns.

Biographical Resources Featuring Ethnic/Cultural Heritage

Who's Who among African Americans provides biographical sketches of prominent African Americans. The main part of this reference work lists each person's personal data, occupation, educational background, career information, organizational affiliations, honors or awards, special achievements, and military service. This resource includes geographical and occupational indexes as well as an obituaries section for people that are recently deceased. This resource is also available as an e-book through the *Gale Virtual Reference Library*. The *African American National Biography* provides substantial, scholarly biographical information on more than 4,100 African Americans. Some of the information comes from the *American National Biography*. The online version is available in *Oxford African American Studies Center*. *African American Biographical Database* brings together historical information from many sources on African Americans between 1790 and 1950, including both prominent leaders and others who are not found elsewhere.

Although very few biographical reference sources exist for individual ethnic groups, many of the electronic reference sources in this chapter can be searched by ethnic groups, allowing the user to find information on contemporary African Americans, Hispanic Americans, Asian Americans, and others.

Collection Development and Maintenance

Selection and Keeping Current

Biographical sources are reviewed by the journals that review reference materials. The librarian can find new biographical resources reviewed in *Library Journal*,

Booklist, *Choice*, and *American Reference Books Annual*. Standard titles are discussed in ALA's *Guide to Reference* and in *New Walford Guide to Reference Resources*.

Evaluating Biographical Resources

Criteria for evaluating biographical resources include the following:

- Scope
- Accuracy
- Length of entry
- Criteria for inclusion
- Audience
- Authority
- Frequency of updates
- Photo
- References for further reading

Scope is particularly important in biographical sources since it applies to the coverage of the resource. Does the resource cover both living and deceased people? Does it only cover certain professions or certain countries? What are the parameters of its coverage? In a library's collection the librarian will want to have biographical sources that describe the lives of well-known people of the past, called retrospective biography, as well as sources that describe the lives of people who are alive today, called current biography. The collection should also have resources with information on people from other countries as well as the United States. Sometimes biographical sources include people from many different parts of the world, whereas others provide information on people from a region or a country.

Attention to accuracy is needed in biographical resources. Fact checking biographical entries is recommended. In addition to checking the birth and death dates against another credible source, the librarian should read some entries in the reference source to see if the entries are objective and comprehensive within the parameters of the entries. If the work is not available, reviews will often point out inaccuracies in a reference work.

The length of the entry is important because sometimes users need a short biographical sketch and sometimes they need lengthy, more detailed information. Libraries will want resources with short and longer biographies.

Criteria for inclusion are of great interest. Perhaps those included filled out a questionnaire or perhaps authors made an effort to find everyone who fit their criteria for inclusion. This is often explained in the preface or introduction to the biographical resource. If, however, it appears that everyone in the book was required to pay to be included, this may not be a very objective source.

The audience for the resource should be noted. Determine the reading level of the biographical source and the intended audience. Some sources provide scholarly biographies, whereas others are more popular in content and tone and are aimed at a general audience.

The authority of the work must be examined, which may be either the publisher or the author. Signed biographies and biographies with a bibliography are good signs of a quality resource. Not all biographical sources are published by major publishers. This does not mean they are not useful additions to a library collection. But it does mean that the librarian should review these resources more carefully.

Determine how often the publisher plans to update the work, especially if most of the people listed are currently alive. Many biographical sources are updated annually. Be aware that many biographical reference sources build on previous volumes and may issue or include an index to assist users to find the needed material. The *Dictionary of Literary Biography* is a good example of this. Multiple volumes are issued in one year with an index providing cumulative indexing. If online, the biographical source can be expected to be updated more regularly. Note if the biographical source includes a photograph of the person. Many sources do not, but it is extremely useful to have biographical sources with photographs since many users are interested in knowing what the person looks or looked like. Finally, it can be useful for the biographical source to include a bibliography of other sources of information about the person to assist in doing more extensive research.

Further Considerations

Biographical information is both easy and difficult to find. Well-known people are listed in many different biographical resources. However, some people can be very hard to locate in biographical resources. It can be useful to narrow the kinds of biographical resources that would possibly be relevant by attempting to categorize the person, assuming the user has some information. First, the user should try to determine if the person is living or dead. If the person is living, for example, the user can eliminate biographical resources that include only deceased persons. The next step is to determine the nationality of the person. This can definitely narrow the number of possible sources as not all biographical sources are international. If the user knows the profession of the person, this can also be useful. Subject encyclopedias can often be useful for finding information on a person known in a particular field. For example, the user could find an extensive biography on Mozart in *Grove Music Online* or a biography of Picasso in *Grove Art Online* (available as *Oxford Music Online* and *Oxford Art Online*). It can be helpful to try large comprehensive resources that cover many resources and provide a single way to identify biographies in multivolume works such as *Biography and Genealogy Master Index*. Sometimes it is necessary to go beyond these biographical sources and try some of the periodical and newspaper databases for information on people currently in the news.

Recommended Resources Discussed in This Chapter

African American Biographical Database. Ann Arbor, MI: ProQuest. http://www.proquest.com/.

African American National Biography. Henry Louis Gates Jr. and Evelyn Brooks Higginbotham, eds. New York: Oxford University Press, 2008.

THE TOP TEN BIOGRAPHICAL SOURCES

Title	Print	Online
American National Biography. 1999. New York: Oxford University Press.	24 volumes	Subscription http://www.anb.org/
Biography and Genealogy Master Index. Farmington, MI: Gale Cengage Learning.		Subscription http://www.gale.cengage.com/
Biography in Context. Farmington, MI: Gale Cengage Learning.		Subscription http://www.gale.cengage.com/
Biography Source. Ipswich, MA: EBSCO.		Subscription http://www.ebscohost.com/
Current Biography. Ipswich, MA: EBSCO.	Monthly	Subscription http://www.ebscohost.com/
Literature Resource Center. Farmington Hills, MI: Gale Cengage Learning.		Subscription http://www.gale.cengage.com/
Marquis Biographies Online. New Providence, NJ: Marquis Who's Who.		Subscription http://www.marquiswhoswho.com/
Oxford Dictionary of National Biography. 2004. New York: Oxford University Press.	60 volumes	Subscription http://www.oxforddnb.com/
Who's Who. 1897–. London: A&C Black.	Annual	Subscription http://www.acblack.co.uk/
World Who's Who. Florence, KY: Routledge.	Annual	Subscription http://www.worldwhoswho.com/

American Men and Women of Science; A Biographical Directory of Today's Leaders in Physical, Biological and Related Sciences. 24th ed. Farmington Hills, MI: Gale Cengage Learning, 2007.

American National Biography. 24 vols. New York: Oxford University Press, 1999. Also available online: http://www.anb.org/.

America's Obituaries and Death Notices. Naples, FL: Newsbank. http://www.newsbank.com/.

Biographical Dictionary. http://www.s9.com/. Free.

Biographical Directory of the United States Congress, 1774 to Present. http://bioguide.congress.gov/biosearch/biosearch.asp. Free.

Biography and Genealogy Master Index. Farmington Hills, MI: Gale Cengage Learning. http://www.gale.cengage.com/.

Biography in Context. Farmington Hills, MI: Gale Cengage Learning. http://www.gale.cengage.com/.

Biography Reference Bank. New York: EBSCO. http://www.ebscohost.com/.

Biography Source. Ipswich, MA: EBSCO. Available online by subscription: http://www.ebscohost.com/.

Biography.com. http://www.biography.com/. Free.

Canadian Who's Who. Toronto: University of Toronto Press, 1980–.

RECOMMENDED FREE BIOGRAPHICAL WEBSITES

Biographical Dictionary. http://www.s9.com/. A source of biographical information that anyone can edit.

Biographical Directory of the United States Congress, 1774 to Present. http://bioguide.congress .gov/biosearch/biosearch.asp. A guide to Congress from the beginning of the Republic.

Biography.com. http://www.biography.com/. A good general biographical source.

Eric Weisstein's World of Biography. http://scienceworld.wolfram.com/biography/. A biographical source for people in science.

Internet Movie Database. http://www.imdb.com/. An excellent source for information on people in the motion picture industry.

National Women's History Museum. http://www.nwhm.org/education-resources/biography/ biographies-home/. Information on outstanding women in history.

Obituaries.com. http://www.obituaries.com/. A good source of obituary information.

Stanford Encyclopedia of Philosophy. http://plato.stanford.edu. Biographies of philosophers.

Union List of Artist Names (ULAN). http://www.getty.edu/research/tools/vocabularies/ ulan/index.html. A good source of information on artists.

Chambers Biographical Dictionary. 9th ed. Edinburgh: Chambers, 2011. Also available online: http://www.chambers.co.uk/.

Contemporary Authors. Farmington Hills, MI: Gale Cengage Learning, 1962–. Also available online as part of the *Literature Resource Center.*

Current Biography. New York: EBSCO, 1940–. Monthly with an annual cumulative volume. Also available online as *Current Biography Illustrated*: http://www.ebscohost .com/.

Dictionary of American Biography, 1927–1936. 20 vols. and index. New York: Scribner. Supplements, 1944–1980 with index, 1996.

Dictionary of Canadian Biography. 14 vols. and index. Toronto: University of Toronto Press, 1966. Also published in French. http://www.biographi.ca/.

Dictionary of Literary Biography. Farmington, MI: Gale Cengage Learning. Also available online: http://www.gale.cengage.com/.

Dictionary of National Biography. London: Smith, Elder, 1885–1900. Supplements 1912–1996.

Dictionary of Scientific Biography. 2007. New York: Simon and Schuster, 2007. Also available online as part of the Gale Cengage Learning *Virtual Reference Library.*

Directory of American Scholars. 6 vols. Farmington Hills, MI: Gale Cengage Learning, 2002.

Encyclopedia of World Biography. 2nd ed. Farmington Hills, MI: Gale Cengage Learning, 1998. Annual supplements.

Eric Weisstein's World of Biography. http://scienceworld.wolfram.com/biography/. Free.

Grove Art Online. In *Oxford Art Online.* New York: Oxford University Press. http://www .oxfordartonline.com/.

Grove Music Online. In *Oxford Music Online.* New York: Oxford University Press. http:// oxfordmusiconline.com/.

Guide to Historical Literature. 1st, 2nd, 3rd eds. New York: Macmillan and American Historical Association, 1931, 1961, 1995 (2 vols.).

Indexes of Biographies. School of Mathematics and Statistics, University of St. Andrews, Scotland. http://www-history.mcs.st-and.ac.uk/BiogIndex.html.

International Who's Who in Classical Music. Florence, KY: Routledge. http://www.routledge .com/. Annual.

International Who's Who in International Affairs. Florence, KY: Routledge. http://www.routledge .com/. Biennial.

Internet Broadway Database. http://www.ibdb.com/. Free.

Internet Movie Database. http://www.imdb.com/. Free.

Jazz Musicians. http://www.pbs.org/jazz/biography/. Free.

Literature Resource Center. Farmington Hills, MI: Gale Cengage Learning. http://www .gale.cengage.com/.

Marquis Biographies Online. http://marquiswhoswho.com/.

Merriam-Webster's Biographical Dictionary. 1995. Springfield, MA: Merriam-Webster, 1995.

Modern and Contemporary Artists and Art. http://www.the-artists.org/. Free.

National Cyclopedia of American Biography. New York: White, 1898–1984.

National Women's History Museum. http://www.nwhm.org/education-resources/biography/ biographies-home/.

New York Times Obituaries Index, 1885–1968. New York: New York Times, 1970.

New York Times Obituaries Index, 1969–1978. New York: New York Times, 1980.

Newsmakers: The People Behind Today's Headlines. Farmington Hills, MI: Gale Cengage Learning. Quarterly.

Notable American Women: A Biographical Dictionary Completing the Twentieth Century. Cambridge, MA: Belknap Press, 2004.

Notable American Women, 1607–1950: A Biographical Dictionary. Cambridge, MA: Belknap Press of Harvard University Press, 1971.

Notable American Women, the Modern Period: A Biographical Dictionary. Cambridge, MA: Belknap Press of Harvard University Press, 1980.

Obituaries.com. http://www.obituaries.com/. Free.

Oxford African American Studies Center. New York: Oxford University Press. http://www .oup.com/online/us/africanamerican/?view=usa.

Oxford Dictionary of National Biography. 60 vols. New York: Oxford University Press, 2004. Also available online: http://www.oxforddnb.com/.

Palgrave Macmillan Dictionary of Women's Biography. 4th ed. Jennifer S. Uglow, Frances Hinton, and Maggy Hendry, eds. New York: Palgrave Macmillan, 2005.

ProQuest Obituaries. Ann Arbor, MI: ProQuest, 1851–. http://www.proquest.com/.

Scribner Encyclopedia of American Lives. Farmington, MI: Gale Cengage Learning, 1998–. Biennial. Also available online: http://www.gale.cengage.com/.

Stanford Encyclopedia of Philosophy. http://plato.stanford.edu/.

Union List of Artist Names (ULAN). http://www.getty.edu/research/tools/vocabularies/ ulan/index.html.

Voices from the Gaps: Women Artists and Writers of Color. http://voices.cla.umn.edu/.

Who Was Who. London: A&C Black, 1897–.

Who Was Who: A Cumulated Index, 1897–2000. London: A&C Black, 2002.

Who Was Who in America. Chicago: Marquis Who's Who, 1897–. Historical volume, 1607–1896.

Who's Who. London: A&C Black, 1897–. Annual. Also available online: http://www .acblack.co.uk/.

Who's Who among African Americans. 19th ed. Farmington Hills, MI: Gale Cengage Learning, 2005–. Annual. Also available as an e-book.

Who's Who in America. New Providence, NJ: Marquis Who's Who. Annual.

Who2? http://www.who2.com/. Free.

World Biographical Information System (WBIS Online). Boston: DeGruyter. http://www .degruyter.com/.

World Who's Who. Florence KY: Europa Publications, distributed by Taylor and Francis. http://www.worldwhoswho.com/.

Recommendations for Further Reading

Beagle, Donald. 2011. "Integrating Digital and Archival Sources in Historical Research: Recovering Lost Knowledge about a Catholic Poet of the Civil War." *The Catholic Library World* 81, no. 3: 201–209. Contains an account of how newly digitized archival sources brought to light previously undiscovered resources that shed new light on the biographical research of a nineteenth-century poet.

Jacso, Peter. 2010. "Metadata Mega Mess in Google Scholar." *Online Information Review* 34, no. 1: 175–191. Addresses the continued issue of large-scale metadata inaccuracy and other problems that impede the usefulness of *Google Scholar* to researchers. The author warns that in its current state, *Google Scholar* cannot be used to find accurate information about an individual's scholarly publishing productivity and impact.

Keiser, Barbie E. 2010. "Free People Searching (With the Occasional Price-tag)." *Online* 34, no. 6: 19–23. Provides an assessment of free and for-pay tools useful for finding contact and biographical information about people, particularly geared toward business.

Soules, Aline. 2012. "Where's the Bio? Databases, Wikipedia, and the Web." *New Library World* 113, no. 1–2: 77–89. Using the names of 500 authors writing in English, compares the biographical information found for each in *Literature Resource Center*, *Biography Reference Bank*, *Wikipedia*, and the web to assess the resources.

Wleklinski, Joann M. 2010. "Get a Life: Comparing Online Biography Resources." *Online* 34, no. 1: 40–44. Compares the search capabilities and content of both fee-based and free biographical resources on the lives of famous people in order to assess their value for library researchers.

Bibliography and Works Cited

Bryant, Eric. 1999. "Assessing American National Biography." *Library Journal* 122 (July): 82.

Fialkoff, Francine. 1998. "Dueling Dictionaries." *Library Journal* 123 (November 15): 54.

LaGuardia, Cheryl. 2005. "Oxford Sets the Bar High." *Library Journal* 129 (October 15): 24–25.

McDermott, Irene E. 2003. "What's What with Who's Who on the Web." *Searcher* 11 (July/August): 49–51.

Rollyson, Carl E. 1997. "Biography as a Genre." *Choice* 35 (October): 249–258.

Schreiner, Susan A., and Michael A. Somers. 2002. "Biography Resources: Finding Information on the Famous, Infamous and Obscure." *College and Research Libraries News* 63 (January): 32–35, 39.

Whiteley, Sandy. 2005. "An Undertaking of Exceptional Magnitude." *Booklist* 101 (January 1–15): 901.

12

Answering Questions about Government and Related Issues— Government Information Sources

Overview

Every level of government, from federal agencies to the local municipalities, publishes. Perhaps unsurprisingly these works are often referred to, in reference services and beyond, as "government documents." In the United States, government publications are defined as "informational matter which is published as an individual document at government expense, or as required by law" (44 U.S. Code 1901). This definition encompasses records of government administrations, research publications including statistics and other data, and popular sources of information on such subjects as nutrition, health, jobs, and travel. They are as varied as "Bee Basics: An Introduction to Our Native Bees" from the U.S. Forest Service and Pollinator Partnership, "A Photographer's Path: Images of National Parks Near the Nation's Capital" from the National Parks Service, "The State of the Hudson 2009" from the New York State Department of Environmental Conservation, and "High Mountain Glaciers and Climate Change: Challenges to Human Livelihoods and Adaptation" from the United Nations Environmental Program. These publications come in many formats: books, CD-ROMs, periodicals, pamphlets, films, maps, and online publications. Every country produces its own government information, and international organizations such as the United Nations and the World Bank also produce many publications. Most of these publications are free if available online, and many are available for purchase at a very reasonable cost.

How Government Publications Are Used

Government publications are an excellent source of information about many important issues. In fact, information on some subjects is only available from government publications and provides primary source material for researchers. If one looks at the array of subjects covered by government departments and agencies, it becomes apparent that the government deals with nearly every part of a citizen's life. For this reason, it is important to know about government publications and how to organize, access, and then add them to a library's collection.

Questions Answered by Government Publications

Q: How can I find National Parks where I can hike in California?

A: Go to the "Find a Park" section of the National Park Service site (http://www.nps.gov/findapark/index.htm), and you will find a list of National Parks in California where you can hike.

Q: Do I need immunizations to visit in Cambodia?

A: Go to the Centers for Disease Control site (http://www.cdc.gov/travel/) and you will be able to find the recommended immunizations for Cambodia.

Q: How can I find out about eligibility requirements for Pell grants?

A: Go to the Department of Education website where you will find a direct link to Pell grants (http://www.ed.gov/programs/fpg/index.html)

Q: How can I find information on small business loans?

A: Go to the Small Business Administration site (http://www.sba.gov/) where you can find out about the services and loan programs that are available and how to apply.

The U.S. Government Printing Office and Its Future

The U.S. Government Printing Office (GPO) is "the Federal Government's primary centralized resource for producing, procuring, cataloging, indexing, authenticating, disseminating and preserving the official information products of the U.S. Government in digital and tangible forms" (http://www.gpo.gov/about/faq.htm). It produces an enormous number of publications annually on every conceivable subject, for example, census information, reports on education, employment rules and regulations, and guidance on health issues. The GPO has changed from publishing most documents in print to publishing them electronically so that the GPO is now basically an online publisher. A selected number of publications will remain in print, but most publications will only be available online. This is a huge change for libraries that have housed vast print collections of government publications. For users it means they can access free of charge most government publications as long as they have a computer and preferably a printer. The government has also put more responsibility on government agencies. The E-Government Act of 2002 mandated agencies to improve public access to their information resources. "Agencies will have to follow standards in organizing information and making it easily searchable, and to provide basic information on agency mission, structure, and strategic plans" (Hernon, Dugan, and Shuler, 2003: 9).

All in all, the face of government publishing has drastically changed. With this new online world, the public and libraries alike must become adept at searching and accessing the information they need. All librarians will want to learn more about government information and how it can benefit their users.

Depository Libraries

Depository libraries were established in their present form by the Printing Act of 1895 in order to keep the citizenry informed and to provide a way to distribute the publications to all parts of the country. These depository libraries receive government information from the Government Printing Office without charge with the agreement that they will provide free access to the public. There are two kinds of depository libraries: regional depository libraries and selective depository libraries. The regional libraries receive all items distributed to the depository system, while the selective depository libraries can receive the materials that meet their needs. Each state can have two regional depository libraries, and each congressional district is allowed two selective depository libraries. There are about 1,250 federal depository libraries including public libraries, academic libraries, and special libraries. The list of depository libraries is available at http://catalog.gpo.gov/fdlpdir/FDLPdir.jsp. Most depository libraries arrange their publications according to the Superintendent of Documents (SuDoc) classification numbers. These numbers are based on a classification system that identifies the name of the agency, the subagency, the publication type, and a cutter number that represents the title. For example, if a publication had the classification C3.134/2:C83/2/994, the C would indicate that it was a Department of Commerce publication, the 3 would indicate that it is a Census Bureau publication, the numbers after the decimal point would indicate the type of publication, and the numbers after the colon would be the individual Cutter number of the publication.

Because the majority of government publications are now available online, the role of the depository libraries is being reevaluated. It is possible that they may take on an enhanced role and that there may not be as many depository libraries. The future of the depository library program is being discussed by the Depository Library Council and librarians administering depository library collections. Charles A. Seavey wrote recently that "we are moving into an era when every library in the country has the potential to become a depository in the sense that each one could potentially provide users with access to government information at a level previously unavailable" (Seavey, 2005: 44).

Major Government Publication Resources Used in Reference Work

Guides to the U.S. Government

Fewer books have been published about government publications in recent years, perhaps due to the fast pace of change. *Fundamentals of Government Information* by Eric J. Forte, Cassandra J. Harnett, and Andrea L. Sevetson (2011) is an excellent new addition to the field of government information for the librarian. *U.S. Government on the Web: Getting the Information You Need* by Peter Hernon and colleagues (2003), which deals with government publications as they appear on the web, remains useful, as does *Managing Electronic Government Information in Libraries*, edited by Andrea M. Morrison (2008) for GODORT.

In addition to books, many good websites link librarians to a wealth of information on government publications. *Core Documents of U.S. Democracy* can be found at http://thomas.loc.gov/. This site leads the user to the Declaration of Independence, the U.S. Constitution, and the Emancipation Proclamation, as well as the

U.S. Code, the *Congressional Record*, and many other key documents. The government documents webpage at the Vanderbilt University Library (http://www .library.vanderbilt.edu/romans/govt/) is an excellent site with a good subject guide to help the librarian or user to find pertinent publications on a wide variety of subjects. Another webpage is housed at the University of Michigan and can be found at http://www.lib.umich.edu/clark-library/collections/government-information. Both are very complete and a good starting place for researching not only U.S. government publications but also state and international publications.

CQ Press Encyclopedia of American Government is a fee-based online resource providing concise information on all aspects of U.S. government, the presidency, the Supreme Court, Congress, and elections. It includes information about the organization and powers of each branch of government as well as current and past presidents, justices, and members of Congress.

Directories

The *U.S. Government Manual* is the best single source of information about the various branches and agencies in the federal government. It provides basic information about each government department and agency and quasi-government agencies including chief officials, addresses, phone numbers, and a summary of the areas of responsibility. It is available in print and online at http://www.us governmentmanual.gov/. The commercial version of this manual is the *Washington Information Directory* (CQ Press), an annual publication available in print and online that provides contact information and a brief description of each government agency or congressional committee. It also includes information on nongovernmental agencies such as associations, lobbying organizations, and foundations.

Each branch of government has its own directory. For Congress, there is the *Congressional Directory* (http://www.gpo.gov/fdsys/browse/collection.action? collectionCode=CDIR), published by the GPO. The *Congressional Staff Directory*, the *Federal Staff Directory* for the Executive Branch, and the *Judicial Staff Directory* for the Judicial Branch are published by CQ Press three times a year with an annual volume. They are all available in paper and online.

Publications by Branch of U.S. Government

To understand the organization of government publications, the librarian must understand the organization of the U.S. government. The U.S. government has three branches: Legislative Branch, Executive Branch, and Judicial Branch. Each branch has many agencies within it. The branches of the U.S. government and their publications are described in the sections that follow. The direct access to the key publications of each branch is the *Federal Digital System* (*FDsys*) (http://www.gpo .gov/fdsys/), *THOMAS* (http://thomas.loc.gov/), or *USA.gov* (http://usa.gov/).

Legislative Branch Publications

The Legislative Branch consists of Congress—the Senate and House of Representatives—and its supporting agencies that include the Library of Congress, the

Government Printing Office, the General Accountability Office, and Congressional Budget Office. The legislative branch of government produces a huge number of publications as it moves from congressional bills to committee hearings and reports to discussions and votes on the floor of the House and Senate and then to the public laws that are eventually written into the *United States Code*. At each step of the way, a document is being discussed and often revised. This legislative process is documented by *THOMAS* (http://thomas.loc.gov/), a database of the Library of Congress named for Thomas Jefferson. With *THOMAS* the user can easily follow the progress of a bill. *THOMAS* provides the text of the bill, its status, committee schedules and reports, the debate in each house of Congress as documented by the *Congressional Record*, the roll call vote, and the text of the public law when passed. Users can search by keyword or bill number. The most important document is the *Congressional Record*, which is the official record of what takes place on the floor of the House and the Senate. Available through *THOMAS*, it is divided into four parts: House of Representatives; Senate; Extension of Remarks, which includes text inserted later and not part of the floor debate; and the *Daily Digest*. Within the *Congressional Record* users can search by subject or by member of Congress. *THOMAS* also provides information about the legislative process and the text of historical publications such as the Constitution of the United States and the Declaration of Independence.

A number of commercially produced publications document the progress of bills through Congress. *ProQuest Congressional*, which now includes the *CIS Index*, provides both historical and current information on Congress. It both indexes and provides selected full text for congressional committee prints, House and Senate documents and reports, hearings, and legislative histories. CQ Press publishes numerous guides to Congress. *CQ Weekly*, an online resource, reports on a weekly basis the activities of Congress. Flexible searching allows the user to search by keyword, date, and so on. This database has expanded to include coverage of the executive branch and government regulations. The annual *CQ Almanac* in its online format provides information back to 1945. *CQ Press Congress Collection*, another online resource, integrates a large amount of information into one database including information on legislation, members of Congress, key floor votes as far back as 1945, and other information about the legislative branch of government. *CQ Researcher*, available in print and online, provides weekly reports on individual topics such as social, political, environmental, and health issues. Each report is about 12,000 words. The *U.S. Serial Set* and the *American State Papers*, available through ProQuest and Readex, provide researchers with access to the congressional legislative history documents from 1789 to approximately 1980.

Executive Branch Publications

The Executive Branch includes the Office of the President and many agencies that report directly to the president, such as the Council of Economic Advisors, the Office of Management and Budget, the National Security Council, and the Domestic Policy Council. The cabinet-level departments, that is, Department of Commerce, Department of Defense, Department of Education, Department of

Health and Human Services, Department of State, and others, are also part of the Executive Branch, as well as a number of independent government agencies such as the Environmental Protection Agency, Federal Reserve, Peace Corps, and National Science Foundation. The White House website (http://www.whitehouse.gov/) provides a guide to information on executive orders and proclamations and issues such as the economy, energy, foreign policy, and immigration.

Two excellent free sources of information on the presidents are *Presidential Libraries* (http://www.archives.gov/presidential-libraries/), which has a link to each of the presidential libraries, and the *American Presidency Project* (http://www.presidency.ucsb.edu/), which includes presidential papers, election information, and an audio and video archive of presidential speeches. Other publications on the presidency include the *Encyclopedia of the American Presidency* by Michael Genovese, which provides information on many aspects of the American presidency from George Washington to the current president. Information is included on the relationship between the presidency and other branches of government and on court cases, elections, and scandals in the *Guide to the Presidency Online Edition*.

The *Federal Register* (http://www.federalregister.gov/), produced by the National Archives and Records Administration, is this branch's most important publication. It provides information on a daily basis about rules and regulations finalized by government departments and agencies, proposed rules, and notices from agencies as well as presidential documents such as executive orders and proclamations This is a good place to look for the guidelines for government-funded programs. The database can be searched by subject or by agency back to 1994. Those interested in proposed rules and regulations can also search http://www.regulations.gov/ where citizens can leave comments about proposed rules and regulations. The *Code of Federal Regulations* (http://www.gpo.gov/fdsys/browse/collectionCfr.action?collectionCode=CFR) codifies the rules and regulations published in the *Federal Register* into broad subject area. It can be found on the home page of *FDsys*. Many rules and regulations are now published on the agencies' websites as a result of the E-Government Act of 2002.

The cabinet-level departments of the U.S. federal government are located in the Executive Branch. Each has its own website. These websites are gold mines of information on all the programs under each department or agency. Because there is so much information, sometimes it takes some hunting to find a particular piece of information. The following is a description of a selection of government departments to provide the reader with a sense of the vast amount of information on these departmental websites.

DEPARTMENT OF EDUCATION

The Department of Education website (http://www.ed.gov/) makes available information on the latest education policies, financial aid information, education publications, grants, and, of course, *ERIC*, the *Educational Resources Information Center* database, which is found at http://www.eric.ed.gov/ (see Chapter 8). Some interesting features are the teaching resources for teachers and parents—Teach.gov (http://www.teach.gov/) on teaching as a profession and the National Center for Education Statistics (http://www.nces.ed.gov/), which provides nationwide statistics on education such as enrollment trends in public and private elementary and secondary schools.

DEPARTMENT OF LABOR

The Department of Labor website (http://www.dol.gov/) provides information on safety and health standards (OSHA); wage, hour, and other workplace standards; labor statistics; information about job seeking and careers; and information for working women from the Women's Bureau. The Bureau of Labor Statistics site (http://www.bls.gov/) is a source of data on employment and unemployment, pay and benefits, and inflation and prices including the consumer price index. The Department of Labor produces many publications including the *Monthly Labor Review*, *Occupational Outlook Quarterly*, and the *Occupational Outlook Handbook*.

DEPARTMENT OF THE INTERIOR

Through the Department of the Interior website (http://www.doi.gov/) one can find information on fish and wildlife, including endangered species and wildlife refuges (United States Fish and Wildlife Service), maps from the U.S. Geological Survey, information from the National Park Service about each national park, and information on Native Americans from the Bureau of Indian Affairs.

DEPARTMENT OF HEALTH AND HUMAN SERVICES

The website of the Department of Health and Human Services (http://www.dhhs .gov/) provides a wealth of information on diseases and medical conditions, safety and wellness, drugs and food, as well as information on aging issues, family issues, and issues for specific populations. This well-organized website provides easy access to many important resources from the Centers for Disease Control and Prevention, Centers for Medicare and Medicaid Services, Food and Drug Administration, and the National Institutes of Health, which publishes *MedlinePlus*, an important source of consumer health information.

DEPARTMENT OF COMMERCE

The Department of Commerce (http://www.commerce.gov/) is a major source of information on the U.S. economy. Commerce includes the Bureau of Economic Analysis, which publishes the journal, *Survey of Current Business*, as well as the International Trade Administration, which provides reports on U.S. trade and the U.S. industry and trade outlook, and the Census Bureau. The Minority Business Development Agency resides here as does NOAA (National Oceanic and Atmospheric Administration). The NOAA site provides weather and climate information including hurricane information and other kinds of weather advisories. The National Technical Information Service (NTIS) is also housed in this department. This clearinghouse for government-funded engineering, scientific, technical, and business-related information has an online library and bookstore. The U.S. Patent and Trademark Office is also part of the Department of Commerce.

DEPARTMENT OF STATE

The State Department (http://www.state.gov/) provides information on U.S. embassies and consulates, travel information, and information on international issues. *Background Notes* is published and updated by the U.S. Department of State.

These publications provide concise information about countries including the land, people, history, government, political conditions, economy, foreign relations, travel, and business and are updated frequently. As of May 2012, they are no longer available as *Background Notes* but will be called *Fact Sheets* and will focus on U.S. relations with each country.

CENTRAL INTELLIGENCE AGENCY
The CIA publishes *The World Factbook*, which provides maps and some general information about 267 countries (https://www.cia.gov/library/publications/the-world-factbook/index.html). This excellent free source, which includes information on geography, people, government, economy, communications, transportation, military, and transnational issues, is current and quite extensive.

LIBRARY OF CONGRESS
The Library of Congress (http://www.loc.gov/) is often treated as a national library, but it is actually the research arm of Congress. Its website states as its mission "to make its resources available and useful to Congress and the American people and to sustain and preserve a universal collection of knowledge and creativity for future generations." The Library of Congress maintains *THOMAS* and houses the Congressional Research Service (CRS). The CRS does research on any subject at the request of members of Congress and produces a report. Many of these reports are available on OpenCRS (https://opencrs.com/) and on the University of North Texas Libraries website (http://digital.library.unt.edu/search/?q=congressional+research+search&t=fulltext). The Library of Congress website includes many useful resources, such as the *American Memory* project, which provides a wealth of digitized text and images on many aspects of American history (e.g., women's history, African American history, immigration, and culture and folk life). The Copyright Office, also housed at the Library of Congress, is of interest to many. Here one can find out how to register a copyright or how to search copyright records.

Judicial Branch Publications

The Judicial Branch consists of the Federal Courts, including the Supreme Court and special courts such as the Court of International Trade. The Judicial Branch contains administrative units such as the Federal Judicial Center. The website for the U.S. Supreme Court (http://www.supremecourt.gov/) contains information about recent court cases, the history of the court, biographies of past and present members of the Supreme Court, and even speeches by members of the Supreme Court. Opinions of the Supreme Court can be found at http://www.supremecourt.gov/opinions/opinions.aspx.

Other sources of court decisions can be found in the subscription databases of *Westlaw* and *LexisNexis*. A commercial online source is *CQ Supreme Court Collection*, which includes information on the history of the Supreme Court, important cases, and the impact of these decisions on American life.

Statistical Resources

Libraries receive many questions about statistics on population, jobs, education, health, crime, income, and much more. Since so many statistics are collected by government entities, this is often a good place to start. The Census Bureau (http://www.census.gov/) has developed a new user-friendly homepage. Pull-down menus by People, Business and Geography list a wide variety of subjects and bring users to the appropriate statistics. For example, under People, the user can easily get to statistics on children, health insurance, or school enrollment, and under Business, the user can find statistics on retail trade, construction, and manufacturing. In addition, on the Census Bureau website, the user can find statistics by state and by county or by city within a state. *American FactFinder* (http://factfinder2.gov/) allows the user to search by combining a subject with a place to find needed statistics. The American Community Survey surveys about 3,000 households annually from every county in the United States for population and housing information and updates census information on a regular basis. The Economic Census is taken every five years. Since 1878, the Census Bureau produced *Statistical Abstract of the United States* annually. This excellent publication gathered U.S. government statistics and some statistics from private organizations to produce a publication providing data on every aspect of American life by subject including agriculture, construction and housing, education, the labor force, and population. The program within the Census Bureau, Statistical Compendium Program, was eliminated at the end of 2011, thus ending the publication of *Statistical Abstract*. Fortunately ProQuest has agreed to pick up this publication as an online publication and Bernan has agreed to publish it in paper format.

For statistics at a national, state, or international level, the best place to turn is *ProQuest Statistical Insight*. It combines statistics from the federal government, state governments, and private sector organizations and from more than 100 international intergovernmental organizations including all major intergovernmental organizations (such as the United Nations, European Union, Organization of Economic Co-operation and Development, and Organization of American States).

Business and economic statistics are available from several sources. The Bureau of Economic Analysis (http://www.bea.gov/) provides statistics such as the gross domestic product, personal income, consumer spending, the balance of payments, and international trade. *USA Trade Online* (http://www.usatrade online.gov/), a publication of the Foreign Trade Division of the U.S. Census Bureau, provides export and import data by commodity. Individuals can subscribe to it for a fee. The Bureau of Labor Statistics (http://www.bls.gov/) provides a wealth of labor statistics including the consumer price index, import/export indexes, wage statistics, demographics about the workforce, and career information. There is also statistical information on a state-by-state basis and for cities. The National Center for Health Statistics (http://www.cdc.gov/nchs/) provides health statistics on all kinds of health issues nationwide such as injuries, infant mortality, and food allergies. These are all examples of the kinds of statistics collected by a government agency and made available on their website.

Historical Statistics of the United States has been updated by Cambridge University Press and is now available in print and online. It includes historical statistics on every aspect of American society from colonial times to the present including population, labor and employment, agriculture, manufacturing, and transportation.

Government Publications by Subject

The government has also made it possible to access information by subject. The overall website, *USA.gov* (http://usa.gov/),was designed to provide access to government publications for the general public. This portal provides gateways by topic and by government agency. Users can search for information by topic such as health, jobs and education, money and taxes, or travel, transportation, and recreation, or by user group such as kids, parents, and seniors. Librarians will find the Reference and General Government section under Topics very useful. For example, users can download forms for jobs, benefits, passports, social security, and taxes. Many subject-specific websites can also be accessed by the public or the librarian, including http://www.science.gov/ and http://www.disability.gov/.

Maps and Geographical Information

The U.S. government is a major producer of maps and related geographical information. Among the agencies producing maps are the U.S. Geological Survey, the Census Bureau, the National Park Service, and the National Oceanic and Atmospheric Administration. These are described in more detail in Chapter 10.

Information on Elections

Elections have become an important part of our national life, as they are in other countries. Many sites provide information on current and historical elections. *USA.gov*, which provides a great deal of user-friendly information, is a good place to start. Another source is the *Federal Election Commission Media Guide* (http://www.fec.gov/), which covers information about campaign finances. The Open Secrets site (http://www.opensecrets.org/) from the Center for Responsive Secrets repackages the FEC information into a more accessible form, tracking campaign money and its effect on elections and public policy. Other sites of interest include America Votes (http://www.americavotes.org/), Project Vote Smart (http://www.votesmart.org/), the League of Women Voters (http://www.lwv.org), and Dave Leip's *Atlas of U.S. Presidential Elections* (http://www.uselectionatlas.org/).

The States

State governments also produce a wide array of interesting and essential publications. They usually have a website that can be checked to find their publications either in print or online. Two useful websites are *State and Local Government on the Net* (http://www.statelocalgov.net/), which is arranged by state and by topic, for example, arts, aging, health, education, and libraries; and *USA.gov*, which has a link to local government information. A state-by-state list of links to state agency databases can be found at http://wikis.ala.org/godort/index.php/State_Agency_Databases. Information on state depository library systems is available at wikis.ala.org/godort/index.php/State_Depository_Library_Systems. *The Book of the States*, published by the Council of State Governments, provides data about state government including articles on trends and issues in state constitutions, the three branches of state governments and major policies and programs, information about legislatures, governors, and other state officials, information on agricultural policy, women in government, environmental spending, education, mental health, and many other subjects.

State Rankings 2011: A Statistical View of America, edited by Rachel Boba and Kathleen O'Leary Morgan, is a commercially published book on the states. It includes tables comparing the states in such areas as education, health, crime/law enforcement, welfare, and taxes.

E-government

E-government is online government services, that is, any interaction one might have with a government agency using the Internet. The access to government information on the Internet has made it possible to provide more government information no matter the library. Although depository libraries are still important, many questions about the federal government as well as state and local government can be answered by any reference librarian. Once a librarian ascertains that a question is related to the government, the first step to finding an answer is to access http://www.usa.gov/ or state or local government websites, where most topics are searchable. Most forms needed by users are available online and can easily be printed.

International Resources

United Nations Publications

Although the United Nations (UN) is the first organization that comes to mind when we say international, there are many other international organizations such as the International Monetary Fund as well as the numerous agencies that are part of the UN worldwide including UNESCO and the International Labour Organization (ILO).

The UN has made its official documents available for free at http://www.un.org/en/documents/. The majority of the documents in this database are from 1993 onward, but older publications are added all the time. The *Official Documents of the United Nations* (ODS Search) "provides access to the resolutions of the General Assembly, Security Council, Economic and Social Council and the Trusteeship Council from 1946 onwards" (http://documents.un.org/welcome.asp?language=E). It does not include the *UN Treaty Series* or the *UN Sales Publications*. The UN publications that are for sale, both print and online, are listed at http://unp.un.org. The *Yearbook of the United Nations* provides data on the world economy, its structure and major trends, population and social statistics, economic activity, and international economic relations. It is published in English and French. The *Demographic Yearbook*, published by the UN, is an international source of statistics that provides basic statistical data on more than 200 countries. The information, presented in tables, includes basic demographic statistics such as population trends and size, fertility, mortality, marriage and divorce, and migration. This yearbook is published in English and French and is available online. The *Population and Vital Statistics Report* is available in print. Libraries can set up standing orders with the UN and can set up alerts for new publications.

UN publications have a similar organization system to the Superintendent of Documents. They are arranged by the issuing body and any subordinate body, and the form and a number for a specific publication. There are UN depository libraries throughout the world. *UNIBISNET* provides free bibliographic access to UN documents and publications from 1979 forward. Check the UN Library site for a wealth of information on the UN at http://www.un.org/Depts/dhl/. *AccessUN* is a subscription database providing access to UN documents and publications.

Canadian Publications

The Canadian government's website for publications (http://publications .gc.ca/site/eng/home.html) provides information about Canadian government publications. Users can search by topic, title, or keyword in a database that lists all kinds of government publications. Users can also access a list of recent releases and information guides. A *Weekly Checklist* of new publications is available online. The only full-text publication is the *Canada Gazette*, the official paper of the government of Canada. Begun in 1841, it publishes weekly information on new statutes and regulations, decisions of administrative boards, government notices, and public notices from the private sector. Similar to the United States, Canada has a library Depository Service Program. Established in 1927 to provide access to federal government information, there are presently 680 depository libraries in public and academic libraries. Of these depository libraries only fifty-two are full depositories and the rest are selective depository libraries. A list of the depository libraries is located at http://publications.gc.ca/site/eng/locating OurPublications/depositoryLibraries/index.html. The selective depositories choose their publications from the *Weekly Checklist*.

Government Publications in the United Kingdom

Information on legislation in the United Kingdom can be found at http://www.legislation.gov.uk/. It is somewhat similar to *THOMAS*. The *UKOP* (http://www.ukop.co.uk/) houses the catalog of official U.K. publications since 1980 and provides access to many full-text documents. The House of Commons Papers and the Command Papers, those presented by a government minister to Parliament "by Command of Her Majesty," since 2005 can be found at http://www.official-documents.gov.uk/. Copies of all government publications can be purchased from the TSO Parliamentary and Legal Bookshop (http://www .tsoshop.co.uk/parliament/). Access to U.K. government information by subject is available through *Direct.gov* (http://www.direct.gov.uk/en/index.htm) which is similar to *USA.gov*.

Collection Development and Maintenance

Selection and Keeping Current

The primary access point for U.S. government publications is *FDsys* (http://www.gpo.gov/fdsys/). This portal provides free access to federal publications produced by the various government departments and agencies. Users can search by branch of government (i.e., legislative, executive, or judicial) or by title or topic.

The *FDsys* (*Federal Digital System*), an online index and database, includes bibliographic records from 1994 to the present as well as full text when available. The print version of the catalog, begun in 1895, was called the *Monthly Catalog of U.S. Government Publications* and is the major access point for pre-1976 documents. Government publications can also be accessed through *WorldCat*, which includes all items from the *Monthly Catalog* and its successors since July 1976.

In order to purchase government publications, the librarian can turn to the U.S. Government Online Bookstore (http://bookstore.gpo.gov/), which allows searching by subject. A weekly list of new publications is also available. Libraries can purchase publications from the GPO by setting up a deposit account or paying by credit card or check.

The Government Documents Round Table (GODORT) on the American Library Asssociation's website is available at http://www.ala.org/godort/. It provides links for the librarian to a great deal of useful information on government publications. It is the best place to start for the beginner and the experienced librarian. GODORT produces guides to government publications and up-to-date information on the status of the Government Printing Office and the Government Depository Library Program.

Evaluating Government Documents

Because government documents are published by a governmental body, they are assumed to provide accurate, reliable, and up-to-date information. For this reason there is less need to apply the usual evaluation criteria. However, since some government information is also published by trade publishers, librarians will want to compare these products to see which will be the most useful to their clientele. For example, material published by a trade publisher might be easier to use, easier to search, or have a more acceptable layout. Cost will enter into the librarian's decision since government publications tend to be less expensive than those published by a trade publisher. Format will continue to be an issue. Librarians should pay attention to which documents remain in print, since at least for U.S. documents, only a small number will continue in print format. The access issue will remain. If important information is not available for a reasonable cost online, librarians must make a case for access. Or if information is made available and is then withdrawn, librarians must call that to the attention of appropriate officials. Even with government information, some evaluation criteria will apply, and librarians must be alert to these issues.

Further Considerations

Having so much information accessible on the Internet has made searching for government publications much easier. Efforts are being made to digitize older legacy material. The *FDsys* (*Federal Digital System*) is the way to begin since it is searchable from a number of access points. However, having some rudimentary knowledge of the organization of the U.S. government will still come in very handy in finding the document needed. Getting familiar with the websites of departments and agencies will also be useful. They are not equally user friendly, and many times the user needs some knowledge to make use of them. The *U.S. Government Manual* is helpful in finding out where a particular agency is housed. This is a time of change in the area of government publications. The librarian must continue to monitor changes as they occur.

TOP TEN U.S. GOVERNMENT PUBLICATIONS	
Title	Online
American Presidency Project	http://www.presidency.ucsb.edu/
Census Bureau publications	http://www.census.gov/
Congressional Record	http://thomas.loc.gov
FDsys	http://www.gpo.gov/fdsys/
Federal Register	http://www.federalregister.gov/
Library of Congress	http://www.loc.gov/
THOMAS	http://thomas.loc.gov/
USA.gov	http://www.usa.gov/
U.S. Government Manual	http://www.usgovernmentmanual.gov/
World Factbook	https://www.cia.gov/library/publications/the-world-factbook/

Recommended Resources Discussed in This Chapter

AccessUN. Naples, FL: Newsbank. http://newsbank.com/.

America Votes. http://www.americavotes.org/.

American FactFinder. http://factfinder2.census.gov/.

American Presidency Project. http://www.presidency.ucsb.edu/.

American State Papers. Available from ProQuest and Readex.

Atlas of U.S. Presidential Elections. Dave Leip. http://www.uselectionatlas.org/.

The Book of the States. Lexington, KY: Council of State Governments, 1965–. Annual.

Canada Depository Libraries. http://publications.gc.ca/site/eng/locatingOurPublications/depositoryLibraries/index.html.

Canada Publications. http://publications.gc.ca/site/eng/home.html.

Code of Federal Regulations. http://www.gpo.gov/fdsys/browse/collectionCfr.action?collectionCode=CFR.

Congressional Directory. http://www.gpo.gov/fdsys/browse/collection.action?collectionCode=CDIR.

Congressional Record. http://thomas.loc.gov/.

RECOMMENDED FREE WEBSITES

FDsys. http://www.gpo.gov/fdsys/. This site provides access to major documents from all three branches of government.

THOMAS. http://thomas.loc.gov/. Housed at the Library of Congress, THOMAS provides access to congressional bills past and present, the *Congressional Record*, and other information on Congress.

United Nations. http://www.un.org/en/documents/. This site provides access to many UN documents.

U.S. Census Bureau. http://www.census.gov/. The website guides the user to a wealth of statistics about the population and economy of the United States.

USA.gov. http://www.usa.gov/. This user-friendly site provides access to government information for all.

Congressional Staff Directory. Washington, DC: CQ Press. Published three times a year with an annual volume. Also available online: http://www.cqpress.com/.

Core Documents of U.S. Democracy. http://thomas.loc.gov/.

CQ Almanac. http://www.cqpress.com/.

CQ Press Congress Collection. Washington, DC: CQ Press. http://www.cqpress.com/.

CQ Press Encyclopedia of American Government. Washington, DC: CQ Press. http://www.cqpress.com/.

CQ Researcher. Washington, DC: CQ Press. Weekly and an annual volume. Also available online: http://www.cqpress.com/researcher/.

CQ Supreme Court Collection. Washington, DC: CQ Press. http://www.cqpress.com/.

CQ Weekly. Washington, DC: CQ Press, 1983–. Also available online: http://www.cqpress.com/.

ERIC (Educational Resources Information Center). http://www.eric.ed.gov/.

FDsys (Federal Digital System). http://www.gpo.gov/fdsys/.

Federal Election Commission Media Guide. http://www.fec.gov/.

Federal Register. http://www.federalregister.gov/.

Federal Staff Directory. Washington, DC: CQ Press. Published three times a year with an annual volume. Also available online: http://cqpress.com/.

Encyclopedia of the American Presidency. Michael Genovese. New York: Facts on File, 2010.

Fundamentals of Government Information. Eric J. Forte, Cassandra J. Harnett, and Andrea L. Sevetson. New York: Neal-Schuman, 2011.

Government Documents Round Table (GODORT). http://www.ala.org/godort.

Guide to the Presidency Online Edition. Washington, DC: CQ Press.http://www.cqpress.com/.

Historical Statistics of the United States. New York: Cambridge University Press, 2006. Also available online: http://hsus.cambridge.org/.

Judicial Staff Directory. Washington, DC: CQ Press. Published three times a year with an annual volume. Also available online: http://www.cqpress.com/.

League of Women Voters. http://www.lwv.org/.

Library of Congress. http://www.loc.gov/.

Managing Electronic Government Information in Libraries. Andrea M. Morrison, ed. Chicago: American Library Association, 2008.

National Center for Education Statistics. http://nces.ed.gov/.

National Center for Health Statistics. http://www.cdc.gov/nchs/.

Open CRS. https://opencrs.com/.

Open Secrets. http://www.opensecrets.org/.

Presidential Libraries. http://www.archives.gov/presidential-libraries/.

Project Vote Smart. http://votesmart.org/.

ProQuest Congressional. http://www.proquest.com/.

ProQuest Statistical Insight. http://www.proquest.com/.

"State Agency Databases." http://wikis.ala.org/godort/index.php/stateagency_databases.

State and Local Government on the Net. http://www.statelocalgov.net/.

"State Depository Library Systems." http://wikis.ala.org/godort/index.php/State_Depository _Library_Systems.

State Rankings 2011: A Statistical View of America. Rachel Boba and Kathleen O'Leary Morgan, eds. Washington, DC: CQ Press.

THOMAS. http://thomas.loc.gov/.

TSO Parliamentary and Legal Bookshop. http://www.tsoshop.co.uk/parliament/.

U.K. *Directgov.* http://www.direct.gov.uk/en/index.htm.

U.K. Legislation. http://www.legislation.gov.uk/.

UKOP. http://www.ukop.co.uk/.

UNIBISNET. http://unibisnet.un.org/.

United Nations *Demographic Yearbook.* http://unstats.un.org/unsd/demographic/products/ dyb/dyb2.htm.

United Nations ODS Search, *Official Documents of the United Nations.* http://documents.un .org/welcome.asp?language=E.

United Nations Publications. https://unp.un.org/.

University of Michigan Government Information Collection. http://www.lib.umich.edu/ clark-library/collections/government-information.

U.S. Bureau of Economic Analysis. http://www.bea.gov/.

U.S. Bureau of Labor Statistics. http://www.bls.gov/.

U.S. Census Bureau. http://www.census.gov/.

U.S. Department of Commerce. http://www.commerce.gov/.

U.S. Department of Education. http://www.ed.gov/.

U.S. Department of Health and Human Services. http://www.dhhs.gov/.

U.S. Department of Labor. http://www.dol.gov/.

U.S. Department of State. http://www.state.gov/.

U.S. Department of State. *Background Notes/Fact Sheets.* http://www.state.gov/.

U.S. Department of the Interior. http://www.doi.gov/.

U.S. Depository Libraries. http://catalog.gpo.gov/fdlpdir/FDLPdir.jsp.

U.S. Government Manual. Washington, DC: Government Printing Office. Annual. Also available online: http://www.usgovernmentmanual.gov/.

U.S. Government on the Web: Getting the Information You Need. 3rd ed. Peter Hernon, Robert E. Dugan, and John A. Shuler. Westport, CT: Libraries Unlimited, 2003.

U.S. Government Online Bookstore. http://bookstore.gpo.gov/.

U.S. Serial Set Digital Collection. Available from ProQuest and Readex.

U.S. Supreme Court. http://www.supremecourt.gov/.

U.S. Supreme Court. Opinions. http://supremecourt.gov/opinions/opinions.aspx.

USA Trade Online. http://www.usatradeonline.gov/.

USA.gov. http://usa.gov/.

Vanderbilt University "Government Information." http://www.library.vanderbilt.edu/ romans/govt/.

Washington Information Directory. Washington, DC: CQ Press. Annual. Also available online: http://cqpress.com/.

White House. http://www.whitehouse.gov/.

The World Factbook. Central Intelligence Agency. https://www.cia.gov/library/publications/ the-world-factbook/index.html.

Recommendations for Further Reading

Bekkers, Victor, and Rebecca Moody. 2011. "Visual Events and Electronic Government: What Do Pictures Mean in Digital Government for Citizen Relations?" *Government Information Quarterly* 28, no. 4: 457–465. Examines the trend of e-government becoming increasingly picture-oriented and explores the question of what the future of visual public space in e-government will mean for citizens.

Byrne, David S. 2010. "Access to Online Local Government Public Records: The Privacy Paradox." *Legal Reference Services Quarterly* 29, no. 1: 1–21. Discusses the complications of providing open access to public records while protecting the privacy of the public. Presents issues and terms relating to privacy rights and public records, along with a case study and comparison of laws in Florida and Rhode Island. Also contains a comparative examination of obtainable personal information in locales within these states.

Cuillier, David, and Suzanne J. Piotrowski. 2009. "Internet Information-Seeking and Its Relation to Support for Access to Government Records." *Government Information Quarterly* 26, no. 3: 441–449. Presents the results of a study in public support for press and citizen access to government records. The study suggests that support for government transparency is not correlated to political ideology, and that the Internet is seen as the best means of accessing public records.

Drake, Miriam A. 2011. "Multimedia, Multilingual Science from Around the World." *Searcher: The Magazine for Database Professionals* 19, no. 7: 16–19, 52. Outlines the functionality and usefulness of Science.gov, which uses federated search technology to access 45 databases and 2,000 websites containing federally funded research from federal agencies. Also profiles WorldWideScience.org, which delivers science research internationally. Both provide a remarkable return on investment for taxpayers.

Hochstein, Colette, Jeanne Goshorn, and Florence Chang. 2009. "United States National Library of Medicine Drug Information Portal." *Medical Reference Services Quarterly* 28, no. 2: 154–163. Outlines the functionality and contents of the NLM Drug Information Portal and provides instructions for the best search techniques within the portal.

Hornung, Heiko, and M. Cecilia C. Baranauskas. 2011. "Towards a Design Rationale for Inclusive E-government Services." *International Journal of Electronic Government Research* 7, no. 3: 1–20. Addresses the issue of e-government framework and design features that may leave some people, such as those with disabilities, behind.

Jaeger, Paul T., and John Carlo Bertot. 2011. "Responsibility Rolls Down: Public Libraries and the Social and Policy Obligations of Ensuring Access to E-government and Government Information." *Public Library Quarterly* 30, no. 2: 91–116. Provides an historic overview of the relationship between public libraries and government information, contextualizing the current dependence on public libraries to provide free access and guidance to e-government resources. The implications of this dependence are that federal agencies reduce cost, while shifting the burden onto locally funded public libraries. The author provides five suggestions for improving the ability of public libraries to maintain this central role in providing access and assistance for government resources.

Johnston, Meredith. 2011. "Availability and Location of Web-Based Government Information Instructional Resources at Academic Federal Depository Library Websites." *DttP: Documents to the People* 39, no. 2: 23–28. Presents an examination of online guides on the websites of federal depository libraries. The study shows that the majority of libraries are presenting government resources through multiple access points, both through generalized government information guides and through discipline-specific guides.

Love, Mark. 2011. "Marketing Government Information Resources to the K–12 Community." *DttP: Documents to the People* 39, no. 2: 14–16. Describes outreach presentations given to K–12 teachers and students highlighting free online government resources. Explains how government information resources can be used to fulfill classroom assignments and meet specific grade-level objectives.

Reinman, Suzanne L. 2011. "The Basics of Patent Resources and Research for Academic Librarians." *DttP: Documents to the People* 39, no. 1: 33–38. A guide to reading patents and searching for them using different tools, with an emphasis on their usefulness in research projects like those typical in an academic library.

Relyea, Harold C. 2010. "Across the Hill: The Congressional Research Service and Providing Research for Congress—A Retrospective on Origins." *Government Information Quarterly* 27, no. 4: 414–422. Provides historical background on the formation of the Congressional Research Service (CRS) at the Library of Congress, from its origins in the Legislative Reference Service in 1914, leading to the current operational status of CRS today.

Scales, B. Jane, and Marilyn Von Seggern. 2010. "Experiencing the Assessment Cycle: Government Document Instruction to Undergraduates." *DttP: Documents to the People* 38, no. 3: 22–26. Describes government information literacy sessions directed at undergraduate students with an emphasis on assessment tools for tracing learning outcomes.

Bibliography and Works Cited

Drake, Miriam A. 2005. "The Federal Depository Library Program: Safety Net for Access." *Searcher* 13, no. 1 (January): 46.

Forte, Eric J., Cassandra J. Harnett, and Andrea L. Sevetson. 2011. *Fundamentals of Government Information.* New York: Neal-Schuman.

Herman, Edward. 1997. *Locating United States Government Information: A Guide to Sources.* 2nd ed. Buffalo, NY: William S. Hein.

Hernon, Peter, Robert E. Dugan, and John A. Shuler. 2003. *U.S. Government on the Web: Getting the Information You Need.* 3rd ed. Westport, CT: Libraries Unlimited.

Johnson, Linda B. 2004. "Electronic Moves Center Stage." *Library Journal* (May 15): 52–57.

Morrison, Andrea M., ed. 2008. *Managing Electronic Government Information in Libraries.* Chicago: American Library Association.

Seavey, Charles A. 2005. "Publications to the People." *American Libraries* 36, no. 7 (August): 42–44.

Smith, Lori L., Daniel C. Barkley, Daniel D. Cornwall, Eric W. Johnson, and J. Louise Malcomb. 2003. *Tapping State Government Information Sources.* Westport, CT: Greenwood Press.

Part III
Special Topics in Reference
and Information Work

13

When and How to Use the Internet as a Reference Tool

The Facts

The most seductive and ubiquitous reference resource to emerge in the twentieth century was the Internet. Virtually unknown to the general population until the advent of the World Wide Web in 1990, the explosion of Internet use in less than two decades has been nothing short of spectacular. It took many centuries for an encyclopedia to be viewed as an all-purpose resource accessible to the common person. In contrast, it has taken less than a decade for almost 100 percent of all libraries to gain access to the Internet (American Library Association, 2010). This access can feed off a stratospheric 888,239,420 IP addresses (Internet Systems Consortium, 2012). With so much material and access freely available, usage statistics are also high. Some 95 percent of eighteen- to twenty-nine-year-olds and 78 percent of adults use the Internet on a regular basis, compared to the year 2000, when the same age groups had Internet usage statistics of 61 percent and 47 percent, respectively (Zickuhr and Smith, 2012). It seems clear then that not only is the Internet here to stay, but there is an upwardly spiraling "insatiable appetite for connectivity" as described in a recent market study (Herther, 2012: 16).

The Puzzle

Despite the insistent evidence of this "insatiable" dynamic, however, reference librarians have been curiously sluggish in wholly claiming, organizing, and charting the course of Internet research.

At the start of the twenty-first century, a fascinating and important study by Ross and Nilsen found that reference librarians "seem to regard the Internet as an external resource that users can search independently...but not as a full-fledged reference tool for which reference librarians have a responsibility to help users search and evaluate" (Ross and Nilsen, 2000: 147). By 2005, the *Chronicle of Higher Education* published a special segment on libraries in which Elizabeth Breakstone, author of the concluding article, wrote, "librarians not only participate in the information revolution but help direct its course" (Breakstone, 2005: B6). However, there were no great moves toward actively "directing the course" of Internet searches. It was only at the close of 2008 that a serious proposal was launched by OCLC and the information schools of Syracuse University and the University of Washington to recast Internet sources as "full-fledged reference tools." The creation of a comprehensive search engine based on librarian recommendations and the automatic gathering of reliable URLs from digital references selected by libraries for their own institutional sites was the underpinning of this venture aptly titled *Reference Extract*. A $350,000 grant from the MacArthur Foundation financed the project, and it remains to be seen whether a search engine trawling for the collective, though restricted, information contained in selected websites is a feasible and effective way to harness the power of web resources without inheriting a large part of its unreliability as well.

Concomitantly, Google appears to be aiming for control over the seeming chaos of web research in its continuing bid to develop the "perfect search engine...that understands exactly what you mean and gives you back exactly what you want" (Carr, 2008: 58). Rather than relying on individually selected web resources, as *Reference Extract* aims to do, Google is refining its internal search algorithms. A systematic analysis of behavioral data is collated as users conduct Google searches, with an aim to create a vast collective artificial intelligence that is larger than the sum of its parts. For example, the Google tool *Flu Trends* appears to supply early detection warnings for regional flu outbreaks at a sustained average of seven to ten days before the venerable Centers for Disease Control makes the announcement. The unintentional behavioral data resulting from individual searches on flu and flu-related words is intentionally collated by *Flu Trends* to produce this nontraditional yet effective way of maximizing Internet research.

Much like the canonical "Hausfrau," reference librarians are using the Internet in any number of ways, without being given the necessary recognition or attention due to a "full-fledged reference tool." Various applications of Internet protocol such as e-mail, chat, remote log-in, and file transfer are being appropriated by librarians to conduct e-mail/chat/instant messaging (IM) reference, launch reference wikis and blogs, and remotely access reference databases. So in addition to the ubiquitous use of websites and search engines, the larger technological domain covered by the Internet is also being used in dynamic and ever-increasing ways, as highlighted in Chapter 21. Some reference librarians are more immersed in Internet reference than others, but no librarian can claim complete immunity.

The Solution

It seems clear that rather than holding on to the tail of the Internet tiger and bumping along wherever it goes, Internet reference must be recognized as a "full-fledged reference tool" so that reference librarians can "help direct its course" in creative ways. This can be achieved through an understanding of the nature of the beast and a considered blueprint for actual use.

Nature of Internet Reference

The portable book was invented in the Middle Ages; throughout all of these centuries, we have developed a visceral acceptance of the strengths and weaknesses of the format. With the Internet, this has yet to happen. Both paeans and dirges are sung with equal passion and sincerity as we grapple with the possibilities and ramifications of the format. A spotlight on the major strengths and weaknesses of the Internet is a step toward understanding the best ways to use the medium to its most effective advantage.

Strengths

Ease

Intuitively, the act of plugging into a universe of information, 24/7, at the click of a finger is enticing. Despite all the wrong or unfiltered information for which the Internet is known, the number of right answers for information that would otherwise have taken extended time, energy, and resources is impressive. The process of getting these right answers is not only trivial, but also instantaneous, handy, and commonplace enough to merit an entire generation being referred to as the "Google Generation" (Randeree and Mon, 2011).

For example, a question like "Who is the person listed at 708-555-1212?" could potentially have been time-consuming for a user. The knowledge that a crisscross directory existed, followed by the search for a library that subscribed to a printed crisscross directory for the 708 area, followed by a study of the arrangement of the directory, would be the minimum requirement to locate the answer. A reverse lookup in Google or any of the online directories is accomplished in a matter of a minute. The Association of Research Libraries (2011) recorded a drop of 5.7 million reference transactions between 1999 and 2009, the same period in which Google saw a rise in the number of searches made each day from 10,000 in 1998 (Google official history) to an estimated 2 billion searches a day in 2008. Ease of use and the potential instant gratification of needs contribute greatly to the perceived strengths of Internet research.

Currency

Internet resources are stereotypically valued for their currency. Print resources, by definition, have built-in time delays to accommodate the vetting and printing process. Even a newspaper takes twenty-four hours to print the day's news. The Internet, on the other hand, can potentially update news as it is made. The print directory listing new Congress members, for example, was published as the *Congressional Directory* in April 2011, four months after the inaugural session of the 112th Congress. In the interim, users wanting to contact a congressional representative or browse the roster had little choice but to consult websites such as the U.S. Senate (http://www.senate.gov/). In a dramatic bid for currency, in 2009, the 100-year-old *Christian Science Monitor* became the first nationally circulated newspaper to shift from a daily print format to a constantly updated online publication in the interests of "improving the *Monitor*'s timeliness and relevance" (Cook, 2008).

Audiovisual Capabilities

Useful or even critical to some research is the need for audiovisual information. The Internet has the capability to provide it in composite forms that can include text, visual, and audio packages. A reference question on the unique positions of

Sirius, Mirzam, Wezen, and Adhara, the major stars of the Canis Major constellation, could be partially answered with a print resource. However, their positions at changing times, dates, and latitudes could only be answered with the interactive simulations of a sky chart provided online at http://www.outerbody.com/stargazer. In children's reference, recurring school projects on country or ethnic studies, for example, gain immeasurably when textual descriptions are enhanced by a rendering of the national anthem of the country, or by videos of the celebration of local festivals and cultural programs. A student presenting a project on Pueblo tribes in the southwestern United States was able to dress and present a truncated kachina dance of the Hopi tribe based on a streaming video found online.

Exclusivity

Given the ease in both entering and accessing information, an increasing number of publications, proceedings, transcripts, and data are available only on the Internet. Conference proceedings, government documents, state job listings and application forms, news blogs, subject wikis, and even professional communications can be found exclusively on the Internet.

The most dramatic example of exclusivity appeared in 1991 when Paul Ginsparg, a physicist at the Los Alamos National Laboratory, launched an online archive of preprint research communications that would, in effect, circumvent print publications. The initiative, owned, operated, and funded by Cornell University, proved to be wildly successful so that close to 80 institutions from around the globe pledged to collaboratively govern and support the initiative from 2013–2017. Acknowledged as a leader in "e-print" service, arXiv, as it is known, attracts monthly submissions numbering over 5,000, a big jump from the less than 500 submissions received in 1991–1992. Reference questions dealing with the cutting edge of physics must frequently be referred to *arXiv.org* (http://arxiv.org/).

Interactivity

Print information informs, but rarely "listens." Internet information has the capability to be interactive. Electronic discussion groups, e-mail newsletters, wikis, Twitter feeds, live interviews, and ongoing comment pages are possible so that an information dialogue can be created. Interactivity in research is quite possibly one of the most dynamic areas of future development in reference librarianship. Even as such major initiatives as *Government Information Online: Ask a Librarian* (http://govtinfo.org/) and *Ask a Librarian: Florida's Virtual Reference Service* (http://www.askalibrarian.org/), for example, are maturing at a hectic pace, IM and short message service (SMS) reference have taken shape as less costly and more personalized alternatives.

My Info Quest is an SMS text message reference service that is staffed by thirty libraries across the nation. Mosio's *Text a Librarian* (http://www.textalibrarian.com/) is used by over 800 U.S. libraries. The extent of IM reference can be seen in the 436 practicing libraries within the United States listed with hyperlinks in *Library Success: A Best Practices Wiki* (http://www.libsuccess.org/). The libraries of the University of Alberta, University of Calgary, University of Toronto, Carleton University, and the Ottawa Public Library are among at least fifteen other libraries in Canada that offer IM reference, as does the Heriot-Watt University Library and the University of Teesside Library in the United Kingdom. Given the unmistakable allure of *Wikipedia*, wiki resources are maturing at an even faster rate. There are now credible moves toward establishing "reference wikis" that are less open than *Wikipedia* and therefore less vulnerable to the charge of being unreliable or inaccurate. The *Psychology Wiki* (http://psychology.wikia.com/wiki/main_page) with over 31,019 articles, the *Thomas Jefferson Encyclopedia* (http://wiki.monticello .org/), and *The Encyclopedia of Earth* (http://www.eoearth.org/) created on wiki platforms as well as the successful *Peer-to-Patent* wiki (http://www.peertopatent .org/) that is speeding the patent review process are examples of authoritative wikis (Bell, 2009).

Another area where interactivity is playing a major role is in statistical information. Websites are beginning to offer data in formats that permit users to transpose data directly onto spreadsheets or Excel and Access programs, to create graphs, or extract selective line data. The National Economics Accounts at the U.S. Department of Commerce, for example, provides "Interactive Access" for all of its tables. A reference question on changes in the market value of goods and services in the American economy before and after the 9/11 terrorist attacks could require multiple printed resources that are relatively difficult to locate. With the "Interactive Access" tables, however, changes in current-dollar gross domestic product can be tailored to fit any selected range of years with the frequency of data tweaked to present annual, quarterly, or monthly figures.

Mass Convenience

Unlike single-book sources, Internet information is accessible to multiple users at the same time. A user spending hours over the *Occupational Outlook Handbook* need not be disturbed if Internet access is available for the 20 high school students with "career assignments" who can do research and access the same resource online at http://www.bls.gov/ooh.

Scope

Reportedly, three new pages are added to the Internet every second of the day. That is a lot of material. Then again, many print resources are published every day as well; so why is "scope" treated so holistically for the Internet? The reason lies in the different forms of print versus Internet resources. The clicking of the same mouse to switch almost instantaneously from one resource to another gives the admittedly misleading impression that the scope of the Internet is one vast composite whole. In reality, the criterion for scope should be applied to each individual site, much as is done for each individual book. However, in terms of the appeal of Internet research, the perception of scope, voiced as "you can find everything," is powerful.

Weaknesses

Given the scope, accessibility, ease, currency, convenience, and value-added features of Internet use, it is curious that the Internet has taken so long to be treated as a full-fledged reference tool. The explanation for this time lag can reasonably be located in the following vulnerabilities peculiar to Internet research.

Lack of Regulated Quality Control

Both the attraction and the detraction of Internet research is that for any and every reason, anyone can write anything, from anywhere in the world, and leave it for any amount of time for anyone to read. With the insouciant littering of information and wisdom, knowledge and factoids, learning and vitriol flung haphazardly into Everyman's existence, it is no wonder that librarians, with their trained beliefs and classical training in classification and subclassification, have indulged in nervous speculation that the end of the information world was imminent (Crawford and Gorman, 1995; Anhang, 2002). Without any checks on authorship, reliability, accuracy, currency, or validity, information can quite literally run amok. The fast-developing Internet religion of the "pastafarians," followers of the Flying Spaghetti Monster, a parodist creation originally designed to mock the inclusion of intelligent design in Kansas school curricula, is a case in point. This illuminating parody can be accessed at http://www.venganza.org/. Actor Sacha Baron Cohen, in keeping with his 2012 film role for *The Dictator*, created an information-rich companion site for the fictitious (and outrageous) "Republic of Wadiya," replete with a map locating it in the Horn of Africa, at http://www.republicofwadiya.com/.

Evaluation Falls to the User

Given the absolute lack of quality control, the onus of evaluating sites falls squarely on the shoulders of the user. Evaluation, as librarians are aware, is a complex undertaking, requiring both the awareness and the skills to navigate between trustworthy and untrustworthy sites. Since users are conditioned to accept all printed material as valid information, the pitfalls of Internet-generated research become more acute. Public librarians faced with the directive to "print something from that Internet" and undergraduates laboring under the IKIA (I Know It Already) syndrome (Wilder, 2005) are daily examples of users being unaware about the fallible nature of Internet information.

Lack of Overview

Thomas Mann, the venerable reference librarian at the Library of Congress, describes how scholarship can be affected in the way information is presented. Direct and physical access to subject-classified shelves can result in information that may not be possible through digital access dependent on the use of keywords because of the following:

1. Researchers invariably do not have all the exact keywords prior to starting the research, but do recognize the information when it is "immediately in front of them within a manageably segregated group of likely sources" (Mann, 2005: 45).
2. Even with the right keywords specified in advance, results cannot "build bridges among multiple sets" so that an overview of the research topic becomes difficult (Mann, 2005: 46).

Mann has a valid point and has voiced a widespread nostalgia for the serendipity of shelf browsing that is so intrinsic to print reference. However, in the place of visual browsing a new set of skills can establish keywords, link words, and search terms to circumvent the apparent lack of an overview. This is outlined in a later part of this chapter.

Overwhelming Results

Oftentimes, the Internet is just not the right resource. Given the powerful belief that all information is available on the Internet, much time can be wasted looking for information that can be found far more efficiently through other formats. In addition to the waste of time engendered by choosing the wrong resource, time can be wasted in sifting reliable from unreliable material, or getting caught in the hop-skip-and-jump allure of hyperlinks. "Relevance ranking" or the ability of search engines to sift through the frequency, uniqueness, and positioning of search keywords and pull those to the top of the returns list, is not always the searcher's best friend. For example, an overly creative title that does not use words directly relevant to the subject matter may receive a lower "weight" and get buried further down the results list. If the file size is small, such as in a brief book review, but uses the search keyword the same number of times as a larger document (such as a literary analysis of the book), it is the smaller book review file that accrues a higher "density" rating. As a result, it is the brief review that gets pushed to the top of the returns list relative to the analysis for which the user may have been searching.

No Guarantee of Free Full Text

Full-text articles from journals are also not always free to the Internet user. Research quality articles have traditionally clustered under expensive subscription databases. This would not ordinarily be considered a "weakness." After all, full-text articles in print journals are also available only through purchase. However, Internet research has accrued the impression of being free. As Joe Thompson of the Baltimore County Public Library laments, "Good information still costs money, and people forget that" (Selingo, 2004: G5). The cost of information, accepted as normal for print, is paid unwillingly for Internet sources, fueled no doubt by the lurking suspicion that the information might indeed be free "somewhere" on the Internet. Increasingly, however, with projects such as Google Scholar's *Print Library Project*, the HathiTrust (http://www.hathitrust.org/) digital repository, which already has the digital equivalent of 121 miles of books on library shelves, as well as the Open Content Alliance scheduled to run Yahoo's library digitization venture, the extent of open access journals has increased.

Spotty Coverage of Historical Material

The presence of historical material on the Internet is relatively limited. Even databases usually do not go far back into archival material so that journal articles prior to the 1980s are hard to find via the Internet. If included, historical coverage tends to be spotty, almost as if it is included only if and when time and personal interest permit such inclusions. With digital initiatives like *American Memory* (http://memory.loc.gov/), Yale University's *Avalon Project* (http://www.yale .edu/lawweb/avalon/avalon.htm), *Gallica* (http://gallica.bnf.fr/) from the National Library of France, the University of Michigan's *Making of America* (http://moa.umdl.umich.edu/), and the *Internet Archive*, the information drought on historical material is lessening.

Volatility

With content being added, modified, deleted, or forgotten, there is a constant level of volatility built into the medium. What was vetted yesterday as being a "good" site will have to be vetted again today before it is used because it might have changed. The *Internet Yellow Pages*, which becomes partially obsolete within the first year of publication, is a prime exhibit of this volatility. Documenting the website to the last letter or number of the URL (uniform resource locator) address is one way of coping with the mercurial quality of Internet-generated answers. While it does not retrieve a lost site, it both testifies and provides clues to the earlier structure of a site. The *Internet Archive* (http://www.archive.org/), with its storehouse of 150 billion pages of dead websites and extinct pages, can also be consulted.

Five Steps to Successful Internet Reference

The Internet is *surfed*. It should be *searched*. Rather than crest every passing "information wave," the following five steps should be followed.

Step 1: Ask Yourself, Is the Internet the Right Medium?

"Type first and think later" has been the instinctive reaction to using the Internet. The considered reaction should be this:

- Is it the best resource to use?
- Is it the only resource to use?

Clarity in the advantages and disadvantages of Internet use is a necessary first step. Being open to a combination of formats can also pay dividends. For example, on the morning of August 29, 2005, when Hurricane Katrina struck the Gulf Coast region of the United States, the website for the American Red Cross was jammed. Loading the page took an average of 25 to 55 minutes, if it opened at all. By contrast, referring users to the information for Disaster Relief at the American Red Cross headquarters, located in such print resources as the *Washington Information Directory*, took a minute. Picking up the telephone or consulting a colleague can also prove to be more efficient in certain situations. A focus group study by Milner Library at Illinois State University found that their chat reference service was proving to be a disappointment primarily because the time it took for a student to complete a chat query was far greater than a one-on-one interaction with a reference librarian in person or over the telephone (Naylor, Stoffel, and Van Der Laan, 2008). The first step, then, involves a clear choice of using the Internet in tandem, or in preference, to print or other information mediums.

Step 2: Select the Right Internet Tool

The second step is using the most efficient Internet search tool—a search engine, a metasearch engine, or a subject directory.

Search Engines

If the question requires a broad overview, single keywords or phrases typed into a search box can provide a flood of hits. This option requires eyeballing a list of random resources that may or may not be productive but, at minimum, helps formulate the research query. General search engine technology, yet in its relative toddlerhood, is growing by leaps and bounds so that various tools are now available to fine-tune the keyword search. Some of the more popular search engines are Yahoo! Search, Google, Ask, DuckDuckGo, Bing, AOL, and Mahalo. Table 13-1 presents a brief overview of some of the major general engines available to users.

For seven-to twelve-year-old users, child-friendly search engines are available. They typically provide a mix of information and ready entertainment. The pages are bright and loaded with contrasting colors and graphics. The sites are usually geared to providing both directories and search engine capabilities. The highly popular *Ask Kids* (http://www.askkids.com/) uses natural language technology so the importance of keywords is lessened. It only accepts links that are "G-rated" and written specifically for children. There is no option for chat. *Yahoo! Kids* (http://kids.yahoo.com/), on the other hand, provides safe surfing guidelines and places the onus of responsibility on parents and the child.

New ways to display results are also appearing, for example: Slikk (http://www.slikk.com/) offers "21st century web search" with blended results that include the web, images, videos, news, blogs, and Twitter feeds. The results appear in multiview format, and an embedded window in the search page allows for a split screen of the actual site pages. Factbites (http://www.factbites.com/) sells itself as a perfectly matched cross between a search engine and an encyclopedia. It provides natural-language sentences for every site listed in the search results so that there is more information on the search page. RedZ (http://www.redz.com/) and Spacetime (http://www.spacetime.com/) provide results in a curving album of webpages that can be flicked through for easy graphic viewing.

Metasearch Engines

Metasearch engines produce far more results, given that they collate sites from multiple search engines. Searches can be overwhelming and search statements can be read differently so that metasearches are best used when a very broad overview of a subject is required. Some of the best-known metasearch engines are KartOO, Ixquick, QueryServer, Mamma, iTools, MetaCrawler, and Dogpile. A brief overview of Dogpile and MetaCrawler is provided in Table 13-2.

Subject Directories

Because directories employ subject headings based on standardized vocabulary, organized by human rather than robotic logic, specific questions can benefit from

Table 13-1. Sample General Search Engines

	Google	Yahoo!	Bing
Debut Year	1998	1994	1998/2009
Site	http://www.google.com/	http://www.yahoo.com	http://www.bing.com/
Name Etymology	From "googol," a number represented by 100 zeros following the numeral 1	Acronym for "Yet Another Hierarchical Officious Oracle"	"Short and catchy" Bing (acronym joke—"Because It's Not Google"), introduced in 2009; originally "MSN Search."
Traffic (ComScore) April 2012	66.2% of U.S. searches	14.1% of U.S. searches	15.2% of U.S. searches
Boolean	Capitalized OR; Default AND	Capitalized AND, OR, AND NOT, NOT	Capitalized OR, AND, NOT
Unique Features	1. Offers at least 44 special features, such as local business listings in the United States, the United Kingdom, and Canada. 2. Provides special tools, such as blogging and services (e.g., a system for organizing medical records online). 3. Sites are "cached" so that if a page is unavailable, the original page can be displayed.	1. Offers both a general search engine and a directory that can be used in tandem. 2. Signature exclamation mark directs users to specific services (e.g., "travel!," goes to Yahoo! Travel). 3. Provides communication services, such as chat, and commerce services, such as investing and personal finance.	1. "Search History" provides chronological links to all previous searches. 2. This is the only engine to provide search display from social networks like Facebook and Twitter. 3. Called a "decision-engine" because it gives more information about search results.
Ranking Algorithm	Page Rank™—general popularity usage calculated from over 100 factors.	Relevancy—through keyword density.	Back-end searching with "Tiger," an index-serving technology, and "Sidebar" for social network searches.

Table 13-2. Sample Metasearch Engines

	Dogpile	MetaCrawler
Debut Year	1996	1994
Site	http://www.dogpile.com/	http://www.metacrawler.com/
Name Etymology	Term used to describe Rugby players piling on top of one another to celebrate	Self-explanatory—designed as doctoral project by Erik Selberg and Professor Oren Etzioni
Metasearches	Google, Yahoo!, Bing, Ask, and content from Kosmix and Fandango	Google, Yahoo!, Bing, Ask, About, MIVA (formerly FindWhat.com), LookSmart
Unique Features	1. Default search settings can be customized to include filtering. 2. Searches can be conducted over ten languages. 3. The fifteen most-recent searches can be displayed at right of page. 4. New search widget features Arfie, the Dogpile mascot, who also functions as a Search Spy, displaying "what the rest of the world is searching." 5. Includes radio buttons for audio, video, images, news, and directories.	1. Potentially explicit material can be filtered from results. 2. Sponsored results are displayed separately from organic web results. 3. Search engines for each result are displayed. 4. Default search settings can be customized. 5. Offers the option to search for web, images, video, news, yellow pages, and white pages. 6. Recent searches are displayed in main page with option to hide.

a directory. Conversely, if users are unclear about search terms within a subject area, the directory supplies terms, much as a thesaurus supplies synonyms. These websites are relatively vetted and therefore produce a more limited, yet pertinent set of results. The directory is also useful in mining the "invisible web," those sites such as specialized searchable databases that are typically not locatable in a general search engine (Devine and Egger-Sider, 2009). An overview of three subject directories is given in Table 13-3.

If the past is a true predictor of the future, search engines, metasearch engines, and directories will morph into sleeker technology and different ranking and selecting systems. Search engine names such as Lycos, Hotbot, and Excite are no longer what they were a few short years ago. Sudden death or transpositions of engine technology and ownership is the order of the day, so that the tables provide a brief, time-bound snapshot of ways to synopsize a tool as and when it appears on the search horizon.

Table 13-3. Sample Subject Directories

	INFOMINE	*ipl2* (2008)	*Open Directory Project*
Debut Year	1994	1993	1998
Site	http://infomine.ucr.edu/	http://www.ipl.org/	http://www.dmoz.org/
Links	Over 100,000 links, of which 26,000 are by librarians and the rest by robots/crawlers	Over 20,000 websites	5,034,762 sites as of May 2012
Boolean	NEAR, NOT, AND, OR are executed in that order.	Default AND. NOT and OR can be used.	Default AND. OR, AND, AND NOT are used.
Unique Features	1. Results include university-level research with sites vetted by librarians from the University of California, Wake Forest University, California State University, and others. 2. It is a rich resource for the "invisible Web" of databases, electronic journals and books, and bulletin boards. 3. Uses nine major subject headings. 4. Offers concise descriptions for each record.	1. Is free of commercials. 2. Sites are vetted by permanent staff and 100 contributors from libraries in California and Washington. 3. Offers free weekly newspaper for resource updates. 4. Uses fourteen primary subject headings and many subheadings.	1. Volunteer editors/net-citizens fuel this open source directory. 2. By May 2012, the directory claimed 95,462 editors and over 1,011,238 categories. 3. Sites can be screened for "kids," "teens," and "mature teens." 4. Handy tab links to metasearch on other engines. 5. "World" category contains 80 non-English sites.

Step 3: Construct the Right Search Terms

The third step, possibly the most critical in establishing the difference between a wild surfing session and a professional search strategy, is in constructing the most effective search terms. To succumb to the siren call of typing in terms as they pop like flashbulbs in one's head is to be vulnerable to a lengthy and possibly frustrating search.

Make a List

Instead, the trained response should be to pick up a pencil and draw up a list. Starting with a blanket strategy, all words and phrases associated with the question should be jotted down in two categories that differentiate between key representative terms and related terms. Once the brainstorming of words is over, a hierarchy needs to be imposed, however tentative the ranking. Stratification would help to both structure preresearch thinking and save an immense amount of time and energy as the research proceeds. Dubious leads can be tweaked and search terms revised based on this list. The goal is to avoid repetition and save time. The Zen insight of finding equal importance in absence as in presence is also instructive in that dead-end terms can throw critical light on the relative relevance of different aspects of a research topic. For example:

Query: *I need to research separatist movements in Sri Lanka.*

Representative search terms: *Sri Lanka, Sri Lanka and politics, Sri Lanka and separatists, Sri Lanka and ethnic conflict*

Related terms: *Ceylon Tamils, Tamils and Sinhalese, LTTE, Tamil Tigers, TULF, PLOTE, EPRLF, Thimpu Talks, Prabhakaran/Pirabhakaran, Sri Lanka and India, eelam, Jayewardene, Kumaratunga*

Hierarchy:

1. *Sri Lanka politics*
2. *Sri Lanka and ethnic conflict*
3. *Liberation Tigers of Tamil Eelam*

Free online tutorials on developing list skills are located at http://www.vtstutorials .ac.uk/, a national initiative in the United Kingdom that presents wonderfully detailed tutorials designed for subject areas ranging widely from engineering to gardening.

Alternate Spellings

In addition to setting up a hierarchy of search terms, an awareness of the syntax, spelling, and alternate spelling of terms can both ease and enhance a search. For example, an Internet search on the history of Myanmar, the Democratic Republic of Congo, Mumbai, or Surinam may be incomplete without using the discarded names of Burma, Zaire, Bombay, and Dutch Guiana. While existing awareness of alternatives is not necessary, it is necessary to be aware of the possibility of alternatives so that clues offered in one search string can be hoarded for another search.

Context

Vague or generic keywords and search terms can result in a frustrating, never-ending, or dead-end search. If a word is generic, the trick to relieve it of its anonymity is to use combination terms that establish the context of the word. For example, a user wanting biographical information on the-artist-formerly-known-as-Prince cannot type a search term as generic as "prince." The results would no doubt cover the singer, but the information would be embedded within millions of sites on the scions of Great Britain, Monaco, the Netherlands, and various

African countries, the history of Russia and the Indian subcontinent, bestsellers from today's Rowling and yesterday's Machiavelli, counties in Maryland and Virginia, and fond owners' descriptions of dogs answering to that name. Combining the term "prince" with "artist" or even searching the notorious phrase "formerly known as prince" provides the necessary limiters to bracket the search.

Step 4: Use the Right Search Operators

Having established the best possible hierarchy of productive search terms, consideration of the most effective search operators is the logical corollary. In theory, Boolean operators, truncations, wildcards, quotation marks or parentheses, and proximity matrices are helpful tools that can streamline the search process or extend it in the right direction. The inclusion of the Boolean "and" between two terms narrows an overlarge search result. If the results are too limited, the use of the Boolean "or" can expand it. For example, a search for <conservatives and republicans> would produce a narrower result than <conservatives or republicans>. Parentheses or quotation marks allow the searcher to nest Boolean operators and refine the search considerably. For example, search strings like <(Clinton and (Hillary or Chelsea)) not Bill> would lighten the search considerably by removing all references to the past president.

In practice, however, search operators vary from site to site. For example, Gigablast accepts Boolean operators AND, OR, NOT, parentheses, and plus and minus signs, while at AltaVista, the Boolean search only works in the Advanced Search page. The best way to take control over idiosyncratic operators is to check the "Help," "About," or "Tip" icons included on each website, directory, or search engine. A comparative chart of the various operators allowed and disallowed by major search engines is provided in effective detail by Greg Notess at http://search engineshowdown.com/features/ and by Joe Barker at http://infopeople.org/search/chart.html. With most searchers favoring one engine over another, it is expedient to be wholly familiar with the effective and timesaving tips provided by each engine. Even trivial shortcuts, such as hitting the "Return" key rather than clicking on the "Search" button as suggested by Google, can shave away search time.

Step 5: Evaluate the Search Results

The moment of truth is at hand. Carefully selected search terms are rewarded with a clutch of sites that can number anywhere from a few pages to thousands. How best to pick the best sites and evaluate them in more detail? Given the complete absolution from traditional vetting agencies such as personal name accountability, publisher standards, editorial expertise, or professional evaluation, all Internet information must be treated as "guilty unless proven authoritative." This sounds harsher than it is. It merely reminds the Internet user to establish the validity of each informational site using some of the same criteria used for print evaluation, along with recognition of the working mechanics of the Internet medium. The need for this is greater when providing Internet reference for minors. A comprehensive checklist of website evaluation for kids can be found at http://gws.ala.org/.

Authority

Placing authorship is a traditional way of establishing the authority of any piece of information. It is no different in the Internet medium, though the ways of gauging the author's reputation may require keener detection.

- Who is the author? Is the work signed, and if so, is the name familiar or well regarded in the field?
- If the name is unfamiliar, is there more detailed contact information about the author? Open accountability can usually be regarded as a sign, though not a guarantee, of reliability.
- Is there any professional review or affiliation of the author provided on the site? Affiliations can provide clues to author validity.
- Is the link that led to this site one that can be trusted? Most trustworthy sites feel responsible about the hyperlinks they allow and thereby act as a vetting agent. Links from libraries are a classic example.
- What appears to be the motive of the author? Is there any indication that the author might be biased? If so, is the bias a necessary part of the research angle or liable to skew the research?
- Does the author exhibit a grasp of the subject, provide an overview of the field, or allude to existing theories in the field? While known authors are reviewed and slotted into comfortable perception fields, unknown web authors must prove their expertise in the field and these exhibits provide some indicators of the level of expertise.

Reliability

Reputable print resources gain stature because of their credentials, authority, and transparent documentation of publishing pedigree. Given that the web is a vast public forum for both individual and institutional output, Internet resources need to be held up to equally strict, and infinitely more creative, indices of reliability.

- Does a known organization or institution sponsor the site?
- If unknown, what does the "About Us" icon say about the organization? This may be termed with alternative phrases such as "Background" or "Our Philosophy." Truncate the URL until it reaches the domain name succeeded by a forward slash, as this is the main homepage of the site and may be the only page containing accountability information.
- Are clear contact details provided? Once again, accountability can vouch for some degree of reliability. If the only contact information is an e-mail address, it should act as a red flag. As a last resort in such cases, e-mailing for more information is advisable.
- Is the URL indicative? For example, when researching for information on Winston Churchill, the reliability of a URL such as http://www.chu.cam.ac .uk/archives/collections/churchill_papers can be considered very high, even without actually delving into the site. Why is that? Because of URL clues such as "uk," which stands for the United Kingdom, home to Churchill; the "ac," which stands for academia much as "edu" does in the United States; and "cam," which stands for the prestigious University of Cambridge. A URL

with a tilde (~) could be a highly useful source of information, but needs a more critical eye as it is the personal site of an individual rather than a known institution.

- The URL is also valuable in establishing the context of the resource. An account of the relevance of insurance ratings by various companies as presented on the Weiss website will quite naturally present a point of view that is favorable to the Weiss ratings system. This is perfectly valid information but must be recognized as information that has a vested interest.
- Another prominent aspect of reliability is accuracy. This is gauged much as it is in print. Is there a bibliography or hyperlinks to other resources with which the searcher is familiar? Does the link seem like a good choice? Is the literature overview or the factual information used correct in the areas with which the user is familiar? If the background research is solid, it is an indication that the rest of the information may be reliable.
- Are quotations, referrals, graphics, or statistical data well documented and fully cited? If statistical data are presented, are the data solid or does the data resort to dubious phrases such as "a majority of" or "a large percentage" or "a significant amount" without any real numbers?
- Are there typos, spelling mistakes, or egregious grammar errors evident throughout the document?

Finally, the wheel need not be endlessly reinvented. Reliable websites vetted by experts have already been listed in *INFOMINE* (http://infomine.ucr.edu/), which is a virtual library of Internet sources relevant for university-level researchers; the *ipl2* (http://www.ipl.org/) that deems "serving the public by finding, evaluating, selecting, organizing, describing, and creating high quality information resources" (as part of its 2008 Vision Statement); the *Language Portal of Canada* (http://www.noslangues-ourlanguages.gc.ca/index-eng.php) that provides links to reputable language resources in both French and English; and *Eagle-i* (http://ials.sas.ac.uk/eagleiproject.htm) in the United Kingdom, which provides a reliable portal to legal researchers.

Currency

Relative to print resources, Internet reference is most valued for providing the kind of currency that print formats cannot possibly supply. Minute-by-minute game plays, hourly stock updates, daily foreign news updates, weekly conference proceedings, monthly cost-of-living estimates—the scope of instant communication of information as provided by the Internet is breathtaking. The relevance of checking for currency in areas where it is required can therefore pose a very important part of evaluation. Follow these steps to check for currency.

- Scroll down to the bottom of the page where a "last updated" message may be provided.
- If unavailable, check the site directory to see the "last modified" date.
- Check for copyright dates.
- Check for statements that verify that the data will be updated on a recurring basis according to a set schedule.

- If no obvious statements of currency are available, check for more subtle signs such as whether a current event or statistic you are sure about has been included.
- Check for giveaway statements that mention the date such as "According to a 2006 study..." or "Next week, the 111th Congress will open..."
- Check for multiple dead links, a sure sign that the site has been abandoned for some time.

In general, if information found on the Internet appears suspicious or dubious, it probably is. Erring on the side of caution is recommended. However, the power of Internet research is irresistible and need not be resisted. Librarians must learn to evaluate resources speedily and effectively so that snap judgments on the millions of available sites become second nature. With this skill, the nature of the medium is accepted, absorbed, and engaged. In addition, establishing a conscientious system of bookmarking favorite websites and creating a "Web-based reference desk" (Sauers, 2001) is an effective way of adding on source-specific searches that are more akin to print research.

Practicing with the excellent *Virtual Training Suite* (http://www.vtstutorials .ac.uk/) of free, interactive tutorials provided by the United Kingdom's *Resource Discovery Network* is a good way to develop evaluation skills. Available at http://www.vtstutorials.ac.uk/, the site has tutorials in various subject areas. Developing a content evaluation tool such as the example shown in Figure 13-1 is another way to practice appraising a site with consistency. Aspects of the criteria

---

Figure 13-1. WWW Cyberguide Ratings for Content Evaluation

Site Title: _____ Subject: _____

URL: _____ Audience: _____

Purpose for exploring this site:
_____

Notes on possible uses of this site and URLs for useful linked sites:
_____
_____
_____

To determine the worth of the website you are considering, evaluate its content according to the criteria described below.

Circle "Y" for "Yes", "N" for "No", "NA" for "Not Applicable"

1. First look

A. User is able to quickly determine the basic content of the site.	Y	N	NA
B. User is able to determine the intended audience of the site.	Y	N	NA

(Continued)

Figure 13-1. WWW Cyberguide Ratings for Content Evaluation *(Continued)*

2. Information Providers

A. The author(s) of the material on the site is clearly identified.   Y   N   NA

B. Information about the author(s) is available.   Y   N   NA

C. According to the info given, author(s) appears qualified to
present information on this topic.   Y   N   NA

D. The sponsor of the site is clearly identified.   Y   N   NA

E. A contact person or address is available so the user can ask
questions or verify information.   Y   N   NA

3. Information Currency

A. Latest revision date is provided. Date last revised _____   Y   N   NA

B. Latest revision date is appropriate to material.   Y   N   NA

C. Content is updated frequently.   Y   N   NA

D. Links to other sites are current and working properly.   Y   N   NA

4. Information Quality

A. The purpose of this site is clear: business/commercial-
entertainment-informational—news—personal page-persuasion.   Y   N   NA

B. The content achieves this intended purpose effectively.   Y   N   NA

C. The content appears to be complete (no "under construction"
signs, for example).   Y   N   NA

D. The content of this site is well organized.   Y   N   NA

E. The information in this site is easy to understand.   Y   N   NA

F. This site offers sufficient information related to my needs/purposes.   Y   N   NA

G. The content is free of bias, or the bias can be easily detected.   Y   N   NA

H. This site provides interactivity that increases its value.   Y   N   NA

I. The information appears to be accurate based on user's
previous knowledge of subject.   Y   N   NA

J. The information is consistent with similar information in other sources.   Y   N   NA

K. Grammar and spelling are correct.   Y   N   NA

5. Further Information

A. There are links to other sites that are related to my needs/purposes.   Y   N   NA

B. The content of linked sites is worthwhile and appropriate to
my needs/purposes.   Y   N   NA

Totals

Based on the total of "yes" and "no" answers and your overall observations, rate the content
of this site as:

_____ Very useful for my information needs   _____ Worth bookmarking for future reference
_____ Not worth coming back to

Source: Created by Karen McLachlan, 2002. Used by permission.

listed earlier in this section are included in the chart. For example, much of the "Authority" factors are covered under "Information Providers" in the chart, whereas "Reliability" is approximated by the "Information Quality" category. However, developing your own ratings using all of the evaluation criteria could be immensely helpful.

Recommendations for Further Reading

Bell, Suzanne. 2012. *Librarian's Guide to Online Searching*. 3rd ed. Santa Barbara, CA: Libraries Unlimited. Written as a textbook, the book is a thorough treatise on how to go about mastering the art of online retrieval. The inherent structure of databases is described as are the arsenal of search tools using Boolean logic, proximity, truncation, and more, in a clear and practical way.

Bradley, Phil. 2004. *The Advanced Internet Searcher's Handbook*. 3rd ed. London: Facet Publishing. The strength of this title, in a long list of titles that hope to enhance the process of web research, is its inclusion of real-life examples for all the techniques provided. Different types of search engines are analyzed by structure to help choose according to individual engine strengths. Tips for searching for multimedia information, the "hidden Web," blogs, and information gateways are also provided along with fifty tips for better searching such as suggestions for truncating an unwieldy URL. The author also keeps up a website with extensive search engine information available at http://www.philb.com/whichengine.htm.

Carr, Nicholas. 2011. *The Shallows: What the Internet Is Doing to Our Brains*. New York: W.W. Norton. In this Pulitzer Prize–nominated book, the elegant and provocative Carr presents a case for the ethics of online information gathering, where optimizing the speedy production and consumption of facts feeds effortlessly into the structuring of knowledge through skimming and widespread scanning. What is lost is the printed book's ability to focus attention. Ultimately, says Carr, "The computer screen bulldozes our doubts with its bounties and conveniences. It is so much our servant that it would seem churlish to notice that it is also our master" (p. 4).

Hacker, Diana, and Barbara Fister. 2010. *Research and Documentation in the Electronic Age*. 5th ed. Boston: Bedford/St. Martin's. This is a classic guide on finding, understanding, and evaluating online resources, with the most recent edition updated by a second author following the death of Hacker. Distinguishing between "narrow," "challenging," and "grounded" research questions, the text is introduced with suggestions for mapping out an appropriate search strategy, and concludes with an extensive annotated bibliography of specialized library and web resources. Newer sources such as blogs and podcasts are also covered in this edition.

Hartman, Karen, and Ernest Ackermann. 2010. *Searching and Researching on the Internet and World Wide Web*. 5th ed. Sherwood, OR: Franklin, Beedle and Associates. The frequently updated book provides a broad overview of finding, evaluating, managing and citing online information. It also addresses searching specialized databases, multimedia, and the use of RSS to keep updated.

Hock, Randolph. 2010. *The Extreme Searcher's Internet Handbook: A Guide for the Serious Searcher*. 3rd ed. Medford, NJ: Information Today. This book has an entire section devoted to "Thinking of the Internet as a Reference Collection." It covers traditional reference resource sources such as dictionaries, encyclopedias, government documents, and so forth, in online format. Directories, portals, and search engines are also covered with the overarching philosophy that the serious searcher requires the "attitude" that marks the lover of extreme sports—the thrill that comes of conquering a challenging and changing environment.

Internet Reference Services Quarterly. http://www.tandfonline.com/toc/wirs20/current. Published four times a year by Taylor and Francis (Routledge), the *Quarterly* is focused on the equation between web technologies and reference services. Its stated aim is to "function as a comprehensive information source librarians can turn to and count on for keeping up-to-date on emerging technological innovations, while emphasizing theoretical, research, and practical applications of Internet-related information services, sources, and resources."

Radford, Marie L., and R. David Lankes, eds. 2010. *Reference Renaissance: Current and Future Trends.* New York: Neal-Schuman. Following successful presentations at a Colorado conference in 2008, this book was compiled and touches upon a number of different trends in the world of reference. Section III.2 provides particularly relevant discussions and ideas on the power of Google searches, as well as the benefits of adding custom search engines to enhance Internet-based reference.

The Scout Report. 2012. http://scout.wisc.edu/. Published by the reputable Internet Scout Project, the weekly report provides an update of new and evolving Internet resources that can be accessed on the web or via direct e-mail. Each resource is annotated. The *Report* is a handy way to keep abreast of new and noteworthy websites.

Spencer, Stephan. 2011. *Google Power Search.* Sebastopol, CA: O'Reilly Media. While even the most basic search in Google spews out pages of results, books such as this one help in taking a simple search to a higher level of refinement. This slim tome introduces the beginner to the value of Google's search operators (e.g., "stocks"; "{area code}"); filtering tools (e.g., "Ads"; "Cached"); and the more dynamic tools and services (e.g., "Real Time Search"; "You Tube/Blogger/Picasa").

Tancer, Bill. 2008. *Click: What Millions of People Are Doing Online and Why It Matters.* New York: Hyperion. "We are what we click" is the interesting basis of this general book on the nature of Internet searching. While ideas range from the peculiarities of the average searcher to pointers for online marketers, the parts that analyze how users navigate the web and search for information can be useful for students of Internet reference.

Bibliography and Works Cited

Abels, Eileen. 2011. "Transforming the Internet Public Library into the ipl2 Virtual Learning Laboratory." *Reference Librarian* 52, no. 4 (October–December): 284–290.

American Library Association. 2010. "ALA Fact Sheet Number 26: Internet Use in Libraries." American Library Association. Last updated July. http://www.ala.org/tools/libfactsheets/alalibraryfactsheet26.

Anhang, Abe. 2002. "Be It Resolved That Reference Librarians Are Toast." *American Libraries* 33, no. 3 (March): 50–51.

Association of Research Libraries. 2011. *ARL Statistics 2009–10.* Association of Research Libraries. http://www.arl.org/stats/annualsurveys/arlstats/arlstats09.shtml.

Bell, Suzanne. 2009. "Wikis for Reference, Enthusiasts, and Government Information." *Online* 33, no. 1 (January–February): 20–24.

Bosančić, Boris. 2010. "A Blueprint for Building Online Reference Knowledge Bases." *Reference and User Services Quarterly* 50, no. 2 (Winter): 152–161.

Breakstone, Elizabeth. 2005. "Libraries." *Chronicle of Higher Education, Supplement*, 52, no. 6 (September 30): B6.

Carr, Nicholas. 2008. "Is Google Making Us Stupid? What the Internet Is Doing to Our Brains." *The Atlantic* 302, no. 1 (July–August): 56–62.

Cook, David. 2008. "Monitor Shifts from Print to Web-Based Strategy." *The Christian Science Monitor* (October 28). http://www.csmonitor.com/ 2008/1029/p25s01-usgn.html.

Coonin, Bryna, and Samantha Hines. 2012. "Reference Services for Distant Students with Disabilities." *Internet Reference Services Quarterly* 17, no. 1 (March): 7–12.

Crawford, Walt, and Michael Gorman. 1995. *Future Libraries: Dreams, Madness, and Reality.* Chicago: American Library Association.

Devine Jane, and Francine Egger-Sider. 2009. *Going Beyond Google: The Invisible Web in Learning and Teaching.* New York: Neal-Schuman.

Duncan, Donna, Laura Lockhart, and Lisa Hamm. 2011. *The New iSearch, You Search, We All Learn to Research: A How-To-Do-It Manual for Research Using Web 2.0 Tools and Digital Resources.* New York: Neal-Schuman.

Frauenfelder, Mark. 2007. *Rule the Web: How to Do Anything and Everything on the Internet— Better, Faster, Easier.* New York: St. Martin's Griffin.

Gil, Paul. 2012. "How to Properly Research on the Internet: Legitimate Methods, Suggested Techniques, Good Sense and Plenty of Patience." *About.com* (July). http://netforbe ginners.about.com/od/navigatingthenet/tp/How-to-Properly-Research-Online.htm.

Helft, Miguel. 2008. "Google Uses Web Searches to Track Flu's Spread." *The New York Times* (November 12): A1.

Herther, Nancy K. 2012. "Ebooks Herald the Future of 21st–Century Publishing." *Searcher* 20, no. 2 (March): 12–54.

Internet Systems Consortium. 2012. *ISC Internet Domain Survey Background.* Internet Systems Consortium. http://www.isc.org/.

MacDonald, James, and Kealin McCabe. 2011. "iRoam: Leveraging Mobile Technology to Provide Innovative Point of Need Reference Services." *Code4Lib Journal* 13 (March): 1–7.

Maceli, Monica, Susan Weidenbeck, and Eileen Abels. 2011. "The Internet Public Library (IPL): An Exploratory Case Study on User Perceptions." *Information Technology and Libraries* 30, no. 1 (March): 16–23.

Mann, Thomas. 2005. "Google Print vs. Onsite Collections." *American Libraries* (August): 45–46.

Naylor, Sharon, Bruce Stoffel, and Sharon Van Der Laan. 2008. "Why Isn't Our Chat Reference Used More? Findings of Focus Group Discussions with Undergraduate Students." *Reference and User Services Quarterly* 47, no. 4 (Summer): 342–355.

Ovadia, Steven. 2011. "Quora.com: Another Place for Users to Ask Questions." *Behavioral and Social Sciences Librarian*, vol. 30, no. 3 (July–September): 176–180.

Peijun, Jia. 2011. "Exploring Google to Enhance Reference Services." *Community and Junior College Libraries* 17, no. 1 (January–March): 23–30.

Pinto, María, and Ramón A. Manso. 2012. "Virtual Reference Services: Defining the Criteria and Indicators to Evaluate Them." *Electronic Library* 30, no. 1: 51–69.

Randeree, Ebrahim, and Lorri Mon. 2011. "Searching for Answers in a Google World." *Reference Librarian* 52, no. 4 (October–December): 342–351.

Ross, Catherine Sheldrick, and Kirsti Nilsen. 2000. "Has the Internet Changed Anything in Reference? The Library Visit Study, Phase 2." *Reference and User Services Quarterly* (Winter): 147–155.

Sauers, Michael P. 2001. *Using the Internet as a Reference Tool.* New York: Neal-Schuman.

Selingo, Jeffrey. 2004. "When a Search Engine Isn't Enough, Call a Librarian." *The New York Times*, February 5: G5.

Spencer, Brett, Lauren B. Dodd, William C. Friedman, and Qiong Xu. 2011. "The Web Beyond Google: Innovative Search Tools and Their Implications for Reference Services." *Internet Reference Services Quarterly* 16, no. 1/2 (January–June): 11–34.

Tyckoson, David A. 2011. "Issues and Trends in the Management of Reference Services: A Historical Perspective." *Journal of Library Administration* 51, no. 3 (April): 259–278.

Veldof, Jerilyn. 2008. "From Desk to Web: Creating Safety Nets in the Online Library." In *The Desk and Beyond: Next Generation Reference Services*, edited by Sarah K. Steiner and M. Leslie Madden, 120–134. Chicago: Association of College and Research Libraries.

Wilder, Larry. 2005. "Changes in Reference Service in Academic Libraries." *Illinois Library Association Reporter* 23, no. 1: 9.

Zickuhr, Kathryn, and Aaron Smith. 2012. "Digital Differences." Pew Internet and American Life Project. April 13. http://pewinternet.org/Reports/2012/Digital-differences/Main-Report/Internet-adoption-over-time.aspx.

14

Readers' Advisory Services

Cindy Orr

Introduction

Many librarians would say that readers' advisory (RA) service requires specific skills and approaches, best delivered in a distinct readers' services department created for this purpose. Others would say that both reference and readers' advisory are simply elements of good public service, which should be delivered by skilled staff members in the reference department, and that, at varying levels, this has been the case for decades.

But no matter how you view the structural questions, RA service has been gaining in popularity and influence in modern times, slowly garnering more attention in the years after Betty Rosenberg's (1982) book *Genreflecting* was published, and gaining speed after Joyce Saricks and Nancy Brown (1989) began codifying the service in 1989 in the first edition of *Readers' Advisory Service in the Public Library* (now in its third edition; Saricks, 2005). It has become an accepted service in public libraries, and its significance has increased among practitioners, if not necessarily in library schools.

The launch of Google in 1998 made it possible for people to begin doing "good enough" reference service for themselves; since then, the proliferation of home-based online computers with fast Internet connections has skyrocketed. A Pew Research study shows that nearly 80 percent of Americans now have a cell phone (Smith, 2011). Of this number, a January 2012 Nielsen survey shows that 48 percent have a smartphone, making Internet access easily available anywhere—a number that is growing quickly, with 69 percent of the 48 percent having acquired their smartphone very recently, in October, November, and December 2011 ("Survey," 2012).

Reference questions in public libraries have decreased, though they are increasingly becoming more difficult to answer, as patrons tend to ask only questions that they can't successfully Google by themselves. Library administrators have begun worrying about a decrease in demand for nonfiction books and reference help, and are concentrating on the importance of offering readers' advisory service to a very significant constituency—those who read for pleasure.

This new attention is also due partially to the fact that adult services librarians who attended graduate school before the 1990s likely had no training in readers' advisory service at all, and even those with more recent degrees may have attended one of the many library schools that still do not offer this service (Orr, 2009). Because of this, deciding to emphasize RA service nearly always requires staff training. Consortia and professional organizations have responded by increasing the workshops and training opportunities available in the field, making readers' advisory services more visible.

We are living in a new time in library history—a post-Google, post-Amazon time—where the public has access to nearly the same information as professional librarians on the topic of new book releases, and where they no longer need to call the library to settle a bar bet. How is this changing the meaning of public library reference and RA service? Before looking at an answer to that question, let's take a brief look at the roots of readers' advisory service.

History of Readers' Advisory Service

Bill Crowley (2005) notes, "It is probably safe to assert that readers advisory existed, even without the name, as long as public and other library staff actually talked about books with patrons, users, or customers" (p. 38). He has summarized the history of readers' advisory service by using the following time periods.

1876 to 1920—Inventing RA

During these years, the educational role of readers' advisory service was emphasized. This made sense, considering that fewer than 25 percent of American children over the age of 14 were still in school. Librarians saw their role as serving the good of the patron and the good of the nation.

1920 to 1940—Privileging Nonfiction RA

"Younger" librarians in the 1920s claimed credit for inventing readers' advisory service as part of the library's educational role. During these years, several major public libraries created full-time positions for readers' advisors, and the American Library Association undertook its Reading with a Purpose program, which identified educational topics, commissioned authors, and published and sold to libraries small books of recommended reading plans for adults. The libraries, in turn, added these books to their collections and sold them to their public. They can still be found in some large public library collections today. This kind of readers' advisory service was not so much about pleasure reading as it was about making reading plans for patrons as part of the library's educational role.

1940 to 1984—RA "Lost" in Adult Services

In *The Public Library in the United States* (Leigh, 1950), results of a huge study of public libraries, the proper role of a public library was seen as a source of reliable information and a center for self-education. The library as a source of recreation or entertainment was seen as a bad thing. In these years, readers' advisory service consisted mainly of informal recommendations given by librarians who had a knack for matching readers with books, but since the primary focus for libraries was to provide information, very little was written in professional journals about readers' advisory service.

1984 to Present—Reviving RA

Crowley sees the current period as a reversal of the earlier emphasis on nonfiction, because at the current time, readers' advisory service concentrates mainly on fiction, though nonfiction books which can be read for pleasure are also included. As Crowley (2005) notes, privileging fiction over nonfiction is a recent phenomenon. "Until the revival of readers' advisory in the 1980s, nonfiction was the intellectual gold standard of adult readers advisory service" (p. 38).

Crowley (2005) marks the beginning of this period with the formation of the Adult Reading Round Table (http://www.arrtreads.org/), a group of Chicago-area librarians interested in readers' advisory service. Since that time, there has been a huge increase in readers' advisory training and programs, a proliferation of publications on the subject, the establishment of RA committees in the American Library Association (ALA) and the Public Library Association (PLA), and the creation of a mailing group called *Fiction_L* (http://www.webrary.org/rs/flmenu .html).

New tools for readers' advisors have proliferated, including print sources, and both subscription-based and free databases and websites. Better subject cataloging for fiction, including links to read-alikes, is now standard in many libraries. (*Read-alike* has become the accepted term for a book that offers a similar experience and appeal as another book the reader has enjoyed.) Therefore, in many ways, the current status of readers' advisory service is better than it has ever been.

Current Status and Importance of RA

Library directors have increasingly realized that patrons primarily identify libraries with reading, and satisfied readers vote for library issues which are essential to the funding of the organization. Demographic studies of library users confirm that "power users" are often readers, and thus administrative support for readers' advisory service makes sense.

RA's Place in the Organization

While some libraries have instituted separate readers' advisory or reader services departments, most expect their reference librarians to also be readers' advisors. This makes sense on several levels. Youth services librarians are expected to be able to serve children's reference needs as well as offer advice in their search for pleasure reading, so this should not be too much to expect from adult services librarians. In this age of budget cuts, the trend is toward fewer service desks rather than more, so it is also likely less expensive to fold readers' advisory service into general reference services.

Another issue is illustrated by the history of RA services. As budgets became tight during and after the Great Depression, early separate readers' advisory departments were closed and had largely died out by the 1940s, so it is not always a good thing to have a separate department which may be seen as a target for budget cuts.

On the other hand, there can be distinct advantages in having a separate reader services department. For instance, it may be easier to recruit staff members who are interested in either reference or readers' advisory service, than it is to find good staff members who can do both kinds of work well.

How RA Service Differs from Reference Service

The reference interview is primarily about thoroughly understanding the informational need of the patron in order to fully answer a question. The readers' advisory interview is more like a conversation, and far less concrete in its goals. While reference questions can occasionally be entertaining, most of the time they are not about recreation. On the other hand, readers' advisory service is usually about reading for pleasure—entertainment, in other words. Both reference and readers' advisory service require the use of good people skills in order to discern the needs and preferences of the patron; readers' advisory service also includes what might be called indirect services, such as the creation of booklists and displays, annotating or reviewing particular titles, leading book discussions, and creating an ambiance attractive to readers.

Current practitioners must provide readers' advisory service while constantly keeping in mind and working to overcome the prejudices of the past—that nonfiction and informational queries are more important than providing entertainment. Readers, too, have dealt with a lifetime of negative messages about reading, and such phrases heard in childhood as "get your nose out of that book," or "why don't you go outside and play," translate into adult messages like "I know I read too much." Research shows, however, that avid readers are actually *more* involved in their communities than those who don't read (Gioia, 2007: 18–19).

These negative points of view can result in the reluctance of readers to ask for help in finding a good book to read. This reluctance may be reinforced by signs that say "Reference," or "Information Desk," implying that only informational queries are appropriate. Even with appropriate signage, readers often feel that asking for help in finding pleasure reading is interrupting the librarian's more important work. Because of this, the readers' advisory librarian must often roam the stacks and ask browsers if they're finding what they need.

Generally speaking, training in readers' advisory service (though it is usually not called RA) is better for youth services librarians, who usually take literature-based programs in library school. But it is important to remember that reference librarians may also often be called upon to help young people find particular types of books assigned by their teachers, so though readers' advisory service is usually identified as being for adult or, at most, young adult readers, librarians should be able to serve children as well.

Another way that RA service interfaces with reference service is that many readers attain cognitive knowledge while reading for pleasure. Catherine Ross's (1999) research with readers along with Kuhlthau's research on the information search process (Kuhlthau, 2004; Kuhlthau, Heinström, and Todd, 2008) show that information seeking has both cognitive and affective components. Not surprisingly, the affective dimension is particularly important for pleasure readers, even though they appreciate the information delivered in their pleasure reading.

A dimension of reading that deserves more research is the risk-taking aspect. Ross's (2006) research shows that the willingness to take on challenging reading decreases based on the level of stress in the reader's life. When the stress level is very high, readers tend to choose unchallenging and familiar reading, even rereading old favorites. This tendency may be generalizable to goal-directed information seeking as well, but more research in this area is needed. In any case, librarians should remember that both information and entertainment are involved in reading for pleasure, with some readers directly expressing their desire to learn while reading for pleasure.

Research on Readers and Reading

Much of the research on reading has been done outside the library community. Library researchers have done very little research on reading for pleasure, and wide-ranging opportunities for researchers exist, though some notable research has been done. Probably the most important research was done by Catherine Ross and reported in her book *Reading Matters* (Ross, 2006) and in her many journal articles. Ross chose passionately avid readers as the focus for her research, hoping to find patterns in their reading experiences that might be used to help less successful readers. She found that avid readers did indeed have some common experiences, including the fact that most read series books avidly as children.

Jessica Moyer (2004) hypothesizes that reading a book can have both educational and recreational outcomes. In her research, she used factor analysis of interview data to show outcomes in four categories. Readers used recreational reading to learn about people and relationships, and other countries, cultures, and time periods. They also used reading to enrich their lives and view the world from different perspectives. Moyer's research seems to point to a false dichotomy between information and entertainment.

Nuts and Bolts—The Readers' Advisory Interview

Leaders in the field of readers' advisory service would say that, while the key to good reference service is the reference interview, the key to good readers' advisory service is the readers' advisory conversation. Joyce Saricks, in the second edition of *Readers' Advisory Service in the Public Library* (Saricks and Brown, 1997), framed the standard conversational opener when a reader wants help finding pleasure reading. She says, "Tell me about a book you have enjoyed." This is the beginning of a conversation that the skillful readers' advisor will steer, in order to discern the "appeal factors" the reader likes.

Catherine Ross and Mary K. Chelton (2001) would add a further question: "Are you in the mood for something similar to that book, or something different?" The basic idea is to use the RA conversation to discern the patron's reading tastes, and in the librarian's knowledge of the literature, to match the reader's moods and tastes with a book that fits those tastes and moods. The readers' advisory librarian needs to develop a good, professional knowledge of books, and the listening and conversational skills to discern the reader's tastes. This is the fundamental concept of the service. Of course, there are many nuances, tips, and tricks that will help improve those skills.

Appeal factors as Saricks (2005) defines them do not mean genre, theme, or topic—though these things are very important to many readers. She defines appeal factors as those features that make up the "feel" of the book—those elements of the work to which the reader relates, such as pacing, characterization, story line, language, and frame—the background of the book, such as the setting, the atmosphere, and the tone. For example, we may say that a book is a quick-paced page-turner, or that it has beautiful evocative language, that it made us feel that we were right there with the character experiencing the story, or that there was a brooding atmosphere over the entire work. There is currently no easy way to get at these kinds of features through subject headings or themes of the book, or even a plot summary. If, for example, a reader says she loved Kathryn Stockett's *The Help*, we can look in the catalog and find the following subject headings:

Civil Rights movements—Fiction
African American women—Fiction
Housekeepers—Mississippi—Fiction
Jackson (Miss.)—Fiction
Mississippi—Fiction

Searching for other books with the same five subject headings leads us to John Grisham's *The Chamber*, *Beloved* by Toni Morrison, a Harlequin novel called *The Tempted* by Amanda Stevens, *Club Dead* by Charlaine Harris, and *As I Lay Dying* by William Faulkner. None of these are good matches for *The Help*.

Saricks (2009) further developed the idea of appeal in her book *The Readers' Advisory Guide to Genre Fiction*. In this book, she arranges genres by appeal. She groups Adventure, Romantic Suspense, Suspense, and Thrillers as Adrenaline reads. Emotions genres include Gentle Reads, Horror, Romance, and Women's Lives and Relationships. As Intellect genres, she lists Science Fiction, Mysteries, Psychological Suspense, and Literary Fiction. In Landscape genres, she includes Westerns, Historical Fiction, and Fantasy. Saricks sees an advantage to arranging genres in this way—providing a broader perspective and not limiting suggestions to one genre.

Still, genre can be very helpful in suggesting titles—especially if it is expanded into subgenres. Some of the most helpful books in the field, the titles in the *Genreflecting* series by Libraries Unlimited, use this approach. Research by Ross (2006) showed that the most often used approach by readers in finding a new book is to first read all the titles by an author whose book they enjoyed. Once they have exhausted the author's output, however, the second thing they do is to look for other books in the same genre. This does not always work well, however, since someone who likes hardboiled, violent, even bloody, mystery novels may not necessarily enjoy a prim, nonviolent cozy mystery set in a slow-paced English village. The *Genreflecting* series addresses this by organizing titles by genre and subgenre, thus listing titles with a similar approach to genre next to each other in this book series.

How do appeal factors and mood affect the outcome? Ross (2006) describes mood preferences along a sliding scale between two opposites: familiarity versus novelty; safety versus risk; easy versus challenging; positive and upbeat versus cynical or ironic; reassuring versus frightening or amazing or stimulating; and confirming values or beliefs versus challenging values or beliefs. Of course, the mood of a person varies from time to time. She found that mood seems to be more important when reading fiction, than when reading nonfiction, for pleasure. This means that after discussing with readers the kinds of books they enjoy, it is important for the librarian to ask whether a patron is in the mood for something similar, or something different.

Another aspect in matching books with readers, and readers with books, could be called "rejection factors." Usually, a person who has strong preferences about what they do not like in books will offer that information without being asked. But the librarian should not be surprised to hear that the reader wants a book with no violence, or no sex, or no bad language, or not set in World War II, or any other factor that they wish to avoid.

Another difference between the RA encounter and the reference interview is that in the reference arena, the librarian can find materials and sources, and then ask the patron whether his or her question has been fully answered. In the readers' advisory conversation, there is no immediate way to assess the suggestions until the reader has actually read the selections. Thus, the best way to end an RA transaction is to invite the reader to come back and let the librarian know how he or she liked the selections.

Common Queries and Unasked Questions

If the reader asks for help, the question is often phrased something like this: "Can you help me find a good book to read?" This raises the question, "What is a good book?" Readers do not usually mean a high-quality, award-winning classic when they talk about a good book. Instead, they mean a book that they will enjoy reading. It is important not to place value judgments on categories or genres of books...or on readers for that matter.

Another common question is asked by readers who have found a favorite author, but have read all of that author's books. They need help in locating other authors whose works might interest them. This question can be answered by thinking of "read-alike" authors—other authors who write similar books with the same feel as the first author. With this kind of question, it is tempting to use electronic tools such as *NoveList*, *Reader's Advisor Online*, *Fiction/Non-Fiction Connection*, *Books and Authors*, or even Google, to find read-alikes for the author or title mentioned. But this is a superficial response. Preferably, the librarian will dig deeper and find out what it is about the favorite author or title that the reader likes before assuming that he or she is looking for something in the same genre. That said, read-alike lists are incredibly helpful in answering this kind of question, especially if they give details about the read-alikes. One way to locate materials if the library does not have access to fee-based electronic RA tools, is to use a search engine to look for "if you like" or "read-alike" along with the name of the author or title in question, but also add the word "library" to the search so that the lists found will most likely have been created by a library, and therefore will be of good quality.

A more common experience is that many readers, if not most, never ask for help at all. This may be because the negative comments they've heard all their lives about reading for pleasure lead them to believe it is not important and surely does not deserve the time of a librarian. Many patrons believe that the library is like a grocery store, in that they are supposed to be able to help themselves. If they do ask for help, they will often begin by saying, "I'm sorry to bother you, but..." The librarian should reassure readers that helping them find a good book is absolutely part of their job, and even their favorite part of the job. Getting over the feeling that the question isn't worthy is imperative if patrons are going to relax and discuss what kinds of books they like to read.

Because this hesitation is so widespread, the librarian should make a real effort not to appear busy when in the public area, as reading reviews, working on the computer, or talking to another staff member will most likely mean the RA patron will decide not to "interrupt." Even this is not enough, though, and another way to overcome this hesitancy is to roam the stacks and ask readers if they need help. Almost always they will say that they do not, but if the librarian then says, be sure to let me know if you need help, this same patron will often come back in a few minutes with "one thing" they thought of that they might need. Even this approach should be undertaken delicately, as when patrons believe they are supposed to help themselves, they may be overly sensitive toward anything that makes them admit they are feeling inadequate. Experienced RA librarians often pretend to be straightening shelves near the browser while they casually inquire, "Are you finding what you need?" This approach has the advantage of removing the barrier of "interrupting" the real work of the librarian and phrasing the question in a way that takes away the stigma of needing help.

The RA Conversation

As mentioned earlier, Saricks (2005), in *Readers' Advisory Service in the Public Library,* suggests that the librarian begin the RA interview by asking the person to tell about a book that he or she has recently read and enjoyed. In her book, she says that the "interview" is more like a conversation. In a later article (2007), she advocates actually changing the terminology to call the transaction the "readers' advisory conversation." One important reason she cites is that a conversation is informal, while an interview implies a formal transaction. Thinking of this contact with a patron as informal may take away some of the pressure that makes many librarians think of the RA question as the scariest reference question there is.

Informality leads to more listening, and give-and-take, allowing for a better transaction, and it encourages the reader to come back for another conversation.

Neal Wyatt, who writes a series of articles called "Redefining RA" in *Library Journal*, agrees. In one of these articles (Wyatt, 2008), she also uses the term "conversation" rather than "interview" for the RA transaction. Wyatt says that "trying to write down the steps of the RA conversation is like trying to write down the moves of the tango" (p. 33). So how should we approach the transaction?

First is preparation. Learn about books and their appeal factors. Remember that the conversation is meant to discern the *reader's* taste. It is not about what the librarian enjoys reading. Try to keep the conversation going by asking open-ended questions rather than questions that can be answered by "yes" or "no." Remember to be respectful and friendly, and to use active listening techniques. Never disparage a reader's taste and be careful not to inadvertently show distaste through body language. Invite the reader back. Don't be afraid to ask for help from colleagues. If a colleague is an expert in mysteries and you have a mystery fan asking for help, there is nothing wrong with telling the patron that you have the perfect compatriot to help. Use readers' advisory tools to help answer the question. If you share your search methods with readers, they will usually be appreciative as most readers are very interested in improving their own selection techniques.

Here are some examples of helpful questions that can be used during the RA conversation:

- Are you looking for something that will keep you turning the pages quickly, or a slower-paced book that you can "live in" for awhile?
- Are there any particular genres or subjects you like or dislike?
- Do you like or dislike books set in a particular time period?
- Can you tell me some of your other favorite authors?

If the reader draws a blank, it sometimes helps to ask for favorite movie titles or to pull some "Best Bets" from the shelf—titles that have been favorably reviewed or singled out as "good reads" by staff members or patrons. For sample questions and detailed approaches to the RA conversation genre by genre, see *The Readers' Advisory Guide to Genre Fiction* by Joyce Saricks (2009).

Common Mistakes and Best Practices

Poor communication and inadequate people skills can result in many mistakes in readers' advisory transactions. It is important to use RA tools but not at the expense of making a real connection with the reader. One common mistake that illustrates this is when a reader asks for help and the librarian immediately turns to the OPAC and begins typing, instead of beginning the conversation. A classic article by Anne May, Elizabeth Olesh, Anne Weinlich Miltenberg, and Catherine Patricia Lackne (2000), reporting on the results of a "secret shopper" exercise conducted in fifty-four libraries by library school students, illustrates some other common mistakes made by librarians, including using body language that conveyed irritation, or saying that helping to find a good book was "a tall order."

One librarian said, "You know this is the query the reference desk dreads," and another said, "I hate this question."

Some other practices to avoid are forgetting to use tools, not conducting an RA interview, showing condescension, recommending whatever book the librarian is currently reading, suggesting one title instead of a range of titles, sending a patron to a genre area to browse alone or simply referring him or her to the OPAC, being unwelcoming, invading the patron's privacy, or just plain panicking. Just as a reference librarian would never tell a customer that he or she can't help the patron find sources on a particular subject because the librarian is unfamiliar with that subject, a readers' advisor should not hesitate to suggest a book just because he or she hasn't read it personally, and the RA advisor certainly should not refuse to help.

A list of best practices may be helpful, in addition to these common mistakes that should be avoided. It is important to prepare by reading widely, keeping a reading log, looking at new books (and noting their appeal factors), restocking themed book displays, taking advantage of training opportunities, and talking about books with other staff members. It is helpful at the beginning of the shift to go through stacks and jot down five or six good titles that are on the shelf and available today.

Preparation is important, but it is also important to be approachable and friendly, walk the stacks and offer to help browsers, listen actively, use RA tools, conduct a good RA interview, and offer a range of three to six choices with reasons why you chose these books. The patron may then want to take a few moments to look at jacket copy or dip into the book to see if it appeals to him or her. Check back to see if the patron is satisfied and remember to invite him or her back to discuss the choices.

Key Works and Tools for Readers' Advisory

The Ideal Tool

The ideal tool for readers' advisors does not yet exist, though tools have greatly improved in the past few years. An ideal tool would have to be electronic in order to include all the necessary elements, and its titles should be linked to the library's catalog. It would have multiple access points, including access by genre, historical time period, setting, award categories, gender, and occupation of the protagonist. Reading level and interest level should be included, and the tool should be kept very current. The tool should cover both fiction and nonfiction and include plot summaries and reviews.

Currently existing subscription databases offer many of these elements, but the ideal tool would also include appeal factors such as pacing (page-turner or leisurely read), characterization (complex characters, several main characters whose stories intertwine, etc.), and story line. It should suggest read-alikes and ancillary reading, including reasons for the suggestions, and should be maintained by experts in the field. The tool should include series and sequels information, with lists of series in the order in which they should be read. It should allow the librarian or end user to suggest read-alikes or additional tags, and it should allow the user to mark titles to be saved to a list to be e-mailed or printed.

Neal Wyatt (2009) suggests that the ideal tool should use appeal tags and an algorithm, in order to operate in a similar way to Pandora, which suggests songs to listeners, and gets better as the listener approves or disapproves of selections. Online movie and music recommenders often also use collaborative filtering to improve the selection. Collaborative filtering assumes that if one person likes a certain list of titles, and another does as well, that they will most likely enjoy all the titles on each other's lists.

Top Tools

Tools for the RA librarian or reader now number in the hundreds, if not thousands. Tools should be evaluated based upon their content, scope, purpose, currency, format, and originator. Some of the most useful tools are listed in this section of the chapter. However, it is important to remember that there are also many useful tools that help with very specific kinds of searches. Expert readers' advisors keep many tools at their fingertips, to be used when the question warrants a precise approach. Examples of some of these kinds of tools include guides to the pronunciation of authors' names (http://www.teachingbooks.net/pronunciations.cgi/), sequels listed in order (http://www.fantasticfiction.co.uk/), the best reviewed new books (http://www.overbooked.org/stars), or books that have been made into movies (http://www.wordandfilm.com/). For this author's RA bookmarks, see Cindy Orr's RA Bookmarks at IKeepbookmarks (http://ww2.ikeepbookmarks.com/browse.asp?folder=1393282).

Many readers' advisory questions fall into a few categories, and certain tools are best in these different areas, but several commercial products can help with many requests, such as these comprehensive electronic tools:

- Bowker's *Fiction/Non-Fiction Connection* (http://www.fictionconnection.com/) (subscription). Bowker's database uses the Aquabrowser interface with high-lighted keywords under the categories of topic, genre, setting, character, location, and timeframe, to allow for a highly visual interface. Users can also enter a title they have enjoyed and obtain read-alikes.
- Gale's *Books and Authors* (http://www.gale.cengage.com/booksandauthors/) (subscription) and the *What Do I Read Next* series (print). Gale's *What Do I Read Next* print series adds a new volume each year with information and read-alikes for books published during that year. The content is very good, though the books are expensive.

    Books and Authors is a fairly new database built to encourage the creation of a community of readers. The interface is customizable and allows readers to create their own personal space called My Reading Room. Users can browse by genre, and by Who, What, Where, When.
- EBSCO's *NoveList* (http://www.ebscohost.com/public/novelist) (subscription). *NoveList* is the most comprehensive RA database available. With over 150,000 fiction titles, over 60,000 juvenile titles, and an optional nonfiction module, its

coverage is impressive. Approximately 20,000 new titles are added per year. This tool offers links to the library catalog, extensive training materials, read-alikes, and searchable reviews, which allows for a powerful retrieval system since often appeal factors are mentioned by reviewers. It includes Lexile scores, award winners, book discussion guides, and much more.

- *FictionDB* (http://www.fictiondb.com/) (free version, but subscription has advertising-free advanced search). *FictionDB* is a comprehensive database with over 250,000 titles and complete bibliographies for over 50,000 authors. It lists series, including Harlequin series, new releases by month for the next year, pseudonyms, and links to ratings and reviews. It allows readers to keep track of what they've read. The advanced search, available only with a subscription, offers the ability to search by genre and subgenre, keywords, time period, and reader rating. While it lists many titles, it has no other readers' advisory materials.

- Libraries Unlimited's *Reader's Advisor Online* (http://www.readersadvisor online.com/lu/RAlogin) (free) and the *Genreflecting* series (print). The *Genreflecting* series is one of the most useful RA tools for librarians. Each book, such as *Make Mine a Mystery*, outlines a particular genre with its sub-genres and lists important titles in each category, so that the librarian or reader can get an overall map of each genre, a description of the characteristics of the subgenres, and find specific titles that fit each of these areas. The overview volume by Diana Tixier Herald (2005) is called *Genreflecting*, and is a standard in the field that has gone through several editions. A new edition is forthcoming in 2012 or 2013.

  The *Reader's Advisor Online* site contains content from the over thirty reference books in the *Genreflecting* series and adds the ability to search by appeal factors, themes, and topics. It also allows browsing by genre and subgenre. It has, unfortunately, not been updated recently. The site is supplemented by the *Reader's Advisor Online Blog* (http://www.readersadvisoronline.com/blog), edited by Cindy Orr. The blog's Monday morning update lists books to be published in the next week, titles new to the bestseller lists, and links to RA news of the week. Libraries Unlimited also publishes an irregular online newsletter called *Readers' Advisor News* (http://www.readersadvisoronline .com/ranews).

- *Which Book?* (http://www.whichbook.net/) (free). This is a refreshingly different experiment on how to choose a book. It's a British site, so titles are skewed toward that direction of the world. Choose from twelve "pull sliders" that allow the user to make choices of content, for example, between happy and sad or funny and serious, and see what books turn up. Choose from various ranges of descriptions of plots, settings, or characters as well.

Other top tools have their niches and can be very helpful in answering common questions:

- *Adult Reading Round Table* (http://www.arrtreads.org/). This is a group of Chicago area readers' advisory librarians who have met regularly for years to work on creating RA training workshops, booklists, and genre studies. They publish a newsletter and lists of resources for the field. Especially useful are their published studies of several genres and their workshop tools, which they offer on their website for free.

- *AudioFile Plus* (http://www.audiofilemagazine.com/audiofileplus.html) (subscription). Many readers enjoy audiobooks just as well as print or electronic reading. *AudioFile* gives access not only to industry news, but over 17,000 reviews.
- *Fiction_L* (http://www.webrary.org/rs/flmenu.html) (free). *Fiction_L* is a discussion group of readers' advisors sponsored by the Morton Grove Public Library in Morton Grove, Illinois. This is an essential site for keeping up with what's happening in the RA world, but it is also a useful tool in itself, especially for indirect readers' advisory services such as making displays and booklists. As mentioned earlier, when stumped by a question, it is perfectly fine to ask for help from a colleague. Posting that stumper on *Fiction_L* is like having 3,000 colleagues to help, and usually the answer comes back within minutes.
- *The Readers' Advisory Guide to Genre Fiction* by Joyce Saricks (2009) is a guide to doing readers' advisory work genre by genre, with detailed tips on the RA interview within each genre. She lists key authors and titles within each genre and includes read-alikes in other genres as well.

Indirect RA

While helping readers find books is important work, it is also true that most readers enjoy browsing for themselves, and libraries can enhance their browsing experience by paying attention to the ambiance of their buildings. If at all possible, the surroundings should be comfortable, pleasant, calm, and attractive. The key is to look at the space from the point of view of a reader, not a librarian.

To enhance the browsing experience, librarians should adopt the best practices from bookstores, including pulling books into themed displays and shelving titles face out whenever possible. Patrons will also appreciate bookmark-sized booklists and attractive merchandising. Placing readers' advisory tools where they are easily accessible to both librarians and patrons is especially useful. Placing magazines such as *Bookmarks*, *Romantic Times*, *Locus*, or *Mystery Scene* near the browsing area makes them accessible to readers who may not be aware that the library has them.

Librarians can emphasize the importance of reading by reviewing books on their website or Facebook page, providing e-mail newsletters about books, bringing in authors to speak, sponsoring book discussion groups, and providing sets of good, discussable titles for reading groups that meet in private homes.

Keeping Current

Learning readers' advisory techniques, practicing them, attending training, and reading widely, will improve the skills of readers' advisors, but the landscape changes quickly, so it is important to keep up with the field. Adopting just a few routines will allow the readers' advisor to keep current.

The wealth of information on the Internet makes it astoundingly easier to keep up now than it was just a decade ago. At the same time, readers have access to those same sources, so it is important for librarians to keep pace with newer technologies and resources. One technique is to use blogs and discussion groups. *Fiction_L*, as mentioned earlier, is essential. In addition, the *Reader's Advisor Online Blog*'s Monday edition each week lists books new to the bestseller lists, titles to be published in the next seven days, and links to relevant news articles. Another resource is *Early Word* (http://www.earlyword.com/), a site for collection development librarians that offers news of upcoming titles, information on what's hot in libraries, and industry news. *Publishers Lunch* (http://www.publishers marketplace.com/lunch/free) and *PW Daily* (http://www.publishersweekly .com/pw/email-subscriptions/index.html) offer daily newsletters for the publishing industry, and *Shelf Awareness* (http://www.shelf-awareness.com/) is a useful daily newsletter for booksellers. All of them are relevant to readers' advisors as well.

Book blogs are another source of current information. A few of the best include *Omnivoracious* by Amazon (http://www.omnivoracious.com/), *Citizen Reader* (http://www.citizenreader.com/) by Sarah Statz Cords, which covers nonfiction, *Jacket Copy* by the *Los Angeles Times*, *RA for All* (http://raforall.blogspot .com/) by Becky Spratford, and *Reading the Past* (http://readingthepast .blogspot.com/) by Sarah Johnson, which discusses historical fiction. *Smart Bitches, Trashy Books* (http://smartbitchestrashybooks.com/) is an irreverent and fun look at romance novels, and *Shelf Renewal* (http://shelfrenewal.booklist .com/) by Rebecca Vnuk and Karen Kleckner looks at good books from the backlist, while *Library Journal's LJ Prepub Alerts* (http://www.libraryjournal.com/csp/ cms/sites/LJ/CollectionDevelopment/PrepubAlerts/index.csp) by Barbara Hoffert highlights new books to be published months in advance. The best-known readers' advisory librarian is Nancy Pearl, and her website (http:// www.nancypearl.com/) is a wonderful source for readers' advisors.

Readers' advisors should be aware of new books on the subject of RA, and watch for current articles in *Library Journal, Public Libraries, Reference and User Services Quarterly* (*RUSQ*), and other library-related journals. Discussing books in staff meetings with colleagues, even for a minute or two, will greatly increase each person's knowledge of titles. Attending workshops and conferences on the local, state, and national level is another way to keep up, but to take it a step further, readers' advisors should get involved themselves. Many of the nationally known readers' advisors are now in their sixties or older, and there is a great need for involvement from younger librarians. The American Library Association and the Public Library Association both have readers' advisory committees which need volunteer members, and the programs for both of their conferences are submitted as proposals by members. Local organizations are always looking for presenters as well, so there is plenty of room for new faces and voices.

Research on readers' advisory services and reading is inadequate, so conducting even a simple research study could mean publication in *RUSQ, Public Libraries*, or other library journals. Many librarians choose a niche that they are passionate about and work to make themselves experts in those areas. Libraries

Unlimited and the American Library Association, as well as other publishers, are open to book proposals on readers' advisory service or one of its aspects.

Conclusion

Readers' advisory service is an important part of reference service; it deserves attention, training, and commitment. Though some people seem to have a knack for suggesting books, there are definitely skills that can be taught and learned. Not enough has been done to increase the level of expertise in readers' advisory service in libraries, and there is much still to be done. There is a great opportunity for new readers' advisors to develop their own expertise and reputations. This is important work. Pass it on.

Recommendations for Further Reading

Baker, Sharon L. 2002. *The Responsive Public Library Collection: How to Develop and Market a Winning Collection.* 2nd ed. Westport, CT: Libraries Unlimited. Baker uses strategic planning methods to anticipate and respond to collection-related needs of patrons of the library. This thorough and outstanding work contains many useful sections for RA librarians, citing the research that has been done on such things as displays, separating genres, using circulation statistics to improve the collection, and much more.

Balcom, Ted., ed. 1997. *Serving Readers.* Fort Atkinson, WI: Highsmith. This is a practical handbook for readers' advisors. Each article by different authors covers an essential topic in the field, from genre studies to services to special groups.

Beard, David, and Kate Vo Thi-Beard. 2008. "Rethinking the Book: New Theories for Readers' Advisory." *Reference and User Services Quarterly* 47, no. 4 (Summer): 331–335. The authors argue for a closer relationship between the research done on reading and readers' advisory service. They believe that focusing on the book rather than the reader is a mistake.

Chelton, M. K. 2003. "Readers' Advisory 101." *Library Journal* 128, no. 18: 38–39. Chelton, a library school professor, has sent her students on secret shopper expeditions to public libraries to ask RA questions. In this article, she lists the common mistakes and the best practices they discovered in their fieldwork.

Langemack, Chapple. 2003. *The Booktalker's Bible: How to Talk about the Books You Love to Any Audience.* Westport, CT: Libraries Unlimited. This book covers all you need to know about telling people about books, whether it be through a formal program or in an informal conversation.

Leigh, Robert Devore. 1950. *The Public Library in the United States: The General Report of the Public Library Inquiry.* New York: Columbia University Press. Following World War II, the American Library Association commissioned a group of social scientists to study the public library in America. This is the final report on that research.

McCook, Kathleen de la Peña, and Gary O. Rolstad, eds. 1993. *Developing Readers' Advisory Services: Concepts and Commitments.* New York: Neal-Schuman. Chapters by several different authors discuss how to implement a strong readers' advisory service program.

Moyer, Jessica E. 2005. "Adult Fiction Reading: A Literature Review of Readers' Advisory Services, Adult Fiction Librarianship, and Fiction Readers." *Reference and User Services Quarterly* 44, no. 3 (Spring): 220–231. This review of the published literature from 1995 to 2003 shows that not enough RA research is being done in the field.

Moyer, Jessica E. 2007. "Learning from Leisure Reading: A Study of Adult Public Library Patrons." *Reference and User Services Quarterly* 46, no. 4 (Summer 2007): 66–79. A research project based on surveys completed by public library patrons yields interesting results on their views about reading, preferences in genre, and more.

Moyer, Jessica E. 2008. *Research-Based Readers' Advisory*. Chicago: ALA. In each chapter, a review of research done in a particular topic pertinent to readers' advisory work, is followed by a reaction to that research from a practitioner in the field.

Nell, Victor. 1998. *Lost in a Book: The Psychology of Reading for Pleasure*. New Haven, CT: Yale University Press. In this book, a psychologist discusses how and why people read for pleasure. He combines his own research with the work of others in a book that a layperson can enjoy as well.

Pearl, Nancy. 2003 and 2005. *Book Lust: Recommended Reading for Every Mood, Moment and Reason*. Seattle, WA: Sasquatch Books. Pearl, in her *Book Lust* series, lists only books that she has identified as "good reads" into various categories so that readers have a catalog of choices from which to choose.

"Recommended Readers' Advisory Tools." 2004. *Reference and User Services Quarterly* 43, no. 4 (Summer): 294–305. *RUSQ* is published by the American Library Association. This article is a compilation of tools nominated by well-known readers' advisors.

Saricks, Joyce G. 2007. "Whole-Library Readers' Advisory." *Booklist* 104, no. 1 (September 1): 51. Saricks argues that libraries should work to create an environment where all library staff members from the janitor on up are comfortable talking about books.

Saricks, Joyce G. 2008. "Readers' Advisory—Flash in the Pan or Here to Stay?" *Booklist* 104, no. 21 (July): 12. RA service has risen to the fore, gone dormant, and been revived again. Saricks believes it is now here to stay.

Shearer, Kenneth D., ed. 1996. *Guiding the Reader to the Next Book*. New York: Neal-Schuman. Shearer gathered several leading names in the RA field to write chapters on various aspects of RA service.

Shearer, Kenneth D., and Robert Burgin, eds. 2001. *The Readers' Advisor's Companion*. Englewood, CO: Libraries Unlimited. This book expands the coverage of Shearer's earlier work (see previous entry). Sixteen chapters cover such subjects as serving young adults, challenges, the future of the field, and best practices.

Smith, Duncan, and Mary K. Chelton. 2000. "Talking with Readers: A Competency Based Approach to Readers' Advisory Service." *Reference and User Services Quarterly* 40, no. 2 (Winter): 135–142. This article discusses different training methods for RA service and argues for competency-based evaluations.

Stover, Kaite Mediatore. 2005. "Working without a Net: Readers' Advisory in the Small Public Library." *Reference and User Services Quarterly* 45, no. 2 (Winter): 122–125. Stover, a practicing readers' advisory librarian, discusses cost-saving ways to provide training and RA service in a small library.

Stover, Kaite Mediatore. 2009. "Stalking the Wild Appeal Factor." *Reference and User Services Quarterly* 48, no. 3 (Spring): 239–242. With the rise in popularity of social media, it's natural to ask how these services can be used by RA librarians. Stover discusses the best-known resources and how libraries can use them.

Trott, Barry. 2005. "Advising Readers Online: A Look at Internet Based Reading Recommendation Services." *Reference and User Services Quarterly* 44, no. 3 (Summer): 210–215. Trott discusses how libraries can offer online RA services.

Trott, Barry. 2008. "Building on a Firm Foundation: Readers' Advisory over the Next 25 Years." *Reference and User Services Quarterly* 48, no. 2 (Winter): 132–135. In this article, Trott describes the RA field and where he thinks it will be in the future.

Watson, Dana, and RUSA CODES RA Committee. 2000. "Time to Turn the Page: Library Education for Readers' Advisory Services." *Reference and User Services Quarterly* 40, no. 2 (Winter): 143–144. The authors argue that since RA service is growing in importance in public libraries, library schools should be more invested in teaching the subject. Their survey showed that only fourteen of fifty-six library schools said they offered courses in RA.

Wyatt, Neal. 2006. "Reading Maps Remake RA: Re-create a Book's Entire Universe Online and Transform Readers' Advisory." *Library Journal* 131, no. 18 (November 1): 38–42. This discussion of how to make a "reading map" for a particular book explains how to map out related works in any format that might lead to further exploration by the reader.

Wyatt, Neal. 2007. "An RA Big Think." *Library Journal* 132, no. 12 (July 1): 40–43. Wyatt introduces the idea of polling several leaders in the field of RA to get their ideas on the topic.

Wyatt, Neal. 2010. "LJ Series: 'Redefining Readers' Advisory': Kissing Cousins." *Library Journal*, 135, no. 11 (June 15): 28–32. Wyatt, a well-known writer on RA service, discusses why reference and RA go hand in hand.

Bibliography and Works Cited

Crowley, Bill. 2005. "Rediscovering the History of Readers Advisory Service." *Public Libraries* 44, no. 1 (January/February): 37–41.

Gioia, Dan. 2007. *To Read or Not to Read: A Question of National Consequence.* National Endowment for the Arts. http://www.nea.gov/research/ToRead.pdf.

Herald, Diana Tixier. 2005. *Genreflecting: A Guide to Popular Reading Interests.* Edited by Wayne A. Wiegand. 6th ed. Englewood, CO: Libraries Unlimited.

Kuhlthau, Carol Collier. 2004. *Seeking Meaning: A Process Approach to Library and Information Services.* 2nd ed. Westport, CT: Libraries Unlimited.

Kuhlthau, Carol C., Jannica Heinström, and Ross J. Todd. 2008. "'The Information Search Process' Revisited: Is the Model Still Useful?" *Information Research* 13, no. 4 (December): paper 355. http://InformationR.net/ir/13-4/paper355.html.

May, Anne K., Elizabeth Olesh, Anne Weinlich Miltenberg, and Catherine Patricia Lackne. 2000. "A Look at Reader's Advisory Services." *Library Journal* 125, no. 15 (September 15): 40–43.

Moyer, Jessica E. 2004. "Learning from Leisure Reading: Educational and Recreational Outcomes of Leisure Reading—A Study of Adult Public Library Patrons" (Certificate of Advanced Study Project Report). Urbana-Champaign, IL: University of Illinois, September 21.

Orr, Cindy. 2009. "Dynamics of Reader's Advisory Education: How Far Can We Go?" *Readers' Advisor News.* September. http://www.readersadvisoronline.com/ranews/sep2009/orr.html.

Rosenberg, Betty. 1982. *Genreflecting: A Guide to Reading Interests in Genre Fiction.* Littleton, CO: Libraries Unlimited.

Ross, Catherine Sheldrick. 1999. "Finding without Seeking: The Information Encounter in the Context of Reading for Pleasure." *Information Processing and Management* 35, no. 6 (November): 783–799.

———. 2006. *Reading Matters: What the Research Reveals about Reading, Libraries, and Community.* Westport, CN: Libraries Unlimited.

Ross, Catherine Sheldrick, and Mary K. Chelton. 2001. "Reader's Advisory: Matching Mood and Material." *Library Journal* 126, no. 2 (February 1): 52–56.

Saricks, Joyce G. 2005. *Readers' Advisory Service in the Public Library*. 3rd ed. Chicago: American Library Association.

———. 2007. "At Leisure with Joyce Saricks: Rethinking the Readers'-Advisory Interview." *Booklist* 103, no. 15 (April 1): 24.

———. 2009. *The Readers' Advisory Guide to Genre Fiction*. Chicago: American Library Association.

Saricks, Joyce G., and Nancy Brown. 1989. *Readers' Advisory Service in the Public Library*. Chicago: American Library Association.

———. 1997. *Readers' Advisory Service in the Public Library*. 2nd ed. Chicago: American Library Association.

Smith, Aaron. 2011. "Americans and Their Cell Phones." Pew Internet and American Life Report. August 15. http://pewinternet.org/Reports/2011/Cell-Phones.aspx.

"Survey: New U.S. Smartphone Growth by Age and Income." 2012. *NielsenWire* (blog), February 20. http://blog.nielsen.com/nielsenwire/online_mobile/survey-new-u-s-smartphone-growth-by-age-and-income/.

Trott, Barry, and Connie Van Fleet. 2008. "Education for Readers' Advisory Service in Library and Information Science Programs." *Reference and User Services Quarterly* 47, no. 3: 224–229.

Wyatt, Neal. 2008. "*LJ* Series: 'Redefining Readers' Advisory': The Conversation 101." *Library Journal* 133, no. 3 (February 15): 33–34.

Wyatt, Neal. 2009. "*LJ* Series: 'Redefining Readers' Advisory': The Ideal Tool." *Library Journal* 134, no. 17 (October 15): 39–43.

15

Reference Sources and Services for Children and Young Adults

Meghan Harper

Introduction

Most public libraries provide specific physical and virtual spaces for collections of reference resources, and design and implement reference services to meet the informational needs of their younger patrons. The reference librarian's skills and knowledge of developmental levels of children and an awareness of characteristics of children are at the heart of efficiently and effectively serving these future supporters and advocates of libraries. Reference librarians must be concerned with what types of resources are provided and how these resources are made accessible and ultimately used by the library's youngest patrons. The development of policies and procedures that guide the compilation of resources and facilitate the acquisition and accessibility of both print and virtual resources should be based on a sound foundation of best practices for serving children in libraries. The provision of resources and services to youth has not been diminished by technological innovation: rather, the importance of providing high-quality resources and instruction in accessing and evaluating authoritative informational resources has increased. The availability of information in a variety of formats can result in "information overload" or, worse, complacency—a settling for the information that is readily accessed, but not necessarily authoritative or designed to meet the specific developmental needs of the child (Brandel, 2008). From traditional print to the latest electronic format, connecting children with high-quality resources is not a new concern; early librarians to the present have been concerned with the provision and accessibility of information. Traditionally, librarians have played a key role in the process of information acquisition and use. Today, librarians can and do play a role that enriches the child's acquisition and subsequent use of information. Now more than ever, children of all ages need guidance in becoming savvy consumers and creators of information.

Reference librarians can draw upon the rich history of providing services to children in libraries. The forward thinking of early children's librarians has led to

This chapter is adapted from *Reference Sources and Services for Youth*, by Meghan Harper (New York: Neal-Schuman, 2011).

the development of standards and guidelines for providing services to youth in addition to the provision of exceptional resources geared for children by providers of informational resources in libraries. Librarians have tirelessly advocated for children to have access to high-quality information and unimpeded access to these resources in school and public libraries. Thus, today, librarians and youth have a wealth of informational resources to choose from, in and out of the physical space. The reference librarian's role as a guide, mediator, and teacher of information literacy skills is more critical than ever.

History and Overview of Reference Services for Youth in America

American public libraries' services to children began in the earliest 1800s with a cadre of concerned individuals developing specialized collections. The mid-1800s saw intermittent funding to begin the development of official school libraries, and the groundwork was laid for the legislation, formal agreements, and standards that act as the foundation for youth reference services today. Specialized training for librarians in children's services began by the late 1860s, and the close of the century saw the establishment of the first children's librarian positions. By the early twentieth century, public libraries had separate physical spaces and collections for children, and collaboration between teachers and librarians began in areas of service, collection development, and literacy. Standards of service developed throughout the 1900s reflect the emphasis on collaboration between public and school libraries in the provision of both materials and guidance in use of informational texts. Early collaborative efforts included the sharing of book collections, presentations by public librarians to schoolchildren on public library resources, organized school visits to the public library, and assignment alerts given to the public library by teachers (Rees, 1924).

The launch of Sputnik in 1957 by the Soviet Union spurred the belief that American schools must be falling behind those of other nations if the United States was not first in the space race. Thus, the late 1900s saw increasing government support for enhancing school libraries with nonfiction materials and an emphasis on providing access to informational texts (Latrobe, 1998). The most significant factor affecting reference services provided to youth in the twenty-first century has been the development of the World Wide Web. The web and other technological innovations have nearly eliminated the constraints of physical space and time on librarians' ability to provide reference services. Today, youth reference services in both school and public libraries are generally focused on supporting the public school's curriculum and improving academic achievement of youth.

Types of Reference Service Transactions for Youth in Libraries

Reference resources and services in public libraries geared for children under the age of five typically focus on the needs of parents or caregivers of these youngest library patrons. These resources are generally characterized by reference resources on building preliteracy awareness and on preparing children for preschool or kindergarten programs. Providing reference services to these youngest patrons usually involves working with their caregivers, parents, and preschool educators to locate resources for individual interests or to support topical units that are presented in preschool. Reference librarians can expect the most common types of reference transactions with youth in grades K–12 to be ready reference, homework help, or research questions that are typically a result of school coursework or class projects. Readers' advisory, or recommendations for reading material to meet either a class assignment or for personal interests, is also an in-demand service. Librarians can prepare to answer ready reference questions by providing a set of resources that address commonly asked questions. Such resources might include informational handouts, directories of community resources, or a topical list of websites.

Youth reference librarians will likely be asked many directional-type questions, for example, "Where is this…?" "How can I find…?" These questions may get tedious when twelve children ask you the same question (Ohio Reference Excellence, 2012). However, librarians should recognize that these types of questions can provide opportunities for instructing children about how the library is organized or for building greater rapport between the children and the librarian. Moreover, some seemingly basic questions may lead to more in-depth reference transactions.

Research transactions generally require the librarian to employ multiple open-ended or clarification questions to determine the breadth and depth of requested information. The librarian may need to share a variety of resources or provide instruction for use and tips for finding and evaluating the requested information. These types of reference transactions often provide a multitude of "teachable moments" for the purpose of introducing or reinforcing information literacy skill acquisition. While directional questions are not considered reference transactions, and may even seem inconsequential, librarians should realize that these simple questions offer an opportunity to establish a child's perception of the librarian as approachable and helpful. Such a positive perception may influence future reference-seeking behaviors.

Readers' advisory interactions require the librarian to be knowledgeable about current literature, the library's collection, and the developmental levels of a child to determine the type, format, and content of a resource that will interest the child. Providing reference services to a youth is not limited to communication exchanged during reference transactions between the librarian and the youth. As noted in the RUSA (2008) definitions, a reference transaction is:

> An information contact that involves the knowledge, use, recommendations, interpretation, or instruction in the use of one or more information sources by a member of the library staff. The term includes information and referral service. Information sources include (a) printed and non-printed material; (b) machine-readable databases (including computer-assisted instruction); (c) the library's own catalogs and other holdings records; (d) other libraries and institutions through communication or referral; and (e) persons both inside and outside the library.

And likewise:

> "Reference Work" encompasses reference transactions and other activities that involve the creation, management, and assessment of information or research resources, tools, and services...[including]
>   • *Creation and management of information resources* includes the development and maintenance of research collections, research guides, catalogs, databases, web sites, search engines, etc., that patrons can use independently, in-house or remotely, to satisfy their information needs.
>   • *Assessment activities* include the measurement and evaluation of reference work, resources, and services.

These descriptions provide direction as well as an expanded view of the activities that comprise reference service in libraries. Some librarians extend reference services and provide independent assistance to students completing homework assignments or conducting independent research by providing a homework center, creating pathfinders for common instructional units (e.g., science fair topics, career exploration, or teen hot topics such as anorexia, alcohol abuse), or establishing an assignment alert process for teachers or a virtual homework help page on the library's webpage.

Homework Centers

Research suggests homework centers have a positive influence on overall academic achievement (Mediavilla, 2001; Walter and Mediavilla, 2011). Homework centers in school and public libraries may look very different from one another. Most homework centers are developed based on the needs of the intended population they are serving. Some homework centers are highly structured, involving multiple personnel, volunteers, or programming, while others are characterized as informal collections of resources that are geared for specific assignments or units in local schools (Mediavilla, 2001).

Homework centers may provide specific programming, such as academic tutoring or literacy instruction, in addition to specialized collections (including web resources) and instructional aids, all housed in one easily accessed location that encourages independent use by youth. Homework centers are typically a win-win program for the library and for the youth involved. They highlight the resources offered by the library and showcase collaborative efforts of the community and library. An example of one such collaborative effort is the Cuyahoga County Public Library System in Ohio that provides homework centers in several of its branch libraries with the help of community partners (Huffman and Rua, 2008).

During some reference transactions that involve homework assignments, librarians will be faced with a difficult dilemma when asked to provide actual answers to the questions. Librarians can be reassured that the limit of their ethical and professional responsibility is to provide resources that will enable the youth to complete the homework assignment independently. In fact, many libraries include a "homework disclaimer" in the library's reference policy that prescribes expectations for librarians and describes the services provided in the library for patrons. For example, the St. Louis Public Library (2002) describes the role of the *homework helpers* available in the library in their reference policy:

> Homework Helpers assist elementary, middle, and high school students with a variety of school assignments. They can help students understand assignments given by teachers. However, interpretation of the teacher's instructions, and completion of assignments, is the responsibility of the student.

Developmentally Appropriate Reference Services

Reference librarians can look to the principles of *developmentally appropriate practice* (DAP) and *developmental assets* to provide a solid, conceptual foundation guiding the provision of sources and services, quality of interaction, and continuing professional development for youth services librarians. Generally, ongoing professional development is needed for those working with youth in libraries in order for librarians to keep up-to-date with hot topics, technologies, and concerns of youth. Most education that librarians have been exposed to has been limited to a child development or a general psychology elective. Thus, most librarians benefit from occasional updates or a refresher on learning characteristics of children. The application of this knowledge to serving children in libraries is critical to the development of effective reference services and the selection and provision of developmentally appropriate resources. The spirit of DAP principles can provide a solid foundation for providing reference services for children pre-K–12.

Developmentally appropriate practice promotes the philosophy that learning will be more meaningful to a child if the instructional practices and environment have been constructed around the age of the child and therefore the specific developmental needs of the child. DAP focuses specifically on "age appropriateness, individual appropriateness and appropriateness for the cultural and social context of the child" (ChildCare Aware, 2012). DAP principles can be adapted to the library setting in the following ways:

- Select age-appropriate resources when developing a reference collection (physically and virtually), that is, those which have additional features such as indices, maps, and photos to facilitate children's use of information.
- Organize resources both physically and virtually using easy-to-understand organizational schemes with visual clues such as color coding and alphabetical, numerical, or topical categories.
- Offer each child a choice of material and/or format to meet children's individual learning needs. Children with limited reading abilities may benefit from audio resources because children often can understand what they hear even though they cannot read the text.
- Be particularly aware of the cultural and social context of the child seeking assistance in terms of the format of available resources. Despite our technologically infused age, some children may lack access to a computer at home, lack peripherals (printers, Internet), have insufficient hardware, or lack a particular software program necessary to access certain resources.

Understanding the sequence of growth and development will assist librarians with providing reference resources and services in a manner that is most helpful for the development of the whole child. Furthermore, knowledge of developmental stages of children can positively influence a librarian's ability to communicate with children in particularly constructive ways.

Table 15.1 provides information on the developmental levels of children ages 5–18 and offers suggestions for librarians providing reference resources and services.

Table 15-1. Developmental Characteristics of Children

Social and Emotional Development	Intellectual Development	Ideas for Librarians
Ages 3–5		
• Can cooperate • Experiences and copes with feelings; emotions appear to be all or nothing • Symbolic representation of self begins • Self-centered egocentric	• Cannot sequence • Understands some abstract concepts • Cannot tell "how many times" • Understands family relations • Can tell a story with a length of 4 to 5 words • Cannot separate fantasy from reality	• Provide activities with simple concepts • Point to text when speaking • Add audio to written directions
Ages 5–7		
• Being friends becomes increasingly important, although feelings of independence continue to develop • Begins seeing things from another child's point of view, but still very self-centered • Finds criticism or failure difficult to handle and may seem very hard on themselves • Views things as black and white, right or wrong, with very little middle ground • Begins to understand consequences of behavior • May become upset when behavior or schoolwork is ignored	• Understands that print "tells" a story • Increased problem-solving ability • Begins to organize information to remember • Can begin to understand time and the days of the week • Develops a basic vocabulary • Asserts personal choice in decision making	• Help children explore their world • Invite community helpers to the library • Provide plenty of failure-free activity choices • Provide open-ended activities • Role model activities • Provide opportunities for practice • Offer limited choices

(Continued)

Table 15-1. Developmental Characteristics of Children *(Continued)*

Social and Emotional Development	Intellectual Development	Ideas for Librarians
Ages 7–9		
• Develops abilities to behave appropriately and gets along with others • Begins to understand consequences of own and others' behavior • Eagerly will take on tasks and activities likely to be successful, but avoids risks • Judges success or failure based on adult responses	• Develops abilities of thinking and speaking • Master reading skills and use math in more abstract ways • Reading may become a major interest and start reading for a variety of purposes • Deepens understanding of cause and effect • Increases ownership in decision making	• Tell stories with lots of details • Work on projects and make things • Provide failure free activities • Allow students to take ownership • Offer multiple choices
Ages 9–11		
• Enjoys being a member of a group • May belittle or defy adult authority	• Interested in reading fictional stories, magazines, and how-to-projects books • Develops special interest in collections or hobbies • May be very interested in discussing a future career • Fantasizes and daydreams about the future • Capable of understanding concepts without having direct hands-on experience • Ability to manipulate thoughts and ideas, but still need hands-on experiences	• Provide opportunities to teach others • Provide opportunities to help out with real skills used in the library • Provide time and space for older children to be alone. Time to read, daydream, or do school-work uninterrupted • Encourage participating in groups to encourage skill developments • Provide opportunities for older children to play games of strategy (checkers, chess, and monopoly) • Provide a wide selection of reading materials
Ages 11–13		
• Develops the ability to work cooperatively, and can see the worth of other's viewpoints	• Does some abstract reasoning • Continues to broaden knowledge	• Wide variety of informational services • Use humor with activities to keep interest

(Continued)

Table 15-1. Developmental Characteristics of Children *(Continued)*

Social and Emotional Development	Intellectual Development	Ideas for Librarians
Ages 11–13 (Continued)		
• Becomes committed to their beliefs and personal views of the world • Starts to question adult authority • Defines self in terms of opinions, beliefs, values and expands sense of self by attempting to copy the culture • Sensitive to criticism and displays feelings of success or failure	• Uses language to clarify thinking and learning, often likes jokes and words with double meanings • Reads for an increasing variety of purposes • Chooses from a wide range of reading materials • Increasingly able to read critically and to detect inconsistencies in argument • Ability to persist with longer and more complex text • Starts plans for the future and career aspirations	• Offer varying levels of text complexity • Provide future and career materials • Offer multiple presentation choices • Offer opportunities to provide input in decision making
Ages 14–18		
• Uncertain about making good decisions and depends on parents to help • Takes on more responsibilities including work and extracurricular activities • Needs time alone and with others • Is not willing to ask for help • Can be very abrupt or have garbled speech	• Thinks more abstractly and understands more complex issues • Plans for the future • Wants information in one or two sources	• Provide opportunities for dialogue • Very important for teens to talk and be listened to • Be sure to follow up and check back with teen library users • Library staff needs to reduce frustration whenever possible • Solicit opinions • Involve in decision making • Offer multiple accessibility options

Source: Compiled from DelCampo, 2000; Ruffin, 2009; Ohio Department of Education, 2010.

Reference Services for Youth with Special Needs

Librarians serving youth will benefit from understanding legislation and professional organization policies that address the provision of services to disabled patrons. The Individuals with Disabilities Education Act (IDEA) identifies fourteen categories of disabilities (NICHCY, 2008a). Librarians should be familiar with these disabilities in order to identify accommodations and/or assistive technologies that will improve the provision of reference services and sources. Providing reference services to special-needs children may be complicated by access and/or communication difficulties or a feeling of stigmatization stemming from the use of assistive technology or a different format of relevant reference resources. Librarians may minimize some of these difficulties by adopting a few simple strategies:

- Librarians can and should make use of assistive technologies and a variety of reference formats for *all* reference services for all children. Many assistive technologies are helpful for all children.
- To better serve children with physical disabilities, the librarian should ensure that both the reference desk and the materials are handicapped-accessible. The overall layout of the library will come into play, as well as having handicapped-accessible furniture and the appropriate assistive technology such as alternative input devices.
- Visual communication may be enhanced by adjusting the print size of signage and/or incorporating icons.
- Library computers may be set up to use text-to-speech, speech-to-text, or screen magnification software, closed-circuit televisions, tactile graphic systems, optical character recognition and reading and writing software. Many devices may be programmed to respond to voice commands.
- The National Library Service for the Blind and Physically Handicapped (NLS) provides a free program loaning recorded Braille books and playback equipment to visually or physically impaired residents of the United States. Often libraries can become the point of contact between patrons and the NLS.
- Children with hearing and speech impairments may have difficulty communicating their reference needs. The librarian should deal with these difficulties by engaging the child in focused conversation, speaking slowly and clearly. If the child has an interpreter, the librarian should address the child rather than the interpreter. Complex requests or instructions should be broken into more manageable segments.
- As some learning disabilities may not be readily visible, librarians should take the time to observe all their patrons so they may still make appropriate accommodations or assist should any difficulties arise.
- A librarian should always be aware of competing stimuli and should try to limit or eliminate distracting noise when giving instructions to help the child focus. The librarian should engage students by asking questions and by engaging as many senses as possible in their instructions (colored paper, icons, hands-on exploration, etc.).
- The librarian should evaluate the appropriateness of the resource or format for the particular child in question. Experience with the resource or format will allow the librarian to better guide the child, prior to the child's independent use of the resource or format.

Librarians can tap into two online resources to begin learning about assistive technology to incorporate during reference transactions; Microsoft and Apple give overviews of products and match disabilities with recommended technology.

Both sites also provide suggestions from implementing changes on the desktop to acquiring additional hardware or software to make technology in the reference area more accessible to youth with disabilities. Tutorials, training guides, and research are also included to provide guidance and knowledge for librarians. Many Apple mobile devices have built-in accessibility features. Reference librarians can provide instruction and guidance to enable youth to maximize use of many of these accessibility features.

Communication in Reference Service

Communication with children when providing reference services requires librarians to exhibit excellent oral, listening, and writing skills. In addition, nonverbal behavior (facial expression, tone, and posture) is also a key factor in communication with children. Children tend to focus more on adult nonverbal behavior than on verbal interaction, so librarians should consciously try to exhibit nonverbal messages that support/complement verbal messages when working with children. "The way you listen, look, move, and react tells the other person whether or not you care, if you're being truthful, and how well you're listening. When your nonverbal signals match up with the words you're saying, they increase trust, clarity, and rapport. When they don't, they generate tension, mistrust, and confusion" (Segal, Smith, and Jaffe, 2012). Children may become confused when nonverbal messages do not match the verbal words they hear (Goode, 2009); for example, when a librarian says, "May I help you?" while frowning or failing to establish eye contact.

Librarians can employ the following strategies when interacting with youth whether it is online, via phone or e-mail, or in person:

1. First contact with a young patron should be a greeting or salutation.
2. Introduce yourself as the "authority figure" or librarian and tell them your role in the information-seeking process, for example, "My name is ___. I am here to help." (Adults often assume that children can discern the difference between young adults, parents, or librarians. Children may assume the "size" of the person indicates age or position.)
3. Make eye contact, smile, and wait for the child to respond.
4. Establish proximity. In person, sit or kneel beside child.
5. Eliminate physical barriers and distance by walking around desks or shelving to stand or sit beside the child.
6. If demonstrating online searches or sharing online resources, be sure the child has a view of the screen.
7. Allow time for the child to phrase his or her question.
8. Don't talk too much or jump to conclusions. This behavior can waste time both for the librarian and the child, leading to miscommunication and time spent finding resources that are not useful.
9. Accompany children to resources in the library; it demonstrates caring and interest and is more productive than pointing or using nonspecific directional terms such as "over there."

10. Avoid the use of sarcasm and figures of speech. Many children interpret sarcasm as "mean." (University of Manitoba, 2007)

Librarians working with multiple children can use eye contact, proximity, or verbal acknowledgment of a question to demonstrate attention and interest in a particular child or teen. Children are more likely to assume a librarian is "too busy" or not interested in providing help and are more likely not to persist in asking questions, whereas teens may assume the librarian is being judgmental. Youth of all ages may focus more on the emotional message they are receiving as a result of observing the librarian's nonverbal behavior. Younger children are more likely to express their emotions, thus librarians can expect children to exhibit exuberance and excitement physically by jumping up and down and exhibit frustration by clenching their fists or stomping their feet (Howard, 2002). Conversely, teens are likely to exhibit the opposite of what they are feeling, speaking loudly or offering their opinions when they may feel insecure, unsure, or embarrassed.

Digital Reference Services

Using online reference resources is a balancing act between providing maximum access to information while remaining vigilant in regard to children's safety. Quality and format are other considerations when looking at any online resource; not only must the information be accurate and authoritative, but it should meet the individual needs of the particular child in question.

The nearly limitless choice of online resources is both the greatest advantage of the Internet and what makes it a particularly difficult realm to navigate. Use of the Internet provides librarians with an excellent opportunity to positively influence youths' acquisition of lifelong information literacy skills. The librarian can serve as a mediator between online information and the child, assisting with access, interpretation, and evaluation of various sources; thus, librarians must possess excellent information literacy skills and be able to assess how to best assist children of all ages.

Online Searching

One of the most important skills librarians can teach children is the difference between search engines, directories, and databases and their limitations and strengths. Unlike search engines, directories are compiled by people rather than automated crawlers. Thus, the information compiled and organized has been evaluated as relevant by someone with some standing as an expert. Most directories are browsable and make use of controlled vocabulary, predetermined by the subject heading under which all documents about a topic are categorized. *KidsClick!* (http://www.kidsclick.org/) is a web directory site designed for kids.

Yahoo! Kids (http://kids.yahoo.com/) is geared for younger children and includes homework help. This search engine would be appropriate for use by upper elementary children and older. Younger students may have better luck with child-focused search engines such as *Yahoo! Kids* or *Fact Monster* or the *KidsClick!* directory, all of which have kid-friendly interfaces and work to limit results and filter out inappropriate sites.

Multimedia search engines are often a first best choice when a multimedia format is needed. Most search engines provide search options for images, but a multimedia search engine is the best bet for finding quick multimedia in a variety of formats. AltaVista also provides a family filter that will stop searches with an alert screen offering the option to continue viewing images with or without photos that contain adult content. Similarly, AlltheWeb provides the option of allowing or blocking offensive content from the results screen.

Teaching students search skills is one step in a much greater information literacy journey. The real challenge comes in teaching students how to evaluate websites, endowing them with the necessary information literacy skills to effectively discern the best results from among the plethora they'll receive from any search engine.

Online Safety

Both the physical and emotional safety of children is a matter of concern when using the Internet. Librarians must be aware of the positive and negative uses of social networking sites and their privacy settings and issues, and they should be able to guide both parents and children to instructional resources on Internet safety. Sexual solicitation, pornography, and virtual bullying are only a few of the harmful situations children might be subjected to online.

Beyond simply understanding the statistics of solicitation, librarians need to become informed about strategies predators implement to gain the attention and trust of their victims. Librarians can then provide relevant Internet safety advice as they guide youth to using the Internet. Many school and public libraries have filtered access to the Internet, preventing access to social networking sites at school or in the library, but this situation may serve only to prevent librarians from modeling safe use of social networking sites. Most children will have access to these same sites at home or elsewhere unsupervised.

As well as personal safety and security issues, librarians should be aware of the risk of technical problems such as viruses or worms. The best way to avoid such malevolent computer programs is to become familiar with prevention and detection software. Librarians may also inform children of these potentially destructive computer programs and how these computer germs can be "caught" on the Internet.

Government Resources

Online government resources are intended to facilitate interaction with the government as well as provide authoritative information. Children will get the most value from these virtual resources if they understand how the government is structured. Government sites often provide access to primary documents, facilitating a unique opportunity to teach children the importance of authority and credibility in the pursuit of information. Government resources provide a good opportunity for the librarian to instruct youth on how to compare and contrast the information found in primary (government) sources with that from secondary sources. Government resources are often particularly well-suited to meeting individual learning needs due to large collections of audiovisual materials (especially useful to children with special learning needs). The following are some government sites librarians can use with children:

- *Kids.gov* (http://www.kids.gov/) calls itself the "official kids' portal for the U.S. government" and is geared for grades K–5, 6–8, and their educators. This site provides an opportunity to teach students about "portal sites" and the evaluation of commercial sites.
- *Ben's Guide to U.S. Government for Kids* (http://bensguide.gpo.gov/) is organized by grade levels K–2, 3–5, 6–8, and 9–12, though there is also a comprehensive index which alphabetically lists all topics addressed with hyperlinks to the grade-level selections. Similar topical information is available in each grade category, while the level of detail of the information increases progressively. Most articles contain hyperlinked cross-references.
- *Find Youth Info* (http://findyouthinfo.gov/) offers activities, resources and information on issues of particular concern to children K–12, providing resources from across the whole of the federal government. The site also includes a searchable database of possible funding sources for running after-school programs.
- *TreasuryDirect Kids* (http://www.treasurydirect.gov/kids/kids.htm) provides downloadable educational materials, games, activities, and information on the U.S. Treasury, as well as acting as a portal to other kid-friendly websites pertaining to the White House, U.S. Mint, Alcohol and Tobacco Tax and Trade Bureau, and more.
- Online collections are composed largely of primary source materials. Perhaps the best such source is the Library of Congress (http://www.loc.gov/). The LOC homepage is organized by user groups. The "Kids, Families" link leads to the section geared for elementary and middle-school children, offering options for exploring American history such as "America's Library" with a treasure trove of links leading to biographies, games, and a digital collection of audio files under the heading "See, Hear and Sing."

See the section Recommended Core Reference Collection Resources later in this chapter for additional government resources. Other resources of interest include the *National Archives* education site (http://www.archives.gov/education), *THOMAS* (http://thomas.loc.gov/), and *USA.gov* (http://www.usa.gov/).

Evaluating Reference Services to Youth

Evaluation of youth reference services requires the librarian to have knowledge of assessment tools, their purpose and implementation, to obtain useful information for the purpose of making decisions regarding the provision of reference services and resources. Librarians must decide on the overall purpose of the evaluation.

Analysis of the data gathered must be conducted within the context of the mission and goals of the library. Librarians must have knowledge of assessment measures to create and implement the measures effectively. Surveys and focus groups are two assessment techniques that can be used effectively with youth to evaluate reference services and sources.

Surveys are commonly used to evaluate services or gather input. Librarians should consider children's vocabulary levels as well as their base knowledge of and prior experience with reference services when creating a survey. Survey length or time needed to complete the survey and format should be developmentally appropriate for the intended age of the survey recipient. Perhaps one of the most common issues is the use of library jargon and library-specific vocabulary; for example, most children do not understand role differentiation among library aides and librarians, or the overall organization of services and departments such as reference or circulation.

Common emoticons can be used to garner the opinions of even the smallest children, while open, closed, Likert, and/or multiple choice questions can all be adapted to meet the needs of any particular age group. The development of Likert scales requires due diligence in the use of any vocabulary that is vague or refers to lapse of time; terms like "often," "sometimes," or "very" might confuse children who are primary through middle school ages because they may have difficulty connecting and recalling the lapse or duration of time and action. Words that require nuanced distinctions such as "very good" and "good" might also be difficult for children to understand. Questions should also avoid emotionally charged language and abbreviations. Librarians creating a survey might find that it's useful to have a child "tester" to assist them with the creation of a child-friendly survey.

Surveys intended for primary-age children should generally follow these formatting guidelines: include ten or fewer questions, use large font, have multiple colors, use graphics, group similar questions together, and sequence questions from general to specific. Surveys should be administered to children individually or in small groups to ensure each child is answering questions correctly, and the writing utensils (e.g., crayons, large pencils, or markers) should be familiar to them (Corporation for National and Community Service, 2009). An oral explanation of the questions or even reading them aloud may be beneficial. To encourage participation, let children know that you will share the survey results with them; this is an opportunity to demonstrate to them that their opinions are valued. Librarians can review general tips for designing surveys in Innovation Network's article "Data Collection Tips: Developing a Survey" at http://www.innonet.org/client_docs/File/Survey_Dev_Tips.pdf. This article presents common barriers to good survey design and provides sample questions for improving survey question design.

Focus groups are another common evaluative method well-suited to younger participants. Focus groups are a type of interview (Patton, 1990) that may be used as a first step in designing a survey or in planning an evaluation. Focus groups involving young children should allow for extra time so that children can ask clarifying questions, but it is also important to keep in mind the general attention span of the participating youth. Librarians should incorporate participation guidelines to ensure feedback is solicited from every individual in the group. Focus group interviews should be limited to one topic, as a diffuse discussion may be hazardous to collecting good data (Archer, 1993).

Librarians searching for more how-to methods of conducting focus groups with children can visit the eHow website (http://www.ehow.com.); searches on using focus groups with children or facilitating a focus group will yield some specific design suggestions. A general manual of facilitating focus groups is available as a downloadable PDF designed by the OMNI Institute, a social science research firm, at http://www.omni.org/docs/focusgrouptoolkit.pdf. A review of the manual's table of contents provides a convenient checklist for considerations of design and facilitation. Librarians will need to adapt these suggestions to incorporate developmentally appropriate practices.

Managing Reference Services for Youth

Effective management of reference services is an essential ingredient in the provision of these services to youth. Decisions regarding allocations of personnel, time, and funds and how these services and resources are implemented, accessed, and maintained are central to facilitating the physical and virtual use of library reference services and sources.

Establishing policies and procedures are typically a first step to promote and ensure access to resources and services. Reference transactions may be the only time librarians and children are engaged in an active, interpersonal communication exchange. Thus, policies should educate children about the value of the library as well as promote the ideals of the library. Policies should be public and known and illuminate a clear course of action for the librarian and provide clear expectations for young patrons.

After policies are determined, the librarian must develop procedures (specific steps, activities, or a set of rules) clarifying how the policies will be fulfilled. Generally, procedures address *who* will be responsible for various policies and *how* the policies will be implemented. Procedures should connect policies specific to one aspect of reference service or provision of resources to the related federal, state, or professional standard or general institutional policy.

Policies specific to the provision of youth services and resources include the following:

- Safety
- Confidentiality (see AASL, 2006)
- Copyright (see ALA, 2012)
- Homework help
- Internet use (see ALA, 2008)

The American Library Association website (http://www.ala.org/) provides sample policies and general guidelines for the development and implementation of policies. The Mid-Hudson Library system website (http://midhudson.org/department/member_information/library_policies.htm) serves as a gateway to sample policies and tips for policy development for public libraries.

Overall, good management practices for providing services to youth include these:

1. Ongoing evaluation of reference services and sources
2. Knowing your audience
3. Awareness of trends and issues in providing services to children

Librarians should consider becoming professionally active in state, national, and international organizations as a first step to keeping up-to-date with technological changes in society, thereby gaining new perspectives and information for managing services and sources in libraries.

The Future of Reference Services for Youth

Speculation about the future of reference services has been an ongoing topic of consideration among librarians, some of whom may wonder if their day-to-day work has been outsourced to one of the plethora of search engines available online. The constant change of technological innovation presents challenges to the three- to five-year technological implementation plans of previous decades. Librarians also must address the characteristics of those who are *born digital*— "those who grow up immersed in digital technologies, for whom a life fully integrated with digital devices is the norm" (Berkman Center for Internet and Society, 2011).

Libraries need to address current trends and issues by developing innovative and effective services to accommodate the exponential increase in availability of and demand for e-content versus print, thereby facilitating information creation and making the library, its services, and its resources integral to the community. Twenty-first-century library services to children should include supporting academic achievement, encouraging information literacy, and making the library a "destination place" (Walter, 2010).

The future success of serving youth in libraries is greatly influenced by the degree to which reference librarians are creatively, proactively, and enthusiastically seeking to engage young patrons in physical and virtual library spaces. Librarians need to develop new types of reference services, provide access to increasingly electronic formats of information, and address the learning styles of the digitally immersed. The future of reference service is likely to support the historically sound tenets of good service; what remains to be seen is how the increasingly mobile and versatile Web 2.0 technologies will affect these services. Many reference services already use electronic mediums to provide service beyond the physical library. As the penchant of youth to access information 24/7 seems unlikely to change, innovations in reference services must continue to develop in conjunction with innovations in technology.

Recommended Core Reference Collection Resources

The core collections described here were developed to address the reference needs of elementary students in grades K–6 and middle school and high school students in grades 7–12. Collection composition is limited to approximately fifty print and electronic resources and is meant to reflect a broad range of titles that would address common informational needs of youth in the given age range. Resources were selected with two primary uses in mind: (1) reference resources that librarians can use to provide answers to ready reference questions and (2) subject-specific references that address typical informational needs of academic projects and units and interest levels of the youth in a particular age group. The scope and selection considerations included the range and format of titles, the ages and developmental levels of the intended audiences, and special features to enhance accessibility and understanding of informational content. Individual titles were evaluated for authority, currency, appropriateness to the audience, and use potential.

Elementary Core Collection for Grades K–6

Students in this age group range from those K–2 students who are just beginning to read to those in upper grades who are becoming savvy consumers and creators of information. Resources for this age range were selected to be both of high interest and to assist students in completing school assignments, bearing in mind that expectations for more detailed research projects may require multiple sources of information for written reports or multimedia presentations.

Dictionaries

The American Heritage Children's Dictionary. 2011. Boston: Houghton Mifflin Harcourt. With over 34,000 words, this dictionary intended for grades 3–6, is a comprehensive reference tool with 1,500 color illustrations and guide words.

Merriam-Webster Visual Dictionary Online. http://visual.merriam-webster .com/index.php. Well-suited for use by elementary-age children and older, this online visual dictionary helps visual learners and promotes further understanding of English words by associating more than 6,000 of them with relevant images. From the homepage children can easily explore by clicking on one of the fifteen major themes, either by name in a left-hand bar, by image in the center of the page, or by an index.

Merriam-Webster Word Central. http://www.wordcentral.com/games.html. This free dictionary website was designed for early elementary to middle school children. The attractive, interactive graphic interface includes such kid-friendly features as games, a daily "buzzword," and a "Build Your Own Dictionary" option, allowing students to use their creativity and participate with a Web 2.0 tool.

Merriam-Webster's Dictionary for Children. 2010. Springfield, MA: Merriam-Webster. Alphabetically arranged entries provide the definition, usage examples, word history, synonym notes, and illustrations for over 36,000 words. A new feature to this edition is pronunciation paragraphs. Intended for grades 3–6.

Morris, C. G. 2007. *Macmillan Dictionary for Children*. New York: Simon and Schuster. This dictionary includes nearly 35,000 entries with over 3,000 illustrations to invite browsing and research use. The layout is visually appealing for children grades 3–6.

Visuwords Online Graphical Dictionary. http://www.visuwords.com/. This online graphical dictionary attempts to show the relationships between words through complex webs showing how one word relates to many others in ways such as "is a kind of" or "is similar to" or "opposes." This tool is excellent for alternative learning styles and should help all children gain a better understanding of words and how they are related.

Encyclopedias

Burnie, David. 2011. *The Kingfisher Animal Encyclopedia.* New York: Kingfisher. This animal encyclopedia exudes visual appeal, with more than 1,000 photographs to accompany the 2,000 animal profiles, making it well suited to students as young as grade 3. The work takes a more scientific approach than most; it is organized first by class, from simpler animals up to mammals, and then each class is organized further by phylum and subphylum.

Encyclopedia Britannica Kids. http://kids.britannica.com/. This online encyclopdedia database is geared for students ages 8 and up. Content includes a broad range of articles from A–Z that include videos, images, and statistics. Additional resources include a dictionary, thesaurus, world atlas, and animated timelines. Research guides and learning activities for English and Language Arts, Mathematics, Science, and Social Sciences enhance the topical coverage. Search options include a search box, topical index, and popular search links. Users can limit their searches by resource type, dictionary and thesaurus, or *Student Encyclopedia* intended for ages 11 and up or the *Children's Encyclopedia* geared for ages 8–11.

Gifford, C. 2011. *The Kingfisher Geography Encyclopedia.* New York: Kingfisher. This fully updated edition of the award-winning *Kingfisher Geography Encyclopedia* includes brief chapters covering the major attributes of each country, arranged by region. Recommended for grade levels 3–6, the country-by-country layout allows for easy navigation while quick reference panels highlight key facts regarding each country.

Khurana, A., ed. 2010. *Children's Illustrated Encyclopedia.* 7th ed. New York: DK Publishing. Entries are organized in alphabetical order from "Abolitionist movement" to "Zoos" and include a single paragraph summary followed by photographs and illustrations with captions highlighting several relevant subtopics. The companion website includes links to relevant, age-appropriate sites so the intended audience (grades 3–6) can conduct further research into particular topics of interest.

World Book Encyclopedia. Chicago: World Book. This twenty-two-volume set covers a broad range of alphabetized topics. Article entries include color photos, charts, statistics, and biographical information. Entries begin with simple information and become more detailed throughout the article. Special features include a guide to using the set, a pronunciation key, a student guide to better writing, speaking, and research skills, and an index.

Atlases

Adams, Simon, et al. 2011. *Children's World Atlas.* New York: DK Publishers. This atlas is arranged by continent; selected countries are highlighted. Plentiful color maps are complimented by satellite images and photographs with caption descriptions of items of interest such as local crops, sports, or cultural attributes. Best suited for grades 3–6.

National Geographic Kid's World Atlas. 2010. Washington, DC: National Geographic. This edition of *National Geographic*'s award-winning atlas includes maps, data, photos, and essays. A universal size in physical and political maps encourages comparison, and all maps include surrounding areas so students might gain context and a full-world perspective. The appealing format and interactivity make this work ideal for any student grades 3 and up.

National Geographic Student Atlas of the World. 3rd ed. 2009. Washington, DC: National Geographic Publishing. Designed for use by middle school (and high school) students, the work is divided into two main sections. An introduction gives an overview of maps and how to read them. The remainder of the work provides information on geologic history, vegetation, climate zones, environmentally vulnerable areas, populations, cities, languages, economies, statistics, food production, energy, and world cultures. The second section offers one chapter per continent, each of which is introduced by an image from space, followed by a wide variety of full-color maps, charts, graphs, photographs, flags, and facts.

Wright, David, and Jill Wright. 2012. *The World Almanac Children's Atlas*. New York: World Almanac Books. Under 100 pages, this concise atlas, filled with color photographs and maps, takes elementary-age children through a brief introduction to our world, one continent at a time. Thirty nations and regions are highlighted with information on the population, topography, culture, religion, climate, and more.

Thesauri

The American Heritage Children's Thesaurus. 2012. Boston: Houghton Mifflin Harcourt. Intended for grades 3–7, this volume contains over 4,000 entries with 36,000 synonyms in alphabetical order. Each entry's common usage is illustrated in a sentence, while synonyms are broken into groups that distinguish between those most closely related and those whose meanings might differ slightly. This feature encourages students to begin thinking analytically about their word choices.

Webster's Thesaurus for Students. 2010. 3rd ed. Springfield, MA: Federal Street Press. This third-edition thesaurus offers over 122,000 synonyms, antonyms, and related words in alphabetically arranged entries.

Almanacs/Random Reference

Brain, M. 2010. *Marshall Brain's How Stuff Works*. New York: Chartwell Books. In more than 100 entries, text and diagrams are combined to explain how stuff works, from antilock brakes to Internet search engines. Readers can use an index or browse by any of the very broad eleven categories (chapters) from "In the Air" to "Around the House." This work is best suited for students in elementary school.

Glenday, C., and Guinness World Records Limited. 2012. *Guinness World Records 2013*. London: Guinness World Records. Intended for readers of any age, this volume is particularly well-suited to browsing. The table of contents organizes the records into broad categories like the Human Body or the Spirit of Adventure, while a subject index allows readers to search for particular records under more specific categories. Record entries include a descriptive paragraph about the record (what was the record, who broke it, how) followed by photographs, generally of the record-holder, often in the midst of breaking the record.

TIME for Kids Almanac 2013. 2012. New York: Time Home Entertainment. Published by *TIME* magazine, this authoritative work is a great resource for elementary school children looking for quick information about countries around the world, interesting facts from various fields of study, or pop culture.

World Almanac for Kids 2013. 2012. New York: World Almanac. This popular full-color reference book of facts includes information on popular subjects such as animals, science, sports, music, and U.S. history, as well as photographs and biographical information on popular sports and entertainment superstars. Information includes homework help and maps with fun activities that include puzzles and games.

(Exclusively) Online Resources

ipl2 For Kids: Internet Public Library. Drexel University iSchool. http://www.ipl .org/div/kidspace/. This site for elementary-age children provides links to information on topics from sports to computers, math, physics, animals, and arts and crafts. Links to further information or outside sites are organized under broad topic headings. Students requiring further direction have an option to "Ask an ipl2 Librarian," an e-mail reference service for children 13 years or older.

World Book Kids. http://www.worldbookonline.com/training/kids/index.htm. This digital reference resource with its highly interactive and colorful interface is intended for children in the younger elementary grades. With thousands of articles for various reading levels, *World Book Kids* includes plenty of textual information, but photos, illustrations, audio clips, and interactive games and activities also abound.

World Book Student. http://www.worldbookonline.com/student/home. *World Book Student* is geared toward middle-school students, particularly to assist them in conducting research. Multiple search features provide a variety of starting points for searching. For example, within the Biography Center, students can search by time period, gender, field of interest, or nationality.

Language(s)/Writing

Janeczko, Paul. 2012. *Poetry from A to Z: A Guide for Young Writers*. New York: Simon and Schuster Books for Young Readers. This is much more than an anthology of poems. Approximately 70 poems in this volume serve as a model for young writers in grades 5–7. Guided poetry writing exercises and explanations of how to write haiku, list poems, and letter poems are included. Organized in alphabetical order by type of poem, children can quickly navigate the text or use the index to go directly to their desired topic.

NoveList K–8 Plus. EBSCO Publishing. http://www.ebscohost.com/novelist/our-products/novelist-k8. The focus of this site is to lead children in grades K–8 toward quality reading materials. Each entry includes suggestions for similar literature. This reader's advisory database can be searched by many qualifiers including age, reading level, subject, and genre.

Terban, M. 2011. *Scholastic Guide to Grammar.* New York: Scholastic. Designed for use by any student grades 3 and up, this grammar guide is color coded and tabbed, allowing for easy navigation. The introduction provides a concise explanation on the importance of mastering the English language and the chapters that follow guide the student through the parts of speech, sentences and paragraphs, spelling, capitalization, and punctuation.

Science/Math

Aguilar, D. 2011. *13 Planets: The Latest View of the Solar System.* Washington, DC: National Geographic Children's Books. This work is a product of collaboration between National Geographic and David Aguilar of the Harvard Smithsonian Astronomical Observatory. This revised edition keeps readers in grades 5–8 updated on the rapidly changing topic of our solar system. This volume uses simple text and the author's own photorealistic computer art to first explain the new planet categorizations and then profile the thirteen planets, the sun, comets, and other space phenomena.

Alexander, B., A. Baggaley, and K. Dennis-Bryan, eds. 2010. *Natural History: The Ultimate Visual Guide to Everything on Earth.* New York: DK Publishing. Intended for grades 5 and up, a cadre of Smithsonian scholars has amassed an international encyclopedia of over 5,000 life forms as well as produced a brilliant visual introduction to the field of natural history as a whole. Broken into six chapters, the work begins with general essays on climate change, evolution, and classification to provide context. Chapters cover "Minerals, Rocks, and Fossils," "Microscopic Life," "Plants," "Fungi," and "Animals."

DeKlerk, Judith. 2009. *Math Dictionary.* New York: DK Publishing. This math dictionary for children grades 3–6 includes over 300 alphabetically arranged entries providing definitions for mathematical terms, phrases, and concepts.

Farndon, J. 2012. *The Great Scientists: From Euclid to Stephen Hawking.* London: Arcturus Publishing Limited. Beginning with Aristotle and ending with Stephen Hawking, this book (part of the popular DK Eyewitness series) introduces students to a brief biography of thirty eminent scientists. Each two-page entry includes a photograph of the scientist, a brief exploration of his or her personal life, an explanation of the contribution to science, and a timeline to orient his or her work in a broader historical context. Intended for grades 3–6.

Fitzgerald, Theresa. 2011. *Math Dictionary for Kids: The Essential Guide to Math Terms, Strategies, and Tables.* Austin, TX: Prufrock Press. Intended for children in grades 4–9, this brightly colored reference work provides definitions for more than 400 math concepts and terms with many problem-solving strategies incorporated into the text to assist students in understanding concepts and applying them to their own math problems.

ipl2 For Kids: Science Fair Project Resource Guide. Drexel University iSchool. http://www.ipl.org/div/projectguide/. This free online resource is geared particularly toward middle school students, with the aim of guiding students through the process of completing a science fair project. The first webpage is a helpful explanation of how to use the Guide and the four steps, "Getting Started," "Choosing a Topic," "Completing the Project," and "Displaying Your Project" are numbered and easy to follow via links from the homepage. The page for each step in the process acts as a hub to a slew of links to other useful sites.

Latham, Donna. 2011. *Endangered Biomes.* White River, VT: Nomad Press. This eight-book series explores the world's endangered biomes, with each book focusing respectively on coniferous forests, deciduous forests, deserts, grasslands and savannas, mountains, oceans, rain forests, and tundra. Each book examines both human and natural threats to these ecosystems and encourages children to consider how their choices might impact the earth.

Parker, Steve. 2010. *100 Things You Should Know about the Human Body.* Broomall, PA: Mason Crest. Intended for grades 3–6, this work contains 100 facts about the human body from the development of the fetus in the womb to the body parts involved in and the body processes of breathing and digestion, to nutrition and general health. A table of contents allows for searching by general topic, or students can use the index to search for specific facts.

PowerKnowledge Life Science Database. Rosen Publishing. http://www.pklifescience.com/. Designed specifically for children in grades 3–6, this subscription science database intends to develop information literacy in conjunction with serving as a science resource. The homepage allows for navigation to 400 articles (with text-to-speech capability) by broad categories from "Animals" to "Green Living" or students can use the search tool.

Science and Technology: Science Online. Infobase Publishing. http://www.infobasepublishing.com/OnlineProductDetail.aspx?ISBN=0816044287. Intended for upper-elementary age children, this science database organizes content by subject area, type of resource, and national and state science education standards. Entries offer article resources, age-appropriate experiments, diagrams, videos and animation, timelines and biographies.

Stoyles, P. 2010. *A to Z of Health.* Mankato, MN: Smart Apple Media. Intended for grades 3–6, this six-volume series answers questions about physical and mental health, from entries on diabetes to jet lag. Different body parts and processes are also explained. Each entry is a brief two pages with a glossary of three to five important terms. This work provides a good starting point for basic health questions.

Social Studies

Alexander, Heather. 2010. *A Child's Introduction to the World: Geography, Cultures, and People from the Grand Canyon to the Great Wall of China.* New York: Black Dog and Leventhal Publishers. Written for grades 3–6, this reference work introduces children to the continents, countries, states, and provinces of our world as well as exploring climates, biomes, terrain, people, cultures, governments, and more. The book begins with a general section explaining overarching topics like Earth's geological history, how to read maps, the diversity of world cultures, and our increasing population density. Part Two introduces children to the various continents; each section is further organized by geographical region.

Bausum, A., B. Obama, and National Geographic Society (U.S.). 2009. *Our Country's Presidents: All You Need to Know about the Presidents, from George Washington to Barack Obama*. Washington, DC: National Geographic. This updated edition begins with a foreword from President Barack Obama, followed by an introduction to the office of the presidency and an initial timeline explaining the context of each presidential term. The bulk of the book is made up of one- to five-page biographical entries on each president in chronological order and divided into six groups by broad historical era.

Ben's Guide to U.S. Government for Kids. http://bensguide.gpo.gov/. *Ben's Guide* is an online portal to free government websites, with specific links on the homepage to take you to further pages specifically geared to grade K–2, 3–5, 6–8, and 9–12 students. The K–2 page, for example, offers the ABCs of government and explains the U.S. symbols (the flag, etc.). The page for grades 3–5 includes an explanation of how laws are made, the division of power between the state and national levels, and the election process. The grades 6–8 and 9–12 pages cover the same topics, but in greater depths, progressively.

Biography Reference Bank. EBSCO Publishing/H. W. Wilson. http://www.ebscohost .com/academic/biography-reference-bank. This subscription-based database contains over 550,000 biographical entries from around the world, spanning ancient to modern times. Entries include photos and full-text articles from journals about individuals both living and dead. Biographies are searchable by name, profession, title, place of origin, gender, race/ethnicity, date of birth, date of death, and keyword.

Blassingame, W. 2012. *The Look-It-Up Book of Presidents*. New York: Random House. Concise biographies of every president from George Washington to Barack Obama are organized chronologically. Entries are complimented by plentiful photos, cartoons, and engravings, making this a suitable book for grades 5–8.

My Guide to the Constitution Series. 2011. Hockessin, DE: Mitchell Lane Publishers. Intended for children grades 3–8, the titles in this six-book series are: *The Legislative Branch, The Executive Branch, The Judicial Branch, The Power of the States, The Story of the Constitution*, and *The Bill of Rights*. Through age-appropriate text and full-color photographs, the books describe the founding of United States, the writing of the Constitution, and how, over the years, the Constitution has acted to keep balance in the government.

Napoli, Donna Jo. 2011. *Treasury of Greek Mythology: Classic Stories of Gods, Goddesses, Heroes, and Monsters*. Washington, DC: National Geographic Children's Books. Intended for children in grades 3–6, this single-volume work contains illustrated retellings of classic Greek myths. A mythological family tree and profiles of each god, goddess, monster, and hero allow children to understand the myths and their characters in relation to one another as well. It's easy to see why this volume was included in *School Library Journal*'s "Best Books of 2011."

Pappas, Lynn, and Molly Aloian. 2012. *Cultural Traditions in My World*. New York: Crabtree. This six-book series describes the cultural traditions, beliefs, and rituals both historically celebrated and still observed today (often in modern festivals and holidays) around the world. Books cover, respectively, Brazil, China, Japan, Mexico, India, and Russia. Intended for K–3 children, the books are sparse on text while providing plenty of photographs to keep younger children interested.

ProQuest K-12. CultureGrams. http://www.proquestk12.com/productinfo/culture grams.shtml. Written for the upper-elementary grades, *ProQuest K-12 CultureGrams* is also available in print editions, though these do not allow for the interactivity of the online editions. The site offers comprehensive information about countries around the world. Individual country profiles feature pictures, videos, data and statistics, and information about political and governmental systems.

Middle School and Secondary Core Collection Grades 7–12

Students at this age level are developing critical thinking skills, becoming interested in popular culture, using mobile technology, and thinking about the future. Academically, students are engaging in more complex research topics. The reference resources recommended here will engage students' interests and assist with the increased demand for more complex research and writing projects. Vetted Internet resources including those with multimedia components are included to address the interests of digitally immersed youth.

Dictionaries

The American Heritage Student Dictionary. 2012. Boston: Houghton Mifflin Harcourt. Filled with nearly 2,000 colored illustrations and hundreds of feature notes, this dictionary is intended for children grades 6 and up. The nearly 65,000 entries are arranged alphabetically following a guide on how to make the most use of a dictionary.

Merriam-Webster's Essential Learner's English Dictionary. 2010. Springfield, MA: Merriam-Webster. This work, designed for non-native speakers of English, offers simplified definitions for more than 54,000 alphabetically arranged English words and extensive examples of usage so non-native speakers might better grasp the words in context. Over 15,000 idioms, collocations, and commonly used phrases are also defined.

Webster's Spanish-English Dictionary for Students. 2010. Bilingual ed. Springfield, MA: Federal Street Press. This bidirectional dictionary for all ages provides definitions for over 40,000 Spanish words, including translations from Spanish to English (and vice versa) and conjugations for Spanish verbs and irregular English verbs.

Thesauri

Merriam-Webster's Collegiate Thesaurus. 2010. Springfield, MA: Merriam-Webster. This alphabetically arranged thesaurus intended for older students contains more than 250,000 synonyms, antonyms, idioms, related and contrasted words, as well as providing extensive cross-references for each selected term. Entries include sample sentences for each synonym listed.

Encyclopedias

Encyclopedia Britannica Deluxe Edition (DVD). 2012. Chicago: Encyclopedia Britannica. Britannica has ceased printing the multivolume set of encyclopedias as of spring 2012. In its place, Britannica has concentrated on providing electronic and digital content of the multivolume encyclopedia set, including over 80,000 articles, 17,000 photos, illustrations, tables, and multimedia resources. Readers can also access the *Merriam-Webster's Collegiate Dictionary and Thesaurus*, research tools, and Book of the Year articles.

Rozett, Robert, and Shmuel Spector, eds. *Encyclopedia of the Holocaust.* 2009. Illustrated ed. Brooklyn, NY: Lambda Publishers. Eight essays on Holocaust topics such as the history of European Jewry and the rise of anti-Semitism provide an overall context of the holocaust. The essays are followed by more than 650 alphabetically organized entries on major subjects of the Holocaust along with over 300 accompanying black-and-white photographs. A day-to-day chronology from 1933 to 1945 provides an overview to place the articles in a historical context.

Almanacs/Other Reference

Chase's Calendar of Events 2013 with CD-ROM. 2012. New York: McGraw-Hill. Described as the "bible of special occurrences" by the *Los Angeles Times*, this guide is the go-to reference resource on special occurrences, holidays, anniversaries, celebrity birth dates, religious observances, and sporting events from around the world. Topics include a major awards section from the previous year in addition to a perpetual calendar and maps of world time zones.

The Knowledge Book: Everything You Need to Know to Get By in the 21st Century. 2009. Washington, DC: National Geographic. This book can serve as either a ready reference tool or simply a browsable tome for interested students. Organized by broad categories such as "Discoveries and Inventions" and "Social Life," the work is then divided by subject areas and further by subtopics. Nearly every conceivable field of study and topic is covered, giving students brief entries and more than 1,000 accompanying color illustrations.

The Old Farmer's Almanac. 2012. Yankee Publishing. http://www.almanac.com/. A free online resource, *The Old Farmer's Almanac* offers traditional almanac information on topics like weather, gardening, astronomy, cooking, birding and fishing, rural real estate, and more. Organization is mainly by broad topics. Note: This site remains free because it has extensive advertising throughout.

Time Almanac 2013. 2012. Chicago: Encyclopedia Britannica. This book of facts includes global and country statistics, a calendar and holiday list, sports results, a website guide, and information about astronomy and space, health and nutrition, business, economy, personal finance, and the Internet. (Description based on print edition.)

The World Almanac and Book of Facts 2013. 2012. New York: World Almanac. Published annually since 1868, this book's long history makes it an authoritative and up-to-date reference guide for general reference questions on history, sports, geography, and pop culture. Special features include a "Year in Pictures" and the U.S. Colleges and Universities section.

Wright, John W. *The New York Times 2013 Almanac*. 2012. New York: Penguin Reference. This approximately 1,000-page paperback book contains data from science and technology to sports, entertainment, maps, and more. An index for navigation purposes is included. Abundant white space and well-spaced text make this more accessible to reluctant readers.

Atlases

National Geographic Atlas of the World. 2011. Washington, DC: National Geographic Society. This authoritative and comprehensive atlas seeks to highlight topics of current interest ranging from areas of civil strife, such as Afghanistan, Pakistan, and Iraq, to hotspots of environmental concern, such as Greenland and the Amazon Basin. Information is organized into critical issue themes, including urbanization, human rights, biodiversity, and energy. Detailed maps of the ocean floor, the moon, Mars, and the Milky Way and satellite imagery present each continent's topography.

(Exclusively) Online Resources

Expert Space. 2012. Scholastic. http://education.scholastic.ca/category/CUR_SCI_ EXPERT_SPACE. Intended particularly for students in grades 7–12, this digital reference resource allows students to develop information literacy skills such as outlining, evaluating sources, citing resources, and more while developing social studies and science content-area knowledge. Entries are organized by broad topics (those most likely to be taught as part of a traditional curriculum). Each individual entry (or "Xspace") begins with a video to attract students' interest followed by an informational article with Lexile reading levels clearly displayed to help guide students to the text best suited to their needs.

Go Grolier Online. 2012. Scholastic. http://go.grolier.com/. For grades 3 and up, this subscription-based online encyclopedia provides a table of contents, links to further reading within each article, and a section explaining how to cite articles. Entries are assigned reading levels.

GovSpot. StartSpot Mediaworks. http://www.govspot.com/. This free portal government site offers access to links to many government department websites, information on the various branches of the U.S. government, a link to the CIA *World FactBook*, frequently updated government news, and more. The homepage allows for navigation by a sidebar that organizes multiple links into broad categories such as "News," "Justice and Military," "Politics," and more.

Issues and Controversies Online. Infobase Publishing. http://www.infobasepublishing .com/OnlineProductDetail.aspx?ISBN=1578520274. This online subscription database provides a balanced discussion of both the pro and con of current events and issues covering topics from politics, business, social, education, and pop culture. Updated weekly, there are more than 1,000 current issues covered through both primary and secondary source documents.

Learning Express Library. http://www.learnatest.com/LEL/. This subscription database provides information, skill-building courses, exercises, e-books, practice tests, and more, all organized into "Learning Centers," which mainly fall into age and grade level categories from "Elementary School" to "Skill Building for Adults."

Opposing Viewpoints in Context. Gale Cengage Learning. http://www.gale.cengage .com/InContext/viewpoints.htm. A subscription-based online bibliographic resource that is subdivided by topic, the Opposing Viewpoints interface is easily navigable. Users can dive right into research from the main page, browsing by "Featured Viewpoints," magazine articles, other reference resources, statistics, or search options for any given issue. All topics are approached as a debate between opposing viewpoints for an unbiased representation.

Pop Culture Universe: Icons, Idols, Ideas. ABC CLIO. http://popculture.abc-clio .com/Authentication/LogOn?returnUrl=%2F. This online subscription database provides access to current information regarding American pop culture icons, idols, and ideas. A portion of the database focuses on historical documents. Students can analyze how past popular culture possibly influenced or contrasted with current trends.

Student Research Center. EBSCO Publishing. http://www.ebscohost.com/schools/ student-research-center. A subscription research collection of databases specifically designed for high school students, the Student Research Center acts as a hub, providing access to content from biography collections, literature and poetry databases, science collections, history collections, image collections, newspaper databases, and more. From the homepage, students can browse by topic heading or use a search tool, limiting their search by type of resource, publication date, full-text only, or even Lexile reading level.

Teen Health and Wellness. Rosen Publishing Online. http://www.teenhealthand wellness.com/. An online subscription resource, *Teen Health and Wellness* offers a comprehensive, categorized collection of information on various issues of health particularly relevant to young adults from body basics to drugs, alcohol, and sex. Informational articles and self-help tools are arranged in broad categories that are then divided by subtopics.

TeensHealth. The Nemours Foundation. http://kidshealth.org/teen/index.jsp? tracking=T_Home. Specifically designed for teens, this website allows students to explore health issues relevant to their lives such as sexual health, food and fitness, drugs and alcohol, mental health, and more. The homepage provides a colorful and interactive interface with hot topics, feature articles, and an expert to answer user questions.

World Book Advanced Online. http://www.worldbookonline.com/advanced/ home. This subscription-based version of *World Book* is designed to address the needs of high school students. Students have access to primary sources, e-books, news articles, a workspace, and multiple research tools, such as a dictionary, an atlas, and world newspapers. To review all of the available editions of *World Book* visit http://www.worldbookonline.com/training/.

World Book Discover. http://www.worldbookonline.com/training/discover/ index.htm. *World Book Discover* is a subscription-based online reference tool intended for use by students reading below grade level due to language or learning difficulties. In addition to *World Book's* usual expansive collection of articles, this resource also includes text-to-speech capabilities, tools such as the "How to Do Research" feature with tutorials, and exercises to help build information literacy skills (from how to find and evaluate sources to how to cite them).

Language(s)/Writing

Hacker, D. 2011. *A Writer's Reference with Resources for Multilingual Writers and ESL.* 7th ed. New York: Bedford/St. Martin's Press. This work is intended to assist all high school students and older with improving their academic writing. The book begins with an explanation of how to use a writing guide, and the table of contents provides easy navigation through the book's organization by broad topics from punctuation and sentence mechanics to research and sections on writing specific types of research papers. This book is especially useful for those students learning the English language.

Lester, James D. 2011. *Writing Research Papers: A Complete Guide.* 14th ed. New York: Longman. Despite its title, this work provides a rubric and resources for writing any type of essay (not just research papers). Intended for high school and college students, the book gives students examples of each type of essay as well as citation styles. The general research writing process is illustrated through a step-by-step format that takes students from selecting a topic to formatting the final paper.

Literature Resource Center. Gale Cengage Learning. http://www.gale.cengage .com/servlet/ItemDetailServlet?region=9&imprint=000&titleCode=GAL30& cf=n&type=4&id=159401. This subscription-based database provides full-text articles from scholarly journals and literary magazines as well as critical essays, work and topic overviews, biographies on worldwide authors, their works, and literary movements from all genres, disciplines, and time periods.

Mango Languages. http://www.mangolanguages.com/libraries/. Designed for use by all ages, Mango Basic and Mango Complete are subscription-based products intended to teach users simple conversational skills as well as more complex conversational skills in Chinese (Mandarin), French, Greek, Hindi, Japanese, Portuguese, Turkish, Spanish, Farsi, German, Hebrew, Italian, Korean, Russian, Thai, or Vietnamese. Mango focuses on practical speaking skills. Languages are taught through an interactive interface visually and through auditory tools. English as a second language (ESL) is also offered.

The Purdue Online Writing Lab (OWL). Purdue University. 2011. http://owl.english .purdue.edu/. OWL is a valuable, free reference resource for writing papers in MLA or APA format. The site provides resources to help students avoid plagiarism, write a good basic business letter, and craft a strong résumé. The most popular resources are highlighted on the homepage as well as suggested resources for particular users, from ESL students to professional writers.

San Jose State University Writing Center. *Writing Resources*. San Jose State University. http://www.sjsu.edu/writingcenter/writingresources/. The San Jose State University Writing Center provides links to resources on a large span of topics for student writers. Though intended for college students, most of these resources are still extremely useful for high school students. Users have the initial choice of choosing the format of informational resources such as handouts, style guides, or video tutorials.

Shabo, Magedah E., ed. 2009. *African American Literature: A Concise Anthology from Frederick Douglass to Toni Morrison*. Clayton, DE: Prestwick House. This book for all ages introduces students to three centuries of African American poems, essays, short stories, speeches, and more. The work is organized chronologically in two parts with timelines to provide historical context and is subdivided by individual authors. Each selection of an author's works is preceded by a brief biography of the author with an accompanying photograph.

Writer's Reference Center. Infobase Publishing. http://www.infobasepublishing .com/OnlineProductDetail.aspx?ISBN=0816081174. This subscription-based resource provides students with assistance in virtually all areas of writing from grammar and usage explanations to vocabulary, word choice, and rewriting advice. One particularly useful feature is a dynamic citation tool for MLA, Chicago, and APA formats.

Science/Math

Access Science. McGraw-Hill. http://accessscience.com/. This online subscription resource grants secondary students access to a vast science collection: encyclopedia articles, news, biographies, images, videos, and much more covering more than 7,000 scientific topics. Students can browse by topic headings, featured articles, or type of resource, or use the search box.

NOVA scienceNOW. PBS Online: WGBH Educational Foundation. http://www .pbs.org/wgbh/nova/sciencenow/. This website is an exciting resource for text-based information and a plethora of audio and visual learning experiences on scientific topics spanning every field of science from "Human Hibernation" to "A One Way Trip to Mars?" Information offered is dense and ideas complex so this source is better suited to older students. This resource includes images, videos, and even interactive features like polls to garner and hold interest in science topics.

Wayne, T. 2010. *American Women of Science Since 1900*. Santa Barbara, CA: ABC-CLIO. This two-volume reference resource provides 500 biographical entries on the most important (though still widely little-known) American women scientists of the twentieth century. Each entry includes black-and-white photographs, a bibliography of further resources, and a mini-biography discussing women's lives and the significance of each individual scientist, their contributions to their particular fields, and the struggles many of these scientists faced as female academics and researchers.

Social Studies

African-American History Online. InfoBase Publishing. http://www.infobase publishing.com/OnlineProductDetail.aspx?ISBN=0816041903. *African-American History Online* is a subscription database covering more than 500 years of African-American history through timelines, essays to explain historical context, biographies, image and video galleries, maps and charts, and entries on particular topics of importance to African American history.

American Indian History Online. Infobase Publishing. http://www.infobase publishing.com/OnlineProductDetail.aspx?ISBN=0816043779. *American Indian History Online* is a subscription database covering 15,000 years of American Indian history and culture. Topical entries, biographies, images and videos, maps and charts, primary sources, timelines, and more are used to provide high school students and up with a comprehensive view of American Indian history. A particular feature of interest may be the "Tribes index" where students may browse through an index covering more than 600 Native American groups.

Biography in Context. Gale Cengage Learning. http://www.gale.cengage .com/InContext/bio.htm. This database provides access to national and international biographical information. Search options include keyword, name, or genre and links give users access to full-text entries of information. An additional feature is clickable categories for browsing of popular searches, such as "Nobel Prize Winners" or "Obama Administration." Pair this database with an online website such as http://www.biography.com/ to find the latest "what's in the news" on famous people. The website is especially good for finding news articles about entertainers and world leaders.

Haywood, John., ed. 2011. *The New Atlas of World History: Global Events at a Glance*. Princeton, NJ: Princeton University Press. Full-color maps depict human history, from 6 million years ago to today. Most maps include detailed illustrated timelines that list important cultures, events, and developments. Maps and timelines include a summary of notable historical and cultural changes. Graphs portray key data on the world's five largest cities and total world population for the relevant year. Glossaries of peoples, cultures, and nations provide helpful context to the maps and timelines.

Purdy, Elizabeth R., ed. 2011. *Celebrating Women in American History*. 5 vols. New York: Facts on File. This five-volume set explores the impact women have had on American history through under-acknowledged roles from colonial times to the present. Each volume addresses a concise era of American history, with an essay introducing each era for context; the chapters are then organized by subject areas such as politics, science and medicine, or entertainment.

Shoulder, K. 2010. *The Everything World's Religions Book: Explore the Beliefs, Traditions, and Cultures of Ancient and Modern Religions*. Avon, MA: Adams Media. Intended for young adults and older, this book explores all major (and many of the minor) world religions from Native American tribal faiths to Judeo-Christian religions to Scientology and even atheism. From ancient to modern religions, each of the fifty entries explores the religion's history, the moral foundations of its major tenets, the rituals, and the cultural convictions associated with the religion.

College/Job Preparation

The Big Book of Jobs 2011–2012. 2011. New York: McGraw-Hill. Intended for anyone seeking a job, this reference work provides detailed information on over 250 careers in an alphabetical listing from architects to zoologists, techniques on how to write compelling résumés and cover letters, and advice on how to navigate the stressful process of job searching.

College Handbook 2012. 2011. 49th ed. New York: College Board. This general reference guide intended for high school students provides a guide to over 5,000 colleges and universities (every accredited college in the United States). Each entry includes information on admission procedures, graduation and attendance statistics, majors offered, tuition and other costs, athletics, on-campus activities, campus commuting, and demographic and geographic information.

Ducat, Diane. 2011. *Turning Points: Your Career Decision Making Guide*. 3rd ed. Upper Saddle River, NJ: Prentice Hall. Intended for all age groups, this work provides a guide to developing networking skills, uncovering job and internship leads, creating résumés and cover letters, and interviewing effectively. It guides readers through exploring their strengths and determining how to use these strengths to effectively reach their career goals, including making sound educational decisions for career development.

Ivester, Matt. 2011. *Lol ... OMG! What Every Student Needs to Know about Online Reputation Management, Digital Citizenship and Cyberbullying*. Las Vegas: Create Space. Intended for today's high school and college students, this work seeks to teach young adults how to manage their online reputation and digital citizenship. Organization by broad topic areas such as "Becoming a Conscious Creator of Content" allows students to easily navigate via the table of contents.

Occupational Outlook Handbook, 2012–2013. 2012. U.S. Department of Labor, Bureau of Labor Statistics. http://www.bls.gov/ooh/. This comprehensive career resource published by the U.S. Department of Labor's Bureau of Labor Statistics includes information about the nature of work, working conditions, and training for hundreds of occupations. It is an excellent resource for career guidance for high schoolers.

Shultze, Q. 2012. *Résumé 101: A Student and Recent-Grad Guide to Crafting Résumés and Cover Letters That Land Jobs*. Berkeley, CA: Ten Speed Press. Intended for recent graduates of high school or college, this book shows students how to craft powerful résumés and cover letters. Readers are guided step-by-step through the process of creating a work portfolio, how to get great references, what to do if your grade point average (GPA) isn't particularly high, and much more. The final chapter focuses on circulating your résumé and how to build a support network.

Tenabe, G., and K. Tenabe. 2011. *The Ultimate Scholarship Book 2012: Billions of Dollars in Scholarships, Grants, and Prizes*. 4th ed. Belmont, CA: Supercollege

LLC Press. This reference work offers information on more than 1.5 million monetary awards, scholarships, and grants to fund higher education, categorized by career goals, intended majors, public service, talents, athletics, religion, ethnicity, and more. This organization allows students to browse by their specific qualifications, ensuring efficiency of use. Each entry includes information on eligibility requirements, how to get more information, how to obtain an application, web listings, award amounts, and application deadlines.

Bibliography and Works Cited

AASL (American Association of School Librarians). 2006. "AASL Position Statement on the Confidentiality of Library Records." American Library Association. http://www.ala.org/aasl/aaslissues/positionstatements/conflibrecds.

ALA (American Library Association). 2008. "Libraries and the Internet Toolkit." American Library Association. http://www.ala.org/template.cfm?section=litoolkit.

———. 2012. "Copyright." http://www.ala.org/advocacy/copyright/.

Archer, Thomas. 1993. "Focus Groups for Kids." *Journal of Extension* 31, no. 1. http://www.joe.org/joe/1993spring/tt2.php.

Association of Specialized and Cooperative Library Agencies. 2008. "Library Services for People with Disabilities Policy." American Library Association. http://www.ala.org/ascla/asclaissues/libraryservices.

Baines, Lawrence. 2008. *A Teacher's Guide to Multisensory Learning: Improving Literacy by Engaging the Senses.* Alexandria, VA. Association for Supervision and Curriculum Development.

Banks, Carrie. 2004. "All Kinds of Flowers Grow Here: The Child's Place for Children with Special Needs." *The Journal of the Association for Library Service to Children* 2, no. 1: 5–10.

Berkman Center for Internet and Society. 2011. "Digital Natives." Harvard University. Last updated March 22. http://cyber.law.harvard.edu/research/youthandmedia/digitalnatives.

Boswell, Wendy. 2012. "The Invisible Web: What It Is, How You Can Find It." About.com. http://websearch.about.com/od/invisibleweb/a/invisible_web.htm.

Brandel, Mary. 2008. "Information Overload: Is It Time to Go on a Data Diet?" *Computerworld* 42, no. 1: 18–23.

Breivik, Patricia S. 2005. "21st Century Learning and Information Literacy." *Change* 3, no. 2: 20–27.

Cassell, Kay, and Uma Hiremath. 2007. "The Future of Reference." *Public Libraries* 46, no. 1: 10–12.

Center for the Digital Future. 2008. "Annual Internet Survey by the Center for the Digital Future Finds Shifting Trends among Adults About the Benefits and Consequences of Children Going Online." University of Southern California. http://www.digitalcenter.org/pdf/2008-Digital-Future-Report-Final-Release.pdf.

Child Development Institute. 2010. "Language Development in Children." Child Development Institute. http://www.childdevelopmentinfo.com/development/language_development.shtml.

ChildCare Aware. 2012. "Developmentally Appropriate Practices." ChildCare Aware of America, National Association of Child Care Resource and Referral Agencies (NACCRRA). Accessed August 16. http://childcareaware.org/child-care-providers/program-planning/developmentally-appropriate-practices.

Conant, Beth. 2010. "Answers to Commonly Asked Questions Concerning Developmentally Appropriate Practice." Early Childhood Educators and Family Web Corner. http://users.stargate.net/~cokids/dapQnA.html.

Cooper, Gregory M., and Michael R. King. 2007. *Predators: Who They Are and How to Stop Them*. Amherst, NY: Prometheus.

Corporation for National and Community Service. 2009. "Administering Surveys to K–5 Children for Post-project Evaluation." ETR Associates. Posted on February 11. http://www.nationalserviceresources.org/practices/19788.

DelCampo, Diana S. 2000. *Understanding Teens*. [Las Cruces, NM]: Cooperative Extension Service, College of Agriculture and Home Economics, New Mexico State University.

Fitzpatrick, Jody, James Sanders, and Blaine Worthen. 2004. *Program Evaluation: Alternative Approaches and Practical Guidelines*. 3rd ed. Boston: Pearson.

Gleason, Paul. 2008. "MySpace—and Yours: Born Digital." *Harvard Magazine*, March–April. http://harvardmagazine.com/2008/03/born-digital.html.

Goode, Caron B. 2009. "What You Say and What Your Children Hear: Why There's a Difference." Healthy Wealthy nWise. http://healthywealthynwise.com/article.aspx?author=Caron%20Goode&title=What%20You%20Say%20and%20What%20Your%20Children%20Hear%20%96%20Why%20There%92s%20a%20Difference&Article=153.

Gorman, Michele. 2006. "'The Terrible Teens': Understanding Adolescent Development Is Key to Successful Teen Services." *School Library Journal* 52, no. 6: 34.

Gorman, Michele, and Tricia Suellentrop. 2009. *Connecting Young Adults and Libraries*. 4th ed. New York: Neal-Schuman.

Harper, Meghan. 2011. *Reference Sources and Services for Youth*. New York: Neal-Schuman.

Hathaway, Kathy. 2006. "How the GPO Got Its Groove Back: Government Printing Office and Government Information on the Internet." *Reference Librarian* no. 93: 109–128.

Howard, Barbara J. 2002. "Communicating with Children." In *Bright Futures in Practice: Mental Health—Volume II. Tool Kit*, edited by Michael Jellinek, Bina P. Patel, and Mary Froehle, 84–85. Arlington, VA: National Center for Education in Maternal and Child Health. http://www.brightfutures.org/mentalhealth/pdf/families/ec/communicating.pdf.

Huffman, Celia, and Robert J. Rua. 2008. "Measuring the Effectiveness of Homework Centers in Libraries." *Children and Libraries: The Journal of the Association for Library Service to Children* 6, no. 3: 25–29.

Jacobs, James A., James R. Jacobs, and Shinjoung Yeo. 2005. "Government Information in the Digital Age: The Once and Future Federal Depository Library Program." *Journal of Academic Librarianship* 31, no. 3: 198–208.

Jaeger, Paul T. 2002. "Section 508 Goes to the Library: Complying with Federal Legal Standards to Produce Accessible Electronic and Information Technology in Libraries." *Information Technology and Disabilities Journal* 8, no. 2: 1–22.

Kern, Kathleen. 2003. "Communication, Patron Satisfaction, and the Reference Interview." *Reference and User Services Quarterly* 43, no. 1: 47–49.

Kostelnik, Marjorie J., Anne K. Soderman, and Alice P. Whiren. 2007. *Developmentally Appropriate Curriculum: Best Practices in Early Childhood Education*. 4th ed. Upper Saddle River, NJ: Pearson.

Kuntz, Kelly. 2003. "Pathfinders: Helping Students Find Paths to Information." *Multimedia Schools* 10, no. 3: 12.

Lamb, Annette, and Larry Johnson. 2008. "The Virtual Teacher-Librarian: Establishing and Maintaining an Effective Web Presence." *Teacher Librarian* 35, no. 4: 69–71.

Latrobe, Kathy, ed. 1998. *Emerging School Library Media Centers: Historical Issues and Perspectives*. Englewood, CO: Libraries Unlimited.

Lee, Deborah O. 2005. "Marketing Resources for the Busy Librarian." *College and Undergraduate Libraries* 12, nos. 1/2: 81–91.

Literacy Builders: For the Love of Learning. 2012. "Conventions of Print." Literacy Builders: For the Love of Learning. http://www.literacy-builders.com/free-resources/156-conventions-of-print-literacy-a-z.

Mediavilla, Cindy. 2001. *Creating the Full-Service Homework Center in Your Library*. Chicago: American Library Association.

Mindtools. 2010. "Active Listening: Hear What People Are Really Saying." Mindtools. http://www.mindtools.com/CommSkll/ActiveListening.htm.

Morgan, Erin, and Angela Huebner. 2009. "Adolescent Growth and Development." Virginia Cooperative Extension, Virginia Tech and Virginia State University. http://www.ext.vt.edu/pubs/family/350-850/350-850.html.

National Association for the Education of Young Children. 2009. *Developmentally Appropriate Practice in Early Childhood Programs Serving Children from Birth through Age 8*. Washington, DC: National Association for the Education of Young Children. http://www.naeyc.org/files/naeyc/file/positions/position%20statement%20Web.pdf.

National Center for Missing and Exploited Children. 2012. "The CyberTipline." National Center for Missing and Exploited Children. Accessed August 16. http://www.cybertipline.org/.

NICHCY (National Dissemination Center for Children with Disabilities). 2008a. "Categories of Disability under IDEA Law." NICHCY. http://www.nichcy.org/Disabilities/Categories/Pages/Default.aspx.

———. 2008b. "Specific Disabilities." NICHCY. http://www.nichcy.org/disabilities/specific/pages/default.aspx.

———. 2008c. "Speech and Language Impairments." NICHCY. http://nichcy.org/disability/specific/speechlanguage.

North Central Regional Educational Laboratory. 2008. "Developmentally Appropriate Practices." North Central Regional Educational Laboratory. http://www.ncrel.org/sdrs/areas/issues/methods/instrctn/in5lk5.htm.

Oesterreich, Lesia. 1995. "Ages and Stages—Six- through Eight-Year-Olds." National Network for Child Care. http://www.nncc.org/child.dev/ages.stages.6y.8y.html.

———. 2001. "9–11 Ages and Stages." Iowa State University, University Extension. http://www.extension.iastate.edu/Publications/PM1530I.pdf.

Ohio Department of Education. 2010. "Your Teen's Development: Grades 9–12." Ohio Department of Education. Last modified May 11. http://www.ode.state.oh.us/GD/Templates/Pages/ODE/ODEDetail.aspx?page=3&TopicRelationID=1530&ContentID=37066&Content=37139.

Ohio Reference Excellence. 2012. "Module 2 The Interview." Ohio Library Council. Accessed August 16. http://www.olc.org/ore/2intro.htm.

Page, Daniel. 2004. "The Importance of Nonverbal Communication in Information Services." *Library Mosaics* 15, no. 6: 11.

Patton, Michael Q. 1990. *Qualitative Evaluation and Research Methods*. 2nd ed. Newbury Park, CA: SAGE Publications.

PBS Parents. 2009. "Talking with Kids: Strategies for Talking with Kids about Everything!" PBS. http://www.pbs.org/parents/talkingwithkids.

Power, Effie. 1930. *Library Service for Children*. Chicago: American Library Association.

Rees, Gwendolen. 1924. *Libraries for Children: A History and a Bibliography*. New York: H.W. Wilson.

Rose, David, Anne Meyer, and Chuck Hitchcock, eds. 2005. *The Universally Designed Classroom: Accessible Curriculum and Digital Technologies.* Cambridge, MA: Harvard Education Press.

Ruffin, Novella. 2009. *Adolescent Growth and Development.* Virginia Cooperative Extension, Virginia State University. http://www.ext.vt.edu/pubs/family/350-850/350-850.html.

RUSA (Reference and User Services Association). 2008. "Definitions of Reference." American Library Association. http://www.ala.org/ala/mgrps/divs/rusa/resources/guidelines/definitionsreference.cfm.

Schwarz, Mattahias. 2008. "MalWebolence: The world of web trolling." *New York Times Magazine.* Available http://www.nytimes.com/2008/08/03/magazine/03trolls-t.html?pagewanted=all.

Search Institute. 2003. "Developmental Assets Lists." Search Institute. http://www.search-institute.org/developmental-assets/lists.

Segal, Jeanne, Melinda Smith, and Jaelline Jaffe. 2012. "Nonverbal Communication: Improving Your Nonverbal Skills and Reading Body Language." Last updated June. http://www.helpguide.org/mental/eq6_nonverbal_communication.htm.

Shellsburg Public Library. 2012. "Reference Policy." http://www.shellsburg.lib.ia.us/library-information/policies/reference.

Siegle, Del. 2010. "Likert Scale." Neag School of Education, University of Connecticut. http://www.gifted.uconn.edu/siegle/research/instrument%20Reliability%20and%20Validity/Likert.html.

Smith, Gregory S. 2007. *How to Protect Your Children on the Internet: A Road Map for Parents and Teachers.* Santa Barbara, CA: Praeger.

St. Louis Public Library. 2002. "Reference Policy." St. Louis Public Library. http://www.slpl.org/slpl/library/Article240097422.asp.

Sturm, Brian. 2008. "History of Youth Services Timeline." University of North Carolina School of Information and Library Science. http://www.ils.unc.edu/courses/2008_spring/inls733_001/history.html.

Torrans, Lee Ann. 2003. *Law for K–12 Libraries and Librarians.* Westport, CT: Libraries Unlimited.

Trief, Ellen. 2007. "The Use of Tangible Cues for Children with Multiple Disabilities and Visual Impairment." *Journal of Visual Impairment and Blindness* 101, no. 10: 613–619.

University of Manitoba. 2007. "Getting Sarcastic with Kids." *Science Daily,* August 9. http://www.sciencedaily.com/releases/2007/08/070803141811.htm.

Walter, Virginia (2010) *Twenty-First Century Kids, Twenty-First Century Librarians.* Chicago: American Library Association.

Walter, Virginia, and Cindy Mediavilla. 2011. "Homework Center Outcomes." UCLA Graduate School of Education and Information Studies: Department of Information Studies. Updated October 25. http://is.gseis.ucla.edu/research/homework/index.htm.

Wemett, Lisa. 2007. "The Building Bridges Project: Library Services to Youth with Disabilities." *Library Services to Children with Special Needs* 5, no. 3: 15–20.

Wertheim, Edward. 2008. "The Importance of Verbal and Nonverbal Communication." College of Business Administration, Northeastern University.

Wikipedia: The Free Encyclopedia. 2012. "Web 2.0." http://en.wikipedia.org/wiki/Web_2.0.

Willard, Nancy. 2007. *Cyber-Safe Kids, Cyber-Savvy Teens: Helping Learn to Use the Internet Safely and Responsibly.* San Francisco: Jossey-Bass.

Willis, Mark R. 1999. *Dealing with Difficult People in the Library.* Chicago: American Library Association.

16
Information Literacy in the Reference Department

Contemporary libraries—whether public, academic, special, or otherwise—are far more than mere storehouses for books and magazines. With few exceptions, today's libraries exist as spaces of dynamic learning in which we actively engage with the products and processes of our culture, exploring the associations and connections between the disparate elements of our changing world. To do so, however, we first need to understand how to use the resources available to us. Many users, daunted by the complexity of our information organizations, give up before reaching this point, content to find what they are looking for in a bookstore or with a quick Google search. Faced with such despair, passionate librarians have an obligation to make the library a less forbidding space.

Reference services are one of the most ideal means to make the library a nonthreatening environment because it is here that we have the opportunity to teach our users how the library really works. This may seem a surprising proposition at first. After all, isn't the primary function of the reference librarian to point users to the information they seek? To some extent, this is, in fact, the case, but reference is also teaching users how to make sense of the library and its resources for themselves—encouraging them to become self-directed, critical thinkers. As has been suggested elsewhere in this book, the reference librarian should be the user's guide on the quest for knowledge, not his or her proxy. We can walk beside our users, but it is rarely a good idea to walk the road for them. In leading them on their path, we can help them find their own sense of direction, developing the skills known as information literacy.

Information literacy is defined as a set of abilities enabling individuals to "recognize when information is needed and have the ability to locate, evaluate, and use effectively the needed information" (American Library Association, 1989). Instruction in these activities evolved from bibliographic instruction (BI), which sought to "meet basic needs and at the same time teach skills that users can transfer to new situations, new information tools, and new environments to help them learn how to learn" (Grassian, 2004: 52). Typical activities of BI included orientations to the library, classes, tours, pathfinders, credit courses, and development of new instructional materials and guides to using reference tools; it also included experiments in integrating bibliographic instruction into the curriculum. Two pioneers in this area were Evan Farber at Earlham College in Indiana and Patricia Knapp with the Monteith College Library Experiment

(Knapp, 1966). Information literacy encompasses and expands the concepts of bibliographic instruction to include outreach, collaboration, and sequenced learning beyond the library (Grassian, 2004).

The American Library Association (ALA) turned its attention to information literacy in 1989, creating a Presidential Task Force on Information Literacy. This led to the creation of the definition cited previously and further resulted in the creation of the National Forum on Information Literacy, an organization of more than seventy-five national organizations. Nine years later, ALA (1998) issued "A Progress Report on Information Literacy: An Update on the American Library Association Presidential Committee on Information Literacy: A Final Report." This report discussed the activities of the National Forum on Information Literacy.

Education organizations and agencies have also been concerned with information literacy, particularly in relation to new technologies. The Committee on Information Technology Literacy and the National Research Council (1999) produced a report on this topic titled *Being Fluent with Information Technology*. The term FIT (fluent with information technology) was used to describe people who have achieved a sufficient understanding of technology to apply problem solving and critical thinking to using technology. It differentiated between information literacy with its focus on content and evaluation and information technology "fluency" that focuses on a more skilled use of technology. The National Council for the Accreditation of Teacher Education has also included information literacy competencies in its standards (http://www.ncate.org/Standards/NCATE/Unit Standards/tabid/123/Default.aspx), as have many other accrediting agencies, including the Middle States Commission on Higher Education (http://www .msche.org/?Nav1=ABOUT&Nav2+MISSION) and the Northwest Commission on Colleges and Universities (http://www.nwcuu.org/StandardsandPolicies/ AccreditationStandards/AccreditationStandards.htm).

In the past few decades, a consciousness of the need to foster universal information literacy has been central to libraries' approaches to user orientation. Instead of focusing only on content, libraries now focus on user outcomes and the need to connect users to knowledge. Whether this involves working one-on-one with users, developing online tutorials, presenting information in classroom situations, or working with teachers and faculty to integrate information literacy skills into their lesson plans, the library has a major role to play in information literacy. In the process, the face of information literacy has changed from simply teaching skills to placing an emphasis on encouraging curiosity and creativity. The ability to think and to evaluate information is at the core of this new information literacy. Randy Burke Hensley (2004) expresses this well, stating, "fostering an individual's sense of curiosity and creativity in tandem with developing his ability to find, locate, and evaluate information is the essence of information literacy" (p. 35).

Standards for Information Literacy

In the past decade, many organizations have developed standards for information literacy. The first were developed by the American Association of School Librarians

(AASL) and the Association of Educational Communications and Technology (AECT) in 1998. "Information Literacy Standards for Student Learning," in *Information Power: Building Partnerships for Learning*, provided standards by competency area for students in K–12, including standards for information literacy (AASL and AECT, 1998). These standards were replaced by *Empowering Learners: Guidelines for School Library Programs* (AASL, 2009) that emphasized the importance of technology and evidence-based learning and the library as a place that is influenced by its surroundings. AASL also developed *Standards for the 21st-Century Learner* as a guide to learning standards for students. In these standards, students use their skills, resources, and tools to:

> Inquire, think critically, and gain knowledge,
> Draw conclusions, make informed decisions, apply knowledge to new situations, and create new knowledge,
> Share knowledge and participate ethically and productively as members of our democratic society,
> Pursue personal and aesthetic growth. (AASL, 2007)

The Association of College and Research Libraries (ACRL) in its 2000 publication *Information Literacy Competency Standards for Higher Education*, defined information literacy as the basis for lifelong learning. These standards were instrumental in providing a framework for a discussion of information literacy within higher education (Arp and Woodward, 2002). The standards define an information-literate person as able to:

1. Determine the extent of information needed;
2. Access the needed information effectively and efficiently;
3. Evaluate information and its sources critically and incorporate selected information into one's knowledge base;
4. Use information effectively to accomplish a specific purpose; and
5. Understand the economic, legal, and social issues surrounding the use of information, and use information ethically and legally. (ACRL, 2000)

Approaches to Information Literacy

Many have outlined the components involved in teaching information literacy. One approach is "The Big 6," which was proposed by Eisenberg and Berkowitz (2000) and is now available at http://www.big6.com/. The authors outlined a practical six-step strategy for working with learners that could be applied equally well to the reference interaction:

1. Defining the information problem
2. Determining the possible sources
3. Locating the sources
4. Using the information and extracting the information needed
5. Organizing the material and presenting it
6. Evaluating the product and process (Big6, 2012)

Another strategy was proposed by Cunningham and Lanning (2002), who presented various approaches for librarians working with faculty to integrate information literacy into the curriculum including information literacy presentations in a class, working as a liaison with an academic department, and providing workshops for faculty. Kobelski and Reichel (1987) defined conceptual frameworks for instruction that included methods such as teaching systematic literature searching, teaching about primary and secondary sources, understanding citation patterns, understanding how different forms of publications are designed, and understanding index structure and how it is designed to describe content.

Reporting on the ACRL Institute for Information Literacy, Susan Barnes Whyte (2001) states, "when we teach, we need to think less about the right way to do research, the right databases. We need to think more about who we're teaching. Ask them what they think they need to know. . . . I think that teaching is a succession of minor epiphanies. . . . It cannot be accomplished in one session or in one year of education. Build upon those epiphanies!" (p. 15). This approach is further supported by Carol Collier Kuhlthau (1999), who stated that a user's needs are best fulfilled by a series of instructional sessions over a period of time rather than just one session. She described the need for the librarian to intervene and help the user when and where the user's need arises and asserts that this is an individual need.

Moving into the digital age, Mackey and Jacobsen (2011) identified the need to fold other types of literacy into information literacy such as media literacy, digital literacy, visual literacy and cyberliteracy, which they call collectively metaliteracy. In this digital world, the user not only must learn to identify the need for information, find it, evaluate it, and use it but also must use the emerging technologies in the information search. The number of choices for finding information has exponentially increased and with it the complexity of deciding which information sources meet the users' needs. Users must also decide how they can produce and share information using the appropriate social media or other technologies.

Information Literacy by Type of Library

Information Literacy in School Media Centers

School media centers try to provide a structured approach to teaching students how to do research in order to prepare them for lifelong learning and for academic research. School media specialists have found that collaborating with teachers is very important to success and that students are best taught using real examples from their school assignments. School media specialists and teachers work together to help students learn to evaluate information sources and to develop search strategies. School media specialists have also found it useful to take high school seniors to a university library and introduce them to the library and its resources. In addition to the AASL standards, school librarians continue to develop and share their strategies for integrating information literacy into new education programs.

Information Literacy in the Academic Library

The academic library is responsible for helping the student to make the transition to more structured research, for example, researching an assigned topic. The academic librarian must begin wherever the school library left off, continuing to blend the skills of structured information seeking with independent information seeking (Hinchliffe, 2003). In order to do this successfully, the librarian must work with the faculty so that the students learn through subject-specific content rather than just through abstract presentations. As is the case with elementary and high school students, the teachable moment is important. The best time for a student to learn is when he or she has a topic to research. In order to make information literacy sustainable in the university setting, librarians must encourage the faculty to take ownership of information literacy (Bridgeland and Whitehead, 2005).

Information Literacy in the Public Library

The public library is often the first library the child encounters. Here the child learns how to use a library and how to use the information technology independently or with the help of the librarian. The introduction may be one-to-one or may be a class visit to the library. The public library provides for children and adults a continuing experience in independent learning. Here they can explore and grow on their own (Hinchliffe, 2003). Public librarians have become more interested in developing their own approaches to information literacy in recent years. They often partner with school librarians to help students learn to use library resources and work with adults returning to school. A library advocacy program developed in 2000 by ALA continued the articulation of information literacy in the public library with this statement: "Librarians will partner with government, education, business, and other organizations to create models for information literate communities" (p. 5). Public libraries have developed structured programs to introduce users to computers and online databases particularly in areas such as health, job searching, and genealogy. Literature in this area of public library information literacy will no doubt continue to increase.

Information Literacy in the Special Library

The special library provides information literacy on a one-on-one basis. Many users of special libraries have already gained some instruction from public, school, or academic libraries. Because special libraries vary widely, the librarian must introduce the user to the library individually (Hinchliffe, 2003). Carmel O'Sullivan (2002) points out the need for information literacy in a corporate setting. She states that many of the skills needed by workers are part of information literacy including advocacy and inquiry, the ability to learn, networking, resource investigation, IT skills, problem solving, and the ability to review risks, opportunities, and successes. O'Sullivan also points out that the librarian must move beyond the walls of the library and "apply corporate terminology to relevant information concepts" in order to work successfully with employees (p. 12). Just as in schools and universities, librarians in a special library setting must make their information literacy relevant to the employees.

Social and Ethical Uses of Information

Plagiarism has become one of the greatest problems in the use of information. Real information literacy is more than the simple ability to find what one is looking for; it is the ability to parse, recombine, and make use of such knowledge. Those who simply appropriate materials without thinking critically about them do not understand how to use information. One of ACRL's (2000) standards states that students should be able to "understand the economic, legal, and social issues surrounding the use of information, and access and use information ethically and legally." *Standards for the 21st-Century Learner* (AASL, 2007) also addresses the social responsibilities of students. Standard 3 states, "Use information and knowledge in the service of democratic values. . . . Respect the principles of intellectual freedom." This standard goes on to say, "Use technology and other information tools to organize and display knowledge and understanding in ways that others can view, use, and assess."

Lynn D. Lampert (2004) has pointed out some of the issues surrounding plagiarism. Often there is no consistent approach by faculty, so the student does not have good guidelines. In other circumstances, it is not clear who is responsible for enforcing plagiarism guidelines, so no one puts them into practice. Finally, Lampert says it is not clear whether the faculty is teaching students to integrate and cite information sources they have used and incorporated into their writing. Arp and Woodward (2002) point out that "technology has blurred the once clearly delineated and separate processes of the use of information and its creation. Cutting, pasting, and cropping are simple keystrokes. The knowledge of when these actions are appropriate or inappropriate is not so easily imparted" (p. 130). Librarians can improve this situation by teaching how to deal with exact citations and with paraphrasing and by providing the faculty with resources for explaining what constitutes plagiarism. Some librarians are now conducting workshops on academic honesty and on plagiarism prevention. Many academic libraries provide information on quoting and paraphrasing on their websites. Some good examples of online tutorials on plagiarism are Rutgers University Library at Camden (http://library.camden.rutgers.edu/EducationalModule/plagiarism/) and the Library at Acadia University (http://library.acadiau.ca/tutorials/plagiarism). The website Plagiarism.org (http://www.plagiarism.org/) is also a good source of information.

One-on-One Instruction

Although we may think of information literacy as a group activity, librarians have traditionally done a great deal of information literacy instruction on a one-on-one basis. In many library situations, librarians use the opportunity of a reference question to provide some individualized library instruction. At times, the help they provide may be as simple as teaching the user how to search the online catalog. Where circumstances permit, they may then move on to instruct the user in how to search a particular index or construct a Boolean search string. Alternately, they might be called on to provide a more in-depth research consultation, allowing them the space and time to educate the user about more detailed but important aspects of doing research in a specific subject area.

Those who recommend making instruction a part of the reference encounter advise that the librarian find out what the user already knows to avoid pedantically reteaching familiar skills. The librarian should query the user as to whether he or she would like to learn more about a database or catalog before proceeding, so as to allow the user to learn at his or her own pace. Beck and Turner (2001) recommend that librarians prepare mini lessons that they can teach at the reference desk, supplementing lessons with handouts. Confronted with those unwilling to listen to more formal lessons, librarians can verbalize the search process so that the user understands the steps the librarian is taking and the decisions the librarian is making.

Librarians should also be aware of "the teachable moment." They must decide if the user is receptive to learning and, if so, use this opportunity to impart appropriate information. Susan Avery (2008) suggests that librarians should be sure that the user is at the computer keyboard since the user will, no doubt, learn more by doing the search himself or herself. This idea of the teachable moment can be extended to chat reference where many librarians mix library instruction with the reference transaction (Johnson, 2003).

Asking questions along the way also helps keep the user engaged in his or her research, thereby demonstrating that the process is as important as the answer. Lisa A. Ellis (2004) describes a topic development exercise that is used in her institution to help students think about their paper topic. This exercise can be done via chat or e-mail. In this exercise, questions are asked about the topic in an effort to further its development. The questions center on what the student already knows and what the student needs to know about the topic. This process helps the student to refine and narrow his or her topic. Jeanne Galvin (2005) suggests that the library should take advantage of out-of-class opportunities to promote and support information literacy. She discusses the use of library pathfinders, individual instruction at the reference desk, instruction in the virtual reference environment, and library webpages. Galvin points out that the use of assignment-specific pathfinders that are readable and accessible and that can be used by students for completing assignments are more useful than more general pathfinders. In addition to pathfinders, LibGuides provide another way to provide guidance by topic. This can be either a LibGuide designed for a particular class or a LibGuide on a subject often requested by users (Mohia, 2012).

For virtual reference, the librarian can develop short scripted messages to include in the interview or to attach to the information that is provided to the user in order to instruct as the question is answered (Beck and Turner, 2001). "Instruction via chat reference is a prime example of 'learning at the point of need' and librarians have found users very open to learning in the chat reference situation" (Galvin, 2005: 355). The fact that the transcript of the chat is sent to the user gives the user a way to refer back to the information imparted.

The librarian can also use the library's website as a way to introduce the students to library resources. They can provide web tutorials or other kinds of web-based instruction, or list good free websites that have been evaluated by the library staff. "A well-constructed and carefully maintained portal would be a good vehicle for breaking down the border between the free Internet resources favored by students and authoritative, scholarly databases not available via Google" (Galvin, 2005: 355).

Information Literacy in a Classroom Setting

School and college libraries and, to a lesser extent, public libraries, have tried to integrate information literacy into the classroom. They have worked with teachers and faculty to teach information literacy at the moment when the student most needs it in order to complete a project. By providing this instruction at such a turning point in the research process, teachers can maximize the learning experience for the students and guide them to appropriate resources. Indiana University librarians have written about their experience attempting to implement a program that integrated information literacy into specific disciplines—in this case social sciences (gender studies) and a hard science (biology). They worked with the faculty to incorporate the information literacy learning into a variety of assignments. The results proved that this new collaboration was successful for the students, instructors, and librarians (Winterman, Donovan, and Slough, 2011).

Molly R. Flaspohler (2003) studied the effectiveness of an instruction program at a four-year liberal arts college. In this study, librarians, working with faculty who taught an introductory course, taught three library sessions focused on active learning and aimed at improving the students' ability to use library resources including online indexes, and to evaluate and identify appropriate periodical literature. This study showed improvement in the ability of the students to use quality academic resources when information literacy skills are integrated into the curriculum.

Many promote the idea of an across-the-curriculum model in which information literacy is fully integrated into the curriculum. In this way, students learn about research and problem solving as part of whatever subject they are learning. The framework should include:

- Recognizing the need for information;
- Developing skills in using information technologies;
- Accessing information from appropriate sources;
- Critically analyzing and evaluating information;
- Processing and organizing information;
- Applying information for effective and creative decision making;
- Effectively communicating information and knowledge;
- Understanding and respecting the ethical, legal, and sociopolitical aspects of information and its technologies; and

- Developing an appreciation of lifelong learning. (Orr, Appleton, and Wallin, 2001: 459)

D'Angelo and Maid (2004) reported on an information literacy program at Arizona State University. In a collaboration between the Multimedia Writing and Technical Communications (MWTC) program and the Library at Arizona State University East, D'Angelo and Maid described a three-credit course, "InfoGlut: Deal with It." The course emphasized how to incorporate new information; how to effectively select information; and how to understand issues related to information, including economic, legal, and ethical issues. They reported that students advocated for the inclusion of information literacy in their program; as a result, other courses were identified in which an information literacy component would be added.

Impact of New Technology on the Teaching of Information Literacy

Through the rise of information technology we have taken great steps to expanding and universalizing our access to knowledge. To many, the way the World Wide Web and other innovations have leveled the playing field seems almost like a utopia, a better world in which all are potentially equal. We must remember, though, that the word *utopia* literally means "no place." The price we pay for living in such a world is the obligation to shape it ourselves, making meaning out of the inchoate mass of information with which we are met. As a result, it has become much more important to be able to critically evaluate information sources in order to select the best. The librarian is challenged daily to present to the user information about reliable sources and the differences between leased electronic resources and sources on the Internet. Information literacy instruction's purpose is to change the way students approach the search for information and to teach them more complex research methods and strategies. This can be done through a variety of instructional approaches including online tutorials (Bloom and Deyrup, 2003: 238). Southeastern Oklahoma State University has developed an interactive tutorial (http://www.se.edu/lib/searchpath/your searchpath/index.html) that helps students to write a paper. It covers areas such as these:

- The types of sources available, such as magazines, books, newspapers, indexes, and the World Wide Web
- Selecting sources, including the difference between library sources and Internet information
- Topic selection and how to narrow the topic
- How to search the catalog
- How to search an index

The University of California at Berkeley Library has developed a tutorial on evaluating webpages for its students to use (http://www.lib.berkeley.edu/ TeachingLib/Guides/Internet/FindInfo.html). The tutorial encourages students to ask questions that will help them to evaluate a webpage and decide whether it is a reliable source of information. The site suggests the following steps:

- Examine the URL to see what it reveals about the site—for example, whether it ends in .edu, .org, or .com.
- Examine who the author is, whether it is current, and the author's credentials.
- Look for indicators of quality information such as footnotes, permissions to reproduce or copyright information, links to other resources, and what other sites link to this resource.

This tutorial shows how complicated it is to examine a site and decide whether it is a good reference to use.

Librarians are also exploring how to integrate information literacy into the various learning management systems such as Blackboard and WebCT. It is clear that a good way to reach students is to have information literacy tutorials embedded in the learning management systems. Pamela Alexandra Jackson (2007) surveyed California State University librarians about their use of learning management systems as a teaching tool. Based on her survey she made several recommendations as to strategies librarians could use. She suggested having a library learning management system liaison, creating a partnership with the learning management system administrator and the faculty involved in using the learning management system, training librarians to be comfortable using the system, developing information literacy packages that can be included in a learning management system, and participating in discussion boards. Jackson gives examples of information literacy packages developed and used at San Diego State University: "Evaluating Information," "Popular versus Scholarly," "Primary versus Secondary Sources in the Sciences," "Developing a Research Strategy," and "Avoiding Plagiarism."

Mobile technology is also being used to provide user instruction. The Sheridan Libraries at Johns Hopkins University developed podcasts to present information about using the library (Murray, 2010). Podcasts can also include walking tours, orientations, and lectures on library resources. Murray State University put Camtasia instruction videos on YouTube (Murray, 2010). Mobile access to library catalogs and databases also provide more access to users.

Assessment and Evaluation of Information Literacy

Teaching assessment and evaluation is equally as important as teaching the basic research skills found in information literacy programs. To judge the effectiveness of the program, learning outcomes must be determined. These outcomes are influenced by the environment, that is, the type of educational institution or library. The use of multiple assessment tools is recommended, including surveys, pre- and posttests, focus groups, and assessment built into the assignments. ACRL's (2003) "Characteristics of Programs of Information Literacy That Illustrate Best Practices" states that the ideal information literacy program is one that "establishes a process for assessment at the outset." The Assessment/Evaluation section identifies both outcomes for program evaluation and student outcomes.

For program evaluation, the recommendation is to use multiple methods for assessment/evaluation, including formative and summative evaluation and short-term and longitudinal evaluation. For student outcomes, the recommendation is to use a variety of appropriate outcome measures, such as portfolio assessment, oral defense, quizzes, essays, direct observation, anecdotal, peer and self-review, and experience to allow for differences in learning and teaching styles.

Molly R. Flaspohler (2003) describes three assessment tools used in her study of the information literacy project conducted at Concordia College. She used an information literacy questionnaire developed by the UCLA libraries, a comparison of the bibliographies of the pilot groups and the control groups to see if the instruction had been successful, and a start/stop exercise that asked the students to write "what they will start doing in the library and what they will stop doing as a result of their session with a librarian" (p. 133). This is a good example of using multiple assessment methods in order to have more than one perspective on the gains achieved.

The most recent information literacy assessment efforts are Project SAILS (Standard Assessment of Information Literacy Skills), ETSs iSkills Assessment, and the Bay Area Community Colleges Information Competency (Larsen, Izenstark, and Burkhardt, 2010). Project SAILS began in 2001 as an initiative of Kent State University. The goal of this project was to develop a standardized test for information literacy skills that would allow librarians to measure the information literacy of groups of students. The three-year research and development project in partnership with the Association of Research Libraries in 2003, with funding from IMLS, produced the SAILS test (https://www.projectsails .org/AboutSAILS). It is a multiple-choice test based on ACRL's (2000) *Information Literacy Competency Standards for Higher Education*.

The work on the ETS iSkills Assessment tool began with an International ICT (Information and Communications Technology) Literacy Panel in 2001. In 2003, a National Higher Education ICT Literacy Initiative was developed that was a consortium of seven colleges and universities working with ETS to develop an assessment test. One of the driving forces behind this effort was the belief of many that the present generation of students are less information savvy and do not have well-developed critical thinking skills. This test is a scenario-based assessment tool that "focuses on the cognitive problem-solving and critical-thinking skills associated with using technology to handle information" (Katz, 2007: 4). The results allow educators and librarians to assess both information literacy and technology competencies.

The Bay Area Community Colleges Information Competency Assessment Project was developed in order to allow students to show information competency in lieu of taking a required course. It is an open source program that maps to the ACRL (2000) information literacy standards (Larsen, Izenstark, and Burkhardt, 2010).

Information-Seeking Behavior

In order to assist users, it is important to understand the stages of the information-seeking process. Carol Kuhlthau's (1993) important research into the information-seeking process has been key to understanding these stages. She describes the users' process from the time they become aware of needing information, to their selection of a topic, their exploration of the topic and its various facets, their formulation of a more focused topic based on their exploration, their actual collection of information for their project, and finally their presentation of the results of their findings. In order to successfully help a user, the librarian must try to understand where the users are in their information seeking. Kuhlthau further defines the various degrees of assistance librarians can offer as they interact with users from simply organizing the materials so the users can work on their own to actual counseling of users in need of more assistance as they progress in the search process.

Further Considerations

Information literacy is an ongoing topic of interest; it is no more likely to go away than the books we store on our shelves. Staying at the cutting edge of this fundamental part of our professional activities, especially as it applies to reference services, is an obligation. Fortunately, many of the leading library publications have taken up the call to provide this information: The *Reference and User Services Quarterly*, *Reference Services Review*, *College and Research Libraries*, and the *Journal of Academic Librarianship* are among the journals that regularly publish articles on information literacy. Articles can also be found in *Knowledge Quest* and *School Library Journal*. AASL and ACRL have an information literacy electronic discussion list to allow librarians to share information.

Concepts regarding information literacy have progressed from a concentration on content to a concentration on how people learn. The idea of presenting information about the library and research in small amounts and integrating it into the curriculum are important new directions for this vital service. Finding quality information can be challenging for the user. Librarians can help the user identify high-quality information sources through well-thought-out information literacy programs.

Recommendations for Further Reading

Bruce, Christine, and Hilary Hughes. 2010. "Informed Learning: A Pedagogical Construct Attending Simultaneously to Information Use and Learning." *Library and Information Science Research* 32, no. 4: A2–A8. A look into the theoretical underpinnings of information literacy instructional models in light of the emergence of informed learning theory. The article includes ideas for implementation, based on the latest developments in this learning theory.

Desai, Christina M., and Stephanie J. Graves. 2008. "Cyberspace or Face-to-Face: The Teachable Moment and Changing Reference Mediums." *Reference and User Services Quarterly* 47, no. 3: 242–254. Presents findings of an empirical study in which levels of library instruction were measured and compared across three reference mediums: instant message, chat, and face-to-face. The findings suggest that patrons desire library instruction in their reference transactions, regardless of medium, and that librarians were providing it in all three mediums.

Gilson, Thomas. 2011. "Reference Services Today and Tomorrow." *Searcher: The Magazine for Database Professionals* 19, no. 7: 32–35. Identifies new tools and service models to alleviate the problem of meeting reference patrons' expectations of immediate results, while teaching them to distinguish between reliable and unreliable sources.

Green, Jeremy, and Troy Swanson. 2011. "Tightening the System: Reference as a Loosely Coupled System." *Journal of Library Administration* 51, no 4: 375–388. A look at the merging and interdependent functions of reference and information literacy instruction from the management perspective. The Moraine Valley Community College Library is described as a "loosely coupled system," held together by and relying upon the knowledge sharing of the librarian.

Harmeyer, Dave. 2010. "Hybrid Reference: Blending the Reference Interview and Information Literacy." *The Reference Librarian* 51, no. 4: 358–362. A personal narrative describing a typical reference interview in an academic library that blended information literacy instruction with traditional reference service.

Johnson, Anna Marie, Claudene Sproles, and Robert Detmering. 2011. "Library Instruction and Information Literacy 2010." *Reference Services Review* 39, no. 4: 551–627. A selective annotated bibliography of resources on the topics of library instruction and information literacy, including books, surveys, and standards. Also contains an analytic overview of publishing trends on the topic.

Mazella, David, and Julie Grob. 2011. "Collaborations between Faculty and Special Collections Librarians in Inquiry-Driven Classes." *portal: Libraries and the Academy* 11, no. 1: 467–487. Discusses how primary source materials can be included in a more advanced and student-curiosity-driven version of the information literacy initiative.

McCallum, Carolyn J., and Bobbie L. Collins. 2011. "Enhancing the Information Literacy Classroom Experience: A Cataloger and a Reference Librarian Team Up to Deliver Library Instruction." *Library Collections, Acquisitions, and Technical Services* 35, no. 1: 10–18. Describes a collaborative instructional model in which a cataloger's insight on subject headings and the structure of citations are shown to enhance the research lesson.

Neely, Theresa Y. 2007. *Information Literacy Assessment: Standards-Based Tools and Assignments.* Chicago: American Library Association. A useful guide that provides librarians with information about using assessment measures in their assignments.

Oakleaf, Megan, and Amy VanScoy. 2010. "Instructional Strategies for Digital Reference: Methods to Facilitate Reference." *Reference and User Services Quarterly* 49, no 4: 380–390. Identifies and defines eight instructional strategies that can be used by librarians in digital reference and assesses how often these strategies are employed in practice. Results show that librarians employed some method of instruction in 62 percent of reference transactions, but that they did not utilize the variety of strategies to their full potential.

Park, Sarah, Lori A. Mardis, and Connie Jo Ury. 2011. "I've Lost My Identity—Oh, There It Is... in a Style Manual: Teaching Citation Styles and Academic Honesty." *Reference Services Review* 39, no. 1: 42–57. Presents the process used in the Library of the Northwest Missouri State University to curb plagiarism and aid students with citing sources. Includes strategies to handle issues arising from international students with different cultural expectations, students with library anxiety, and the use of new types of electronic resources.

Bibliography and Works Cited

AASL (American Association of School Librarians). 2007. *Standards for the 21st-Century Learner.* Chicago: American Association of School Librarians.

————. 2009. *Empowering Learners: Guidelines for School Library Programs.* Chicago: American Association of School Librarians.

AASL (American Association of School Librarians) and AECT (Association of Educational Communications and Technology). 1998. *Information Power: Building Partnerships for Learning.* Chicago: ALA Editions.

ACRL (Association of College and Research Libraries). 2000. *Information Literacy Competency Standards for Higher Education.* American Library Association. http://www.ala.org/acrl/standards/informationliteracycompetency.

————. 2003. "Characteristics of Programs of Information Literacy That Illustrate Best Practices: A Guideline." American Library Association. http://www.ala.org/acrl/standards/characteristics.

ALA (American Library Association). 1989. "Presidential Committee on Information Literacy: Final Report." American Library Association. http://www.ala.org/acrl/publications/whitepapers/presidential.

————. 1998. "A Progress Report on Information Literacy: An Update on the American Library Association Presidential Committee on Information Literacy: Final Report." American Library Association. http://www.ala.org/acrl/publications/whitepapers/progressreport.

————. 2000. *Library Advocacy Now! Action Pack: A Library Advocate's Guide to Building Information Literate Communities.* 2000. Chicago: American Library Association.

Arp, Lori, and Beth S. Woodward. 2002. "Recent Trends in Information Literacy and Instruction." *Reference and User Services Quarterly* 42, no. 2 (Winter): 124–132.

Avery, Susan. 2008. "When Opportunity Knocks: Opening the Door Through Teachable Moments." *The Reference Librarian* 49, no. 2 (#102): 109–118.

Beck, Susan E., and Nancy B. Turner. 2001. "On the Fly BI: Reaching and Teaching from the Reference Desk." *The Reference Librarian* no. 72: 83–96.

Big6. 2012. "Big6 Skills Overview." Big6. Accessed August 17. http://www.big6.com/pages/about/big6-skills-overview.php.

Bloom, Beth, and Marta Deyrup. 2003. "Information Literacy across the Wired University." *Reference Services Review* 31, no. 3: 237–247.

Bridgeland, Angela, and Martha Whitehead. 2005. "Information Literacy in the 'E' Environment: An Approach for Sustainability." *Journal of Academic Librarianship* 31, no. 1 (January): 54–59.

Committee on Information Technology Literacy and National Research Council. 1999. *Being Fluent with Information Technology.* Washington, DC: National Academies Press.

Cunningham, Thomas H., and Scott Lanning. 2002. "New Frontier Trail Guides: Faculty-Librarian Collaboration on Information Literacy." *Reference Services Review* 30, no. 4: 343–348.

D'Angelo, Barbara J., and Barry M. Maid. 2004. "Moving Beyond Definitions: Implementing Information Literacy across the Curriculum." *Journal of Academic Librarianship* 30, no. 3 (May): 212–217.

Eisenberg, M. B., and R. E. Berkowitz. 2000. *Teaching Information and Technology Skills: The Big 6 in Secondary Schools.* Worthington, OH: Linworth Publishing.

Ellis, Lisa A. 2004. "Approaches to Teaching through Digital Reference." *Reference Services Review* 32, no. 2: 107.

Flaspohler, Molly R. 2003. "Information Literacy Program Assessment: One Small College Takes the Big Plunge." *Reference Services Review* 31, no. 2: 129–140.

Galvin, Jeanne. 2005. "Alternative Strategies for Promoting Information Literacy." *Journal of Academic Librarianship* 31, no. 4: 352–357.

Grassian, Esther. 2004. "Building on Bibliographic Instruction." *American Libraries* 35 (October): 51–53.

Hensley, Randy Burke. 2004. "Curiosity and Creativity as Attributes of Information Literacy." *Reference and User Services Quarterly* 44, no. 1 (Fall): 31–36.

Hinchliffe, Lisa Janicke. 2003. "Examining the Context, New Voices Reflect on Information Literacy." *Reference and User Services Quarterly* 42, no. 4 (Summer): 311–317.

Jackson, Pamela Alexondra. 2007. "Integrating Information Literacy into Blackboard: Building Campus Partnerships for Successful Student Learning." *Journal of Academic Librarianship* 33, no. 4 (July): 454–461.

Johnson, Patricia E. 2003. "Digital Reference as an Instructional Tool: Just in Time and Just Enough." *Searcher* 11: 31–33.

Katz, Irvin R. 2007. "Testing Information Literacy in Digital Environments: ETS's iSkills Assessment." *Information Technology and Libraries* 26, no. 3: 3–12.

Knapp, Patricia. 1966. *The Monteith College Library Experiment*. Metuchen, NJ: Scarecrow Press.

Kobelski, Pamela, and Mary Reichel. 1987. "Conceptual Frameworks for Bibliographic Instruction." In *Conceptual Frameworks for Bibliographic Education: Theory into Practice*, edited by Mary Reichel and Mary Ann Ramey, 3–10. Littleton, CO: Libraries Unlimited.

Kuhlthau, Carol Collier. 1993. *Seeking Meaning: A Process Approach to Library and Information Services*. Norwood, NJ: Ablex Publishing Corp.

———. 1999. "Accommodating the User's Information Search Process: Challenges for Information Retrieval System Designers." *Bulletin of the American Society for Information Science* 25, no. 3 (February–March): 12–17.

Lampert, Lynn D. 2004. "Integrating Discipline-Based Anti-plagiarism Instruction." *Reference Services Review* 32, no. 4: 347–355.

Larsen, Peter, Amanda Izenstark, and Joanna Burkhardt. 2010. "Aiming for Assessment." *Communications in Information Literacy* 4, no. 1: 61–70.

Mackey, Thomas P., and Trudi E. Jacobsen. 2011. "Reframing Information Literacy as a Metaliteracy." *College and Research Libraries* 72, no. 1: 62–78.

Mohia, Rosemary, and Rhonda Rolen. 2012. "LibGuides: Improving Student and Faculty Access to Information Literacy." *Codex* 1, no. 4: 37–45.

Murray, Lilia. 2010. "Libraries 'Like to Move It, Move It.'" *Journal of Library Administration* 38, no. 2: 233–249.

Orr, Debbie, Margaret Appleton, and Margie Wallin. 2001. "Information Literacy and Flexible Delivery: Creating a Conceptual Framework and Model." *Journal of Academic Librarianship* 27, no. 6 (November): 457–463.

O'Sullivan, Carmel. 2002. "Is Information Literacy Relevant in the Real World?" *Reference Services Review* 30, no. 1: 7–14.

Whyte, Susan Barnes. 2001. "From BL to IL: The ACRL Institute for Information Literacy." *OLA Quarterly* 7, no. 2 (Summer): 14–15.

Winterman, Brian, Carrie Donovan, and Rachel Slough. 2011. "Information Literacy for Multiple Disciplines; Toward a Campus-Wide Integration Model at Indiana University, Bloomington." *Communications in Information Literacy* 5, no. 1: 38–54.

Woodward, Beth S. 2005. "One-on-One Instruction: From the Reference Desk to Online Chat." *Reference and User Services Quarterly* 44, no. 3 (Spring): 203–209.

Part IV
Developing and Managing Reference Collections and Services

17

Selecting and Evaluating Reference Materials

Of all the sections of a library collection, the reference collection must be the most focused, specific, and selective. Although far smaller than circulating collections, the works they contain are often more expensive than those found elsewhere. Consequently, developing a reference collection must be carefully orchestrated, each step requiring great thoughtfulness and care. To stay balanced and keep the collection from toppling over into the abyss of redundancy and irrelevance, the materials selector must combine knowledge and experience to great effect. Each choice must be made with care, allowing the library to best leverage its resources and ensuring that the reference collection funds are well spent. As has been suggested in the previous chapters, thoughtful evaluation of relevance and currency is crucial with each individual purchase, but those responsible for development must also possess the following:

- Knowledge of the library's community of users and their needs and interests
- Knowledge of how different types and formats of reference materials are used
- Knowledge of subject areas and how much updating they need
- Knowledge of how to evaluate reference materials

More often than not, these areas are interdependent. Note, for example, that an understanding of the library's users often goes hand in hand with the type of library and the educational level of the community it serves.

The takeaway point here is that selectors must be willing to think outside of the box and look beyond their immediate spheres of influence. Thus, academic librarians must take the various disciplines studied at their university or college into account when considering purchases. The needs and interests of this community are defined by the college's or university's curriculum as well as the research needs of both students and faculty. As the curricula change, the academic library must respond by adding new reference resources that will meet these new needs. Likewise, public libraries must respond to the requests for information from members of their communities. The response should reflect users' wide-ranging information needs and interests from educational and career interests to hobbies and leisure reading. Public libraries have the most diverse user body. Their audience includes children, teens, and adults of all ages and all backgrounds. Consequently, reference collection development must take into account the widest possible range of users. School libraries serve a community of students and faculty. They tailor their collections to the subject areas being studied in the school as well as the interests of their user group. Special libraries serve the needs of their community of users, be they museum curators, hospital employees, business people, or others. Their users have very specific information needs and interests that may change over time.

The ways in which knowledge is sought out and used by a library's patrons also plays a crucial part in the shaping of the reference collection. If the users tend toward factual information, the library may acquire ready reference materials or build a ready reference section on its website. If queries tend more toward in-depth research, the library should concentrate on databases, indexes, and other reference sources that lead the user to full-text information. Sometimes libraries will need specialized materials such as maps or government documents. Alternatively, they may need collections of directories to meet certain kinds of requests.

By understanding characteristics of specific types of materials, librarians can tailor their collections to meet user needs. Formats of reference materials are much more important than ever before. In particular, libraries are moving their reference collections to e-resources. The choices and rate of change may be based on the way the library's users request and utilize materials or the most suitable format for particular types of material. In general, there is now less demand for print resources since users tend to prefer e-resources. Alternative media, such as audio and video, may also be selected in some circumstances if they add needed dimensions to the information provided.

A comprehensive knowledge of relevant subject areas will help the librarian decide how much material is needed to cover fully any given topic. Again, it is helpful here to think in terms of what users need and want. Sometimes, if demand is low, a single book, e-book, or database is sufficient coverage for a given subject area, while other subject areas require multiple titles to support the user requests. Returning to the question of formats, note that frequent content changes in such subject areas as the sciences, technology, and business may call for the purchase of or subscription to online resources that are regularly updated.

Finally, as should by now be obvious, knowing how to evaluate reference materials is key to the success of a reference department. This requires both knowledge of how reference materials are used and knowledge of the subjects of the materials. Careful examination of the many important criteria is essential, as well as identifying for a particular work what the most important characteristics are. For many subject areas, there may be more than one choice. Knowing the library's users ensures that the librarian can select the materials best suited to this particular audience.

Although reference collection development may appear to be one-dimensional, it actually includes a number of different tasks, such as these:

- Identifying new reference material
- Management of the reference budget, including approval plans, standing orders, exchange agreements, negotiation with vendors, and cooperative collection development

- Ongoing assessment of the reference collection
- Weeding the reference collection
- Writing and updating a reference collection development policy
- Promoting and marketing new reference materials to the library's users

Identifying, Selecting, and Evaluating New Reference Materials

Some reference materials are published both in print format and electronically, whereas others are available in only one of these formats. Since most reference collections can acquire only a selection of the available titles, all decisions must be made carefully and thoughtfully. Reference materials should be selected either through reading reviews, personal examination, trial online subscriptions, reference to literature produced by the publisher, or some combination.

Sources of Reviews

Reviews are one way of obtaining information about reference materials. *Booklist*'s "Reference Books Bulletin," *Library Journal*, *School Library Journal*, *Choice*, and *Reference and User Services Quarterly* are the review sources most frequently consulted by librarians searching for reviews of new reference titles.

Booklist is published by the American Library Association twice monthly, September through June, and monthly in July and August. "*Booklist* magazine delivers over 8,000 recommended-only reviews of books, audiobooks, reference sources, video and DVD titles each year" (http://www.ala.org/offices/publishing/booklist). Resources are recommended especially for use in public libraries and school library media centers. "Reference Books Bulletin" is a section of each issue of *Booklist* devoted to reference sources that will be of interest to public libraries and school media centers. The reviews in "Reference Books Bulletin" are prepared and critiqued by members of the editorial board and by contributing reviewers and represent the board's collective judgment. Each issue includes reviews of adult and youth reference titles. The reviews are well written and thorough. Occasional special sections on types of material or one subject area such as an annual review of encyclopedias or a page devoted to science databases are among the best to be found. This review source is available online at http://www.booklistonline.com/.

Reference and User Services Quarterly (*RUSQ*) is published by the Reference and User Services Association of the American Library Association. This journal is devoted to articles on all aspects of reference services. Each issue includes a "Reference Books" column that reviews twenty-five to thirty reference titles. The signed reviews both describe and critically evaluate each work.

Library Journal (*LJ*), a publication of Media Source, is published semimonthly, and monthly in January, July, August, and December. A "Reference" section in each issue looks at about fifteen to twenty reference titles with a recommendation as to whether the title is recommended and for what type of library. An "eReviews" column in each issue reviews one or two subscription databases in depth. *LJ* also regularly publishes many reviews of e-reference materials on its website (http://www.libraryjournal.com/).

School Library Journal (SLJ), also published by Media Source, is a magazine for librarians who work with young people in schools or in public libraries; in it are two reference-related columns, "Digital Resources" and "Reference Reviews." Suggestions as to which titles should be purchased are clearly made. *SLJ* also publishes reference reviews online (http://www.schoollibraryjournal.com/).

Choice is published monthly by the Association of College and Research Libraries. It is a review service designed to support academic library collections. *Choice*'s reference reviews are divided into General, Humanities, Science and Technology, and Social and Behavioral Sciences. More than sixty reference titles are reviewed in each issue. These reviews are written by academic scholars and librarians and, similar to the other titles discussed in this section, include a recommendation as to whether the text should be purchased and the types of libraries for which it is recommended. Electronic resource reviews are integrated with the print material reviews. Each issue includes a bibliographic essay pointing to resources in a particular subject area. *Choice* reviews are also available online (http://www.cro2.org/).

ARBA (American Reference Books Annual), available from Libraries Unlimited in print and online, reviews all new reference works in print, online, or on CD-ROM published in the United States and Canada during the year. The reviews are arranged by four broad subject categories—general reference, social sciences, humanities, and science and technology. It is an important and fairly comprehensive source of information about reference materials published during a particular year and includes reviews of some professional materials. The online version (http://www.arbaonline.com/) covers 1997 to date and is updated monthly with 100 to 150 additional reviews.

In addition to the publications described previously, a number of annual lists of recommended reference titles are produced by committees and publications. These include "Outstanding Reference Sources," a list compiled annually by a RUSA committee and published in May in *American Libraries*, and "Best Reference Sources," an annual list compiled by *Library Journal* and published in the April issue. Reference reviews also appear on the Gale site (http://www.gale.cengage .com/reference/) under "Guest Columnists." The four columns are "Péter's Digital Reference Shelf," in which Péter Jacsó, a professor at the Library and Information Science Program at the University of Hawaii Department of Information and Computer Science, reviews online and CD-ROM products; a review of public and academic reference resources by John R. M. Lawrence, a librarian at the Joyner Library, East Carolina University, called "Lawrence Looks at Books"; "Reference Unbound" by Wendy Stephens, a librarian at the Buckhorn High School Library in New Market, Alabama, that reviews print and online resources for K–12; and "Doug's Student Reference Room" by Doug Achterman, a library media specialist at the San Benito High School, Hollister, California, that reviews both print and online resources for K–12 as well as a "Reference Archive." Other important and highly authoritative retrospective guides to reference materials include *Guide to Reference*, a guide to reference material updating the *Guide to*

Reference Books, edited by Robert Balay; the *New Walford Guide to Reference Resources* (three volumes), a guide to reference sources published in the United Kingdom but international in scope and organized by subject; *Recommended Reference Books for Small and Medium-Sized Libraries and Media Centers*, a list of best titles compiled from those reviewed in *American Reference Books Annual (ARBA) Online* and *Reference Sources for Small and Medium-Sized Libraries*, a list of useful and affordable reference titles for libraries serving populations of under 100,000.

Evaluation Criteria

Since reference budgets are tight these days, selection decisions have become more difficult. Despite increasing user demands, no library can afford to buy or subscribe to every reference source, so choices must be made. Evaluation criteria provide guidance and rationale for selection decisions. In order to determine which reference materials to purchase, the materials must meet certain evaluation criteria. Most of these criteria apply to both print and electronic materials and are discussed in this section of the chapter. Criteria specific to certain types of reference sources are mentioned in the appropriate chapter.

- Scope
- Quality of content
- Authority of author and/or publisher
- Accuracy of content
- Currency
- Ease of use, including usability, searching capabilities, and response time (for electronic resources)
- Arrangement of material
- Appropriateness to the audience/meeting of user needs
- Format
- Cost

Scope

When evaluating a reference work, it is important to understand its scope and purpose. In printed works the author usually discusses this in the preface or introduction. This should include a discussion of what the work covers, including topics such as how comprehensive it is, whether it covers allied fields, the dates covered, and whether the work includes only information from the United States or is international in scope. Referring to this information will give the librarian a way to compare this work with similar reference works on the same subject and to decide if this title is a necessary addition to the collection. Determining the scope of an electronic database is often more difficult, as there is rarely a direct equivalent to the preface and access to nonsubscribers may be limited. Often the printed material from the publisher describing the electronic database includes information on scope, and the website of the company may also be a source of information. In electronic versions of print resources, coverage is still an issue, as it is important to determine whether the digital version offers anything newer than the print version and, if so, what time period it covers. Questions of duplication are critical because most libraries cannot afford to have identical print and electronic resources.

Quality of Content

The quality of the content has become particularly important in e-resources because the librarian appears to have less control over what content the publisher chooses. Quantity is not as important as quality here. Quality content can be defined as accurate, up-to-date information of sufficient depth for the intended audience. Given the diversity of reference titles on almost every subject imaginable, librarians must try to distinguish between the good and the bad. A close examination of a title will reveal whether it has current material on the subject, whether it is similar to other titles on the same subject, or whether it has unique material. If it is current and has unique material, this would be a good reason for purchasing this title.

Authority of Author and/or Publisher

The authority of the reference work is evaluated by the qualifications of the author or the publisher. The author may be someone known for authoring reference materials or may be an expert in a particular field. Some publishers have a good track record in a certain area of reference material such as Merriam-Webster for dictionaries, National Geographic for maps and atlases, and Oxford University Press for biographical dictionaries, meaning that the selector can begin the examination of the work with some confidence that the publisher will produce a credible work.

Accuracy of Content

Even the most seemingly authoritative work still needs to be examined for accuracy. Accuracy can be tested by comparing it to other works on the same topic. Although not the easiest of tasks, it is important to try to determine whether a reference resource is providing accurate information.

Currency

Currency can be tested by checking to see if recent information on a specific topic is included in the work and checking the dates of resources cited. It is also important to note the cutoff date in relation to the publication date for this reference work. To test this, in the case of e-resources, choose a current topic or a recent world event and see how current the information on that topic is.

Ease of Use

E-resources should be examined for usability. Here, the most relevant factors are whether the program is easy to search and how quickly it responds to commands and queries. In addition, the resource should be examined to see if it can accept Boolean operators, whether it has both basic and advance search capabilities, and whether it can easily be browsed. These issues of manipulating the database are one set of criteria that applies exclusively to e-resources. The electronic resource should also provide a "Help" option and a "How to" guide.

Arrangement of Material

Examining the arrangement of the reference work will determine whether its sections are organized and indexed in such a way as to facilitate easy access to the information it contains. Good organization separates a truly useful reference work from a text or simply a well-written work on a subject. The print reference work needs to have good page layout with many headings to make it easy to scan the pages. A sufficient amount of white space is needed, and a typeface that is clear and easy to read. The reference work must also have a good table of contents and index with cross-references where appropriate. An electronic work should use a thesaurus or accepted list of subject headings such as the Library of Congress Subject Headings as well as cross-references to enable the user to find the information easily. An intelligible interface and searchable "Help" files are equally significant ways to enable the user to understand how to search the database easily. When making purchase choices of materials available in multiple formats, it is important to consider the format that will best convey a title's content. Some information is still appropriately in print format whereas other material lends itself to electronic format. If the content changes often, it will be best as an e-resource since the updates are easily made online. Periodicals and newspapers are far superior as e-resources since new material is being indexed constantly. Directories are another good candidate for the electronic format since addresses, phone numbers, e-mail addresses, and so on, are constantly changing. Some reference works may be best or very acceptable in print. These include atlases, reference materials that are based on historical information, and any reference work for which the information changes infrequently.

Appropriateness to the Audience

The audience for the reference work must be considered in purchasing. A good reference work that is not directed at the audience of a particular library is not a good purchase. For example, a science handbook that is aimed at a university or professional audience will not be appropriate in a high school library. Reference works on the same subject are usually available on a variety of levels so that there is an appropriate title for the library's audience. On this account, it may be helpful to consider where in the professional literature a work has been reviewed. A resource spotlighted in a school library publication will probably be inappropriate for the main research library of a large university. An astute selector should be able to determine this information independently, however, as it should be clear on examination of the text.

Format

Format has been a tremendously complicated issue for librarians as reference sources have changed from print to electronic. The choices continue to be complex for a variety of reasons. First, not all reference sources are available in both print and electronic versions, so librarians who need a particular work must acquire it in whatever format is available. Second, if both print and electronic versions are available, the choice will depend on the library's user population and the library's budget. Academic libraries, for example, want most reference sources in electronic format since much of their user population wants off-site access. Public and school libraries have more choices since they have users who want print and users who want electronic. Also, public and school libraries do not always have a large enough budget to support a large number of e-resources. Third, some reference resources are very acceptable in print such as atlases and large maps.

Cost

Cost may be the final determination as to whether to purchase a specific reference work. For most subjects several good quality reference works are available online as well as in print, and the librarian can choose based on any or all of the criteria above. But in the end—all other factors being equal—price may be the determining factor. In the case of e-resources, the library may want to be part of a consortium in which it can share costs to afford the more expensive e-resources. One problem with subscriptions to e-resources is that the library must pay annually to continue the subscription. Even if the library buys an e-resource, there may still be an annual maintenance fee.

Choosing Between Print and Electronic Resources

Many factors go into the decision as to which format to buy. Usually it is a decision based on the library's own needs. Some factors that may influence a library's decision are how often the resource is updated, whether everything in the print version is included in the electronic version, the years of coverage, the ease of use, and whether the resource is compatible with the library's technology infrastructure. For most academic libraries, e-resources are the best choice for many materials since students want to use the resources outside of the library and at any hour. In public libraries, the choice may not be so clear since most public libraries have a wide range of users—many of whom are probably not accustomed to doing all their research electronically or simply prefer print resources. Sometimes the decision must be to duplicate the resource in print and electronically because it is so heavily used that it makes sense to have both. Encyclopedias are an example of a resource that is useful to have in both print and electronic format, as the print set will accommodate more users at one time. A few reference materials may really still be best in print if the digital conversions are not as good as their original sources. The best example is atlases where large maps are not as easy to read on a computer screen. Materials where visual browsing within the text is useful may be better in print. Although there is not a large place for CD-ROMs in the library today, there may still be occasions when it makes sense to buy a CD-ROM. Some examples of this might be a seldom updated bibliography or a dictionary.

Management of the Reference Budget

Librarians must learn to manage and maximize the library's reference budget. Reference departments typically have a specific annual budget. Depending on the size and administrative complexity of the institution, this may be one budget or it may be divided into a number of categories such as print, electronic, approval plans, standing orders, and specific subject areas. Either way, the staff must make a plan at the beginning of the year as to how the budget will be distributed. In academic and large public libraries, approval plans and standing orders play a major role in the reference budget. Money must be allocated at the beginning of the year to pay for these plans. Reference works may come as part of a larger library approval plan, or the library may set up approval plans with reference publishers. E-resources may include contracts paid for by the library and cooperative arrangements with library consortia. Most libraries have found it economical to join or form consortia for the purpose of purchasing e-resources. This has made it possible to buy more titles for a more reasonable price.

Ongoing Assessment of Reference Collections

Collections should be assessed on a regular basis to ascertain whether the materials meet the needs of the users and whether the selections are worth the cost. This is a two-pronged process that involves both determining gaps in the existing collection and evaluating the quality of available resources. On the former count, the library might want to look at the questions it received and could not answer and the interlibrary loans placed because the material was not available at the library. In addition to this, it is wise to browse the shelves to see if the collection appears balanced in relation to the current interests of the library's users. Is there too much material on subjects no longer of interest to the users? Is more material needed on subjects that have recently become more popular?

Collections may be assessed in a number of ways. For example, the staff could check the collection against standard lists such as the *Guide to Reference*, *Resources for College Libraries, Recommended Reference Books for Small and Medium Sized Libraries and Media Centers*, or *Reference Sources for Small and Medium-Sized Libraries*. Alternatively, the staff could use the conspectus approach developed by the Research Libraries Group, which evaluates the level of materials in each subject area (i.e., 1 is the minimal level, 2 is the basic information level, 3 is the instructional support level, 4 is the research level, and 5 is the comprehensive level) and whether the level reflects the emphasis and interest in the subject area as reflected in the use of the materials. Third, the library could compare its holdings with comparable libraries using OCLC's WorldCat Collection Analysis or comparable programs. User satisfaction can also be ascertained by questionnaires to the library's users—in person, by mail or e-mail, through interviews, and through feedback at the reference desk.

Weeding the Reference Collection

Weeding or deselection is an important part of reference collection development. Reference collections by their very nature must have the most current information to accurately answer users' questions. Anything less than the most current information possible is simply not acceptable. Accordingly, removing dated materials from the collection must take high priority. Current thinking dictates that print reference collections should be smaller since many materials are available electronically and are much more suitable in that form.

The criteria for weeding reference materials in any type of library are as follows:

- The content is no longer up-to-date or accurate.
- A new edition is available.
- The reference work is seldom used.
- The information is duplicated in another reference work.
- The book is physically damaged.

Libraries may want to use the same guidelines for weeding reference materials as for circulating nonfiction. Libraries will want to identify subjects that date quickly and weed those areas more often. History, art, literature, philosophy, and religion are seldom weeded, whereas science, medicine, and some of the social sciences require continual updating. Libraries do not necessarily replace all annuals each year. Because of the cost considerations some annuals are replaced every two or three years. Encyclopedias are often rotated out of the collection; five years is the longest an encyclopedia should be kept in a reference collection (Nolan, 1998: 162–163). Cumulative sets such as *Current Biography* are usually maintained unless they become available online at an affordable price.

It is important to have an organized approach to weeding so that within a particular time period all materials have been reviewed. A weeding team is a good approach so that materials in question can be discussed and decisions made as to whether to discard, move to the circulating collection, or put in storage. It is also essential to approach weeding with the knowledge that some users do not understand weeding and are critical of library weeding projects. Nicolson Baker's attack on the weeding practices of the San Francisco Public Library in *Double Fold* illustrates this issue (Baker, 2001).

Writing a Reference Collection Development Policy

Indiana University–Purdue University Fort Wayne provides this statement about the reference collection:

> The reference collection supports the research needs of IPFW students, faculty and staff. It contains such materials as abstracts and indexes, encyclopedias, dictionaries, atlases, directories, bibliographies, statistical compilations, and handbooks. The reference collection primarily supports IPFW academic programs. Reference works that provide basic bibliographic access to or an overview of other academic disciplines are also selected. (Walter E. Helmke Library, 2008)

The Morton Grove Public Library includes this information about reference materials in their collection development policy.

> The Morton Grove Public Library's Reference Department contains materials that cover the entire range of the Dewey Decimal Classification System.

These materials vary in degree of difficulty from a basic introductory level to a beginning research level. The goal of the Library's Reference Department is to provide current information on all subjects and historical information in areas where previous questions and experience indicate that it is likely to be in demand. Materials formally cataloged for reference comprise only part of the collection. (MGPL Webrary, 2005)

Reference collection development policies provide a way to document current practices in a reference department and to set directions for their future development. This is useful for guiding the present staff in their work, orienting new staff, and providing information to the users. It also provides consistency and continuity within the library as staff changes. Although the reference collection development policy need not repeat details about collection development that have already been documented in the library's overall collection development policy, it does help to document separately the collection development activities of the reference department, especially as it reflects some practices that differ from the rest of the library. The primary parts of this policy should include the following:

- Introduction that describes the library, its clientele, and its areas of research or reference service
- Description of the scope and size of the collection
- Formats of materials collected, with a separate section on electronic resources
- Collecting levels by subject
- Types of reference materials collected
- Description of the responsibilities of staff and others for selection
- Criteria for selection, assessment, and weeding
- Sources of funding
- External relationships with other libraries, consortial arrangements, and resource sharing
- Policy for dealing with challenged works and censorship

In the *introduction* the policy should describe briefly the library, its goals, and its clientele. This introduction should also provide an overarching statement about the goals of the reference collection, which might be to provide accurate, up-to-date information or to support educational and informational needs. If nonprimary clientele are allowed to use the library, this should be mentioned, as well as how the library serves them. For example, some university libraries are open to the general public as well as to the school's employees and students. With the increase in distance learning, the policy might want to discuss how the library serves this part of its users.

In the *description of the scope and size* of the collection, the library should describe the subject areas covered by the reference collection. This may be different from the circulating collection or may mirror it. In any case, it is important to describe what the collection does and does not include. For example, the library may not buy textbooks or may not purchase materials in certain subject areas. The size of the collection is equally important. Today the size must include both print and e-resources, so the description may begin to differ from previous policies.

The *formats of materials* collected should be outlined. Here the library should discuss how it decides whether to buy a reference work in print or as an e-resource and when it might buy both. It is also important to state whether microform collections continue to be maintained and whether CD-ROMs continue to be purchased. Since e-resources have become an important part of the collection, guidelines must be set up to help staff and users understand how these decisions are being made. Some of the issues that need discussion are whether e-resources will be offered for remote use, criteria for purchase of e-resources, and consortial relationships. Future plans for e-resources might be outlined here.

Subject collecting levels and the *types of reference materials* collected reflect the use of the reference collection. The subject levels might be explained using the Research Library Group system or another system that describes subject levels. The library might also want to list some specific types of reference materials it collects, such as government documents, maps, and so forth. The reference collection is developed and maintained based on user requests and interests. This can change over time as user needs move in new directions.

Staff often have *specific collection development responsibilities*. Each staff member may be responsible for a certain area of the collection. In an academic library the faculty as well as the library staff may have some responsibility for collection development. Some libraries use committees to discuss proposed additions to the reference collection. This may be particularly true for e-resources, since their cost is often so much greater than that of a print reference book.

The library should outline the *criteria used for selection and for weeding*. General guidelines are discussed elsewhere in this chapter.

It can be helpful to discuss in general terms the *funding of the library's collection*. Many people have no idea how a library is funded and the limits of its budget.

Finally, the policy should discuss *relationships* that the library has with other libraries, such as the consortia agreements between academic institutions discussed throughout this chapter. The policy will document whatever agreement has been developed with other libraries, whether for print or e-resources.

Promoting and Marketing Reference Materials to Library Users

Promoting and marketing reference materials have recently increased in importance because of the advent of electronic resources. These new resources often remain hidden from users unless they are making extensive use of the library's website. Most libraries believe that their e-resources are underutilized by their users. In the hopes of rectifying this situation, many have begun to take more active steps to increase the visibility of these resources among library users. Two important areas must be addressed in promoting these resources: The first is the staff. Many e-resources are added to the collection in a short time such that the staff does not have much time to get acquainted with them. It is important to go back and refresh the staff's knowledge of these databases. Some libraries send out a write-up on a different database each week or month. Other libraries ask staff members to each study a particular database and then make a presentation. Second, for the users, the library can feature a "database of the week" or month on the library's website. The librarians can feature databases in newsletters, on bookmarks, on their Facebook page, on Twitter and blogs, and they can encourage staff to routinely tell users about the e-resources.

Regardless of the approach taken, it is crucial that the contents of the collection be advertised to the library's users. Reference work is, after all, predicated on service, and unless the collection is put to use in real, practical scenarios it does little good.

Recommendations for Further Reading

Beals, Jennifer, and Ron Gilmour. 2007. "Assessing Collections Using Brief Tests and WorldCat Collection Analysis." *Collection Building* 26, no. 4: 104–107. A report on using the Brief Test approach to collection evaluation.

Boissy, Robert, and Bob Schatz. 2011. "Scholarly Communications from the Publisher Perspective." *Journal of Library Administration* 51, no. 5–6: 476–484. An evaluation of current trends and crises in scholarly communications, from a publisher's perspective. Addresses the issue of open access publishing and information stewardship. The article advocates for the role of the publisher in e-resources by explicating the value that publishers have had in vetting and marketing scholarly materials.

Crosetto, Alice, et al. 2007. "Assessment in a Tight Time Frame: Using Readily Available Data to Evaluate Your Collection." *Collection Management* 33, no. 1/2: 29–50. The William S. Carlson Library at the University of Toledo needed to move the reference and circulation collections to make room for an information commons. This proved to be an opportunity to evaluate the collection.

England, Lenore, and Li Fu. 2011. "Electronic Resources Evaluation Central: Using Off-the-Shelf Software, Web 2.0 Tools, and LibGuides to Manage an Electronic Resources Evaluation Process." *Journal of Electronic Resources Librarianship* 23, no. 1: 30–42. Describes the evaluation process in use at the University of Maryland University College library. The process involves using a LibGuide to collect and organize evaluative input from disparate sources within the library.

Farmer, Lesley S. J. 2009. "The Life Cycle of Digital Reference Sources." *The Reference Librarian* 50, no. 2: 117–136. Describes strategies for working with subscription electronic reference sources from assessment and collection to archiving, preservation, and deselection.

Hjørland, Birger. 2011. "Evaluation of an Information Source Illustrated by a Case Study: Effect of Screening for Breast Cancer." *Journal of the American Society for Information Science and Technology* 62, no. 10: 1892–1898. Makes the argument that, when evaluating reference sources, information professionals ought to evaluate them in relation to contemporary research and scientific controversy at the forefront of the field. Hjørland uses the example of controversy in breast cancer screenings to trace the treatment of the topic in various encyclopedias, including *Wikipedia.org* and the *Encyclopedia Britannica*.

Johnson, Peggy. 2009. *Fundamentals of Collection Development and Management*. 2nd ed. Chicago: American Library Association. An excellent recent addition to the literature on collection development.

Kahl, Chad M., and Stephanie R. Davis-Kahl. 2010. "Human Rights Reference Sources: A Critical Annotated Bibliography." *Behavioral and Social Sciences Librarian* 29, no. 1: 32–64. Responding to an increase in depictions of torture in popular culture, the authors provide an extensive annotated bibliography of sources for research in human rights. Methodology is described and primary, secondary, and tertiary sources are included.

Lafferty, Meghan. 2009. "A Framework for Evaluating Science and Technology Electronic Reference Books: A Comparison of Five Platforms in Chemistry." *Issues in Science and Technology Librarianship* 59. Considers users' needs in online science and technology reference. Develops unique criteria and evaluates five e-reference sources in science and technology for ease of use.

Pickett, Carmelita, Jane Stephens, Rusty Kimball, Diana Ramirez, Joel Thornton, and Nancy Burford. 2011. "Revisiting an Abandoned Practice: The Death and Resurrection of Collection Development Policies." *Collection Management* 36, no. 3: 165–181. According to a literature review conducted by the authors, written collection development policies have been neglected in many universities in the recent past. This article documents the systematic process implemented by Texas A&M University's librarians for revising existing written policies and creating new policies where none existed.

Singer, Carol A. 2008. "Weeding Gone Wild: Planning and Implementing a Review of the Reference Collection." *Reference and User Services Quarterly* 47, no. 3: 256–264. Describes a review of the reference collection at the Jerome Library at Bowling Green State University because of the proposed move of the science reference collection to the Jerome Library.

Tucker, James Cory, and Matt Torence. 2004. "Collection Development for New Librarians: Advice from the Trenches." *Library Collections, Acquisitions and Technical Services* 28, no. 4: 397–409. Practical advice on collection development for the new librarian.

Tyckson, David. 2005. "Reference Classics Ahead of Their Time." *Against the Grain* 17, no. 4 (September): 22–28. Based on an ALA program in 2005 that discussed what makes a reference classic.

Wilkinson, Frances C., and Linda K. Lewis. 2005. "Reference eBooks: Does an eBook on the Screen Beat One on the Shelf?; Discussion on Electronic Reference Books with Seven Academic Librarians." *Against the Grain* 17, no. 4 (September): 1, 18, 20, 22. This article explores the rapidly changing world of reference books—the ways that electronic reference books are being selected, purchased, and budgeted.

Bibliography and Works Cited

Baker, Nicolson. 2001. *Double Fold*. New York: Random House.

Doll, Carol A., and Pamela Petrick Barron. 2002. *Managing and Analyzing Your Collection: A Practical Guide for Small Libraries and School Media Centers*. Chicago: American Library Association.

Kieft, Bob, ed. *Guide to Reference*. Chicago: American Library Association. Available: http://www.guidetoreference.org/HomePage.aspx.

MGPL Webrary. 2005. "Collection Development Policy." Morton Grove Public Library. http://www.webrary.org/inside/colldevadultref.html.

Nolan, Christopher W. 1998. *Managing the Reference Collection*. Occasional Paper #27. Chicago: American Library Association.

O'Gorman, Jack, ed. 2008. *Reference Sources for Small and Medium-Sized Libraries*. 7th ed. Chicago: American Library Association.

Perez, Alice J. 2004. *Reference Collection Development: A Manual*. 2nd ed. Chicago: Reference and User Services Association.

Walter E. Helmke Library. 2008. "Collection Development Policy." Indiana University–Purdue University Fort Wayne. http://www.lib.ipfw.edu/2909.0.html.

18

Ethics in Reference

Angela Ecklund

As long as libraries remain one cornerstone of a free, democratic society, the ethical principles of our profession continue to be of the utmost importance. Unbiased and equitable services, matched with the promise of confidentiality and the safeguarding of intellectual freedoms, are unique and vital offerings that librarians bring to the age of information. As a profession, we are energized by the intrinsic value of goodwill and constructive action.

The adherence to a shared code of ethics is one of the most significant factors distinguishing a librarian as a professional from a layperson. The internalization of the code of ethics that occurs during library education is often cited as a reason to require that job candidates possess an ALA-accredited master's degree in library science. As professionals, we are expected to regulate ourselves and to act with accountability. Standards of ethics, once eroded, may be difficult to re-establish. And unlike many actions that librarians are responsible for, reference takes place in public, where interactions may be overheard. The consequences of misconduct or irresponsible corner-cutting in reference interactions may easily spread.

While the average librarian may not spend much time day-to-day thinking about ethics, the ethical principles of our profession should be the spirit behind the policies within which we work on a daily basis. An understanding of these principles will empower the policy discussions between library staff and users. For example, understanding a library's ethical obligation to provide equitable access will help to explain why the library spends money on classes in literacy and computer skills, or why the library provides computer access to the homeless.

Our Professional Codes of Ethics

In 1903, as librarianship was developing standards of practice consistent with the societal values of the time, Mary Plummer spoke to the Illinois Library Association. She made one of the first formal statements on ethics in the library profession, speaking in terms of personal attributes: the essentials of dignity, humility, a willingness to learn, and a belief in the work of the library (Preer, 2008: 6). Other early discourse-situated ethics within an institutional framework included obligations to trustees, library users, and library staff. While both personal attitudes and institutional obligations remain an integral aspect of library ethics today, standards and customs in libraries have evolved significantly. One trend has been the shift from emphasis on service to providing unfettered access. It could be argued that in the digital age, service and access have grown closer together, or that access, and knowledge of how to access, is the main service demanded of all librarians. Another trend is a reflection of the changing mission of libraries. In 1911, John Cotton Dana recommended against expending time on answering reference inquiries that were "personal and dilettante" or "obviously frivolous" (p. 108). Many libraries now, especially public libraries, implicitly accept recreation and casual curiosity as legitimate, and even central, to the purpose of a library.

In 1939, a professional code of ethics was adopted by the American Library Association (ALA) Council. This code was revised several times: in 1981, 1995, and 2008 (ALA, 2008; ALA, 2012c). This code stipulates the following:

I.   We provide the highest level of service to all library users through appropriate and usefully organized resources; equitable service policies; equitable access; and accurate, unbiased, and courteous responses to all requests.

II. We uphold the principles of intellectual freedom and resist all efforts to censor library resources.

III. We protect each library user's right to privacy and confidentiality with respect to information sought or received and resources consulted, borrowed, acquired or transmitted.

IV. We respect intellectual property rights and advocate balance between the interests of information users and rights holders.

V.   We treat co-workers and other colleagues with respect, fairness, and good faith, and advocate conditions of employment that safeguard the rights and welfare of all employees of our institutions.

VI. We do not advance private interests at the expense of library users, colleagues, or our employing institutions.

VII. We distinguish between our personal convictions and professional duties and do not allow our personal beliefs to interfere with fair representation of the aims of our institutions or the provision of access to their information resources.

VIII. We strive for excellence in the profession by maintaining and enhancing our own knowledge and skills, by encouraging the professional development of co-workers, and by fostering the aspirations of potential members of the profession. (ALA, 2008)

The ALA code is accompanied by a statement, which asserts that the practical interpretation of these principles must be dictated by individual circumstances; they are intended as "a guide to ethical decision making." The four basic obligations addressed in the code are to protect confidentiality, to provide a high level of service, to avoid conflicts of interest (including censorship and threats to intellectual freedom), and to provide access.

Other professional library associations, including the American Society for Information Science (ASIS), the Society of American Archivists (SAA), the Association of College and Research Libraries (ACRL), the Medical Library Association (MLA), and the American Association of Law Libraries (AALL), maintain their own codes of ethics adapted from the ALA code. The code of ethics maintained by ACRL is written specifically for librarians working with Special Collections, and emphasizes the importance of caring for cultural property and supporting scholarship.

If these codes of ethics are our guides to "ethical decision making," the implication is that, as librarians, we are capable of thinking ethically, and of making sound decisions based on that thinking. So, what are ethics and what is ethical thinking?

A distinction can be drawn between morals and ethics. Morals are your personal sense of right and wrong, derived from your upbringing and life experiences, and perhaps some innate characteristics of personality. You are using moral thinking when you intuitively interpret new experiences vis-à-vis the actions you have seen in the past or actions you have taken yourself. Your morals serve you well in your everyday life, but when unfamiliar circumstances arise, they may be inadequate. When faced with the unfamiliar, such as our profession is in the digital age, ethical systems are most useful to us (Severson, 1995: 13). Ethical codes, like those published by ALA and the other associations listed previously, systematically articulate the principles behind moral judgment; we can use them to extend our application of moral reasoning to the unfamiliar.

Ethics are a topic of growing concern to the profession because of the rate of change affecting our work. Our collective understanding of traditional issues such as equitable access and copyright must be drastically reevaluated and reinterpreted in the digital age. Professionals in the library field have responded to this need by producing a robust and growing body of scholarship that applies ethical principles to the practice of librarianship in our changing environment. It would not be possible in this chapter to exhaust the possible applications of the ethical framework of our profession. Instead, the major issues are identified and discussed.

Service Ethics (aka Doing a Good Job)

How can a reference librarian maintain the highest possible standards of diligence under time restraints that often require compromise? Professional librarians operating under difficult conditions often face this question. Charles Bunge (1999) recommends creating a mental imprint of an effective service transaction and measuring one's service against this standard in order to make the behavior habitual (p. 32). In order to aid in the creation of an imprint of the ideal service, it helps to take notice of library colleagues and of the tasks in which they excel. Another way to keep personal standards high is to refer to professional competencies, such as the guidelines provided by the Reference and User Services Association (RUSA) division of ALA, in particular the "Professional Competencies for Reference and User Services Librarians" (RUSA, 2003). The following sections examine aspects of these competencies in more detail.

Knowledge Base

It is an ethical obligation that the reference librarian "not attempt to provide information of a sort he or she is not competent to provide and that the reference librarian be as competent as possible in providing the information that he or she and the employing agency purport to be able to provide" (Bunge, 1999: 29). Keeping one's skills and knowledge current is an implicit component of the ethical obligation to provide the highest possible level of service and removing barriers to the access of materials. Reading journals and blogs, attending conferences, webinars, and workshops are common ways of keeping current. A related obligation mentioned in both the ALA code and the RUSA professional competencies is that of collegiality with peers and encouraging their professional development. Developing one's own areas of expertise and sharing knowledge can be personally rewarding, but it also serves the greater good of the profession. For a reference librarian, taking advantage of the latest tools such as Google search and *Wikipedia* has both constructive uses and limitations. Maintaining an up-to-date ability to distinguish what those uses and limitations are, and being able to communicate these to users, is part of staying current in the digital age.

Misinforming a library user can have serious consequences; for this very reason there is a proscription against reference librarians providing legal or medical advice of a personal nature. In such a case, librarians should help users of the library to understand that, while the library attempts to provide access to the most reliable and current material, it is advisable to consult a medical or legal professional.

Collaboration

Collaborating with colleagues, users, and individuals and entities outside the library is a good way for reference librarians to optimize their effectiveness. RUSA's competency guideline states that in the reference interview, users should be treated as partners or collaborators. Working effectively with colleagues within the institution as part of a team is another element of collaboration. Forming relationships with colleagues both inside and outside the profession can lead to mutually beneficial improvements in service and access.

Equitable Access

First let's look at the provision of access as a professional competency. Later on, we will examine equitable access as an ethical principle. The need to balance obligations in a busy library can lead to discrimination between users or reference questions, whether in person or in a virtual reference environment. A librarian may lack the time to bring each transaction to the destination envisioned at the outset. Equitable service does not mean that each user will receive an equal amount of time with the librarian. Rather, it means that the time spent will be proportional to the needs of the user and the probable benefit he or she will receive from the interaction. In order to avoid personal bias when dividing one's attention, it is necessary to consider the missions of the library. Considering the primary role of the library can help the librarian determine which user will derive the greatest benefit from the collection, based on his or her information need. Furthermore, the goal of providing equitable access may require spending more time with the users who most need help accessing materials. Rather than rushing from one user to the next and leaving many users unsatisfied with their transactions, assisting a single user to his or her destination point will result in that user having a higher level of satisfaction with the service that was provided (Bunge, 1999: 32). This way the librarian's competency to provide a high level of service will not be questioned, and the fact that the library is short-staffed will be registered instead.

Outreach

Effective communication and outreach help users to realize the nature of the services and resources available to them, which is an essential aspect of equitable access. If users are unaware that the library has digitized its collection of local postcards, or if they are unaware of how to view them, access to the digitized collection may as well not exist. Outreach methods may include lectures, programs, classroom visits, the use of social media, posters, mailings, and even press conferences. Outreach needs must be identified by determining which services require the most promoting and to whom they should be promoted. After a strategy has been implemented, an evaluation of its effectiveness should be completed.

Evaluation and Assessment

Assessing the effectiveness and necessity of library instruction and reference services within the context of user needs is another obligation taken seriously by librarians. Sometimes, the possibility of eliminating reference functions is broached in the profession. In 2002, Robert Hauptman wrote about the next generation of library users: "as children of the computer generation, they will become extremely proficient at locating materials.... [T]o continue to insist that sophisticated and esoteric research services are required ... is to act unprofessionally and unethically" (p. 67). Many would strongly disagree with this statement, including Joseph Aubele, Susan Jackson, and Lesley Farmer (2008), who write, "although technically adept, they do not understand the research process ... that research takes time ... [or] the thought process necessary for research" (p. 4). Still, it is characteristic of our profession that we feel obligated to debate the necessity of our own work in its current state. Adapting our skills and finding new and diverse ways to make ourselves useful in a changing environment is both practical and responsible.

However, ethical issues will arise in the planning and implementation of an assessment. The use of "mystery shopping" or videotaping as assessment tools, for example, can lead librarians to feel that they have been deceived by their administration. Involving reference librarians in the formation of the rubric that will be used to assess reference services, and keeping them informed about the time frame in which the assessment will take place, will allow librarians to voice any objections and to prepare mentally. Any type of assessment of services should be fair and involve enough reference transactions to ensure a representative sampling.

Equitable Access to Information

Who does the library serve? In the days of subscription libraries, the answer to this question was those with a paying membership. In later years, reference librarians working with closed stacks, especially in archives or special collections, traditionally played the role of gatekeeper, vetting researchers to determine which material and how much of it they would be able to see. Partly in response to societal change, and partly thanks to the advent of digital collections, reference librarians today are more likely to be promoting material than trying to protect it. In tax-supported libraries, the potential user base includes all members of the community, and as the "Library Bill of Rights" specifies, "library resources should be provided for the interest, information and enlightenment of all people of the community the library serves" (ALA, 1996).

Conceptually, equity of access means that everyone has the right to unfettered access to library resources, irrespective of who they are, their status, their income, or where they live. Equity of access is a fundamental right, an ideal of social justice and fairness. Equality in practice is another matter, as Michael Gorman (2000) suggests: " An ideal world of equality of access is out of reach, but a world in which librarians and library users have achieved a far greater state of fairness than now obtained is by no means impossible" (p. 131). Barriers to equity of access may be personal, such as a lack of mobility or literacy; they may be institutional, such as too few staff or inadequate equipment; or they may be societal, such as unequal funding of public service (p. 135).

Librarians cannot serve each user equally, but they must strive to do so fairly. Combating inequity requires us to distinguish those inequities that we may reduce from those over which we have no control, so that we can direct efforts effectively. Librarians should be aware of the special needs of people with disabilities and users from other cultures. In cases of unruly or objectionable library visitors, it is important to devise a policy that can be enforced consistently. Policies that are established in advance, clearly stated, and applied consistently will be treated with greater respect.

Technology has reduced some kinds of inequity while creating new forms. For instance, while the Internet has been a boon to access, not all users have Internet access and functioning computers at home, or the knowledge of how to use them. The substitution of digital reference works for print reference works with print versions will have the effect of making them easier for many users to access, while effectively making them invisible to others.

Charging fees should be avoided whenever possible, because fees present an unequal barrier to information. What may seem a reasonable fee to one person may overwhelm another, and certain types of research projects may require a high volume of access to resources that require a fee.

Academic librarians often assist patrons who are not associated with the institution as a matter of courtesy, and as Still and Kassabian (1999) point out, "Most public colleges and universities have several legal or moral commitments or ties to the community around them" (p. 9). Even so, the noble, egalitarian "concept of the library as a place that serves all people must be tempered by the academic library's mission, which gives priority to the needs of students, faculty, and staff" (Lenker and Kocevar-Weidinger, 2010: 421). Developing the policies governing this access requires ethical decision making. While in the past unassociated users may have been welcome to the print collection, the shift to electronic databases and Internet resources necessitates a more careful consideration of the conditions under which an open-door policy is an advisable extension of service. Use of electronic resources by unassociated users may increase expenditures and require a cutback in services to associated users, and that should be avoided. Librarians also have an ethical obligation to honor contractual access restrictions under which many electronic resources are now licensed.

The "Library Bill of Rights," issued by ALA in 1939 and revised six times, most recently in 1996, provides guidelines for services based on the concepts of equitable access and intellectual freedom:

> The American Library Association affirms that all libraries are forums for information and ideas, and that the following basic policies should guide their services.
>
> I. Books and other library resources should be provided for the interest, information, and enlightenment of all people of the community the library serves. Materials should not be excluded because of the origin, background, or views of those contributing to their creation.
>
> II. Libraries should provide materials and information presenting all points of view on current and historical issues. Materials should not be proscribed or removed because of partisan or doctrinal disapproval.
>
> III. Libraries should challenge censorship in the fulfillment of their responsibility to provide information and enlightenment.
>
> IV. Libraries should cooperate with all persons and groups concerned with resisting abridgment of free expression and free access to ideas.
>
> V. A person's right to use a library should not be denied or abridged because of origin, age, background, or views.
>
> VI. Libraries that make exhibit spaces and meeting rooms available to the public they serve should make such facilities available on an equitable basis, regardless of the beliefs or affiliations of individuals or groups requesting their use. (ALA, 1996)

Confidentiality

The right to privacy is highly valued, and often assailed, in an age of social media and information security breaches. Although reference desk "queries are not usually sensitive and though it is often feasible to move to a more secluded location or a private office, very few patrons or librarians avail themselves of this possibility" (Hauptman, 2002: 62). More so than the occasional reference question, electronic records, records of online searches, and personal data should be protected. However, several professionals have raised the question of whether collecting specific user data anonymously for the purposes of improving library systems is actually unethical. In any case, the transfer of this user data has been established as unethical, as can be seen in the profession's response to attempts by the federal government to obtain personal records of users. The Federal

Bureau of Investigation's secret Library Awareness Program, designed to identify subversives by their use of unclassified material available in academic libraries, was discovered by the public in 1987 following an incident at Columbia University. In response to the events of September 11, 2001, the federal government placed restrictions on information seeking that many felt seriously threatened civil liberties: actions affecting "access to information on terrorist and immigration proceedings, restrictions placed on biochemicals and toxic agents research, restrictions placed on foreign students and scholars, restrictions placed on journalists covering the wars in Afghanistan and Iraq, and the use of military tribunals" (Martorella, 2006: 111). Controversy surrounding the USA PATRIOT Act has recently highlighted the conflict between the country's duty to protect its citizens from threats and its duty to protect civil liberties.

Conflicts of Interest

Corporate sponsorship is generally considered a respected and mutually beneficial arrangement, not often interfering with the basic ethical tenets of librarianship. Still, caution and judgment must be exercised. Financial conflicts of interest may occur when relations with one vendor precludes doing business with another, who may have a better or equally good product. Another potential conflict may arise when a corporation offering an endorsement may have a product which in some way offends the user population. Transparency with regard to the library's dealings should work as a corrective to potential conflicts.

Copyright and Intellectual Property Rights

> We're the nation that put cars in driveways and computers in offices; the nation of Edison and the Wright brothers; of Google and Facebook. In America, innovation doesn't just change our lives. It is how we make our living.
>
> —Barack Obama
> State of the Union Address, January 25, 2011

Copyright issues are among the most debated ethical challenges to librarianship today. As librarians, we remain intermediaries between creators and other copyright holders, whose intellectual and legal rights we value, and users, for whom we seek to provide simple and equitable means of access. As specific lawsuits and legislation have the potential to alter the legal landscape in which we work, technological advances alter the means by which librarians practice within that landscape.

The constitutional framework behind copyright policy is that "Congress shall have Power... To promote the Progress of Science and useful Arts, by securing for limited Times to Authors and Inventors the exclusive Right to their respective Writings and Discoveries" (U.S. Const. art. 1, § 8). In other words, copyright was conceived as a way to protect the economic incentive of creators by granting them monopoly rights on their own works for a limited time. Individuals and society alike have much to gain from the protection of Intellectual Property Rights. This has not changed with the advent of digitally distributable material.

Copyright Exceptions and Limitations

The following issues are among the areas of copyright most often discussed in libraries. Decisions about how copyright is interpreted will differ from one institution to another and are made on the administrative level, usually with legal advice from a copyright expert. Reference librarians should be aware of the policies of their institution and should enforce and follow them.

Public Domain

Some notable exceptions to the protection of copyright are ideas, facts, and government works. These belong to *public domain*. Works for which the copyright terms have expired are also in public domain, unless the copyright holder has renewed and extended the copyright. Chapter 3 of the U.S. Copyright Act of 1976 (17 U.S.C.) outlines the duration of copyright, which depends on the date and origin of publication. A general understanding of the types of information in the public domain will enable a reference librarian to direct patrons to material that can be used for presentations, posters, and other projects for which public domain material is needed.

First Sale Doctrine

The *first sale doctrine* allows libraries to lend books and other materials that it has purchased, an essential element in the library's balance between rights holders and the public. Digital distribution of material has created an increase in the ease of access and reproduction of the material lent by libraries, which many believe has undermined the balance of the system. It is possible to create an unlimited number of digital copies of an e-book with little effort. Providing the greatest ease of access has long been a traditional goal of library service, but protecting the rights of creators is a concern of equal importance. The status of the first sale doctrine as it applies to digital objects is the subject of intense debate, one to which librarians are obliged to pay close attention. Library patrons are understandably curious about this issue, especially as it relates to e-resources. A patron may ask why he or she cannot "keep" an e-book indefinitely or share it with a relative. Another frequent question is why there are virtual queues for popular e-book titles. The reference librarian's ability to provide a reasoned answer to these types of questions may significantly affect the library's reputation in the community.

Fair Use

Fair use allows for the use of copyrighted materials without permission under certain circumstances, including those of research and nonprofit education. Photocopying and electronic reserve functions in libraries rely on fair use. The four basic criteria to consider in determining fair use are as follows:

(1) the purpose and character of the use, including whether such use is of a commercial nature or is for nonprofit educational purposes;
(2) the nature of the copyrighted work;
(3) the amount and substantiality of the portion used in relation to the copyrighted work as a whole; and

(4) the effect of the use upon the potential market for or value of the copyrighted work.

The fact that a work is unpublished shall not itself bar a finding of fair use
if such finding is made upon consideration of all the above factors. (17
U.S.C. § 107)

The distinction between infringement and fair use is not clearly defined. For
example, the third consideration does not specify a number of lines or pages or a
ratio to the whole. For this reason, interpretation of fair use varies by institution.
This statement published online by the American Library Association sums up
the current spirit of thought on the matter:

> Each institution's combination of practices reflects its tolerance for risk
> against the background of prevailing beliefs about fair use. Understand-
> ably, "not knowing" makes many people uncomfortable, so Congress
> explicitly addressed this aspect of fair use. Section 504(c)(2) of the Copy-
> right Act provides special protection to nonprofit libraries, educational
> institutions and their employees. When we act in good faith, reasonably
> believing that our actions are fair use, in the unlikely event we are actually
> sued over a use, we will not have to pay statutory damages even if a court
> finds that we were wrong. This demonstrates Congressional acknowl-
> edgement of the importance of fair use and the importance of our using it!
> (ALA, 2012b)

Section 108 Exceptions

The U.S. Copyright Act of 1976 (17 U.S.C. § 108) expressly provides for libraries and
archives to make reproductions of copyrighted works without seeking permission
from the copyright holder for the purposes of preservation of unpublished works
and the replacement of published works. Any digital copies made are not to be
displayed publicly.

Orphan Works

Orphan works are works that are in copyright, but for which the copyright holder
can't be found or identified. They are in copyright "limbo." Libraries cannot
make these works available publicly because they could be sued for statutory
damages of up to $150,000 per work (ALA, 2012a). Orphan books have been getting
attention lately because of Google's plan to scan a copy of every book ever
published, which they began implementing in 2004. The "Google Books Settlement,"
which was made public in 2008, was the result of negotiation between Google,
the Authors Guild, and five major publishers. It would have allowed Google to
scan the works, sell online copies, and share the profit with copyright owners.
Copyright owners would have to "opt out" to keep their works from being sold,
but of course by definition, the copyright owners of orphan works can't be
found. Both Google and the libraries would have been granted immunity for
their parts in the scanning under the settlement. However, the federal court
rejected the settlement in March 2011 (Grimmelman, 2012).

In the summer of 2011, HathiTrust members created the *Orphan Works Project*,
which aimed to identify works as orphans and make them available for digital

viewing. In September 2011, the Authors Guild filed a lawsuit against HathiTrust and five member libraries. This suit, rather than seeking damages, is seeking a declaration of wrong-doing, an injunction against further scanning, and the right to lock up all digital copies already made. If the Authors Guild wins the suit, digital preservation efforts in libraries could be adversely affected. If the suit is decided in favor of HathiTrust, libraries could potentially start making orphan books available digitally more widely. In either case, the operations of the newly formed Digital Public Library of America (DPLA) will be affected (Grimmelman, 2012).

Open Access

Open access allows for the free access of published material through openly accessible digital repositories. Some open access agreements allow just for the removal of pricing and registration barriers, while other agreements may additionally allow for redistribution, adaptation, and text mining. Often the author is required to pay up front, a situation that is inspiring some colleges and universities to collect pools of money to cover the expense. A list of open access scientific and scholarly journals can be found at the *Directory of Open Access Journals* (http://www.doaj.org/). Reference librarians should be aware of how to direct users to open access resources. This is often an issue with independent scholars and researchers without an affiliation to an institution that provides access to subscription or otherwise restricted-access databases.

Creative Commons

Creative Commons is a nonprofit organization that provides a set of copyright licenses and tools allowing creators and copyright holders to incrementally waive their own rights to works they have created. This provides more options than the "all rights reserved" of traditional copyright. Currently, there are six levels of licensing, which allow for various combinations of sharing, commercial or noncommercial use, and the creation of derivatives. All require attribution, and each license is accompanied by a symbol. In addition to these options, the CC0 designation allows creators and owners of copyrighted material to waive their intellectual property rights as completely as possible, effectively placing their work in the public domain and setting their work free for mass dissemination. It should be noted that "no tool, not even CC0, can guarantee a complete relinquishment of all copyright and database rights in every jurisdiction" (Creative Commons, 2012). The Creative Commons Public Domain Mark, aka "No Known Copyright," is for labeling items that are already believed to be in the public domain. Libraries have been able to make extensive use of this label in the online environment, because it most often applies to works that are too old to be covered by any copyright provision. Library users can benefit from an understanding of Creative Commons licensing and how to find materials with particular licensing labels, especially when creating multimedia projects with image or audio components. The benefits of Creative Commons licensing and labeling tools in the digital environment will likely make it an even more popular option in the future.

Library Instruction and Intellectual Property

> We need to better understand this generation of students. . . . Where my generation made the occasional mix tape for a friend, theirs is being sued for mass distribution of copyrighted music and file-sharing. I find it hard to believe that these students intentionally try to breach a previously defined code of ethics. I have to believe that they know right from wrong in the general sense; technology however has allowed us/them to blur that line. (Jacobs, 2008: 216)

The previous quote was written by an instructional librarian. Librarians are in a unique role to inform and provide guidance to students about copyright violations and how to avoid liability. Many students have never heard discourse on the topic from an authority. Some may be accustomed to cultural permissiveness toward appropriation, and certain online communities thrive on sharing.

Library instructional sessions generally include discussions of academic integrity and the ethical use of information. Traditionally, library instruction on the topic of intellectual property rights has focused on the prevention of plagiarism, that is, the appropriation of the written word without acknowledgment. As Rebecca Tushnet (2012) of the Georgetown University Law Center writes, "Copyright is literal. It takes the written word as its model and tries to fit everything else into the literary mode" (p. 684). Plagiarism of the written word negatively affects the integrity of scholarship and is an important topic to address with students. Librarians should recognize that plagiarism often arises from a lack of understanding and confidence in the academic support system by users, and that other copyright violations, such as the appropriation or unlicensed copying of images and music, are also, to some extent, due to a lack of understanding. The librarian's role in preventing copyright violation is an educational one. As Robert Hauptman (2002) wrote, "Reference librarians are not trained to police, nor should they do so, but they must also avoid helping the dishonest" (p. 63). If a librarian is aware of a clear case of plagiarism being enacted, it is his or her responsibility to educate the user about the nature of the infraction, to suggest alternative courses of action, and to make the user aware of the potential consequences of plagiarizing.

Digital Rights Management

Digital rights management (DRM) is a method by which copyrighted works may be enabled to police themselves. DRM technology is designed to track and limit the uses of digital material, in order to protect intellectual property. DRM technology is usually embedded as code within an item and remains there after the consumer has acquired it, which raises the possibility that privacy could be violated. The use of DRM technology could potentially impact libraries' provision of e-books as it could eliminate the use of the doctrine of first sale and fair use, enforce the necessity of a "pay-per-use" model, and impose time limits for usage, outside the control of the library.

Intellectual Freedom and Human Rights

> We significantly influence or control the selection, organization, preservation, and dissemination of information. In a political system grounded in an informed citizenry, we are members of a profession explicitly committed to intellectual freedom and the freedom of access to information. (ALA, 2008)

As a profession, librarians have long felt a sense of social responsibility toward the protection of *intellectual freedom*, defined most simply by the American Library Association as the freedom to express one's own ideas and the right to read those expressed by others. According to the *Intellectual Freedom Manual* (ALA, Office for Intellectual Freedom, 2010), this freedom can only be achieved "where two essential conditions are met: first, that all individuals have the right to hold any belief on any subject and to convey their ideas in any form they deem appropriate, and second, that society makes an equal commitment to the right of unrestricted access to information and ideas regardless of the communication medium used, the content of work, and the viewpoints of both the author and the receiver of information."

Censorship

Defending First Amendment rights concerning the freedom of speech and protecting against *censorship* is a primary tenet of intellectual freedom. Censorship can affect policy, selection of materials, access to materials, and the diversity of materials, staff, and users. "The Freedom to Read Statement" (ALA and Association of American Publishers, 2004) declares that "the freedom to read . . . is continuously under attack." Librarians may be called upon to distinguish between obscene and offensive material. We may have to consider the overall merits of a work over salacious excerpts and may find it necessary to defend the right to collect books representing politically controversial ideas.

In his presidential address to ALA in 1908, Arthur Boswick said, "Let us admit at the outset that there is absolutely no book that may not find its place on the shelves of some library and perform there its appointed function" (p. 257). As developers of collections, librarians make value judgments with every purchase, but it is not necessary for them to endorse the values of what they collect. As "The Freedom to Read Statement" declares, "We trust Americans to recognize propaganda and misinformation, and to make their own decisions about what they read and believe" (ALA and Association of American Publishers, 2004).

Internet filtering in public libraries to block offensive materials is another issue confronting library policy makers. In 2001, ALA issued a statement in opposition to federally mandated filtering in libraries, based on the tenets of intellectual freedom. In practice, libraries have developed a variety of ways to allow access to the Internet while fulfilling the guidelines developed by ALA.

Public libraries in particular consider minors an important group to serve, and fostering their development is understood to be a fundamental part of their mission. Children complicate the issues of censorship and confidentiality in library policy because their guardians may want to control and survey their borrowing habits. Decisions about accommodating this are made on the basis of an individual community.

Neutrality

A long-standing public service role for libraries has been to provide materials of a variety of viewpoints, including that of the minority or fringe groups. It is always difficult to present all points of view on every topic, but presenting a plurality of opinion has been considered a matter of professional pride in many libraries. As budgets are cut and the volume and variety of production increases, presenting the full range of minority points of view becomes even more challenging. ALA continues to embrace the ideals of objectivity and political neutrality.

Practical neutrality must naturally be tempered by good judgment. For instance, neutrality may not apply when a reference librarian strongly suspects that information provided will cause imminent harm. To illustrate, we may look at the classic case of Robert Hauptman's experiment in 1975, in which he posed as a user and asked reference librarians in six public and seven academic libraries for specific information on how to build a small bomb, the chemicals needed, and "whether a small amount [of cordite] will blow up, say, a small suburban house" (Hauptman, 1976: 626). In such a scenario, he concludes, the reference librarian "must refuse to cooperate" (Hauptman, 2002: 63).

What, besides homemade bombs, can cause harm? "Matters concerning human rights and freedom of expression are central to the ability of librarians and libraries to serve the needs and interests of their users world-wide" (ALA, 1997). IFLA's human rights resolutions should be heeded by information professionals "to avoid becoming a tool in the hands of those who seek to manipulate others, and in order to support core library values, as well as giving due attention to global democratic and human rights" (Samek, 2007: xxiii). Human rights may seem far divorced from the day-to-day practice of working in a library, and most librarians rarely engage in work that provides opportunity to defend or promote human rights. This should not be a deterrent to staying apprised of world events and the terminology requisite to speaking knowledgeably on the topic. IFLA and ALA are not sanctioning entities; they are leaders. Librarians can fill the same role in their professional interactions (Samek, 2007: 9). It is an ethical imperative that librarians maintain a trusted, well-selected, organized, preserved, and openly accessible foundation of knowledge for the future's journalists, scholars, and policy makers. This foundation, and the principled reference services which connect it with the user, will serve as a safeguard to a just and reasoned civil discourse.

Bibliography and Works Cited

ALA (American Library Association). 1996. "Library Bill of Rights." American Library Association. Reaffirmed January 23. http://www.ala.org/advocacy/intfreedom/librarybill.

————. 1997. "Resolution on IFLA, Human Rights and Freedom of Expression." American Library Association. http://www.ala.org/offices/iro/awardsactivities/resolutionifla.

————. 2001. "Resolution on Opposition to Federally Mandated Internet Filtering." American Library Association. Adopted January 17. http://www.ala.org/offices/oif/statements pols/ifresolutions/resolutionopposition.

————. 2008. "Code of Ethics of the American Library Association." American Library Association. Last updated January 22. Available: http://www.ala.org/advocacy/proethics/codeofethics/codeethics.

————. 2012a. "Copyright: Orphan Works." American Library Association. Accessed July 18. http://www.ala.org/advocacy/copyright/orphan.

————. 2012b. "Fair Use and Electronic Reserves." American Library Association. Accessed July 18. http://www.ala.org/advocacy/copyright/fairuse/fairuseandelectronic reserves.

————. 2012c. "History of the ALA Code of Ethics." American Library Association. Accessed July 18. http://www.ala.org/advocacy/proethics/history.

————. Office for Intellectual Freedom. 2010. *Intellectual Freedom Manual*. 8th ed. Chicago: American Library Association.

ALA (American Library Association) and Association of American Publishers. 2004. "The Freedom to Read Statement." American Library Association. Amended June 30. http://www.ala.org/offices/oif/statementspols/ftrstatement/freedomreadstatement.

Aubele, Joseph, Susan Jackson, and Lesley Farmer. 2008. "Technology Impact on Information Needs and Behaviors of the Academic Community." In *The Human Side of Reference and Information Services in Academic Libraries*, edited by Lesley Farmer, 1–17. London: Chandos.

Boswick, Arthur. 1908. "The Librarian as Censor: Address of the President, American Library Association, Lake Minnetonka Conference, 1908." *Library Journal* 33: 257–264.

Bunge, Charles. 1999. "Ethics and the Reference Librarian." *The Reference Librarian* 31, no. 66: 25–43.

Creative Commons. 2012. "About CC0—'No Rights Reserved.'" Creative Commons. Accessed July 18. http://creativecommons.org/about/cc0.

Dana, John Cotton. 1911. "Misdirection of Effort in Reference." *Public Libraries* 16: 108–109.

Gorman, Michael. 2000. *Our Enduring Values: Librarianship in the 21st Century*. Chicago: American Library Association.

Grimmelman, James. 2012. "The Orphan Wars." *EDUCAUSE Review* 47, no 1. http://www.educause.edu/ero/article/orphan-wars.

Hauptman, Robert. 1976. "Professionalism or Culpability? An Experiment in Ethics." *Wilson Library Bulletin* 50: 626–627.

————. 2002. *Ethics and Librarianship*. Jefferson, NC: London: McFarland.

Jacobs, Michelle L. 2008. "Ethics and Ethical Challenges in Library Instruction." *Journal of Library Administration* 47, no. 3–4: 211–232.

Lenker, Mark, and Elizabeth Kocevar-Weidinger. 2010. "Nonaffiliated Users in Academic Libraries: Using W.D. Ross's Ethical Pluralism to Make Sense of the Tough Questions." *College and Research Libraries* 71, no. 5: 421–434.

Martorella, Georgina. 2006. "Libraries in the Aftermath of 9/11." *The Reference Librarian* 45, no. 94: 109–137.

Preer, Jean. 2008. *Library Ethics*. Westport, CT: Greenwood.

RUSA (Reference and User Services Association). 2003. "Professional Competencies for Reference and User Services Librarians." American Library Association. http://www.ala.org/rusa/resources/guidelines/professional.

Samek, Toni. 2007. *Librarianship and Human Rights: A Twenty-First Century Guide*. London: Chandos.

Severson, Richard. 1995. "The Recovery of Ethics in Librarianship." *Journal of Information Ethics* 4, no. 1: 11–16.

Still, Julie, and Vibiana Kassabian. 1999. "The Mole's Dilemma: Ethical Aspects of Public Internet Access in Academic Libraries." *Internet Reference Services Quarterly* 4, no. 3: 7–22.

Tushnet, Rebecca. 2012. "Worth a Thousand Words: The Images of Copyright." *Harvard Law Review* 125, no. 3: 684–759.

U.S. Copyright Office. 2012. *Copyright Law of the United States*. U.S. Copyright Office. Accessed July 18. http://www.copyright.gov/title17/.

19

Managing Reference Departments

Of Car Designs and Learning Styles

In 2012, the Chairman of the "new" General Motors (GM) stated, "we win when the customer says we win." This was in stark contrast to little over a decade ago when GM, once the largest employer in the United States, had the thankless job of announcing the layoff of 30,000 workers, just prior to the Thanksgiving holiday of 2005. Many of those workers, according to a commentator, "were its best and most productive. Their bosses simply couldn't give them a car to build that Americans really wanted to buy" (Bai, 2005: 15). In other words, despite stellar staff and a conscientiously produced product, it was management that had failed in its primary duty of making effective business decisions. The fallibility of their decision making was further traced to an inability or unwillingness to "let consumers drive its designs."

Library management has traditionally looked to corporate management for guidance. For reference managers of the twenty-first century a clear cautionary tale can be salvaged from both GM's managerial pileup, as well as its subsequent resurgence. The consumers of reference services are information seekers, and information is mined according to their individual learning styles. Do information seekers of the twenty-first century have learning styles that are intrinsically different from the past? If we peer through the mists of time, we can see Socrates surrounded by a group of students who have presumably traveled from many directions to quite literally be at the feet of the master in their search for answers.

If we flip forward two and a half millennia to the Simon Fraser University in Canada or Harvard University in Boston, we see reference librarians toting tablets, iPads, or mobile apps that are primed to instantaneously assist students in their search for answers. So yes, the "design" has changed and there is such a thing as a twenty-first-century learning style. It is a style that has developed a muscular expectation for rapid and "anytime, anywhere" information services. Fueled by this expectation, the organization of reference delivery and access continues to change in many ways. The reference manager of the twenty-first century must not only be acutely sensitized to the evolving environment but also be prepared to ably administer and manage dramatic new service models, information delivery systems, and innovative staff configurations. All of this must be done while both gracefully accepting the additional new roles thrust upon them by the continuing changes and becoming proactive change managers themselves.

Organizing Reference Departments

Traditionally, the management of reference departments has cohered to a hierarchical principle that upholds a scalar chain of command. While elements of that chain continue, the hierarchy is perforce flattening out to accommodate the vibrant new roles and services necessitated by the new learning style (see Table 19-1).

Table 19-1. Changing Paradigms in Reference Management		
Traditional	**→**	**Emerging**
Hierarchical	*Organization*	Flattened
Stationary	*Service Delivery*	Spatial
Specialized	*Staffing*	Multidisciplinary
Isolated	*Work*	Integrated
Independent	*Structure*	Interdependent
Inductive	*Logic*	Deductive
Materials	*Mission Focus*	Users
Status Quo	*Attitude*	Innovate

Self-directed or team-based management has made some inroads into traditional hierarchies. In 1998, the Ohio State University Health Sciences Library instituted the Reference and Information Services Team (RIST), a "self-regulating management team" that adopted a system of rotating coordinators rather than a head of reference to manage the team. All members of the team were given the opportunity to learn one another's jobs with the idea of making reference services more integrated (Bradigan and Powell, 2004). The Valley Library at Oregon State University subscribed to "team-based management" that employed work groups and coordinating advisory councils to replace top-down decision making (McMillen and Rielly, 2003).

Various persuasive analyses have also appeared in the professional literature attesting to the intrinsic value of self-managed teams. It has been argued that "members feel a moral sense to make the approach work so as not to let down other members" (Young, 2004: 185); there is flexibility in being able to respond quickly to problems without consulting a chain of authority (Poon-Richards, 1996); it increases the effectiveness of organizational practice (Yang and Guy, 2011); and the opportunity exists to provide professional development for a wider swathe of reference librarians (McMillen and Rielly, 2003).

However, these are all perceived advantages accruing to nonhierarchical administrative models in any scenario, not specifically the one facing the twenty-first-century reference manager. The reason these models are appearing in the current environment is *because* of the current environment. The explosion of changing technology requires a far more diverse body of talents and experience. In addition, the rapid change in service needs demands a higher degree of coordination and "synergistic problem-solving" (Kelly, 1998: 8) or "hybrid services"

(Radford and Vine, 2011: 79). These have combined to limn the advantages of flexibility, dimensionality, and personal motivation inherent to self-directed management. A survey of libraries showed "a general trend of technical services in academic libraries to reorganize into teams" (Zhu, 2011: 69).

By logical extension, once the environment is not marked by such intense flux and changing expectations, the relevance of self-directed teams could dim. This in fact already holds true for smaller public libraries, where the change in user needs and the induction of technological innovations is more gradual. The emergence of self-directed teams is, not surprisingly, dominant in academic libraries, where both the expectation and delivery of changing technologies is most insistent. A study covering changes in the role of academic librarians found that the highest percentage of change in both job activities and reference tools was a spin-off of changes in technology.

Electronic collection development, virtual reference, online searching, and designing webpages marked the largest changes in job activity. Online databases, the World Wide Web, e-mail, and electronic dictionaries and indexes counted for the most dramatic changes in reference tools used (Cardina and Wicks, 2004). Additionally, social media initiatives have introduced yet another pressing element of service to reference staff responsibilities. The onus of keeping up with the ever-hungry appetites of Facebook, Twitter, and blog audiences cannot be underestimated. Finally, the expansion of online technology has increased the numbers of distance-learning students who, in turn, further raise the need for online resources and virtual reference from academic and public libraries (Nicholas and White, 2012).

Organizing Staff

Given that staff costs account for up to 70 percent of a library's operating budget (Davis, 2010), the onus of providing the wisest possible allocation of staff time lies heavily on the head of the reference manager. According to an earlier time management analysis, "reference desk scheduling is one of the most challenging tasks in the organizational structure" (Sciammarella, Fernandes, and McKay, 2008).

The Reference Desk

In 1967, a minimum standard for staffing public libraries was published by the American Library Association (ALA) such that x number of staff, y number of books, and z square footage of building per capita was deemed as necessary. The logic girding this prescriptive and quantitative model did not prove very effective. Currently, and in the foreseeable future, the staffing of reference derives from the type of deductive logic provided by confirmed user needs.

For example, at the University of South Florida Library, Desk Tracker, an online tool was adapted to collect statistics on reference desk usage. The collected data were key in reenvisioning staffing patterns at the reference desk (Todorinova et al., 2011). *Staffing for Results*, published as part of the PLA (Public Library Association) Planning for Results series, also subscribed to deductive principles of staffing so that the number and type of staff was presented as a function of proven local needs and priorities rather than a formulaic allocation based on a priori assumptions (Mayo and Goodrich, 2002). Faced with a shrinking budget, the University of Minnesota's Bio-Medical Library created a medley of staffing initiatives that included fee-based reference services, trained undergraduate reference assistance, and interdepartmental staff coverage options (Aho, Beschnett, and Reimer, 2011).

In many cases, the primacy of the reference desk as the nexus for all information needs is consciously muted. As Karyle Butcher (1999) presciently stated over a decade ago, "The physical reference desk has become the place where librarians catch their breath between patrons. It is less and less the place where actual reference service takes place" (p. 351).

In the academic libraries of Pennsylvania's York College and Dickinson College, the Merced Library at the University of California, and Northwest Missouri State University, for example, the reference desk was completely phased out and reference librarians are seen by appointment. Ready reference questions are handled at a general-purpose desk that covers circulation and the more basic technological problems faced by users. This model has taken on different variations in different institutions. The medical library at the Johns Hopkins University and the Arizona State University West libraries staff the all-purpose desk with paraprofessionals. Brandeis University libraries employ graduate students. The University of North Carolina at Charlotte uses both paraprofessionals and student assistants to staff routine queries complemented by referrals to more in-depth research by professional reference librarians (Bailey and Tierney, 2002). At the University of Arizona, if ready reference at the general-purpose desk is not what is required by the user, a subject specialist is either called or the user fills out an online form for the specialist who will then get back to the user (Bracke, Chinnaswamy, and Kline, 2008). The Ohio State University Health Sciences Library has adopted PICS (Personalized Information Consult Service) that provides reference services only by appointment (Schulte, 2011). While acknowledging that "one size does not fit all," a report noted that "reference service is not only possible, but can thrive without the desk" (Arndt, 2010), while another evidence-based study concluded that "interactions with patrons in librarians' offices—either in person or virtually—remain substantial even without a traditional reference desk" (Lederer and Feldmann, 2012: 6).

The model of an "Information/Learning Commons" aims to integrate all reference activities into a one-stop shop, so that students and faculty are provided with a "seamless continuum...from planning and research through presentation into final product" (Bailey and Tierney, 2002: 284). Further discussion on how such models feed into a viable picture of the future of reference is found in Chapter 22.

Managing Service Delivery

Service delivery has undergone perhaps the most dramatic transformations. With the growing pervasiveness of digitized information, electronic databases, the all-consuming Internet, podcasting, blogging, RSS (really simple syndication), SMS (short message service), virtual, live chat, and IM reference, teamed with the ubiquity of desktop, tablet, iPad, laptop, and notebook computers, wireless networking, and mobile technology, the delivery of reference services is at a whole new level.

Roving or Mobile Services

Traditionally, the term "roving reference" implied a model whereby reference librarians were encouraged to be less stationary in their traditional posts behind a reference desk and more proactive in approaching users. As Suzanne Tronier, the manager of the East Millcreek Library of the Salt Lake County Library System, succinctly explained in a Publib Listserv exchange (December 22, 2005):

> Our librarians are expected to contact people in the library during the first part of their roving shift, helping as needed. After that they provide back up for the reference desk, put out new arrivals and straighten displays; they can weed or do other projects in the stacks and otherwise make themselves available for questions. In some areas of the library...just working in that area will invite questions.

Reference librarians at the Salem–South Lyon District Library in Michigan have found it effective to carry a tablet PC with them as they rove the stacks and help patrons as they browse (Hibner, 2007). At the Southern Illinois University–Carbondale, librarians carry an iPad to assist students and find that it also helps "as a badge and initiator for roving reference. The iPads give the impression that the librarian is technically accessible and 'cool'" (Lotts and Graves, 2011: 219).

A more dramatic interpretation of roving librarians has them ranging far beyond the confines not only of the desk, but of the library building as well. At Harvard University, the roving librarian provides "reference on the road" by strategically roving the undergraduate student center with laptop in hand. Given the wealth of electronic databases and online resources available, these librarians are able to either answer or direct a large part of the research interests of the students milling around the center. Similarly, the "Ask Us Here!" initiative at the Bennett Library of the Simon Fraser University in Canada has two choice "service locations" with a "high volume of pedestrian traffic" (Wong and O'Shea, 2004: 91). Here the research needs of students are either referred appropriately or answered by reference librarians with wireless laptops. The librarians at the University of Montana subscribe to "outpost reference," which involves roving around student dormitories and the student union. The student union was the more effective venue because there was more consistency and reliability in location and schedule (Hines, 2007).

Virtual Services

The successful integration of remote access to reference information and services has created an important additional responsibility for reference managers. Hiring or training staff to provide this service, apportioning staff time, effectively evaluating the services provided, and staying on top of the quicksilver advances in remote access technology must all become part of the management environment.

Anytime, Anywhere Access

The most robust form of virtual reference has been live, 24/7 "anytime, anywhere" access, that is, "chat" reference. Recent literature on the provision of this form of virtual reference suggests that its cost-effectiveness can vary dramatically from one institution to another. While individual libraries that provide virtual reference can pay up to $12,000 annually for merely retaining the infrastructure, consortial arrangements can whittle down the cost to $3,000 (Bailey-Hainer, 2005). A study at an academic library found that the cost of answering a chat reference by a reference librarian ranged from $37 to $439 per question (Bravender, Lyon, and Molaro, 2011), though other equally convincing studies point to its cost-effectiveness (Tenopir, 2004). As concluded in a national survey of academic libraries conducting chat reference, the success of it, "like all reference services,...is community specific" (Devine, Paladino, and Davis, 2011). Reference managers following the debate may also want to track the developments of various national and statewide collaborations, some of which are listed in Table 19-2.

Table 19-2. Select Examples of Collaborative Virtual Reference Services

Service	URL	Area	Activated	Libraries
ASKaLibrarian	http://askalibrarian.org/	Florida	2003	120
AskColorado	http://www.askcolorado.org/	Colorado	2003	74
AskUsNow	http://www.askusnow.info/	Maryland	2003	39
KnowItNow	http://www.knowitnow.org/	Ohio	2004	77
L-net	http://www.oregonlibraries.net/	Oregon	2003	40
My Info Quest	http://www.myinfoquest.info/	USA	2009	50
NCknows	http:www.ncknows.org/	North Carolina	2004	120
QuestionPoint: 24/7 Reference	http://www.questionpoint.org/	Global	2001 (merger 2005)	Nearly 1,500

The attraction of virtual reference collaborations can also be traced internationally. The *People's Network Enquire* is a U.K. initiative that has been put together by over 80 public libraries under the sponsorship of the Museums, Libraries and Archives Council. The *ZLB* (*Zentral- und Landesbibliothek*) of Berlin provides e-mail reference in German and multiple languages through active partnerships with other libraries in Europe and QuestionPoint. These collaborative ventures, then, appear to be the most viable models of 24/7 virtual reference access (Kaufman, 2012).

Reference managers wanting to organize virtual reference services for their institution can refer to ALA's guidelines at http://www.ala.org/rusa/resources/guidelines/virtrefguidelines. Helpful survey planning documents describing the initiation of these services can also be found at the URLs given in Table 19-2. Project management software tools, such as MSP2000 (Microsoft Project), are handy organizers to both scope and monitor the introduction of such services. A study by Zhang and Bishop (2005) provides an example of the use of this tool.

"Ask A" Services

In addition to virtual reference offering both e-mail and live reference services through statewide collaboration, a dizzying variety of individual initiatives are available to the reference manager:

- IM and chat reference services are not only offered by many libraries, but are being constantly fine-tuned to remain attractive to increasingly sophisticated users. An entire study has been devoted, for example, to the training of "the millennial generation of reference workers," to ensure that chat reference does not devolve into casual colloquialisms (Langan, 2012). The addition of videos and screenshots on the fly through screen capture tools like Jing and Snagit have added to the impact of communication via IM reference (Sekyere, 2010).

- SMS, the mobile cousin to IM, is also evolving along with the meteoric takeover of wireless phone technology. Despite the ability to concatenate messages, carriers typically allow for up to 160 characters per SMS message. Texting as a reference service is recognizable through initiatives such as Mosio's *Text a Librarian* and Cha Cha. The chat-based reference service offered at the University of Little Rock in Arkansas, *LibraryH3lp* (http://libraryh3lp.com/), is an open source alternative that aims to unify chat across web, texting, and IM. The recognized value of SMS reference can also be detected in consortial undertakings such as *My Info Quest* that includes close to 50 public and university libraries (Brannon, 2011).

- The Orange County Library Systems of Florida were the first public library system to adopt RSS to enhance its content distribution and have been followed by thousands of other libraries. The Pepperdine University Libraries, MIT Libraries, and Baylor University Libraries, for example, offer RSS feeds for newly cataloged titles. The Hennepin County Library and the Seattle Public Library provide feeds for items checked out and titles on hold. The new generation of feeds also includes audio files (Podcasts) and video files (Vodcasts).

- Reference libraries are also including special enhancements to web contact center software such as VoIP (voice-over Internet protocol); "knowledge bases" that hold frequently asked questions and answers; and improved co-browsing even with proprietary databases (Coffman, 2001). Given that the number of smartphones will be greater than personal computers (Booth, 2010), the Ohio University Libraries have developed Skype-based reference service; and the Salem–South Lyon District Library in Michigan has inducted VoIP among reference staff (Hibner, 2007). One of the earliest and most comprehensive "knowledge bases" can be seen in "Start," created by a member of MIT's InfoLab Group at the Artificial Intelligence Laboratory and accessible at http://start.csail.mit.edu/index.html.

Increasingly, almost all libraries, be they academic, public, corporate, special, or school libraries, are setting up websites with some form of "Ask a Librarian" service.

New Roles

A study of the Executive Leadership Institute instituted by the Urban Libraries Council to develop strong future managers found that successful participants were, among other things, "intrigued by recreating libraries through new business models" and "comfortable with messy, complex partnerships" (Nicely and Dempsey, 2005: 3–4). As outlined earlier in this chapter, new business models marked by a flattening of the hierarchy, multiprofessional staffing, and innovative service delivery systems unrestricted by stationary physical locations are par for the course being followed by reference managers of the twenty-first century. In addition, though, is the recognized value of getting comfortable with "messy partnerships." Some recurring areas requiring reference managers to get "messy" are in the field of electronic resource management, web management, and reference marketing.

Electronic Resource Management

"Buying electronic information is more expensive and more complicated than purchasing print information" (Butcher, 1999: 350). While this truism was offered over a decade ago, the amplitude of its resonance has increased for the reference manager who must plan, choose, negotiate, and finally budget for every database that is purchased from a frequently bewildering array of pricing options. "Big deal" packages commonly offered by major publishers, "little deals" or "pay per view" arrangements, and open access content are some of the creative models for pricing of electronic resources (Bosch and Henderson, 2012). Guidelines for implementing collection development policies, such as whether a print resource needs to be replaced or complemented with an electronic counterpart, must be prepared. Given that academic libraries reportedly budget 61 percent of their resources on electronic material (Albanese, 2004), planning a reflective and judicious budget can be a demanding task, requiring a change in traditionally held collection policies and dexterity in choosing the best option.

Vendor negotiation and long-term vendor viability have evolved into art forms demanding far greater sophistication on the part of the reference manager (Williams, 2010). The variety and scope for negotiation tends to fracture into as many possibilities as vendors available to provide them. Given this, decisions on whether and how to join the simplifying construct of a consortium become relevant (Hiremath, 2001). Consortial initiatives such as the International Coalition of

Library Consortia (http://icolc.net/); the Washington Research Library Consortium (http://www.wrlc.org/); or the Statewide California Electronic Library Consortium (http://scelc.org/), to name just a few, have the potential to exponentially power both the breadth and depth of access to electronic databases for individual libraries. Future developments in groundbreaking digital consortiums such as the HathiTrust and 2CUL (http://2cul.org/) require "radical collaboration." Legal issues of copyright compliance need to be mastered and conveyed to users in effective ways, given that "interactive services increase the chance of patrons violating copyright law" (Wyatt and Hahn, 2011: 303).

Selecting and utilizing the most effective software platform to host electronic resources is also expanding into a multiple-choice option. Library-specific systems and software are no longer the natural choice as proven by the creative use of Drupal, a free content management system, at Eastern Kentucky University libraries. The libraries at Stanford University and the University at South Florida have also adopted "mainstream technologies to create new approaches to managing electronic resources acquisitions, workflows, and metadata" (Wilson, 2011).

Web Management

A library's website is both the introductory façade to the institution and the user's first step to dipping into the library's reference services and tools. It is no wonder then that the responsibility of website content invariably falls on the reference department. Managers of the twenty-first century must be geared to either take on—or at minimum, share—the task of developing and maintaining websites.

A survey of the Association of Research Libraries found that 98 percent of reference librarians worked at web content (Ragsdale, 2001). "Reference librarians are no longer expected to simply answer questions.... They are rather expected to promote, teach, design websites and online tutorials"(Bronstein, 2011: 803–804). Depending on the size, structure, and motivations of the library, the management of web projects can take on many permutations, from the employment of a single webmaster to a web committee, to a distributed system involving input and coordination with collection development staff, catalogers, and bibliographers. The reference manager must also prepare for messier strains of web responsibilities. As pointed out by Butcher (1999), with the digitization of information becoming a rising expectation, "faculty look to librarians to participate in campus partnerships concerning the storage and retrieval of information" (p. 351).

The soaring popularity of Web 2.0 social networking tools has further complicated the content management of library webpages. Increasingly interactive online experiences have conditioned users to expect a site that is not only informative, but also personalized to their needs, capable of active bidirectional communication, and collaborative. Next-generation web management must necessarily incorporate the idea that what was once "a solitary experience has become a social one" (Del Pinto, 2009: 41) and both design and manage library websites accordingly.

Reference Marketing

Although nonprofits have been using marketing techniques in recent decades, libraries have been slow to realize the need to market reference resources and services. Relative to Google and *Wikipedia*, electronic resources are invisible to most users. This feeling of invisibility has caused librarians to ensure that their users are more aware of what they have available by creating "an E-Buzz" that uses new technologies to both market and promote resources in strategic and creative ways (Dubicki, 2008). "Marketing" is a broad term that includes public relations, advertising, contacts with community groups, and more. Marketing can involve a cost to the library or can be almost cost free.

Developing a plan for the reference marketing project is the first step. For a public library, it will be necessary to define a target audience, which might include students, senior citizens, teachers, businesspeople, freelancers, government officials, professionals, and so on, while for an academic library it would be faculty, students, and administrators. The library's market could also be defined by demographics such as age, gender, income, education, occupation, ethnicity, and so forth. The next step is to list the reference resources and services that the library offers and wishes to promote to its users. This could include electronic databases, the library's virtual reference service, or the library's e-book collection.

Many strategies can be used to promote these resources and services. Consider both the low-cost and more costly possibilities. These range from brochures, newsletters, newspaper articles, newspaper ads, direct mail, radio and TV advertising, and promotion on the Internet. For potential users, the library could develop subject pathfinders in print or on the web that will bring an awareness of relevant and available electronic databases. Information on any reference resource or service can be highlighted on the library's website homepage. The Internet is an inexpensive and powerful way to provide information to the library's users; for example, online newsletters can be sent to users on a regular basis. A simple bookmark or QR (quick response) code with information about reference resources and services can also serve as a reminder to library users. The library's public relations office may want to place news stories or articles about the library's reference resources and services. Staff can promote reference resources by making presentations to community groups, faculty or student groups, or to the employees of local institutions and organizations. With a budget for paid advertising, the library can promote its reference services and resources through newspaper ads and radio or TV spots. It's important to define what results are being sought before beginning, so there is a way to measure success.

Although general marketing of services and resources is effective, libraries can also consider the techniques of niche marketing, which is aimed at a specific audience such as senior citizens, students, businesspeople, and so forth. By using niche marketing, the message can be made more detailed and specific. To do this, the reference manager will need to focus on a particular resource or service (or a group of them) and consider who might benefit from these resources and services (Walters, 2004). For example, a message aimed at the business community could discuss the kinds of information available through electronic databases that identify new places to advertise, new audiences for their products, and new advertising techniques that are cost-effective.

Relationship marketing is another technique that reference managers should consider. This kind of marketing goes a step beyond traditional marketing by developing interactive programs that highlight individual staff expertise to cater to specific user needs. This is an excellent technique for reference libraries because it allows long-term partnerships based on listening closely to user needs and developing strategies that respond to those needs. In this kind of marketing, all staff members play a role in carrying the library's message to raise awareness among users (Nunn and Ruane, 2011).

Virtual Reference Service Evaluation

In addition to evaluating traditional reference services, one of the new duties demanded of the reference manager is to administer and evaluate the many permutations of virtual reference (VR) services. Whereas in-person reference transactions quite naturally focus on the reference interview and answer, VR has a dual focus. Both human interaction and digital competency vie for attention. A successful VR transaction is highly dependent on effective chat software, bandwidth speed, a robust workstation, as well as interpersonal and query clarification skills (Radford et al., 2011).

The ability to cobrowse so that the librarian can directly demonstrate a search to the user; page-pushing software that can transfer files and screenshots without cutting and pasting; file sharing from proprietary databases; the ability to archive pages; concurrent usage with more than one user at a time; customizable user and library information; queuing options such as call selection; scripted messages; transference of active sessions; provision of final transcripts with hyperlinks; in-built statistical assessment tools and surveys; and troubleshooting assistance are just some of the cogs that keep the wheels of VR moving smoothly. These are also some of the criteria for initial selection of software technology, as are cost and staffing models.

In addition to the choosing, assessing, and constant upgrading of virtual technology, managers are responsible for relatively involved logistical factors. Collaborative virtual services, such as those listed earlier in this chapter, are increasingly becoming the norm. The parameters of individual contributions have to be decided, effective liaison procedures need to be instituted, and the scheduling of staff time, training, and evaluation slotted into place.

The training of reference librarians in the art and science of VR requires constant vetting, fine-tuning, and improvement. Whether it be "query clarifications" (Radford et al., 2011) enshrined in the give-and-take of chat transactions or the ongoing collation of handy local information in the knowledge bases available to librarians working within large VR consortiums (Bishop, Sach-Silveira, and Avet, 2011), the need for calibration is ever-present. Continuing assessment also becomes a "necessary good" (Logan and Lewis, 2011) at all times during this ongoing process.

Further Considerations

In their text on the management of libraries and information centers, Stueart and Moran (2007: 15) present five "functions common to all managers":

1. Planning
2. Organizing
3. Staffing
4. Directing
5. Controlling

For reference managers, technological innovations of tsunami proportions have compulsively created changes in all five functions. *Planning* of both strategic and long-term reference services and tools must necessarily incorporate the expectations of a demanding new learning style typical of users of the twenty-first century. The learning style, in turn, has fed into new experiments with the *organization* of reference departments so that a variety of models leaning toward lateral coordination can facilitate quick information services, rather than pyramidal hierarchies that are typically less flexible. *Staffing* must necessarily be more multidisciplinary to cater to different varieties of reference service delivery ranging from traditional in-person desk reference to 24/7 remote access services. Reference managers, faced with rapid changes, must be motivated to take on new and unexpected *directing* roles that could involve "messy partnerships" with players as varied as web developers, electronic database vendors, and statewide consortia. Finally, the *control* of reference services is best maintained through a canny mix of effective marketing and vigilant evaluation.

Recommendations for Further Reading

Aguilar, Paulita, Kathleen Keating, Suzanne Schadl, and Johann Van Reenen. 2011. "Reference as Outreach: Meeting Users Where They Are." *Journal of Library Administration* 51, no. 4 (May–June): 343–358. The article supplies an instructive description of the move away from traditional desk reference to the evolution and adoption of reference instruction and aggressive outreach. Reference managers introduced satellite reference centers that were physically located in relatively marginalized spots such as multiethnic centers on campus; as well as virtual reference services, and a new liaison program at the University of New Mexico University Libraries, with the aim of "meeting users where they are."

Brevig, Armand. 2008. "Getting Value from Vendor Relationships." *Searcher* 16, no. 9 (October): 28–34. Managing e-content is a major responsibility for all reference managers. This article clearly lays out strategies for assessing collection goals and vendor relations in order to develop excellence in the art of negotiation. Real-life examples are helpfully provided by the author from his library at AstraZeneca, the Anglo-Swedish pharmaceutical company that has directly linked corporate strategy with an information acquisition vision for the library's e-resources. This is a stimulating article for reference managers ready to face their first vendors.

Collins, Tim. 2012. "The Current Budget Environment and Its Impact on Libraries, Publishers and Vendors." *Journal of Library Administration* 52, no. 1: 18–35. Based on extensive

EBSCO surveys, the article provides an interesting overarching view of the general migration to electronic formats that aims to feed the "latest advancement in research—discovery" (p. 19). Discovery solutions and discovery services that allow reference users to find resources so that actual usage is increased and user experience is improved, is the common goal of libraries, publishing houses, and information vendors.

Electronic Resources and Libraries. 2012. http://www.electroniclibrarian.com/. Annual conferences held since 2006 focus on the collection, management, and maintenance of electronic resources, as well as discuss the constantly changing landscape of the online environment and encourage the cross-pollination of ideas across various fields. The sessions are recorded and archived for free and easy access. For reference managers, the site offers a useful overview of ongoing issues and innovative ideas to manage the shape-changing field of electronic resources.

Fritts, Jack E., Jr., ed. 2010. *Mistakes in Academic Library Management.* Lanham, MD: Scarecrow Press. While aimed at incoming directors of academic libraries, the chapters on information technology, future planning, staff, and communication issues, provide useful cautionary notes to new reference managers as well.

Kern, Kathleen M. 2009. *Virtual Reference Best Practices: Tailoring Services to your Library.* Chicago: ALA Editions. The book provides a basic primer on defining the many iterations of virtual reference; followed by its implementation, policy-setting, software selection, staffing models and training, cost calculations, collaborations, marketing, and evaluation. The guiding purpose is for managers to be able to find a "perfect fit" for their library and the community it serves.

Kinkus, J. 2007. "Project Management Skills: A Literature Review and Content Analysis of Librarian Position Announcements." *College and Research Libraries* 68, no. 4 (July): 352–363. Given the increasing complexity of the library world, the author argues that expertise is needed from multiple departments. This, in turn, argues for a strong need to place project management as a core requirement in new library management skills, much as it is in professions such as construction, pharmaceuticals, finance, and the software industry. The author reviews the content of 1,180 library job advertisements and library curricula to support the contention that project management is an increasing requirement for all successful library managers and must become an integral part of basic training as well.

Koehn, Shona L., and Suliman Hawamdeh. 2010. "The Acquisition and Management of Electronic Resources: Can Use Justify Cost?" *Library Quarterly* 80, no. 2 (April): 161–174. An interesting case study of the Tulsa City-County Library that reports on collection development issues related to the acquisition, retention, and management of expensive digital databases, from the perspective of a public library.

Resnick, Taryn, Ana Ugaz, Nancy Buford, and Esther Carrigan. 2008. "E-resources: Transforming Access Services for the Digital Age." *Library Hi Tech* 26, no. 1 (Winter): 141–157. A thought-provoking case study of new styles in staffing management tried out at the University Libraries of Texas A&M found that the reference experience for users of electronic resources was greatly enhanced by the inclusion of reference librarians who were adept at managing and licensing electronic resources. The importance of technical service librarians who can keep up with the explosion of database resources was suggested by this study.

Tyckoson, David A. 2011. "Issues and Trends in the Management of Reference Services: A Historical Perspective." *Journal of Library Administration* 51: 259–278. A succinct overview of the management of reference services through the years is provided in this article, along with an annotated and chronological bibliography. Focus is on staffing needs and ongoing training, service models, communication formats, information resources, and assessment issues.

WebJunction. http://www.webjunction.org/management. Subtitled the "learning place for libraries," this site has an interactive and vibrant resource-sharing section on library management. It broadly divides management issues into sections such as budgets and funding, community relations, facilities, marketing, policies, personnel, and so on. Be prepared to get immersed as you move from one interesting link to another, given the easy access to past webinars that are available as videos and podcasts.

Wikoff, Karen. 2012. *Electronic Resources Management in the Academic Library: A Professional Guide*. Santa Barbara, CA: Libraries Unlimited. The author, a long-time manager of electronic resources (and a former professional football player!), provides a very readable, step-by-step guide that cover the five stages of management involved in the making of a successful electronic resource collection. From acquisition of resources and linking technologies, through providing easy access, sustained administration, troubleshooting, and evaluation of these resources, the guide is helped along by samples and assignments.

Bibliography and Works Cited

Aho, Melissa K., Anne M. Beschnett, and Emily Y. Reimer. 2011. "Who Is Sitting at the Reference Desk? The Ever-Changing Concept of Staffing the Reference Desk at the Bio-Medical Library." *Collaborative Librarianship* 3, no. 1: 46–49.

Albanese, Richard Andrew. 2004. "The Reference Evolution." *Library Journal* 129, no. 19 (November 15): 10–12, 14.

Arndt, Theresa S. 2010. "Reference Service Without the Desk." *Reference Services Review* 38, no. 1: 71–80.

Bai, Matt. 2005. "New World Economy." *New York Times Magazine* (December 18): 15.

Bailey, Russell, and Barbara Tierney. 2002. "Information Commons Redux: Concept, Evolution, and Transcending the Tragedy of the Commons." *Journal of Academic Librarianship* 28, no. 5 (September): 277–286.

Bailey-Hainer, Brenda. 2005. "Virtual Reference: Alive and Well." *Library Journal* 130, no. 1 (January 15).

Bishop, Bradley Wade, Diana Sach-Silveira, and Traci Avet. 2011. "Populating a Knowledge Base with Local Knowledge for Florida's Ask A Librarian Reference Consortium." *Reference Librarian* 52, no. 3 (July–September): 197–207.

Booth, Char. 2008. "Developing Skype-Based Reference Services." *Internet Reference Services Quarterly* 13, no. 2/3: 147–165.

Booth, Char. 2010. "IP Phones, Software VoIP, and Integrated and Mobile VoIP." *Library Technology Reports* 46, no. 5 (July): 11–19.

Bosch, Stephen, and Kittie Henderson. 2012. "Coping with the Terrible Twins: Periodicals Price Survey." *Library Journal* 137, no. 8 (May): 28–32.

Bracke, Marianne Stowell, Sainath Chinnaswamy, and Elizabeth Kline. 2008. "Evolution of Reference: A New Service Model for Science and Engineering Libraries." *Issues in Science and Technology Librarianship* no. 53 (Winter–Spring). http://www.istl.org/08-winter/index.html.

Bradigan, Pamela S., and Carol A. Powell. 2004. "The Reference and Information Services Team." *Reference and User Services Quarterly* 44, no. 2 (Winter): 143–149.

Brannon, Sian. 2011. "SMS Reference." *The Reference Librarian* 52: 152–158.

Bravender, Patricia, Colleen Lyon, and Anthony Molaro. 2011. "Should Chat Reference Be Staffed by Librarians? An Assessment of Chat Reference at an Academic Library

Using LibStats." *Internet Reference Services Quarterly* 16, no. 3 (July–September): 111–127.

Bronstein, Jenny. 2011. "The Role and Work Perceptions of Academic Reference Librarians: A Qualitative Inquiry." *Libraries and the Academy* 11, no. 3 (July): 791–811.

Butcher, Karyle. 1999. "Reflections on Academic Librarianship." *The Journal of Academic Librarianship* 25, no. 5 (September): 350–354.

Cardina, Christen, and Donald Wicks. 2004. "The Changing Roles of Academic Reference Librarians over a Ten-Year Period." *Reference and User Services Quarterly* 44, no. 2 (Winter): 133–142.

Cassell, Kay Ann. 1999. *Developing Reference Collections and Services in an Electronic Age: A How-To-Do-It Manual for Librarians.* New York: Neal-Schuman.

Coffman, Steve. 2001. "Distance Education and Virtual Reference: Where Are We Headed?" *Computers in Libraries* 21, no. 4 (April): 20.

Davis, Denise M. 2010. "Academic and Public Librarian Salaries and Staffing Expenditure Trends, 2000-2009." *Library Trends* 59, no. 1/2 (Summer): 43–66, 374.

Del Pinto, Frank. 2009. "Trends and Observations: Adapting to Needs of the New Consumer (EMC: Web Content Management)." *EContent* 32, no. 1 (January–February): 41.

Detmering, Robert, and Claudene Sproles. 2012. "Reference in Transition": A Case Study on Reference Collection Development." *Collection Building* 31, no. 1: 19–22.

Devine, Christopher, Emily Bounds Paladino, and John A. Davis. 2011. "Chat Reference Training: The Results of a National Survey of Academic Libraries." *The Journal of Academic Librarianship* 37, no. 3 (May): 197–206.

Dubicki, Eleanora I., ed. 2008. *Marketing and Promoting Electronic Resources: Creating the E-buzz!* New York: Routledge.

Hibner, Holly. 2007. "Reference on the Edge." *Public Libraries* 46, no. 1 (January–February): 21–22.

Hines, Samantha Schmehl. 2007. "Outpost Reference: Meeting Patrons on Their Own Ground." *PNLA Quarterly* 72, no. 1 (Fall): 12–13, 26.

Hiremath, Uma. 2001. "Electronic Consortia: Resource Sharing in the Digital Age." *Collection Building* 20, no. 2: 80–88.

Johnson, Wendell G. 2011. "The Evolution of the Reference Librarian." *Community and Junior College Libraries* 17, no. 2 (April–June): 91–103.

Kaufman, Paula. 2012. "Let's Get Cozy: Evolving Collaborations in the 21st Century." *Journal of Library Administration* 52, no. 1 (January): 53–69.

Kelly, Graham. 1998. *Team Leadership: Five Interactive Management Adventures.* Hampshire, UK: Gower.

Kennedy, Marie. 2011. "What Are We Really Doing to Market Electronic Resources?" *Library Management* 32, no. 3 (May): 144–158.

Kennedy, Scott. 2011. "Farewell to the Reference Librarian." *Journal of Library Administration* 52, no. 4 (May–June): 319–325.

Langan, Kathleen. 2012. "Training Millennials: A Practical and Theoretical Approach." *Reference Services Review* 40, no. 1: 24–48.

Lederer, Naomi, and Louise Mort Feldmann. 2012. "Interactions: A Study of Office Reference Statistics." *Evidence Based Library and Information Practice* 7, no. 2: 5–19.

Logan, Firouzeh F., and Krystal Lewis. 2011. "Quality Control: A Necessary Good for Improving Service." *Reference Librarian* 52, no. 3 (July–September): 218–230.

Lotts, Megan, and Stephanie Graves. 2011. "Using the iPad for Reference Services: Librarians go Mobile." *College and Research Libraries News* 72, no. 4 (April): 217–220.

Luo, Lili, and Emily Weak. 2012. "Managing a Text Reference Consortium: The My Info Quest Experience." *Reference Services Review* 40, no. 2: 311–325.

Mayo, Diane, and Jeanne Goodrich. 2002. *Staffing for Results: A Guide to Working Smarter.* Chicago: American Library Association.

McMillen, Paula, and Loretta Rielly. 2003. "It Takes a Village to Manage the 21st Century Reference Department." *Reference Librarian* 39, no. 81 (January): 71–87.

Nicely, Donna, with Beth Dempsey. 2005. "Building a Culture of Leadership." *Public Libraries* 44, no. 5 (September–October): 297–300.

Nicholas, Pauline, and Thelma White. 2012. "e-Learning, e-Books and Virtual Reference Service: The Nexus between the Library and Education." *Journal of Library and Information Services in Distance Learning* 6, no. 1 (January–March): 3–18.

Nunn, Brent, and Elizabeth Ruane. 2011."Marketing Gets Personal: Promoting Reference Staff to Reach Users." *Journal of Library Administration* 51, no. 3 (April): 291–300.

Pinto, María, and Ramón A. Manso. 2012. "Virtual Reference Services: Defining the Criteria and Indicators to Evaluate Them." *Electronic Library* 30, no. 1: 51–69.

Poon-Richards, Craig. 1996. "Self-Managed Teams for Library Management: Increasing Employee Participation via Empowerment." *Journal of Library Administration* 22, no. 1 (April): 67–84.

Radford, Marie L. 2012. *Leading the Reference Renaissance: Today's Ideas for Tomorrow's Cutting-Edge Services.* New York: Neal-Schuman.

Radford, M. L., Lynn Silpigni Connaway, Patrick A. Confer, Susanna Sabolcsi-Boros, and Hannah Kwon. 2011. "'Are We Getting Warmer?' Query Clarification in Live Chat Virtual Reference." *Reference and User Services Quarterly* 50, no. 3 (Spring): 259–279.

Radford, M. L., and S. Vine. 2011. "An Exploration of the Hybrid Service Model: Keeping What Works." In *Reference Reborn: Breathing New Life into Public Services Librarianship*, edited by Diane Zabel, 79–89. Santa Barbara, CA: Libraries Unlimited.

Ragsdale, Kate. 2001. *SPEC Lit 266: Staffing the Library Website.* Washington, DC: ARL Publications.

Schulte, Stephanie. 2011. "Eliminating Traditional Reference Services in an Academic Health Sciences Library: A Case Study." *Journal of the Medical Library Association* 99, no. 4 (October): 273–279.

Sciammarella, Susan, Maria Isabel Fernandes, and Devin McKay. 2008. "It Is Not Just About the Schedule: Key Factors in Effective Reference Desk Scheduling and Management." *Community and Junior College Libraries* 14, no. 4: 277–289.

Sekyere, Kwabena. 2010. "Less Words, More Action: Using On-the-Fly Videos and Screenshots in Your Library's IM/Chat and Email Reference Transactions." *Community and Junior College Libraries* 16, no. 3 (July–September): 157–161.

Stormont, Sam. 2010. "Becoming Embedded: Incorporating Instant Messaging and the Ongoing Evolution of a Virtual Reference Service." *Public Services Quarterly* 6, no. 4 (October–December): 343–359.

Stueart, Robert D., and Barbara B. Moran. 2007. *Library and Information Center Management.* 7th ed. Englewood, CO: Libraries Unlimited.

Tenopir, Carol. 2004. "Chat's Positive Side." *Library Journal* 129, no. 28 (December): 42.

Todorinova, Lily, Andy Huse, Barbara Lewis, and Matt Torrence. 2011. "Making Decisions: Using Electronic Data Collection to Re-Envision Reference Services at the USF Tampa Libraries." *Public Services Quarterly* 7, no. 1/2 (January–June): 34–48.

Walters, Suzanne. 2004. *Library Marketing That Works!* New York: Neal-Schuman.

Williams, Virginia Kay. 2010. "Assessing Your Vendor's Viability." *Serials Librarian* 59, no. 3/4 (October–December): 313–324.

Wilson, Kristen. 2011. "Beyond Library Software: New Tools for Electronic Resources Management." *Serials Review* 37, no. 4 (December): 294–304.

Wong, Sandra, and Anne O'Shea. 2004. "Librarians Have Left the Building: Ask Us HERE at Simon Fraser University." *Feliciter* 3: 90–92. Also available through the Canadian Library Association website: http://www.cla.ca/.

Wyatt, Anna May, and Susan E. Hahn. 2011. "Copyright Concerns Triggered by Web 2.0 Users." *Reference Services Review* 39, no. 2: 303–317.

Yang, Seung-Bum, and Mary Guy. 2011. "The Effectiveness of Self-Managed Teams in Government Organizations." *Journal of Business and Psychology* 26, no. 4 (December): 531–541.

Young, William F. 2004. "Reference Team Self-Management at the University at Albany." *Library Administration and Management* 18, no. 4 (Fall): 185–191.

Zhang, Ying, and Corinne Bishop. 2005. "Project Management Tools for Libraries: A Planning and Implementation Model Using Microsoft Project 2000." *Information Technology and Libraries* 24, no. 3 (September): 147–152.

Zhu, Lihong. 2011. "Use of Teams in Technical Services in Academic Libraries." *Library Collections, Acquisitions, and Technical Services* 35, no. 2–3 (June): 69–82.

20
Assessing and Improving Reference Services

Why Assess

There is an unwritten assumption that libraries, like Mom and apple pie, will always be there. One of the more impressive buildings in an academic campus, for example, is invariably the library building. With an estimated 121,785, libraries in the country, even Anytown, USA, usually has a town hall, a post office, and yes, a library. In Canada, the 14,069 libraries in the country constitute three times the number of McDonald's restaurants. In the United Kingdom, public libraries have existed for more than 150 years and currently number 4,517 not counting the national, academic, specialized, and school libraries.

However, times are changing and the very existence of physical libraries is being questioned, even as funding for libraries is habitually finding a position at the bottom of the totem pole. Despite an astonishing 1.5 billion visits to public libraries in the United States by adults, major library systems are seeing dramatic downgrades, ranging from reduced hours (Knox County Public Library System, TN), job elimination (Newark, NJ), and budget cuts (Los Angeles, CA) to proposed branch closures (Detroit Public Library, MI). With budget cuts is the unsettling parallel development of a quantum increase in funding resources required for erupting electronic information formats and resources essential to every modern library institution. Caught between spiraling costs and continued funding invisibility, library managers are fast jumping into the ethos of the business world. Terms like "ROI" (return on investment), "performance indicators," "institutional accountability," and "outcome-based evaluations" are finding expression through increasingly sophisticated tools of survey and multivariate analysis.

Traditionally, library feedback has been strong in the realm of library material and usage. Circulation statistics and turnstile counts are an integral part of many libraries. Both provide direct indicators of the number of people entering a library and borrowing material from the library collection. Libraries have been content with these few areas of quantification. The value quotient of a library has drawn legitimacy from these numbers. This is no longer enough.

In 1993, the U.S. government passed the Government Performance and Results Act (http://www.whitehouse.gov/omb/mgmt-gpra/gplaw2m), which mandates federal agencies to "establish specific objective, quantifiable and measurable performance goals," thus setting the goal of accountability for all institutions. Academic libraries are increasingly accountable to regional accrediting agencies. Corporate libraries must demonstrate ROI on a recurring basis. Public libraries are also finding it beneficial to establish an ROI on every dollar spent. An economic impact study of the Free Library of Philadelphia found that in FY2010, the library created over $30 million worth of value to the city and that homes within a quarter-mile radius of a library branch were typically worth almost $10,000 more (Penn Fels Institute of Government, 2010).

Even school libraries are feeling the need to rely on more than historical precedent to justify their existence. Statistical truths and the institutional reliance on numbers are being used by all kinds of libraries across the nation both as validation and as a way to support changes, modifications, and additions to library services. Reference rooms do not have the backing of circulation statistics and are particularly vulnerable to marginalization if no clear mandate for their purpose and performance is readily available.

What to Assess

Every reference environment has three aspects that can and should be evaluated:

1. Reference collection
2. Reference staff
3. Reference services

Given the time and commitment levels required, the question naturally arises: is the assessment of a reference environment really necessary? Most town libraries, for example, tend to rely on multitasking librarians so that a day in the life of a reference librarian could involve computer troubleshooting, calming disturbed patrons, sorting personnel problems, mopping unfortunate spills, conducting diplomatic conversations with unexpected visitors from Town Hall, and sweating over an antique copier, tweezing out inky papers accordioned in the machine. In the midst of such busy days, is it any wonder that service assessment is more a theory than a practice?

Traditionally, reference staff has also relied heavily on the accuracy of a strong reference collection. The process of building up a good reference collection has been established in the field. Library literature is replete with monthly broadcasts of "best of" lists and "core collection" choices. But for who are these collections "best" and to what end? Do the small-town public library and the large college library choose their selections because they are, after all, "the best of reference" or because their customers have a proven need for these specific materials? "A measure of library quality based solely on collections has become obsolete" (Hernon and Dugan, 2001: 119). It is becoming increasingly so in the context of the current dynamic and interactive reference universe, where missions such as "facilitating knowledge creation in their communities" is being held as a core mission (Lankes, 2011).

Furthermore, the formats in which collections are being accessed are multiplying at a dizzying rate. Do users prefer electronic to print resources? Is remote access to sources essential? A pressing challenge for each reference librarian today is to align quality of reference materials, formats, and service so that the fundamentals of what constitutes a "core" reference collection are constantly being questioned and molded in accordance with reference needs. To benefit from feedback, a reliable reference services assessment is essential.

Finally, the funds for setting up and supporting a reference room are increasingly propelled by an assessment of achievement levels in the provision of reference services. If an actuary can convert the value of missing eyes, limbs, and even thumbs to specific dollar amounts well within the purview of community understanding, surely the library can convert the value of reference services into calculable numbers—or so seems to be the thinking of the day.

How to Assess

The evaluation of reference services is of predominant importance simply because it gauges the satisfaction of the end user, with the collection and the staff as the critical means to attain satisfying end-user service. In that sense, an assessment of reference services encompasses the collection and the staff as well.

The evaluation of services is also abstract. Reference service requires multi-dimensional approaches for a reliable assessment. In many cases, there are little or no direct tracings of service activity so that evaluative indexes must be devised to accurately reflect user satisfaction. Given the need to establish convincing evaluative techniques, a number of strategies have evolved over the past few decades. It is incumbent on each reference manager to be familiar with all the following techniques so that the right combination of techniques can be selected, appropriate to the assessment at hand. The most prominently used methods are discussed in this section along a continuum of simple to complex requirements:

Suggestion boxes > Surveys > Interviews > Observations > Focus groups > Case studies

Suggestion Boxes

The most basic attempt at assessment is via feedback channels such as the humble suggestion box. Whether a generic container with a slot for slipping in suggestions; a book for writing in suggestions and comments; an online box for keyboarding in suggestions; an e-mail address for sending in suggestions; or enabling text messaging for mobile feedback, the intent is the same. "Tell us what you think, or want, or hate, or love about anything and everything" is the simple appeal of the ubiquitous "box."

The advantages of this method are ease of access for the user and simplicity of design and implementation for cash-strapped reference managers. John Lubans Jr., for example, introduced his wildly popular "Suggestion Answer Book" at both the University of Colorado and Duke University. In his experience, the thousands of suggestions entered in the book were used to leverage "improvements in facilities, services, policies, and staffing." Equally important, he notes, the "desire to help...was made manifest" to the users (Lubans, 2001: 240–245). Text message feedbacks are possible through innovations such as Mosio's Mobile PRM (patron relationship management), which allows for real-time interaction (Thomas, 2012).

One of the strictures of the format is the lack of accountability inherent in answering random suggestions. The very randomness of the suggestions tends to feed more easily into tweaking improvements, rather than any systemic planning. Idiosyncratic feedback can spark insights but is less amenable to detecting a pattern or trend in general reference user needs and assessments. While the importance of user needs and assessment is openly and consistently upheld with the provision of an ongoing feedback channel, a more formalized format would need to be instituted for a reference assessment requiring depth.

Surveys

One such format is the age-old survey method. A survey is simply a set of questions asked of a defined community in order to get a quantitative handle on community values, activities, qualities, or perceptions. Since the purpose of a survey is to tap into people's individual preferences, the method is most appropriate when personal information is required: "Were YOU satisfied with the help you received today?" or "Did YOU find the information you wanted?" or "Do YOU think the reference room should be open on Sundays?" Surveys are also helpful when information is required about community characteristics. Demographic information, the mainstay of collection developers, is, after all, derivative of the king of all surveys, the U.S. Census. Age, education, ethnicity, and affluence are critical survey results that undergird the shaping of library collections.

The rules of logic suggest that a response to survey questions provides a direct and effective way of assessing reference services, yet the reality and complexity of human behavior suggests otherwise. Users who answered they were "very satisfied" with the help they received at the reference desk may still not have found the answer to their question, but are responding instead to the strenuous efforts of a charming reference librarian. The seemingly innocuous structuring of survey questions so as to elicit the desired area of response is a tricky business. Users who want "more hours" available at reference may be users who never really utilize those extra hours. The chasm between stated perceptions and actual behavior is well documented. Surveys then are an intuitive, age-old method of collecting data on a community of users, but they gain in value when supported with collaborating data on observed behavior or when teamed with reasoned treatises.

Once conducted, surveys tend to develop a life of their own. They act as powerful, persuasive, and recurrent sources of justification for arguments, additions, or modifications made in the library world. The whole idea for roving reference librarians, for example, emerged when surveys showed that users were reluctant to walk up to a reference desk. Hernon and McClure's (1986) survey, which claimed that the average percentage of reference questions answered correctly in a library was 55 percent, has clung onto professional memory long after it was undermined on several counts and by several authorities (Richardson,

2002). Given the power of surveys, a number of formats have emerged through which a survey can be conducted. The primary choice of the twenty-first century appears to be the online survey; the following sections cover some common formats in use by libraries.

In-House Surveys

In-house surveys have been the most common method utilized by libraries. The advantage of such surveys is that they are relatively inexpensive and can be administered by staff as part of their daily routine. The staff of the Leavey Library at the University of Southern California, for example, describes an in-house survey that cost less than $250 (Eng and Gardner, 2005). According to the results of a College Library Information Packet Note venture that studied 214 colleges, "the most common instrument developed in college libraries is the self-administered user satisfaction survey" (Adams and Beck, 1995). Since they are administered on the spot, the rates of response are high. The assessments given out following an Internet instruction session, or after concluding a reference transaction, or using a new electronic database are all commonly used surveys. The Yuba County Library's Reference Department, for example, has conducted various in-house surveys to gauge patron satisfaction and collection usage. Figure 20-1 shows an example of a survey conducted.

Figure 20-1. Reference Department Survey

Yuba County Library
Reference Department

Please take a few minutes to complete this survey so that we can enhance our services. All individual answers will be combined with others, thus remaining confidential.

1. Have you ever used any of the Reference Department's services?

   __ Yes   __ No*

   *If no, please stop here

2. Which of the services have you used in the past year?

   __ Reference Librarian   __ Brochures and fliers at the reference desk

   __ Small Business Resources   __ Reference collection

   __ Nolo press legal references __ Law Library computers

   __ *Buzz* newsletter   __ *Ping* newsletter

   __ ALP newsletter   __ Adult Literacy

3. If you have made use of the Reference Librarian's services, how was your "case" handled?

   __ In person   __ E-mail   __ Phone

4. Overall, what is your impression of the Reference Librarian and his/her service?

   __ Poor   __ Adequate   __ Good   __ Excellent

(Continued)

Figure 20-1. Reference Department Survey *(Continued)*

---

5. If you used any of the brochures and fliers available at the reference desk, please list as many as you can remember on the back.

6. If you used the Small Business Resources collection, please give your evaluation by filling out the last page of this survey.

7. If you used our Reference collection this past year, please give us your overall opinion of the quality and usefulness.

    ___ Poor   ___ Adequate   ___ Good   ___ Excellent

8. If you used our reference collection, what materials or subject areas do you feel need improvement?

9. Have you ever used our collection of Nolo press legal materials?

    __ Yes   __ No

    If yes, which materials?

10. Have you ever used our Law Library computers?

    __ Yes   __ No

    If yes, what is your general opinion of the computers, their programs, etc.?

11. Have you ever seen a copy of the *Buzz* newsletter? If you have, please fill out the last page of this survey.

    __ Yes   __ No

12. Have you ever seen a copy of the *Ping* newsletter?

    __ Yes   __ No

    If yes, what is your impression of the newsletter? Please give us ways to improve.

13. Have you ever considered participating in our Adult Literacy program, either as a tutor or a learner? (For more information, please see the Reference Librarian.)

    __ Yes   __ No

Please return this survey to
the Reference desk

Thank you very much.

Source: Survey provided by Yuba County Reference Librarian Regina Zurakowski, Yuba County Library, Marysville, California. Used by permission.

Telephone Surveys

Ironically, the advantages of telephone surveys appear suspiciously close to their disadvantages. The telephone indisputably provides direct and instant entry into every household, qualities that appeal to every serious surveyor. However, that very aspect can lead to criticism from those being surveyed (for being too intrusive), and result in unwilling or less-than-sincere responses. The nature of the format also defines and limits the depth and breadth of questions. By definition, telephone surveys would be limited to relatively shorter questions and responses that require minimal or no relative rankings. While this increases the speed of responses, it limits the depth and variety of questions. Telephone surveys, while widely used in the past, enjoy less legitimacy in the aftermath of intrusive telemarketing and the subsequent law allowing households to block calls or monitor incoming calls through caller identification.

Mailed Questionnaires

Mailed questionnaires are the most nonintrusive way of conducting surveys. The time to fill out a survey and the inclination to complete one are left entirely up to the respondent. However, this could lead to low response rates as well as slow return rates. The cost required for postage is also relatively higher than other formats, especially since self-addressed, stamped envelopes are usually included in a survey package to encourage a return from the chosen respondents.

E-mail/Online Surveys

The online survey is undoubtedly becoming the primary tool of choice for all types of libraries. Given the ubiquity of chat and virtual reference sessions, instant surveys that pop up at the end of each session are par for the course, and user receptivity is high to answering the required question on whether the session was useful. More elaborate online surveys are also conducted either by contracting with professionals or through easily available software applications such as *Zoomerang* (http://www.zoomerang.com/) and *Survey Monkey* (http://www.surveymonkey.com/).

Survey Monkey, the "intelligent survey software for primates of all species," is a globally popular, flexible, and intuitive online survey tool used by reference managers in a range of libraries such as the Marygrove College Library, Michigan, the Texas State Law Library, Texas, and the California State University libraries, California. Academic libraries in New Jersey used *Zoomerang* to conduct an extensive survey to explore the use of traditional and nontraditional forms of reference services being offered (Dawson, 2011). Software to create personalized online surveys is also available, such as the Remark Web Survey, which allows for highly flexible formatting without the need for HTML expertise. The LibQUAL+ survey developed by the Association of Research Libraries is a handy tool for all kinds of survey assessments. Overall, the survey method is advantageous in that "information is gathered, summarized, analyzed, and put to use in a short amount of time" (Everhart, 1998: 4).

Federal regulations mandate that surveys which require data to be gathered from human subjects must undergo a review process both before and during the survey process. This is typically undertaken in academic institutions by "an appropriately constituted group" commonly referred to as the Institutional Review Board (IRB). Libraries that are less familiar with the review process can refer to the specific code (45 C.F.R. 46.116) available at the Department of Health and Human Services at http://www.hhs.gov/ohrp/humansubjects/guidance/45cfr46.html.

Interviews

Surveys are often supplemented with another method of assessment, that is, the individual interview. Interviews are used to either help in the making of survey questions, or to add depth and anecdotes to the quantitative parsimony of a survey. They are useful tools to collect personal experience and perception that can lead to meaningful assessment information. They can be conducted face-to-face or via telephone or e-mail. Much as in the survey method, the questions must be designed to take advantage of the insight and experience of individual users. A preguide that frames the interview assessment is recommended to ensure the integrity of the interview process, the unbiased selection of interviewees, and consistency in both questions and answer ratings.

Observations

An observation is the seemingly simple act of recording what took place. Did the reference librarian answer the question correctly? Did the reference user approach the desk for assistance? Are reference sources easily accessible to the user? A live transaction is recorded and evaluated in accordance with preset questions and expectations. The method is most applicable when actual behavior as opposed to values and perceptions is the required area of assessment. Whatever the area of assessment, there are three distinct types of observational methods: direct observation, hidden observation, and self-imposed observation.

Direct Observation

The most intuitive method is through *direct observation*. An activity or service is monitored and the observations are recorded. However, as Newton's humble apple can testify, the simple recording of an activity can lend itself to relevance only if it is placed within a context of well-developed suppositions and expectations. In the case of reference assessments, a set of clear questions needs to establish the grounds for observation. A sampling plan needs to set the periodicity of the observation. Finally, a plan for analyzing the data gathered through observation must be in place so that the criteria for observation are fully answered.

The Pennsylvania State University Libraries, for example, undertook direct observational analysis of the usability of a new online catalog introduced in 2001 and known as CAT (Novotny, 2004). A clear set of questions and rationale for analysis was prepared in advance. As can be seen in Figure 20-2, in order to add more dimension to the observations, users were not only observed but were also asked to "think aloud" as they searched.

The method is attractive in that the results resonate with the sincerity of direct observation. On the negative side, the procedure can be intrusive; reference staff or reference users are aware they are being watched constantly. Human subject permissions and informed consent from each participant are required in advance. The verbalizations of participants have to be recorded, even as the observations recorded can be potentially colored by the biases and idiosyncratic perceptions of the all-too-fallible human observer. The quality of the questions

---

Figure 20-2. Trigger Questions Used in a Protocol Analysis Study

---

1. A friend recommends that you read a book called *History by Hollywood*. Does the Penn State Libraries have this book?

   Question Rationale: *To examine how users search for known items and whether they could locate a book when they knew the title. The title was chosen so that the broadest keyword search resulted in fewer than fifty matches.*

2. Please use the library catalog to ask for a copy of the book *History by Hollywood*.

   Question Rationale: *This task was designed to see if users could determine how to use the "I Want It" button in CAT to request materials. Analysis of e-mail queries revealed that many users were unable to determine how to request materials.*

3. The article you need is in the journal *Kansas Law Review*, volume 49, issue 5, June 2001. Is this issue of the journal in the Penn State libraries? If so, where is it?

   Question Rationale: *A unique title was chosen so that users retrieved only one match regardless of which search type was selected (keyword or browse). The research team was interested in determining how users interpreted a serials record.*

4. Another article you need is in a journal called *Civil Engineering*. Specifically, you need volume 70, December 2000. Is a copy for this year available on the University Park campus? If so, which library can it be found in?

   Question Rationale: *To see how users navigated a potentially complex search. The default keyword search options results in over 2,000 matches. The record display includes multiple holdings, with the UP copy at the bottom of a very long record.*

5. You have been assigned to write a paper on the topic "Efforts to combat teen smoking." For this paper, you need to find four books at the Penn State Libraries. Please note the call numbers and locations of four books on this topic.

   Question Rationale: *To see how users search for materials on a subject. The topic was constructed so as to make it likely that multiple strategies would be required. Teen smoking as a keyword only retrieves two of the necessary four matches. The LC subject heading is Teenagers-United States-Tobacco-Use-Prevention, but other keywords would also work: teens, adolescents, smokers, and so on.*

Source: Eric Novotny. 2004. "I Don't Think I Click: A Protocol Analysis Study of Use of a Library Online Catalog in the Internet Age." *College and Research Libraries* 65, no. 6 (November): 537.

---

and the strictures of plan analysis methods can skew observational studies. Relying on a tried and tested question plan can dilute some of the methodology angst.

Hidden Observation

A variation on direct observation is the method of the *hidden observer*. A frequently used method, the modus operandi is inculcated right from library school, when students are asked to observe and record reference interviews being conducted by librarians at their neighborhood library. In this method, the same set of predetermined questions and plan of analysis need to be in place, but the staff is unaware that they are under scrutiny. The rationale is that the results would mirror more typical behavior, much as naturalist portrait photography claims to be a more profound presentation of the "true" person, than does a formal studio photograph.

For example, the University of Arizona libraries evaluated reference service as a function of both approachability and reliability that was evaluated through a three-step approach involving a survey questionnaire, observation, and focus groups. According to the coordinator of this assessment, "most of the important information the team uncovered was from the unobtrusive observation" (Norlin, 2000: 553). The questions structuring the observation are given in Figure 20-3 as an example of how to plan hidden observations.

Although the claim of veracity might make this a more appealing form of observation, the use of this method must be tempered by questions of ethics and accuracy. Staff that is subsequently told they were under observation may feel embarrassed or upset. Proxy questions that required staff time in research may be considered a waste of time and energy and engender hostility. Studies that have circumvented this problem have typically involved large, multibranch libraries where the identity of the observed librarians can be kept anonymous.

Figure 20-3. Unobtrusive Observation Worksheet

UNOBTRUSIVE OBSERVATION WORKSHEET (QUESTIONS)

1. Observe the reference desk for approximately two to five minutes (incognito). What are the reference staff members doing? (Write down everything.) Do they look approachable?

   Yes   No   1   2   3   4   5

2. How long is the average wait for service?

3. Which person are you going to approach? Why?

4. What is your research question? (Write down the general idea.)

5. What did the person say when you initially asked the question?

6. What was the person's attitude while you explained the problem?

7. Which resources did the person recommend?

8. Did you find the resources useful?

   Yes   No   1   2   3   4   5

9. Did the sources directly answer your question?

   Yes   No   1   2   3   4   5

10. Would you approach the same person again? Why?

11. Did the person follow up to see if you needed additional help?

Take this time out to list two strengths and two ideas for improvement about the reference/service.

Source: Elaina Norlin. 2000. "Reference Evaluation: A Three-Step Approach—Surveys, Unobtrusive Observations, and Focus Groups." *College and Research Libraries* 61, no. 6: 546–553.

Online reference transactions that apply hidden observation techniques are also relatively easier, given the invisibility of the assessor. In 2001, for example, a set of specific assessment questions were sent to 111 sites of the Association of Research Libraries that offered e-mail reference services. The unobtrusive study allowed comparisons across institutions and could lend itself to a wider and more comprehensive assessment of e-mail reference in general. Timeliness, scope of answer, and policy statements versus actual delivery were some of the aspects of e-mail service that were studied through this method (Stacy-Bates, 2003: 59–70). When a study of such scale is required, unobtrusive online observation can be the best method available.

Self-Imposed Observation

Transaction diaries, journals, preset forms, and reference activity notebooks are all examples of *self-imposed observations* (see Figure 20-4). The most basic observation is the number and general type of reference question answered. Almost all libraries have or should have a recording of this. The use of hash marks to denote reference, directional, or technological queries was instrumental in providing the foundation for the innovative Brandeis Model of reference service whereby staff (Herman, 1994) were apportioned to graded levels of service.

Figure 20-4. Reference Transaction Diary			
DAY	**TELEPHONE**	**IN PERSON**	**COMPUTER**
MONDAY			
TUESDAY			
WEDNESDAY			
THURSDAY			
FRIDAY			
SATURDAY			
SUNDAY			
COMMENTS:			

A more intensive format for self-imposed observation is a preset transactional form that not only records the number and type of questions but also provides information on how the question was answered or referred. Such observational data can be highly useful in a number of assessment scenarios. The reliance on one format over another, the efficacy or inefficacy of one source over another, and the success of one reference librarian's search strategy over another are all areas where preset transactional forms can throw evaluative light.

Many librarians also use unformatted reference activity notebooks. Given hectic schedules at a reference desk, a hurried scrawl on the text of a question is sometimes the only record that a librarian is physically able to manage. Analyzing such notebooks is far more challenging, but great utility is found in such books, because the reference manager has more than individual memory to back up a statement like "we get a lot of health questions during winter." Figure 20-5 shows the transcript of a page from the reference desk notebook of West Orange Public Library, New Jersey.

Diaries and journals are the hardest self-observation tools to institute, decipher, and present as a consolidated finding. However, they are rich sources of information that can supplement or fill in the blanks left by other more succinct modes of observation.

Focus Groups

A focus group involves the creation of a setting and agenda calculated to elicit a group response on any issue. Like the individual interview method, the focus group aims at probing community experience and perceptions. Unlike individual interviews, the responses are a function of individual thoughts tempered or

---

Figure 20-5. Reference Desk Notebook, Sample Page

Monday, 4/18/2005

• Bergen's 'Record'	• Writing a screenplay
• Ledger—March 27th—'Detailer' ad?	• Reviews of Guare—six degrees of sep
• T-bills—tax considerations	• e-mail reviews of Gilead to xxxxxxxx
• Out of print books—how to purchase?	• Lemony Snicket pseudonym
• Assertiveness training	• Japanese population in NJ
• Math review for aptitude test	• Montessori
• How to teach an adult to ride a bicycle	• Slavery in north vs. south
• Fashion during Harlem Renaissance	• Johnnie Cochran—bio
• Business plan for screen script	• Scholarly articles on HIV/AIDS
• Microsoft Publisher	• Historic real estate values
• Jane Watson—nursing?	• AIDS in Africa

Source: Transcript of page from the Reference Notebook of the West Orange Public Library, New Jersey.

catalyzed by group dynamics. Focus groups act like old-fashioned butter churns, stirring up the most resonant or democratically held values and perceptions curdling in a group.

When does a focus group become the most useful tool available? Typically, the format serves best in the following situations:

- Immediate follow-ups on responses would provide a richer study. (For example, when a preliminary survey conducted by the Microsoft Library found that users needed more in-depth technical data, a follow-through focus group was organized to "drill down" into the exact kinds of data required. The survey set up the area of priority and the focus group honed down the exact nature of the library's user needs.)
- Individual surveys are hard to carry out for logistical or other reasons.
- Statistically larger data are required in a limited time slot.
- Group consensus on issues is as valid as or more valid than individual preferences.
- Existing data are puzzling and require community interpretation.
- Areas of modification or change are unclear so that a preliminary sense of group priorities is required.
- Community investment is an issue that needs to be jump-started or fanned into greater intensity.

Overall, because group interpretation is the purpose of the format, it has been most beneficial when used as an exploratory tool or when an issue needed further clarification or interpretation. For example, after three SERVQUAL surveys were administered by the Texas A&M University Libraries, it was clear that a gap existed between user expectations and perceptions; but details remained unclear. A final series of focus groups was held, which the researchers found "useful for identifying areas of improvement" (Ho and Crowley, 2003: 86). The librarians at the New Jersey Institute of Technology (NJIT) at Newark conduct a focus group every year to explore different aspects of reference service. A draft of the questions asked is posted in Figure 20-6.

Though a pedestrian format that has been frequently used by many different types of libraries and institutions, focus groups are challenging to organize. As in the interview method, the elaboration of questions and their interpretation can be complex. For example, one of the questions at a focus group aimed at assessing "technostress" at the reference desk was, "Your job today is to paint the reference desk and everything on it. What colors will you use?" (Rose, Gray, and Stoklosa, 1998: 311). How would stippled sage be interpreted? It boggles the imagination.

There is also the additional complexity of training facilitators, as the success of a focus group depends largely on the expertise of the facilitator in both moderating the discussion and recording what transpires. The very creation of a focus group requires a high level of preplanning. Random sampling is not conducive to productive discussion, so by definition group members must be selected on the basis of their interest or experience in the issues under consideration. The "snowball technique" is frequently used to develop further focus groups based

Figure 20-6. Focus Group Questions Draft

2005 NJIT Library Focus Group Questions—DRAFT

February 3, 2005

Unless otherwise noted, every question is to be posed to all focus groups (faculty, graduate students, undergraduate students, architecture students).

Website

1. How frequently do you use the library website?
2. How effective are you at finding what you need on the library website?
3. What did you use the last time you were on the website?
4. What have you looked for on the library's homepage that you have had trouble finding?
5. What are your suggestions for improving the library website?
6. What's the best place you go to when looking for a journal article?
7. Where do you go to do your current awareness reading? Do you have trouble finding full text? (fac)
8. Where do you start when you have a research project?
9. What have your experiences been with the following: Renewing books online? Placing a hold on a book? Checking your library accounts? Discuss your successes/difficulties in finding a book in the catalog. Finding a journal?
10. Have you used the library website at Rutgers? What other libraries' websites do you use?
11. What have your experiences been using databases on site and remotely?
12. When you use the library website, do you feel certain that you've found what you're looking for or not? (excl arch)
13. *Have moderator go down the navigation bar and ask for each item:* "What do you use this for? What else?" (arch, grad and undergrad) (note for arch moderator: use arch website)
14. How often have you used the Image database? Did it suit your research needs? (arch)

Source: Richard Sweeney, University Librarian, New Jersey Institute of Technology, 2006. Used by permission.

on the suggestions of initial participants who may know others in the community who are interested or experienced in the issue area.

Despite these challenges, the focus group format continues to be used by many different libraries because of the rich dividends it tends to yield. Academic libraries such as Texas A&M have used it to set priorities, and corporate libraries such as the Microsoft Library have used it to add depth to an existing study.

Given its popularity and usage, the ideal dimensions of a focus group have been increasingly identified as follows:

- Unbiased, un-self-conscious, and trained facilitators
- Six to twelve participants in each group
- Forty-five- to ninety-minute sessions

- Six to ten questions
- A minimum of three groups for a preliminary investigation, with the understanding that the larger the number of groups the greater the relevance of the method

Brown University Library hired a professional firm "for several thousand dollars" to conduct its focus groups and found that the data was well worth the investment; it "helped the Library build a case with university administrators to fund specific projects for improvement" (Shoaf, 2003: 130). The University of Arizona effectively used focus groups to evaluate the reference needs of the College of Pharmacy for the stated goal of designing new and improved library services (Kramer et al., 2011). At Kent State University, user expectations and use of mobiles to access reference resources and services was studied with the help of student focus groups. The study found students far more interested in using their mobile devices than was anticipated (Seeholzer and Salem, 2011).

Case Studies

Case studies are much like magnifying glasses. They focus on one aspect of librarianship, which is then studied in expanded detail. The case study method has a venerable history that traces its ancestry to the law schools of 1870 that first introduced case method as a system of learning. What was initially a system of learning has now extended into an accepted tool of assessment in a number of social sciences.

Unlike the other methods outlined so far, the instrumentation used in this method is nonspecific. Whereas surveys use questionnaires and focus groups use mediators, case studies use any or all of the other methods to reach a conclusion. The primary imperative in this method is to posit the case. Once the magnifying glass has settled on a case, it is studied from all angles with whatever means available or possible. The method serves as an excellent organizing tool for in-depth evaluation, especially if "no one tool is perfect for any assessment project" (Gerlich and Berard, 2010: 116).

Does nonverbal communication affect patron perceptions of a reference interaction? How well does collaborative digital self-service work? Are student workers effective at reference desk service? Annotated cases can be found in *Evaluating Reference Services* (Whitlatch, 2000). The methods employed in these cases included surveys, interviews, direct observation, and diaries. Why then are they case studies? If more than one tool is used to study the same issue, then it becomes a case study. The difference is one of detail and emphasis rather than the adoption of an entirely different evaluation tool. Since the case study poses the imperative of focus and in-depth evaluation, the method is distinguished by the following:

- Multiplicity of assessment instruments
- Greater depth of evaluative understanding
- Greater reliability
- Relatively limited replicability

The results following a case study are invariably less "catchy" than those following a quantitative survey. Unlike a pithy percentage or number, the case study relies on triangulating the results of different assessments to best approximate the workings of a reference service or initiative. The results, by definition, are less succinct and far denser.

Case studies are most effective in the following situations:

- A single survey method is unconvincing.
- A novel service or new collection is being introduced.
- Staff has the time and expertise to expend on multiple assessments and analyses.
- Advance weighting is attributed to each method in case of discrepancies between two results.

Acting on Assessments

At a first level, assessments allow a reference manager to follow the dictum of "knowing thyself." In this knowledge lies the potential ability to establish priorities, scrape away redundancies, allot proper funding, allow new initiatives, and provide defensible institutional justification. All of the assessment techniques covered previously are important as a means to the end of "knowing thyself." Given that a great deal of time, energy, finances, and effort go into the completion of an assessment, it is imperative that a reference manager, having gained the necessary knowledge, should act on it. Microsoft Library conducts an annual survey of user needs with the express guideline that "all questions must lead to potentially actionable results" (Plosker, 2004: 50).

The New Americans Program at the Queens Borough Public Library found direction in both funding and programming through the survey analysis conducted by its Information and Data Analysis Librarian, Wai Sze Chan ("Better Service," 2004). Ms. Chan mapped ethnic correlates extracted from the census to create neighborhood profiles that in turn fed into relevant collection development and program initiatives. It is unlikely that something as exotic as a "Toddler Learning Center in Bengali" for the children of recent immigrants from Bengal could have been planned and funded by an external grant without strong survey analysis and presentation.

After a three-step survey of reference services was conducted at the University of Arizona Libraries, a roving reference librarian was introduced to enhance services; signage was improved including name tags on staff; and referrals for technology were organized since that was an area that students had found weak. The coordinator found the results of the assessment study to be "very meaningful" (Norlin, 2000).

The business of "knowing thyself" never quite concludes, as evaluation must follow implementation on an ongoing basis. As stated in a chapter of *Reference Reborn*, "Assessment is useful only as part of a cycle that includes data gathering, data analysis, and the implementation of changes based on the data. Once changes are made, the assessment cycle begins again" (Gedeon and Salem, 2011: 168).

Quantify

If major funding is at stake, a statistical analysis of collected data goes a long way toward exciting external support. However, statistical analyses will invariably involve ancient mathematical beasts such as factor analysis, Likert scales, data reduction tools, chi-squares, and measures of association. Trivial to the average statistician or statistically inclined librarian, data analyses, even through the simplifying construct of programs such as SAS and SPSS, can be daunting to many a stouthearted reference manager. At this point, investing in a professional surveyor, or locating a statistically endowed colleague, or purchasing a preset service such as LibQUAL+ is money and time well spent. Information about the LibQUAL+ kit is available at http://www.libqual.org/, including the 2011 ALA Midwinter Meeting presentation by Michael Maciel, "12 Years of LibQUAL+ at the Texas A&M University." Older surveys of libraries that have used the kit can be found in *Libraries Act on Their LibQUAL+ Findings* (Heath, Kyrillidou, and Askew, 2005) as well as in the ten-year longitudinal research done at the University of Mississippi (Greenwood, Watson, and Dennis, 2011).

Strategize

Absolute clarity in assessment needs also goes a long way toward choosing both the level and type of assessment technique. Some questions to ask are these:

- *Do you want to launch a new reference initiative?* For example, do you want to start 24/7 virtual reference services or live online reference or tiered reference? Survey methods have worked well when broad information on subjective preferences is required.
- *Do you merely want to get a "pulse" on user needs and expectations?* For example, are patrons satisfied with the answers they have found to their reference questions? Are databases useful? Are reference hours satisfactory? Suggestion boxes and observation methods have succeeded in opinion-based studies such as these.
- *Do you want to reprioritize funding allocation?* For example, will information assistants suffice for basic reference questions? Should print resources be diverted to electronic purchases? Should a certain area such as local history or small business be given special financial focus? For analytical studies, individual opinions are rarely enough. A focus group that forces deeper interpretations would be far more effective.
- *Do you want to attract new funding?* For example, will bibliographic instruction in computer technology enhance the reference profile? Will adding lifelong learning commitments to traditional reference add value to overall services? For diagnostic studies that aim to improve services, opinion-based studies alone present relatively feeble input. Case studies that incorporate both subjective opinions and objective quantification are best suited.

Visualize

The following are scenarios that you may face as a reference manager:

- The vice president of your graduate college has made several unsubstantiated remarks about faculty having to look elsewhere for their higher research needs. How would you convince her that the reference department is indeed serving the needs of the staff?
- Professional literature claims that 24/7 virtual reference is the library of the future. How would you design a technique to assess whether such services are necessary to your particular library?
- You have just been appointed as the supervising reference librarian of a multibranch county system. Your "feeling" is that annual updates of online general encyclopedias are preferable to purchasing the more expensive print updates. What assessment or data would you use to test your instinct?
- You are the head of reference at a medium-sized public library. Your director claims that the following year's budget will be much lower and would like you to reduce reference standing orders by 10 percent. What would you discard and how would you justify your decision?

Ongoing Assessments: An Imperative

Time-consuming though they may be, ongoing assessments of the reference environment are an imperative. Especially given the current diversity and flux in reference services, formats, and information expectations, each reference library will of necessity need to establish as conclusively as possible what makes the current reference environment successful and what to project as long-range reference needs.

Librarians can keep up with assessment tools on the Internet; one place to monitor is *LibraryAssessment.info*, "a blog for and by librarians interested in library assessment, evaluation, and improvement" (http://libraryassessment.info). This site is supported by the Association of Research Libraries (ARL). Another ARL-supported activity is the biannual Library Assessment Conference; information about upcoming meetings is located at http://libraryassessment.org/.

Referring to libraries as a whole, the authors of *Future Libraries* state, "The surest path to irrelevance is to allow yourself to be defined by someone else" (Crawford and Gorman, 1995: 182). Although the statement sounds suspiciously close to something heard on *Oprah*, it is a valid observation in a world of shifting reference environments. The level of digitized reference material required by a law library may not be anywhere near the level required by a rural public library. The definition of a roving reference librarian could mean anything from moving out from behind the desk to laptop-toting reference librarians positioned strategically within academic departments, as practiced at Brandeis and Harvard; to mobile outdoor "reference stations" assembled at university campus hot spots, as at the University of Florida; to librarians embedded in classroom instructions such as at Capella University in Minneapolis (Bennett and Simning, 2010). The need and extent of reference services requiring virtual/chat software can also range widely among different types of libraries serving different communities.

The evaluation and assessment tools described in this chapter are just that: tools. They are a means to an end. The end to keep in mind at all times is that assessments are well-thought-out, and thereby convincing measures of performance. The very act of assessing one aspect of reference swivels focus on that aspect. The focus can then lead to a compelling argument for:

- evaluating practices, performance, procedures, and services of the existing reference environment;
- foreshadowing reference services, formats, and practices of the future; and
- marketing the value of reference services to others, such as the community at large, funding agencies, and even the reference staff itself.

The pivotal role played by assessments cannot be underestimated. Assessments affect a decision maker who must decide which of multiple alternatives is the best choice; a manager who must allocate resources to one reference activity over another; and a spokesperson for a reference room that needs to attract legitimacy and funding from external sources.

Recommendations for Further Reading

American Library Association. 2012. "Measuring and Assessing Reference Services and Resources: A Guide." Last modified February 7. http://connect.ala.org/node/97245. This comprehensive guide developed by the Reference Services Section of the American Library Association's RUSA group, provides a sweeping bird's-eye view of assessment definitions, measurement tools, and an updated bibliography. The descriptions, while brief, are a useful first step for those beginning to think about assessing reference services.

Cobus, Laura, Valeda Frances Dent, and Anita Ondrusek. 2005. "How Twenty-Eight Users Helped Redesign an Academic Library Web Site: A Usability Study." *Reference and User Services Quarterly* 44, no. 3 (Spring): 232–246. The authors provide compelling evidence that usability testing, with even a small sampling population, was not only instructive, but provided sufficient insight to effect concrete changes. A comprehensive list of similar studies, distinguished by their small sampling populations, can be found at http://www.jkup.net/terms.html.

Diamond, Tom, and Mark Sanders, eds. 2006. *Reference Assessment and Evaluation*. Binghamton, NY: The Haworth Press. University and college libraries are the target audiences for this collection of ideas, methods, and case studies for evaluating digital reference, staff training, desk staffing, and other reference activities.

Dudden, Rosalind Farnam. 2007. *Using Benchmarking, Needs Assessment, Performance Improvements, Outcome Measures, and Library Standards: A How-To-Do-It Manual for Librarians*. New York: Neal-Schuman. The examples provided in this book are presented with the clear aim of allowing replicability in both small and large libraries. Dudden's work is focused on those institutions that acknowledge the importance of constant evaluations and assessment of reference services in theory, but end up giving it low priority in terms of actual practice.

Fink, Arlene. 2009. *How to Conduct Surveys: A Step-by-Step Guide*. 4th ed. Thousand Oaks, CA: SAGE Publications. This is not a manual for reference libraries per se; however, it contains a pragmatic and comprehensive guide to all kinds of surveys with examples of real surveys that have been used in a variety of institutions that can be adapted to reference services as well.

Heath, Fred M., Martha Kyrillidou, and Consuella A. Askew, eds. 2005. *Libraries Act on Their LibQUAL+ Findings: From Data to Action*. Binghamton, NY: The Haworth Press. This title is invaluable for reference departments interested in using LibQUAL+ to conduct surveys. The experiences of more than two dozen college, university, health sciences, and consortial libraries are presented, so that the survey tool has an immediacy not found in the many structural descriptions of LibQUAL+.

Hernon, Peter, and Ellen Altman. 2010. *Assessing Service Quality: Satisfying the Expectations of Library Customers*. 2nd ed. Chicago: American Library Association. Winner of the 1998 Highsmith award, this updated classic includes the use of new technologies and extends the definition of library customers to include distance learners.

Hubbertz, Andrew. 2005. "The Design and Interpretation of Unobtrusive Evaluations." *Reference and User Services Quarterly* 44, no. 4 (Summer): 327–335. The author supports this assessment tool by presenting it as a standardized test method. Such a method, he argues, is potentially valuable for establishing relative rankings across libraries. The (mis)use of this tool to assess overall service quality is deemed improper.

Lyons, Ray. 2011. "Statistical Correctness." *Library and Information Science Research*, 33, no. 1 (January): 92–95. This article is a rather blunt statement on the misleading propensity of library surveys that do not use "probability sampling." Instead, the widespread use of "convenience sampling" results in research conclusions that the author believes are no better than "fabricated data."

Maness, Jack, and Sarah Naper. 2007. "Assessing Inappropriate Behavior: Learning from the AskColorado Experience." In *Virtual Reference Service: From Competencies to Assessment*, edited by David Lankes, Scott Nicholson, Marie L. Radford, Lynn Westbrook, Joanne Silverstein, and Philip Nast, 91–104. New York: Neal-Schuman. The chapter specifically studies "trends in inappropriate behavior" during virtual reference transactions and traces these trends across markets. The somewhat novel goal of the chapter is to assess bad practices, rather than best practices, with an eye to improving the virtual reference experience for both users and staff.

Matthews, Joseph R. 2007. *The Evaluation and Measurement of Library Services*. Santa Barbara, CA: Libraries Unlimited. Matthews tailors the book around the single question of what differences libraries make in the lives of their patrons and whether these are quantifiable through various measuring techniques. The book is a general exposition on evaluating library services as a whole; however, a great part of the material is devoted specifically to reference services. He also argues that traditional measurements such as number of reference transactions are less effective unless teamed up with customer-centric metrics such as whether the reference patron was satisfied by the transaction.

McLaughlin, Jean E. 2011. "Reference Transaction Assessment: Survey of a Multiple Perspectives Approach." *Reference Services Review* 39, no. 4: 536–550. Reference transactions are complex interactions that are difficult to assess through simple tabulations. In this article, a decade-long survey of assessment studies that focus on reference interaction are reviewed, with an eye to highlighting challenges and problems, as well as tools to improve assessment models.

Novotny, Eric. 2002. *Reference Service Statistics and Assessment*. Washington, DC: Association of Research Libraries. Published as part of the SPEC Kit series (#268), the survey of seventy-seven member libraries provides a highly useful compilation on the various methods used by research libraries of all sizes. An interesting general observation by Novotny states that the high level of activity in reference departments, juxtaposed against data that show a decrease in the number of transactions, appears to be fostering a growing opinion that data collection techniques should be revamped.

Novotny, Eric, ed. 2007. *Assessing Reference and User Services in a Digital Age.* Binghamton, NY: The Haworth Press. Both best practices and case studies are explored by various authorities in this compilation of e-reference evaluation in academic and public libraries. Topics include the effective evaluation of chat reference, online instruction, electronic resources, budgets and consortial undertakings, and the VET or Virtual Evaluation Toolkit.

Proceedings of the 2010 Library Assessment Conference: Building Effective, Sustainable, Practical Assessment. 2011. Steve Hiller, Martha Kyrillidou, and Jim Self, eds. Annapolis Junction, MD: ARL Publications. The *Proceedings* provide a convenient compilation of over sixty wide-ranging presentations on assessment strategies, tools, and case studies. It also includes conference posters, workshops, and keynote speeches. As a whole, it provides an in-depth view of the main topics related to evaluation and assessment in all kinds of libraries.

RUSA RSS Research and Statistics Committee. 2012. "Reference Research Review: 2011." American Library Association. http://connect.ala.org/node/180163. A rich resource that is updated annually by the Reference Services Section, this is an annotated and selective list of up-to-date statistical analyses of reference services. For example, newer assessment tools that use ethnographic methods associated with anthropological research can be found in this listing, as can controversies on the meaningful use of statistics.

Zabel, Diane, ed. 2010. *Reference Reborn: Breathing New Life into Public Services Librarianship.* Santa Barbara, CA: ABC-CLIO. This collection of more than twelve essays by over thirty authors makes for thoughtful reading. Among other subjects, it also stresses the importance of tracking data from external environmental scans such as the Pew project and OCLC and investing in systematic data collection to combat the increased scrutiny on return-on-investment evaluations of library services.

Bibliography and Works Cited

Adams, Mignon, and Jeffrey Beck, compilers. 1995. *User Surveys in College Libraries.* (CLIP Note #23). Chicago: Association of College and Research Libraries.

Agosto, Denise E., Lily Rozaklis, Craig MacDonald, and Eileen G. Abels. 2011. "A Model of the Reference and Information Service Process: An Educator's Perspective." *Reference and User Services Quarterly* 50, no. 3 (Spring): 235–244.

ALA (American Library Association). 2010. "Quotable Facts about America's Libraries." American Library Association. http://www.ala.org/offices/ola/quotablefacts/ quotablefacts.

———. 2012. "Public Library Funding Updates: Funding News at Your Library." American Library Association. http://www.ala.org/advocacy/libfunding/public.

Bennett, Erika, and Jennie Simning. 2010. "Embedded Librarians and Reference Traffic: A Quantitative Analysis." *Journal of Library Administration* 50, no. 5/6 (July–September): 443–457.

"Better Service Through Data Numbers—Wai Sze (Lacey) Chan." 2004. *Library Journal* 129, no. 5 (March 15): 34.

Bravender, Patricia, Colleen Lyon, and Anthony Molaro. 2011. "Should Chat Reference Be Staffed by Librarians? An Assessment of Chat Reference at an Academic Library Using LibStats." *Internet Reference Services Quarterly* 16, no. 3 (July–September): 111–127.

Chang, Jung-Jung, and Chyan Yang. 2012. "Viable or Vital? Evaluation of IM Services from Patrons' Perspectives." *Electronic Library* 30, no. 1: 70–88.

Citti, Alessandra, Angela Politi, Fulvia Sabattini, and Chiara Semenzato. 2012. "User Satisfaction Surveys as Decision Making Resources at the University of Bologna." *Library Management* 33, no. 3: 142–150.

Crawford, Walt, and Michael Gorman. 1995. *Future Libraries: Dreams, Madness, and Reality.* Chicago: American Library Association.

Dawson, Patricia H. 2011. "Are Science, Engineering, and Medical Libraries Moving Away from the Reference Desk? Results of a Survey of New Jersey Libraries." *Science and Technology Libraries* 30: 343–353.

Eng, Susanna, and Susan Gardner. 2005. "Conducting Surveys on a Shoestring Budget." *American Libraries* 36, no. 2 (February): 38–39.

Everhart, Nancy. 1998. *Evaluating the School Library Media Center: Analysis Techniques and Research Practices.* Englewood, CO: Libraries Unlimited.

Gedeon, Julie A., and Joseph A. Salem Jr. 2011. "Reference Quality: A Primer in Methods and Tools for Assessing Reference Services." In *Reference Reborn: Breathing New Life into Public Services Librarianship,* edited by Diane Zabel, 155–172. Santa Barbara, CA: Libraries Unlimited.

Gerlich, B. K., and G .L. Berard. 2010. "Testing the Viability of the READ Scale (Reference Effort Assessment Data): Qualitative Statistics for Academic Reference Services." *College and Research Libraries* 71, no. 2: 116–137.

Greenwood, Judy T., Alex P. Watson, and Melissa Dennis. 2011. "Ten Years of LibQual: A Study of Qualitative and Quantitative Survey Results at the University of Mississippi 2001–2010." *The Journal of Academic Librarianship* 37, no. 4 (July): 312–318.

Herman, Douglas. 1994. "But Does It Work? Evaluating the Brandeis Reference Model." *RSR: Reference Services Review* 22, no. 4 (Winter): 17–28.

Hernon, Peter, and Robert E. Dugan. 2001. *An Action Plan for Outcomes Assessment in Your Library.* Chicago: American Library Association.

Hernon, Peter, and Charles R. McClure. 1986. "Unobtrusive Reference Testing: The 55 Percent Rule." *Library Journal* 111, no. 7 (April 15): 37–41.

Ho, Jeannette, and Gwyneth H. Crowley. 2003. "User Perception of the 'Reliability' of Library Services at Texas A&M University: A Focus Group Study." *Journal of Academic Librarianship* 29, no. 2 (March): 82–87.

Kramer, Sandra S., Jennifer R. Martin, Joan B. Schlimgen, Marion K. Slack, and Jim Martin. 2011. "Effectiveness of a Liaison Program in Meeting Information Needs of College of Pharmacy Faculty." *Medical Reference Services Quarterly* 30, no. 1 (January–March): 31–41.

Lankes, David. R. 2011. *The Atlas of New Librarianship.* Cambridge, MA: MIT Press.

Lewis, Janice S. 2011. "Using LibQUAL+ Survey Results to Document the Adequacy of Services to Distance Learning Students for an Accreditation Review." *Journal of Library and Information Services in Distance Learning* 5, no. 3 (July–September): 83–104.

Lubans, John, Jr. 2001. "'Where Are the Snows of Yesteryear?' Reflections on a Suggestion 'Box' That Worked." *Library Administration and Management* 15, no. 4: 240–245.

McLaughlin, Jean E. 2011. "Reference Transaction Assessment: Survey of A Multiple Perspectives Approach." *Reference Services Review* 39, no. 4: 536–550.

Norlin, Elaina. 2000. "Reference Evaluation: A Three-Step Approach—Surveys, Unobtrusive Observations, and Focus Groups." *College and Research Libraries* 61, no. 6 (November): 546–553.

Novotny, Eric. 2004. "I Don't Think I Click: A Protocol Analysis Study of Use of a Library Online Catalog in the Internet Age." *College and Research Libraries* 65, no. 6 (November): 523–537.

Penn Fels Institute of Government. 2010. *The Economic Value of the Free Library in Philadelphia.* Free Library of Philadelphia. http://www.freelibrary.org/about/felsstudy.htm.

Pinto, Maria, and Ramon A. Manso. 2012. "Virtual Reference Services: Defining the Criteria and Indicators to Evaluate Them." *The Electronic Library* 30, no. 1: 51–69.

Plosker, G. 2004. "Learning from Best Practices." *Online* 28, no. 3: 50–52.

Read, Eleanor J. 2007. "Data Services in Academic Libraries Assessing Needs and Promoting Services." *Reference and User Services Quarterly* 46, no. 3 (Spring): 61–76.

Richardson, John V. 2002. "Reference Is Better Than We Thought." *Library Journal* 127, no. 7 (April 15): 41–42.

Rose, Pamela, Sharon A. Gray, and Kristin Stoklosa. 1998. "A Focus Group Approach to Assessing Techno-Stress at the Reference Desk." *Reference and User Services Quarterly* 37, no. 4 (Summer): 311–317.

Seeholzer, Jamie, and Joseph A. Salem Jr. 2011. "Library on the Go: A Focus Group Study of the Mobile Web and the Academic Library." *College and Research Libraries* 72, no. 1 (January): 9–20.

Shoaf, Eric C. 2003. "Using a Professional Moderator in Library Focus Group Research." *College and Research Libraries* 64, no. 2 (March): 124–132.

Stacy-Bates, Kristine. 2003. "E-mail Reference Responses from Academic ARL Libraries: An Unobtrusive Study." *Reference and User Services Quarterly* 43, no. 1: 59–70.

Thomas, Lisa Carlucci. 2012. "The State of Mobile in Libraries 2012." *The Digital Shift*, February 7. http://www.thedigitalshift.com/.

Whitlatch, Jo Bell. 2000. *Evaluating Reference Services: A Practical Guide.* Chicago: American Library Association.

21

Reference 2.0

Changing Vocabulary Attests to Changing Times

More than two decades ago we entered a new world where a mouse no longer referred to Mickey; a floppy rarely described a hat; and Apple and BlackBerry became proper nouns. We have now entered a universe where "twittering" is no longer the preserve of birds; communication in addition to food is "Delicious"; and to have an avatar in a Second Life does not require the penance of an Asian mystic. We have, in short, entered the universe of Reference 2.0.

This universe has moved at such a fast clip that defining it and understanding its ramifications continue to skitter across many viewpoints. The goal of effective reference remains timeless, namely, the satisfaction of the user. However, the dramatic technological tools thrown up by Web 2.0 in which mass participation and web socialization have become both the norm and the expectation have added a new dimension to business as usual.

In the world of reference, information is increasingly more than a one-way delivery of facts from those who know to those who seek to know. It is a multi-way, interactive dialogue, drawing from a vast anonymous social network that believes the sum to be greater than its parts. Users expect information to be individually developed so that the uniqueness of the user's needs are both acknowledged and satisfied. This information delivery system is expected to reach out and connect with users wherever they are rather than remain in the static splendor of a physical site. It is not a simple change where information is being provided in a new format brought about by new technology as has been the case ever since the clay tablets of Mesopotamia, the scrolls of Alexandria, the quipa of the Incas, and even the advent of print. The informational model for all formats grew unchallenged from the central premise that information was to be collated in a central place or format that people could access.

In the brave new universe of 2.0, the focus is on social networking—leading to "designer information." This chapter touches upon some of the more vigorous tools being utilized by reference librarians across the globe. They have been selected to underlie what currently appear to be the four main sounding notes of the 2.0 universe: collaboration, social networking, customization, and seamlessness.

What Is the 2.0 Universe?

Even at the end of 2008, *Library Journal* was already prophesizing the imminence of "Reference 3.0" and the possible routes it might follow. Collaboration, spontaneity, customization, and multimedia formatting were all part of the future as defined by selected librarians and publishers. It was less clear in what ways Reference 3.0 was different from 2.0. More interesting still was the fact that no single definition of 2.0 had really emerged in any definitive way. As passionately argued and elaborately substantiated by Walt Crawford (2006), the term "Library 2.0" had sixty-two views and seven different definitions befuddling the concept, leading him to the generalization that 2.0 "encompasse(d) a range of new and not-so-new software methodologies" (p. 31). Lankes, Silverstein, and Nicholson (2007) also characterized the whole notion of a Web 2.0 as "an aggregation of concepts" (p. 9). Reference 2.0 as well is really a congregation of concepts variously approached and rated by different practitioners.

With the fast-spreading viral quality of new technology associated with 2.0 developments, the necessary distance to catch one's breath and view the change has really not existed and will not exist for some time to come. Yet waiting for that distance before trying to come to a comprehensive definition does not make sense either, given the active use of flourishing tools such as wikis, RSS feeds, blogs, widgets, podcasts, streaming videos, mashups, and wildly popular sites such as Facebook, Flickr, LinkedIn, Pinterest, and Twitter. Caught in the maelstrom of expanding Internet capabilities and user curiosity and maturity, it is possible to find patterns in what makes 2.0 such an attractive tool to the traditional reference arsenal, even if a complete definition remains ambiguous. Copious examples of how these tools are currently being used provide an experiential alternate to the holistic picture typically afforded by time and distance.

The following sections outline the four most prominent patterns found in the Reference 2.0 universe:

1. *Collaboration* refers to cooperative content creation. Tools used for this include wikis, blogs, microblogs, folksonomies, and podcasting. Sites like MediaWiki (http://mediawiki.org/), Bloglines (http://bloglines.com/), Twitter (https://www.twitter.com/), Delicious (http://delicious.com/), LibraryThing (http://librarything.com/), GoodReads (http://www.goodreads.com/), Bookcrossing (http://www.bookcrossing.com/), and Shelfari (http://www.shelfari.com/) are all representative of this aspect of Reference 2.0.

2. *Social networking* is associated with the outgrowth of online communities that are relevant for reference outreach—"where people are." Sites such as Facebook (http://facebook.com/), LinkedIn (http://www.linkedin.com/), Myspace (http://www.myspace.com/), and Google+ (https://plus.google.com/) are prime examples of social networking.

3. *Customization* is also a strong corollary to social networking; tools like widgets, RSS feeds, mashup initiatives like *Google Maps* (http://maps.google.com/), Facebook Plug-ins, and Meebo IM (https://www.meebo.com/), and creation sites such as Ning (http://www.ning.com/) and Wordpress (http://wordpress.org/) are important components of Reference 2.0.

4. *Seamlessness*—global, transparent platforms that allow for seamlessness between mediums is evident in environments like Second Life (http://secondlife.com/); and multiformat reference through IM (instant messaging), SMS (short message service or text messaging), and mobile reference.

The tools themselves overlap over all four pattern categories so that providing Meebo IM reference, for example, testifies both to seamlessness in allowing for a creative combination of traditional reference data mashed up with the functionality provided by a 2.0 tool like Meebo. The University of Calgary Library in Canada, for example, started a successful Meebo IM reference service in late 2007. The New City Library in New York experimented with both Meebo and Trillian to add easy-to-access chat-based reference (Reynolds, 2011). Reference initiatives launched in Second Life can be perceived as collaborative (as evident in the sprawling *InfoIsland Archipelago*), customized (as in the art-imitating-real-life library buildings populating the eerily familiar Second Life topography), and a product of the new seamlessness (as made startlingly clear by the talking, visually arresting 3-D librarian avatars of Second Life). The patterns, then, are not hitched exclusively to one tool, but stand as broader and calming descriptive harnesses to the welter of "shiny toys" (Crawford, 2009) inundating the 2.0 landscape.

Cooperative Content Creation

Reference Wikis

Imagine for a minute that you are sitting with a book, highlighting in yellow marker the sentences that you want to remember and jotting in the margins the thoughts and associative knowledge that the reading material has inspired in you. Imagine then that your jottings and highlighting are absorbed into the pages of the book so that they merge to create a new book, one that has incorporated your wisdom and knowledge into its pages. Whereas the print medium would have to view such a scenario as pure fantasy, the online medium has realized it in the form of a "wiki." Wikis are quite simply interactive sites that can be asynchronously amended, corrected, or expanded by the user. The further glory of the wiki dictates that no user needs to master web technology to be an active wiki player. Wiki engines such as MediaWiki (http://www.mediawiki.org/), Traction TeamPage (http://www.tractionsoftware.com/), and PmWiki (http://www.pmwiki.org/) provide the software; Google Sites (http://sites.google.com/), and PBworks (http://pbworks.com/) can act as hosts so that the user is left to focus on the material and interaction with the material. Since its inception in 1994, wiki implementations have expanded exponentially so that they now come in all types and can be attached to just about any system.

How can the inherent structure of a wiki lend itself to enhancing reference services? Though "wikiwiki" started as a Hawaiian term for being super fast, the defining quality of a wiki is not so much speed as the ability to be cooperative and interactive. As usage around the nation and the globe attest, it is this interactivity that is being mined in various, creative ways by reference institutions.

Ready Reference

Given that instant updates are the hallmark of a wiki product, ready reference is one of the prime areas where the technology can flourish. The most popular and dramatic ready reference tool online is the much-debated *Wikipedia*. As elaborated in Chapter 5, *Wikipedia* draws its greatest strength and its most acute vulnerability from the same feature, namely its openness to content collaboration. A global community of almost 800 million monthly visitors and its consistent reign as one of the top ten most visited sites in the world (Alexa, 2011) attests to its success as a wiki resource of uncommon popularity. In the United Kingdom, *h2g2* (http://www.h2g2.com/) aims to provide encyclopedic wiki content to "life, the universe, and everything." Small-scale ready reference by individual libraries is also played out with notable success by many institutions. *Andover Answers* (http://www.mhl.org/answers/), run by the Memorial Hall Library in Andover (MA), hosts a public ready reference wiki on the town's history and social, cultural, and economic establishments. The Burbank (CA) Public Library hosts a local community wiki at http://burbank.wikidot.com/; however, the wiki is closed to instant editing and all changes must be submitted by e-mail.

Subject Guides

The Camden County (NJ) Library has more than fifty pathfinders and subject guides available on its website. The New York Public Library has almost 100 research guides on its site. Libraries have traditionally created these guides to aid their users. The onus of continuously updating all these guides is a requirement of good reference service. Wikis can assist in the process as seen in a number of examples. QuestionPoint (http://wiki.questionpoint.org/readyref), the 24/7 reference service provided by the Library of Congress and OCLC, has a subject wiki for chat librarians "to provide quick, authoritative starting points for librarians." The Grand Rapids (MI) Public Library hosts a whole collection of subject guides that can only be updated by reference librarians within the library system at http://www.grpl.org/wiki/index.php/.

Discussions and Proceedings

Reference librarians have also been using wiki formats to keep an ongoing, interactive record of meetings, conference proceedings, and staff discussions. The ALA Annual Conferences, for example, host a wiki at http://presentations.ala.org/ that is open for posts from all attendees and exhibitors. The Oregon State Library uses Confluence to provide an ongoing source of internal information for its reference librarians. The issues of "reference desk managers," "subject research guides," and "digital access services" are all contained in "spaces" that the librarian can consult to get a sense of what has been discussed both longitudinally across time, latitudinally across committees, and annotated by staff through wiki access. A representative example from this wiki can be seen at https://wiki.library.oregon state.edu/. The Albany County (WY) Public Library staff aim to capture the elusive institutional wisdom of their system by documenting "how to do things" via a wiki at http://albystaff.pbwiki.com/.

Reference Instruction and Manuals

Wikis are potentially capable of reducing the constant reinvention of the wheel with regard to instruction manuals. Reference librarians looking to create how-to manuals for basic computer classes, class syllabi for bibliographic instruction, or handouts dealing with information literacy are well served with wiki versions that can be updated and repackaged in keeping with the times and the institution using it. "Using a wiki to integrate the library instruction knowledge of many librarians enables a library instruction program to better meet our patrons' needs," states reference librarian Charles Allan (2007: 242). An example can be seen in the Library Technology Training Wiki (http://trainingwiki.pbworks.com/) that provides comprehensive tutorials on how to conduct an online survey and make a wiki. A useful list of "wiki-based opportunities" can be found at http://statelibrary.ncdcr.gov/ld/education/elearninglinks.html.

Project Management

Wikis can be useful tools of knowledge management for specific projects. In trying to improve the computer services offered by the reference department at the Durham County (NC) Library, the staff became part of a larger Strategic Plan Wiki that aimed at both informing and encouraging active participation from the library board, trustees, the town government, and the community at large to effect a public transformation of the library system. The site, now retired, can still be seen as a historical snapshot at http://dclstrategicplan.pbworks.com/ and testifies to the successful use of wiki technology to further the goals of a reference project. The University of Connecticut Libraries' Staff Wiki was aimed at creating a comprehensive, updated, and reliable source for over 500 Library Documents and was made accessible to staff via password at http://wiki.lib.uconn.edu/index.php/Main_Page.

Reference Blogs, Microblogs, and Podcasts

In the early 1990s, the term "Weblogs" was used to loosely describe online postings or logs on a website. In less than a decade, the expansion of the tool led to a contraction of the word, and "Weblogs" was reduced to "blogs." The popularity of blogs and the rich variety of blog formats, in turn, gave birth to a host of corollary words such as bloggers (those who blog), blogging (a verb describing the act of posting a blog), microblogs (really short blogs), blogosphere (the universe of blogs), blogrolls (list of links to other blogs), blog search engines (engines that search blog postings and content), trackbacks (acknowledgment of communication between blogs), vlogs (video blogs), qlogs (question-and-answer blogs), MP3 blogs (music blogs), and podcasts (audio blogs). As of 2008, a reported 1 million posts were being added each day in 81 different languages across the globe (Technorati, June 2008). As of 2010, corporate bloggers were receiving an average of over 300,000 unique visitors per month. As of 2012, there were 1,301,733 blogs recorded by Technorati.

Blogs are frequent posts made on a site, with the posts typically listed in reverse chronological order. There is nothing very new about this act. In the world of print reference, columns titled "What's New in Reference" or "Reference Updates" held the basic ingredients of a "blog." How then are blogs different? For one thing, blogs are not static columns, but actual websites navigable through hyperlinks. This allows blog sites to link with other blogs, accept online discussion and commentary, and archive past blogs so that the site is marked strongly with its own rugged personality. Topic, genre, content structure, motivation, media type, and composing device all play a role in marking the individualistic world of blogging. Hyperlinks, feedback, and open discussion forums accentuate the distinctiveness of blogs, even as they harness the 2.0 hallmarks of dynamic collaboration, networking, and cooperative content creation. A working paper on blogging conducted by the University of Essex in the United Kingdom refers to it as a means of "public knowledge-building on the web" that creates "self-organizing communities" (Brady, 2005). The world of reference blogs has been developing a great many such "self-organizing communities."

Reference Blogs as Campus Newsletters

The Lillian Goldman Law Library at Yale Law School in New Haven (CT) has a *Reference Blog* that serves as a catchall for things that may be pertinent to the academic law community ranging from global and national news bulletins to in-house library acquisitions and bibliographic instruction (see Figure 21-1). A cloud of hyperlinked subject tags brackets the blog, serving as an index that the user can instantly click to retrieve blogs of personal interest.

Reference Blogs as Readers' Advisory

In years past, *Genreflecting* was a classic printed reference tool supporting readers' advisory. The publishers of the series now offer a blog, *Reader's Advisor Online*, that collates a weekly synopsis from hundreds of advisory blogs at http://www.readersadvisoronline.com/blog/. The Bensenville (IL) Community Public Library hosted a website rich in blogs directed at readers' advisory for all ages (see Figure 21-2). In July 2012, Credo Reference, known primarily for its collection of reference e-books, launched a weekly readers' advisory blog called *Required Reading* at http://blog.credoreference.com/category/required-reading/. The personalized selectivity required of readers' advisory appears to lend itself to the chatty intimacy of the blog format quite effortlessly.

Reference Blogs as In-House Communication

Internal blogs are handy tools to enhance communication within a busy or wide-ranging reference department. Not only is the original message or update open to all staff, but also changes over time or other viewpoints can be incorporated or appended to the blog. "Blogs are a crucial element of the Web 2.0 landscape not just for the information they publish, but for the spider web of relationships they spawn," observes Funk (2009: 4), and this holds very true to in-house reference blogs. The Barnard College Library (NYC) blog (shown in Figure 21-3), the *Librarians' Blog* at Hennepin County (MN) Library, the *Science Updates* at Washington and Lee University Libraries (Lexington, VA), and the *Public Services and the Trade Bazaar Blog* at Kansas State University (Coleman, Theiss-White, and Fritch, 2011) are all examples of blogs used in interesting ways to keep reference librarians on the same page. Issues as small as a consistent way to report problems with the local printer to long-term issues of digitizing the local history collection are examples of subjects; the efficacy and nature of an in-house blog is very much a function of institutional requirement and staff commitment.

Figure 21-1. Screenshot of *Reference Blog* at the Yale Law Library

Source: Screenshot reproduced with permission from Yale Law School.

Figure 21-2. Readers' Advisory Blog at the Bensenville Community Public Library

Source: Printed with permission from the Bensenville Community Public Library District.

Figure 21-3. Blog as In-House Communication at Barnard College Library

barnardrefdesk

THIS BLOG SERVES TO KEEP BARNARD LIBRARIANS POSTED ABOUT REFERENCE DESK GOINGS ON.

Tuesday, March 24, 2009
Student access to fax machines
Basically, there is no student access to a fax machine on campus. (I called office services; their fax machine requires an administrative code for use.)

However, there are tons of free fax services online, where you upload your file and they send it to the recipient's fax machine. Some have ads or require registration or other pesky things. If anyone has a recommendation about one service over another. Please post it in the comments.

Labels: fax machine

// posted by Jenna @ 1:06 PM 0 comments

Monday, March 16, 2009
REFERENCE SYMPOSIUM: FRIDAY MARCH 13, 2009

The 7th Annual Reference Symposium, "The Making of a Reference Librarian" was held on Friday March 13. Thanks to colleagues who helped the reference librarians by taking additional reference hours. Many of the papers and presentations are available on the symposium's website with more to come this week:

Source: Used by permission of Barnard College Library.

Reference Blogs as News Bulletins

Mainstream newspapers, with their guiding principle of providing updates on news, are fertile ground for blogging. In fact, 95 percent of the top 100 newspapers have reporter blogs (Technorati, 2011). Concurrently, large news blogs such as the wildly successful *Huffington Post* (http://www.huffingtonpost.com/) have taken on the persona of mainstream newspapers so that the boundary between the mainstream print sites and blog format is merging. Reference librarians, especially those connected with special interest collections, have been quick to emulate the trend. News blogs, aimed at specific constituencies, can be seen in the field. The Government Documents and Reference Librarian at the Mansfield Library, University of Montana-Missoula, for example, has collaborated with staff to create a news update for "recently published government information" in blog form accessible at http://montanagovinfo.blogspot.com/ (see Figure 21-4).

Reference Blogs as Personal Statement

In 2006, *Time* magazine selected "You" as its "Person of the Year" based on the wildfire appeal of blogging and related user-created websites. Blog software is simple enough that publishing web content, formerly the preserve of a technical department, is accessible to all. Personal blogs are the most common form of

Figure 21-4. Blogs as News Bulletins at the University of Montana

GOVERNMENT NEWS FOR MONTANA

RECENTLY PUBLISHED GOVERNMENT INFORMATION
SPONSORED BY THE MANSFIELD LIBRARY AT THE UNIVERSITY OF MONTANA,
WITH SUPPORT FROM MONTANA GOVERNMENT INFORMATION PROFESSIONALS

WEDNESDAY, MARCH 25, 2009

Montana Bill on Stimulus Funds

From the *Missoulian*: "Capping more than a week of marathon committee sessions and one-on-one negotiations among its members, a key legislative panel Tuesday approved the bill outlining how to spend Montana's $870 million share of federal economic 'stimulus' money."

The House Appropriations Committee passed House Bill 645, Implement receipt of and appropriate federal stimulus and recovery funds, yesterday. You can find the latest text of the bill on the Montana Legislature website. The bill now heads to the floor of the Montana House.

Source: Dennison, M. (25 March 2009). "Legislature 2009: Key panel approves stimulus measure." *Missoulian*. A1.

Labels: budget, legislature, Montana, recession

POSTED BY J. BURROUGHS AT 12:59 PM   0 COMMENTS

Contact a Government Information Librarian for Assistance

Jennie Burroughs, University of Montana
jennie.burroughs@umontana.edu

Carol Jestrab, MSU-Northern
jestrab@msun.edu

James Kammerer, Montana State Library
jkammerer@mt.gov

LINKS

Montana State Website
USA.gov
GPO Access
THOMAS
About the FDLP

PREVIOUS POSTS

Montana Bill on Stimulus Funds
GAO Report on the Labor Department
NIOSH Vermiculite Study

Source: Government News for Montana, sponsored by the Maureen and Mike Mansfield Library of the University of Montana, http://montanagovinfo.blogspot.com/.

blogging to be found and also the most vulnerable to abandonment over time. A study in 2006 found more than 200 million dead blogs (Funk, 2009). Despite this high fatality rate, personal blogs have found favor with reference librarians both as personalized commentary and as institutional branding tools, most typically presented as library director blogs. Paul Courant, the University Librarian and Dean of Libraries at the University of Michigan, for example, has been writing *Au Courant*, a personal blog on topics related primarily, though not exclusively, to the library universe at http://paulcourant.net/. The University Librarians' Blog, posted by Yale University Library, functions as a personalized branding tool for the library. Each post describes some special exhibit or feature of the library as seen in Figure 21-5.

Microblogs

Microblogs are exactly what they sound like, blogs that inform, update, comment, or notify users in pithy form. The most popular version of a microblog is Twitter, which claims a total of 500 million registered users (Barnett, 2012). Twitter's limit to a text-based post is a maximum of 140 characters. In a 2.0 world where fact is frequently stranger than fiction, it would have been hard to predict that the sending of 140 characters, or "tweets," could become a viable reference tool. Yet tweeting has been recognized as an efficient way to provide quick updates, bulleted information, enhance publicity, or reinforce library messages. From the Library of Congress (see Figure 21-6) to academic, public, and small-town libraries, tweeting is currently used for a variety of purposes. The Casa Grande (AZ) Public Library uses it to provide program updates; the Perkins Library Reference Desk at Duke

Figure 21-5. Blogs as Personal Statement

Yale University Library

RESEARCH TOOLS   LIBRARIES & COLLECTIONS   ABOUT THE LIBRARY   LIBRARY SERVICES

Departments & Staff / Working at the Library / Giving to the Library / Access & Use / Computers in the Library / Ask! a Librarian

University Librarian's Blog

February 9, 2009

Celebrating the Power of Ideas

The first weeks of 2009 mark some extraordinary anniversaries, each one with a heightened resonance in the context of the seismic changes that are going on in the economic and political life of the nation. Martin Luther King, Jr. would have been eighty years old, Abraham Lincoln was born two hundred years ago, and we are also celebrating the bicentenary of Lincoln's exact contemporary Charles Darwin. The Library will celebrate Black History month, and so honor Dr. King, with a notable trio of lectures coming up. Abraham Lincoln's anniversary will be celebrated across the campus in many different forums, classes, and symposia. Charles Darwin, meanwhile, that reclusive and reflective scientist and man of letters, never visited North America, but the impact of his work on this country's political, philosophical and theological discourse, let alone our science, continues to animate controversy and passions that Darwin himself might never have imagined.

Though he did not visit, Darwin corresponded at length with scientists in North America, including Yale's James Dwight Dana, Silliman Professor of Natural History and Geology. Darwin's and Dana's association as explorers, scholars, and pioneering scientists fostered a rich and rewarding correspondence between 1849 and 1863 and the display of Darwin's letters to his friend and mentor (which are part of the collection of Manuscripts and Archives) in Sterling Memorial Library is one of a group of exhibits in different parts of the Library system, celebrating the Darwin bicentenary. Kline Science Library has mounted two displays, and there are others at the Medical, Music, and Divinity Libraries. They provide between them some fascinating insights, based on Yale collections, into Darwin's own life, times, and thought, and into the reception of his theory of evolution in the one hundred and fifty years since he published On the Origin of Species. They also give food for thought about the way ideas are transmitted, and the power of one man and his book to transform the world's view of itself.

Posted by Alice at 1:48 PM | Comments (0)

Alice Prochaska

FEBRUARY 2009
Sun Mon Tue Wed Thu Fri Sat
1 2 3 4 5 6 7
8 9 10 11 12 13 14
15 16 17 18 19 20 21
22 23 24 25 26 27 28

ARCHIVES

Source: Screenshot reproduced with permission from Yale Law School.

Figure 21-6. Twitter Account at the Library of Congress

Login Join Twitter!

Hey there! **librarycongress** is using Twitter.

Twitter is a free service that lets you keep in touch with people through the exchange of quick, frequent answers to one simple question: What are you doing? **Join today** to start receiving **librarycongress's** updates.

Join today!

Already using Twitter
from your phone? Click here.

 librarycongress

C-SPAN posted a series of vignettes with our curator about Lincoln-exhibit objects -- the next best thing to being there! http://is.gd/oXGc

Name *Library of Congress (librarycongress)*
Location *Washington, DC*
Web *http://www.loc.go...*
Bio *We are the largest library in the world, with millions of books, recordings, photographs, maps and manuscripts in our collections.*

0
following

4,446
followers

201
updates

Updates

University in Durham (North Carolina) tweets out answers to reference questions, bibliographic updates, and even the library room temperature; Maryland's cooperative 24/7 online service, *AskUsNow!*, offers tweets for quick question-and-answer sessions; the Nebraska Library Commission provides ready reference through its Twitter account. Examples of reference questions answered through tweets at the commission's site (http://twitter.com/NLC_Reference) shows how microblogging is capable of providing ready reference.

> Q: *Where can I search to see who owns a particular corporation in Nebraska?*
> A: *Tweet: http://tinyurl.com/384na4*

> Q: *Where are the state statutes online?*
> A: *Tweet: http://tinyurl.com/b4px4w*

Podcasts

Much like blogs, podcasts also provide updates over the Internet, except they are audio files. The same structure of web syndication and feeds allows podcasts to be accessible effortlessly to vast numbers of users linked to a single site. Reference libraries have used podcasts to conduct tours of the collection, distribute reference programs to a wider audience that could not attend an in-house session, and deliver bibliographic instruction. The Claude Moore Health Sciences Library of the University of Virginia, for example, has open access to podcasts of its health lecture series. Those interested in these podcasts can either subscribe to receive them as an automatic feed, or opt to listen to any one of the podcasts offered at their website (http://www.hsl.virginia.edu/historical/lectures.cfm). The Sheridan Libraries of the Johns Hopkins University in Baltimore (MD) uses podcasts to assist its constituency in effectively navigating the library's reference resources. Instructive podcasts on *JHsearch*, a metasearch platform for searching through multiple library databases, "Ask a Librarian" services offered by subject specialists, and mapping software available to analyze geospatial data and create customized maps, are part of the repertoire on bibliographic instruction offered by the library (see Figure 21-7).

Reference Folksonomies

Another dramatic manifestation of cooperative content creation has been in the area of socially tagged informational sites. The classification of information, far from being slotted into traditional subject indexing, develops taxonomy based on keyword usage from multiple folks; hence the term, "folksonomy." The visual display of this form of keyword indexing is popularly projected through graphical words or tag clouds, where words used most often by the user community have larger fonts, and correspondingly, words with lesser usage are displayed in smaller fonts. All the variously sized words are typically hyperlinked so users can drill down into the subject in which they are interested. The familiar hierarchy or connecting relationship between terms, which constitutes the bedrock of subject classification, is simply nonexistent in folksonomies where keywords float in their own user-created space.

Figure 21-7. Podcasts at the Sheridan Libraries, Johns Hopkins University

JOHNS HOPKINS UNIVERSITY | THE SHERIDAN LIBRARIES

STAFF DIRECTORY | PERSONS WITH DISABILITIES | CONTACT US | SITE MAP | HOURS

HOME | LIBRARY SERVICES | ONLINE RESOURCES | CATALOGS | RESEARCH HELP | COLLECTIONS

ASK A LIBRARIAN ?
HOW DO I...
FORMS
MY ACCOUNT
ABOUT US
INFO FOR
GIVING
SEARCH
NEWS & EVENTS
LIBRARY BLOG

SPOTLIGHT

2009 Homewood Student Video Contest

Prizes include $200 for best library-related video. Deadline: March 25, 2009. More...

Archives

Home > Podcasts > Sheridan Libraries Podcasts

Printer-friendly Version

Sheridan Libraries Podcasts

Listen to our podcasts to learn about library collections, services and people, and get tips for making the most of your library.

#4: How to Make Maps

Length: 23:06
File size: 21.1 MB

"About 80% of the data [collected] in the world is related to some place on the earth's surface," says Jim Gillispie, head of the Government Publications/Maps/Law Library (GPML). Jim talks with Andrea Bartelstein about ArcGIS, mapping software that enables users to analyze geospatial data and create their own custom designed maps. "Maps are not about answering your questions, but [...] giving you all the details for you to ask more questions of the map. ...What's kind of neat is you get to choose what components you want to bring to the map."

Click on the podcast link to listen on your computer, or right-click to download the file.

Automatically download new podcasts from this site to your mp3 player or other portable device by subscribing to the RSS feed. What is RSS? RSS

Click on the orange RSS icon and copy the URL or shortcut into your feed reader.

Source: Used with permission of the Johns Hopkins University Sheridan Libraries.

Flickr (http://www.flickr.com/) is one of the most popular online photo management and sharing application sites that is freely available to all users. Libraries interested in maintaining a visual profile have been quick to upload institutional photographs on Flickr. As with all public images that are used for library marketing, the convoluted laws of patron privacy need to be followed (Carson, 2008). In Figure 21-8, the photos associated with the University of British Columbia in Canada have developed a folksonomy that is graphically depicted with a tag cloud. The majority of photographs appear to describe the "campus," the "library," and "ubc" (given that the fonts for these words are the largest in the cloud). Clicking on any one of these indexing words would lead the user to see the associated photographs.

Dropbox and Delicious are widely used social bookmarking services that allow all users to freely tag and save sites that they choose in order to share them with others at a future date. Unlike the old system of having to save such sites on individual computers as "Favorites," this service manages saved webpages from

Figure 21-8. Folksonomy of the University of British Columbia Graphics in Flickr

UBC Library Graphics' photostream
Sets **Tags** Archives Favorites Profile

Jump to: [   ] **GO**

aarp advising advisor architecture architecure archives asian asianlibrary assistance astronomy auditorium barber bike biker biking black books business campus center centre chapman christmas chung class classroom clock cold collection college commerce commons computer david desaturated desk desturated dlam dodson entrance exhibit exterior fog foggy german glasssculpture group hall help holidays homework human ice ikblc info information irving koerner lab lam leam learning learningcentre lecture librarian library lounge main museum newspaper nice orrery park parliamentary program rare reading reference research resources ridington room sauder scene school shelves snow student students studies study studying teach teacher teaching theatre tower tree trees ubc ubclibrary university universityofbritishcolumbia vancouver victoria volume wagon wheels white winter woodward xmas

Source: Meredith, M. 2009. UBC Library Graphics' Photostream—Tags (http://www.flickr.com/).

a centralized source that can be accessed from anywhere. In Figure 21-9, the Witkin State Law Library in Sacramento (CA) has pertinent sites bookmarked. The popularity of the subject matter is indexed in a folksonomy with a tag cloud in which "California" has the largest collection of bookmarked sites. Drilling down in the hyperlinked tag allows the user to encounter the sites seen in the next graphic: "How To File A Claim," "California Codes," "LA Law Library," and so on (see Figure 21-10).

Figure 21-9. Cloud Tag for the Witkin State Law Library

delicious Home | Bookmarks ▼ | People ▼ | Tags ▼

Witkin State Law Library of California's Tags
Bookmarks | Network | **Tags** | Subscriptions

Also try exploring Popular tags

csllaw ▸ [Type a tag]   Tags **56**

Sort: Alphabetically | By size

agencies analysis archives bills briefs business California Canada cases catalogs citations cities codes constitution consumer counties courts decisions dictionaries directories elderlaw elections employment executive familylaw federal forms fulltext government guides history initiatives international landlord-tenant lawreviews laws lawyers legal legislative legislativehistory libraries local Mexico news notonlawref propositions publications publishers referral regulations reports research selfhelp states taxes USA

Figure 21-10. A Drill-Down of Single Tag for the Witkin State Law Library

Social Networking

Facebook and Myspace

Much like Flickr, which is a media site, Facebook (http://www.facebook.com/), Google+ (https://plus.google.com/), LinkedIn (http://www.linkedin.com/), Myspace (http://www.myspace.com/), Bebo (http://www.bebo.com/), Friendster (http://www.friendster.com/), StudiVZ (http://www.studivz.net/), hi5 (http://www.hi5.com/), and Orkut (http://www.orkut.com/) are social sites that are structured to facilitate online user interaction and the open sharing of data. Given the emphasis on providing timely reference "where the users are," attention to these social networking sites has risen amongst reference librarians because of the rising popularity of these sites. By January 2012, for example, Facebook had posted over 845 million active users. Within these millions of users, interest groups voluntarily coalesce based on stated interests and invitations to be part of the group. Each group features a "profile" with information on the group or institution, and a "wall" with threaded discussion lists and scrolled messages allowing for data collation and interactive discussion.

For reference librarians, the sites provide yet another online space in which to offer services. "Ask A Librarian" groups, book discussion groups attracting outlier populations that may not visit a physical library, and professional consultation groups that are able to discuss database vendor negotiation, conference proceedings, or library best practices are some of the iterations playing out in these relatively early days of social networking site usage amongst reference librarians.

Public libraries like the Denver (CO) Public Library (http://myspace.com/denver_eVolver); the Houston (TX) Public Library (http://www.facebook.com/houstonlibrary); and the Hennepin County (MN) Library (http://www.facebook.com/hclib) among many others, have set up a presence in these sites. Academic libraries like Mississippi State University Libraries (http://www.facebook.com/

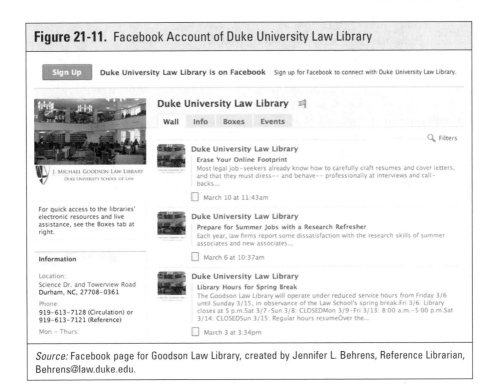

Figure 21-11. Facebook Account of Duke University Law Library

Source: Facebook page for Goodson Law Library, created by Jennifer L. Behrens, Reference Librarian, Behrens@law.duke.edu.

msulibrary); the Brooklyn (NY) College Library (http://www.myspace.com/brooklyncollegelibrary); and the Duke University Law Library (Durham, NC) (see Figure 21-11) have accounts. Larger professional groups such as *Librarians and Facebook*, *Library Applications in Facebook*, the *Libraries without Walls* conference group, and the *University College and Research* group can all be located in Facebook.

As may be seen in the Duke graphic, in addition to information about the Duke University Law Library's contact information and hours of service, the potential user can also click on the "Boxes" link and directly launch into *WorldCat* and catalog searches, chat with a reference librarian, access *LexisNexis* and other databases, and use the "Ask-a-Librarian" service, all without leaving the site. Herein lies the potential attraction of social networking sites like Facebook. Much like iPad- and laptop-toting reference librarians who try to catch the physical user in high-traffic areas such as the student community area (as discussed in styles of roving reference [Chapter 19]), Reference 2.0 aims to catch tomorrow's user at online high-traffic areas.

Customization

Widgets Used for Reference

"Gadgets," "snippets," "modules," "add-ons," and "plugins" are some of the other terms used for widget technology. Widgets are miniscule programming codes that can be easily plucked and inserted into a larger webpage so that the page becomes more interactive and customized to user preferences. Reference libraries have used widgets as well as offered widgets to their users for accessing library services in innovative ways.

A prominent use of widgets by reference librarians has been in the field of chat reference. Chat widgets such as Qwidget (http://www.qwidget.com/), Plugoo (http://www.plugoo.com/), and Digsby (http://www.digsby.com/) have become prominent tools for chat reference. The University Libraries at the Pennsylvania State University attached chat widgets on various pages of its website so users can access it at the point of need. The "Ask-a-Librarian" page, course guide pages, subject guide pages, and subject library homepages all have embedded chat widgets for speedy and anonymous reference interactions.

The University of Texas Libraries has a family of widgets that are helpfully divided into search widgets, information-organizing widgets, and collaboration widgets (see Figure 21-12).

- *Search* widgets include a Toolbar Button that allows Google users to add a button for the library catalog on their Google page; a web browser add-on that allows users to search the University of Texas Digital Repository; and a widget that opens up the possibility of using iPhones to search for material in the closest library through *WorldCat* searches.
- *Information organizing* widgets include a Facebook application that creates APA (American Psychological Association), Chicago Manual, MLA (Modern Language Association), Turabian, and Harvard citation styles for material found in *WorldCat*; a Flickr Uploader that organizes photographs on the web; and Zotero (http://www.zotero.org/), a widget that helps users to collect, manage, and cite research sources.
- *Collaboration* widgets include a widget that helps "clip out" material from webpages to then share with others through blogs, e-mails, and printouts;

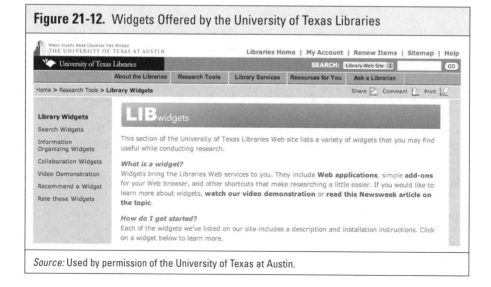

Figure 21-12. Widgets Offered by the University of Texas Libraries

Source: Used by permission of the University of Texas at Austin.

and PBWiki (http://pbwiki.com/), which allows users to set up their own free, hosted, password-protected wiki in the time it takes to make a PB (peanut butter) sandwich.

RSS Feeds Used for Reference

In 2005, the powers that be at Firefox and Internet Explorer collaborated in an effort to standardize a little orange logo with white wavy lines rippling outward, denoting the "broadcasting of content." This was to become the ubiquitous RSS logo that stands for really simple syndication. What is really simple about this customization tool is its ability to automatically view breaking new content from any number of websites in one single interface, without having to search each site independently. Since 1999, when RSS first originated, the software (feed reader or aggregator) used to read the feeds has expanded so that it can be web based, desktop based, or available through mobile devices. Whereas the current family of Internet browsers has built-in RSS readers, accessing feeds is limited to the computer in which it is saved. On the other hand, web-based feed aggregators such as Google Reader (http://www.google.com/reader) and Bloglines (http://www.bloglines.com/) are free, easy to use, and accessible from any computer with Internet access, key considerations in the popularity of 2.0 tools.

For reference librarians, RSS feeds can be used to alert patrons about new books, articles, library news and happenings, blogs, and even tables of contents from new journals (see Figure 21-13). The custom of updates, however, has far predated RSS technology and, in fact, continues through e-mail notification in a

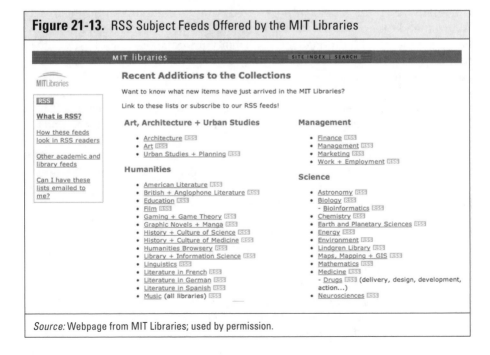

Figure 21-13. RSS Subject Feeds Offered by the MIT Libraries

Source: Webpage from MIT Libraries; used by permission.

great many libraries. Why then is the popularity of RSS feeds gaining so rapidly in so many environments, including reference libraries? The answer may be contained in some of the functional differences between e-mail and RSS alerts. Unlike receiving updates via e-mail, RSS feeds allow for customizable formatting; the items are automatically deleted or marked as "read"; subscription to an RSS is typically anonymous; and updates are kept sacrosanct from the flotsam and jetsam populating the standard e-mail account. An in-built elegance to RSS updates for both the sender and the receiver promises its continued expansion in user base.

Mashups

Mashups are creative enterprises. They describe a single graphical interface for a distinctive service that is created when content and functionality from more than one web application are brought together or "mashed up." Why would reference librarians want to mash things up?

First, mashups continue the traditions of good reference in allowing services to develop based on patron-driven wants. If the reference user is able to find peer-based and professional reviews of books on a single site such as Amazon.com, the likelihood of that site being used for evaluating the product is greater than if the user had to toggle through two or more sites to collect the same information. Hennepin County (MN) Library, for example, has mashed its integrated library system (ILS) with its customer book review database so that its constituency now enjoys a compelling and popular new product, namely, a catalog that can also provide side-by-side comparative reviews of books by contemporaries. At the University of Huddersfield in the United Kingdom, the ILS is mashed with Amazon and other external data sites so that a search in the catalog not only brings up the usual locational and availability information, but a host of other user-focused tools. The user can rate and comment on the book as well as check out reviews by peers, see the cover of the book, instantly link to social bookmarking sites like Delicious, sign up for RSS feeds to be alerted of all new acquisitions in that call number category, and visually browse through a virtual bookshelf holding similar material (see Figure 21-14). An "Ask a Librarian" link completes the page for every single search made in the library catalog.

Second, mashups involve merging and can be used to foment cooperation between different entities. For example, at the University of Rochester (NY), course management has benefited from a well-conceived mashup between reference library resources and the course system as a whole. When professors structure their courses, a feed is sent to the library, which then proceeds to match library resources with the course syllabus. As stated by Susan Gibbons, vice provost of the River Campus Libraries at the university, "mashups provide us an opportunity to better integrate the library with the rest of campus, so that our resources are not siloed but seen as part of an integrated whole of the University" (Storey, 2008: 9).

The Southeastern Libraries Cooperating (SELCO) in Minnesota, a library consortium, mashed up its website with both *Google Maps* and MapBuilder.net (see Figure 21-15). With the mashup, library users could immediately connect their

Figure 21-14. Catalog Search Result Page at the University of Huddersfield

Source: Screenshot of University of Huddersfield Library catalog; used by permission.

library to the pertinent legislator of that legislative district. The legislator list was also linked to individual photographs and official sites of the legislative body. In addition to added value for the user, it turned out to be a great way of setting up linkages with the legislators themselves, some of whom had no idea of the number of libraries, in addition to the obvious public library, that they represented.

Figure 21-15. Mashup of SELCO Library Consortium Site

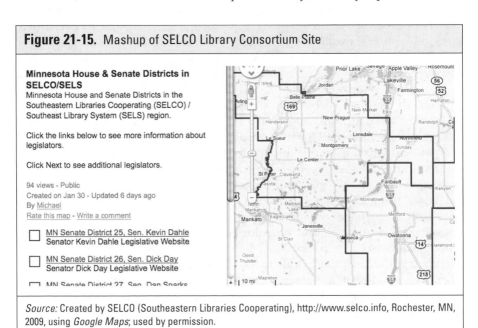

Source: Created by SELCO (Southeastern Libraries Cooperating), http://www.selco.info, Rochester, MN, 2009, using *Google Maps*; used by permission.

Finally, as with a great many 2.0 tools populating the library universe, some mashups require relatively basic technical knowledge and can be built by leveraging existing software and sites. In sum, mashups are technologically accessible engines of innovation and can quite simply create a more resonant product and a more unique user experience.

Seamlessness

A glowing orb acts as a liaison to a virtual reference librarian, flying cars provide tours of reference facilities, and books can be searched or questions can be answered in real time by texting through a mobile device: we have entered a certain level of technological seamlessness in the continually emerging world of Reference 2.0. The drive "to make quality information available anyplace, anytime, and for everyone" (Robinson, 2008: 4) undergirds the restless desire to keep experimenting with new forms of media formatting and interactivity, so that there is a palpable sense of increasing transparency between mediums.

Reference in Virtual Worlds

Drawing from realistic three-dimensional (3-D) modeling tools, and underwritten by the assumption that the one life lived physically is not quite enough for the imaginative genius of humans, a wildly popular online virtual world was created in 2003. Second Life (SL), as it was so aptly termed, used the compelling lure of 3-D to help its "residents" create an expanding digital world filled with people/"avatars," a thriving environment, and online experiences. Participants, both individuals and institutions, could buy land, build library buildings, set up reference desks, and hold discussions or answer questions in a somewhat surreal, cartoon-like virtual world that, nonetheless, mirrors real-life environments. Basic entry into this world and the setting up of an avatar to represent the user is free and easily accessible at http://www.secondlife.com/.

Hundreds of university, college, and public libraries were established on SL, with one of the more spectacular initiatives being the InfoIsland Archipelago, where the user could "talk" in real-time, synchronous interaction with a visually solid reference librarian. However, students at San Jose State University found out quite early that navigating through the SL world was clunky, required a steep learning curve, and left one with the perception that in this early stage, SL was more immersed in the "gee-whiz aspect...like building neat-o buildings and fountains" (Gerardin, Yamamoto, and Gordon, 2008: 324) and less successful at establishing a viable and vibrant reference presence. "Maybe 3-D online environments are just one of those technologies that sound cool but never fully materialize, like personal jetpacks," was Jeffrey Young's (2010) comment. Yet, the ongoing appeal of virtual worlds for the reference librarian is secured more by what may come about in the future than by what is currently evolving. As pithily stated by Hurst-Wahl (2007: 53), "By being a part of SL now, librarians believe they are positioning themselves for the tools, services, and user environments that will come after it." And in fact, newer ventures such as Open Cobalt at Duke

University (Durham, NC), stand-alone versions of SL at Case Western Reserve University (Cleveland, OH), and the creation of Open Simulator continue to testify to the attraction of reference in virtual worlds.

Mobile Reference

Although virtual reference has been discussed in other parts of the book, it is being highlighted in this chapter both to emphasize its vital role in the 2.0 landscape, as well as its continuing expansion from online, e-mail, chat, and IM reference to the world of mobile devices such as iPods, BlackBerrys, PDAs, MP3 players, notebooks, iPhones, and iPads. Personal digital devices are on their way to becoming popcorn technology: easy to use, cheaper to buy, and accessible to more than a few. Equally important, the Millennials and NextGen generations appear to interact through e-mail, texting, chat, and Skype and regard mobile devices as an integral part of their persona. As Google CEO Eric Schmidt stated at the Web 2.0 Expo in San Francisco, "The biggest growth areas are clearly going to be in the mobile space.... And the reason is people treat their mobile phones as extensions of their person" (Claburn, 2007). At the start of 2012, there were an estimated 6 billion cell phone subscriptions around the globe according to the International Telecommunication Union. For this ever-growing world of users, the traditional use of the cell phone as a communication device has rapidly expanded to include instant information as well. A 2007 survey of Harvard Medical School (Boston, MA) found that 52 percent of the students had PDAs that were used primarily (26 percent) for accessing reference information (Lippincott, 2008).

Libraries, especially academic institutions, are working toward mobile-ready reference services in different ways. The University of South Dakota offers reference books that are preloaded on PDAs. The University of Alberta in Edmonton, Canada, has a PDA Zone (see Figure 21-16) with technical support, reference bibliographies, and downloadable text from databases such as *Access Medicine*.

Libraries are creating websites and OPACs that are mobile friendly. Libraries at the University of Virginia, University of Richmond (VA), Ball State University (Muncie, IN), the Grainger Engineering Library (Urbana, IL), Wayne State University Library (Detroit, MI), North Carolina State University Library, and the Boston (MA) University Medical Center have established "mobile libraries." Staff and students at the Boston University Medical Center, for example, can access the *MEDLINE* database, check out e-books, and use a hyperlinked directory of library staff and services via the mobile library interface (see Figure 21-17).

Whereas some libraries have adopted SMS or text messaging to deliver due notices and interlibrary loan request updates, other libraries such as those at University of California at Los Angeles, New York University, Yale Science Libraries (New Haven, CT), and the Worcester (MA) Public Library offer text-messaging reference. The Ohio University Libraries offer Skype reference via calls, video calls, or text messaging. Reference librarians from New York University studied more than 300 of their SMS reference sessions in 2008 and produced

Figure 21-16. PDA Zone at the University of Alberta, Edmonton, Canada

This site provides access to resources and library services that are available for users of handheld devices known as **Personal Digital Assistants (PDAs)**.

PDA Library Resources and Services

- Wireless PDA Support
- MDC Mobile - MDConsult's information service for PDAs
- PDA Bibliographies
- PEPID
- PICOmaker
- Access Medicine

PDA Guides

- Health Sciences Resources
- PDAs in Education
- Ressources en franiɔ½ais
- E-Book / E-Text Sites for PDAs
- Downloading Library Resource Guides To Your PDA

 UNIVERSITY OF
ALBERTA Learning Services | Privacy Policy | Site Map | Site Search | RSS

Source: Reprinted with permission from the University of Alberta Libraries.

Figure 21-17. Mobile Library at the Boston University Medical Center

Boston University Medical Center Mobile Library

Medline: PubMed [Handheld]

Subject Guides
A - C | D - H | I - O | P - Z |

Library Directory

Search

E-Book Titles

(Search) Use operators: **AND, OR, NOT**
Truncate with an asterisk *

M-Th: 7:30AM-12AM
Fri: 7:30AM-10PM
Sat: 10AM-10PM
Sun: 10AM-12AM
Holiday hours may differ

72 E. Concord St., 12th Floor
Boston, MA 02118
(617) 638-4232

some interesting analyses. Questions that began as SMS queries could very easily develop into other venues more suitable to the depth of the question. Despite the nature of SMS, which is predicated on short questions and answers, actual usage involved single interactions marked with a furious volley of back-and-forth transactions. The University of California, Merced, not only offers SMS reference but also maintains cell phones at the reference desk so that the librarians are not tied to the spot. Embedded chat reference through *MeeboMe* (George Mason University Library [Fairfax, VA] and Darien [CT] Public Library), *Plugoo* (Brigham Young University Library [Provo, UT] and University of Wisconsin Law Library), *LibraryH3lp* (Baylor University [Waco, TX] and Rochester [NY] Public Library), and *Chatango* (http://www.chatango.com/) (Oregon State University Libraries and University of Calgary in Canada) are also found in all kinds of reference libraries.

The Athabasca University Library in Canada, cosponsor of the 2012 Fourth International m-Libraries Conference on mobile devices, has a mobile-friendly Digital Reading Room where the campus community can access course readings and mobile language websites such as ESL and accent reduction. The Roehampton University in London created a Green Room in 2008 for staff to experiment with mobile devices and exchange best practices in the active use of such technology. The Open University in the United Kingdom, a distance learning institution with more than 260,000 students, has a similar initiative that they call the Digilab. It is becoming increasingly apparent that the "combination of mobile librarians, mobile patrons, and mobile content provides an opportunity to move closer to the ideal of the ubiquitous library" (Barnhart and Pierce, 2011).

Concluding Remarks: The Tree of 2.0 Knowledge

A full-page advertisement in the *New York Times* (February 22, 2009: A26) displays a colorful iPhone3G, with 20 modern pictographs touting apps (widgets). These apps provide everything from Shazam ("Ever hear a song and wonder who sings it? Just hold your iPhone up to the music and, in seconds, you have the name, artist and album, plus a link") to RunKeeper ("GPS to track your run, hike, or walk. See your routes on a map, record time and distance and more"). The advertisement goes on to offer tens of thousands of such apps. And you thought a phone was a mere communication device.

President Barack Obama had more than 1.5 million friends on Facebook, more than 165,000 Twitter followers, a YouTube channel (http://www.youtube.com/) with more than 1,800 videos, a Flickr stream with more than 50,000 images, and an associated community-organizing website called BarackObama.com (Steins, 2009). His unqualified success at attracting campaign funds from the "little person" and establishing a groundswell of popular opinion around the nation has been attributed in large part to successful strategizing and use of 2.0 tools.

In December 2008, Linda Braun of Librarians and Educators Online (LEO) presented a 2.0 workshop at the Boston (MA) Public Library titled "Meeting Customers on Their Own Turf" (with the unwritten but stated subtext that "the library webpage is dead"). Susan Gibbons of the University of Rochester (NY) echoed that approach with her observation: "The wider the gap between the passive experiences of library Web sites and the interactive ones, the more ripe libraries are for replacement by disruptive technologies and services that we may not even be able to yet imagine"(Storey, 2008: 11).

As a testament to the increasing use of 2.0, the Kingston Frontenac Public Library in Ontario, Canada, put out an advertisement for a full-time "Librarian 2.0 in preparation for the 2.0 World" (see Figure 21-18).

From the everyday use of telephones to the organization of a presidential campaign, Web 2.0 is a recognizable presence. Within the field of librarianship, simple professional workshops as well as institutionalized structures such as reference librarian job requirements are also marked by the 2.0 universe. The onrush of 2.0 technology in everyday life is both insistent and ubiquitous. Cartoonish words like Plugoo and Digsby, words conjoined like centaurs such as Facebook and folksonomy, and a forest of acronyms such as MMOGs, SaaS, API, and XML are all linguistic markers to the emergence and settling-in process of this bustling new technology.

It is quite possible that sections of the community are "punch drunk" with the availability of "shiny new toys." It is quite possible that large chunks of this new technology will glitter for a period and fall away into oblivion. It is even possible for reference departments to continue with business as usual, much as there are libraries that continue to use card catalogs.

What is not possible is to pretend that it is not happening. Having eaten from the tree of 2.0 technologies, there is no turning back. Getting intimate with

---

Figure 21-18. Screenshot of Librarian 2.0 Position Announcement

Kingston Frontenac Public Library
Career Opportunities
http://www.kfpl.ca/

LIBRARIAN Permanent Full-Time

KFPL is a progressive, innovative, multi-branch library system with a mission to provide exceptional customer service within the context of a warm and welcoming environment. To this end, we are seeking a dynamic, creative individual to develop and promote the library as a continuous learning organization.

We are looking for a Librarian 2.0 in preparation for the 2.0 World

Are you an information specialist with a combined reference and technological orientation who will:
- Lead our virtual reference team, implementing transformative technology such as IM, podcasting, and streaming audio/video as well as participate in our traditional reference services
- Recommend and implement new and developing technologies such as wikis, blogs, etc.
- Contribute to the development of the library's website
- Contribute to our virtual services offerings, such as web 2.0, federated searching, open URL resolver, etc
- Provide training and support for other librarians in new technologies
- Manage our electronic resources and online databases, explore and recommend new online resources, and negotiate contracts with consortia and vendors
- Collaborate with other librarians to provide community development and outreach, particularly in regard to our virtual services.

Source: Used by permission.

the arsenal of tools available is good reference behavior. It allows the luxury of forgetting to innovate for the sake of innovation and continuing to focus on what is important, namely, the provision of stellar and resonant reference service to end users.

TOP TEN REFERENCE 2.0 TOOLS
Apps
Blogs
Instant Messaging/SMS
Mashups
Microblogs
Podcasts/Video Sharing
RSS Feeds
Social Bookmarking
Social Networking
Wikis

TOP TEN REFERENCE 2.0 SITES	
Bloglines	http://www.bloglines.com/
Facebook	http://www.facebook.com/
Flickr	http://www.flickr.com/
LinkedIn	http://www.linkedin.com/
MediaWiki	http://www.mediawiki.org/
Pinterest	https://www.pinterest.com/
Skype	http://www.skype.com/
Twitter	https://twitter.com/
WordPress	http://wordpress.org/
YouTube	http://www.youtube.com/

Recommendations for Further Reading

Bradley, Phil. 2011. *How to Use Web 2.0 in Your Library, Revised Edition*. London: Facet Publishing. A practical, how-to book on using Web 2.0 tools in libraries, the author also provides helpful illustrations and step-by-step instructions on setting up various initiatives. A companion website with author podcasts enhances the text version.

Braun, Linda. 2011. "The Enablers." *School Library Journal* 57, no. 9 (September): 40–46. This is a succinct and practical article on the ever-expanding world of apps. While a number of practical apps that can help the reference librarian make the most of social media are annotated, there is a valuable section devoted to "App Awareness," which lists indices of evaluation to keep in mind when choosing an app.

Farkas, Meredith (creator). 2005–. *Library Success: A Best Practices Wiki*. http://www.lib success.org/. Launched in 2005 following the Chicago ALA meeting, the wiki was designed to provide a general and freely accessible repository for innovative ideas coming out of libraries. Farkas reports approximately 8,000 visitors a month, and deservedly so, as the wiki provides a wide-ranging list of real-life examples that are illuminative. The sections on "Implementing Tech in the Library" and "Information Sharing and Education" are relevant for this topic.

Farkas, Meredith. 2007. *Social Software in Libraries: Building Collaboration, Communication, and Community Online*. Medford, NJ: Information Today. A comprehensive overview and explanation of 2.0 tools, heavily supplemented with examples of usage by different kinds of libraries. The book is strongly supported by a companion website at http://sociallibraries.com/. The site includes "Five Weeks to a Social Library," a dynamic initiative that was initially taught to forty students online; it provides freely accessible course content to learn about 2.0 tools and their use in libraries. The tools covered are blogs, RSS, wikis, Second Life, social networking, Flickr, social bookmarking, and selling social software at your library to get past staff resistance to 2.0 changes.

Godwin, Peter, and Jo Parker, eds. 2008. *Information Literacy Meets Library 2.0*. London: Facet Publishing. Twelve experts discuss the use of 2.0 tools by library patrons and students and then go on to suggest ways in which libraries can integrate usage patterns with technology.

Kroski, Elyssa. 2008. *Web 2.0 for Librarians and Information Professionals*. New York: Neal-Schuman. A comprehensive survey of 2.0 technology is provided along with real-life examples of its use in various types of libraries.

Peltier-Davis, Cheryl Ann. 2012. *The Cybrarian's Web: An A–Z Guide to 101 Free Web 2.0 Tools and Other Resources*. Medford, NJ: Information Today. For reference librarians looking to implement 2.0 services, this how-to guide will prove valuable. It covers everything from blogging and hosting photos to micropublishing and streaming live videos.

Rheingold, Howard. 2012. *Net Smart: How to Thrive Online*. Cambridge, MA: MIT Press. See also http://rheingold.com/netsmart. "All of us can be smarter than any of us" is the underpinning of social media advancements. The author makes a compelling case for mastering Web 2.0 in a mindful, intelligent, and ethical way so that the barrage of advancements are augmentations of the mind rather than endless distractions and society as a whole benefits from the "architecture of participation." A clarifying and philosophical read when inundated with Reference 2.0 choices.

Sanchez, Joe. 2009. "Implementing Second Life: Ideas, Challenges, and Innovations." *ALA Library Technology Reports* 45, no. 2 (February/March). The author, a doctoral candidate at the University of Texas at Austin, provides a broad context for Second Life by giving a detailed history of the evolution of text-based games to 3-D social virtual worlds. The pedagogical applications of digital storytelling, role-playing, community engagement, and working with teen populations are suggested. Guest author Jane Stimpson provides real-life examples of public libraries that have apparated into Second Life and discusses the large numbers that have dissipated into "ghost sims."

Steiner, Sarah K., and M. Leslie Madden, eds. 2008. *The Desk and Beyond: Next Generation Reference Service*. Chicago: ACRL/ALA. Thirteen chapters by different experts on various 2.0 technological tools and newly defined reference services, with a focus on moving "beyond the walls of the library."

Technorati. http://www.technorati.com/. *Time* magazine had the comment that if Google was the web's reference library, Technorati was becoming its coffeehouse. It is the preeminent blog search engine and provides substantive information about the blogosphere.

Wood, M. Sandra, ed. 2007. *Medical Librarian 2.0: Use of Web 2.0 Technologies in Reference Services*. Binghamton, NY: The Haworth Press. Edited by a medical reference librarian of many years' experience and authored by both bloggers and well-known health science specialists, the book provides an interesting focus on the impact of 2.0 technology on medical librarianship.

Bibliography and Works Cited

Alexa. 2011. "Top 500 Global Sites." Alexa Internet. Accessed January 27. http://www.alexa.com/topsites/.

Allan, Charles. 2007. "Using a Wiki to Manage a Library Instruction Program: Sharing Knowledge to Better Serve Patrons." *College and Research Libraries News* 68, no. 4 (April): 242–244.

Barnett, Emma. 2012. "Twitter to Hit 500 Million Registered Users." *The Telegraph*, February 22. http://www.telegraph.co.uk.

Barnhart, Fred D., and Jeannette E. Pierce. 2011. "Becoming Mobile: Reference in the Ubiquitous Library." *Journal of Library Administration* 51, no. 3 (April): 279–290.

Brady, Mark. 2005. "Blogging: Personal Participation in Public Knowledge Building on the Web." *Chimera Working Paper*. Available as archived material: http://www.essex.ac.uk/chimera.

Braun, Linda. 2007. *Listen Up! Podcasting for Schools and Libraries*. Medford, NJ: Information Today.

Carson, Bryan. 2008. "How-To Laws for Using Photos You Take at Your Library." MLS: *Marketing Library Service* 22, no. 5 (September-October). http://www.infotoday.com/mls/sep08/Carson.shtml.

Claburn, Thomas. 2007. "CEO Eric Schmidt Presents Google's Friendly Face at Web 2.0 Expo." *Information Week*, April 17. http://tinyurl.com/djmkkh.

Coleman, Jason, Danielle Theiss-White, and Melia Erin Fritch. 2011. "Social Software for Training and Managing Reference Staff." *Indiana Libraries* 30, no. 1: 40–48.

Crawford, Walt. 2006. "Library 2.0 and 'Library 2.0.'" *Cites and Insights* 6, no. 2 (Midwinter): 1–32.

Crawford, Walt. 2009. "Shiny Toys or Useful Tools?" *Cites and Insights* 9, no. 3 (February): 1–9.

Farkas, Meredith. 2007. *Social Software in Libraries: Building Collaboration, Communication, and Community Online*. Medford, NJ: Information Today. Companion website: http://www.sociallibraries.com/.

Funk, Tom. 2009. *Web 2.0 and Beyond*. Westport, CT: Praeger Publishers.

Gerardin, Julie, Michelle Yamamoto, and Kelly Gordon. 2008. "Fresh Perspectives on Reference Work in Second Life." *Reference and User Services Quarterly* 47, no. 4 (Summer): 324–327.

Hall, Hazel. 2011. "Relationships and Role Transformations in Social Media Environments." *Electronic Library* 29, no. 4: 421–428.

Hammond, Sarah. 2011. "Social Media and Librarianship: A Whistle-Stop Tour." *Refer* 27, no. 2/3 (Summer/Autumn): 60–65.

Hurst-Wahl, Jill. 2007. "Librarians and Second Life." *Information Outlook* 11, no. 6 (June): 44–53.

International Telecommunication Union. 2012. "The World in 2011: ICT Facts and Figures." International Telecommunication Union. http://www.itu.int/ict.

Lankes, David R., Joanne Silverstein, and Scott Nicholson. 2007. "Participatory Networks: The Library as Conversation." *Information Technology and Libraries* (December). http://www.ala.org/lita/ital/files/26/4/lankes.pdf.

Lippincott, Joan K. 2008. "Mobile Technologies, Mobile Users: Implications for Academic Libraries." *ARL* no. 261 (December): 1–4. http://www.arl.org/bm~doc/arl-br-261-mobile.pdf.

Needham, Gill, and Mohamed Ally. 2012. *Transforming Libraries with Mobile Technology*. London: Facet Publishing.

Reynolds, Veronica. 2011. "I've Seen the Future and It's Surprisingly CHEAP!" *Computers in Libraries* 31, no. 10 (December): 10–14.

Robinson, Kathryn. 2008. "Multimedia." Comment in "Future-Present: What's Possible Now and Coming Soon in Reference." *Library Journal* no. 19 (November 15): 4–5.

Sauers, Michael P. 2010. *Blogging and RSS: A Librarian's Guide*. 2nd ed. Medford, NJ: Information Today.

Shapiro, Samantha. 2009. "Revolution, Facebook-Style." *New York Times* (January 25): MM34, NY edition.

Smith, Justin. 2009. T*he Facebook Marketing Bible: 40+ Ways to Market Your Brand, Company, Product, or Service Inside Facebook*. 2nd ed. http://www.insidefacebook.com/category/opensocial/.

Steins, Chris. 2009. "Obama, Web 2.0 and Planning." *Planetizen*. January 19. http://www.planetizen.com/node/37013.

Storey, Tom. 2008. "Mixing It Up: Libraries Mash Up Content, Services, and Ideas." *Next Space* no. 9 (June): 6–11.

Technorati. 2008 and 2011. *State of the Blogosphere*. November 4. http://technorati.com/social-media/article/state-of-the-blogosphere-2011-introduction/.

Young, Jeffrey. 2010. "After Frustrations in Second Life, Colleges Look to New Virtual Worlds." *The Chronicle of Higher Education*, February 14. http://chronicle.com/.

22

The Future of Information Service

Libraries in the twenty-first century are evolving at a rate that would have been unimaginable to Samuel Green when he first proposed the notion of a reference department well over a century ago. The rapid rate of change is reflected in almost every sector of society from the economy to technology. Libraries are not an exception. As new technology makes its way into our lives, libraries are quick to use it. As our users adopt social software and mobile devices, libraries want to use them to reach our users. Libraries are now on Facebook; use Twitter, instant messaging, and text messaging; have blogs, wikis, and RSS feeds; and are developing mobile apps.

Change does not, however, entail an outright rejection of all that has come before. Basic elements of libraries and their services to users remain, but the ways of delivering the services continue to evolve. Change has come rapidly to libraries and reference departments in the past decade. Reference services and sources must change to meet new user interests and needs. In this chapter, we will attempt to map the winds of change while acknowledging that many principles of good reference service remain.

As one standard definition has it, reference work is "reference transactions and other activities that involve the creation, management and assessment of information or research resources tools and services" (RUSA, 2008). Although this description is accurate, reference services continue to change dramatically. Advances in computing technology, the rise of the Internet, the advent of *Wikipedia*, and the popularity of social networking have led to irrevocable paradigm shifts in the work of library and information science professionals. Crucially, such developments are not static, and the growth of the technological sphere is ongoing. A Pew Internet and American Life survey released in February 2012 indicated that 66 percent of Internet adults use social networking sites (Brenner, 2012). Librarians must, by consequence, now focus on what technology their users have adopted and how they can use that same technology in the library to better support patron needs. The ease of using Google and question-answering systems such as Cha Cha (http://www.chacha.com/) has made it hard for users to understand that all information is not the same and that search engines and question-answering systems do not always supply accurate or complete information. This is an ongoing challenge to librarians who have turned to a more active role in information literacy to try to help users understand how to evaluate and handle the information they find. Technology and easy access to information are part of the challenge facing librarians as they reassess their role in reference service. Librarians now realize that they must make their resources and services as easy to use as these simplified online portals.

Many experts have sought to provide us with a view of the future of reference. David Tyckoson (2011) believes that we still perform the four basic functions outlined by Samuel Green in 1876—teaching people how to use the library and its resources, answering information questions, recommending information sources, and promoting the library. He goes on to say that "by establishing a service model and staffing patterns, developing a manageable collection of information resources, adopting the appropriate communication tools for the local community, providing useful continuing education opportunities and continually collecting assessment data, reference managers can keep their services purring" (p. 277).

Joseph Janes (2003) suggested that librarians should continue to work in areas where their strengths lie. These, he suggested, are

> concerns about evaluation and quality of information sources, sophisticated tools and techniques for searching, understanding the nature of users, their communities, their needs and situations, compiling and organizing and packaging information resources for their use, helping them to understand how to help themselves and how to use and evaluate information. (p. 24)

Janes (2003) also envisioned a future that focuses

> less on the answers to specific questions and more on providing assistance and support to people with more detailed, more demanding, more comprehensive information needs of all kinds. (p. 24)

Last, Stephen Abram (2008) stated:

> In 2008 we are seeing the real action in our world of libraries move from the back office to the front desk. We are moving from a technology-centric strategy to one in which the real needs of our clients must predominate. Aligning technology with user behavior no longer suffices to ensure success. We need to understand, and understand deeply, the role of the library in our end-users' lives, work, research and play.

New Ways of Doing Business—Reference 2.0

As the Internet has become part of our daily existence, libraries have chosen to compete by adding e-mail reference, chat reference, and IM (instant messaging) and text messaging. E-mail reference was a simple addition. Using basic e-mail software, librarians began to communicate with their users outside the confines of the library. Though it is harder to conduct the reference interview using e-mail, libraries have developed forms for users to fill out to assist in ascertaining the exact question. Though it can be an uneven service, as some e-mails are answered quickly and others take several days, it can be quite satisfactory; it gives the librarian a chance to think about the question and provide a more thorough answer.

Chat reference was patterned after some of the commercial enterprises already using this technology, such as L.L.Bean, who has a "Live Help" site where customers can chat with a customer representative. The software has improved and has been made more usable for libraries, although the best of it is expensive. The advantage of chat reference is that it is done in real time, is interactive and immediate, and enables the librarian to do a better reference interview. Chat reference can be done through a consortium or regionally to spread the expense and allow the libraries involved to offer more hours of service. Some consortia offer chat reference 24/7. One of the early services was a pilot project set up by the Library of Congress called the Collaborative Digital Reference Service (CDRS). Its software, QuestionPoint, was then adopted by OCLC (Online Computer Library Center). Many libraries have chosen to use the QuestionPoint software while others use LibraryH3lp or other free software.

Instant and text messaging have been adopted especially by academic libraries because they appeal to their user population. This type of communication is immediate and interactive and can be done from any location. Libraries staff IM during regular hours or can add additional hours if needed. A successful IM project was reported at the Kansas State Libraries at the Reference Renaissance conference in 2008. This IM and text messaging reference project began using Meebo, and later the library moved to the open source LibraryH3lp, which allowed multiple operators and more flexibility (Theiss-White et al., 2008).

All of these new services continue to develop as librarians gain experience using them. There are definitely audiences for these new ways of communication, and the services continue to grow. Much of their success or failure may simply revolve around the marketing issue and whether the marketing is continuous. Nevertheless, it is an important effort to reach a mobile and diverse library user population. One way to continue to support this service is to make it a service of a consortium such as: CleveNet's *KnowItNow* in Cleveland, Ohio; Maryland's *AskUsNow!*; and *AskColorado*.

Providing New Materials and Formats

Though print materials will always remain part of the reference picture, digital versions of print titles and new materials in digital format only have flooded the market. Slowly, reference titles available only in print are receding and digital titles are multiplying. Although this seems like a wonderful world for the library user, it is actually a complex world that is not easy to maneuver. In fact, the user often turns to Google or Yahoo!, assuming equal quality rather than using the library's databases. Libraries have taken many approaches to encouraging the use of their online bibliographic and full-text databases from online tutorials and pathfinders to information literacy programs and marketing. They have added new software to aid users. The article linker software, for example, makes it possible for a user to find the full text of articles in another database owned by the library when there is only a bibliographic citation. Federated searching software makes it possible for users to search across several databases on a topic rather than having to identify which database should be used.

More access to online databases is available beyond the library. Thus, the library's users can access the databases from home, in their office, on mobile devices, or elsewhere. This improved access makes it easier for the user who finds it inconvenient to visit the library during its hours of service. The library's website provides access not only to the databases leased or owned by the library but to other information gathered by the library such as guides on how to research a term paper or a list of reliable Internet sites. A dynamic library website can engage library users in the use of many excellent sources of information.

Providing New Service Models

Face-to-face reference service has declined in the past few years as the Internet has become a more prominent part of users' lives. Library statistics, especially academic library statistics, show a decrease in reference transactions in the past decade. Use of public libraries has remained more stable. Libraries have also noted a decline in the number of ready reference questions and an increase in more complicated questions. Users only consult the reference librarian after trying unsuccessfully to find the information on the Internet. New models of reference service have emerged as libraries have reached out to new user groups in an effort to compensate for this decline in face-to-face reference (see Table 22-1). Many libraries have opted not to have a reference desk but rather to have librarians available in their offices, by phone, by e-mail, chat, and text messaging. Others have consolidated library services into one desk that provides reference service, photocopying services, and assistance with computing. Some libraries are replacing the reference desk with more active participation in classes where they can respond to student and faculty needs.

Librarians have developed roving as a way to talk informally to users who do not approach the reference desk. Public libraries have always done outreach, but now academic librarians are developing new outreach models. The State University of New York at Buffalo Library developed an outreach model that can be adapted by others. Its plan included getting office space in academic departments and arranging for Internet access (Wagner and Tysick, 2007). Librarians also have to provide access through the web to the library and its resources in order to reach users wherever they are. This calls for continual user-friendly upgrades to the library's technological infrastructure and designing systems. Librarians must find easy-to-use ways to present quality information. It is important to tailor the information to users' needs.

What Will Librarians Do? Competencies Needed

This newly defined reference service means that the role of the librarian must change. Among the competencies that twenty-first-century librarians will need are these:

- Ability to provide information using Reference 2.0 technologies
- Knowledge of how to select electronic resources
- Online searching expertise
- Desire to share knowledge through teaching

Table 22-1. Models of Reference Service

Type	Description	Pros	Cons
Traditional reference desk	Librarian serves user at the reference desk	Easy to staff—one service point	Only serves users who come to the desk
Reference consultation model	Complex questions are referred to a consultation service	Uses librarians for complex questions	Limits the number of users that can be served
Tiered reference service	Three levels of service—information desk, general reference desk, and consultation service	Users consult librarians for complex questions	Must train staff to do appropriate referrals and limits the number of users that can be served
Team staffing	Librarian and paraprofessional work together at reference desk	Librarian available to answer more difficult questions	Paraprofessional must make appropriate referrals to the librarian
Integrated service point concept	Integration of reference and circulation desks	Only one point of service for users	Requires ongoing training of staff
Roving	Librarians circulate throughout the reference area	Reach users who have not approached the reference desk	May require additional staffing
Virtual reference	Librarians answer questions by e-mail, chat, SMS, etc.	Users assisted who cannot visit the library	Technology still needs improvement
Outreach model	Librarians reach out to departments, groups, and organizations	Can reach new audiences	May require additional staffing
Reverse-tier service model	Librarians work within classes and organizations as the first step in providing reference service	Users can get answers for "at the moment" questions	Requires more staff to provide this service
No reference desk	Users can make an appointment with a librarian or contact them by telephone, e-mail, chat, or SMS	More flexibility for librarians and users	May be confusing for users who expect a reference desk

- Readers' advisory skills
- Knowledge of how to develop an effective web presence
- Appreciation of the importance of marketing a program
- Familiarity with research on assessment and evaluation
- Interpersonal skills
- Ability to adapt to change
- Enthusiasm for career-long learning

Of course, librarians will continue to answer reference questions, although they may encounter fewer ready reference requests and more complex questions. Many of these requests will be made online or from mobile devices rather than in person (though users will continue to come to the library). Librarians may want to take on more of a consultation role to better help users with complicated questions that require more time and perhaps follow-up. Whitlatch (2003) suggests that "answering questions requires more focus on instruction in search strategies and other elements related to the basic information competencies of identifying the type of information needed, and finding, evaluating, and communicating the information successfully" (p. 30).

Librarians need to understand how Reference 2.0 technology works and to keep abreast of changes and innovations. They also need to evaluate the potential of using Facebook, Twitter, blogs, wikis, tagging, RSS, podcasting, widgets, and so forth. These social networking technologies help libraries connect with users and potential users "where they are."

Librarians will continue to do collection development. With less print to order, librarians will concentrate their attention on the evaluation and selection of electronic resources. Each new resource added must then be fitted into the library's electronic collection. The new resources must also be introduced to the users for whom it is intended and marketed to an even broader audience. Along with the selection goes the ability to excel in online searching. As all librarians know, a well-planned search can yield much better results. Librarians owe it to their users to help them search effectively and efficiently.

Librarians will engage in more information literacy instruction—both one-to-one and in groups. Users need to learn to use electronic resources, the online catalog, and other databases that are available. The complexity of the library's resources, especially the online databases, has made it imperative that users receive assistance. Information literacy instruction may be one-to-one at the reference desk or in an e-mail or chat session; or it may be a class—either a one-shot class to get users started or part of a collaboration with a teacher or professor to help students begin a particular assignment. E-learning is another important aspect of information literacy as librarians learn to insert learning packages into learning management systems such as Blackboard or hold an online discussion about research methods.

Librarians will develop their readers' advisory skills to provide more person-alized service to their users. Readers' advisory services now include nonfiction as well as fiction. Librarians will also spend time creating finding tools to guide their users in the ever-more-complex world of information resources. Finally, they will continue to develop webpages to organize and present information to their users in a form that is easy to use and understand, such as pages on how to do research in general or guides to research on particular subject areas.

Librarians will learn more about marketing. "As part of their marketing competencies, library professionals must have the skill to systematically assess the information seeking needs and habits of their primary clientele" (Whitlatch, 2003: 29). These skills will be learned in library school or in a continuing education course.

Assessment and evaluation will be practiced on a much more regular basis by librarians. Decision making will be based on the results of surveys, questionnaires, and focus groups. Programs and projects will be based on both quantitative and qualitative information. Librarians have done a great deal of evaluation of their services. An article documents a multiple-methods study done at Villanova (PA) University and its Falvey Memorial Library. The library used focus groups, benchmarking, surveys, transaction analysis, activity mapping, and secret shoppers to evaluate library service. The study resulted in the consolidation of the service points into one single large desk from which all services are available, the installation of a print center in the library in partnership with the university's graphic services, and the creation of a multipurpose instructional computer lab (Stein et al., 2008). Evaluation can take many forms, but the need for continual evaluation of reference services is a necessity.

Interpersonal skills will remain essential in this changing world. It has for many decades distinguished libraries and librarians and will continue to do so. The ability to change and the enthusiasm for lifelong learning will continue to mark the route of this profession. Libraries and librarians must continue to respond to the needs of their users and to be alert to changes in the world that will affect libraries. The role of reference librarians will change as reference continues to evolve. Reference work will become more collaborative. It might mean that more than one librarian will contribute to the response to a user or that several libraries will work collaboratively to respond to reference questions such as is done now on chat reference. The librarians' new role will be multifaceted and more proactive than in the past. They will work to design better systems that meet their users' more personalized needs.

Planning the Future

In a recent article, Terence K. Huwe (2009) posed a series of diagnostic questions to help libraries stay on top of change. These questions can be a way to guide future planning.

- Is the library following the interests of its community? Huwe suggests keeping current on what technologies are being used in the community.
- Is the new technology something that should be implemented immediately or should it be tested carefully first? Huwe says that sometimes it's good to adopt a new technology immediately and other times to move more cautiously and look at the pros and cons of it.

- How does a new technology impact on existing library services? Huwe says, for example, that new technology can increase use of other library services.
- How does a new technology link to other existing technologies? Huwe says that often people move between various technologies, so it is important to see how they link together. People may use, for example, wikis and e-mail interchangeably.
- How do librarians keep themselves prepared and informed about new technologies? Librarians must keep up with what is happening around them and try new technologies.

What Will the Future of Reference Look Like?

Reference in the future will be less attached to a particular location no matter what type of library, but its focus will be user-centered. In a library building there will no doubt be one desk that serves a variety of functions such as assisting users to identify, use, and evaluate electronic resources and helping them with various software packages. Users can reach librarians for assistance by making an appointment to meet with them or contacting them by phone, e-mail, chat, IM, or text messaging.. This gives the librarians more flexibility to do other projects rather than staffing a desk and gives the user more choices. Most library reference work will be transacted virtually in the future.

Librarians will spend their time providing instruction in the use of resources. They will also develop tutorials, LibGuides, and FAQs for the library's website. They will spend a great deal of time putting resources needed by their users on the web and adding and subtracting information to keep the website timely and current. For example, librarians put up lists of resources on their websites after the 9/11 terrorist attacks, and in March 2009, librarians developed a list of resources titled "Economic Crisis Reference Guide." Librarians will plan outreach services to reach prospective users—either in physical locations or virtually. Librarians will evaluate their efforts to judge what projects are most effective so they can use their funding wisely.

Does Reference Have a Future?

Questions about the ongoing relevance of all aspects of our profession have likely been ongoing concerns since Samuel Green established reference service in 1876. Although libraries are certainly subject to change, we need not fear their dissolution. Comparatively speaking, reference service is a new dimension of our institutions, but as we grow both more complex and more open, it increasingly seems certain that this service is here to stay. Far more productive, then, may be to ask how that future should be approached. James Rettig (2003) has suggested that libraries must respond to their users' values, which are "immediacy, interactivity, person-alization, and mobility" (p. 19). As to immediacy and interactivity, using chat reference, instant messaging, and text messaging is an attempt to meet this user need as well as provide reference 24/7. Personalization has been implemented by personalizing the library's website to users' needs. The need for mobility has been responded to by making the library website and its resources available wherever the user is and at any hour. Rettig (2003) has also challenged librarians to become "expert anthropologists of our user communities" in order to serve them well (p. 20).

Marketing is another important component of the library's future. As with any profit-making or nonprofit organization, libraries must make their present and potential users aware of their products and services. Marketing need not be terribly expensive, but it must be effective. Libraries offer a wide range of materials and services that are often not obvious to the users unless they are highlighted. Because so many of the resources and services are online and often remote, libraries must use a variety of media to market themselves—flyers and brochures, the library's homepage, newspapers, radio and television, websites, and social networking sites such as Facebook.

The future of reference is best summed up as "high tech and high touch." Librarians will continue to change their service model. They will strive to meet user needs at the first point of contact whether it is in person, online, from a mobile device or even from an audio/video source such as Skype. They will develop a variety of services which are not tied to a service point. Libraries are "increasingly…a platform for getting things done. Library users are empowered as never before to explore, research and uncover new patterns in the world of recorded knowledge" (Kennedy, 2011: 324). Reference service will be integrated and seamless such that it will be provided to match the user's needs no matter where he or she enters the library's sphere. The personal aspect of library service will continue to distinguish itself from other institutions and will separate it from its competition and fill the needs of its users.

Recommendations for Further Reading

Anderson, Rick. 2011. "Collections 2021: The Future of the Library Collection Is Not a Collection." *Serials* 24, no. 3: 211–215. Predicts that in the next ten years library collections will be drastically altered by moves toward patron-driven acquisitions, print-on-demand, and full-text search. Library services will become indistinguishable from educational services, while the academic library's educational mission will ironically put it at a disadvantage in competition with other information providers.

Arlitsch, Kenning. 2011. "The Espresso Book Machine: A Change Agent for Libraries." *Library Hi Tech* 29, no. 1: 62–72. Considers the impact of the print-on-demand model of service on academic libraries in terms of comparative costs and potential benefits to users.

Bronstein, Jenny. 2011. "The Role and Work Perceptions of Academic Reference Librarians: A Qualitative Inquiry." *Portal: Libraries and the Academy* 11, no. 3: 791–811. Results of a survey show that the core values and skills of the academic reference profession have remained the same over the past 30 years despite the dramatic changes in information technology and the nature of reference inquiries. Future reference librarians are envisioned as guides and motivated learners, who still have much to gain from those in the field today.

Davidson, Sara, and Susan Mikkelsen. 2009. "Desk Bound No More: Reference Services at a New Research University Library." *The Reference Librarian* 50, no. 4: 346–355. The opening of a new campus library at the University of California provided the opportunity to experiment with a model of research services that excluded the reference desk. Student workers at a service desk fielded questions that would have fallen to professionals, but, overall, the experiment is deemed by the authors to be a success in terms of quality of service. It is also acknowledged to be a practical necessity due to limited resources.

Jones, Edgar. 2010. "Google Books as a General Research Collection." *Library Resources and Technical Services* 54, no. 2: 77–89. An attempt to qualify the extent to which Google Books has created a serviceable general research collection in pre-1872 public domain material. The experiment leads the author to question, "What is a collection?" The results conclude that Google Books does approximate the pre-1872 content available at a major research library but with some drawbacks: poor scanning, missing pages, incorrect metadata, and other quality control issues.

LaGuardia, Cheryl. 2011. "Library Instruction in the Digital Age." *Journal of Library Administration* 51, no. 3: 301–308. An update to the author's own article, written in 2003: "The Future of Reference: Get Real!" The author discovers that the need for library instruction has grown since her earlier article, due to increased complexity in the online environment and online catalogs that confuse users. Decreased staffing and increased demand has led to librarians experiencing burnout. Standardized information literacy programs are criticized.

Little, Geoffrey. 2011. "The Book Is Dead, Long Live the Book!" *The Journal of Academic Librarianship* 37, no. 6: 536–538. An assessment of the current and future importance of the e-book in academic libraries. While e-book platforms and models of access leave much to be desired at present, the author provides reasons why the e-book will become increasingly attractive to both libraries and their users.

Peters, Thomas A. 2010. "Left to Their Own Devices: The Future of Reference Services on Personal, Portable Information, Communication, and Entertainment Devices." *The Reference Librarian* 52, no. 1–2: 88–97. A guide to running a successful mobile reference service. Greater portability and improvements in information literacy and online systems are expanding the nature of reference and will have significant effects on its future, but will never entirely replace other established modes of reference, such as the desk, chat, or phone.

Reynolds, Veronica. 2011. "I've Seen the Future, and It's Surprisingly Cheap!" *Computers in Libraries* 31, no. 10: 10–14. Describes low-cost, experimental projects utilizing open source software in a public library.

Thomsett-Scott, Beth, and Frances May. 2009. "How May We Help You? Online Education Faculty Tell Us What They Need from Libraries and Librarians." *Journal of Library Administration* 49, no. 1–2: 111–135. The growth in distance and online learning necessitates outreach to faculty and students. The responses to a survey conducted by the authors reveal that instructors of online classes are often unaware of the services offered by instructional librarians, but that they do perceive a need for them.

Trott, Barry, and Jack O'Gorman. 2009. "What Will Become of Reference in Academic and Public Libraries?" *Journal of Library Administration* 49: 327–339. A good overview article on what is changing in reference work.

Wolfe, Judith A., Ted Naylor, and Jeanette Drueke. 2010. "The Role of the Academic Reference Librarian in the Learning Commons." *Reference and User Services Quarterly* 50, no. 2 (Winter): 108–113. Reference librarians use their skills in a variety of reference service models which range from the traditional to the tiered to the information commons to the learning commons. Libraries might use one form of any model, a hybrid model, or a model in the process of transformation. Some libraries are adopting the learning commons model with good results.

Bibliography and Works Cited

Abram, Stephen. 2008. "Evolution to Revolution to Chaos? Reference in Transition." *Searcher* 16, no. 8: 42–48. http://www.infotoday.com/searcher/sep08/Abram.shtml

Brenner, Joanna. 2012. "Pew Internet: Social Networking." Pew Internet and American Life Project. http://www.pewinternet.org/Commentary/2012/March/Pew-Internet-Social-Networking-full-detail.aspx.

Ferguson, Chris. 2000. "'Shaking the Conceptual Foundations,' Too: Integrating Research and Technology Support for the Next Generation of Information Service." *College and Research Libraries* 61, no. 4 (July): 300–311.

Flanagan, Pat, and Lisa R. Horowitz. 2000. "Exploring New Service Models: Can Consolidating Public Service Points Improve Response to Customer Needs?" *Journal of Academic Librarianship* 26, no. 5 (September): 329–338.

Huwe, Terence K. 2009. "Reference Diagnostics for a Virtual World." *Computers in Libraries* 29, no. 1: 27–29.

Jackson, Rebecca. 2002. "Revolution or Evolution: Reference Planning in ARL Libraries." *Reference Services Review* 30, no. 3: 212–228.

Janes, Joseph. 2003. "What Is Reference For?" *Reference Services Review* 31, no. 1: 22–25.

Kennedy, Scott. 2011. "Farewell to the Reference Librarian." *Journal of Library Administration* 51: 319–325.

Rettig, James. 2003. "Technology, Cluelessness, Anthropology and the Memex: The Future of Academic Reference Service." *Reference Service Review* 31, no. 1: 17–21.

RUSA (Reference and User Services Association). 2008. "Definitions of Reference." American Library Association. http://www.ala.org/rusa/resources/guidelines/definitions reference.

Stein, Merrill, Theresa Edge, John M. Kelley, Dana Hewlett, and James F. Trainer. 2008. "Using Continuous Quality Improvement Methods to Evaluate Library Service Points." *Reference and User Services Quarterly* 48, no. 1: 78–85.

Tenopir, Carol, and Lisa A. Ennis. 2001. "Reference Services in the New Millennium." *Online* (July–August): 41–45.

Theiss-White, Danielle, Laura Bonella, Jason Coleman, and Erin Fitch. 2008 "'r u there? I need help:' Virtual Reference at Kansas State University." Presented at the Reference Renaissance Conference, August 4 and 5. Denver, Colorado.

Tyckoson, David A. 2011. "Issues and Trends in the Management of Reference Services: A Historical Perspective." *Journal of Library Administration* 51: 259–278.

Wagner, A. Ben, and Cynthia Tysick. 2007. "Onsite Reference and Instruction Services; Setting Up Shop Where Our Patrons Live." *Reference and User Services Quarterly* 46, no. 4: 60–65.

Whitlatch, Jo Bell. 2003. "Reference Futures: Outsourcing, the Web, or Knowledge Counseling." *Reference Services Review* 31, no. 1: 26–30.

Wilson, Myoung C. 2000. "Evolution or Entropy? Changing Reference/User Culture and the Future of Reference." *Reference and User Services Quarterly* 28 (Summer): 387–390.

Appendix

RUSA Outstanding Reference Sources 2007–2012

The Reference and User Services Association (RUSA) of the American Library Association uses twenty-two criteria to select the best reference publications to recommend for small and medium-sized libraries. A committee made up of reference librarians from different kinds of libraries is responsible for final selections, a practice that has continued since 1958. Previous selections can be accessed through the RUSA site at http://www.ala.org/.

The list provides a handy focus on the extraordinary variety of reference resources available to users—and the breadth of familiarity required of reference librarians. "Best of . . . " lists are expedient ways to keep abreast of titles that will be popularly requested.

2012

- *The Encyclopedia of Political Science*. George T. Kurian, editor-in-chief. CQ Press, 2011. (9781933116440)
- *The Civil War Naval Encyclopedia*. Spencer Tucker, ed. ABC-CLIO, 2011. (9781598843385)
- *Competing Voices from the Russian Revolution: Fighting Words*. Michael Hickey, ed. Greenwood, 2011. (9780313385230)
- *The Oxford Encyclopedia of the Books of the Bible*. Michael D. Coogan, ed. Oxford University Press, 2011. (9780195377378)
- *Concise Encyclopedia of Amish, Brethren, Hutterites, and Mennonites*. Donald B. Kraybill. The Johns Hopkins University Press, 2010. (9780801896576)
- *The Polish American Encyclopedia*. James S. Pula, ed. McFarland, 2011. (9780786433087)
- *Green's Dictionary of Slang*. Jonathon Green. Oxford University Press, 2010. (9780550104403)
- *Encyclopedia of Sports Medicine*. Lyle J. Micheli, ed. SAGE, 2011. (9781412961158)
- *The Encyclopedia of Literary and Cultural Theory*. Michael Ryan, general ed. Wiley-Blackwell, 2011. (9781405183123)
- *The Homer Encyclopedia*. Margalit Finkelberg, ed. Wiley-Blackwell, 2011. (9781405177689)
- *The Grove Encyclopedia of American Art*. Joan M. Marter, ed. Oxford University Press, 2011. (9780195335798)

2011

- *The Oxford Companion to the Book.* Michael F. Suarez, S.J. and H.R. Woudhuysen, eds. 2 vols. Oxford University Press, 2010. (9780198606536)
- *Encyclopedia of Identity.* Ronald L. Jackson II, ed. 2 vols. SAGE, 2010. (9781412951531)
- *Encyclopedia of Geography.* Barney Warf, ed. 6 vols. SAGE, 2010. (9781412956970)
- *The Oxford Encyclopedia of Ancient Greece and Rome.* Michael Gagarin, ed. 7 vols. Oxford University Press, 2010. (9780195170726)
- *The Encyclopedia of Religion in America.* Charles H. Lippy and Peter W. Williams, eds. 4 vols. CQ Press, 2010. (9780872895805)
- *Off Broadway Musicals, 1910–2007: Casts, Credits, Songs, Critical Reception and Performance Data of More Than 1,800 Shows.* Dan Dietz, ed. 1 vol. McFarland, 2010. (9780786433995)
- *Encyclopedia of World Dress and Fashion.* Joanne B. Eicher, ed. 10 vols. Oxford University Press, 2010. (9780195377330)
- Berg Fashion Library. http://www.bergfashionlibrary.com/. Oxford University Press, 2010.
- *Chronology of the Evolution-Creationism Controversy.* Randy Moore, ed., et al. 1 vol. Greenwood, 2009. (9780313362873)
- *The Oxford International Encyclopedia of Peace.* Nigel Young, ed. 4. vols. Oxford University Press, 2010. (9780195334685)
- *21st Century Economics: A Reference Handbook.* Rhona C. Free, ed. 2 vols. SAGE, 2010. (9781412961424)
- *Encyclopedia of Political Theory.* Mark Bevir, ed. 3 vols. SAGE, 2010. (9781412958653)
- *Encyclopedia of Group Processes and Intergroup Relations.* John M. Levine and Michael A. Hogg, eds. 2 vols. SAGE, 2010. (9781412942089)

2010

- *Archaeology in America: An Encyclopedia.* Francis P. McManamon, ed. 4 vols. Greenwood, 2009. (9780313331847)
- *Encyclopedia of African American History: 1896 to the Present.* Paul Finkelman, ed. 5 vols. Oxford University Press, 2009. (9780195167791)
- *Encyclopedia of Modern China.* David Pong, ed. 4 vols. Charles Scribner's Sons, 2009. (9780684315661)
- *The Encyclopedia of the Spanish-American and Philippine-American Wars.* Spencer Tucker, ed. 3 vols. ABC-CLIO, 2009. (9781851099511)
- *Encyclopedia of Environmental Ethics and Philosophy.* J. Baird Callicott and Robert Frodeman, eds. 2 vols. Gale Cengage, 2009. (9780028661370)
- *Encyclopedia of Human Rights.* David Forsythe, ed. 5 vols. Oxford University Press, 2009. (9780195334029)
- Social Explorer. http://www.socialexplorer.com/pub/home/home.aspx. Social Explorer, 2009.
- *Broadway Plays and Musicals: Descriptions and Essential Facts.* Thomas S. Hischak, ed. 1 vol. McFarland, 2009. (9780786434481)

- *American Countercultures.* Gina Misiroglu, ed. 3 vols. Sharp, 2009. (9780765680600)
- *Encyclopedia of Gender and Society.* Jodi O'Brien, ed. 2 vols. SAGE, 2009. (9781412909167)
- *Encyclopedia of Marine Science.* C. Reid Nichols and Robert G. Williams, eds. 1 vol. Facts on File, 2009. (9780816050222)

2009

- *Books and Beyond: The Greenwood Encyclopedia of New American Reading.* Kenneth Womack, ed. 4 vols. Greenwood, 2008. (9780313337383)
- *Encyclopedia of Taoism.* Fabrizio Pregadio, ed. 2 vols. Routledge, 2008. (9780700712007)
- *Encyclopedia of the First Amendment.* John R. Vile, David L. Hudson Jr., and David Schultz, eds. 2 vols. CQ Press, 2009. (9780872893115)
- *Greenwood Encyclopedia of Folktales and Fairy Tales.* Donald Haase, ed. 3 vols. Greenwood, 2008. (9780313334412)
- *Encyclopedia of Education Law.* Charles J. Russo, ed. 2 vols. SAGE, 2008. (9781412940795)
- *Climate Change: In Context.* Brenda Wilmoth Lerner and K. Lee Lerner, eds. 2 vols. Gale Cengage, 2008. (9781414436142)
- *Gale Encyclopedia of Diets: A Guide to Health and Nutrition.* Jacqueline L. Longe, ed. Gale Cengage, 2008. (9781414429915)
- *New Encyclopedia of Orchids: 1500 Species in Cultivation.* Isobyl la Croix. Timber Press, 2008. (9780881928761)
- *Encyclopedia of the Arab-Israeli Conflict: A Political, Social and Military History.* Spencer C. Tucker, ed. 4 vols. ABC-CLIO, 2008. (9781851098415)
- *African American National Biography.* Henry Louis Gates Jr. and Evelyn Brooks-Higginbotham, eds. 8 vols. Oxford University Press, 2008. (9780195160192)
- *Oxford Encyclopedia of Women in World History.* Bonnie G. Smith, ed. 4 vols. Oxford University Press, 2008. (9780195148909)

2008

- *APA Dictionary of Psychology.* Gary R. VandenBos, ed. American Psychological Association, 2007. (1591473802)
- *Encyclopaedia Judaica.* Staff, ed. Macmillan Reference U. S. A. 22 vols. Rev. ed. Gale, 2006. (0028659287)
- *Blackwell Encyclopedia of Sociology.* George Ritzer, ed. 11 vols. Blackwell, 2007. (1405124334)
- *Encyclopedia of Body Adornment.* Margo Demello. Greenwood, 2007. (313336954)
- *Encyclopedia of Race and Racism.* John Hartwell Moore, ed. 4 vols. Gale, 2008. (9780028660202)
- *The Oxford Encyclopedia of Maritime History.* John B. Hattendorf, ed. 4 vols. Oxford University Press, 2007. (9780195130751)
- *Schirmer Encyclopedia of Film.* Barry Keith Grant, ed. 4 vols. Gale, 2006. (0028657912)

- *Encyclopedia of Asian Theatre.* Samuel L. Leiter, ed. 2 vols. Greenwood, 2007. (03133529x)
- *Brave New Words: The Oxford Dictionary of Science Fiction.* Jeff Prucher, ed. Oxford University Press, 2007. (0195305671)
- *Postwar America: An Encyclopedia of Social, Political, Cultural and Economic History.* James Ciment. 4 vols. ME Sharpe, 2007. (079568067x)
- *Oxford Companion to World Exploration.* David Buisseret, ed. 2 vols. Oxford University Press, 2007. (019514922X)

2007

- *Colonial America: An Encyclopedia of Social, Political, Cultural, and Economic History.* James Ciment, ed. M. E. Sharpe, 2005. (0765680653)
- *Crusades: An Encyclopedia.* Alan V. Murray, ed. 4 vols. ABC-CLIO, 2006. (1576078620)
- *Encyclopedia of Swearing: The Social History of Oaths, Profanity, Foul Language, and Ethnic Slurs in the English-Speaking World.* Geoffrey Hughes. M. E. Sharpe, 2006. (0765612311)
- *Encyclopedia of the American Revolutionary War: A Political, Social, and Military History.* Gregory Fremont-Barnes and Richard Ryerson, eds. ABC-CLIO, 2006. (1851094083)
- *Encyclopedia of the Developing World.* Thomas M. Leonard, ed. 3 vols. Routledge, 2005. (1579583881)
- *Encyclopedia of US Labor and Working Class History.* Eric Arnesen, ed. 3 vols. Routledge, 2006. (0415968267)
- *Encyclopedia of Western Colonialism Since 1450.* Thomas Benjamin, ed. 3 vols. MacMillian, 2007. (0028658434)
- *Encyclopedia of Women and Religion in North America.* Rosemary Skinner Keller, ed. 3 vols. Indiana University Press, 2006. (0253346851)
- *Historical Statistics of the United States: Earliest Times to the Present.* Susan B. Carter, Scott Sigmund Gartner, Michael R. Haines, et al., eds. 5 vols. Cambridge University Press, 2006. (0521817919)
- *Insects: Their Natural History and Diversity.* Stephen A. Marshall. Firefly, 2006. (1552979008)
- *Oxford Encyclopedia of British Literature.* David Scott Kastan, ed. 5 vols. Oxford University Press, 2006. (0195169212)
- *Oxford Encyclopedia of Children's Literature.* Jack Zipes, ed. 4 vols. Oxford University Press, 2006. (01951146561)
- *Qu'ran: An Encyclopedia.* Oliver Leaman, ed. Routledge, 2005. (0415326397)
- *Right, Wrong, and Risky: A Dictionary of Today's American English Usage.* Norton, 2005. (0393061191)

Index of Reference Resources

Page numbers followed by the letter "f" indicate figures; those followed by the letter "t" indicate tables.

Subject Index

Page numbers followed by the letter "f" indicate figures; those followed by the letter "t" indicate tables.

About the Authors
and Contributors

Kay Ann Cassell received her BA from Carnegie Mellon University, her MLS from Rutgers University, and her PhD from the International University for Graduate Studies. She has worked in academic libraries and public libraries as a reference librarian and as a library director. Ms. Cassell is a past president of Reference and User Services Association of ALA and is active on ALA and RUSA committees. She is the editor of the journal *Collection Building* and is the author of numerous articles and books on collection development and reference service. She was formerly the Associate Director of Collections and Services for the Branch Libraries of the New York Public Library where she was in charge of collection development and age-level services for the Branch Libraries. She is now a Lecturer and Director of the MLIS Program in the School of Communication, Information and Library Studies at Rutgers, the State University of New Jersey.

Uma Hiremath is Executive Director at the Ames Free Library, Massachusetts. She was Assistant Director at the Thayer Public Library, Massachusetts; Head of Reference at the West Orange Public Library, New Jersey; and Supervising Librarian at the New York Public Library where she worked for five years. She received her MLS from Pratt Institute, New York, and her PhD in political science at the University of Pittsburgh.

• • •

Angela Ecklund holds an MLIS from Rutgers University and an MPhil in English from the CUNY Graduate Center. She has worked as a reference and instructional librarian at Rutgers University Libraries and is a part-time lecturer of literature at Hunter College. She also serves as assistant editor for the journal *Collection Building*.

Meghan Harper, PhD, is an Associate Professor at Kent State University in Kent, Ohio. Dr. Harper serves as the Coordinator of the School Library program and currently teaches three courses in the area of Youth Services in the School of Library and Information Science. Her research areas include school library administration and evaluation. She is author of *Reference Sources and Services for Youth* (Neal-Schuman, 2011) and the forthcoming *Cataloging for School Librarians*

(Neal-Schuman, 2013), along with numerous articles, book chapters, and reviews. She has been an invited speaker at numerous state, national, and international conferences. Dr. Harper is co-director of the Virginia Hamilton Multicultural Literature Conference, the longest-running national conference of its kind.

Cindy Orr has held various positions in public libraries, including reference librarian, department head, deputy director, library manager, collection manager, and interim technical services director and has worked in two very large star-rated multibranch urban and suburban public libraries, as well as a smaller suburban library and an exurban system. She is currently a library consultant with over thirty years of experience in public libraries. She consults with libraries and vendors, speaks extensively on the subject of readers' advisory service, collection development, and technical services, teaches a class on readers' advisory service at Kent State University's School of Library and Information Science, and edits the monthly "Collection Development" columns in *Library Journal*. She is the editor of the *Reader's Advisor Online Blog* and was the 2004 winner of the ALA/RUSA Margaret E. Monroe Library Adult Services Award.